The Helen Rose Scheuer Jewish Women's Series

Streets: A Memoir of the Lower East Side
by Bella Spewack

The Maimie Papers: Letters from an Ex-Prostitute
by Maimie Pinzer
edited by Ruth Rosen and Sue Davidson

A Cross and a Star: Memoirs of a Jewish Girl in Chile
by Marjorie Agosín
(forthcoming 1997)

*"This picture of me and Poke
was taken in San Antonio, Texas,
in the summer of 1909."*

The Maimie Papers

Letters from
an Ex-Prostitute

MAIMIE PINZER

Ruth Rosen, Historical Editor
Sue Davidson, Textual Editor
Introduction and New Afterword by Ruth Rosen
New Literary Afterword by Florence Howe

Published by The Feminist Press
at The City University of New York
New York

in cooperation with
The Schlesinger Library of Radcliffe College

DEDICATION

Helen Huntington Howe
1905–1975

Published in 1997 by The Feminist Press at The City University of New York,
311 East 94 Street, New York, New York 10128-5684.
(Originally published, excluding afterwords, by The Feminist Press in 1977.)

Library of Congress Cataloging in Publication Data

Pinzer, Maimie, 1885–

Letters written 1910–1922 chiefly to Fanny Quincy Howe. Includes index.

1. Pinzer, Maimie, 1885– 2. Prostitutes—Pennsylvania—Philadelphia—
Correspondence, reminiscences, etc. 3. United States—Moral
conditions—Sources.

I. Rosen, Ruth. II. Davidson, Sue.

III. Howe, Fanny Quincy, 1870–1933. IV. Title.

HQ146.P4P56 301.41'54'0924[B] 77-21693 ISBN: 1-55861-143-6

02 01 00 99 98 97   4 3 2 1

Steven H. Scheuer, in memory of his mother and in celebration of her life and the
100th anniversary of her birth (1995) has been pleased to announce a substantial gift
to The Feminist Press to endow the Helen Rose Scheuer Jewish Women's Series.
The Maimie Papers is the second named book in this series.

For permission to use the photograph of Maimie, The Feminist Press
acknowledges the Arthur and Elizabeth Schlesinger Library on the
History of Women in America, Radcliffe College.

Cover Design: Tina R. Malaney
Text Design: Susan Trowbridge
Printed in the United States of America on acid-free paper by BookCrafters.

TABLE OF CONTENTS

LIST OF PAPERS

ACKNOWLEDGMENTS

The Maimie Papers owes its existence to several prescient individuals, two feminist institutions, the generosity of the National Endowment for the Humanities, and all those who have worked to plan and produce the book. Before it became a book, it was an idea; before that, it was a bundle of letters kept for more than half a century by Fanny Quincy Howe, and then passed on to her daughter, the late Helen Howe, who had also, as a child, corresponded with Maimie. In 1971, Helen Howe donated the letters to the Schlesinger Library at Radcliffe College.

The idea first made its way to The Feminist Press in the summer of 1974. Ruth Rosen had come upon Maimie's letters while doing research for her dissertation at the Schlesinger Library. She communicated her enthusiasm about the letters to Ellen DuBois, a historian who serves on the Reprints Advisory Board of The Feminist Press. The Reprints Advisory Board, a group of historians and literary scholars, read Maimie's letters in holograph and recommended that the Press make them available to the broadest possible audience. The Reprints Advisory Board has continued, through the life of what became "the Maimie Project," to take an active interest in its plans and progress.

In the spring of 1975, Florence Howe for The Feminist Press and Patricia Miller King, Director of the Schlesinger Library, wrote and submitted to the National Endowment for the Humanities a proposal to fund the Maimie project. Support from the Endowment was to be responsible for the production of a complete typescript now available to scholars using the Schlesinger Library, and for the production of an edited manuscript making the letters accessible in a single volume to general readers, and to students and scholars of social history. The controlling idea of this proposal, given the literary quality of the letters, was that the volume might resemble a restored autobiography.

Two editors were chosen by the co-directors of the Maimie project: historian Ruth Rosen for her knowledge of the subject and the period, Sue Davidson for her literary judgment and editorial skills. Up to that point, those who had read the collection of letters in holograph had been uncertain that none was missing, since they were not in chronological order, and many lacked dates or had become separated from date-bearing envelopes. Once Davidson had placed the letters in chronological order through the use of internal evidence, however, there emerged a complete account, not only of the twelve years during which the letters were written, but of the preceding twenty-five. When the letters had been cut and edited, the original idea of recovering a lost autobiography became a reality. With an introduction by Rosen, setting the letters in their historical context, the Maimie project became *The Maimie Papers*.

Special acknowledgments are due other individuals. The accurate typescript of the handwritten letters was prepared by Amanda Bennet, Hester Fuller, Susan Jane Liguori and Anne Whittington. Susan Trowbridge of The Feminist Press designed the volume and coordinated its production. Co-editor Sue Davidson was also the in-house Press editor. Proofreading was done by Millie Hawk Daniels and Jeanne Ford, and the index was prepared by Maro Rio Francos. We are also grateful to Charlotte Davis McGhee and Harriette Walker of Radcliffe College; and to Phyllis Arlow, Brett Harvey and Corrine Lucido of The Feminist Press for their assistance.

The content of this volume does not necessarily represent the views of the National Endowment for the Humanities.

Florence Howe
Patricia Miller King

INTRODUCTION

Until recently, history has been written largely from the viewpoint of the classes that were its beneficiaries. Inevitably, then, historians have failed to provide us with a reliable account of "ordinary" and powerless people. They have given scarcely any account at all of the working-class women who faced the difficult task of surviving in early twentieth-century America.

Prostitution, the so-called "oldest profession," and a frequent means of survival for working-class women, has been especially neglected. As part of an "historically inarticulate" subculture, prostitutes, like other working-class women, remain excluded from traditional accounts of history.[1] One very real obstacle to such scholarly inquiry has been the lack of accessible sources which can document prostitutes' origins and consciousness. Leaving few personal records of their own, prostitutes have often remained a footnote in the histories of famous men's flirtations with "ladies of the night." Yet, the famous courtesans briefly mentioned in history texts represent but a fraction of the vast majority of prostitutes who have led far less auspicious lives. They, like other working-class women, have a history of their own. How did working-class women live during a period of history characterized by great industrial exploitation and institutionalized sexism? Who were the prostitutes of the past? What was their economic and social background? Why did some women choose to become prostitutes, while others did not?

Due to the lack of authentic memoirs written by prostitutes, the attempt to answer these questions has remained a formidable task.

Literate middle- and upper-class women frequently kept diaries and letters which are now enabling historians to offer new perspectives on women's historical experience.[2] The greatest challenge, however, is the attempt to document the historical experience of women in the poorest classes—many of whom were unskilled workers and prostitutes.

"The Maimie Letters," written by a former prostitute, who also supported herself by other means available to working-class women of her period, is therefore a unique document and source in the history of women.[3] Through Maimie's vivid and precise rendering, we are offered a unique view of the "underside" of American culture and society, and of the options and obstacles which faced working-class women in their struggle for survival.

It is important to note that "The Maimie Letters" constitute an unquestionably authentic handwritten document. Many so-called "memoirs" written by prostitutes appeared during the early twentieth century. Unfortunately, most of these "memoirs" must ultimately be judged inauthentic because they are typescripts with no parent manuscript. Furthermore, most of these memoirs were written as moralistic tracts by "purity crusaders" who wished to advance their anti-prostitution movement. Like the "slave narratives" written by zealous abolitionists in the nineteenth century, these memoirs read like evangelical sermons on the evils of vice.[4]

What are "The Maimie Letters" and to whom were they written? The letters were written by Maimie Pinzer to Fanny Quincy Howe, from 1910-1922. After losing an eye, possibly to syphilitic infection, Maimie was helped by a Philadelphia social worker, Herbert Welsh, to reconstruct her life. She first fought a successful battle against morphine addiction.[5] It was during that crucial struggle that Mr. Welsh, in his effort to prevent Maimie from returning to her life as a prostitute, asked Mrs. Howe, a prominent and socially concerned Bostonian, to write Maimie. As a result of this suggestion, a remarkable correspondence between the two women continued over a decade.

One can hardly imagine two more unlikely correspondents than Maimie Pinzer (1885-?) and Fanny Quincy Howe (1870-1933). Yet the correspondence, which continued at an active and often frenetic pace for twelve years, is characterized by genuine affection and mutual concern. Maimie, the product of a broken and quarrelsome Jewish family, spent much of her youth learning to survive through prostitution. Intent on self-improvement, Maimie wished to live as a "lady." Fanny Quincy Howe, in contrast, was made a "lady" by the circumstances of her birth and upbringing.

Although Mrs. Howe's half of the correspondence has apparently not survived, she is no stranger to historians of the period. She belonged to that special breed of Americans which her daughter, Helen Howe, described in a family biography as the "Gentle Americans."[6] According to the Howes' daughter, the family was neither "long tailed nor short." They were a proper, but unstuffy Bostonian family marked by originality and creativity.

Fanny Quincy was a member of that class of Americans whose financial and social security permitted them to devote their lives to artistic, literary, and humanistic pursuits. "All the Dear People," as Helen Howe wrote, "were born into a tradition concerned with ethical living, plain living and high thinking."[7] It was considered improper to direct one's energies toward "trade" or commercial ventures. Also taboo was the conspicuous consumption or display of one's wealth. These were the children of a long and rich heritage—the Puritans, the Transcendentalists, and the Abolitionists. In the early twentieth century, many of them became Progressive reformers. In an increasingly industrialized and commercialized society, Fanny Quincy and her contemporaries were fast becoming an "extinct" breed.

"Like a proper Henry James Heroine," Fanny journeyed in Europe for two years. Soon after, she met and married Mark Howe in 1899, whereupon they withdrew on an extended "wedding journey." ("Gentle Americans," Helen Howe reminds us, "never embarked on as crude an interlude as a honeymoon.")[8]

Fanny's young husband Mark Anthony De Wolfe Howe (1864-1960) came from a Bristol, Rhode Island, family which enjoyed "un-Bostonian kisses" as well as a lively and robust vitality. Having decided upon a life devoted to "letters," Mark Howe attended Harvard University in preparation for a career as a gentleman scholar. During his lengthy and productive career, Mark A. De Wolfe Howe was characterized as a Boston "radical" as well as "the Dean of Boston Letters." A biographer and historian, Mark Howe passed his days working in the Boston Athenaeum, lunching with other Boston literati at the Tavern Club on Boylston Place, and receiving literary luminaries into his home. For his precise attention to historical detail and artful writing, he received many literary awards, including the Pulitzer Prize.

For most of their marriage, Fanny and Mark Howe resided at 26 Brimmer Street, Boston, a genteel, but not "too fashionable" address. Their six-storied home housed three Irish maids, a laundress, a French governess, and a kitchen staff which prepared meals "downstairs." It was to this splendid home that Maimie Pinzer's frequent letters arrived. During the summers, however, Maimie wrote Mrs. Howe at the Cotuit, Cape Cod, home. In Cotuit, the Howe family, along with other "old moneyed" families, quietly passed the summers engaged in sailing and other summer sports.

Among other subjects, the topic of money was carefully avoided in the Howe household. Trying to describe her parents' financial status, Helen Howe wrote,

According to the standard of the time and place, we lived modestly, but comfortably. Money was a subject that was taboo as being vulgar so I have no idea what my parents' income was at any time during their lives, although each had a little something with which to supplement Father's modest professional salary and income from writing.[9]

Although the Howes avoided the conspicuous consumption which marked the "new commercial interests," a refined and understated elegance characterized both their home and life style. Entertainment of friends, guests, and famous literati such as William and Henry James or Dr. Charles Putnam was set off by "delectable dinners." Oysters, fish mousse, filet mignon with mushroom sauce, homemade rolls, and meringues accompanied by fine champagnes and wines graced the Howe table.

Above all, the Howe home was marked by a literary atmosphere. As Fanny Howe observed, books seemed to multiply on the shelves and tables. On Sundays, Mark Howe read poetry aloud to his family. "As children we accepted the written word as a basic Fact of Life," Helen Howe recalled.[10] Even the family dog was named "Brownie" after Elizabeth Barrett Browning.

Like her husband, Mrs. Howe directed her energies toward literary pursuits. With her husband at work, her three small children at school, and her home efficiently run by servants, Mrs. Howe was a "lady of leisure" who chose to avoid the social occasions enjoyed by other women of her class. Instead, she spent a great deal of time preoccupied with writing. "I am sure," wrote her daughter, that Mother's most intense inner life came into focus when she was seated at her desk—placed between the windows of the "back parlor." It was seated there, her straight back not touching the back of her chair, that she poured herself out in letters.[11]

In addition to her frequent correspondence with Maimie and other friends and relatives, Mrs. Howe wrote essays and short stories which were published in the *Atlantic*, *Scribner's*, and the *New England Magazine* under the *nom de plume* of Wilmot Price or Catherine Russell. During the early years of her marriage, Mrs. Howe anonymously published her only novel, *The Opal*, to which Maimie refers many times in her letters. For the "Contributor's Club" of the *Atlantic*, Fanny Howe also wrote a series of anonymous essays which appeared in book form as *Notes about Nothing by Nobody*. Like many women writers during this period, Mrs. Howe was too modest and self-effacing to write under her own name. Under the name "Mrs. Grundy," she penned a column about the post-war generation in the *Atlantic*.

To those who knew Fanny, she *appeared* predictably Bostonian. "It was not only her speech which is recognizably Bostonian," recalled her daughter. "For all her wit and beauty and warmth of heart there is a certain Yankee crispness."[12] In portraying her mother, however, Helen Howe described Fanny as a melancholy and reserved woman known for her "acerbity and warmth, aloofness and passion, sensitiveness to the suffering of others and an icy barrier of reserve around her own." It was characteristic of Fanny to empathize deeply with those less fortunate than herself. "Mother's temperament," her daughter remembered, "was slanted far more toward feeling the sorrows of others as though they were her own."[13]

Fanny Quincy Howe, however, was not simply another charitable Bostonian lady motivated by a sense of *noblesse oblige*. A deep pessimism and sense of tragedy characterized this unusual woman's daily perceptions of the human condition. Although nominally a Unitarian, Mrs. Howe tended toward a "deeply ingrained agnosticism." Despite her secure background and environment, she experienced a "general distrust of life" and tended to perceive "the only reality in life as unhappiness—the stretches of happiness between being only parentheses." It was this particular sensibility that enabled Mrs. Howe to understand and gain the confidence of Maimie Pinzer.[14] In attempting to explain her mother's strong affinity to Maimie, Helen Howe aptly quoted Isak Dinesen, who wrote that "only the true aristocracy and the true proletariat of the world understand tragedy. The bourgeoisie of all classes deny it because it represents 'unpleasantness.' "[15] Though worlds apart, Mrs. Howe and Maimie became united by their common perception of the human condition.

Although they met only twice during the twelve years of their correspondence,[16] Mrs. Howe and Maimie came to respect and admire each other as genuine friends. Helen Howe accurately characterized their relationship:

What could have rippled on as a conventional correspondence on one side and mock gratitude on the other, flowered instead into an interchange between two remarkable women who grew in respect and affection for each other.[17]

Due to their frequent correspondence, Maimie and Mrs. Howe became increasingly important presences in one another's lives. Mrs. Howe, for example, discussed Maimie's struggle for survival with her family, genteelly censoring parts of Maimie's story: "Being the children of the Gentle Generation," Helen Howe recounted,

We children were kept in rather hazy ignorance as to exactly what kind of "hard time" Mother's offstage friend had had.[18]

Nevertheless, as a child Helen understood that

. . . as a woman she [Maimie] had "lived." The shape of that living was far removed from us not only geographically but in the depth of experience. It is equally certain in 26 Brimmer Street she also lived—as a vital and breathing Presence.[19]

For Maimie, Mrs. Howe became an equally if not more important presence in her life. Distrustful of Mrs. Howe's first letter, Maimie shrank from the possibility of personal rejection and condescending charity. Gradually, however, Maimie came to trust Mrs. Howe's concern and affection for her. As Maimie was herself aware, Mrs. Howe became a diary for her, the one person to whom Maimie could honestly relate her fears and anxieties, her struggle to survive without "going back." Although Mrs. Howe provided a significant amount of financial support to Maimie over the years, Maimie clearly valued her affection and friendship more than the gifts and assistance she received. Throughout the letters, there is abundant evidence of Maimie's deep emotional need for Mrs. Howe's acceptance, advice, and respect. Many of the letters, for example, were written late at night or early in the morning hours, when Maimie felt most troubled by unresolved problems. At times, the letters cover thirty to forty pages of lengthy introspective descriptions of her life in an "array of handwritings that would confound an expert, as each one seems to have been written by somebody else."[20]

These are not the letters of a manipulative charity seeker. On several occasions, Maimie admitted that she was tempermentally incapable of writing "duty" letters. "When I am worried," Maimie explained, "then I feel most that I want to write to you."[21] Trying to extricate herself from a past characterized by deceit and deception, Maimie was elated by the possibility of an honest relationship with Mrs. Howe. "You see," she wrote, in an early letter,

when I write you, I write everything, and mostly the things that trouble me and that is because I love you and don't stop to think whether it would be better to write this or that—but just keep on writing what is on my mind—things that I have always had to keep to myself for I never trusted any other woman.[22]

On another occasion, Maimie again explained that she was unable to censor her letters to Mrs. Howe. "I hesitate about calling a spade a spade and yet I enjoy telling you about my affairs as I would tell them to myself."[23] Thus, Mrs. Howe became an important outlet for Maimie's deepest feelings and concerns. Maimie even wondered whether she would be able to communicate the "truth" after their first meeting in person.

To Maimie, who felt unloved and unprotected by her own family, Mrs. Howe's letters meant a great deal. The correspondence provided her with a sense of self-importance, as well as a much needed source of nurturance and affection. Of Mrs. Howe's letters, Maimie wrote, "I unconsciously made them a live friend, and we, the letters and I, were in league against all these ugly conditions and the letters were the only things I discussed my hatred to of things."[24] Alienated from her family and frequently lonely in large cities, Maimie found Mrs. Howe's letters an important source of sustenance. "I did not eat lunch today to write this," Maimie wrote Mrs. Howe in one letter, "but to write you is like a good meal, especially when I get fat letters—they make me so happy, and are so satisfying."[25]

In 1922, the correspondence between Maimie and Fanny ended. After her marriage to Ira Benjamin in 1917, Maimie began writing less frequently to Mrs. Howe. With her husband available to provide the support, intimacy, and friendship which she had shared with Mrs. Howe, Maimie found less urgency to write as frequently.[26]

In most of her letters to Mrs. Howe, Maimie shared her financial worries, described her relationships with her family and recounted her frequent interventions into the lives of other "unfortunates." Maimie was aware, however, that the majority of her letters focused on her daily difficulties. Quite candidly, she admitted,

I have a faculty for wanting to tell you mostly things that make me appear a martyr & one whose lot is pitifully hard where in reality it isn't a bit so, only somehow I like to make you feel sorry for me and then to sympathize with me. . . . I notice I've only told the good things to the family and to you only the ugly things.[27]

Does Maimie's statement diminish the credibility of her tales of hardship? On the contrary, one must understand that Maimie was simply aware that she permitted herself to "beef" to Mrs. Howe about her real struggle for survival. On occasion, Maimie may have exaggerated her difficulties in order to gain needed compassion and sympathy. To the family who rejected her as a moral misfit, however, Maimie wished to present an image of success. It was to Mrs. Howe, then, that Maimie expressed her most authentic feelings—her anxieties and insecurities, as well as her hopes and her dreams.

An important reason for Maimie's transformation of Mrs. Howe into a mother, friend, and advisor was that her early youth was characterized by estranged and hostile familial relationships. Much of Maimie's early life is known through the descriptions in her correspondence. She was born in 1885 of immigrant Polish-Russian parents; and her family apparently enjoyed a modest degree of comfort during her early childhood in Philadelphia. Her home, for example, boasted two servant girls. At the age of thirteen, however, Maimie's life underwent a radical transformation. Her father, whom she apparently adored, was "brutally murdered." Neither the reasons for the murder nor the murderers were ever discovered.

The death of Maimie's father adversely affected the Pinzer's modest financial stability. Without her husband's income, Julia Pinzer faced the formidable task of providing for five children. The family economy of an upwardly mobile lower-class family was at best precarious during this period. The death or desertion of a working parent frequently plunged a family into a real state of poverty. Maimie's struggle for survival began at age thirteen.

Although she was an enthusiastic student, Maimie's studies ended when her mother ordered her to assume fulltime housework. Like many young women who later became prostitutes, Maimie deeply resented her mother's refusal to give her any spending money in return for the drudgery imposed upon her.[28] To improve her situation, Maimie began earning an independent wage at a department store.

It is important to note that many concerned reformers of the period regarded the department store as a steppingstone to prostitution.[29] There, poor young women became exposed to a materialistic splendor which they had never before known. In essence, such work often created rising expectations among the youthful saleswomen. A study of department store employees confirmed the fact that rising expectations often led saleswomen to prostitution: the highest paid saleswoman, not the lowest paid employee, more frequently turned to prostitution.[30]

As a department store "salesgirl," Maimie followed a typical pattern of behavior described by many reformers. She met and dated the young men who hung about much of the day, flirting with the young department store employees. Estranged from her mother, Maimie, like so many other young women of the period, sought emotional companionship with the young men she dated. After staying over at one young man's house for several days, Maimie returned home and was arrested on the request of her mother. Despite Maimie's desperate pleas, Julia Pinzer permitted her daughter to be placed in prison. Ironically, Maimie found herself in a prison to which her father had donated books in Yiddish for the benefit of Jewish prisoners.

Maimie's terrifying experience in prison, along with her painful recognition of her mother's hostility toward her, helped to crystalize a cynical perspective toward survival:

I was terrified and pleaded to be taken out of there. It was only after I permitted one of the men who seemed to be in charge at the time, to take all sorts of liberties with me that I was permitted to come out of the cell and I sat up for the rest of the night in the room where he too sat all night. The man was perhaps 50 or even older.[31]

Along with her mother, Maimie's uncle requested that Maimie be declared an incorrigible child. This was a particularly bitter experience for Maimie, since this uncle was "the same one who did me the first wrong when I was a tiny girl and any number of times since then."[32] As a result of the two adults' position, Maimie was sent to a Magdalenian home, "a mild sort of reform school for girls who have gone astray." There, Maimie passed her time teaching other inmates to read. As was typical of the period, however, she received no rehabilitative skilled training. More than likely, Maimie learned more about the subculture of prostitution than she had ever known before.

For four years after her release from the home, ages fourteen to eighteen, Maimie lived with a lover in Boston. At five feet six inches and 133 pounds, Maimie "cut" an attractive figure. Furthermore, she early learned how to parlay her attractiveness into a decent standard of living. During this period she also worked on the stage and as a nude model for art classes.

Due to infection, however, Maimie's left eye was removed, leaving her without eyelids and with an eye socket incapable of retaining a glass eye. Physically exhausted and wrecked from over thirty surgical operations, Maimie decided to marry Albert Jones, a laborer, in hopes of finding economic protection and security. Instead, Maimie and Albert, like many working-class couples, faced constant unemployment and consequent poverty. To support herself and her frequently unemployed husband, Maimie "dated" other men. When again hospitalized for morphine addiction, Maimie, with the encouragement of Mr. Welsh, began to consider a new direction for her life. It was at this point that Maimie's correspondence with Fanny Quincy Howe began.

An important theme weaving throughout Maimie's letters is her estranged relationship with her family. At Mr. Welsh's request, Maimie reluctantly agreed to see her mother after avoiding her for eleven years. Maimie's relationship with her mother, however, continued to be characterized by strongly ambivalent feelings:

I have ever since becoming freindly [sic] with my mother tried to make beleive [sic] there was some feeling of Love that she had for me and tho a great many things made me doubt it, still in a measure I pretended not to see or notice the things that made me doubtful & too, I'd always excuse anything that stuck out too prominently by saying "well she hasn't an idea how to be Motherly kind."[33]

At crucial moments when Maimie requested her mother's help, she was coldly refused. Maimie's anger and hurt, as well as her mother's rejection of her "unnatural" daughter, helped to create an extremely precarious relationship. "We get along most serenely," Maimie explained on one occasion, "because we never scratch thru the veneer."[34]

Characteristically, Maimie alternated between angry feelings toward her mother and doubts of her own self-worth. "When I look on this woman," Maimie confided to Mrs. Howe,

and I force myself to keep in mind that I was born of her, that I lay in her arms as a baby, nursed of her breast and was at one time her chief interest, I listen for a cry in my heart for her and there isn't any. I look at her and feel toward her only coldness. This I am sure is unnatural and I feel sure I am to blame. Don't think that I bear her any ill will for wrongs, fancied or real—I don't. I want so hard to love her—or even like her and I can't.[35]

The rest of Maimie's family hardly qualified as the stereotyped, close-knit, traditional Jewish-American family. Neither religious inter-marriage nor geographic mobility was unheard of among the children of Jewish immigrants. Nevertheless, this family was atypical in the extent of its religious departure from Hebrew traditions, physical separations from the family home, and unsupportive and distant relationships.

Rachel, Maimie's younger sister, suffered from tuberculosis and was a permanently institutionalized mental patient at an insane asylum. More frequently than other members in her family, Maimie visited and cared for this sister. At one point, she even considered returning to prostitution in order to resume her former support of her sister's needs.

Maimie's oldest brother, Sy, who scarcely knew Maimie, avoided all contact with her simply on evidence supplied by their mother. Partially blinded from a gun accident, Sy was nevertheless a successful businessman who combined the further odd achievements of being a devoted socialist married to a Catholic wife and living in Memphis, Tennessee. Maimie's younger brother, Sam, studied chemistry at the University of Pennsylvania. He then left the family to pursue his career as a chemist in California, where he converted to Christian Science. James, the only brother who continued to reside near his mother in Philadelphia, also married a Gentile wife and was the proprietor of a grocery store. Like his mother, James could not seem to forgive Maimie for her "past." Even when Maimie began school, assisted in his store, and demonstrated her endless devotion toward his children, James assaulted his sister with accusations and insults.

Unfortunately, Maimie's family was not unique in their lack of forgiveness. Many prostitutes during this era—particularly in Jewish, Irish and Italian families—were permanently rejected by their families for prostitution or even for overt sexual promiscuity. Disowned by their families, young women faced a difficult struggle for survival. Not surprisingly, their new friends in the bars and brothels of the tenderloin subculture offered an important source of emotional and economic support.[36]

Certainly, Maimie's family contributed little to the restoration of her self-esteem. Each time she returned to Philadelphia, Maimie experienced great apprehension at being held accountable, once again, for her "past." As always, the prostitute, and not the customer, suffered community ostracism.

As a victim of this double standard, Maimie was never forgiven by her family. On one occasion, she wrote Fanny, "they all hate me. I know I must be somehow at fault or why doesn't one of them like me?"[37] In despair, she added, "I've got three brothers, a mother and many uncles and aunts and I can't turn to one of them and my brother said he'd consider I'd done the family a kindness if I would get off the earth."[38] With the help of Mrs. Howe and Mr. Welsh, however, Maimie's self-esteem was repaired. At times she could then view her family with greater objectivity:

There is something so empty in their relationship with me that I think it folly for me to force it any longer. This condition exists not only with me but between themselves. Their love for each other (if it could be called that) is absolutely hollow.[39]

It is significant to note, however, that during several family crises, hostile factions of this "hollow" family converged to aid one another through illness and death. In particular, Maimie, a most forgiving and generous person, frequently rushed to help those who refused her similar assistance.

Without the help of her family, then, Maimie had to survive by her own efforts. Through her descriptions of this struggle we are drawn into the world of early twentieth-century American working-class women. There are many ways, of course, in which

Maimie is not "typical" of this particular social group. Maimie, for example, originally came from a modestly comfortable home in which learning, education, and upward mobility were emphasized. Furthermore, most of Maimie's family eventually achieved a degree of middle-class comfort. Maimie, too, received a substantial degree of financial assistance from Mrs. Howe and Mr. Welsh during desperate periods of poverty.

Yet, there are also important ways in which we may characterize Maimie as typical and representative of women in the lower classes during the same historical period. Most significantly, Maimie, like most working-class women, was forced to choose her means of survival from a position of socially structured powerlessness. She faced the same limited options of fulfilling her economic, social, and psychological needs: prostitution, marriage, and unskilled menial work. In a sense, then, through Maimie's life, we can observe the choices which working-class women confronted in their struggle for survival.

Maimie's first choice for survival was through prostitution. In their struggle to survive, many poor women chose to enter prostitution. I say "chose" because prostitutes were not and are not the passive victims of impersonal economic or social forces. From a variety of grim alternatives, women chose their means of survival. The reasons for their choices varied. Some came to "the life" out of sheer destitution. Many came out of rising expectations, or through a search for companionship. Others drifted into prostitution after "giving it away free for years" and "getting wizened up." Still others perceived prostitution as the best means of survival.[40]

Was Maimie a "typical" prostitute? Like others who entered prostitution, Maimie came from a "broken" home in which death, desertion, or divorce of parents caused a sudden disturbance in the family income. The sudden decline in family income frequently meant that a young woman like Maimie had to leave school to help support the family.[41] Maimie's family conflicts, too, were frequently echoed by interviewed prostitutes of the period.[42]

It is important to recognize that several forms of prostitution existed during the early twentieth century. During the late nineteenth century and the early years of the twentieth century, a system of openly tolerated red-light districts flourished in nearly every American city. There, bars and brothels created a virtual subculture of de facto legalized prostitution. Reflecting the different class status of American males, brothels and prostitutes appealed to differing specific clientele. A few exclusive "houses" offered sumptuous surroundings and special services to politicians and wealthy gentlemen for five to ten dollars. Other houses, serving a more middle-class clientele, charged one to two dollars a "trick." In the shabbiest tenement brothels, called "cribs," the oldest and least attractive prostitutes charged fifty cents for a few seconds' service. Streetwalkers, although less common than today, also inhabited such tenderloin areas.

In addition to these women of the red-light districts, there existed the so-called "occasional" prostitutes, women who supplemented their meagre wages or survived seasonal unemployment through sporadic involvement in prostitution. Such women drifted in and out of prostitution as economic survival demanded.[43]

Among such occasional prostitutes, there were women like Maimie, who often made their own private connections with gentlemen of means and managed to achieve a degree of upward mobility with a minimal amount of public visibility as a prostitute. In describing her past to Mrs. Howe, Maimie carefully distinguishes herself from other prostitutes. Once, Maimie assures Mrs. Howe that no public disgrace will occur if she returns to her former life:

...you need never fear that I would get into some public place; I don't have to do that; I wouldn't ever have to do that. As long as I have my mind and can use my tongue, such extreme measures are unnecessary. I never did that before, never did anything even 1/10 as low and consider that the last gasp. I never associated with low women—I don't think I ever met to talk to the second time a woman who was publicly known to live other than she should. I shun such people. Even girls who did no worse than I couldn't claim acquaintance with me.[44]

Such "class snobbery" was not unusual among prostitutes. Each group regarded the others as "trash" who lowered the profession.

A second and viable means of survival for young working-class women was marriage. During the early twentieth century, most young women regarded marriage as the most likely and respectable means of achieving economic security. Vicariously achieved security, however, could become a fragile achievement, with the withdrawal of the husband's economic support. Having viewed marriage as a method of achieving security, Maimie was deeply disappointed when Albert faced frequent unemployment. "When I married him," Maimie candidly explains,

I knew exactly what for—it was as a sort of anchor. I was living more or less uncleanly; I had lost my eye and weighed 96 lbs...and I reasoned it all out as one would a business proposition.[45]

Later, when Albert failed to supply Maimie with economic support, she came to recognize the futility of her marriage.

When I saw how useless trying to use him to earn any more than a bare, meagre livelihood was, I gave up in disgust and as I began to see that I was still attractive to men, I began to use what charms I might possess to make it possible to have a few of the luxuries which had become necessities.[46]

As far as Maimie was concerned, her loveless marriage, or "business proposition," seemed worse than her life as a prostitute. As she explained, all it gave her was the "respect of people I don't give a hoot for."

When Maimie rejected both her former life as a prostitute and her husband, she found her third choice as a working woman unbearable. Like other young women of the period, Maimie found it impossible to survive economically unless she lived with her family. Most prostitutes interviewed in this era were unskilled workers who, prior to entering prostitution, had earned a weekly wage of four to six dollars.[47] But authorities generally agreed that a woman living without a family needed a weekly wage of nine dollars.[48] How then was a woman without a family to survive? Both unions and employers refused to train women for the more highly paid skilled jobs. Industrialists justified their subsistence wages by arguing that most females worked only for "pin money" and were already supported by husbands or by families.[49] In fact, however, because of the great social pressure against women working outside the home, the overwhelming number of working women were those whose wages were their sole source of support or were an essential part of the family income. The 1916 United States Bureau of Labor Statistics *Summary Report on Women and Child Wage Earners*, in fact, found that women's wages represented from one-fourth to two-fifths of their families' entire income.[50]

Like other working-class women, Maimie's employment opportunities were bleak. Working-class women were concentrated into unskilled factory or domestic work. Factory employment meant long, monotonous and grueling work which frequently deteriorated a woman's health and spirit. It also meant extremely low pay without any prospects of upward mobility.[51]

Domestic service, in which a majority of young working women were employed, provided room and board in addition to a small salary of two to three dollars. The domestic servant, however, became a virtual slave to her employers' needs from sunrise to sundown. Many young prostitutes expressed their hatred of domestic work precisely because they possessed no time to join other young women and men in evening social activities.[52]

During the early years of Maimie's youth, office work was becoming an increasingly available form of female employment. In contrast with other forms of "women's work," office work offered better salaries and a greater chance for upward mobility. Such employment, however, required skilled training in typing or in stenography. Without these skills, Maimie found that she could not support herself on wages earned at the only jobs she could find—addressing envelopes or soliciting ads for companies.

Like many other prostitutes, Maimie refused to consider domestic and factory work as a way of earning her livelihood. Recognizing her intelligence, her desire for self-improvement, her ability to speak five languages—German, French, English, Yiddish, and Russian—Maimie sought employment consistent with her capabilities and her desire for a decent standard of living. Maimie saw nothing "respectable" about poverty and menial labor. "Respectability too often means a cheap room with cheap surroundings," she observed.

Maimie's feelings toward traditional "women's work" were echoed by many interviewed prostitutes who found prostitution far more lucrative as well as "easier" than other available forms of employment.[53] As a prostitute, a woman's earnings soared. On the average, prostitutes in American cities during the first fifteen years of the century earned from fifty to four hundred dollars a week.[54] As a reformer and crusader for better wages for women, William Stead observed, "The peculiar temptation of a woman is that her virtue is a realizable asset. It costs a man money to indulge in vice but for a woman it is money in the pocket."[55]

As an unskilled office worker, Maimie found little "money in the pocket"; she was exhausted and impoverished. Endless discussions of her financial difficulties fill her letters. As she anguished over the possibility of "going back," Maimie regarded her new "respectability" with a degree of cynicism. To Mrs. Howe she confided, "I just cannot be moral enough to see where drudgery is better than a life of lazy vice."[56] Tired of worrying about laundry bills and insufficient meals, she wrote, "I am absolutely honest with you....I can't stand this any longer. It is a struggle each day...."[57] "My trouble," she admitted, "is that I am a working girl who has lived like a 'lady' and it's hard to curb my desires and live as the working girl should."[58] Constantly in debt, disgusted with living from hand to mouth, she captured the plight of many young working-class women in the early twentieth century in a few eloquent lines: "When the seasons change as they are doing now—I feel the smallness of my life and I get terribly discouraged for need of many things makes me wonder if after all it is worthwhile to struggle as I do."[59]

Without her "new" friends' assistance and encouragement, Maimie might not have resisted the "easier" life she had formerly known. Their trust and expectations became a strong source of support and motivation for her. Nevertheless, Maimie even questioned the "respectability" of being a recipient of their charity. "It is too cheapening," Maimie confided to Mrs Howe.

I feel like some miserable parasite and for what? Just sustenance? It is not worth it especially since I frankly admit that I would love to live decently if I could in comfort...this life is a living Hell.[60]

When Maimie temporarily decided to abandon this poverty to live with her former childhood sweetheart, Ira Benjamin, she again explained her own views of "respectability." Ecstatic over her comfortable and aesthetic new environment, Maimie defended her decision to live with Ira while still married to Albert Jones:

I considered them [divorces] a lot of foolishness and a marriage ceremony the worst lot of cant I ever heard. That is my honest opinion and why bother about it? I could go deep into that subject to show why I have arrived at such an unusual conclusion but I will simply say because of observation of the various marriage contracts I know intimately about, my own, my sister's, my mother's and a host of others.[61]

Despite Maimie's defense of her unconventional behavior, however, she remained emotionally ambivalent. It is clear that, from her viewpoint, even a stable living arrangement with her friend Ira—who loved and respected her—was equivalent to prostitution. After a brief, idyllic interlude with Ira, Maimie left him, making a conscious decision to try to improve her chances for an independent livelihood. With tuition raised by several benefactors, she enthusiastically enrolled in a secretarial school. There, she hoped to offset the numerous obstacles hindering her employment opportunities—including her visual handicap—through new skills.

Ambitious and talented, Maimie encountered a great deal of cultural and institutionalized sexism in the business world. The obstacles she described accurately reflect the problems which working women daily faced in American business offices. Because of Maimie's eye patch, she was not sufficiently "attractive" for public relations work. On one occasion, Maimie used her writing talent to re-write a poorly worded form letter—for which her male boss then took public credit. In another situation, Maimie found herself sexually assaulted by an employer who demanded sexual submission in exchange for Maimie's paycheck. Such sexual blackmail was not an uncommon part of women's employment. Factory workers and domestic servants especially mentioned sexual assaults from their employers.[62]

Women's exclusion from the professions is also underscored in the failure of Maimie's friend Jean Holland, a talented writer, to find work as a journalist. Instead, Maimie and Jean ambitiously created their own business, the Business Aid Bureau of Montreal. Predictably, they encountered various forms of resentment and hostility from businessmen. "It seems," Maimie lamented at one point, "all the forces of the business world in Montreal are arranged against a woman developing a real business—in spite of that I am going to work up a real business that will be a big money maker."[63] Unfortunately, the economic chaos which followed Canada's entry into the First World War halted Maimie's initially successful business.

Despite Maimie's persistence and determination, she recognized that her goals and dreams were limited by her gender. In a moment of despair, Maimie voiced the envy that many women have experienced when limited by the fact of their sex: "I wish I was born a man," Maimie fantasizes. "I know what I'd do this morning. I'd button up my coat and jump on the tail end of a train and steal a ride to wherever it was going and then when I'd get there I'd stop to consider, 'What next?' "[64]

Unable to live out her fantasy, Maimie did create a niche for herself, a place where she was free to be "Maimie." After her business faltered, Maimie conceived of helping the "younger

Maimie's" who roamed Montreal's streets. With assistance from several benefactors, Maimie informally transformed her apartment into a halfway house for young, would-be and actual prostitutes.

It was not at all the first time that Maimie had assisted those in need of moral and practical support. Indeed, she was almost incapable of resisting any spoken or unspoken appeal for help. Her letters reveal her energetic intervention in the lives of the poor with whom she generously shared her own slender means.

Through Maimie's description of the young prostitutes who wandered in and out of her life, we are introduced to many of the problems which caused Maimie, as well as her "girls," to enter the "life." Severe economic need is clearly an omnipresent cause. Maimie also recognized, however—as did Jane Addams and other enlightened reformers—that many of these young girls suffered from overly strict families who prevented them from enjoying a normal social life and who also refused them a few cents to fulfill necessary adolescent vanities and fantasies.[65]

Maimie was similarly sensitive to the emotional deprivation from which many of these young girls suffered. Families marked by death, illness, impoverishment, desertion, and divorce did not seem particularly "deviant" to Maimie. She was equally understanding of the young women's search for emotional companionship with young men in their own neighborhoods. But their own families, once they had stigmatized the young women as "whores," frequently "locked them out."

Since many young women during this period encountered poverty and family conflict—particularly in the ethnic neighborhoods where Maimie lived—one must ask why some young women turned to prostitution while others did not. The answer, of course, is complex. Many factors caused women to turn to prostitution.[66] According to Maimie, an important deterrent to prostitution appeared to be the presence of a family or an adult who demonstrated loving and compassionate acceptance. Maimie, at least, felt this was true for herself and for many of the girls she helped. "I am sure I lacked love," Maimie recalled.

Many girls before they give themselves over to the sinful life, have the love of their parents, but people of the sort they spring from—as were my people—are singularly undemonstrative and often it isn't for lack of love, that the girls go astray, as much as for some evidence of it, which in the sinful life, they get in abundance—of a sort of course.[67]

In Maimie's opinion, then, the presence or absence of such demonstrated family love was a crucial factor in determining a woman's choice to turn to prostitution. On one happy occasion when Maimie felt enveloped by the warm atmosphere of the Arons family, she wrote,

Do you know it isn't a bit hard to stay "good"?—I used to admire the women who stuck to the "path" & wonder how they had the courage etc. but I found out it is all humbug. It's really only the way one gets started. The girls who have the right sort of parents no matter how poor or even ignorant they are have no difficulty in staying "good" because it is just how they get started.[68]

Maimie believed that her ability to reconstruct her own life was due to Mrs. Howe's affection and the high expectations of Mrs. Howe and other supporters. When her benefactors raised tuition for Maimie's secretarial lessons, Maimie declared that it was this demonstrated belief in her, rather than the tuition money, that changed her life-chances. "I feel this is the beginning of a new era," she wrote Mrs. Howe,

for I am not only being educated in a sense...but it will be the means of my being above living questionably or accepting favors. When I walk around town now I am a different person—for my future looms up large. It is a question with me why I did not do this long ago, for certainly at various times I have had large sums of money that would have amply paid for the lessons, but my life being such an irregular one, my desires were not the same as now. I had ambitious thoughts but they would come and go—for I had no one to help me. I did not have anyone that cared whether I earned my living one way or the other and I lacked sufficient backbone to want to do things just for myself.[69]

In looking back upon her life as a prostitute, Maimie was aware that prostitution had appeared to offer the promise of upward mobility. Both young men and women were exposed to the American ideals of economic and social upward mobility. Young girls, however, were not expected to fulfill this dream by their own efforts. Instead, most women expected to vicariously achieve the American Dream by marrying Horatio Alger and becoming Mrs. Horatio Alger.

Many women could and did accept their blocked mobility. On the other hand, many poor women more ambitious, rebellious, or talented than their sisters, found certain "illegitimate" means—such as prostitution—to achieve the socially "acceptable" goals of economic security and social status. That Maimie experienced constant frustration in the face of her limited economic and social mobility is clear from many of her letters.

I feel a gnawing discontent all the time because I see so much that I desire and I envy the women I see on the streets and I haven't even the courage to work in the office with the clerks there who are all so well dressed.[70]

Maimie's yearning for the "good life," however, was more than a matter of desiring proper dress. Very early she set out on a quest for self-improvement aimed at elevating her social surroundings and status:

I can recall distinctly that I was ever on the alert as a girl to learn the things that distinguished "nice" people from the other kind. I don't know just why I thought this desirable in as much as I didn't show any desire to live as "nice" people did—but I can recall hundreds of times when I would meet a man—son of "nice" people—& he, thinking to come down to the level of a girl of my sort would either express himself coarsely or in language that would not be considered good English by "nice" people—and I would take great pleasure in correcting him, thinking to show that it wasn't necessary to come down—I would come up. In this way, I learned much—often it wasn't their speech, sometimes their mannerisms at or away from the table—but I knew all this because I wanted to know and nothing escaped me.[71]

Through her contact with Mrs. Howe, Maimie increasingly aspired to a gentle and refined life. In describing a book she had read, Maimie wistfully wrote, "It has only everyday incidents in it but they are such lovely people. The kind I'd give half my life to mingle with just a while."[72]

Although Maimie dreamed of an unattainable future, she was not one to deny her "past." With characteristic candor, she avowed,

I am what I am. It sticks in one's throat at first to admit it, but it gets easier and when, as people sometimes say, "Oh but you're different," I get so tired and say I am not, it was just that I was just given a chance and I took it.[73]

As a result of her frankness and comprehension of the life of prostitutes, Maimie was remarkably successful in attracting and helping "younger Maimies" who inhabited her halfway house.

In contrast, most of the social reformers who financially assisted Maimie's "mission" viewed prostitutes' problems through a religious or moralistic perspective. Canadian reformers, like their counterparts in the United States, failed to understand the economic and social needs of prostitutes, and defined prostitution in terms of moral degeneracy.[74] Even before her mission work forced her to deal regularly with the typical attitudes of reformers, Maimie, like many other prostitutes, had felt occasional hostility toward her well-intentioned benefactors. For instance, she bristled at the fact that Mr. Welsh and social reformers such as Miss Outerbridge regarded her as their "work." She felt betrayed when her letters were openly shared and read aloud by such people. Angered at their breach of confidentiality, Mamie confided to Mrs. Howe, "It makes me feel as if I am Exhibit A."[75] Refusing to play the role of "an object of charity work," Maimie explained that she was unwilling to write "to persons that I feel are not interested in me as a person but in me as a question (if you know what I mean)."[76]

Mamie basically distrusted reformers' capacities to comprehend the perspective of the prostitute. Of Miss Outerbridge, for example, Maimie observed,

She has beautiful ideals and lives the life of the characters in the Sunday story books. . . .if I wrote her as I do you, she would think I had gone completely daft.[77]

Maimie also resented social workers' "impracticality," namely, their emphasis on religious conversion and their frequent indifference to the long-range economic difficulties faced by working-class women. Although an increasing number of reformers during the early twentieth century adopted an environmentalist perspective toward social problems, Maimie's particular benefactors were of the "rescue and redeem" religious variety. In essence, they asked her to relinquish her economic independence as a prostitute and to submit her "will"—to God, to the Church, to life with an alienated husband.

Maimie's differences with her "new" friends (with the exception of Fanny Howe) became increasingly obvious as she established her shelter for young prostitutes. Having lived the "sporting life," Maimie understood women's reluctance to be labeled as moral deviants. When her financial backers wanted to name Maimie's shelter, "The Montreal Mission For Friendless Girls," she wrote to Mrs. Howe, in utter disgust,

I thank God you are not friendless, but if you were—and were 18 years old—you would no more admit it than any girl does. The kind of girl—the human jelly fish—that is willing to be classed as "friendless" I haven't much time for....and I'd like to see the place I'd have walked into when I was a young girl that was known to be a haven for friendless girls.[78]

Maimie continually resisted the social workers' attempts to transform her informal and loosely organized apartment into a more religious and impersonal institution. Quite emphatically, Maimie insisted that "...prisons and institutions for reform should not be tolerated by Christian people."[79] Confident of her own attitudes and behavior with prostitutes, Maimie vigorously defended herself:

I would prefer not to write this for it sounds ridiculously egotistical but I believe I am correct and it is, that I can do more, given the time, with a girl who is on the street, toward getting her to go to work than any 10 ladies whose methods of procedure is along the lines laid down by Rescue Workers.[80]

In effect, Maimie treated prostitutes as she wished she had been received ten years earlier. In one memorable passage, Maimie revealed her means of gaining prostitutes' trust. In approaching a young and ailing syphilitic prostitute named Lillian, Maimie introduced herself in the following manner:

Come now Lillian, tell me what you are thinking? Well, you needn't tell me. I know. You are thinking that I am going to pull a long face & ask a million questions and then read you a tract and preach a little, leave my card and tell you that I'll come again tomorrow. But you're all wrong. I'm going to do nothing of the sort. In the first place, I am Maimie Jones, I don't own a card. I'm not connected with the Charity Organization, I don't pull long faces and I hate tracts and lectures myself tho Goodness knows I've had enough of them. Besides I laugh at everything and chatter everyone to death. I don't ask questions either because I know more than you do why you are sick, alone, etc. because I've been all that myself.[81]

With her emphasis on non-institutionalized, personal interaction and her frank admission of her own past, Maimie became a social worker years ahead of her own time. Fully fifty years before the development and adoption of what has come to be known in social work practice today as "peer counseling," Maimie expounded this concept in her letters and implemented it in her approach to the young women whom she endeavored to reclaim from prostitution.

In addition to Maimie's observations of the subculture of prostitution, her letters also provide continuous commentary about the society in which she lived. Indeed, Maimie's letters are a unique source of American social history. Characteristically, Maimie reminds us of the ways in which historical "dry" facts affected the daily lives of ordinary people, such as an influenza epidemic or the closing of the red-light districts. Due to the passing of the famous anti-trust laws, for example, Maimie's employers were forced to close their office. As a result of Canada's entry into the First World War, Maimie's own business was forced to close. A water famine and war-time riots in Canada similarly reveal the often neglected "homefront" history of the war. Even more significantly, the continual seasonal layoffs faced by Maimie's first husband and many working women underscore an important and frequently neglected aspect of labor history.

Because of her Jewish background, Maimie's letters also provide intimate views of the Jewish immigration and acculturation experience in early twentieth-century America. Despite Mr. Welsh's attempts to bring Maimie into the Christian fold, Maimie is as unmistakably "Jewish" as Mrs. Howe is "Bostonian." Throughout her letters, Maimie describes important Jewish rituals which commemorate birth, betrothal, and death. While living in Canada, she befriended several members of the Montreal Jewish community. As a result, her letters provide a unique portrait of their cafe culture, Jewish customs, and community life.

In addition to their obvious historical significance, Maimie's letters are also important for their literary value. Although her formal education ended at age thirteen, Maimie clearly had the ability of a gifted writer.

On occasion, Maimie's letters read like a historical novel in which Maimie is the main protagonist. Readers will delight in Maimie's uncanny ability to capture the precise atmosphere of an event or the perfect expression of an individual's personality and values. By focusing on significant and symbolic details, Maimie printed indelible images of the people she encountered. In describing two women with whom her first husband had consorted, she writes:

They are of a good sort the women but horribly plebian, [sic] big knotty fingers with large rings & yellow diamonds and nails bitten almost to the quick with huge pompadours and big hips and all that goes to make up the ordinary sort of women who have a little money enough to take them out of the class of wash woman.[82]

In her last letter, Maimie evokes an entire atmosphere when she writes that she and Ira are staying at a hotel "patronized by big, fat, Jewish ladies and their thin nervous husbands."[83]

In another memorable letter, Maimie created an unforgettable portrait of Mary Antin, a well-known novelist of the period. After meticulously describing the furnishings and atmosphere of the writer's home, Maimie focused on the novelist herself. In one of her finest descriptions of the many people who parade through these letters, Maimie sarcastically writes,

Her smile seemed to break her face all up & did not seem real & one felt instinctively that the smile would not just fade away naturally but that as soon as she released the string, the features would snap back to the same sharp look we saw at the door and sure enough it did.[84]

In addition to Maimie's ability to perceive and express human foibles, she is also an extremely gifted storyteller. Her tale of "Brownie" (a neighborhood dog), her powerful recreation of her experience in jail, and her episodic accounts of a variety of adventures and misadventures are characterized by superb suspense, absorbing plots, and vivid realizations of the main characters.

As active writers themselves, both Fanny and Mark Howe admired Maimie's special gift for writing. After several years of correspondence, in fact, they asked Ellery Sedgwick of the *Atlantic* to consider publishing Maimie's letters. Sedgwick was clearly impressed with both the style and content of Maimie's letters. "They are most remarkable," he wrote in a letter dated March 10, 1915, to the Howes. "Her clear critical insight is highly exceptional, and, of course, quite outside of the inherent pathos of the narrative, her gift for telling a straightforward story is most captivating to a reader."

Despite his admiration for Maimie's writing, however, Ellery Sedgwick decided against publishing the letters. In his own words, he felt the effect "on Maimie herself would be unfortunate." Furthermore, he worried that "a considerable minority of readers would misinterpret the magazine's motives in printing the letters, and I am inclined to think (although I am not sure) that their appearance in the *Atlantic* would be a blow not to our circulation, but to our influence."[85]

Although the Howes' attempt to publish Maimie's letters failed, Mrs. Howe continued to encourage Maimie's writing talent. Periodically, Maimie considered expanding her literary pursuits. To one of her roommates, she confided, "I expect some day to write short stories successfully tho to date I have never tried to write one single word."[86]

Given Maimie's gift for writing, one is tempted to imagine the literary career she might have pursued and enjoyed had she lived under different circumstances. Accustomed to a daily struggle for survival, Maimie could barely imagine such a life. When Mrs. Howe suggested that Maimie write her autobiography, Maimie responded,

I had wanted to write about the possibility of writing my autobiography as you suggested but as I couldn't seem to feel sure of my own opinion on the subject, I didn't write. There seems so many reasons why I could not do it. For instance the little time, even if it only took 15 min. a day is so hard to spare. There are so many tasks—stockings always to be darned, letters to write, sometimes work for the office—that I don't feel I could accomplish much if I did start. I really feel I could write it, if I could write it a bit at a time and maybe I will try it and if it goes easy, keep on with it.[87]

Maimie apparently never wrote an intentional biography, probably for the reasons she outlined above. Nevertheless, Maimie's letters—written "a bit at a time"—do in fact constitute a kind of autobiography. As an episodic narrative of her life history, Maimie's letters contain many of the elements of a conventional autobiography—as well as of the epistolary novel.

However we may classify them, Maimie's letters eminently succeed in re-creating the Life and Times of Maimie Pinzer Benjamin. Most strikingly, Maimie created an unforgettable character in her "autobiography": herself. With unusual candor, sharp observation, and insightful introspection, Maimie presents a magnificently multi-dimensional *persona*.

Maimie's *persona* was rich in contradictions and complexities. Manipulative and cagey, Maimie was also generous to a fault. At times sentimental, she was also a realist who could perform gruesome and odious tasks. She was at once a sympathizer with the downtrodden and an instinctive aristocrat, genuinely offended— sometimes to the point of snobbery—by the manners of the lower classes. "I find," she wrote, "that instinctively I avoid being where I have to mix and mingle with the half-bred, the half-souled and half-educated—they seem to offend my spirit."[88] Yet this same "offended spirit" actively, selflessly gave of herself to syphilitic prostitutes and other poor and diseased friends. Most significantly, Maimie never ignored the needs of the "half-bred and half-educated" as she sought to improve her own life.

In roughly the first half of the correspondence, Maimie again and again presents herself as a self-effacing, childlike seeker of advice and acceptance. As her "autobiography" unfolds, however, Maimie gradually changes, growing in confidence and self-respect. By the end of the letters, the "old" Maimie has nearly disappeared, replaced by a strong woman with a dignity all her own. Maimie was herself very much aware of this growth. In her younger days, as she told Mrs. Howe, she had refused to take full responsibility for her own actions, even assuming an alternate personality, the childishly amoral "Mimi," on whom she blamed her "sporting life." "Mimi," Maimie explained to Mrs. Howe,

was supposed to be another personality of mine and I got so, that I found it quite convenient to heap on Mimi all the *dirty* contemptible things that Maimie did....And now I realize that was all bally rot....I decided "Mimi" was a sloppy excuse for a weak kneed individual, and I've never stood for another one of those silly excuses for doing wrong....I alone was to blame for anything I did.[89]

Unfortunately, Maimie's story ends with her last letter in 1922 at age thirty-seven. There is no information available to document the remainder of her life. Having suffered a miscarriage, Maimie last appears in Chicago with her second husband, Ira Benjamin. Still seeking to fulfill her unrealized potential, Maimie confides to Mrs. Howe that she wants to return to school "to take up the study of something." Although she expresses some insecurity about her ability to pursue a formal education, her maturity and intelligence are altogether evident. With these final words of wisdom: "I know what I have yet to know," Maimie closes the last page of her "autobiography."

As the central figure of her "autobiography," Maimie is an extraordinary and fascinating individual. Her search for understanding reveals a sensitive and spirited intelligence assaulted by the traumas of twentieth-century urban life. "I felt so alone and useless in this big world," she wrote in a moment of existential despair.[90] With her sense for the absurd and her gentle humor, however, Maimie avoided constant self-pity or perpetual despair.

Maimie's letters will invite laughter and tears, and perhaps a sense of hope. Through her letters she affords us a view not only of her own struggle, but that of obscure people like herself, to whom she has given life, breath, and voice. Like Maimie, they impress themselves upon us as they endure—and even sometimes overcome. At the end, we know that they and Maimie, her life and her world, have become a permanent and sustaining aspect of our own experience.

Ruth Rosen
Berkeley, California
August, 1976

1. The majority of historical studies on prostitution have tended to be weak in conceptualization as well as anecdotal, and span nearly all of human history. Examples are Vern Bullough, *The History of Prostitution* (New Hyde Park, New York: University Books, 1964), George Scott, *History of Prostitution* (London: T. Werner Laurie, 1936), Ivan Block, *Die Prostitution*, 2 vols. (Berlin: L. Marcus, 1912).

For a critique of sociologists' writings about prostitution, see Marcia Millman, "The History of the Sociology of Prostitution" (paper presented to the Second Berkshire Conference on the History of Women, October 27, 1974).

The following are some of the better articles which have appeared in recent years which add to a more sophisticated knowledge of society and prostitution: Robert Riegel, "Changing American Attitudes Towards Prostitution, 1800-1920," *Journal of the History of Ideas* 24, pp. 437-452; Egal Feldman, "Prostitution: The Alien Woman and the Progressive Imagination, 1910-1915," *American Quarterly* 30 (Summer, 1967).

For insightful work on prostitutes' lives themselves, see Judith Walkowitz, "'We are Not Beasts of the Field': Prostitution and the Campaign Against the Contagious Diseases Act, 1869-1886" (doctoral dissertation, University of Rochester, New York, 1973-74); Kate Coleman, "Carnal Knowledge: A Portrait of Four Hookers," *Ramparts* 10, No. 6 (December, 1971).

2. See, in particular, the work of Carol Smith Rosenberg, "Puberty to Menopause: The Cycle of Femininity in Nineteenth-Century America" in *Clio's Consciousness Raised*, ed. by Mary Hartman and Lois Banner (New York: Harper and Row, 1975), and her recent article, "The Female World of Love and Ritual: Relations between Women in Nineteenth-Century America," *Signs* (Autumn 1975), pp. 1-31.

3. "The Maimie Letters" were donated to the Arthur and Elizabeth Schlesinger Library on the History of Women in America, Radcliffe College, by the late Helen Howe, the daughter of the recipient, Fanny

Quincy Howe. The source of *The Maimie Papers* is the typescript of the handwritten "Maimie Letters." See "Acknowledgements" and "Textual Note."

4. Such typescripts or published documents were frequently passed around in suffragist circles to elicit sympathy for the anti-prostitution campaign of the Progressive era, 1900-1917, as well as to warn young girls of the hazards of unvirtuous behavior. Two typical examples I have encountered are Lydia Taylor, *From Under the Lid, An Appeal to True Womanhood* (n.p., 1913), and Margaret Von Staden, "My Story," Harriet Laidlaw Papers, Schlesinger Library, Cambridge, Massachusetts.

5. Maimie specifically denied that the loss of her eye was related to syphilitic infection (Letter 97, p. 270), but gave no alternate explanation in her abundant references to her handicap. Similarly, the letters offer no clue to the genesis of her addiction to morphine. However, since the operation on Maimie's eye was the first of thirty-one surgeries, and since it is possible to become addicted to morphine after weeks of its administration for medical care, it is not unlikely that Maimie became an addict through her hospital experiences. On the other hand, the use of drugs by prostitutes was common, then as now.

6. Helen Howe, *The Gentle Americans: Biography of a Breed* (New York: Harper and Row, 1965).

7. *Ibid.*, p. 166.

8. *Ibid.*, p. 80.

9. *Ibid.*, p. 98.

10. *Ibid.*, p. 11. The three Howe children were frequently mentioned in Maimie's letters. Quincy Howe (1900-1977), the eldest, became a writer, author of numerous books including *England Expects Every American To Do His Duty* (1937), *Blood Is Cheaper Than Water* (1939), *The World We Lost* (vol. I, 1949; vol. II, 1953); an editor of *Living Age*, editor-in-chief of *Atlantic Monthly* and, for many years, of Simon and Schuster; and a news analyst for CBS (1942-1950). Helen Huntington Howe (1905-1975), with whom Maimie exchanged letters, became a writer, her books including, besides *The Gentle Americans*, *We Happy Few* (1940), *The Whole Heart* (1943), *The Flies of Autumn* (1959). She also wrote character sketches which she performed in theaters in New York and London. Mark De Wolfe Howe (1906-1967), a graduate of Harvard Law School, served as secretary to Justice Oliver Wendell Holmes and as professor of law at Harvard and the University of Buffalo. He edited the *Holmes-Pollock Letters* (1941), *Touched With Fire: Civil War Letters and Diary of Oliver Wendell Holmes* (1946), *Readings in American Legal History* (1949), the *Holmes-Laski Letters* (1953), and Holmes' *The Common Law* (1963).

11. *Ibid.*, p. 263.

12. *Ibid.*, p. 5.

13. *Ibid.*, p. 274.

14. For detailed characterization of Fanny Quincy Howe, see *ibid.*, pp. 268, 277, 343.

15. *Ibid.*, p. 277.

16. Although Helen Howe believed that her mother and Maimie met only once, Maimie mentioned in her letters that she was visited twice by Mrs. Howe—once in Philadelphia and once in Wilmington, Delaware.

17. *The Gentle Americans*, p. 150.

18. *Ibid.*, p. 156.

19. *Ibid.*

20. *Ibid.*, p. 150.

21. *The Maimie Papers*, Letter 55, p. 150. Page numbers as given here refer to this volume. Quotations in this introduction, however, are unedited, conforming to the typescript of "The Maimie Letters" in the Schlesinger Library. See "Textual Note."

22. *Ibid.*, Letter 20, p. 49.

23. *Ibid.*, Letter 6, p. 9.

24. *Ibid.*, Letter 27, p. 82. Partially unpublished.

25. *Ibid.*, Letter 72, p. 188.

26. *Ibid.*, Letter 137, p. 403.

27. "The Maimie Letters," Letter 71. Partially unpublished.

28. In this introduction, there will be many comparisons made between Maimie and other prostitutes of the period in which she lived and wrote. This comparison is based on a study of over two thousand prostitutes who lived during the Progressive era (1900-1917), a period in which reformers attempted to close down the openly tolerated red-light districts in American cities. The study, entitled "The Lost Sisterhood: An Analysis of the Causes of Prostitution," is a chapter from Ruth Rosen, "The Lost Sisterhood: Prostitution During the Progressive Era," (doctoral dissertation, University of California, Berkeley, 1976). The study, based on surveys conducted by thirty-six vice commissions, created a profile of the background and consciousness of prostitutes, as well as the causes which prompted them to enter prostitution. It is impossible here to cite all the primary sources used to compare Maimie's particular life with those cited in the study. Interested readers should consult the original study for the entire list of primary sources consulted.

29. See, for example, Committee of Fourteen in New York, "Department Store Investigation Report of the Sub Committee" (New York, 1915).

30. *Ibid.*

31. *The Maimie Papers*, Letter 75, p. 193.

32. *Ibid.* One assumes from this statement that Maimie was in some way sexually assaulted by this uncle.

33. "The Maimie Letters," Letter 72. Partially unpublished.

34. *The Maimie Papers*, Letter 93, p. 251.

35. *Ibid.*, p. 250.

36. A well-known novel which depicts this common occurrence is Stephen Crane's *Maggie*, published in 1893. Social workers, too, found that families disowned "wild" daughters.

37. *The Maimie Papers*, Letter 97, p. 270.

38. *Ibid.*

39. *Ibid.*, Letter 85A, p. 227.

40. For a detailed discussion and data on prostitutes' reasons for

entering prostitution, see George Kneeland, *Commercialized Prostitution in New York* (1913 Reprint; Montclair: Patterson and Smith Reprint, 1969), pp. 235, 251, 259; Fred Johnson, *The Social Evil in Kansas* (Kansas, 1911), p. 16; Vice Commission of Chicago, *The Social Evil in Chicago* (Chicago: Gunthrop Warren, 1911), pp. 167, 173; *Report and Recommendations of the Bridgeport Vice Commission* (Bridgeport: 1916), pp. 76-77.

41. In comparing my own study of two thousand prostitutes with the women workers profiled in the *Report on Condition of Women and Child Wage Earners in the United States*, 61st Congress, Senate Document, no. 645 (Washington, D.C.: Government Printing Office: 1911), I found that a statistically significantly higher percentage of prostitutes came from such broken families.

42. Hartford Vice Commission, *Report of the Hartford Vice Commission* Reprint (Hartford: Connecticut Woman Suffrage Association, 1913), p. 57; Al Rose, *Storeyville, New Orleans, being an authentic, illustrated account of the notorious red-light district* (Alabama: University of Alabama Press, 1974), p. 155; Illinois Senate Vice Committee, *Report of the Illinois Senate Vice Committee* (Chicago: Allied Printing Company, 1916), p. 328.

43. See Rosen, "The Political Economy and Subculture of Prostitution," in "The Lost Sisterhood."

44. *The Maimie Papers*, Letter 27, p. 77.

45. *Ibid.* Letter 21-22, p. 51.

46. *Ibid.*, p. 52.

47. United States Department of Labor, Bureau of Labor Statistics, *Summary Report on Condition of Women and Child Wage Earners in the United States* (Washington, D.C.: Government Printing Office, 1916), pp. 218-224; *Report of the Senate Vice Committee* (Illinois), p. 34.

48. *Ibid.*, p. 921.

49. Elizabeth Beardsley Butler, *Women and The Trades: The Pittsburgh Survey Findings in Six Volumes*, Paul Kellogg, ed. (New York: Charities Publications, 1909), p. 346; *Report of the Senate Vice Committee* (Illinois), p. 34.

50. *Summary Report*, p. 84.

51. See *Summary Report* for greater detail of women's involvement in factory work.

52. Helen Campbell, *Prisoners of Poverty* (Boston: Roberts Brothers, 1887), p. 226; Robert Smuts, *Women and Work in America* (New York: Schocken, 1971), p. 90; *Report on the Senate Vice Committee* (Illinois), p. 818.

53. Rosen, "The Lost Sisterhood," p. 282.

54. *Report and Recommendations for the Wisconsin Legislative Committee to Investigate the White Slave Traffic and Kindred Subjects* (Madison: 1914), p. 23; *Report of the Hartford Vice Commission*, p. 53; Kneeland, *Commercialized Prostitution*, p. 231.

55. William Stead, *If Christ Came to Chicago* (New York: Living Books, 1964), p. 255.

56. *The Maimie Papers*, Letter 2, p. 4.

57. *Ibid.*, Letter 21-22, p. 56.

58. *Ibid.*, Letter 52, pp. 141-42.

59. *Ibid.*, Letter 67, p. 179.

60. *Ibid.*, Letter 25, p. 67.

61. *Ibid.*, Letter 27, p. 81.

62. *Report of the Hartford Vice Commission*, p. 51.

63. *The Maimie Papers*, Letter 83, p. 219.

64. *Ibid.*, Letter 21-22, p. 50.

65. See Jane Addams, *A New Conscience and An Ancient Evil* (New York: Macmillan Company, 1912), as well as Rosen, "The Lost Sisterhood," p. 282.

66. For a study of the answers of over two thousand prostitutes to the question of why they entered prostitution, see Rosen, "The Lost Sisterhood," p. 282.

67. *The Maimie Papers*, Letter 113, p. 333.

68. *Ibid.*, Letter 52, pp. 142-43.

69. *Ibid.*, Letter 43, p. 109.

70. *Ibid.*, Letter 56, p. 156.

71. *Ibid.*, Letter 98, p. 277.

72. "The Maimie Letters," Letter 39. This letter is not included in *The Maimie Papers*.

73. *The Maimie Papers*, Letter 126A, p. 373.

74. For an insightful study of Toronto reformers as well as a profile of the women who worked as prostitutes, see Lori Rotenberg, "The Wayward Worker: Toronto's Prostitute at the Turn of the Century," in Janice Acton, Penny Goldsmith, Bonnie Shephard, eds., *Women at Work: Ontario, 1850-1930* (Toronto: Canadian Women's Educational Press, 1974).

75. "The Maimie Letters," Letter 91. Not included in *The Maimie Papers*.

76. *The Maimie Papers*, Letter 104, p. 285.

77. *Ibid.*, Letter 9, p. 22.

78. *Ibid.*, Letter 118B, p. 340.

79. *Ibid.*, Letter 93, p. 257.

80. *Ibid.*, p. 253.

81. *Ibid.*, Letter 122, p. 355.

82. "The Maimie Letters," Letter 32. Not included in *The Maimie Papers*.

83. *The Maimie Papers*, Letter 140, p. 416.

84. *Ibid.*, Letter 58, pp. 161-62.

85. Letter from Ellery Sedgwick to Mrs. Mark A. De Wolfe Howe, March 10, 1915, Helen Howe Papers, Schlesinger Library; also partially quoted in Howe, *The Gentle Americans*, p. 150.

86. *The Maimie Papers*, Letter 71, p. 187.

87. *Ibid.*, Letter 75, p. 199.

88. *Ibid.*, Letter 54, p. 149.

89. *Ibid.*, Letter 126A, pp. 372-73.

90. *Ibid.*, Letter 73, p. 189.

TEXTUAL NOTE

The Schlesinger Library typescript of the handwritten "Maimie Letters" runs to 934 pages, including 143 letters, all but nine of them Maimie's. For the purposes of this volume, we have cut 270 typescript pages, including twenty-four letters.[1] It was a painful operation, but one we believe Maimie Pinzer would have understood, and approved.

Very early in the history of this undertaking, we began to regard Maimie as a person who had become, through the legacy of her letters, the writer she aspired to be. The obstacles to printing the complete letters, at first financial, ended by seeming an opportunity to give Maimie—like other published writers—the advantages of an editorial blue-pencil. For the letters, while they do "constitute a kind of autobiography," were not written for publication. Thus, in the course of them, there is thematic over-repetition; there are details of household budgeting that would strain a reader's attention, references to some persons and events that have no context, and errors of the kind many literate writers make in informal correspondence.

Our editorial aim has been to present those letters and parts of letters that are both important as social history and, where possible, "best" from a literary standpoint. In addition, Maimie's personal fortunes and history, the complexities of her relationships with her family, with those she befriended and those who befriended her—above all, the changing nature of her attachment to Fanny Howe—had to be preserved. We were also concerned that the impressive development of Maimie's thought and character over the years be clearly evident. Finally, we wanted continuity in the "story." Remarkably, in spite of gaps of months, even years, in the extant letters, the 119 presented here required no editorial bridges. Where time-gaps occur, they only serve to heighten that suspense Maimie herself often deliberately created, with no loss in continuity.

Less successful was the attempt to present in print all parts of the letters that have literary worth. This is in large part due to Maimie's fecundity as a story-teller. The correspondence is richly strewn with vignettes, dramas, mini-histories tossed out by Maimie in mid-passage. Where they unduly interrupted the progress of the "autobiography," we were forced to part with them.

Beyond the cutting, some additional discrepancies between this volume and the Schlesinger typescript require comment.

Because some letters have been eliminated, the numbering of the letters in this volume is not unfailingly consecutive. Letters bear the numbers given to them in the Schlesinger typescript. Dates in this volume, however, do not always correspond: some dates have been corrected on the basis of internal evidence that conflicts with the typescript, while missing dates have been supplied on a best-guess basis, also from internal evidence.

We agreed that the published text should be conventional in its approach to punctuation and spelling, although we have left some few anachronisms untouched, for the sake of conveying the flavor of the period, and have preserved some informalities common to personal correspondence—such as abbreviations—as authentic ear-marks of this *genre*.[2] Maimie's grammatical lapses were rare; such as they were, they have been allowed to stand, unaccompanied by the distraction of *sic*.

It was, however, in part to avoid distracting the reader, in part to avoid enormous proofreading difficulties, but above all to do justice to Maimie herself that we decided to regularize punctuation and spelling. The punctuation of Maimie's letters to Mrs. Howe is functional—only rarely does error interfere with immediate understanding—while Maimie's command of spelling, especially considering the ambitiousness of her vocabulary, was somewhat better than that of today's average college graduate. Among her misdemeanors, she was fairly consistent in confusing the possessive *its* with contractual *it's*, as well as in reversing *e*'s and *i*'s (*recieve, beleive, shreik*)—although Mrs. Howe quickly became and always remained "my dear *friend*." But while the hasty compositions to her dear, understanding Mrs. Howe contain more errors than are reflected in the present text, the few extant letters that Maimie intended "for show" are virtually without a slip. It was the painstakingly composed, typewritten letters—such as that reporting on the mission's first year, and those models of care sent to the young Helen Howe—that made us feel that an uncorrected text would be unfair to an author who so evidently respected formal rules of usage.

In no case have we altered the order of words, sentences, or paragraphs, although we have made a few changes in the breaking of paragraphs. The rare insertion of a word or phrase is indicated by brackets, as is standard; and deletions, except those at the beginnings and closes of letters, are indicated by ellipsis points, also standard. The only liberty occurred in dealing with some of Maimie's series of compound-complex sentences strung together with the conjunctions *and, so, but*. The extent of the tampering was the placement of a period and the capitalization of the conjunction that followed. Maimie's original form comes off well in single letters; it seemed taxing when encountered throughout an entire volume.

Many of the "characters" in Maimie's letters appear here under fictitious names—beginning, not unexpectedly, with Maimie Pinzer Benjamin herself. Street and apartment numbers have been excised. The changes here are identical with changes made in the typescript at the Schlesinger Library.

This book is perhaps more remarkable for what has not been changed than for what has been edited or disguised. If Maimie's gifts as a writer called for only the lightest of editing, so, too, have we presented the struggle of her social sensibilities without varnish. That struggle was an upward one, but incomplete in ways that may occasionally offend readers. We have not attempted to pretty up Maimie's social attitudes by excising her slighting references to Jews and blacks. Her bias against blacks was perfunctory, without emotional investment. But toward Jews—at least, toward those Jews who lacked "refinement" and charity—she was unfriendly: as she felt this "class" of Jews had been to her. On the other hand, she fully identified herself as a Jew, taking pride in Jewish cultural and intellectual achievement, and the tenderest care of such poverty-stricken "fine" Jews as the Arons and the Goldsteins. We are tantalized by the suggestion, in her final letter of 1922, that by then her bias against "fat Jewish ladies" had become perfunctory, while her tenderness had grown to encompass the Filipino hotel porter to whom she was giving English lessons. Where did the amazing growth of this amazing woman end?

Or—was she amazing? Perhaps it is another kind of bias, growing out of the historical ignorance in which we have all lived, that makes us think so. How many other poor and working-class people—women especially—may there have been of Maimie's caliber, whose passions and opinions historians, scholars, editors have not seen fit to consult, encourage, or preserve? The inquiry into those vanished lives is only now beginning. We would do well to be aware, with Maimie, of what we have yet to know.

Sue Davidson

1. Following are the letters not included in this volume: numbers 32, 33, 39, 59, 60, 64, 65, 74, 78, 86, 89, 91, 94, 95, 101, 102 (void), 108, 112, 114, 116, 118A, 119, 123, 128, 139. Three letters not written by Maimie are included: they are numbers 63, 121, 125.

2. Like most letter writers, Maimie was not consistent in her use of abbreviations. We have preserved the inconsistencies in her abbreviations of months and of days of the week, except in the headings of the letters.

A number of idiosyncratic capitalizations have also been allowed to stand; however, it is often difficult to distinguish lower-case from capital letters in Maimie's hand. When in doubt, we choose standard forms.

Our text also reflects Maimie's nearly unvarying choice of figures rather than words for dollar amounts and other numerals.

CHRONOLOGY

July 14, 1885: May (Maimie) Pinzer born, Philadelphia, to Julia and Morris Pinzer.

1897-1898: Morris Pinzer is "brutally murdered." Survived by wife and five children. Maimie is made to leave high school in order to help keep house. Frequent, violent quarrels with Julia.

Maimie goes to work as a saleswoman at a downtown department store, begins going out with "boys." Following several days and nights away from home, she is arrested upon the complaint of her mother and an uncle who had molested Maimie sexually when she was a child. Maimie goes first to prison, then to Magdalen Home for wayward girls.

1899: Released from Magdalen Home. Returns to department store work. Attends business college for three weeks. Makes a decisive break with her mother.

1899-1903: Goes to Boston with lover Frank Sloan. Lives with him throughout this period. Works as an actor at Columbia Theatre and as nude model for art classes.

1904-1905: Hospitalized in New York, possibly for venereal disease. At a charity hospital, her left eye is removed, the first of thirty-one surgical operations. The entire year spent in various hospitals in New York and Philadelphia.

May 30, 1906: Married to Albert Jones.

1909: Hospitalized again in St. Louis, Maimie is befriended by visiting Philadelphia social worker Herbert Welsh. Rejoins Albert in Oklahoma. Begins correspondence with Welsh.

Spring, 1910: Brought by Welsh to Philadelphia to be treated for morphine addiction at the Orthopedic Hospital. At the suggestion of Welsh, Fanny Quincy Howe writes to Maimie during her hospitalization.

Summer, 1910: Cured of morphine addiction, Maimie is released from hospital and obtains work soliciting ads. Resumes her friendship with Ira "Bennie" Benjamin, a sweetheart of her adolescence.

November 29, 1910: First extant letter of Maimie to Fanny Quincy Howe.

Winter, 1911: Albert and Maimie frequently unemployed; Maimie considers "going back" to former life.

Spring, 1911: On Maimie's initiative, she and Albert separate.

July, 1911: Despondent at her inability to get employment and at Mr. Welsh's financial desertion and withdrawal of emotional support, Maimie joins Ira in New York.

Mid-Autumn, 1911: Returns to Philadelphia to live with youngest brother, James; his wife, Caroline; their baby daughter, Sarah (Potsy). Mrs. Howe contributes support of five dollars weekly. James continues long-standing abusive treatment of Maimie.

December, 1911: With assistance of money raised by Welsh, begins stenography school. At Welsh's urging, renews relationship with her mother.

April, 1912: Moves first to Port Chester, New York, then to White Plains, New York, to take stenographic job with a meat packing firm. Lives with, and begins financially assisting, the Aron family.

Visits writer Mary Antin, with an introduction from Mrs. Howe.

August or September, 1912 — July, 1913: Moves to the New York City office of her firm. Begins sharing quarters with co-worker Frances McCoy.

Moves, with Frances, to Wilmington, Delaware office of her firm.

August, 1913: Moves to the Montreal office of her firm. Assists the Goldstein family and Ethel Holmes, immigrants.

Winter, 1914: In partnership with Jean Holland, advertising woman and translator, starts the Business Aid Bureau, a letter-writing and duplicating service.

Summer, 1914: Ira Benjamin moves to Montreal, where he attempts to establish himself through a series of business ventures.

Autumn, 1914—Winter, 1915: Housing and personal problems, wartime cutbacks in the economy, force the closure of the Business Aid Bureau.

Maimie begins to befriend young prostitutes.

Summer, 1915: Takes favorite protégée, Stella Phillips, to Philadelphia for treatment of venereal disease. Recovery of Stella.

Autumn, 1915: Begins divorce proceedings, in order to be able to marry Ira. Begins correspondence with Helen, daughter of Fanny Quincy and Mark A. De Wolfe Howe.

Through adroit management of small contributions, Maimie founds the Montreal Mission, a halfway house for young prostitutes.

January 1, 1916: Issues report on Montreal Mission and twenty-three young women being assisted at that time.

January, 1917: Married to Ira Benjamin in Philadelphia.

Summer, 1917: Rents a country cottage in Lachine, near Montreal, as a vacation retreat for the mission women.

Autumn, Winter, 1917: Inadequate funding, police harassment, other problems force the closing of the mission. Maimie and Ira move to a hotel room, Maimie continuing the mission through visiting the women.

Becomes pregnant, but loses the child.

October, 1918: Returns to Philadelphia during the influenza epidemic, to assist the stricken family of James. Death of her beloved friend and sister-in-law, Caroline. Maimie cares for the children, Sarah and David, with increasing interference by Julia.

March 6, 1922: Mamie and Ira residing at a hotel in Chicago. Last extant letter to Fanny Quincy Howe.

THE MAIMIE PAPERS

PART ONE: 1910-1913

Mrs. Mark Howe
Brimmer Street, Boston   *Broad Street, Philadelphia*
My dear Mrs. Howe—   *November 29, 1910*

I HAVE THOUGHT OFTEN OF YOU SINCE HEARING FROM YOU WHILE I WAS 1 ⟨⟩
in the hospital and have wanted to write, but some inexpressible
feeling that I made myself so very ridiculous while I was in the
hospital in my letters to you has prevented the writing thus far. I
have heard of you and sort of kept in touch with you through our
friend Mr. Welsh. He told me of how ill you were, and I was
genuinely and sincerely sorry; and when I learned you were well, I
wanted to write but did not because of the same feeling that I had,
right along, that you thought me particularly silly and very rude.
All that feeling of resentment that I nursed against those who were
kindest to me has all gone, and I am now deeply grateful to them
and to you, too, for insisting on being friendly to such a "chump"
(that is the only word I know, in the English language, that exactly
expresses what I am). In the past week, you have been in my mind
very often—and I wanted to write but that same obstinate feeling
comes to me, and I ask myself all sorts of questions as to why you
would want to hear from me. I am writing now, anyway—

Since leaving the hospital, I have kept very well and busy. I
found employment with the *North American*—a morning newspaper—in the advertising department, soliciting for them, and
worked steadily every day from August 10 until Nov. 18 —then
quit, as the pay was inadequate for the work I did, and while I was
taken on with the understanding that I should be advanced accord-

ing to my ability, I was advanced in position but not in salary—
which might be satisfactory for a person to whom money is not a
vital issue but was most unsatisfactory to me. I was given an office
to myself, and a roll-top desk, and a stenographer and nine dollars
a week in "real" money. I am now sort of working about, soliciting
ads for an agency on a commission basis, but hope by the first of
the year to locate somewhere. It is much better that I hold a position where I am obliged to be at work at certain hours, for, to be
perfectly frank, I am not the most responsible person in the world,
and I really need to feel that I am obliged to do things at certain
stated times to make my work pay anything. I have nothing
definite in view but hope to get something by the first of the year. I
like the newspaper work, and would like to work on the reportorial
side of it, but all that requires preparation and means.

I have written so much about myself—but then, that was all that
I thought would interest you.

I hope you have entirely recovered from your severe illness and
have avoided catching cold, which seems so prevalent in this
section. . . .

Mr. Welsh, as you perhaps know, has been in Italy since
October. For some reason I do not hear from him, and I cannot
understand it entirely. He possibly is kept busy with so many more
important duties—still, I can scarcely believe that he would cease
writing to me. I must not write further on that subject, as it tends to
depress me, and I think it is "up" to this letter to be cheerful,
considering the other "mails" I sent you last summer.

With kindest regards to Mr. Howe and trusting that some time
when you are not busy you will write me, I am

Yours sincerely,
Maimie Jones

My dear Mrs. Howe,

Broad Street, Philadelphia
December 9, 1910

⚜ 2   YOU HAVE NO IDEA HOW SURPRISED I WAS TO HEAR FROM YOU SO SOON—
I was glad, too.

Isn't it strange that in the same mail came a letter from Mr.
Welsh, from whom I had no letter since he arrived in Italy in
October? Of course, I was delighted to hear from both you and him
—but wished afterward that they had come at least a day apart, for

I could have been happier longer. I love to receive letters—especially from those in whom I am especially interested—and believe should I receive one each day, I would never feel gloomy. It gives me a sense of importance and makes me feel that at least the writer of the letter knows of my existence.

Your letter is so cheerful, I should never suspect that you had sustained so great a loss, had you not told me so. Perhaps, though, you feel about death as Mr. Welsh does; for he wrote about the death of his daughter Bessie, "Could we catch a glimpse of the life beyond, we would not grieve, but rejoice, when our loved ones are taken away." I do not know if I quote that verbatim, but it is the sentiment anyway. My own father had a horrible death, he was brutally murdered by persons even-as-yet unknown. I do not feel it very keenly, as I was very young at the time, but I cannot [but think that] had he lived I should not have had such a rough road to travel in my twenty-five years. My mother is living in this city but I have not seen her in eleven years. You did not say in your letter whether your maternal parent was still living, but somehow I judge she is not. Will you tell me in your next letter whether she is or not, and also what your age is? That sounds very personal and I suppose rather rude, but I want to know and don't know of any other way to find out except to ask you.

I am not working at anything, and I am ashamed to admit it, for I always felt that if a person sincerely wanted to work they could readily find work, even though it was not exactly the sort of work they prefer, and I still believe that, so the plain truth must be that I do not sincerely want work. In my mind, I explain my inability to get work this way. I am not fitted for any work that is a trade, as stenography, etc.; and as for the sort of work that a general education and some "horse sense" fits you for, I cannot work at [that], for that is almost always clerking in the public stores, and where they see me they will not employ me because of the appearance I present with this patch on my eye. I am invariably told that they will be glad to take me on when I—or rather my eye—"get well." Of course, there is scrubbing of floors and dishwashing to be considered—and since I wouldn't do that, it is plain to be seen I do not *sincerely* want to go to work. I could not need money any worse than I do, and yet I would not do work of that sort, so I must admit that I am not serious when I say I would do any sort of work. You know, Mrs. Howe, that had I never had any luxuries, and been

3

reared a domestic, that would not seem so absolutely not-possible, but I lived in a luxurious home until I was sixteen, and then for years after that had the easy life that immoral living brings, and I just cannot be moral enough to see where drudgery is better than a life of lazy vice. I don't quite understand why I tell you all this (I do not want you should let your husband see this), for perhaps I simply write this and yet would not do what I say I would. If I knew you—or, rather, had we ever met—I know I should not write this way; for, knowing you, my wits would immediately work almost automatically to write the sort of letter that would make you pleased with me; if you were a man, my fingers would make my pen write things that I never really felt. So as this is the first time I have carried on an extended correspondence with a person of my own sex whose mind I do not really know, it is a comfort to write just what I say to myself. Again, I feel "silly" and "ridiculous," but that is a chronic condition with me. I always feel I am misunderstood by women. I am never absolutely sincere with anyone except Mr. Welsh, not even with myself—that is perhaps why I always feel "silly" when I am not "acting up" and "making believe." I am always sincere with Mr. Welsh.

This room is cold and my fingers are almost rigid—I know this letter is scarcely legible and perhaps incoherent, for I really don't know what I'm driving at, myself. I think it is perhaps a clumsy attempt to excuse my laziness.

It is even nearer Christmas than when I wrote before, so if you are busy making ready for Christmas, don't feel obliged to write until you are at leisure. Very Sincerely yours, May Jones

Broad Street, Philadelphia
My dear Mrs. Howe, *December 14, 1910*
℘ 3 I WAS QUITE SHOCKED AT THE THOUGHT OF SEEING YOU SO SOON. OF course I want to see you; indeed, very much. As to whether it—that is, knowing you personally—will make any difference, I do not know. I feel just now as though it couldn't possibly. For I seem to know you now as well as though we had met, and I couldn't possibly bear to think of your being here and my not seeing you; but should it make any difference I will not know until after I do see you. Of course, nothing is impossible, and it may be that I would be perfectly natural with you, as I am with Mr. Welsh—though if I did, you would be the first person of my own sex to whom I did not

lie a straight streak; and I am so heartily tired of it, until now I occasionally tell the outright truth to see how I can startle folks. Still, Mr. Welsh is also the first man that I ever found I did not find it necessary to deceive.... I wonder if I met you face-to-face could I really be "what I am," without the slightest subterfuge. I have "acted up" so often that I began to have a secret admiration for myself as a second "Rebecca" or "Rachel" (I forget what was the name of that famous actress). At times, after certain meetings with various folks, in which I was just what they liked best in me, I would marvel at my own cleverness; and the thought would come to me that I outclassed Maude Adams or Bernhardt, for while they were clever actresses, still their audiences knew they were "making believe," whereas I not only had to be as much somebody else as they do, but also had to make my audience think I was just what I was acting. And I do that every day, and—to use the vernacular—"I get away with it."

I had no plans for this Sunday, so I will be glad to await your coming. I visit my sister every second Sunday. She is an inmate of the State Insane Asylum, at Norristown. But as I was there last Sunday, I will be at home Sunday. I am so glad you decided to make the trip. At any rate, I have something to anticipate between now and Sunday. Yours sincerely, May Jones

Broad Street, Philadelphia

My dear Mrs. Howe, January 7, 1911

I DON'T KNOW WHY I DIDN'T ACKNOWLEDGE THE RECEIPT OF YOUR GIFT— **4** ✺ the tie—before. I think perhaps I was waiting to receive a letter from you. I liked the little tie and wished I could have kept it to wear, but I made a present of it to my cousin for Christmas. I had promised her that she should have something, for she was very kind in coming to see me very often while I was in the hospital last spring, and as I did not receive any other gifts and had no money with which to buy her one, your little tie had to go—for she likes that sort of ornament. She is 16 years old. Albert said I should not do it, but I felt it was mine: you gave it to me, and I could do as I saw fit; and I tell you of it because I don't think you will mind. I was glad to get it because I needed it to give her.

I received your letter yesterday in the forenoon and in the afternoon took your note of introduction and went to see Mr. Morgan. He was very nice to me, but I do not think understood exactly how I was situated. I imagine he thought I was one of the many who think they are cheating the public by not writing for publication. I enlightened him, and he seemed very much relieved. He told me the conditions as they exist on any newspaper, and I knew then that I was not in for much. To give me a position with a salary was impossible; and the columns of the newspaper are open to anyone at the rate of $5.00 a column; and even the better and well-known writers scarcely get more than a ¼ column, every other day or so, accepted by his paper. I told him I had no experience in that line, so had better not expect to do anything. If there was some way I could get onto the ropes, I've no doubt I could command a salary the same as other women do—but as he explained it, I had little or no chance. He was extremely kind and nice to me, and not in a patronizing way, either, but in a manner most flattering. I told him I would go down to see their advertising manager, and Mr. Morgan insisted that he go along, and he did, and I was introduced all around, and then he left me to talk with them and he returned to his office. Mr. Donnelly, the *Record* ad man, listened to all I had to say. I explained the system used by the *North American*, for whom I worked, and showed him how his ad columns could be increased by the use of their system. He seemed impressed and told me he would talk and think it over and would let me know. Of course, I can't tell whether it will bring a position, but I can only hope for the best and thank you very much for securing the assistance of Mr. Morgan. I intended to write you ere this, but I was busy day and night and I will tell you how.

When you were here, I don't know if I told you that I had been to see about doing some addressing of New Year's cards, for which a fine Spencerian hand was necessary. Addressing generally pays 75 cents a thousand envelopes, and only the most experienced can write almost a thousand in a day. So when I sent a sample of my best Spencerian hand, I received a reply saying that they would engage me for the two weeks preceding New Year's, at $5.00 a thousand. I thought that was almost too easy, and started in—only to learn that the $5.00 was for a thousand envelopes addressed in full, no abbreviations, and the average one was something like this:

Messrs. William A. Anderson, and Sons,
Milk Street, Boston, Massachusetts
c/o The United States Mercantile Company

Then the name had to be filled out on an engraved card. As each card cost 32 cents, an error meant the loss of that amount to the writer. So you know there couldn't be much speed, and that sort of writing takes so much time. The envelopes were 8½ by 10½, and the writing had to be twice the size of the above. At any rate, I soon learned my job and was no sinecure, and as they permitted men to work at night, I did too, and by not even getting up to eat luncheon or dinner, but bringing it with me, and working from 9:00 A.M. to 12:00 midnight for the week before Christmas and New Years I managed to earn $13.51. As my husband had no work in all that time, he borrowed money from Mr. Suiffen, Mr. Welsh's secretary, and I paid it with that money. So you can see I was kept busy and hated to lift a pen up except for that purpose. My arms ached at the shoulder, and even while I was glad to earn that money, I wouldn't do it again, for my eye burned all the time and I had headaches.

Mr. Suiffen, Mr. Welsh's secretary, who up to now I went to see occasionally . . . is going to Arizona this week, and I will no doubt be obliged to call on the monkeys in the zoo for want of someone to talk with.

Now I believe I've told you how things "are" with me, as you asked me to do in your letter. I don't know whether there is much else to write about. I, too, enjoyed your visit, although I felt embarrassed because I felt very small and insignificant, knowing that you knew me for what I am. I don't think I said or did anything to deceive you while you were here, but I think I would if I saw you often, for my pride would not permit me to be open and honest about the vile things I might do. I found it was awfully hard to be honest with you, for even though you do not moralize, I instinctively know by looking at you that you do not do things that are not clean and right. I didn't have any recent act to be ashamed of when I saw you but I felt very picayune, and doubt whether I could be as honest with you face to face as I am on paper. As yet I have stayed clean and decent . . ., and not for any object or purpose—just to be honest with you. But I am also going to be frank and tell you that possibly before this letter reaches you, I won't be. I hope you won't think I am crazy for writing you like this, but somehow I want to tell you, and perhaps you will be glad to know that I experience a great dread when I think of it, for I have kept absolutely straight since last March, almost a year.

Perhaps I ought to tell you that I do not write any more to Mr. Welsh; I did not answer the letter I told you he wrote me some time ago when your letter came—so it is nothing that he will know about through me. But I would not care if he knew—only I would hate it awfully if he knew it, because it would distress him so. I don't know again whether I've made myself plain—I sound horribly confused. I was trying to say politely that I would not care for him to know, not that I want to deceive him, but because it would hurt him so.

Goodbye Mrs. Howe, I am very nervous today and you must pardon this illegible writing, but I knew unless I wrote today, I would perhaps never write. Yours sincerely—Maimie

My dear Mrs. Howe,   *Philadelphia, January 11, 1911*

∞ 5   I WAS ON MY WAY OUT WHEN YOUR LETTER WAS HANDED TO ME, AND came back to write you a few lines to tell you that I had received your letter. I want to write at length, and will, but can't just now, as I am going to my brother's to dinner and it is almost dinner time now. You can't possibly know how good it is to know you care.

You haven't an idea what a bunch of inconsistent feelings I harbor, but from observation I think everyone is the same. Hastily scanning your letter downstairs, when I came to the offer of a loan, I unconsciously felt angry—then when I came up here and calmly read it, it came to me that you would be a poor friend if you didn't offer it, and it was the very thing which down deep in my heart I held against Mr. Welsh. And with all my "beefing" and "bewailing of my fate," I don't need the $25.00 or 25 cents—and don't really know what I do want. I can't write coherently to you, it seems. When I am known to be an excellent letter-writer, that seems strange. I think it must be because of the conflict between my desire to be honest with you and my long standing habit of writing what is only so much "gaff."

I will write tomorrow, but must tell you that we moved Monday. We had been in the other place seven months and have a receipt for every week paid in advance—and when we did not have it to pay, for the first time Monday, we were ordered out. I am glad, though, that we have gone. More anon, in the morning, when I shall be quieter and can write [in an orderly way]. Your letter moved me very much and I feel better. Yours sincerely, Maimie

I WROTE YOU YESTERDAY AND HAVE ONLY A VAGUE IDEA OF WHAT THE 6 ✖
letter was about. I know if I persist in writing you confused letters,
you will think I am not entirely right in my mind. I don't know why
my letters to you seem so disconnected and incoherent. Perhaps it
is because I hesitate about calling a spade a spade, and yet I enjoy
telling you about my affairs as I would tell them to myself. That
must be the reason I get so frightfully bawled up.

I was very glad to get your letter. Do you know, when I try to
recall just how you look, I can't seem to see anything but your
crinkly golden hair. I wish I knew if you colored it or if it is so
always. Now that I've written that, it sounds impertinent. I am
writing just as I would talk if you were sitting here, and I don't
think it would sound ugly if I asked it, and yet it does read silly, I
know. I often wondered how an intelligent person of sound mind
could keep a diary to record every small event, and thought. It
seemed such a ridiculous thing, almost asinine. I think now that I
have hit on the very reason why they do it, and what for. It must be
that, while they are the only ones that see them, they are
unconsciously addressing another person, a second self, who is
interested in the minutest detail concerning the writers' life; and in
writing down each thing, it sort of clears the mind each day and
leaves it free for a new set of perplexities.

When I was in the hospital during the years of 1904-1905, when
I lost my eye, I had all sorts of time for retrospection. Would I have
been able to read, I would have had something constantly before
my eyes, and my mind on anything else besides my personal
troubles; but, without sight the thirty-two weeks I was in the Post
Graduate Hospital in New York and eleven weeks in the Sydenham
Hospital in New York and fourteen weeks in the Germantown
Hospital in this city, you may well imagine how busy my brain was
with the past up to that time. And oh! what a jumble it all was. I
can't begin to write you of what my thoughts were; but I know I
had a half-formed idea of living better if I came out alive, blind or
with sight. And I did, when I came out in the world again. I don't
exactly know whether that was due to circumstances or desire on
my part; at any rate, either the loss of the good looks or the time
spent in retrospection subdued me very much. Before that, I had no
care about anything; and afterwards I found I stopped to consider

before going into things. Of course I was getting older, and that helped some. I lived very much more moderately and even married Mr. Jones, so that I would be obliged, in a certain sense, not to be too free about, and with, my manner of living.[1] And yet I could not buckle down to cutting out entirely all the things I had summed up while in the hospital as being empty and not worthwhile. At times, I would go all over the thoughts that passed through my mind while in the various hospitals and would decide that I would keep my word to myself and cut it out. Of course, the attending luxuries that go with loose living I did not want to give up. But, summed all up, it is anything but a pleasant road to travel; and I saw how the few luxuries did not make up for the indignities offered me and the cautious way I had to live. As, for instance, I love women—that is, I would like to have women friends—but I can't have; or rather, I couldn't have. I avoided them, even though very often I would meet one who would want to be friendly, and even now, the habit is so strong in me that I never encourage any advances from them—much as I should like to—for I couldn't find any enjoyment in being on friendly terms with a woman who lived a sporting sort of life, and the others, I dreaded would find out, perhaps inadvertently, something about me, and perhaps cut me, and I couldn't stand that; so I always repel any advances they make—so much so, that Mr. Jones thinks I am rude about it. When we lived in Enid, Oklahoma, a small town of 12,000 people, I had an occasion to look up a lady who owned a Boston Terrier, and I took quite a fancy to her and she did to me. She had a very beautiful home and was very wealthy. For once, I permitted myself the luxury of accepting her invitations to little luncheons to be partaken only with her. She seemed to enjoy talking with me, and although everything I talked about was superficial and mostly lies, I too enjoyed going to her home. As we had been there almost six months when I met her, and I had never done anything wrong in the town, I hadn't much to fear, although I used to go to Oklahoma City about once a month to meet a man I knew there. So for six months I was very friendly with her and two other younger girls—the daughters of the local banker—when one day, like a bolt out of a clear sky, this lady's father (she was unmarried and about thirty-five years old—she kept house for her father) called to see me and in very terse language told me I must not continue my friendship with his daughter. It afterwards developed that a young man who called on one of these younger girls knew something ugly about me and told it to their father, who in turn told it to Mr. Kemble, who told his daughter. But she would not believe it at first, but must have later—for when her dog saw me on the street some time later and came to me, she called him away and cut me direct. At any rate, we left town the following week—although Mr. Jones was business agent for the carpenter's Union, receiving $25.00 a week without having to do any manual labor. I could not stand living there longer; and since then, with the exception of being "charming" to some friends of Mr. Welsh's who knew all about me, I haven't ventured to know any women except you—and that's different, of course.

When I was in the hospital in St. Louis in 1909, again I came to the conclusion that I would live right and perhaps be happy. I thought my mode of life explained why I was lying there all alone, without the visits of a human being other than the general nurse and no word from anyone—besides the letters from my husband, which are always the very kindest and affectionate. I would see all about me at the visiting hour people hurrying and scurrying to the various beds to see the other patients, bringing them fruit and flowers and magazines. I don't think I ever wanted anything in my life so much as I did some grapes while I was there, but I had no friends to bring or send them to me. Then the conviction was strong in me again that it was surely my fault that I was so friendless and that I would surely try living straight and start to make friends that were real. But, while I had that thought in my brain, I tucked it conveniently out of my road—and hadn't been out of the hospital three weeks before I went to San Antonio, Texas, with a circuit attorney of St. Louis who too had been ill in the St. Agnes Hospital when I was, and who had the same doctor. The doctor ordered the trip for his health and I went along, writing my husband some absurd story about my uncle Louis who lives thirty miles out of San Antonio sending me the ticket to go there. (Fact of the matter was, when I did go to this small town to visit my uncle whom I hadn't seen in ten years, he treated me as one would an acquaintance and never even asked me to stop for a meal.) At any rate, when I returned from San Antonio, went to Oklahoma City to join Mr. Jones, I was again thoroughly and heartily weary of my precarious way of living, for I had another belittling experience in San Antonio. And then I just sat down and waited.

For what, I didn't know, but I had an idea that I wasn't going to meet anyone and would just cut it all out. Then came Mr. Welsh's first letter; and no sooner was that correspondence started than I knew why, before that, I could only *think* to live decent. For I found that which is the reason people keep diaries. It records these thoughts, and once they are carefully taken apart and written, you can follow the lines of your thoughts more clearly; and then it is a clearing-house, and from one writing to the next, one's brain is cleared, ready to follow out the line of thought or perhaps start a new line of thought. In that way, Mr. Welsh helped me most, for I kept a sort of diary in my letters to him of my thoughts as they came to me each day. And then, when I felt I was responsible to a real live father for my actions, I was very careful as to what I did. And I never did anything (even the most ridiculous detail) that I didn't write to him of it; and I was happier than ever before in my life. And because I believed in him, he readily convinced me that I had a Father in Heaven; and when I think back to the first few weeks I was in the hospital last spring, I doubt whether it was really I who had such childlike faith in prayers. I haven't even the slightest atom of that left, but I wish I had. It was very comforting. In a measure I'm like a child for I love to show off, provided I have the right sort of an audience. I know when I procured the work at the *North American*, it was because I wanted to show everyone how clever I was; and then when Mr. Welsh left and I had no one to applaud, I quit being clever. You know, I've told you how hard I've looked for work. Well I have, in a halfhearted sort of a way and with the feeling: "Oh! What's the use—for I don't propose to get up at 6:30 to be at work at 8 and work in a close, stuffy room with people I despise, until dark, for $6.00 or $7.00 a week! When I could, just by phoning, spend an afternoon with some congenial person and in the end have more than a week's work could pay me." Doesn't that sound ugly—and it feels ugly—but they are my thoughts. I had them very persistently when I ceased writing regularly to Mr. Welsh, and you don't know how I miss writing my thoughts to him. I feel perhaps that is why I wrote you the day I was so very despondent. As yet, they are still thoughts—

I will have to stop writing soon, as it is getting very late, and write again tomorrow. You will wonder when you see this what I could have found to write so much about. Today I went to a matinee performance, a benefit given by the various theatre people for the families of the firemen who were killed (thirteen of them) in a fire here a few weeks ago. It was given in the Academy of Music and, as it was all for charity, the programmes had a great many advertisements on them. Among other advertisers were two full page ads that each of my uncles paid $150 a page for. They were each given two seats in the loge boxes for the performance. One of my uncles left on Monday with his family for a month's stay in Cuba, where they go each winter, and as I knew he had the tickets, I asked for one and got it. The performance started at 12:50 P.M. and lasted all afternoon until twenty minutes of seven. It was splendid, every theatre in town sending its representative people, among whom were some of the best talent in the U.S. I did not have any breakfast before going—I did not feel like it, although there was a pint of milk here, which I usually drink—so before half the afternoon was over, I had an excruciating headache. There were all sorts of pretty girls, dressed elegantly, selling flowers, candies and even the programmes for 25 cents! As I had no money, I could not buy one. Sitting beside me was a lady whom I at first admired because she was dressed so elegantly, yet quietly. She was about your age and size, and I soon thought she was like you, for she had a very soft, gentle face. During the performance there was a three minute intermission, and as she sat there with her programme in her lap, not looking at it, I asked her if I might look at it. The moment I did, I knew she wasn't like you, and I could have bitten my tongue off, for she handed it to me without a smile or a word; and when I began to turn the leaves, she said in a very querulous tone of voice, "Please don't lose the place." I handed it immediately back to her and noticed for the first time how very hard my head was aching.

I think perhaps using the opera glasses so much tended to aggravate the headache. When I reached home, Albert helped me to undress and lowered the lights, and I went to bed, remaining there quietly until eleven o'clock—when I got up, feeling very much better, to write you. It is now one o'clock; so I will have to go to bed and write tomorrow.

It is Friday noon. I went this morning to see Dr. Chance, who is an eye specialist and such a fine gentleman. He was the doctor that really cured me when I had the infection in the eye socket, although he is not the man that removed the eye. I went to a hospital dispensary [in Philadelphia] soon after leaving the New York hospitals, and Dr. Chance was the attending physician and was good to me beyond words. He had me to visit him at his private office and asked no pay, which he knew I couldn't afford. When I returned to Philadelphia this spring, Mr. Welsh told me of how he had arranged for me to call on an eye specialist—and it developed that it was this same Dr. Chance who had befriended me. I went to see him this past fall three times, each time because I had a cinder in my eye; and as his office is but three blocks away, I did not hesitate to run in; and he then sent me a bill for $15.00 which I have paid—and since then have been removing my own cinders. This morning I called on him, though, because I am such a coward about impairing the sight of my remaining eye, and I was some-what alarmed because I suffer so much with these headaches, which seem to be relieved when I stay in a darkened room. He gave me a prescription for an eyewash which he says will help me very much if I use it three times daily. I haven't gotten it yet, as I did not have the money to have it filled, but hope to, by tomorrow night.

I think I told you we had moved. They would not permit us to remain because we did not have the money to pay them. Even through our run of bad luck through the holidays, I managed to get the money for them, although except for the money I earned addressing the envelopes, there wasn't a penny earned by either of us in more than eight weeks. During that time, I borrowed the $10.00 we paid them in advance: twice from a man I just slightly knew, and still owe it to him; once from my brother and haven't paid him—and that worries me more than that which I borrowed from the stranger, because I hate to admit to him that I am in want. Many a time recently I have been hungry—not later than yesterday I went to bed without anything all day, except a pint of milk, to eat—and yet I could get all the food I could carry off, from my brother's store, if only I could tell him that I was hungry. I borrowed $10.00 from Mr. Suiffen but returned that, as I did not want him nor Mr. Welsh to think I was taking advantage of Mr. Welsh's interest in me. Then, another week, I was obliged to pawn my clothes for $5.50—all except the one skirt that I had on when you were here—and they are still there. I did not pawn my fur coat, as I had to keep that to go out in. Then I pawned my wedding ring, Kodak, grip, umbrella and silver toilet articles—for $8.75—which are also still unredeemed. In all that time, I dug up the money, never asking any favors of these people from whom we rented—until last Monday, when I asked them to wait until Sat. for their money. As we paid in advance, we owed them nothing; but they would not hear of waiting until Sat., and as I had nothing else to pawn and could not without humbling myself ask it of any one, we had to get out. They told us at six o'clock that the room had to be vacated that night. I thought I should go frantic. It was so hard for me, as we didn't have a nickel. But there was 50 cents coming to us that we had deposited for our night keys; and I thought we should use that to procure a place of some sort to stay Monday night, and Tuesday I would just have to ask aid of some of my various kinfolks—of whom I had never asked a penny. I knew we should have money Saturday—for Albert had procured work of a sort and would have some pay by Sat.—so I hated so badly to have to go for help when we wouldn't need it if we could only wait until Sat.

Fortunately, the people with whom we are now staying had a vacant room and told Albert of it. They run a small cigar and newspaper shop, and Albert had come into their store to buy a paper to see where we could get a room for the night. He told them we would pay them Sat., and they were satisfied; but as they furnish no meals, it was pretty hard. Fortunately, as it was very mild this week, Albert pawned his overcoat—for $2.50, to buy food and car fare for this week—until Saturday, when he will take it out immediately he is paid.

Now I believe I told you all, and it is off my conscience; for I believe though I try to be absolutely honest with you, I can't help but let some deceit creep out. I know I wrote you that I did not need anything—and it is because it is galling that I do. I don't mind the sordidness of it all as much as the thought that I can't help myself.

I believe I've told you everything except of the work Albert is doing. He saw an ad in the paper for a millwright, and although he had not done such work before, he applied for the position. I believe it has something to do with carpentering. He has the alarm clock to call him at five, as he has to get breakfast and go 'way out to the suburbs and be on the job at seven o'clock. He works until six o'clock and will receive $12.00 for it Saturday. The work is to last four or five weeks, and while it is terribly hard and such poor pay, still I hope that in four weeks spring will be almost here, and building work opened up....[Carpenter work] pays $4.00 a day for eight hours, from 8 A.M. to 4 P.M. You know, this is awfully

15

hard for him, but he doesn't complain, as he is glad to make even that much.

I want to tell you before I close that I did not do what I wrote you I might. That is, I haven't so far. I'll tell you about it. I know a man in Phila. with whom I used to go out years ago on rare occasions, and when he saw me last fall on my way to lunch while I was working, he used to offer to buy my lunch; but I refused him, and was happy to get my 10 cent lunches. Then, later, when I had no work and was starved for something good and clean to eat, I phoned him and went to luncheon, but refused to go further than that. He then took me again to luncheon, and I returned home immediately after the luncheon, absolutely refusing to go elsewhere, and telling him that I was absolutely straight. He seemed to admire that; and when I had to get money for our rent, and everything was pawned, I phoned him and borrowed $10.00, telling him I would pay him in a week. But I didn't have it to pay—the next week I was just as bad off, and knew it was almost useless to ask him for some more money unless I would consent to go out with him. The afternoon I wrote you as I did, I had an engagement with him for three o'clock, and I intended to give in, as I just had to have the money. When I met him, though, I just could not do it. . . . [He gave me] the money anyhow . . . and really and truly, when I came home with the $10.00 and I hadn't done anything for it, I felt almost like the winner of some grand prize. Of course, I had to trick him, but I hope some time to pay him; or if I don't hold out much longer, I can then go out with him to wipe off the debt.

While the place we are living in now isn't quite as nice in some respects as the other house was, still, it is very much cleaner in the small things, and as the room is as large as the other one and [is] a front room with bath adjoining, I am pleased. The furniture is even better than in the other room. Perhaps we could get a room lots cheaper—but oh! I will destroy myself if I ever have to live in a dirty, smelly place. I would far rather go hungry and live in a pleasant place.

It is now Saturday, and I will bring this to a close and mail it when Albert returns at three—for I had no stamp, but will have, by then. I suppose you will think it queer that I write you so much that is so trivial. I used to write like this to Mr. Welsh, and it makes me feel better now that I've written. I wrote each day since getting your letter, but had no stamps to mail each day's writing with, so will put it all in one envelope at three o'clock and mail it. I do not talk to anyone, day-in-and-out, but my dog, who is so much a friend of mine. When my husband comes home at seven, he is so tired that as soon as he has something to eat, he goes to bed—and leaves before daylight, while I am sleeping. Even when he is home, we do not talk—for, you know, it is all deceit and farce; and I am so heartily tired of that sort of conversation.

So far, the *Record* man has not written me, so I imagine there is no chance there. I am going out Monday to make another try to find something to do. I haven't felt like looking for weeks, and haven't, because I was so depressed and hungry half the time; but Monday I am going to make an earnest effort and show you that I am in earnest. I think perhaps this damp, sultry weather has added to my depression. So now, perhaps next week, with a cold dry change that is promised and the thought that you will be waiting to know if I was successful, I may summon up the courage to ask for work. I don't know why it is that it is always that all the hard luck comes at once. I am having more now than I ever did, except when I lost my eye. In today's mail came a note from Mr. Suiffen's stenographer. As long as Mr. Suiffen was here, I knew I could go to him—at least to talk occasionally—and now he has gone. Although he promised to see me before he left, he never did. I just wrote him a note telling him we were obliged to move and enclosed a letter to Mr. Welsh telling him the same, but had no 5 cents to buy a stamp. . . .

I am going out in a few moments to help my brother in his store, where I go each Sat., and although I will have to walk there, at least I know I will get a clean dinner of the best food that money can buy. They eat only "kosher" meat, although my sister-in-law is a Gentile, because kosher meat is absolutely the cleanest and freshest and costs 5 cents more on each pound.

Would you send me a dear little bit of a picture of you? I hadn't the courage to ask you before, but I just found a picture of myself, and. . .if you have some sort of an inexpensive one that looks as you do now, I would be awfully happy to have it. This picture of me and Poke was taken in San Antonio, Texas, in the summer of 1909.

I wish you were coming here again tomorrow. I have arranged my room so pretty and clean, and I am "playing" that I am going to have some ladies call—and it is pretty enough for anyone. Sometime when I haven't written such a fearfully long letter, I will tell you just what is in the room and how Albert and I fixed it up. Goodby for this time. I will buy two or three stamps today so I can write you oftener this week—as of course I will be "busted" again by Monday or Tuesday. I am surely going to go for work next week. Yours sincerely, Maimie

Will you write me something about your home? If you have a dog, and what kind—or something I can place around you, as I only can think of you now in that chair with your hat on, and that sort of awes me. M.

Walnut Street, Philadelphia
January 23, 1911

CЗ 7   THIS CARD [IS] TO LET YOU KNOW I RECEIVED YOUR LETTER AND THE enclosure. I thank you for it. I was agreeably surprised to learn about the children, but shocked that one is ill with a sickness that seems to be a dread one. I hope it is all over by now. I have so much to tell you, and—among other things—that I am moving again. I have written it all in detail in the letter which will reach you soon. Address is now Walnut St.

Walnut Street, Philadelphia
January 27, 1911

CЗ 8   FIRST OF ALL, I MUST TELL YOU ABOUT THE CHECK. I AM DEEPLY grateful. At first I thought I should keep it, but not cash it unless it was vitally necessary that I use it, and that perhaps I shouldn't have to use it at all, and then I would return it to you. Not that I wouldn't accept money from you, but I should have liked not to have needed it. So, for almost a week, I kept the check uncashed in my purse; and you haven't an idea what a help it was all week. It actually made a difference in my appearance. That sounds ridiculous, but it is so nevertheless; for somehow when I have some money, I feel independent, and naturally I walk and act differently. Then came the opportunity to get the place where we are now, and the check had to be cashed, for it is necessary to pay these people in advance for one month, and it makes the rent cheaper. So I cashed the check, after all, and used $20.00 for our rent and $5.00 for some shoes. I was a little bit puzzled, at first, as to whether you meant that I must use it to pay back toward the $20.00 debt, or only suggested it. I thought it was better to use it as I did; and I went to see the man who let me have $10.00 twice, and I don't think he believed me when I told him I would return that money—but I will, nevertheless.

Now I must tell you why I moved again. You know, we left the place where you called in such a hurry that we had no opportunity of finding out anything much about our new place at South Broad; and since it was scrupulously clean and the furnishings very nice, I thought we should like it; but somehow I did not put my "house in order," because I was not entirely satisfied. I despise moving, so thought I should put up with it; but it proved impossible. . . . My chief objection to the place was that the people from whom we rented were Jewish of a very low order, and they persisted in being friendly to such a degree that I had no privacy; and while I have complained to you that I was miserably lonesome, still, I prefer to be entirely alone than to associate with plebeian people. I also objected to the very pungent odors that came up from the kitchen. They use garlic and onions and cabbage in their food, and I could not stand it, for it always permeated my room as well as the halls. Then someone told me of this place—but because it is in the most exclusive section of Phila., I did not dream I could afford to rent it, until I learned all the conditions—And then I went to see the man, and we took the place, and I am so very satisfied. While the rent is not excessive, still, I could not take it if I hadn't had the check you sent me, for it has to be paid an entire month in advance. The house is in the same block as Bellevue-Stratford, only on the other side, and—my room being the third floor front—you have no idea how much satisfaction I derive watching the elegantly gowned women coming and going from there. . . .

The room has been freshly painted with a thick white enamel, and every speck of woodwork is painted with it, and the new paper is of a subdued shade in grey and silver. There are no colors to worry me. The rug is dark green, and then the sides of the floor are stained. The furniture is of an excellent sort, I don't know what you call it, but it's a reddish brown in color and, [there are] a rocker, two chairs, a bed, a bureau, a chiffonier desk and a rattan couch. And with nice white curtains at the windows, the place is as pretty as a picture. The sun comes in all day, and with my pictures and some books around the room, I am very happy. I only wish you could call now to see me. I would like to see you sit in this low

19

rocker and look about and see how clean I live. I need a couple of cushions to put on my couch, which is of the sort they put on porches in the summer. I am going out to my brother's tomorrow, to help in the store, and I intend asking his wife whether she will make a pillow for me, or show me how to make it. I know you would be glad if you could see how nicely everything is arranged here; and the house is of such an elegant order that it makes me happy to come in and out—for they have a liveried servant at the door, and I certainly do like airs. If I had your picture, I would get a frame for it and put it on the top of my desk.

Albert is working every day, but he only is earning $12.00 a week—still, that is $12.00 more than nothing, and at least I have had food every day since he has been working. He earned $6.00 this week, doing a small job for the owner of this house. He did it in two evenings and he gave me the money, which I put away toward the rent which will be due in a month again. I am hoping that soon work will open up so that he can make $4.00 a day, as he usually does. Two doors below here, there is an addressing company, and I went to see the man who conducts it, and he said that beginning Monday, he would give me work to do, from time to time, at my own desk—that is, bring it home. The pay is ridiculously small, 75 cents a thousand envelopes. I couldn't possibly do a thousand a day, but having it here in my own room to do, I could do, between times, a thousand every two days or so and earn at least $2.25 a week, if not more. That seems ridiculous, but it seems as though I can't get anything that pays better. I went out yesterday in answer to an ad that called for a young lady to make herself generally useful around an office and they said I could come, and the pay was $4.00 a week—hours from eight to six. With 60 cents a week for carfare, I refused to work for $3.40 from sunup to sundown. So, you see, I am really little better off than I was before. Still, I feel better, because I am living in such a desirable place.

I was thinking, had I been in Boston, I could have assisted you with those poor sick babies, for I love them, and I really can do almost any work that a child's nurse does, for I have helped so often with them. I hope they have entirely recovered. Do you know, I feel differently about you since I know you are a mother? I can't explain it but I do. . . . Mr. Welsh did not mention the fact [that you had children], nor did you, in your letters, or when I saw you. I used to think of you and try to place you in your surroundings, and I couldn't seem to, exactly, and that is why I asked you if you had a puppy—I wanted to know how you were placed. And now that I know, I can see you, and feel I am not far wrong. I would like to have a picture of you and the children, then I could think of them, too. My sister-in-law is going to have a baby in about April or, I hope, earlier. I can scarcely wait until it comes. It is going to be a boy—or, rather, I want it to be a boy—and as I am going to take care of her house, and help in their store during the time she will be in bed, I will be with the baby lots of the time. It is too cunning to see all the little things she is making. I can't sew—that is, I can't fashion anything—but I can make hems that do not show stitches; and so she makes it all—that is, the slips and dresses—and I hem them at the bottom. I wish I could sew something for you. I could make hems in tablecloths and napkins, or hemstitch them, if you would let me. I would be happy if I was able to do some service for you.

I am going to have a large family of my own soon, for Poke will have five or six puppies in about three weeks; and while I look forward to it with dread, still, I derive lots of pleasure puttering about with the poor little things. They get to be very cute; and my great trouble is that I dislike to part with them, but I always do, so soon as possible. I keep them three weeks, no longer. Of these, one male must be given for the mating, and two more are promised— one to a cousin and one to my brother—and the other two or three I sell for $10.00 to $15.00 and I intend to use that money to pay the $20.00 that I owe. I want to mend some stockings today, as tomorrow—Saturday, all day—I am a grocer's clerk; so I will close. . . .

I hope the babies are better—or, better still, entirely well. Will you write me their names?

Walnut Street, Philadelphia

My dear Mrs. Howe, *February, 1911*

I RECEIVED YOUR LETTER AND THE LITTLE PICTURE—AND IT IS ALREADY 9 ◌ in a round, old-fashioned walnut frame. I am very glad to have it; and while it doesn't look as I picture you from my impression that afternoon, still, I can catch the expression when I look at it intently; and then, anyhow, I know it is you, and soon I will have you looking just like that picture in my mind's eye. . . .

I watch these ladies pass here and wonder if I couldn't do

something that they wouldn't want to bother to do themselves and yet which wouldn't require any great skill, for you know I am not skilled at all. I know this will sound ridiculous but I must tell you that I've often wished I could do things for well-bred people of your . . . sort, just so as to have dealings with them, even if it didn't bring any income. I'd rather do it than work that paid well for low-born people . . . .

I wrote to Miss Outerbridge, who is a friend of Mr. Welsh . . . a maiden lady of perhaps forty or forty-five . . . .[2] She is one of those people that I wrote you about some time ago—to whom I lied so much until I grew tired of her. She is very sweet, and Mr. Welsh asked me to confide in her and make her my friend during his absence, but I couldn't. She has never had any of the real experiences of life and lives in the clouds. She has beautiful ideals and lives the life of the characters in the Sunday School story-books. When I was sick in the hospital, she came twice and brought books and then some more books. No one loves books better than I do; but it was the spring—or, rather, early summer (in June)—and there were roses in abundance, and I wanted them, and next to that, I wanted some cherries to eat, and she never thought of that. Had I told her, she would have brought them in a moment; but I couldn't bring myself to do it, so I accepted books. Then, when Chrismas came, she never even thought to send me a card, but I sent her one—and by New Year's, she sent me a book! It has about twenty pages of reading matter and no pictures, and the print is as large as your fist. It is really a child's book—but as it has a white and gold cover, it looks pretty on my table. I know it isn't "good form" to make these criticisms, but I have thought them, and somehow want to tell you, to show you what manner of person Mr. Welsh expected me to make a confidential friend of. She is such a well-bred lady, and so beautiful, and just the sort of person I like to look at—but if I wrote her as I do you, she would think I had gone completely daft. I received a letter from her this week, and she wrote that she learned I had moved, and said if I would appoint an hour, she would call. I haven't answered it and dread to, because she is so earnest, honest and altogether sweet, and I am heartily tired of "playing" up to her ideal. Still, if I don't answer she will be hurt, and I would not like to do that either. I wish it was you that wanted to come.

I know she is puzzling her head about what I am doing at Walnut Street. Bet she thinks someone left me a fortune. . . .

Before I go further I must tell you that when I wrote you last, I wrote that I was glad Albert was working even if he was only earning $2.00 a day. . . . Sat. he found other work which is eight hour work instead of eleven hours, and the pay is $3.25 a day! He started to work yesterday; and this work will last indefinitely—that is, as long as he does the work to suit them—and maybe I'm not relieved, for soon I will get some of my things back. You haven't an idea how horrible I feel not to have all my nice things around me, especially in this pretty room that has so many places for nice things. I may, when I have the money, get a coffee arrangement and get Albert's breakfast on it. Up to now, he left too early for that; but now he has to be there only at eight o'clock (regular banking hours!), and as the work is a block from here he leaves at quarter to eight. . . .

I have no addressing now to do—and I wish I had, for I would like to earn some money. . . .

I hope you avoid [the measles] and that the children are almost well. You have troubles enough, it seems, without burdening you with mine, only your troubles don't seem to depress you, and I am glad for you. . . .

We have cousins. . . married about eight years and never had a child, and are devoted to children. Some time ago, it developed that Cousin Iris was pregnant and there was great joy. . . . Then a few weeks ago. . . the doctor pronounced her too ill to be up, and ordered her to bed, and said she too had pneumonia. . . . Then. . . Iris [delivered] twins. It was a premature birth. . . and while the twins were alive when they were born, they died. . . . I [had] offered to remain there and take care of them. . . but Cousin Iris wouldn't have it. . . . She has never been nice to me, claiming that my having been "bad" was an awful blow to her reputation because I was her cousin—and sick as she was. . . she made it plain that she had to have a *decent* person in her house. I don't feel a bit hurt by it, for I consider and pardon her poor narrow mind, but it is only an example of how they all treat me; and that is how I excuse myself in my own mind for not wanting to live entirely clean, and be like her. . . .

With much love. I am yours sincerely, Maimie

Walnut Street, Philadelphia
February, 1911

CR 10 I FOUND THE PICTURE OF YOU AND THE BABIES AWAITING ME. I AM SO glad. The picture of you is exactly how I picture you, and I can even see your hair and the crinkles in it. . . .

Cousin Iris took a turn for the worse. . .she died in my arms at 4:25 P.M. . . . She had all her faculties to the end, and she begged me to forgive her for some things she had said of me. . .that were not true. . . .I feel it all so keenly. . . .I have thought and thought since, until my head is bursting. . . .

You are so good to me. I don't know if I deserve it all, but I'd like to. I won't say I'll try to, for that would be almost maudlin— for I would do as I liked whenever the occasion demanded—but I do feel as though I could do almost anything or do without almost anything if you personally asked it. That must be Mark on your lap—and while their faces look like two peas in a pod, I like his eyes, for they look as yours do. . . .

I wish I could write you about the story that goes in my mind with each of your pictures. That is, my relation to you in each of them. I don't mean I wouldn't tell you—but I couldn't; for written down, it would be too silly, as it is all "make-believe."

Walnut Street, Philadelphia
February, 1911

My dear, dear Friend,

CR 11 I JUST CAME IN AND READ YOUR LETTER. . . .I LOVE YOU SO MUCH tonight. You make me feel so much at ease. I am tired because I was shopping today—just imagine! Hunting bargains, as it were. Albert was paid yesterday and gave me $3.00 to spend on some things we have needed, so I was as important as anyone else, buying things today. I love pretty things. So much, that we came mighty near doing without our necessities when I saw a beautiful bronze statuette that was $25.00 and had been very badly damaged, but not so as to spoil its prettiness—and it was marked "as is" for $2.50. I managed to resist the temptation and bought our little necessities.

I must tell you of a predicament I am in. It is peculiar how, when one starts to lie, they absolutely must keep it up or go in over their head. When I first came to Phila. last spring, Miss Outerbridge asked me if I could sew—i.e., embroider. I told her I never had, but thought I could—thinking she wanted me to do something for her, which I would be happy to do. The next visit, she brought along a sofa-pillow top, and it was a bright mauve. It seems she bought it to embroider and present to her brother when he graduated from "Penn" in 1900. She had it scarcely begun, and then neglected it—as most of that sort of work is. Personally, I have never cared for that sort of thing, for I would rather use that time reading, and buy things embroidered by machine—which is generally lots better looking. Miss Outerbridge happened to think of it at the time, because my own brother was then graduating from "Penn." (I showed him the cushion, and he said if I dared to present it to him, he'd cut me out of his will.) At any rate, I told her I'd be glad to work it, and with the silk she furnished, I did. By picking out the 0 in 1900 and substituting the 1—for 1910—the cushion was finished. And it sure was "some" cushion cover. It was a fright—although "if I say it as shouldn't," the part I worked was the better of the two, because it looked the same on both sides. Miss Outerbridge was "deelighted," and on the next trip, she was to bring the cushion that was to go in it. Then she went to Canada and forgot all about it. In the interim, Brother graduated and went to California, taking a position as a chemist in a cement factory. Recently, in our talks on one of her visits, Miss Outerbridge asked me if Bro had taken the cushion along. I answered "no"—and she, I suppose, took it for granted that I had it. But I had not. For I gave it to a young boy who is a student at "Penn." (He works at night in a drug store—that is how I knew him—and attends "Penn" during the day.) . . .He is only nineteen. . .and he was made very happy with it. Then Miss Outerbridge called the other day. . .and dwelt long on that pillow. . . .I wouldn't dare to tell her I gave it away—and now it will have to be another big whopper of a lie!. . .

Before I forget it, I must tell you that I shall be glad to get the book you wrote. I never before knew anyone who wrote a book, and wished I might, so that I might judge if persons who wrote, generally, were like their books—that is, whether they thought and lived as they idealize.

Before I close, I must tell you about the funeral [of Cousin Iris]. . . .I have had so little experience with the death of near ones, that I haven't given "death" much thought. My father died when I was a child of twelve, and Iris' death is the only near one since then. I could not feel solemn, and I hope you won't be shocked when I tell you I was quite amused at some things. As, for instance, when I got there almost everyone was assembled—standing, from the front door to her coffin, mostly in single file against the walls on each side. Starting at the door, I spoke quietly to each one as I came thru, saying just their names, hardly audibly, and bowing my head—"Uncle Sam, Cousin Alex, Cousin Max, Aunt Fanny, Cousin Naomi," so on, and so on. Some of them I hadn't seen in ten years, perhaps, but remember them, nevertheless, as I have a most retentive memory for faces. And then came my mother, who was near the coffin. Of course, I was the cynosure of all eyes—and quick as a flash, when I saw my mother, although she does not speak to me, nor do I to her, it occurred to me that I must not make this apparent at such a time before all the kin. So I nodded to her, in turn, and said "Howdo do Mother"—or something like that. And while each one had said something—scarcely audible, except for "Maimie"—she turned completely around, ignoring me. Then, a few minutes later, the body was to be taken out, and there was much crying—and loudest and most insistent of all, the wailing of my Mother could be heard. She is qualified to be a professional mourner, for she sure can make a racket. Now, this is what I was amused at—for, in view of the fact that my mother had not spoken with or to Iris in twelve years, and they hated one another cordially, the wailing was so funny to me. I said, later—after the body had gone and my mother was still in the room—that I had derived a great deal of happiness in coming to this funeral. This being a rather peculiar remark to make, my Cousin Esther said, "Why Maimie?" And I said, because I knew that, at any rate, those who refused to speak to me now would shed bucketsful of tears when I died, for there were there a few persons who hated Iris and never spoke to her, and yet they cried copiously at her funeral. The shaft struck home; for she fussed around a second more and then flounced out of the room. The men, only, went to the cemetery, as it was miles and miles away, and because of the snow, it was almost impossible to get there in less than five or six hours. It was in the same cemetery my father was buried in. I have felt the effects of being with her when she expired, all week feeling very depressed.

I must retire, as my eye feels tired. I will write you again Monday, as tomorrow, Saturday, I must, of course, sell mackerels and cheese all day; and Sunday I am going to Norristown to see my poor sister.

I hope the children are fast getting well and that you spare yourself. Yours sincerely, Maimie

I HAD QUITE A DAY, VALENTINE'S DAY....THE FIRST MAIL BROUGHT your postal, my only valentine, and I was very happy....I went down to the door...at five minutes of one, and the mailman brought my second Valentine gift—*The Opal!* I uncovered it and was reading it, or, rather, looking it over, for I am intensely interested in seeing what you would write....[3] When I returned to my room, imagine my surprise to find another visitor, Mrs. Geddes. Oh! How I wish I could tell you all about her....

First, I must describe her. She is about thirty-two or thirty-three; five feet eleven inches tall, and without a single ounce of flesh; light hair of no decided shade; light eyes (of no decided shade); large mouth with perfect teeth; large hands, and abnormally large feet. Her eyes have deep sockets, and her cheek and jaw bones are very prominent. I met her when I was staying at the little studio of Mr. Welsh, prior to going to the hospital—for she lives in the next door house.

She is married, and her husband can be summed up with a few words: a handsome, well-set-up chap, of no antecedents and little education, who earns a small but regular salary as a customhouse officer. He has absolutely no character and no strength of mind— so while he is a good man, it is because he couldn't be a bad man. He works at night and sleeps all day. His only advantage is—like Albert—he has nothing to say; and one can't even be annoyed by his illiteracy. But when she is about, Robert is brought out astonishingly well.

As for her, she is of a little better than middle-class people, with an ability to do anything—everything—that is useful, and she does it. I think that was brought out by the fact that her family were always poor and, finding it necessary to keep up appearances, Sophia can do everything. Her one ambition in life is to be thought artistic—and to my anything-but-artistic mind, she is as artistic as a mule. Her happiness is being in contact with the socially elect and giving out the impression to such humble creatures as I, for instance, that she is of them, and that both she and Robert are of old aristocratic families—and I think Robert's people are of the "poor but honest" class, while hers just escaped that. They have an old humble cottage with quite some grounds. Being so far out, and yet not far out enough to be "stylish," the place rents for about $18.00 a month. They—or, rather, she—has turned it upside down, until she brought about the idea that they took the place because it is "quaint" and so "darling old-fashioned," to quote her. She is a carpenter, a painter, a baker. . .and she is really good at it all. She buys ratty old things in secondhand places and fixes them up until they would defy the best "antique" connoisseur. Then, she goes in for painting; and the nudes thrown around her walls with reckless abandon always make me think of these pictures that the quacks use to depict the deformities of their patients before taking their cure-all. And she sings. But I have never heard her—only that she has about four million copies of old sheet music, yellow with age, of all the classic songs. I think she came across them at an auction sale and bought them—and then the "voice" came soon after. She has no piano; she has, instead a tuning fork, which she says all real artists use. And four dogs, all collies—with, of course, priceless value—and a cat which sits right smack on the table while they eat, and "impudently snatches a mouthful here and there during the progress of the meal." (That is supposed to be a part of an artistic life—as are, also, unwashed dishes and unswept rooms.)

She has about forty books of no kind: that is, I mean that when I looked them over, I couldn't decide what sort of reading she cared for, for they were of so many, varied subjects; and each of them has her book—?—something-or-other, the exact word has escaped me, but it is a huge black cat sprawled on a table laden with books—which she draws herself. Then, last but not least, she is *a* actress. Charles Frohman has offered her no end of a good inducement, but that is all out of the question. I really believe though, that she is pretty clever at that sort of thing, for all the real society people here ask her to appear with them whenever they have a play, and she always does, which I think is all responsible for her "aristocratic ideas." She is to appear in a play today at Ten South Broad, in which the really socially elect are the patronesses, etc., and that is why she dropped in en route to the theatre. Of course, no one in the play is any good, and she is terribly ashamed to be seen with such "rotters," but then what would you?—without her they would have been in a frightful hole.

And now, can you tell me what she can find in me to appeal to all her high class tastes? For goodness knows I am "common" enough, and the wife of a carpenter. But she persists in keeping up our friendship—and with it all, I rather like her, although I secretly am heartily amused at her. I permit her to think, though, that I am terribly impressed, and I think she likes that. Oh! if you could only hear her rant about her various successes in almost anything that you might mention. Fidgety and nervous—she can't remain still one second. This is not exaggerated. So after she trotted around my room, forty times in that many minutes, she left. I hope I haven't given you the impression that she is ridiculous, for she isn't. For she carries it all off very well, and talks like chained lightning. She is very sure she will die of galloping consumption, although so far there have been no symptoms.

I intended writing you Mon., but I am anxious to read the book. So I will mail this, and "in our next chapter," I will tell you all about six wee litta bitta puppies wot I have got.

Ca. February 23, 1911

MY TROLLEY IS TWISTED AGAIN; THAT IS, I AM "OFF AGAIN," AND THAT   13 ✗ means I can't think but that everything is going to the bow-wows. I think it's a scurvy trick on my part to write you in this mood, but I just can't or won't help it . . . .

On Saturday of last week, Albert came home with the glad tidings that work was over, and I don't know of any time, before, that news broke me up so. You see, we have been here a month, and our rent was due today again. I had $12.00 saved, and as there was one more "pay day" before "rent day" (which was today), I expected to surely have it, and was comfortable, in consequence. The news that there was no work, of course, brought visions of the hurried exit from Broad Street and all its wretched details, due to not having the rent. My mind became filled with one idea, and that was how to get the remaining $8.00, and also to live, until Albert got to work—which I hoped would be the next day. The week passed and yet not a hopeful sign of work; and we had spent $2.50 of my $12.00—leaving $10.50 [*sic*] and then, today, the bill for the rent was shoved under our door. In the afternoon I went to Brother's, expecting to borrow the money from him, much as I hated to, and almost would prefer being dispossessed than admit to him my need. At any rate, I left there without borrowing it, although just one word would have done the trick; but his smug satisfied manner made the saying impossible. And while I was downright hungry when I got there, and there was food of every sort and description there, I ate nothing, because it was in-between their regular mealtimes, and I could not let them know I had no

29

lunch nor breakfast. When I left them, I went to a restaurant—and while I had bought no food all that forenoon, knowing I was going [to Brother's] and would eat there, when I didn't eat there and found myself in a restaurant, I attacked the menu card with a vicious delight, and ate 75 cents worth of food. Somehow it gave me new courage; and I looked up a man who wants to buy two of my puppies. And while they are much too young to sell, I suggested that if he paid for them now, I'd sell them for $15.00 for the two, instead of the $20.00 I had priced them, and would keep them for two months more. He could not be made to see it my way; and I came home Thursday night no better off, and if anything worse, due to my extravagant meal. Believe me, I was almost frantic. And Albert—I pitied him, for he seemed so frightened about what would happen on rent day, which was two days off. I wish I had gotten a letter from you Friday, but I didn't; so I just kept on going with no definite aim or reason in thinking I would be any better off by going out than by staying in—so I went out. I went to the Photographic Art Society's Exhibit, and on my return, I was terribly hungry for some good food; and as I had given over the money to Albert—for fear I would get another crazy notion to eat expensive meals—I only had a dime in my pocketbook, and my appetite felt that the 10 cents wouldn't even take the edge off of it. And then I felt I must eat some good steak in a first class place where they served sweet butter and sweet clean bread. Then I used a nickel to phone a young boy I used to know well, intending to get him to meet me—as he had often asked me to—and I was told he was in Salem Beach with his family. And then I just had to phone the man I had borrowed the $20.00 from. I don't try to excuse myself, but I was terribly hungry—and my appetite has a contemptible trick of getting very lively just when I am without funds. So he came to meet me at five o'clock and brought his brother, a young fellow of twenty-six years. The one I knew couldn't stay—a prior engagement—so the younger one did; and I frankly told him I was hungry, after he had bought two cocktails apiece. I did not know it at the time—but I do now—that liquor taken when one's stomach is empty is sure to knock one out. At any rate, I ate my dinner with an uncomfortable feeling, but did not recognize that it was due to the liquor—for I drink rarely, ever, but when I do, I can drink without much effect. That is, I used to; and since that was the first time I had tasted liquor since being rid of the M——, I

attribute my not feeling the liquor, before, to being a M—— user.[4]
At any rate, some light wine went with the dinner, and then some liqueur—yellow chartreuse, I believe—and then I knew I was horribly, frightfully, disgustingly intoxicated. Thank goodness the man wasn't a rotter, but much of a gentleman, and tried to fix me up to send me home. But there wasn't any use—I just could not revive, though he walked with me blocks and blocks. I had all my faculties, but could not control my feet—and then, I was very sick. It grew late. . . . I disliked going home to Albert in that condition, for I did not know what to tell him, as he had never seen me in so sorry a plight before. But I did manage somehow to get to the third floor at 1:00 A.M.—and he was almost wild with worrying as to what had become of me. When he saw my condition, he grew angry and loud, at first. But I settled that in short order, and he helped to undress me. In the morning, I told him just what did happen, telling the unadulterated truth; and he has been crying and acting the fool all day today in consequence. Now I have told you—and you don't know how humiliating it all is. I wish I could have done without telling you—but somehow I couldn't. It is the first bad thing I've done since last March—a year, lacking a week—and I feel so small.

As a sequel, I must tell you that I lost in the shuffle, somewhere, a fur piece which belonged on my coat. You see, my coat is worn, directly in front, and last year when I had money, I purchased a big flat bow which I pinned across the front. It looked smart, and it covered the worn places—and now it is gone. Can you imagine how I hate myself? Today was spent in bed. I asked Albert to go out all afternoon, and stay out, as I wanted to be alone. He took some fool notion that I intended taking my life, which was never a moment in my thoughts. So after reassuring him, he went, and did not return until seven-thirty. About five o'clock I phoned my cousin Alex. He is a young boy of sixteen years who has been in this country, coming from Russia, thirteen months. He is really a "greenhorn," but a very eager boy to learn, and I have been giving him English lessons all winter, and it is marvellous how he progresses. I know that he has been saving a small sum out of his weekly earnings to save enough so that he might send the money to bring his widowed mother to this country. And altho he only earns $5.00 a week, I know he saves $1.00 each week by the most rigid economy. I frankly told him my plight—and without the slightest hesitation, he gave me the entire savings, which were $15.00. And I felt so cheap to take it. But he knows it is as safe as though it is in the bank, and before he has the whole amount, I will repay the $15.00. Doesn't it seem strange that I could not ask my own brother to lend me the money—and yet had no hesitation about asking Alex?

If I was "blue" all week, last night's sweet escapade has given me a monopoly on all the Blues in the world. Somehow I feel I ought not tell you all this, for I think it will pain you; but then, I don't want to keep that one ugly thing out. For I have said all along to myself that I was writing you—my other self—just as I would write were I keeping a faithful diary.

I would like to read your mind when you read this letter. I don't think you would be angry, but still you might be disgusted. It surely doesn't seem as though your and Mr. Welsh's encouraging letters helped me much. Well, there is no use sitting here condemning myself. I am to you what I am to myself; so it is rank waste of time expressing my opinion of myself, when you know my worth—or, rather, worthlessness—just as well as I do. I wonder whether you knew I was off again, when you did not hear from me.

I will go to bed now, as it is twenty-five minutes of five and I am sleepy; but I wish I could end this appropriately—cleverly I mean—as you do in the letter in *The Opal*.

Perhaps after all I had better say goodnight.

February or March, 1911

CЗ 14   I WAS SO GLAD FOR BOTH YOUR LETTERS TODAY. I WAS ANXIOUSLY awaiting the mail that would bring your letter. I did not think you would scold; still, I was somewhat uneasy, for I am so disgusted with myself that I should have expected that you would be, too. It is 1:30 A.M.—and again I am wakeful, although I have had about three hours' sleep. After I have written you my mind will be clear, and I will soon sleep.

I think I shall first answer the questions you ask in your letter. As to why Albert had to stop work: He was working for a contractor who had "weather strips" to put on each window and door for one of the largest estates in this city and probably in the U.S.A..... The estate is divided into sections, and the men finished one section Saturday week, and they were told to report Monday morning at a second section. When they came, they found they could not go on, as the "Weather-Strip" had got mixed up into some "red tape"...and the men were all laid off and told they would be notified by letter as soon as the work started in again. Of course they all are looking for other work, as this may mean six months waiting....

Now as to the job I wrote you I thought I might get. It was a correspondent's position with Curtis Publishing Company, answering letters to persons making inquiries about wanting to sell the *Ladies Home Journal* or the *Saturday Evening Post*. I felt I could do that work satisfactorily, so when I was asked to call, I went; and the manager told me that out of twenty-five or thirty answers he had received in answer to his ad, he had only written four of the applicants to come in. I made out a general application, and then I was given three letters to answer, just the main facts being given to me; and while they told me the other three girls would have to answer the same letters, all other things being equal, the girl answering the letters best would have the position. Somehow, I felt the job was mine, such was my confidence in my answers—and sure enough, the next day, in the first mail, I was told to come in "prepared to go to work provided my references were satisfactory." I then went the day following and had to go through a lot of red tape, and answered almost a hundred questions. You see, they keep a close account of each of their employees. On the top of this printed employees' record was a bunch of printing in reference to the Curtis Publishing Company, but I did not stop to read it. I handed in my "record," and when the manager said, "Did you get it all filled out?" I said, "Yes, although I had to leave several questions unanswered because either I do not know just what to say, or for obvious reasons." He then glanced down it and came to this:

Are you married or single?—*Married.*
How long have you been married?—*5 years.*
Are you divorced?—
Are you suing for divorce?—
On what ground?—
How long is it since you have not been living with your husband?—

Of course I left the above questions unanswered for obvious reasons. The manager then said: "Now, here are some you overlooked," and I explained that I hadn't, but that since I was living with my husband and there was no separation of any sort, I did not answer the questions. He looked at me so strange then, and said, "Did you fill out one of the employee's applications for positions when you came to apply?" and I told him I had. Well, he then told me that had I read the list of rules which the Company had, I would understand his astonishment, for there was quite a few of them printed on the application. He then got [the application] and imagine my disappointment when he pointed out a rule which was somewhat as follows—"The Curtis Publishing Company under no conditions will employ a woman who is married and still living with her husband." That is why their questions read as they did, for it was taken for granted that I knew their rules. Of course, that let me all out, and I was terribly disappointed, for somehow I had made up my mind that the position was mine—for it was one I could have held better than any other sort. . . . I told this to Miss Outerbridge and she said she was glad I had not lied. I was obliged to tell her that I am afraid had I seen this printed rule, I should have lied—for I wanted the work so badly, and coming just as it did when Albert lost work again.

It is morning now, 10:30, and I will resume. I believe what I wrote in the night covers the questions you asked. Now as to applying to James for assistance, that is entirely out of the question. . . . I prefer far better to get along "somehow" without his charity. If I were to tell you some of the recent indignities I suffered at his hand, you would appreciate how I feel—although if he knew my position, he would treat me better; but I do not care for his or anyone else's patronage.

I went the other night to call on them, with the real object of bringing away a basketful of groceries for which I would pay him at some future date—which would not seem strange as I have done it before. He never greeted me when I came in—and that is ignorance, not arrogance. He knows in his heart how superior I am to him in every way, and he resents it. Whereas some brothers would be proud of it—to think that a sister born of the same mother and father and without much education, can converse with people, etc.—he resents it. (As, for instance, a great many professors at the University buy at his store, and while helping them on Saturday, I sort of got acquainted with them. And with my desire to know such people and perhaps learn something from them, I became quite friendly—so much so that one of these men, Mr. King, brought his wife over to the store to see me, and then she asked me to call and dine with them Sunday. Now, James knows that people of that sort wouldn't invite him in a million years—and that his wife, whose English is a crime, couldn't hope to know such people.) So, to continue: when I walked in, he never raised his head nor smiled a greeting, and I went back in the house. In the store were two customers, a man and lady. They were dressed too much like gentle people to be gentle, so I just drifted right by without even looking at them. James' wife greeted me with effusion and, as they were just getting ready to eat dinner, I sat down with them, as I am not on ceremony there. He came in and said, "You almost knocked that man down." I didn't answer. Then he said, with a chuckle, "Oh! he is a big society man and lives at the Chermont—If you had known that, May, I guess you wouldn't have been so rude." I didn't answer that either. And later his wife, who served the steak, cut a large piece off for him with the carving knife, and then another for me, and then proceeded to calmly eat out of the platter, using the carving knife and fork for utensils. Of course, I never noticed it, but Brother jumped on her with both feet—"For God's sake Caroline, don't do such things! Can't you learn something from May? See how she cuts each piece off at a time before taking it to her mouth. And don't bite off that whole slice—break it, as she does, and butter each piece as you break it." The poor girl—she was almost paralyzed, and did not eat any more—while he kept on reading the paper, thoroughly satisfied with himself. Then I could not contain myself any longer, and as he is younger than I am, I proceeded to tell him what had been in my mind for months. I said "James why couldn't you reserve that call-down for after I left, when you are alone, which is the proper time for all domestic quarrels and corrections. When you married Caroline, you knew she hadn't any refined table manners—for certainly in the three years you courted her, you must have noticed it—and if you intend to teach her any, it would be a good idea if you knew something about it yourself. Everything you pointed out to Caroline you do yourself—and you wouldn't have noticed it on her, if the contrast between my eating and hers wasn't so evident. You have now more food in your mouth than you should have, for your cheeks protrude in eating; and that is worse than what

Caroline did. And your teaspoon in your cup with one finger draped about it to keep the spoon from sliding into your stomach is anything but elegant. Your knife resting on the table and the plate is way off: it should be flat on the plate. Then, if you would carry your food to your mouth instead of your mouth to your food—it would perhaps be possible for you to criticize others." The silence was ominous—and he soon left the table. She seemed very grateful, without speaking—for I've no doubt that he is very high and mighty in his manner toward her, even though he loves her devotedly, and I imagine that when I am not there, he is always setting me up as a paragon.

At any rate, it was not congenial to stay there, so I said I would go call on the Kings, my new acquaintances, who live one block away. When I left it was 8:15. I stayed an hour, returning at 9:15. Brother never has, to my knowledge, closed before ten or eleven during the week, but when I came in he said, "I thought you were going to stay all night. I want to close, and have been awaiting your return." I knew it was just a lie to make me feel he had inconvenienced himself on my account, so I said, "Well, I want to get a few things, and then I will go." He said nothing, but stood there sullenly while I packed a small basket. The things I had to have, to live on. Still, he did not know that; so I selected only things to make him think it was for between-meal bites and light lunches, and for that reason, had to take things other than I really wanted. I should have liked to take homelier things, but instead took delicacies. In the meantime, Caroline came out; and as I did not know the prices of everything, I asked him, and he did not answer, but she did. While I was sort of picking around, he said, "May, didn't I tell you I want to close, so hurry and go?" Just imagine the coarseness of such a remark to me—when Albert and I had stayed there for three weeks prior to his opening, Albert carpentering and making the fixtures, and I staining the wood! As Albert was working at the time, he did all this work for Bro at night, staying until one and two every morning, then riding a hour in the cars and getting up again at six to go to work, for which he received not one penny. In fact, money couldn't pay for it—and at that time, it meant lots to Bro, for he had no money to spare. Anyway, when I got all the things together it came to $3.40. I said, "Goodness, how shall I carry this?" He came over and put it all in a thin paper bag. I said, "Won't that break?" He shook his head, meaning "no." I knew better; and just as I stepped off his step, the bag broke, smashing a jar of preserves that cost 40 cents. And I left it lying there for him to see in the morning, and I carried the rest of the stuff to the corner grocery, and they wrapped it properly. Just as he would have done, for anyone but me. To return to my leaving—As soon as he handed me the bag, he put the light out, leaving us in almost pitch darkness. Now, Caroline always—invariably—comes forward and kisses me goodnight, while James simply says goodnight. So as I started to the door, he did too; but she never stirred. And I looked at her, and she had her head bowed. And he evidently had told her not to kiss me any more, and she was visibly agitated. So I said, "Good night, Caroline," while he held the door open in a most insulting manner, just as much as to say, "For goodness sake, *get* out." She murmured good night, and he never said a word, and as I placed my feet off the sill, he banged the door a frightful bang and clicked the key in the lock. And I sat down on the steps and cried—although he, of course, didn't see me, as he went directly into the house. It was after I got up again that the bag broke.

Now you may judge from that whether I would care to apply to him for aid. Of course, that was the worst I had ever received from his hands. So I shall never go there again. Albert made me promise that, although I am going to see her when the baby comes, regardless. You may imagine that I have caused him to act like that through some act of mine, but if you understood him as I do, you would see it is not anything which I do or did that I can help. Before he became prosperous, he was very affable; and now, because he is the youngest and is doing so well, he doesn't want anyone to imagine it is "luck," or "opportunity," or because he happened to strike a good place, but because he is so all-fired clever. Never before did he have anything, and was a "drummer," and was obliged to fawn on everyone to get anything; and now that he is making money so fast, he thinks it is only right that he show everyone that he doesn't need them—and his manner is so contemptible that I cannot understand ladies, real ones, buying of him more than once.

I wanted to write you in detail about him, so that you would not attribute my refusal to go to him for assistance as false pride....

I never wrote you about my thoughts about *The Opal*, and I am not going to, until circumstances are different and I don't feel depressed—even if that doesn't happen for a fortnight—because I am not my real self and am mostly cynical and pessimistic at this time. If one could firmly and surely believe in a Heaven where there would be all the things that go to make up the sort of Heaven we each would want, I would perhaps be less fretful and calmly await my reward in Heaven for sitting tight and being good. But I don't feel that way, and while I don't do things, it is for a combination of reasons: because I am out of the running and too lazy to get back in, and then I value your and Mr. Welsh's and a few others' friendship and good opinion—and perhaps other reasons that I can't define. . . .

I wish I knew why I feel so badly. I believe I will lie down—

My very dear Friend,   *March, 1911*

☙ 15   IT IS SUCH A PERFECTLY BEAUTIFUL DAY THAT "BY RIGHTS," AS THE KIDS say, I ought to go out into the air. It is so balmy. But having nowhere to go, I will remain in and write you . . . .

Right now I will say that of course I will be glad to have the dresses, provided, of course, you can't use them yourself. . . . As for the money, I do feel differently about that. I read to Albert the portion of your letter offering to send me another check, and he begged me to write you that we would not need it, as he feels it dreadfully—that work is so scarce. He got some work last week but it snowed hard the next morning and it was all off again. . . . But Tuesday night a gentleman called and it seems he is the foreman of a large company for whom Albert worked all last summer. And they sent him to get Albert to sign up with them to work starting April 15, for six months—for as I told you before, carpenters are in great demand then, and Albert being such a steady, reliable man, they were anxious to secure his services for the season. Albert seemed elated; but I stepped in and delivered a lecture to this young man, and told him that as they had the best service from Albert all summer, and then when work was scarce they turned him adrift while they kept on men less capable—that this summer Albert could only work for a contractor who would guarantee to keep him at work at least part of the winter; and I felt that I could bring such a guarantee about. He explained that this firm was forty years in existence and that the men they retained through the winter were men that had been in their employ for years and years. I told him: if he was maintaining an old men's home, he couldn't expect Albert to idle all winter and then pitch in and give him the best of his energy to make up for the poor material in the shape of carpenters that he was obliged to work with; and that the firm had the right idea and should take care of its old men, but should pension them off without work. He hadn't much to say, then. I told him that if he would give Albert employment now until April 15, on that date Albert could sign up with him in a six month contract. So he finally agreed to that, and Albert goes to work Monday, and I hope that means until next winter without hitch. . . . If only I could earn regularly $10.00 a week, I would be very comfortable. As for your giving me more aid—I don't think we will need that, except in this way: If you send it, this time it would have to be a loan, provided I could feel I could pay it back when I was able, and small parts of it at a time—as, for instance, a dollar every other week. In that way, there would be no question but that I could pay it, and I would not have much trouble after Albert works steadily, and right now it would help lots. . . .

I have written but little that I had in my mind, but I am just a tiny wee bit depressed. Just you see when I am cheerful again—you will not know I am the same writer. Then I will tell you all about Poke's puppies. . . and about Opal—Oh! I have such a joke to tell you—It is that I imagine I am the Opal in your book—not that I prefer her character to Mary's, but that I feel were I to live their lives, I should have been like Edith. Mrs. Geddes is reading it now. She knew all about it, having heard it discussed in very fashionable circles. That is what she says, but I believe she read the criticism somewhere, as she doesn't really go into fashionable circles. . . .

Goodbye—It is getting cold now; I must close the windows—

March 16, 1911

I HAVE THOUGHT MUCH ABOUT WHAT YOU SUGGESTED—THAT IS, MY **16** trying to write something marketable—and I only wish I could have the confidence in myself that you have in me. Sunday night I went to a typical Jewish wedding, among the real Jews, and I only wish I could depict that as I saw it—it was so very interesting, and amusing as well. I feel perhaps I could tell you about it in a letter; but to write about it, there's the rub—I would not perhaps do as well. Again, I have it in mind that when I am not so hampered by small worries and needs, that I will try that: writing to you what I see among my friends of that class, and then perhaps compiling them and try making a short story of it. But now I couldn't possibly, for I am so upset all the time. . . .

∞ 17   I HAVE BEEN WORKING. REALLY AND TRULY, AS YOU KNOW, I HAVE BEEN answering ads right along; and in most instances the reason I could not get employment was because of my appearance; but somehow this man seemed to have been satisfied. The work is soliciting ads for a programme of a benefit performance to be given at the Metropolitan Opera House for some charitable organizations. It is something very different than was ever held in this city, for it is to be a colossal affair, 820 Philadelphians of the best society being the performers. The patronesses are the best known ladies in Phila. and of course that carries some weight in soliciting the ads. I carry credentials from them with me. The only trouble is that Phila. is always having something of this sort, although nothing anywhere in this class. Still, the merchants don't know that, for as yet it has not been advertised, and soliciting is no easy work. So far, since Tuesday afternoon when I started, I have earned $11.50, and believe me, I worked some to get it. I would not hold out on it, only that I need money so very badly. It may get easier, later, when it is advertised, but now it's the hardest kind of plugging; and it is such a drag to be on one's feet; and the people you meet are not always the kindest in the world. Still, I will keep at it until something else turns up. The performance is to be held May 1, so I have until then to do some good work. When I come home at night, my feet burn and ache, but perhaps that is due to my not being accustomed to it. That is why I have not written sooner, for I was so tired. Any sort of work is hard, I guess, provided you do it properly; and on the whole, any work that saves my eyesight is best . . . .

I don't remember whether I thanked you for the checks, and if not, I must, for it was such a relief not to be worried. I gave Alex his money and he was very pleased. I gave him an extra half dollar. He is so saving. Sometimes I wish I could be as he is; then again, I am glad I am not. Goodness, I never let money worry me—the lack of it sometimes does. We paid our rent, and now got started paying up a debt of Albert—to the union. He is working but is losing time, because the building they are working on is a concrete one, and all the carpenters do is make the moulds; but due to the cold weather, they lost two days last week and two-and-a-half this week, because the cold makes the cement too hard to run, and all work ceases. So instead of bringing home $22.00 Sat. afternoon, he only drew $16.00.

Mr. Suiffen wrote in the early part of the week that he expected to be home on the twenty-fifth—that was Saturday (yesterday), but as yet I have not heard from him. I probably will tomorrow. I rather like him—but then, not particularly. He is one of those very nice men whom one never could speak for or against. I think when a man has been a secretary for twenty-five years to one man, especially a man like Mr. Welsh, he loses his own identity; and not being a strong enough character to absorb Mr. Welsh's, he is just neutral. He never offers any advice or suggestions, but listens to anything you might say very attentively, just as a phonographic record would; and then he tells or writes it to Mr. Welsh. His return, then, as you may judge, doesn't mean very much to me. I told you I heard from Mr. Welsh, and since then, I have received still another letter. You asked me whether hearing from him is a help to me. I am sorry to say that it isn't much, not now, at any rate. In the beginning when I first heard from Mr. Welsh, while I was still in the West, I believed in whatever he wrote as being the very thing to do in every case; but since knowing him and what a pure, perfect person he is, when I read his experience and advice, I don't feel as though they could mean anything to me, who is so totally different from him. He is so unselfish and pure. Reading his letters is like reading books gotten up for Sunday School purposes, with the characters just such good Boys and Girls as no one ever knew. While I love him, I can't ever imagine being like him. He is so very kind and sympathetic—but so was Christ, and while everyone loves Him, they all don't do as He would have them do. I regret most that I can't feel as Mr. Welsh does about some things; and I regret it most when I am writing him, for then I would like to write the things I know would make him most happy and pleased with me. When you wrote that you would like me to make you a promise, I found there was nothing new in the thought, for evidently without our ever speaking it, I have made some such promise to myself, something after this fashion: that I wouldn't do anything that would grieve Mr. Welsh if he knew it. And as I wrote you each time, I was happy that there was nothing very ugly that I would have to report to you. I did not make any promise to Mr.

Welsh other than that I would "try" to remain clean; and other than what I wrote you—the twice I drank—I have tried to be good and decent. I promise you now, though, Mrs. Howe, that until Mr. Welsh returns, I will *not*, *absolutely*, do anything that would grieve him when he would have to hear it, on his return. As I have written him that I love you so much, and that you are good to me and write me so often, he, I know, sort of feels that you will take care of me, not to let me fall back; and now I must be more careful than ever, for I wouldn't want that he or anyone else should think the interest you have taken in me has been without result. No matter what anyone thinks, it wouldn't change the absolute fact that, hadn't it been for you, the night we were ejected from the Broad Street house, I would have certainly fallen back—and then right along for a few weeks about the same time, when I was hungry all the time and went to bed each night thinking that I would do wrong the next day; and the "next day" did not come. I have not written in answer to Mr. Welsh's recent letter as yet, but I will tomorrow, especially now that I have work to report that will please him. I have written this in bunches, so if it is rather disconnected, you will understand. It is Monday morning now and I am going to work presently. I hope you and the "childer" are all well.

My very dear Friend,   *March 31, 1911*

℞ 18   I AM NOT GOING TO TRY TO ANSWER YOUR LETTER, FOR I AM IN A HURRY, and the letter I received yesterday, I feel was too lovely to be answered in a hurry. I am to report at the office at nine, and it is eight o'clock now and I am in my birthday clothes. I felt I must write you today to let you know what is doing— That sounds slangy, but I don't mean it that way, for there are really things doing with me, for the first time in months. I am still soliciting ads, with much success, averaging $5.00 a day for "yours truly."

Somehow I got it in my head while you were in the country, that I'd give anything to be there—or somewhere away from the strife and turmoil of this big city—but, of course, it was just wishes with me. Now, since I have been working, I am dead tired and want to go to a real country [place] for Sunday; and as I have $20.00 of my own money, I am going. . . . Albert is going to Norristown to visit my poor sister on Sunday; but I, for once, am going to be alone and have plenty of time to think, with sufficient food. . . . I am almost crazy to

42

go. And I will take a long walk Sat. and Sun., and I will think of you; and I know you will be happy Sunday, for I expect to be happy. Am I crazy? I wonder, but it seems I can smell the country even as I write. I will write you directly I return, all about my trip, and until then believe me to be— Sincerely, gratefully and cheerfully yours, Maimie

This letter seems an insult after the letter I received yesterday, but I certainly don't mean to be anything that is ugly to you, for I worship you and I will prove it.

April, 1911

I HAVE SO MUCH TO TELL YOU—BUT FIRST I MUST TELL YOU OF MY TRIP. I   **19** ✖
left Saturday, April 1, and took Miss Poke along. It was a very mild day when I left, but that night it became very cold, and I was mighty glad I had brought my fur coat along, which I did not think I would need. The next day, Sunday, was beautiful but no milder, but I was determined to take that walk. So I went, and it was the most delightful experience of months. I can't explain why, but since receiving your letter telling me of your walk along the country roads, I have thought of nothing else; and when I was soliciting for the ads, I would keep that object in view, hoping I would earn enough so that—even though it seemed folly to spend money on such things—I would have enough to buy some few absolute necessities and also pay for the trip. The first walk, Sunday morning, was all that I anticipated. Everything smelled fresh and virgin, and while there wasn't much green, still, here and there were tiny buds and live things. I even found some peculiar blossoms which I suppose, had I ever studied botany, would have meant something to me. As it was, it just looked like a degenerate flower here and there on the roadside. And Miss Poke, perhaps she didn't just have the time of her life. She has a wonderful imagination and chased everything imaginable, until she was so tired that she would select a sunny spot and lie down, and I'd have to coax, cajole and then threaten, before she'd decide to come along. Then when I was "dog tired," too, we returned, and I ate—or, rather, devoured—five boiled eggs which had only been laid a few hours before, and cream, and butter—that I know about but seldom have—and then real biscuits, made while I waited. It was all so good.

I expected to return Monday; and as I didn't,[5] Mr. Towne—for whom I had worked soliciting the ads—wrote suggesting that since I wasn't far off, why didn't I run over to Atlantic City and see what I could do toward getting some of the larger hotels to advertise? I thought his suggestion a good one and believed that getting those hotels would be almost too easy; and there, too, I had the added pleasure of being by the seashore, which made my little trip seem more like a holiday. Tuesday, then, I started for Atlantic City; and on the way it started to pour; and I arrived in the wettest rain storm I ever experienced.

I had some difficulty finding a place within my means, and as I had to foot the expenses of the Atlantic City trip, too, my means necessarily were very limited. But I found a room, clean and desirable, but, oh! so bleak, compared to my pretty place here. The lady promised that it would be heated at once, but it never was, all the time I was there; and you know how damp a cottage at the seashore must be, especially as *it rained all the time, day and night, that I was there.* At the start, I developed a very bad sore throat, and it was with me until the day I returned, although I fought it assiduously with my old friend, "Perry Oxide." Then, of course, I sat down and waited for the rain to desist, for it was impossible to go about, as it came down in torrents; and now I know that rain is wetter at the seashore than inland. Each day, I decided to wait until the next day to write you, for of course each day the weather prophet forecasted, "clear weather" on the morrow—and then I hoped to get some ads and have something worthwhile to tell you. Then something happened which I shall write of later that gave me an awful jolt. But by Sat., I decided I would wait no longer, but return, and made arrangements to come. And then Sunday the sun came out, and it could not have been a more perfect day. But I was discouraged and sick, for with the sore throat, I developed something wrong which I don't know much about—but the lady in whose house I stayed said she thought it was a "cold in the ovaries," and that I must have gotten it walking about in the rain when my feet were always sopping wet. I only had a room in her house and was obliged to go out to eat, and without rubbers I just couldn't help getting my feet wet. So even though Sunday promised a beautiful week, I decided not to remain, for with the fact that it is Easter season, the managers would no doubt be hard to approach. So home I came, without having made one penny in Atlantic City, and the trip cost me—that is, just the Atlantic City trip—$13.00.

As I told Miss Outerbridge when she was here yesterday, while I was awfully depressed on my return, the clouds all cleared away when I saw the box you sent me and found that the dresses fitted so perfectly. I had the blue polka-dotted one on when she was here, and she said she had been admiring it before I spoke about it, and she was, too, surprised at how perfectly they fit. I kept the dress on, and later, when she left, went out to my brother's house—the first time since I wrote you, when he was so overbearing. Albert told me on my return that "Katie" (James's wife—Caroline is her name, but he has changed it to "Katie"), had phoned twice, so I phoned her, and she said she wanted me to come out so much. I asked about her condition, and when I learned that the baby is expected next week, I could not resist going. She seemed so happy when I told her I would come that I felt sorry that I had stayed away so long. And Brother was so very careful to be polite and all was very pleasant. I stayed to dinner, and the table manners of both were things of beauty and a joy forever. I know they were both so careful that they couldn't enjoy their food. . . .

While I think of it, I want to tell you about that which you wrote about last—in reference to what I told Albert as to my life prior to my marriage to him. He knew I had lived with a man, the man I first left my home with, Frank Sloan of Boston, and that I lived with him as his wife for nearly four years. But really, the things that were the ugliest I have done mostly since my marriage, which will be five years the thirtieth of May. But all that he knows is about Mr. Sloan, which I told him.

There is something I want to tell you, that has shocked me so that I can't even think about it. Before I tell you about it, I will tell you some things relative to it. You know, as I told you, about what Albert's earning capacity is, for while he does earn a fair wage all summer, it is at that time that he must have clothes, shoes, underwear, etc; and as his mother is a sufferer of hay fever, she goes away each August, and I always permit him to contribute toward the expense of the trip, which is generally $5.00 a week and $5.00 toward the fare going, and $5.00 returning. As she stays a month, it meant each summer $30.00 at the least for her. So you can see how almost-impossible it is for me to save anything from what he earns

45

in the summer to live in the winter, during which time he doesn't earn his salt. So, of course, up to last spring, I would get money in various ways, sometimes working, and when I wasn't, I would tell him I was, and in many ways make it possible for both of us to live. Most of the time when I would get money, he would share it with me, for I could never see him want. Of course, I always pretended to work for it. Now I do not want to pose as a martyr or as being entirely unselfish, but when I tell you I do not love him, and have no feeling other than a certain amount of respect for him, you can see that I was unselfish in a measure. And even since I have not received money in ugly ways, I worked, and worked mighty hard, and have done without food [some] days so that he could have it. And then I would maneuver different ways to pay our way, so that he always should have a little change in his pockets. Even the money you sent me went right into the rent, and personally I had no benefits from anything that I have worked for this winter, as it has all gone toward keeping us. If I didn't help or couldn't help, I have never even imagined what would happen. Either he would have to find a way or instead of keeping him and myself, I could just take care of myself. At any rate, those things have never occurred to me. I just did the best I could, looking out for him at all times just as though he was part of me—or better still, much as a mother would a child. Even though he is so very much older than I, I have in reality been as a mother to him, for his mind is not much more developed than the average child's. When he does anything, it is as I direct, and—I do not say this to be facetious—if I did not tell him when to take a bath, I don't know how long it would be before he would do it. And then I always credited him with being straight-forward and simple as a child in every small or large matter—until now, when I am all up in the air and I don't know what to think. I will tell you the whole thing, and then I am going to ask you to write me what you think of it.

When I left here Sat., I counted just what I thought my expenses would be, figuring very close, so that I could leave him with as much money as possible, for I had put the money we both earned that week in a general fund. As it had been cold to freezing point two days and a half that week, he only earned $12.00. You see, what that means—when he says he earns $4.00 a day—something happens each week, until I am almost frantic hoping that some week he will put in a full week. At any rate, when I left, I left him all I could spare, which was $4.30. As he had to pay $1.00 of that for the union (which is a weekly debt) and 40 cents for laundry and then carfare and his food, I knew that it wouldn't be enough to last the week out, so I assured him, by mail, when I decided to go on to work Atlantic City, that the first ad I received I would instruct Towne to send him $5.00 to last until pay-day. He answered in the letter that the money was almost gone, but that he would wait until Mr. Towne sent the money—for of course he was sure as I was that I would secure plenty of ads in Atlantic City. Then when it began to rain, and rained steadily all day Tues. and Wed.—by Thursday morning I was frantic. Believe me, not for myself, but for him; for I was buying 5-cent pieces of cheesecake to make out lunch with, and things like that, but I was so sorry for him—especially as it rained here in Phila. all week, and I knew that he wasn't working and without money for food. My heart ached for him. After considerable thought, I devised a plan to help him. I phoned to Phila., over long distance, calling up the brother of the girl at whose house I stayed in the country, and I told him that I was in need of a loan: He is a very young boy, not over twenty-three—and he has a good position with an insurance company, and I know that he is, in secret, supposed to be in love with me. His two sisters make quite a joke of it, but in threshing over in my mind someone to go to, I thought of him. So I told him that I needed some money immediately and thought of him, knowing he would lend it to me. I then explained that I didn't want Mr. Jones to know anything about it. . . . This young fellow assured me that he would let me have it. The amount was $10.00, and he said since I seemed to be in such a hurry for it, he would phone it to me, which he did. . . . He had the money to me by 8:15 A.M., I kept $5.00 for myself and phoned Albert $5.00. I then got Albert on the phone to tell him it was coming, and as it was still raining, he was at home. I asked him what his finances were, and he said he had 9 cents in his pockets, and I said to "cheer up," that I had done some work and collected $10.00, $5.00 of which he would receive in a very short while. He thanked me most effusively, and that ended it with me—except that now I had to more-than-ever get out and do some work, so as to pay the $10.00. For, you see, I did not even tell him where I got the $10.00, for as usual I was saving him the worry and mortification that I imagine he would feel if he knew to what ends I often go to make him comfortable. Then, here is the climax.

About noon, this same young fellow called me up from Phila., asking me if I got the money all right; and then he said that he wanted to explain something about the money: that he did not happen to have any on hand. . .and as I phoned him so early in the morning. . . . he had difficulty finding anyone that he could borrow it from, and then he thought of Albert. . . . As he knows Albert very well, he decided he would phone him, and although Albert was in bed at the time, 7:30 A.M., he told him to come over; and he (Albert) loaned him the $10.00! (Of course, Albert didn't know what he wanted it for.) You may know I was speechless then—and I am yet. In fact, I can't think. I am almost afraid to think. It seems horrible. . . . He said Albert certainly loaned him $10.00 at 7:30 A.M. Thursday morning—and here I hadn't slept Wed. night worrying if he had to go to bed hungry while I had spent that money to go to the country. I asked this boy if Albert had any more money, and he said he seemed to have two or three more bills. And only an hour later, he told me he had 9 cents in his jeans. I can't tell you, for I really don't know the extent of it myself, what this all means to me. I *never*, not once, ever caught him even in a white lie before, and this seems such a heinous one. I never asked Albert a thing about it—really I am afraid to, for if he would lie to me, I don't know what I would do. For you see, my life up to now has never meant any happiness because of him, but I thought I made him so happy; and yet if he has been lying, cheating and stealing—for that is what it would amount to—what reason would I have for keeping this farce up? Well, I am in a worse muddle than ever, and it seems a pity to drag you into it. But I don't see what else to do, for if I went to Mr. Suiffen, I know he would say just to keep on as I have, and to trust him (Albert), that everything is all right—and yet unless I lie to myself I don't see how it can be. I wish you would write me what you think of it. Of course, you may think I may not be justified in placing so much importance to it; but think as I will, I don't see how I can avoid it. It opens up so many avenues for deceit in him that I never dreamed of before, and makes all the effort and energy I have expended not to worry him seem as a joke. I am all perplexed, so I will bring this to a close. I hope you don't object to the use of this paper. Somehow I like it, it is so honest and without any attempt at anything but to be useful. I haven't the courage to write many people on it but I seem to know to you it won't make any difference. I hope your children are all well—oh yes! and your husband, too. I seem to forget you have one. Yours lovingly, Maimie

I am so tired.

April 22, 1911

...YOU SEE, WHEN I WRITE YOU, I WRITE EVERYTHING, AND MOSTLY **20** ✷ the things that trouble me, and that is because I love you and don't stop to think whether it would be better to write this or that, but just keep on writing what is on my mind—things that I have always had to keep to myself, for I never trusted any other woman—and then even if I did tell them, I wouldn't feel it has helped matters any. Of course, the pleasant things I sometimes write you about, but not often, because my few pleasant experiences I tell and re-tell to so many people that I couldn't possibly tell anything else to. But to you I tell the real things...and while your letters to me are generally about myself, I felt that you told me the "real things" also....

So when you wrote that you were going to the hospital in the course of a few days and, as I thought, to undergo a serious operation, and only spoke of it most casually, I was hurt—for I thought you didn't think it was any of my business. But I feel better now. Your husband wrote to me how you were, and it was written as though it was indeed some of my business as to your condition; and I know he only could feel that way because you do....

...We have a baby, a sure-enough one. A " 'itty, bitty Katie," for that's it's name. I could write volumes about that baby, but won't bore you. It is a blonde with large blue eyes, and weighed eight pounds at birth. I was in the room when it was born, and as it is the only child I ever saw born or in fact that ever was so near to me, I feel it is the "wonderous" thing in the world....

I received another letter from Mr. Welsh, and just now, as I think of it, I want to tell you something. In your letter, you wrote of Mr. Welsh sending some money. Soon after he left, his son sent a check for $7.00, made out to Albert, and [they] came for four weeks. Then, with the last check came a note saying: this is the last of the checks. Remember, they weren't sent to me, but to Albert;

49

and *I never touched a penny of it.* In this letter which came today, Mr. Welsh wrote he hoped things were easier for me now that the winter is practically over, and if so, would I please instruct his son not to send the checks any longer! Albert used the money, of course, to pay both our expenses. That's true; but he considers it a loan—and if I told you why that whole thing incensed me, you would surely think I was crazy. I do hope this finds you out of pain.

    With much love, I am yours sincerely, Maimie

I am sending a "Dog Book"—edited by myself—under separate cover.

Walnut Street, Philadelphia
May or June, 1911

☙ 21-22   I AM VERY GLAD YOU ARE HOME [FROM THE HOSPITAL].[6] I WISH YOU were where I could wheel you about in a big rolling chair, during these fine days. You have no idea how strong I am; and I am thoroughly appreciative of the fact. It occurs to some people that since I am admittedly so strong, that I'd make a good laundress or "scrub-lady"—since physical strength seems my only strength. But I guess it's because I am lazy that I refuse to do that sort of work, and not because it's beneath me—for what right have I to consider anything beneath me? I wish I was born a man. I know what I'd do this morning. I'd button up my coat and jump on the tail end of a train and steal a ride to wherever it was going—and then when I'd get there, I'd stop to consider "What's next?" As it is, in the first place I couldn't steal the ride; and even if I went the regular way, how could I manage without "things"—which would mean a trunk; and then Miss Poke—Oh, I guess I couldn't think of such things! Whatever I do will have to be regular and thought out, and I despise that. For I have no regular idea of what I want to do—only that I must do something, and that, right away. I have drifted all my life and expect I'll keep that up until the end of the chapter. Since last spring, I—to use a common slang—"kidded" myself that now I was living with a purpose.... I thought I really was going to be like the average decent woman, with a circle of friends for whom one keeps up appearances; and even though it seemed silly—still, it's what everyone else does, and why not fall in line? During this winter, I felt how terrifying such a life would be to me, even if I was successful in keeping in the circle of friends. If it had not been for you and Mr. Welsh, I'd have had to do something real wicked to make up for the terrible monotony of my existence. All this would not have been so horrible if, as a compensation, my husband was a man that even in the slightest degree interested me. I suppose that is my fault, for other women seem to like him, and to me—oh, I can't express it! It is silly for me to write that other women of my class like him—they like what I make him appear to be. They never meet him without me, and of course I make him appear at least desirable, since without me he would be what these artificial diamonds are without the mirrors, black velvet, and the strong electric lights. I would be willing to be all these things to him indefinitely, if there was something to be gained outside of what seems to be small compensation: that is, the respect of others—people that I don't give a hoot for. And now I've come to where I must make a stand.

Albert went to Atlantic City to procure work, and was successful; and I have been here alone for two weeks. Saturday night he came home, to remain over Sunday, and I don't know what possessed me—the "Old Nick," or what—but I came out in the open with him; and instead of keeping up this silly subterfuge that nothing could be gained thereby, I was open and aboveboard. He heard the truth for the first time in five years—and it sent him packing. I am a "widow-woman" now, and the aspect does not seem so alarming. Why should I persist in living with him? When I married him, I knew exactly what for—it was as a sort of anchor. I was living more or less uncleanly; I had lost my eye, and weighed ninety-six pounds, which at that time I seemed to think was the end of all my attractiveness; I was mentally very low, and I reasoned it all out as one would a business proposition. I saw that he was not blessed with much gray matter and that he was in awe of me, and I intended to always keep him that way. I didn't imagine there was much chance of marrying the sort of a man I could love, for with the loss of my eye, I thought I had lost everything—which I found a mistake, for since I have been married, I could have married, had I been single, one of three men who have proposed to me, not knowing I was married, and any one of them were gentlemen born, and all with considerable money. Prior to Albert's proposal, I had never had a man ask to marry me. Of course, I was only nineteen years past when I went to the hospital; and all of three years I was sick; and then prior to going to the hospital, I lived almost four years with one man; so it is not altogether strange that no man but Albert proposed to me. I decided to marry—and thought I could use Albert's simplicity of manner and appearance, and my tricky brain, to make it possible for him to do something beside pound nails. After years of effort I found that useless, as he would never consent to tell even a white lie to men, and unless I stood like a prompter in the wings, he couldn't remember for two minutes things which I had rehearsed with him hundreds of times. When I saw how useless trying to use him to earn any more than a bare, meagre livelihood was, I gave up in disgust; and as I began to see that I was still attractive to men, I began to use what charms I might possess to make it possible to have a few of the luxuries which had become necessities. And by insisting that Albert study, through me, all the little niceties of manner and speech and dress, I gave out the impression that Albert was the businessman he appeared to be, and that all I had, I got from him. To him I explained that things cost less, and that Brother sent me this, and Sister sent me that, and Uncle the other things. And when I wanted to go on a trip, I'd concoct some fairy tale about a position in the other city. And so I kept it up, using him to cover up things, and then sharing with him—for every winter has been as this one was. And I would dig up the money, but I did not regret it, as of course I had to have some respect from people; and it was given to him. . . . Outside of using him as a cloak, I had absolutely no reason to live with him whatever. He doesn't utter over ten words a day (that seems ridiculous and exaggerated, but it is an absolute fact), and they are generally about: where is such and such a thing? If you ask him to do anything, it is as good as done, if it is in his physical power—for of course he has no other—so I also benefited by having a sort of general servant. Then, may I speak of something else? I will try to make you understand: As for any relations that might exist because of the fact that we were man and wife, he did not interest me at all; so whenever it was necessary, I went almost frantic, although he never knew it.

When Mr. Welsh started to interest himself in me, I wrote him just what Albert had meant to me, and when I ceased living immorally I could see no use in living further with Albert. I must say, I did never think if I left him, that he would care much, for he is such a phlegmatic person that he would accept it, knowing that nothing he could do would affect my feeling in the matter—and he would go on as he [had]. For really I wasn't with him more than four months in the year, for on some pretext or other, I'd get away. I'd have gone mad if I had to live with him as do most wives with their husbands. So as I thought this, I wrote it to Mr. Welsh, and he seemed to think it was possible to leave him. . . . And when I began to make arrangements to come East, I never included him in any of them, and he never asked even one single question. Mr. Welsh's idea was that as soon as I was cured of using the M——, some work would be procured for me, and thereby I could earn my support. At that time, I was trying so hard to believe in Jesus Christ, and I succeeded in a measure which now seems astonishing. Mr. Welsh even wrote that when I left Albert, it must be with the thought that I would never marry again, and believe me, I was willing.

Then I came East, and do you know that from the start Mr. Welsh was disappointed in me? I won't explain why, although I think in a general way I know why. Somehow, from my letters and that casual glimpse and my pictures, he had evidently made of me a person entirely different than what I really was, and he was sorely disappointed. I don't think he knows himself why, but he really was very disappointed, and I knew it.

In cutting out the life I had been living and starting in on this new one, I was determined to do away with these petty lies and Machiavellian methods of gaining people's favor. I saw immediately that Mr. Welsh is a man to whom everyone in my position bows, and rather than cross him they would do everything according to his views. I was through with all that. Mr. Welsh does not throw away his money—and if I wanted to keep up that sort of thing, I could gain more from the very people that I had thrown out. So I was honest and asserted myself and refused to fawn on him. Of course, we had some differences of opinion, a thing evidently Mr. Welsh was not accustomed to, for he was used to everyone fawning on him—and then, away from him, saying he was not entirely sane. Anyway, I soon realized what he, in his really innocent, childlike mind had made of me; and I could have fitted into that character like the paper on the wall—for that had been my business for years, and I was most proficient, and could have readily taken Mr. Welsh in. But I had just got thru with that kind of business and was taking real interest in Jesus Christ—or rather in God as the Jews see Him for I couldn't, try as I would, see Jesus as Mr. Welsh saw Him; and I knew you couldn't fool God and I didn't try to. So even in the smallest degree I was myself; and I was not what Mr. Welsh could have wished. To substantiate the above—I had hardly been in Phila. a week before Mr. Welsh told me he thought I had better return to the West, and offered me the money. I know I had done nothing except be myself. Of course, I wasn't all that was desirable and what Mr. Welsh would have liked—but isn't that what I was supposed to come East for? Instead, when I did not come up to the mark he was ready to send me back to my dirty mode of living in Oklahoma City. At any rate, I didn't go. I refused to, for I saw no rhyme nor reason for it.

Later, through not knowing just what better to do, I submitted to Albert's suggestion that he come to Phila., which he did while I was in the hospital. While I worked, things were bearable in a measure. But when I had nothing to do, and work for Albert was as hard to be found as the proverbial needle in a haystack, it was agony indescribable to live with him. Of course, the fact that I was living decently kept me home with him all the time, and I can't understand how I stood it the entire winter.

You know how I suffered privation and want; and even when I suppose I should have looked for work, I didn't at all, but just let things drift. The worst of it was that, before, when I was not doing right, I was independent in my manner, and that was of course because I had money always in my pocketbook, but this winter I even had to be agreeable and fawning in my manner to him to make living with him possible. Oh, it all seems like a horrible nightmare! I don't know, I can't imagine why I submitted without making some effort to get away from him. For since I was living respectably, I could not use him for any purpose, for I did not need him as a cloak, and he couldn't possibly interest me in any other way. It was really that he was a drag on me, for what little I earned or managed to get I had to use to take care of him, and for what? So when I went to Atlantic City to work, I caught him at that miserable trick—and then when he got home that Saturday, his manner was so arrogant and aggressive; and he had spent money which we could ill afford on things which he would not tell me about; and altogether I was thoroughly disgusted, until I ordered him out. As I afterwards learned, he left that night and became intoxicated in some horrible place—and a lot of ugly things which sicken me to think about. It only proves conclusively that try as one might, one can't change a leopard's spots.

Then here I am—and that is all. I haven't looked ahead, and in truth haven't any idea as to what is next, except that I feel like a person who has been ridded of an enormous white elephant that has been sitting astride of my chest. I even breathe more freely. I know you are thinking, "What next?"—but there isn't the remotest idea in my mind of the "next," as yet. It seems so good to be alone here—and to know that the "alone" is for good, and that I won't have to be worried that in a day or a week or a year—for I am absolutely through—he will return to get on my nerves.

THE FOREGOING HAS BEEN WRITTEN SOME TIME, AT LEAST TWO WEEKS— and I can't say just why I got no further, except that I didn't know further. To be honest, my time has been full, what with really and sincerely looking for work (a little which I managed to get), and with slight sick spells, due to the excessive heat. I just came in from an enforced visit to an uncle's house where they have seven orphan children, of whom I have already written you. . . . I told you they were motherless, and the father, hoping to procure a caretaker for them, recently married; and as one of the girls expressed it tonight: "Pop got a crate of lemons when he married her." He surely did. Oh, it was horrible! When we came we went into the yard, lying about was refuse, and a general disorder which made me feel warmer and stickier than I had before I came in. . . . If only they would try to be clean, and in the summer eat food that is not greasy nor spoiled. But I can't revolutionize the world, and while I make an effort every time I go there to have them [behave] differently, it has little or no effect. The youngest one, a baby of perhaps five who attends kindergarten, told me they were told to buy and bring to school a toothbrush, but that their father wouldn't give them the money, as he thought it foolishness; so they are learning to keep their teeth clean with their fingers and a rag. I then gave Alex (the cousin whom I wrote you of, who lives there with them) a dime and told him to go to the drug store and bring a toothbrush, which he did. And the child showed me how they were taught to use it. . . . My attention was called away . . . and when I returned to the subject of the toothbrush, they had it out on the front steps with a cup of dirty soapy water, washing the teeth of a crowd of kiddies who stood about waiting to have their turn to have Yetta use this wonderfully strange brush on their teeth. . . .

I can't write much, as I just came in and it is 11:20, and if I want to get up to be at work by eight o'clock, I had better turn in. You must have received my card and know I found some work. I am so glad, it gives one so little time to think.

I want to tell you about Albert— Anyway, when he returned home from Atlantic City—after having worked there for two weeks—without any funds, and admitted having earned two full weeks' work, and refusing to give an account, my patience gave out and I ordered him out. I don't know whether I wrote you this before in the body of the letter—I think I have. Then I had no plans, and have none now. Mr. Suiffen paid my rent for me this month and gave me small sums to live on—but I hate that. I feel like a yellow dog, and don't intend to put up with it much longer. If I wait, it will only be until Mr. Welsh's return. I shall *absolutely* refuse to eat charity bread after he returns, and if I don't find work that has possibilities—at least to enable me to keep myself from actual want—I shall just have to cut loose. I hate to write this to you—and I've thought and thought until my brain is weary and fagged out. I can't stand it—It is bad enough in the wintertime, but it is unbearable in the summer. I am wearing heavy winter boots and heavy stockings. If it wasn't for the clothes you sent me, I could certainly not manage; and as it is, I don't wear the white skirt, as it means too much for laundry bills—and only yesterday, I stood near a printing press and ruined the green plaid dress all up the front. I doubt whether it can be cleaned, as I worked on it Friday with gasoline and couldn't budge it. Oh! it almost drove me frantic, as these two dresses looked so well on me, and I would have liked to keep the one I have on now—the polka-dot dress—for best. I am absolutely honest with you—I can't stand this any longer. It is a struggle each day, for hot weather takes the starch out of me. But I shall hang on until Mr. Welsh comes; then, I don't intend to tell him—as of course he would try to persuade me to do otherwise—but I am going to leave Phila. and probably go to New York, though I am not decided just where. I am fully decided to go. I don't have to tell you, I think—for I believe you believe in me—that I hate to do it. But I don't hate it half as much as suffering the consequences of hot weather without the comforts that make hot weather bearable. I want lots of linen, and not to be afraid of laundry bills, and ice water to drink, and comfortable outer garments that are presentable—and I know I can't get that with the $4.00 I can make in a week at this work, and nothing better am I fitted to do. If you will want my friendship after I break away, I will write to you and hang on to you until I die—but I think perhaps it would be better if I dropped out of sight. I intended to do it, at first, without telling you, but somehow I didn't feel right about that. And I guess I'm reluctant about giving you up. I know you will tell me to keep in touch with you—and I know if you say it, you mean it—but I know I shouldn't take advantage of it, and ought to gracefully drop out while I am at least fit to write to you. I am very sleepy, so shall close—and go to bed. It is so warm here and that, too, just knocks me out. I hope you are now fully recovered and have regained your strength.

Mrs. Mark Howe
Cotuit, Massachusetts   *June, 1911*

TONIGHT I FEEL A LITTLE MORE CHEERFUL THAN USUAL, SO WANT TO   23 &
take this opportunity to write...for I am weary of writing my same old tale of woe....

I sent you a card today from Keiths—How I did enjoy myself![7] It was an unexpected pleasure....At 1:15 I went to my box and found only one envelope—which had a [complimentary] ticket for Keiths enclosed!...I felt I had no reason not to go, especially as I had nothing to do and am a great lover of the theatre. The show was generally good; and Irene Franklin, who was the headliner, was simply immense. In her last song, she had on a shabby suit and worn shoes and a fuzzy tam-o'-shanter, and with her own hair hanging in two long braids, she told that she was "bringing up the family." She looked very winsome, albeit she was so untidily dressed, and the song was very touching. It was about a girl of fourteen whose mother had died, and the father was incapable, and this child was bringing up a family of six young'uns. It made me think of my poor little cousins, so...I went to their house. I bought some fruit and a handful of magnolias on my way up...and found things about the same as before when I wrote you....

I left there at eleven o'clock, and Alex took me home, and we were obliged to walk, as Miss Poke was along and we couldn't take her in the cars. It is about twenty blocks, and it was about 11:45 when we neared home. As we came up to the Forrest Theatre, we saw quite a mob, and when we investigated we found that the "Divine Sarah" had played there and they were waiting for her to come out on her way back to her hotel.[8] And although I never did such a thing before in all my life, I waited, too—and although I was dog-tired, I thought she was the one person that a glimpse of would be some satisfaction. I was waiting at the door for quite awhile; then a happy thought struck me, and I went down to the curb where the auto was waiting. In a few moments, out she came, wrapped in a chinchilla mantle. And to my surprise, was not feeble and disabled as report has it. She got in the car smiling and bowing; and as I stood directly next to the door, she happened to look squarely at me and, I suppose, was attracted by my patch, and smiled directly to me. And impulsively I put out my hand, and she took it and clasped it in a warm and sincere manner. Then she said something in French to me, which of course I did not understand; and as I looked puzzled, she again took my hand. And then I leaned over and kissed her hand. And oh! how graciously she smiled! All I can remember is how very bright her eyes are, and how warm and firm her handclasp was. She is very attractive and doesn't look over forty-five—I think, though, that all her upper teeth were false. All this time, the man—the chauffeur—was preparing to go. But after the crowd saw her give me her hand, they crowded close, and she waved and waved to them and kissed her hand to them—but though their hands were extended, hundreds of them, she didn't take any of them. So I feel good tonight. You haven't an idea how friendless I feel almost all the time; and while I am grateful to be able to stay in my pretty room, it is very monotonous to have no one to talk to but Miss Poke—sometimes for days at a time. So, you see, I had two kindnesses shown me today—and honestly I don't deserve them. Why I do get them is a mystery, for while I do no wrong, I do no good. I wonder if there was any reason for both those occurrences today? Do you think there is any significance to be attached to it, coming just at this time—just when I have decided that those little things aren't worthwhile? I read and reread your letter to me most carefully, and it gave me much to think of, but I could not come to any conclusion as yet. But the return of Mr. Welsh in a few days brings me to where I will just have to do something. . . .

Now I am going to write you just what I have thought:

Of course, Mr. Welsh does not know the finale—that is, Albert going—and he will learn it, no doubt, from Mr. Suiffen on his arrival, even before I see him. Now, I really do love Mr. Welsh. This is not written for effect or for a purpose. I do love him—less like a child loves its father, but more like a father or mother loves its child. I hate, I loathe to pain him. In this letter, he said I had not written how I was keeping on with my attendance at church, etc. The fact that I made no mention of anything of that sort since 'way before Christmas should give him to understand that I have ceased going entirely; and if it was anyone else, I would think he knew that, but was evading the obvious, to sort of make me go. But I know very well that Mr. Welsh would not do that, so it must be that he thinks I still go to church as regularly as I did, when I don't go at all. My not going is for no other reason than lack of interest. When he was here, I knew my attending made him happy—so I was happy—and while I should have felt that way in his absence, I didn't. For I felt how very ridiculous to sit thru what seems to me like a lot of cant—for while I am not a scoffer or an unbeliever, to go through a lot of religious ceremony seems like child's play; and as long as I was not genuine about it and Mr. Welsh was not here for me to please, I ceased going and preferred to remain in bed Sunday and read. Now, when I have to tell him all that, and all about Albert, I know I shall give him great pain—and how disappointed he will be! Do you know, for the first time since I have known him I am tempted to deceive him? Really, I am afraid I can't tell him, it will be just like deliberately slapping his face. I don't know what to do. If I tell him all I have written you—in my last letter—he will perhaps ask me to pray—and I have no faith. Oh! I don't know what to do! If I say I will, that will be deliberate deceit, and I might have spared him the revelations in the first place; and if I say I won't or can't pray, won't he think I am deliberately disobeying him? In this letter from him, he said he would stand ready to help me to find happiness through the Lord; and then—to quote him—"To help you a little with my purse to get over the rough places." I hope you won't misunderstand me when I tell you about that. In all probabilities, he will advocate my permitting Albert to return—and I shall absolutely refuse that. Then of course it will be prayer, and then work, because I know he will not think of my going back to my former life. As to work: Unless it would be

59

the work of a menial sort, I don't see how he could procure that for me any better than I could for myself, for anyone must see that I am not fitted for work that requires training; and then my appearance handicaps me in trying to get jobs where training is not necessary and which is not in the menial class. So if I do go to work, it will be to please Mr. Welsh—it will be, I am sure, work that will be most distasteful to me. And since I have decided not to have to go through any more of the sort of thing I have in the past year, what can I do other than come right out and tell Mr. Welsh that I am going back—or go back, and just drop out of sight and leave him in ignorance as to the real situation? As to the money from him, there are reasons why I should not like to keep that up; even outside of those that make it undesirable to be dependent. In the first place, when Mr. Welsh has expended moneys on me, he always got it from three or four sources who gave it to him to be used for me out of a sense of pity, the same as any other charity. Now, really, I do not need charity, because I am big and strong and capable of earning a living if I was willing to earn it at any old thing; and, of course, you have no idea how it belittles me in my own opinion to have to accept that money. Now, if Mr. Welsh had out of his own private purse seen fit to make things more comfortable for me, I should have seen no reason to object, for that puts it in a different light. Just like the money you sent me—I did not feel cheap or small in using it, for I have often had a little more than I needed; so I shared it with others less fortunate. But if you were a stranger, and the money had been collected because of a sense of pity for me, I would not have taken it. If I should remain, and Mr. Welsh would see fit to take care of me, and I had the feeling it was given because of a love for me and a desire to see me comfortable and happy—as a father would his child—I would remain until the end; and going back to my former life would be out of the question. But it would not be like that. Chances are Mr. Welsh would get some of his wealthy friends to contribute small amounts—and it would be mighty small, just enough to keep me from actual starvation, and feeling like a beggar with a tin cup. Before I went to the hospital, I had a taste of what that should be like, as I remained at Mr. Welsh's studio in the care of an old lady for about four weeks—and if I thought I had to live like that indefinitely, I'd die. I bought my own provisions; and Mr. Welsh questioned each item, even 2 or 3 cents, until I almost jumped out of my skin in aggravation. I ate as little as possible and I bought what cost the least; and yet Mr. Welsh seemed to think it was a large sum. When I came from Oklahoma, the money was sent by Mr. Welsh, although three or four people contributed the sum—$55.00. The fare was nearly $50.00, and with food, etc. for a four day trip, the $55.00 was spent. I knew that would not be enough; and just before leaving sold some remains of my finery—three dresses—for $15.00, and took that along, also. As I had never been in Chicago, I stopped over for two days—and, anyway, by the time I got to Pittsburgh, I hadn't a penny; and as Mr. Welsh and my brother Sam met me at the depot, I had to ask them for the money to pay the baggage man for Poke's fare from Pittsburgh, which was 25 cents. Then, a week or so later when we were talking my trip over, Mr. Welsh asked me how much money I had left from the $55.00 that was sent to me. I did not tell him of the extra $15.00 I had—but when I explained my expenses, I felt surely he would see that I did wonders to make it on $55.00. But he couldn't and said I was extravagant. That I only tell you to show you how next to impossible it would be for me to accept my living from Mr. Welsh and have no other source of income.

I never was so muddled as to what to do. He will be here in a day or more and I am at sea. If I tell him all this, it will not remedy things. It may be that he will insist on my leaving the room here and going to live in some family cheaply—and I am *not* going to live that way. I cannot see what it would benefit me by staying, for I know by heart what he will advise—I don't intend to live in misery longer. I have, for more than a year, and I can't see when I have benefited myself any. The only thing I can see to do, is not tell him anything at all, and let matters drift—and then get ready in a week or two, and just drop out of sight, sending him a letter in explanation, but cutting out the entire thing, and dropping completely out. I wish I knew what to do. I wonder if you understand my predicament? Would you send me a small letter at once and tell me—shall I tell Mr. Welsh any or all of what I have told you? Mind, I am sure there is nothing, I think, that he could say that would alter my opinion that I have to break away, that I can't see anything to be derived by my accepting favors any longer, especially since I admit to you that I am not very gracious about it. You know it is not to be thought of that Mr. Welsh will give practical advice, and what he will suggest, I don't want to do—and if I don't, and deliberately disappear, I think it would hurt him less than if I remained and disobeyed him. Even if, out of my love for him, I would say I was willing to do work that would almost kill me, I know I would not last at it long. If I were a Believer and did it to please God, and had the faith of Mr. Welsh, I could derive some satisfaction from that—but as it is, it would only be to please Mr. Welsh, and I know that would not be lasting; for I cannot but see a future ahead like this winter I have just passed—and I know I am not going to live thru much more like that. I wish you would write me whether you think I ought to tell him, and then absolutely refuse to pray and do other things that Mr. Welsh might think would relieve the situation, or whether I should say nothing and then just pass out, leaving him only a sort of explanatory note. You asked me if I had a friend here that I could go to. No—there is no one that I would tell my affairs to. The only one that I told is Miss Outerbridge, and I only told her in part. And she is as impractical as Mr. Welsh, only not so kind. You see I have become a cynic, but I have to smile at Miss Outerbridge. Until Albert left, she came once in awhile—about once a week—and talked with me. Her last visit was when Albert was gone but a day or two; and when she was here, of course I told her what was uppermost in my mind: Albert's going, and my plight, etc. When she was about to go, she fumbled about her purse and said that she would leave me a dollar to help me until I found some employment. I could have fallen thru the floor, because I never dreamed she would do that—and I refused it, and lied and told her that I did not know that I had given out the impression that I was in immediate need, and that I had quite a little money just then—although I think I had a dime at the time. She took back the dollar and has never come here since! She phoned twice and asked how I was getting along, and once sent a letter that was so general that the heading could have as well been Mr. Doe, or Mrs. Miller, or in fact, anyone—it was so strictly impersonal. So you see, I could not go to her for advice and it seems there is no one else but you. I am so undecided about what to tell Mr. Welsh that I wish you could advise me so that I would know what to do by Tuesday, when I think I shall see him. I am getting so sleepy and I am making so many errors that I will close and go to bed. I hate dreadfully to burden you with my petty annoyances and troubles, but in this instance I just can't see my way clear as to what I shall tell Mr. Welsh. Goodnight.

June 20, 1911

I just returned from a visit to my poor sister, and felt "down in **24** ✑
the mouth" until I opened my mailbox and found your letter. You
always make me feel important. Though I think Mr. Welsh has
returned, I haven't seen him as yet, but no doubt I will tomorrow—
and I do not look forward to it with the same pleasure I would if I
did not have to tell him what I feel, etc.

My sister was worse today than I found her on a great many
visits—that is, mentally—and it almost drives me insane to see her,
as I know she is just sitting there waiting for the years to go by that
she might die; and I can't help her. You see, they have so many
thousands that they can give them but little attention. Her condition is another strong argument that makes "going back" seem
easier, for I used to be able to do more for her. She asks me for
shoes, and how can I buy them, when my own are without soles,
and so on?—and yet she thinks that I just won't spend the money. I
bought her some in December, but they are practically gone. And
when I asked some of the family to assist me in getting things for
her, they say that if I don't take them out to her, the institution will
provide them, whereas if I do take her all she needs they will think
we are people of large means and ask us to pay more, etc. The logic
is the same kind that has made my life a wreck—but I can't
revolutionize the world, so I don't even comment on it. They asked
me today at the hospital if I could pay $7.50 toward having her
teeth attended to, as she suffers so much. So I said I would—I
haven't as yet the remotest idea where I will get it. Oh, yes! While I
am wailing, I will also tell you of what may be good news. On my
way out this morning, I found a postal in my box from the people I
did this last work for. It asked me to call as soon as possible, so I
am going as soon as I finish this; and it may mean work—I do hope
you won't think this untidy letter is the result of carelessness—it is
haste, as I want to get over there as soon as possible. I will write
you as soon as I see Mr. Welsh. Yours affectionately and sincerely,
Maimie

I wonder do you know anything that will remove printer's ink from
that green dress? I have asked in so many drugstores, but they say
there is nothing—and I am so miserable about it, as I have no
change now; and the other one that I have on is going to pieces
under the arms. I tried so many things, but not any budged it. I

wonder if you have any of the material left. I believe my sister-in-law could patch it. It is inked about 5 inches wide, to 8 or 9 inches long—That is, I smeared it that much in trying to clean it.

Letterhead:
The Continental, Philadelphia
Frank Kimble Mgr.   *June 23, 1911*

CX 25   I JUST LEFT MR. WELSH'S OFFICE AND CAME IN HERE SO I COULD WRITE
you at once and without going back home. I received your letter on
my way out; and I decided, after all, to come right out with it all to
him—although the thought of it alone was terrible, and while I was
talking to him I wished that I had not told him, for I am such a
coward and hate to face the music. First, I must tell you that he
greeted me very formally, and until the end one would never dream
that I knew him but very slightly, as he was very cold and formal. I
had just seated myself when he asked me to tell him about my
affairs. I told him I was very well, physically, which was about all I
could say. Then he asked about my going to church, etc., and
appeared to be shocked when I told him I did not go to church. I
also told him that while I hadn't done anything bad since he left, I
hadn't, either, done anything good. Somehow I could not talk to
him as I can write to you, and I don't think he understood, but
rather thinks I am just perverse. I told him as best I could, but not
much. And then he began to tell me what he thought about it.
Among other things, he spoke of his kindness to me as "work"—
that in itself is exactly what makes me hate my condition so. He
said—as he has often said before—"You know, Maimie, how I am
on all sides talked to by my family to keep out of this *work*." Now
do you see what I mean? Then, when I told him that I simply ate
and slept, he judged that I wanted more money, and said—as he
also had said before—that he was not a rich man; and that he had
many calls on him; and that several things he had money in had
failed, so his income was greatly reduced; but he would do what he
could to keep on as he had done, provided, etc.—So, you see, it is
just as I wrote you. When I told him, as I did you, how I despised to
feel that I was living on charity, he said he didn't see why I should
feel that way, when I knew it was given with affection, etc.—Then—
As I was dressing to go to see him, I thought much about the hat
question, knowing how my hat once before annoyed [him]. . . . You
recall the incident with the hat and the bird of paradise—So after

64

that, whenever I went out, I wore a hat bought two years before (last summer). It was a small, dark-blue turban with a flat velvet bow of the same color, and Mr. Welsh was pleased. I happened to keep it because it was always so neat looking. Then, this summer, I wore it until it looked so shabby that I hated to go out. So I got a hat and turned it myself. A large black shape, and a bow with three loops wired and standing up, and the rest flat. As I only purchased two and one-half yards of the ribbon, it couldn't be very large (the bow); and the ribbon is black and white silk, with a narrow edge of red velvet. To me it does not look loud, as I haven't even drawn the ribbon all around the hat, but just made the bow. And I thought Mr. Welsh would like it, as I often used to wear a red tie, a real bright one, with a white waist, and he remarked how well I looked. But just as I was dressing, I decided to put on the little blue hat—but then didn't, as it seemed like petty deceit—and put on the large one. Then—Mr. Welsh remarked that I was dressed too loud. So I said I had on only the dress you sent—the dotted one. Then he said the dress was all right, but the hat was frightful—and he spoke of it again and again during the interview. He told me he thought I ought to go to a hospital and let them try to make it possible for me to wear a "glass eye." Really, if I thought there was half a chance, wouldn't I be only too glad?—but it is impossible. True, Dr. Chance says he will "try." And that would mean my lying about in hospitals, with the possible result of wearing an eye just stuck in my head—for I have no eyelids, or lashes, or anything that looks like anything that generally holds an eye in place. To go thru such an ordeal when I know full well the impossibility of ever arriving at anything seems ridiculous, and yet Mr. Welsh said that I should go regardless of what I personally think, as long as he wanted me to. As I said before, his talk to me was most formal, and his offer of assistance was such that it appeared as though he felt he wanted the peace of mind to know that at least he had offered me assistance. It was all so terribly formal; and then, in conclusion, he said he hoped I would change my mind and not "go back," but if I did "go back"—that before I did, he suggested that I should return to him the letters he has written me, which he knows I still retain. He brought special emphasis to bear on that point—that I should deliver up to him in person these letters, should I go back—then he dismissed me by telling me to think it over, and opened the door for me to go without even a goodbye handclasp. It was all so horrible.

You see, like him, I, too, have conjured up pictures of how Mr. Welsh would [be] when he met me on this return trip—and it all went to pieces, and I am not yet recovered my breath. You see, in almost everything I did, I felt I [acted] to please or displease Mr. Welsh; naturally, then, he became very near to me, and I felt as anyone would feel who was going to see their very own father—and you can imagine how I feel now. When he returned from Lake Sunapee last fall, he kissed me and remarked about how I looked, and was very intimate—and the same when he went away to Europe. Hadn't it been for that, I shouldn't have hung on as I did (although perhaps I would anyway, on your account), for I thought it was just so important to him about even my smallest doings. And then the great stress he put on the return of those letters makes me feel that perhaps he regrets writing them, and that perhaps later, after I went back, I might use them for some nefarious purpose. I know it will make me seem such a dreadful ingrate for not feeling such deep gratitude for past favors, that I wouldn't dream of finding fault, but really I can't tell you what a blow this was to me. It doesn't seem as though I had really seen Mr. Welsh, for he isn't the man that I have kept ever before me as the person I wanted to please. Of course, I am just as much up in the air as possible, only more so than before. For while I said there didn't seem anything else to do, before, still deep down in the innermost recesses of my heart, I felt that something would happen with the return of Mr. Welsh. As it is, there seem but two ways open to me, as he plainly told me. One to submit to what I know is a rank waste of time and would only jeopardize my present good health by going to a hospital, and go under a great many operations—minor ones, of course, but still operations—which, if I do, Mr. Welsh will retain his interest in me, and make it possible for me to sleep, and eat some sort of food, provided too that I return to church-going and prayer. If I don't do that, then of course I must "go back"—for I have no other means of a livelihood—and then return to Mr. Welsh his letters, which he will understand means that I have given up. Certainly I never was in a worse predicament. I think I shall go home and get together Mr. Welsh's letters and return them thru Mr. Suiffen, anyway, so that Mr. Welsh can rest easy on that score. I do not know that he is uneasy...but one in my position is generally very sensitive, and I shouldn't care to retain them if he didn't want me to for any reason, anyway.

I am grateful to you for your offer to help me thru school. I think you know I'd gladly accept if it was possible, but you can readily see why it wouldn't be. For even should Mr. Welsh care to help me learn, I would have to live in the meantime; and I just couldn't have any interest at my work if I had to keep on living as I do now and have for a long time now. It is too cheapening. I feel like some miserable parasite—and for what? Just sustenance? It is not worth it, especially since I frankly admit that I would love to live decently if I could in comfort—but without comfort, this life is a living Hell.

I am going home now and shall finish there.

Home—1:30 P.M.

I have reread your letter and want to say in answer that since Mr. Welsh paid my rent for one month, until July 23, I might as well stay here. I do not know if I will get the check each week or not—for I do not intend to submit to the operations, nor do I intend to promise to go to Sunday school and church and that sort of thing. But I will have to begin to look about for the making of a change. For should the check not come, I would be in bad shape; and since Mr. Welsh told me it would be one or the other thing, and I do not intend to submit, I must begin to prepare to get away. You see, even when one lives in the other world, there are different classes; and the condition of my clothes would put me among different sort of people than I used to associate with.

Of course, I will "hang on" a while longer, for having been out of things for so long a time, I feel like a novice and don't know just how to start, especially since I truly loathe to do it. But really, Mrs. Howe, I will have to make some sort of a break; for while it will, as I know full well, lead to destruction—what will this life, with no friends, no interest, no comforts, no anything else that is desirable lead me to? No self-respecting person could keep on as I have, eating the bread of charity and not even feeling very grateful for it. I am literally all run-down at the heels and walking on the bare bricks—for my shoes have holes as big as silver dollars in them— and when I contemplate the many really necessary things I need before I can "go back," I can't think how I will get them. So I am between the devil and the deep sea—I can't stay and I can't go. I know one thing a person can always do, and that is die; and yet even that takes courage which I don't begin to possess. Of course, I wouldn't do such a thing, but it does seem such an easy way to solve all these miserable perplexities. You know, I am truly grateful to you for your honesty in admitting you understand me. I don't think there are many who don't—only they won't.

I was glad to get the kiddies' pictures. How very much Helen looks like you. They seem so affectionate toward each other. Goodness, I don't really know why you want to bother with my small troubles, when you have such sweet babies and could spend your time entirely with them. I believe I wouldn't be so kind to you if I was happy and the positions were reversed—for I'd spend all my time enjoying my happiness. Of course, now I sometimes mix up with people in great stress, but I think it is because misery likes company.

I must close now, although I wanted to write you of the interview with the lady who sent for me—although it was not about work. I will write you of it again.

Wednesday, June 28, 1911

C⅔ 26   I JUST RETURNED FROM ATLANTIC CITY AT SEVEN THIS EVENING AND found your letter awaiting me, so hastened out to mail you two post cards, one to your Boston and one to your Cotuit address. After I mailed them, I recalled that the one to the Cotuit address was an ornate card and that I had neglected to stamp it, so I sent another.

You don't know—you can't imagine—how torn I am between the desire to do what is right and the absolute necessity of doing that which is wrong. Your letters always stir up in me any good which is there—and then other forces bring out the other side of me. There is so much I want to tell you. My letters to you always seem so long, and I fear to bore you—but then I also feel you want to know. And I can't tell you things without going into detail, for I want you to see what brings me to these conclusions. You know after my visit to Mr. Welsh's office how I felt. All my thoughts, when they became troublesome, I had quieted with the thought that with the return of Mr. Welsh my troubles would practically be at an end—and then you know how I was awakened out of that dream. I knew it was up to me to make some definite move, as Mr. Welsh had told me plainly what to expect. So I decided to cut it all out here; for while there were hundreds of reasons I should "go back," there were only a few general ones that would affect my future that urged me to remain. As I wrote you, it was as hard to go back as anything I had ever contemplated, but to go on accepting Mr. Welsh's kindnesses—I couldn't. So, as a starter, I decided that I would have to give Poke up. And you can't imagine what that means to me—for, I hope you won't feel insulted by being classed with her, but you and she are the only two in my life who seemed to thoroughly understand me. She is as human as anyone, only she can't speak with her mouth. But to take her with me is an impossibility for many reasons, and as she is growing quite old, she is set in her ways and hates changes. So out of kindness to her, too, I thought I should have to give her up. And while I know a man in this city who would give me $50.000 for her at any time, I wouldn't sell her, but would rather Albert had her, as he is as devoted to her as though she were a child and is very anxious to have her. I haven't heard from him in a little while. The last time I had heard, he wrote a very impertinent letter, among other things mentioning that he had found a friend—a lady—who lived in the same place he did, and that they had congenial times together. And as I know it was the truth, I answered at length, telling him that if he had a spark of manhood he would share his prosperity with me—for had I not made it possible for him to exist all winter? And then I wrote—that, forgetting that I was his wife and had provided for him practically for five years, with the exception of a few weeks each summer—if any woman or man had been kind to him for months, working hard, very hard, and not only sharing, but giving him the larger half—wouldn't it be the natural thing, that now when he is enjoying some prosperity and this other person was in want, to share as before? And that letter brought no reply. So some little time went by; and then when, as I said, I decided to let him have Poke. I wrote him and asked if he would care to have her. Of course, he was willing. . . . so I wrote I'd bring her down, provided he would send the expense, which would be $2.75. He sent me a money order with a terse note reading to let him know when I was coming—which I did, writing I would leave here Tuesday eve. Which I did, arriving 7 p.m.—and no sign of Albert at the station. Oh! how provoked I was at him. Knowing, though, where he lives, I went there in a bus—and found it the worst place I ever put my foot in. It was a miserable-looking hovel with a large sign reading "Meals 15 cents" before it. Just imagine! And as it was suppertime, standing about were half-a-dozen or so hard, rough-looking men of the coarsest kind— Words fail me. I walked into what was the dining room and asked for him, and they said he had gone out directly after he had eaten. Oh! that dining room—the odor, the filth, the uncleanly women working there—and just think of my being married to a man who would live at a place of that sort. I couldn't stand it, so came out on the sidewalk until the proprietoress asked me if I cared to come in and sit down. And then she showed me Albert's room. I will never forget it. It was the size of a pantry, it being half of a small-sized room, the partition being a sheet hung over a line—and oh! that sheet! In the part that was Albert's was two beds—a large one, and then a sort of camp cot. The linen on both beds was unspeakably filthy, and flies buzzed about as in a butcher shop; and on the floor were seven or eight little baby kittens about three days old—their birthplace being under the bed. As there was only one window, which was in the part of the room that was not Albert's—you can imagine the rest. Do you wonder I shrink from respectability when it means things of that sort? God—how I loathe it! And then, how I felt after seeing that I can't tell you. Anyway, I came out at once and walked up the street—just anywhere—and met Albert coming up, just out of a barbershop, looking quite spick and span, with a new shirt and new shoes and new entire outfit. And here I was, with shoes on that are without soles—and he looked very prosperous. The idea of living in a place of that sort, and buying new clothes! If necessity drove him there because he had no means!—but a place of that sort costs just as much as a cleaner place in a quiet laboring man's family, which is easy to get. He seemed surprised to see me, and said he had read the letter to mean I was coming on Wednesday. Just like everything else he ever did in his life, he naturally didn't see right. That carelessness explains why he can't do anything else besides knock nails. The letter read *Tuesday* very plainly. It was written like this: *Tuesday*. And he read that *Wednesday*. So he told me he was just on his way to meet a man on business, and he was obliged to go. So we took Poke back to his *hotel*, and then he bought me a ticket to a vaudeville show and he left, saying he would call for me. When I came out, imagine my surprise to find him standing there with Mr. Suiffen beside him. Mr. Suiffen then explained that he had come up for a few days' rest *and had run into Albert on the Boardwalk*. We stood and talked a few minutes. Then he left—not before he made an appointment to see Albert the next eve, so as to spend it together, as I expected to return the next day to the city. I forgot to say that prior to leaving for Atlantic City yesterday, I received a letter from Mr. Welsh—one-page letter—telling me I ought not to "go back" because of my love for Christ, and if not for that, then out of a sense of gratitude to him. The letter was very brief, and he casually told me he was leaving that night for his summer home in Sunapee—and, in conclusion, that I must not destroy his letters. I really feel that he is quite alarmed about those letters, and wish you would tell me what to do about them, as I should be glad to return them at once—only I shouldn't want him to feel any insecurity about them. What should I do? I wish you would advise me in this matter, also. You see, I was not wrong in what I said—that Mr. Welsh has no personal regard for me. Last year before leaving, he came and spent awhile with me, and bought me some peaches: and then kissed me again and again; and wrote me two postals en route and a letter quite often; and in July, on my birthday, selected a scarf and a sweet-smelling grass box for me—and then, see the difference now. Well, I am not altogether to blame for being so surprised, since there is such a difference. But I had nothing to do with the change, since I have done nothing so far to merit it. To return to Albert and Atlantic City: After Mr. Suiffen left, we started to walk; and as he had not said a word about supper and I hadn't had anything since early morning, I called his attention to it; and we went to a restaurant. And when he paid the bill, he pulled out a roll of money—perhaps twenty or thirty dollars. Of course, he knew I wouldn't stay at the place he lives, so he took me to a nice hotel; and when I was handed the pen to register, I said "Are you going to stay here too Albert"? And he said, "No, I shall go to my own room." Then we went out on the porch and sat there. You see, I knew that if I wanted to, in about two minutes' time I could have made him willing to give me every penny in his pockets—but, oh! I despise that game, it is so sickening. It is just what I will have to do when I go back, and I loathe it. And yet that is what I always had to do to make living with him possible. To fawn on him, and pretend to be very much in love with him, and to suffer gross indignities all the while—and for what? And while I knew it would have been child's play for me to get that money—which goodness knows I need desperately—I sat there stolidly, with my hands in my lap, discussing the most impersonal things. And tonight I feel sorry that I didn't. Goodness,

71

how I hate to!—but when I look at myself and see what a help toward a better appearance that money would have been, I regret not having gotten it. At any rate, after awhile he took himself off with my poor little Poke—which was like parting with my teeth— and I went to bed heartbroken, for I am fond, very fond, of that poor little dumb animal. I awakened at ten o'clock—or, rather, was out by that time—and while I should have liked to have gone on the Boardwalk, I didn't, for the women looked so fresh and pretty, and I feel so miserable. And then, I love to bathe but can't any more, as the water wetting the patch makes that impossible. So I left at once, arriving in Camden at 12:30. I spent the afternoon visiting Caroline's (my brother's wife's) aunt who lives there, and then came home at seven o'clock to find your letter awaiting me—with so much in it that makes me love you, and deeply grateful, but as undecided as ever. Of course, . . . another bridge [is] burned, and still less to go over, to "get back"—for, like in Mr. Welsh's case, when I felt his coming would make such a difference, I also felt this visit to see Albert would have some desirable effect—which you see it didn't. I forgot to tell you that he after- wards admitted that the "man he had to see on business" was Mr. Suiffen, who had written to him making the appointment; and that instead of it being an accidental meeting—as Mr. Suiffen plainly told me—it was a cut and dried one; and that Mr. Suiffen did not meet him accidentally on the street, but he went to his hotel. I believe wonders will never cease. I could not have been made to believe that Mr. Suiffen would stoop to such petty deceit—and then, his meeting Albert, apparently surreptitiously, makes it appear as though he was in league with Albert against me. Oh, it is all so disillusioning compared to what I had all figured out, until Mr. Welsh's return. It seems that if he—Mr. Suiffen, as Mr. Welsh's representative—had my interest at heart and believed in me, he would have told me he intended seeing Albert for my interest, instead of all these suspicious actions. Albert also told me that Mr. Suiffen asked him if he thought that I still used the M——. And Albert said it surpised him—so that he thought probably I had returned to the use of it since his leaving. So he said he didn't know. And then Mr. Suiffen said that Mr. Welsh, or he (I don't know which), thought at first perhaps I did; but since Mr. Welsh saw me, he didn't think so. Then Mr. Suiffen said that Mr. Welsh was determined that I have a glass eye; and Albert also told him how absolutely impossible that was. Then another thing: This question of learning stenography came up; and Mr. Welsh or Mr. Suiffen thought that, rather than expend the money that it would cost to learn stenography, that this next month in July—when Miss Muteer, the bookkeeper in Mr. Welsh's office, is going on her vacation—that I come there daily and remain all day; and as Mr. Suiffen finds a minute here and there, he could teach me all I ought to know. Now, that sounds all right, and I ought to be deeply grateful—and yet I can't be. And I am ashamed of it, but still I am not going to pretend I want to, when I don't. The idea has absolutely no attraction for me, for being so close with them, I could not get along unless I kept up that ridiculous pretence of believing in the church, etc., as Mr. Welsh does. I know the situation thoroughly, and unless I do, it will be impossible to stand it. Don't I know, had I kept up a lively correspondence with Mr. Welsh, going to church every Sunday and detailing all the events, and reading a lot of stuff that bores me and pretending to be interested—Mr. W's attitude toward me on his return would have been as it was when he left, and everything would have been lovely? But since I had elected to be honest in all my dealings with him, I come out the loser in the end. And then, besides that reason, I shouldn't—in fact, I couldn't—go into that right now, feeling as I do. I am thoroughly depressed; and before I could get into the right state of mind to do anything worthwhile, I would have to mingle with people and feel as they do. To start right in, to go to that dull office and learn under Mr. Suiffen would madden me. While he is a very fine man and an able stenographer, he would get on my nerves. He learned stenography twenty-five years ago and like old doctors, he hasn't an idea of up-to-date systems, etc.—so that I don't see how he could teach me any too well, so I could cope with positions in this wide-awake field where there are hundreds of applicants for each position. The aspect is anything but alluring; and though I should not refuse—since it might be beneficial to me—yet I don't think I could stand it. Whereas if I went to a modern school, with other young people about me, and they not regarding me as "Exhibit No. 1," or something other than the rest, I should be fired with my usual ambition—as I always do when I am around others in the same position as I, to show them how much more clever I am than they are—and in so doing, I should learn so much quicker. They accept pay guaranteeing to teach for so much, so that it is up to the pupil as to how soon they get through. Why Mr. Suiffen should want to bother to teach me when he has so much to do he hardly gets a breathing time in a day—unless it is because of the money involved—I do not know.

This brings me to your generous offer in the letter I received tonight, and I don't know what to say. Looking at it dispassionately, it seems just the chance for me. The one chance—but then how can I accept it? You see, I am not absolutely sure of myself, and if I went into this, I would like to go into it feeling that I was perfectly satisfied. I look at it this way: Forgetting that it is your offer, and as though I had a certain amount of money in the bank, just enough to pay for the course and my living while learning, I would not hesitate, but jump at [it] at once, as a means for a livelihood in the future without going back. And I truly do not feel about your assistance as I always did about Mr. Welsh's—and then as he himself expressed it—as "work." But the fact still remains that it is not my money that is in the bank, but yours; and I am afraid to go into it. If I hadn't gone thru this wretched winter as I had, and then the insecurity of the summer as far as I've gone, I would not hesitate. For I would not have tasted the sordidness of such living and, having started—which would be like giving my word to do something—I should certainly stick it out. But now I dread it. For a moral life to me, now, seems wearing clothes a little longer than I should like to because of the expense of washing; eating food that I hope is cleanly, but not that I am sure of; and suffering every known inconvenience—with only the reward that the world at large respects me. Since Albert has gone and the duties he performed about the place are being done by another, I have to pay $20.00 a month for this room; but it is too sweet, and altogether lovely—and then, when Albert was telling me what Mr. Suiffen had to say, he also said that Mr. Suiffen said Mr. Welsh would no longer, *under any circumstances*, pay the rent of this room. You see, they did not tell me that—so I am supposed to go on in sweet innocence. Then the news, I suppose, will be broken to me at the last minute. The thought, as he told me, that I couldn't have this room frightened me, for it is the last hope I have of hanging on. I will have to go back then—for I should refuse to go to some cheap or cramped place thru the hot months, or even after that. Then, you see, the same idea presents itself when I think over the ways and means of your offer. To live as I should like to live—unham-

pered, thru the time I should have to learn, by the fact that I have
to skimp on that and save on this—and be altogether uncomfortable because it is not my money, makes the thing unbearable—
especially so, since it's you, and I care so much about you that I
would perhaps be always worried that I was not doing enough. Oh!
it is such a worry. The facts are that I hate, I despise to go back;
and I loathe to remain, if I have to suffer inconveniences even
worse than I so far have had to—and yet, what a nerve I should
have to expect anything else. Just now, the most desirable thing in
the world seems to be to have money in my pocket all my own,
sufficient to buy some decent-looking clothes, and to feel clean,
calm, and not continually perturbed by the thought that each day is
the last of this mode of living, and then what? It seems the devil is
right behind me to make the way easier. I used to know a man
whose home is in Boston; he is with the "Bostonian Shoe" people. I
met him first in San Antonio, Texas; and then by accident in Waco,
Texas; and then by appointment in Kansas City, and a year later in
Chicago; and then by accident here in Phila. 'way last fall. Our
acquaintance has lasted five years, and he is a good sort—although
I am no more interested in him than in anyone else. Up to now, he
has been the Texas and Kansas representative for his house, and
now he has been given a "home" position in Boston. And since I left
Albert, I wrote him—so he has offered to take care of me if I come
to live in Boston. His people live in Brockton now, and in a recent
letter he said they were moving back to Boston. He knew I used to
live at North Wait Street in Boston when I was with Frank Sloan.
So he told me he looked it up, and found that the same flat I had
was vacant, and if I would come, he would furnish it. And while I
suppose parts of it is, and would be, disgusting and make me so
tired—yet when I think of that beautiful flat and the white,
perfectly-fitted bathroom and kitchen, I can't seem to get my mind
adjusted to the advantage of respectability in a cheap room with
cheap surroundings—

I have written so much and arrived at nothing. You must see
what I mean—I should love to take advantage of your kindness,
and it is even more than that to me—but how can I? I know I am in
a horribly depressed state of mind—never was like this before. I
seem haunted by the different evils, no matter which way I choose.

You know I appreciate your thought in getting me a dress,
especially since it is not given conditionally. Am I not awfully

particular for a beggar? But I just can't help it. I cannot cringe and fawn on people.

As to whether you should write to Mr. Welsh—I should rather that you do as you would feel you wanted to do, feeling free to write what you please. Only I shall hope that you will understand that I write you freely, as I would to anyone who didn't even know Mr. Welsh, and not with the thought that you would intercede for me. I am going to bed now. I am so tired and it is so quiet without Poke. Goodnight.

My very dear Friend— *July 12, 1911*

℘ 27 THERE IS SO MUCH I WANT TO WRITE YOU—BUT FIRST I MUST THANK you for the dresses, which I liked so much. The blue one, particularly, looks great on me and fits to perfection. It only needed shortening, and my sister-in-law did that. But the other one requires much alteration and will have to be done by a seamstress. I took it to one who wanted $2.00, so I will wait and have it done later. The ribbon, too, is so sweet. I put a cheap white washable belt under it and wore it on the white shirt you sent me. It is so good of you, that I wish I did not appear such an ingrate. I am so ashamed of my apparent ingratitude; and yet, not to do what I want to do, puts me back in the hypocrite class. . . .

I have come to a more definite idea of what I should do. I have as yet not moved, but I shall do so Saturday the 15th. You know Mr. Welsh sent me a weekly check and paid my rent. He gave me no sign that he should not continue doing so; but after my meeting with him, and when I learned how I stood, I knew he would not do so much longer. I asked Mr. Suiffen, and he said, yes, that Mr. Welsh had said he wouldn't pay my rent any longer. I knew then that I was just obliged to make some sort of a move. Then, today, I received a letter from Mr. Welsh. . . and I feel that this is his last letter to me, for he summed things up generally: that I should return to Albert; should join the church, give up my own will and submit to others—and much about accepting the Saviour; and that I should have something done to make a glass eye possible; and that he would continue sending the check until August 1, but no longer—that after that, I must not expect help from him, as he had suffered much loss of money—and, last but not least, the old story of the "gay clothes," and that I had added to "nature's tint in the cheeks." It would make me so cross if it wasn't so very ridiculous.

All my grown life I have had one prolonged fight with my natural complexion because of its high color, which I have always considered an evidence of plebeian birth, and have used every known thing to bring it down to the general pale tints of other girls'. Years ago when I was silly, I remember eating arsenic tablets, which someone told me makes one pale—so, in the face of that, do you wonder this latest accusation makes me smile? But then, all that is trivial, except that it has brought me to a true realization of where I stand. I have been backed up into a corner, and know it is up to me to make a break for liberty, taking the first course that seems the best. As for the idea of going to Boston, I have given that up. . . . I will be frank with you; the reason that I would not care to go there. . .is because you are there. I know you would not trouble me, but I know myself. I know I should feel ashamed, and because of that would go out and get work of some hateful, uncongenial kind that would pay $5.00 or $6.00 a week—even if I did let Arthur help me—just to keep up appearances. And I would be hating it dreadfully all the time. And then, I'm not terribly fond of him. I want to tell you, though, that you need never fear that I would get into some public place; I don't have to do that; I wouldn't ever have to do that. As long as I have my mind and can use my tongue, such extreme measures are unnecessary. I never did that before, never did anything even one-tenth as low, and consider that the last gasp. I never associated with low women—I don't think I ever met, to talk to the second time, a woman who was publicly known to live other than she should. I shun such people. Even girls who did no worse than I, couldn't claim acquaintance with me. So, you see, it is never to be feared that I should do anything of that sort. If I may say it, I am too smart for that.

On Saturday, July 15th, I shall send all my things to Bro's, and I shall go to New York. Before I forget, I want to mention that I shall tell no one but you where I am going, as I would rather they should not know—and particularly Albert, for I fear him, more or less; and I think if he thought I wasn't doing just right, even if he wouldn't help me himself, he would make it ugly for me. So this will be "entre-nous," for awhile, anyway.

I will explain why it is New York: Years ago when I was about fifteen, I went with a Jewish boy about seventeen; and we liked each other, but could not meet openly, as my mother had a man who was a butcher—a widower with two children, about thirty-

77

five years old—that I was to marry because he had fifty thousand dollars—perhaps. So the mere sight of this boy infuriated my mother, and in time we had to cut it all out, although I liked him fairly well, and he was real silly about me. He has since then had quite an eventful life, leaving home at about that time and knocking about here and there, and getting an education much as I did mine. About four years ago, on a visit to Phila., his people arranged a *shiddach* for him—which is Jewish for a "match"—having a girl selected whose father was willing to give the man $3,000 as her dowry. This is the regular way among the Orthodox Jews. And he had been knocking about doing fairly well—only at times he was tired of it, and willing to settle down. So he agreed to marry her—mind you, sight unseen. This thing was very opportune, for his father was just at that time in a tight place, and the marriage of his son would help him. For he had a business that was on its last legs that the son offered to take over for $2,000, enabling the father and the mother to move out on a farm with a large family of five daughters. At any rate, when he saw the girl, he knew it would be anything but possible for him to love her; but as she was sweet, and apparently clean and sensible, he thought he could make it possible for them to live at least in peace. So the marriage took place; the money was turned over; the business was bought; the family went out on the farm, and they prepared to live happily ever after. She turned out to be most slovenly and, from what I heard, the filthiest woman in the world. He worried along with her for almost a year, and then a baby came; and after she was up and about three months, her absolute disregard for cleanliness disgusted him; and as she didn't seem to be over-fond of their baby, a little girl, he sent her back to her home. And as she didn't want the baby, he took it, sold out the business and went with his baby to the farm. I can't tell you, it would take too much time, about the sort of woman this was. I know the type well. It is encountered quite often among a certain class of Jews. Perfect morally—but the last word when it comes to being a companion, a mate, and all the other things a wife should be. At any rate, she is with her people in Trenton, and he never sees her, and she doesn't trouble him. The baby is on the farm with his mother and sisters, and he has since then done quite a few things—mostly selling, as he is a very capable salesman.

When I worked on the *North American*, I met Lina, his oldest sister...we had been friends years ago....I ran into him...three or four times, but I never encouraged him, because I had grown out of his class. For while he had been able to educate himself somewhat, it was not along refined lines, and he looked and was quite rough, and knew nothing of the "nice" things that men of better birth do instinctively.... He had been selling celluloid starch to the retailers, meeting the smaller and necessarily the more ignorant class of grocers, so he had nothing much to learn from them. So when I talked with him, I showed him how he was going after such small game when he might as well be after larger. On several occasions he took Albert and I to the theatre, but would never accept our invitation to call on us—which I didn't understand, at the time. So about the time I quit the *North American*, he quit the starch people and tried out two or three things, but all where he only interviewed the cheaper element. Then, I, of course, knew that I was the "wonderful girl" in his mind, but I never gave him a serious thought, for he is three years younger than I in years—and thirty in actual life. And yet, I somehow took delight in ordering him to change some part of his rather loud apparel, or to use better English, to taboo slang, to eat more quietly and nicely—and the thousand-and-one things which I had been six years teaching to Albert, and which Ira learned in that many weeks, for he wanted to know so much. Then, when Albert left and I was left alone, Ira's sister came up from the country and stayed two nights with me, and I told her how I was situated. Almost the earliest he could get here after his sister's return, he came; and being young, and not having known any designing, calculating women very much, he was very enthusiastic and most anxious to begin right away to take care of me. He said that he would begin to save and work ten times as hard, and in two years' time he would accomplish all this: earn and save sufficient money to buy two divorces, and have $1000 to give me in my name, if I would marry him. Of course, he was so intense that I couldn't laugh in his face, but it did seem so ridiculous. And yet, when I looked at his face—which is very ugly, but very strong—I knew he was capable of doing it, provided I was the incentive. But I had no such plans, for I was fully aware of the fact that I don't care for him. When I told him that, he said he didn't care, for he was willing to love me and wait on me. At any rate, I thought it was all just boyish exuberance, and rather than say "No"—which I would do if I took him seriously—the thought came to me that perhaps it would be a big thing for him to have a prize to strive for—for with his naturally quick wit and a strong [goal] that he took seriously, he would do wonders for himself. So I made a sort of vague promise that if in three months he had a position that was dignified and was earning $50.00 a week, or $200.00 a month, I would give him, starting from then, some of my time. Oh! he could do that readily, as he said, as he was earning $125.00 at the time. So that way, I thought, little by little, step by step to bring him up; and as he went up, perhaps he wouldn't be so repulsive to me. But in fairness to myself, I don't think I once expected to derive any benefits from it personally. Anyway, since that time—or almost the same week— he went to New York and tried two other things, before he hit on selling a high-grade proposition. I put the idea in his head, for I had met one of their salesmen in my uncle's store. It is the "Protecto-graph" which protects a check from being erased. They sell for $30.00—the agent gets $10.00 for each he sells. He made a big suc-cess of it right from the start, selling three machines his first day. In the meantime, I kept up a dilatory correspondence with him, although he wrote or sent a post card each day. In one of his recent letters he told me of being in second place that week, ahead of men two and three times his age who had been with these people for years. His letters bubbled with enthusiasm—and being so depressed myself, it was so refreshing. He told me that in the week he got into second place, he earned $120.00 net, and said he was ready now, but he would stick it out the three months to show me how he could do what he said he could—the three months not being up until July 25, and he had $250.00 toward the expense of the divorces, etc. It was really quite laughable until he showed me that he wasn't to be laughed at. Then, as I felt things closing around me, I thought of him as an avenue of escape. But it seemed like "taking candy from babies," and somehow I couldn't take advantage of his sincere, honest purpose. Then, when I decided—as I wrote you—not to consider going to Boston, I decided to send for him. He came Sunday, 9 A.M., and came directly to Brother's who is a great friend of his. He brought me a beautiful box of flowers—some long-stemmed pink rosebuds. Then, a bunch of sweet peas and a small brooch pin of gold with three small diamonds, the pin being worth around $25.00. It was so long since I had received any such attentions that I felt foolish. After dinner, we went to the park and I told him then the exact truth of my condition. He was somewhat surprised, because heretofore I had been deceiving him—for as I never took him seriously, I saw no reason for divulging everything. Anyway, his idea was for me to go to his mother's, and he would come to see me every weekend. Now, I know how pleasant that would be. For his people "funned" along with me about him, because they knew I didn't take him seriously—but if I go there now, acknowledging that I am taking advantage of his success, they would despise me. Because now, since his success, they have large plans for themselves and benefits they will derive, as he is very generous to those he cares for. Of course, I feel the success he has made has been largely due to my "kidding" him along, so I don't feel so badly about using him now in my need. At any rate, he said he would do anything I suggested, but he would tell me frankly that he has to take care of his family—mother, sisters, and baby. And I think I will see that they get more than ever before. Of course, he was surprised when I told him I was willing to live with him regardless of divorces, etc.—that I considered them a lot of foolishness, and a marriage ceremony the worst lot of cant I ever heard. That is my honest opinion, and why bother about it? I could go deep into that subject to show why I have arrived at such an unusual conclusion; but I will simply say: because of observation of the various marriage contracts I know intimately about—my own, my sister's, my mother's, and a host of others. Anyway he returned to New York—or, rather, left here Sunday night and went to his home, and then to New York Monday morning. Between now and Sat., he will find a two-rooms-and-bath apartment that is spacious and airy and thoroughly up-to-date and modern in everything—one that is furnished—and I will come over Sat., and if I like what he selects, I will stay right on. If not, I will go to a hotel and then Monday look for a place. I shall take along just necessities and clothes, sending the rest to Bro's, as I may not like this arrangement and may come back. He was alarmed that his mother might refuse to take care of his daughter if he did as we proposed doing. But he wrote me she cried a little and begged him not to do it—she said nothing about the baby. I was hoping she would refuse to care for her longer, for I'd like to myself. He said I might have her after she is a little older.

Now I believe I have told you all, in full detail, so you could see for yourself how this came about. Oh, yes—I forgot to tell you his name! It is Ira Benjamin. They are Russian Jews; and when the father came to this country, he engaged in the grocery business and, as do most of the ignorant Jews, they thought the use of a Jewish name would be a detriment to trade. So they just took the name of Benson—and the father, whose name is Aaron Benjamin in Jewish, translated that into "Bernard Benson," and the girls—all of them go by that name. Then, among other things that I taught this boy, was how silly it was to take a good, strong family name and change it into a mere appellation that means nothing—as, for instance, his own Jewish [name is "Ira"]...and they call him "Henry." So he took my advice, and when he went to New York to engage in business, he used his own given name and right family name—and no one can dispute that Ira Benjamin sounds better than Henry Benson.

Oh, it has been suffocating here, and this room with the sun pouring in all day makes sleep impossible. It is 4:30 A.M. and I am wide awake. I am going to write Mr. Welsh before I go, and of course thank him, for he was truly very kind to me. There are some things I cannot understand, but I presume it is not necessary that I do. And he is human, too, and liable to do as other humans do— although to me he was God himself. You would laugh outright if you knew of the place I thought I had in Mr. Welsh's affection— But I shall not go into that. As I said, I shall thank him and just give him a vague idea of what I am going to do. Since I am going back into the lying business—for it is one lie after another—I might as well lie a little here, before I leave, and tell him that I have had a position offered to me and that I am going to work. Then I shall also return his letters.

Now I will close, but not before wishing I had a more adequate way than just saying "thank you" to you for your letters, which were the best friends I had for six months or more. To be silly, effusively so, or express a lot of cheap sentiment is not possible for me when I am sincere, but I will say that I would feel happy if I could do something for you. Some real thing to prove to you, and as satisfaction to myself, how deep is my gratitude to you. Not so much for your aid when I was in need as much as for the regular letters. I unconsciously made them a live friend, and we, the letters and I, were in league against all these ugly conditions. . . . I carried always one or two of your letters in my pocketbook; and when I had to bear things and accept indignities, I would often think of the letters being there, and how they sympathized with me; and often when I pretended to be as meek as Moses, later I'd get my letters out and pat them, knowing they alone knew how superior I am to those who belittled me....

I think I shall let Poke remain where she is this summer, and then in the fall I will take her to me. For it is really much better for her there, where she takes a sea bath each day....

I shall keep on writing you from New York....I will also send you my N.Y. address. And I shall write you how I get along, if you are sure you want me to. Yours very sincerely and deeply grateful, Maimie

Hotel Richmond, New York
July 27, 1911

IT SEEMS STRANGE TO WRITE YOU WITHOUT MY USUAL TALE OF WOE, AND 28 ⊠ no doubt it will seem such a change for you. Well, I finally got away Saturday, without telling anyone anything; and as the train came to Newark, N.J., Ira got on, and I was much relieved—for I felt like a country girl coming to a large city. Sunday, we got this little apartment, which is almost like a doll's house, it is so pretty and small. It is in a large eleven-story hotel—right in the heart of the city, but Ira selected it because he thought it would be better for me to be close in, until I got tired of seeing the "bright lights" and going to shows and the elegant restaurants, etc. The hotel is so swagger looking from the outside and in the lobby, that it makes me feel like somebody to come in and out. We have one large sitting room, and a smaller alcove bedroom, and a bath leading from that, which is almost too pretty to use. I couldn't begin to tell you of the various things that delight me—but a few are the elevator service and the bellboys in pure white uniform— Then, my sitting room has light-green summer wicker furniture and shiny floors with Persian rugs. The wallpaper is also a delicate green, and everything harmonizes. I have a brass desk-set which looks great on this green desk; then I have a Haviland china breakfast-set, which is an apple green, and it looks great on the oval green table. Then, the bed is the most comfortable I ever slept on, as it has a box spring and a hair mattress. We have a telephone, and the exchange is in the lobby. The ice water is filtered and brought to your room whenever I ring. And the bath—that is the main joy of my life here — I wonder if this—writing of my life here—is in bad taste. I sort of feel that it is—or would be, only that I regard you so intimately that I would not hesitate to tell you of even the most intimate of intimate things...

I did not write [Mr. Welsh] of my expected leaving. When I heard from him last, he said that I must not expect help from him further; so I felt free to do as I please, as he no doubt expected me to do. I don't think I need tell you that I should have preferred doing "right," had all things been equal; but as they were not, I choose this life. And knowing I couldn't, if I wrote reams about it, make Mr. Welsh understand, I decided not to write him at all....

I recall when I first wrote Mr. Welsh when I first knew him, and wrote the most intimate things—my surprise when coming to Phila. to learn that he had permitted every and any sort to read them. I had not thought it necessary to write that no one should see these things, for I never dreamed but that was something unheard-of among a class of people such as Mr. Welsh belonged to....It naturally put me on my guard, and thereafter I wrote Mr. Welsh only what I felt the world could see for all I cared....

So again I wrote vaguely, telling him I had come to New York...I will never fully admit the facts; and while he may, and others may guess at the truth, I shall admit it to absolutely no one. Excepting, of course, you—and you are one and the same as me. Is that grammatically proper?

I am so contented and pleased. I have gotten some new clothes that I needed, and now feel so much more like myself when I am on the street. We have been to three shows, and they are the good ones and I surely do love them. I have my chafing dish here, and prepare my breakfast now, because Ira located a place where fresh eggs are sold not later than twelve hours after laid. This is bona fide, and they are delicious. They cost 10 cents apiece but are well worth it, and it is so nice to prepare my own breakfast. He gets his in the cafe downstairs, where they serve a club breakfast. It is all so nice that I feel like Alice in Wonderland.

New York, while it is up-to-date, doesn't appeal to me as well as Phila. There are so many things to divert one—but to find friends here would be impossible. One thing that I don't like is the number of "bad women" one sees on the street. They are "bad" in every sense of the word, and they have it written across their faces. Such style of dress, too! They wear décolleté and the most glaring combination of colors, right on the street, in the morning or afternoon, just as though it was a ballroom.

I started this letter some few days ago and have added to it every time I had a few moments to spare, for I go out so much, just to walk on Fifth Avenue or go to a matinee. It is all such fun, and I love to see the windows on Fifth Avenue. I secured a card—in fact, two, one for each of us—to use books from the big new library, which is magnificent. I have your two pictures over my desk, there in the middle, in a little *passepartout* frame, the snapshot you sent of Helen and Mark. I have an electric iron, and as we send our clothes to the laundry, I kept the small pieces—handkerchiefs, stockings, hose, undervests, etc.—and washed them in the bath tub and will now proceed to press them. It is all so lovely here that I take pleasure in all these things. With much love. . . .

Hotel Richmond, New York
August 1, 1911

I HOPE YOU AND THE CHILDREN ARE WELL. I AM ENCLOSING A POST CARD   29 ᘓ
for them. I think it is so dear. I am well and spending a great lot of my time reading, as we have both taken out cards to this magnificent new library that is an inspiration in itself. As we only live a few blocks from it, it is very convenient. I have outlined some reading for Ira and have made it so attractive by reading it together and discussing it, until he is almost as omnivorous a reader as I am.

Hotel Richmond, New York
August 23, 1911

IT SEEMS SO LONG SINCE I HAVE WRITTEN YOU THAT I AM ASHAMED OF   30 ᘓ
myself, for you will surely think I am negligent. It isn't that, really—it is just that I procrastinate, and nothing gets done when I am at home; and the rest of the time I am either hurrying to work or to the theatre. I am still a "cloak model," but Saturday terminates that work—and I'm somewhat glad, in a measure, as it has been very warm and it is no easy job to stand around with those hot suits on, with as much as three or four people pawing over you at one time.

Last Sunday week we went over to Brooklyn to visit an aunt of mine, a poor old lady, my father's sister. She has three daughters at home and they live in three rooms on the top floor of a dwelling in the most congested part of the Brooklyn ghetto. It is over a grocery store of the unspeakable kind. . . . One cannot understand why they persist in living in such places, because for the same rent they could I know live in a suburban cottage. I think it is because they like to live among their own kind, and then too, being Orthodox Jews, they must not be separated by more than a minute's walk from the rabbi's dwelling. I found my little cousin Alex from Phila. there visiting them. . . . He is a clean boy in every respect, and thoroughly Americanized, although he is only here from Russia but a short while. . . .

Do you know that Mr. Welsh never answered the letter I wrote him? It rather surprises me for I felt he would interest himself in trying to make me return to Phila. Mr. Suiffen wrote that one typewritten and short note I wrote you of and since then he also has not written. I heard from Albert and he writes he thinks Poke is due to have some puppies. . . .

Before I forget, I want to tell you about what we read. In the first place, Ira, even before I came to New York, subscribed to the *Philistine* and the *Fra*. He admires the ideas of this man Hubbard.[9] Personally, I can't say just where I stand on the subject. Immediately after reading something he has written, I admire him immensely; but afterwards, when I think it all over, it strikes me that he is not sincere and that he is a trickster with words, knowing human nature very well and knowing how to appeal to me. But Bennie is entirely wrapped in him. Prior to my coming, Bennie smoked cigarettes; but after reading Elbert Hubbard's *Cigarrthist*—which I sent for—and at my request, he desisted.[10] Then imagine the inconsistency of it all when later we saw an ad in the *Fra* written by "Elbert" himself, "bragging" about Pall Mall cigarettes. I wish you would tell me what is the general opinion among right-minded educated people about this man. Sometimes his poses seem so cheap and flimsy to me. Anyway, we read the two magazines each month and such other literature as they send us. His "little journeys" to the homes of people worthwhile are fascinating reading. Then, I got the life of Napoleon for Ira. He admires him, so I got him the biography—and as most of our reading is done by me aloud, he doesn't get far into it, as I stop to talk it over. But I will renew it every two weeks until finished. I bought a small bronze head of Napoleon for Bennie, and also a print of the Napoleon picture called the "snuff box picture." Then for myself I get books that I have often wanted to read, and books that I hear quoted and feel I ought to read. Just now I have a very interesting book by Israel Zangwill, who personally attracts me because of his being a Hebrew.[11] If you haven't seen this book and have the time, I wish you'd get it. It is called *Without Prejudice.* It is a collection of articles once published in *Pall Mall,* and [they] are on the order of essays on various subjects, mostly with a humorous turn.[12] Some of it is so subtle, and yet so sharp, and I am very glad I selected it. I do not get two books in turn by the same writers, so last week read *The Tale of Two Cities* and some short stories by Frank Stockton, which I didn't care for. I got the book so as to read "The Lady or The Tiger," to which I had often seen references.[13] The story did not impress me greatly, nor did any of the others. I am going to the library today. I wonder—if you have in mind any stories I should like, would you tell me of them? While they have an enormous amount of books, they taboo certain ones, but I find plenty for me to select from. I like books of modern society like *The Opal* or *The House of Mirth;* but when I come across one, unless it is one I have heard of as being good, I am loathe to waste my time reading it, for I am afraid they are not of much value.[14] I had the pleasure of reading *The Opal* all over again, as I read it aloud to Bennie Sunday—and do you know, I changed my opinion about two things since the second reading? Both about the characters of Edith and Mary. Prior to this second reading, I thought Edith a silly girl—but I don't know whether it wasn't because she was very wise, that she did what seemed so dastardly in the first reading. I have promised myself to read it again to myself, giving it the benefit of my changed views, and see then whether each speech has a different meaning to me. Did you know that they have the art galleries in the new library? And oh! how exquisite some of the paintings are. A visit there is a double pleasure, because after selecting our books we go up to the galleries and look at the pictures. And Bennie has found a painting of me. He insists it is me, and I can't swear that it isn't, because I used to pose for the man that paints it—Carl Blemmer. It is really very real, and Bennie went to find this artist to ask him, but it appears he is not in New York. You may know that when the artists engage a model, they don't tell you what for, and they may only use your upper lip or ear, and you never see what they are painting—that is, if you are a "strictly-business" model. And this picture is surely my profile and nose and eyes and mouth, but I am not positive—and Bennie goes to it every time we go to the library, and informs everyone in the neighborhood of the picture that it is me. We have the *Life of Henry Stanley* picked out as the next reading—thanks to your suggestion....[15]

Now I must tell you of my friend. Her name is Mrs. Gregory. I will tell you from the very beginning of how I know her.

When I was on the stage in Boston playing at the Columbia Theatre, this lady's son Gilbert Gregory had the star part. I just knew him—that's all. Then when I was in the Post Graduate Hospital in New York City, four years later, after losing my eye and while I was recuperating...they brought an old lady into [the bed next to me], seventy years old, who was to be operated on for appendicitis....Her son came to see her, and I recognized him as this Gilbert Gregory...and he introduced me to his mother. Of course, no one thought she should ever survive the operation; but she did and we became very fast friends, lying there side by side for more than two months. I thought it strange that she should be obliged to be in a ward when her son earned such a large salary, perhaps $500.00 a week—and he never brought her any of the things we all craved, such as fruit, etc. Anyway, she left, and after a few more months I was brought to Phila. to another hospital, and in that way did not see her again. In 1907 I saw her son in New Orleans playing with Geo. Cohan in *The American Idea.* I purposely called on him at his hotel to ask after his mother. He said she was in New York and not very well. I thought of her quite often after I came to New York this time, and even made inquiries of some theatrical people I know about Gilbert Gregory; and somehow no one seemed to know where he was, they hadn't heard of him in years. Then about a week ago—we were going to see *Get Rich Quick Wallingford*—and I saw Mr. Gilbert Gregory and asked after his mother —really not having the least idea she was alive—and he told me she was well and gave me her address. So the next morning I called on her, and she was so glad to see me and to know, as she expresses it, that someone wanted to see her. She is perhaps seventy-eight or eighty years old. I was astonished to find her in a little hall bedroom not large enough for a human to live in. Of course, I was astounded and she saw it, so she explained. It seems this son never did for her. Every dollar was spent on riotous living with fast women. She was the mother of ten children, and they all died after attaining full growth and this son is all that is left of them. She had a little money, a very little saved up, and as she worked right along, sewing fancy things on the church things for the Little Church Around the Corner, she managed to live and have a bit put by. Then what with drink, etc., the son soon lost his position in the theatrical world, and prior to 1909 stayed here in N.Y. for *eight months* living on *this old lady's earnings.* The saved-up money gave out about the same time as her work did—the church people giving it over to a large firm who contracted with all the churches by the year. After several months spent in vain attempts to get paying work, she accepted a position with a dressmaker at $5.00 a week. Of course, when her store gave out, she saw no more of the son, and finally he went out West and stayed *two* years....He never wrote a word and no one knew of his whereabouts. Then four weeks ago he turned up. In the meantime—you know the poor old lady couldn't do much with $5.00. She pays $1.50 a week for her room and cooks her own meals and does her own washing and ironing. Just think, in all that sleet and ice and cold last winter, she walked every day, never missing a day in *two years* to her work, which is at 41st St.—and she lives at 63rd, a matter of twenty-two blocks. She told me she had no friends, as in New York people do not make friends unless they can have good times. She hasn't even a winter coat, and last winter wore a thin gray sack and a sweater —a man's sweater—under it, which someone gave her....She isn't working now, as this firm closes down for the summer— so she saved $1.00 a week to meet this contingency, and now this son has *borrowed* it to use *toward* buying a suit which he told her he had to have in order to make an appearance so that he may get a job. He doesn't tell her what he did while away, and in fact I went with her to meet him last week, and he treats her like a cur. Of course, I am in no position to do much for her, but I feel so sorry for the poor old lady, and we take her to dinner every night. It is surprising how able she is to get about, and sprightly, and eats heartily. The poor soul. We have had her with us every night since I called on her about eight or nine days ago, and she has taken luncheon with me several times. I thought I'd make inquiries in Sept. when people are all back to see if I couldn't get some wealthy philanthropic person to do something toward making this winter a more comfortable one for her.

I have written so long my fingers are cramped, so I will close now, even though abruptly, and send this along.

Hotel Richmond, New York
August 26, 1911

§ 31 THIS IS JUST A LINE TO TELL YOU OF GOOD NEWS. I AM GOING tomorrow, Sunday, to Atlantic City to stay a week. The visit is to get Miss Poke—who, by the way, is Mrs. Poke, for she has three babies. Albeit mites, they are very pretty, and although their birth was an accident, they look like thoroughbreds. I expect to tell Albert the truth about New York and Bennie and I don't think it will have anything but a good effect. Bennie thought as long as I was going, I should make a holiday of it; so I shall stay a week and only bring one pup back with Pokes. From Atlantic City, I will go to Phila. and visit with my Bro and see the Wonder Baby. I am taking it a present which I bought in the Gorham Silver Company, a silver outfit—brush, comb, napkinring, pushes, etc.—eight pieces in all. I paid $15.00 for it. Then I shall go to Norristown to see my unfortunate sister, and be back here in ten days. I am very happy to see them all, and I thought it would make you happy to know....

I have turned Bennie over to [Mrs. Gregory], and he promises that she shall take dinner every night with him. Poor old lady—I wish you could see her, she is so pretty—really pretty—anyway, in my eyes.

Hotel Richmond, New York
September 9, 1911

§ 34 I RECEIVED A LETTER FROM MR. SUIFFEN IN WHICH HE SAID MR. WELSH had written me and I hadn't answered it. I get all mail in the name of *Jones* at a newspaper store which a second cousin of mine operates, and get many letters, but think due to Mr. Welsh's rather illegible hand, the letter didn't reach me. In this letter, Mr. Suiffen quotes part of Mr. Welsh's letter in which he wrote that he had $50.00 which he had *"collected"* for Maimie, which she could have to help pay her expenses at a business college this fall. I was surprised, and yet don't know what to do. As far as going to school is concerned, I am very eager to go. I have wanted to all the time, but never broached the subject to Bennie, as he is up to his neck in expenses, what with his sisters continually at him, and that which he wants to get me, because he loves to give me things. I never inquired what a course would cost, but intend to in the next day or so. I rather dislike the way Mr. Welsh gets the money to help me. Somehow it makes me furious. I guess you can't understand that. I ought to be grateful, but I can't be, under the circumstances. I feel like a street corner beggar, and I worry as to what arguments Mr. Welsh puts forth that makes people give him money for me. I think he uses my eye—or lack of eye—as the thing to excite sympathy, and I can't bear that. Well, what's the use. I can either take it and learn what I am crazy to know, or reject it and kick myself afterwards. I know nothing whatever about the cost of a course. Whether $50.00 would pay it, or whether that's just a drop in the bucket. I wouldn't ask Ira to pay toward it, as I'm sure he'd say that I will never have to earn a living for myself; but I would like to have the knowledge anyhow.

Ira's mother and stepfather are coming to New York to remain four or five days. I do not know. I did not ask him, but I think it is at his invitation—and oh! how I shall hate it; but of course I won't let him know that. I do not know if I have told you that he is very temperamental. So much so that I have to be so careful—for one or two careless words before he leaves means that he will do no business that day. I attribute this run of bad business to his state of mind, which began a few days before my trip to Atlantic City—and even though I have been back a few days—rather, almost a week—he hasn't returned to his normal state. . . . I am going to get seats for a lively show tonight that may help some.

I must conclude now as the maid has come in to give the room its weekly good cleaning and use the vacuum on the floor, etc. . . .

I want though to explain something about the $12.00 night-dresses. . . . Bennie. . . pictured me in the pretty, filmy nightdresses he used to see on women in places such as he frequented, of course before he knew me, and that is why he bought the prettiest he could find. . . . He also buys ribbons; almost every other day he will bring home a bolt or piece of pretty ribbon, and I make bows and string them all over me, and he is pleased. Doesn't that sound silly? But then, he is such a boy. He has another notion, shall I tell you? And that is I must wear stockings, pink silk ones in bed. . . . Poor dear Poke. She inhabits the bath tub with her son—and such a big bounder he is, since he alone has all the good milk intended for three. We call him "Rummy"—

My Dear Friend—   *September 9, 1911*

☎ 35   WHEN ONE IS HAPPY—OR RATHER, WHEN I AM HAPPY—I FEEL I MUST
talk to someone about it. And I have no one to tell, that I care for,
but you. This is it: Bennie didn't sell a machine all week, and in
consequence was very despondent—especially so because his
mother is due for a visit. . . . Yesterday afternoon he came home
feeling very blue. He and I went to a show and it helped some. I
awakened this morning at three o'clock and wrote him a note—or
rather, a six page letter, telling him all sorts of encouraging things,
and on the envelope cautioned him to read it at his breakfast this
morning. He did, and just now came back—Sat. half-holiday—and
had sold six machines! Four to one firm, and one each to two
others, making for his half-day's work $60.00. Isn't that almost like
a fairy tale? And I feel that now he will be himself again. He is
jumping around here like a boy of eight—and I'm so glad for him,
even more than for what the money means. I know you will be
glad, too. We are going out to buy my Bennie's mother a present,
and for him, a fall hat. He is looking over my shoulder and tells me
to tell you that he is going to buy me a pair of white gloves.
Goodbye—Your loving friend, Mamie

New York, September, 1911

☎ 36   I SHALL WRITE MR. WELSH THAT I WANT TO LEARN VERY MUCH, AND
then I shall tell him of Ira—but must admit that I shall tell him that
my relations with him are only recent ones; that is, I shall infer so
because of Mr. Suiffen, to whom I have been writing and have not
said a thing about it. I shall tell Mr. Welsh that I would like to go to
school—provided he would send me there knowing what I am
doing. I believe that Mr. Welsh is to be in Boston some time soon
and perhaps then you shall see him. His letter to me awakens all the
deep feelings I had for him when I loved him and believed in his
love for me—and I feel like I wish I wasn't living this way, knowing
that it will hurt him. Of course, I know that I was fairly driven to
this—for I held out and worried along, being cold and hungry
almost to desperation, all last winter. But no doubt he won't
consider that. . . .

I have received a letter from [Albert] saying he had gone to
Phila. and has a job there. . . . I promised him that if he ever had

$1000.00 saved up and a permanent position or a business that netted him at least $100.00 a month, I would return to him. He may never make it but it won't hurt him to try . . . .

Will you write me when you have a birthday? I am making something for you and I don't want to wait until Christmas to give it to you.

New York, October 5, 1911

I MUST TELL YOU NOW ABOUT MR. WELSH. SATURDAY NIGHT AFTER A **37** 🕮
walk with Ira and Poke, I found Mr. Welsh's letter in our box. I opened it with a feeling of dread, for I somehow felt that he would scold me no matter how kind his letter was—for in a way, I felt I deserved it. I cannot tell you then how I felt, then, when I opened it . . . to find peeping out a few simple little buttercups, still quite fresh. I felt differently then—I knew the letter would be kind. And I don't know why I should have dreaded it so, since he was always kind to me, except when he returned from Europe, and perhaps I didn't understand. The letter was very very kind and I felt so grateful . . . . The letter recounted somewhat my experiences and his, since he has known me; and he feels that I have shown much progress . . . and that his efforts were not in vain. It may sound silly, but I really am a better woman than when he first knew me; and he is really responsible for it. He said that I cared so much for you, and your friendship argued well for me. At any rate, I loved him so much for the letter and told him so. He even asked kindly about Ira, and Ira is elated. He knows that I am very much affected by your and Mr. Welsh's opinion; and now he feels easier, as do I, about Mr. Welsh. I have a very good picture of Mr. Welsh, in a simple brass frame, and I used to keep it on my desk opposite yours and your children—but somehow, after that memorable visit to his office, I couldn't bear to keep it there. Not that I didn't care for him, but when I would see it, it would recall that day which I hated. So I placed in the frame in front of his picture one of a girl friend. Then Sat. night, after reading the letter, I wanted to see his face, so got the picture out—and how different it now seems. It is now in its place opposite yours, and I can see it now, and you, too. I love your picture, too.

[Albert wrote me] that he was going to Newark, N.J. . . . to sell some contrivance which is very new, to clean silver . . . . He hoped it would prove a success, then he would branch out by going to a Western city. I surely hope he is successful, and write him encouraging letters.

New York, Thursday Night, October 12, 1911

CS 38 YOUR LETTER CAME TODAY—THIS IS NOT TO ANSWER IT, RATHER TO ASK something of you. It is to do with my reading, of which I am doing a great deal lately. Prior to this, the heat made reading less of a pleasure than now. Contrary to the general belief about one who reads a great deal, I read intelligently, absorbing new things and teaching and benefiting myself—not the least of which is increasing my vocabulary. During the last two years, I have read more with a view to entertaining myself than to educating myself—although prior to that time, all my reading was done with the latter object in view. At that time, when I came to references or words that I had no knowledge of, I had recourse only to a well-worn book which I still have and prize. I bought it in an old bookstore in Phila., years ago, when I first had the idea of educating myself through reading. It is a rather meagre dictionary, and also has a few pages devoted to French, Italian, Latin, German and Spanish familiar phrases that one meets with often in books, and then a small part given over to the explanation of some of the better-known fables and persons in history. I think you will know the sort of book it is, and it has been truly my school; but the provoking part of it all is that just when I want to know about something or the meaning of some word—it isn't in my book. At various times I have thought to buy something—perhaps even only a fuller dictionary—but heretofore have been reluctant to buy, because of my peregrinations, which makes anything bulky undesirable and means "excess baggage." Now, more than for some time, have I felt how inadequate is my "Little Red Book," for in some of my recent readings—especially a book by Henry James, and even Hardy—I have had that same experience which makes me so vexed with my "Little Red Book" (a name given to it by Albert when trotting me about my authority on any subject), to find what I am looking for is not there. . . . Perhaps hidden away somewhere among your shelves is a dictionary, better than mine and yet one that you or your husband may have laid aside for a more recent and better one. . . and if you have such a one that you really are not using and perhaps won't use, I should like to have it, either as a loan or a gift. . . .

94

Tonight we started to go to a show, but got as far as the library to get some books—and I became interested, as did Bennie, and we gave up the show. We expected to see *The Woman* but I'm just as well pleased we didn't go. What with winter, which means higher rent, starting since October 1, and Ira's overcoat, and various other things—besides, the girls at his home have to be helped to get their winter things—it is nip and tuck....We took out *John Percyfield* by C. Hanford Henderson and *The Beloved Vagabond* by Locke (the latter at your suggestion)....For poetry we got *Poems* by Geo. Meredith and *Collected Poems* by Dr. S. Weir Mitchell.[16] I always read the poems to Bennie as he is falling to sleep, and he said he thought he could *sleep better with Geo. Meredith as an accompanying lullaby*....[17] Will you tell me about Hardy? He is living, or is he not? I somehow have the impression he is. And is he considered a standard writer—and with what sort of writers that you think I would know, is he ranked? I liked *Tess of the D'Urbervilles*—did you read it?—but it was too tragic and left me sad for several days.[18] Tell me what you think of Hardy. Will you?

Chester Avenue, Philadelphia
October or November, 1911

IT SEEMS MONTHS SINCE I HAVE WRITTEN YOU, BUT WHAT WITH MY   **40** ✪
being laid up and then making the change (for I'm in Phila.), I haven't had much time to write. I did not get out of bed until Saturday of last week; and as my being sick was such an expensive experience coming right on top of Ira's trouble with his work, I thought I would come to my brother's for a visit—which would give Ira a chance to get on his feet again. Besides, I wanted to get some winter clothes I had here, and lay aside some of the summer ones. It was getting very hard for him, as his sisters had taken to sending telegrams collect, for they could not be made to believe that his money was held up—and rather than try to educate the world, I always cheerfully step aside and let them have it their way. Life is indeed too short to be continually trying to explain things to people who are not educated up to a certain point.

The fact that he sent them, from the time I joined him, from 100 to 150 per cent more money that he ever did before, doesn't appeal to their intelligence as meaning anything in my favor. Of course, this was up to the time [Ira's firm] refused to advance commissions. As we expected the money from day to day, they didn't feel the pinch (until just now); and I pawned both the ring and pin Ira bought me—first for a small amount, and then had another advance made on it, to the full amount they would lend me—and I sent every cent of it to his home. And we lived almost niggardly, up to the time I got downright sick. Then we had to spend money, and even that little bit of sickness cost around $50.00—for I first had a doctor in that told me I had appendicitis and must be operated on at once, and was for at once giving me an injection of morphine. I got so provoked at him, I almost threw him out. Even when I insisted I had my appendix removed, he advocated an operation, insisting I had appendicitis. When he spoke of morphine it was like waving a red flag before a bull. Ira ran him out. Then we called in a doctor that we had to pay $5.00 a visit, and he was of course a sure-enough doctor. He was such a gentleman, too, that it soothed me to have him about. He was so much like Dr. Wistar whom I knew well thru Mr. Welsh. Of course, not knowing us, we had to pay after each visit; and what with medicines and a visiting nurse every day to do for me while Bennie was gone out to chase down the elusive dollar, we were at a large expense. We are in debt, of course, but I suppose that is all in a lifetime. I thought coming here for a couple of weeks would keep some; besides, I wanted so much to see this Big Bouncing Baby, and to go out to the hospital to see my poor sister; and this would be as good a time as any to do it in. We owe a hundred dollars at the hotel, for they helped Ira when I became ill. They were very lovely, and we could have stayed there until Ira got on his feet. But I could not bear to keep up such an expensive place while Ira was not earning so much—for as yet he has not settled down definitely to anything, for the vacuum cleaners require too many visits to close a sale. So he is just working at it in the afternoons, while in the mornings he is looking into other things; and he makes an occasional sale of the cleaners— enough to keep himself going. Besides what we owe the hotel, we borrowed $100.00 on my jewelry and Kodak. So we went into the hole $250.00, and Ira has that much coming to him, if he ever gets it. We feel confident he will, only that it will come in $5.00 and $10.00 payments, weeks apart, and not do as much good as if he got it in a lump sum. I worried a great deal while I was in N.Y., but since coming here—for I got here Sunday night—I've been kept so busy I haven't had time to worry.

It's so strange to me, about my people. This brother here, for example. He seems to care for me, and yet he never questions how I manage to live, or if I live at all. Of course, I never told them about Bennie, and they don't know a thing about it. True, they know I see him, but I know they never dream about his taking care of me, because they know his responsibilities at home, and never knew him to make enough for that—to say nothing of taking care of me. My brother abhors a woman who is lewd, and I know he doesn't think I live that way, for as much as I am his sister, he wouldn't permit me to sleep under his roof if he thought that. Last summer I showed him Mr. Welsh's letter that told me he could not give me further help, even the small amount he did send me weekly. He knows Albert has no resources and can scarcely support himself, and that I am not working. I really would like to know how he thinks I live. Perhaps he doesn't care—or, in fact, none of them do. They could—any one of them—afford and never miss it, to give me $5.00 a week. True, I never asked it, but I could always be independent with it. And yet they never say a word as to what I do to live. My fur coat and muff and scarf I pawned, last summer, for $5.00, when I was in straits—but really only borrowed enough so that it would be stored away for the summer, for they protect it as much as any fur-storing concern does. Last night, as I wanted to go to the corner, I asked my sister-in-law to put on her coat, as I have no other but that fur one. My Bro remarked, "Where's your fur coat?" I explained I had borrowed $5.00 and had it stored—not in a regular pawn shop, but in a place that makes a business of taking care of furs—and that I would have to pay $7.50 to get it. He said I had better get it, if that was the only coat I had, as it was getting too cold to go around without any, as I was doing. I answered I would, as soon as I had $7.50. It really would be funny, if it wasn't that he is my Bro—for he answered, "Well, now, as soon as you get your money, get it—or you'll have another cold." Just as though I had a regular income. Just for curiosity's sake, I said: "What do you mean by 'when I get my money'? What money?" He said—"I don't know, but what I suggest is that you get it soon, for I hated to see you coming from New York, as cold as it was Sunday, without a coat and in that thin waist." And that ended the conversation, for he walked out. I tell you this to show you what a queer lot my people are. I know I should never rest if I thought any of them needed for a coat to keep warm—and yet he never considered to offer to get my coat. That seems strange to me—and yet it is strange that I notice such things, when I have had such experiences from them ever since I became more or less incapacitated when I lost my eye. At that time, while I was in the hospital, the authorities there insisted that I give them the name of my people, so they could wire them that I was in such a dying condition. I finally did—and no one came, just as I expected. And since [then, when] I have talked about it, this was the explanation: That I was in a hospital, and they couldn't do anything better than that—and as it would cost $5.00 to go and come, they didn't see any use in expending that amount. It isn't strange, then, that no questions are asked. It is only strange that I keep on letting it trouble me—but I can't keep it. And this morning I am more bitter than usual—and I am sorry that you have to bear the brunt of it, because I insist on talking about it.

To change the subject, I will tell you about the baby—who is so sweet and dear that I forget some of the things about here. I wonder, when I play with her, whether she will grow up as selfish as her father—who just this minute scolded me, because I am writing so long, when I could be out in the store—where I have been since Monday morning, without stopping but just long enough to catch a bite to eat. He employs a clerk and a boy, and Monday he discharged the boy, explaining to me that he has been wanting to let him go for a couple of weeks, but couldn't spare him. But now that I am here, he let him go, and he will advertise for another (*soon*) and experiment with them until he gets a good one. And I am doing the boy's work in the meantime. I am perfectly willing to, for I am never here that I don't work from the time I arise at 7:00 or 7:30, until 11:30 when he closes the store—but I do think it seems presumptuous on his part to suggest such a thing.

I am feeling good—for mercifully lots of work keeps one from thinking about being sick. I am sorry to have to give up any reading, but I hope it won't be for long. I want to thank you for the dictionary, which is more than I looked for, but am sorry you bought it. I would have felt more comfortable about having asked for it if it was a discarded one of yours or your husband. It is so much more of a dictionary than my "Little Red Book" that I feel I was stupid not to have secured one long ago. I hope you and your family are well, and that you will excuse my "beefing" again in this letter; but I guess you are used to it by this time. Someday, I intend to be able to write you at length and have no reason for the least bit of wailing.

Chester Avenue, Philadelphia
November 14, 1911

SUCH A TIME AS I DO HAVE TO GET A LETTER WRITTEN! I SIT DOWN AT THE **41** desk and it's either the baby or the store that requires my attention. Then I put the sheet away with the few lines on it, intending to finish it when I get a chance; but when I return to it, the part written seems to be anything but what I want to write you—and I destroy it and start anew. This is the fourth start—almost like the way proposals are written, according to some novelists. I may get this through, this time, as I have the baby on my lap and she seems quiet, [content] just to watch the pen bob about, since it is a red pen-holder and attracts her eye.

I received your letter just as I was leaving to go to Norristown to see my poor sister Rachel in the asylum. I read and reread your letter on the train, and it helped to divert my mind; for generally that trip to see her is always so sad and distressing. I found her mentally about the same, but physically not looking so well. It makes me so miserable, because I am so helpless. In so many ways she is all that is to be desired—and just that one little something wrong in the great machine that makes all the trouble. I stayed with her all afternoon, about five hours, and worked very hard to keep her mind on sensible things, and she did very well. I did not notice how fatiguing it was to keep that up, so persevered. I had no breakfast nor lunch, for when I have to anticipate that trip, I can't possibly eat. About five o'clock, while with her, I felt very faint, but gave it no thought, just kept on getting sensible answers from her. Then I prepared to leave; and as usual the parting was very hard—for she clings to me, crying and pleading piteously that I should remain—and before I had any idea what was going on, I had fallen and fainted. And when I revived, I was very much surprised. When I thought I was able to go, I did, suffering no ill-effects at the time, nor since. She looked as though she had not been well, and said she had been in bed for some time, but I could not learn what was wrong with her. Oh! so much misery as there is out there. It depresses me, naturally, to see poor Rachel—but the sight of so many old ladies who have sat there for years, waiting to

99

die, makes me feel even more miserable. A visit there depresses me for weeks—yet I suppose I have to go. She begs so hard I should come often, as she sees no one else—as my mother and brother go once every year at *Rosh Hashona* (that is the Jewish New Year, when one is supposed to make all such visits in preparation to asking to be forgiven for their sins a week later—the Day of Atonement, *Yom Kippur*).

I noticed, in your letter, your suggestion that I call on or communicate with Mr. Welsh and Mr. Suiffen. That seemed strange, at the first reading, for that was the very first thing I did—wrote to Mr. Welsh and then to Mr. Suiffen, and have since seen Mr. Suiffen. On second thought, I knew why you thought I might not—because I wrote how hurt I was at some things that happened last summer. Truly, I had no right to be, for no one in all my life has been as kind to me as Mr. Welsh. Perhaps that is why I feel hurt—because he was always so good to me and so interested, I became spoiled; and when he returned from Europe and I saw him, I thought he was cold to me. As I think about it now, perhaps I should not have been hurt. I think I was hoping that Mr. Welsh would insist that I do nothing nasty and save me from myself. All of the time when I was nursing this hurt feeling, I would consider these past two years and the difference in my thoughts, and the fact that I now have some sincere friends—and I knew it was something more that I owed Mr. Welsh. I was almost afraid, then, to write of my life in New York—for I feared he would not ever care for me again. It was then I realized how deep my affection was for him. For after I wrote, I could scarcely contain myself until I had his reply. I wrote you then of his letter and the pressed buttercups—

Three days have elapsed since I wrote the foregoing. Somehow I can never concentrate my mind while I am here, even when I do have the time. . . . I want to tell you more of Mr. Welsh. As I wrote you, I communicated with him; and he asked me to stay at my Bro's, and until such time that I could do something, he would send me $5.00 a week. This was not part of his "work," but because he truly cares for me—as I wrote him late one night, and the next afternoon at three o'clock brought his reply and kind offer. I had no thought of refusing it, for I know why he offered to help me, whereas last summer it was different—yes, very different, and I can tell instinctively. . . . You cannot imagine how independent the

$5.00 makes me. I am giving it to my brother for board, and also [I am giving] my services—and it makes my stay here very different. Caroline is always the same, as dear and kind to me as she is to her own child, and she never varies. She accepts the fact that I have to stand for my brother's unkindness and tries to make it easier for me in every possible way.

It seems I will never get this letter finished, as it is now eight hours since I wrote the foregoing—I suppose you would like to know about Ira. He is selling stock in the John Kramer concern. I think it is a malt extract. I am not at all sure what it is, but he reports he is very enthusiastic about it and is meeting with much success....I don't think I shall go back to him for I would rather not have to live that way if I can help it. As you said, my "going back" didn't relieve me much, but I knew that was possible when I went. For I undertook to make something of him, doing something that was commendable, in a measure—whereas had I "gone back" to a cut-and-dried condition such as it would have been had I gone to Boston, it would have been an entirely different thing. In a way, I worked as hard as though I had a position, for I had a lot to learn and a whole lot to unlearn, and the same can be said of Ira. I taught him many things, most important of which was to keep clean his person. He was a boy of the type that read only the headlines of the newspapers and the sporting news, but now he is almost foolish in his love for poetry—especially about the sea, and of course about love. A letter of his now generally is three-fourths quotations— poetry and prose from books he is reading. He still borrows books from the library and writes that he spends much time there reading, as he finds it pleasanter than the little inexpensive hall bedroom he now occupies. Poor boy. I pity him, for he misses my care of him, especially as to his clothes, etc. Since starting this letter it has turned quite cold and I am happy to say I have my coat, as Mr. Welsh got it for me. Do you think I was inconsistent in saying last summer that I would not live again on charity—calling it by that name—and then the moment I was in need—urgent need—accepting Mr. Welsh's kindness, calling it by another name? I can't tell you why the discrimination, but it is different, just the same, and I can tell it as readily as black from white.

I now have "Treasure Island"—that's the Baby—on my lap, so will at last come to a close. I hope you will pardon this scrappy letter, but I can't do as I want here. Mr. Welsh asked me not to conflict with my Bro—that it pleased him to know that I am here, and to keep up agreeable relations with him—even though I am paying for my keep, as it were. I have to keep constantly busy—and thus keep him from being ugly in his manner to me. When you are quite thru with your *Atlantic* (there is no hurry) send it here, and after I read it I will send it to Ira, who asked me about it in a late letter.[19] I hope your brood are all well and you and your kind husband are, too.

Philadelphia, December 9, 1911

CS 42 TODAY I WENT TO MR. SUIFFEN'S OFFICE AND JUST CAME HOME WITH THE little gift box you sent me by Mr. Welsh...I thank you— Why you are so good to me, I don't know. Mr. Welsh (whom I saw today) also told me that you were truly fond of me. He told it as though it was a grand piece of news, but somehow it didn't startle me, for I knew it—only I am glad that Mr. Welsh knows it. I think prior to this, he thought you were "interested" in me (goodness, how I despise that word!) somewhat after the fashion of Miss Outerbridge, and that it was only me that benefited by our friendship.

You see how I feel about it. I think you must really enjoy reading my letters, or you wouldn't encourage me. If you just wanted to read letters, I am sure there are no end of "Letters" publisehd that would be far better reading than mine. I told Mr. Welsh that I knew you were fond of me—and he insisted I don't know the extent of it, but I think I do. He told me to bear it in mind, but I guess you know I don't need any reminders, for I haven't had such a horde of friends among women in my life that I am likely to forget in a hurry. I recall when I was in the hospital in N.Y. in 1904, after a cruel round of experiences—such as doctors refusing to operate on me because I had no money—and I suffered so much, then at the point of death I was taken to the Charity Hospital. And the "big" doctor—the one who had untold wealth but was one of the good men of the world—came at 4 A.M. to operate and remove my eye and save my life. He was very very kind to me in a thousand ways, coming to the hospital every day to dress my wounds, when that was usually left to the interns. On one occasion when I had to go thru a minor operation—one of no less than thirty that I had to go thru—I took a notion that I was afraid of the ether cone. The truth was that the nurses administered the ether, but Dr. Douglas always performed the work—but I would never see him for he would not appear until after I was anesthetized (? as to spelling—my dictionary is downstairs with a new book Mr. Welsh loaned me). Now I did not know this all along, until a nurse told me. So when it came to the ether part, I cried and carried on until they sent for Dr. Douglas, who immediately appeared. He always petted me and talked to me as though I was a little better than the rabble who lie in the wards of a charity hospital. When he came, I had to still pretend to be afraid so that he would not see thru my game. So he said I should hold his hand and look into his eyes, and then asked if I thought he would let any harm befall me. I was satisfied, then; so hanging on to his hand and without a murmur, I took the ether. The next day in the ward as he stood by my bed, I told him how I had fooled them; and he said he knew it all the time, but he did not think I knew I was fooling, and that he thought I was afraid, but that he knew I just wanted him to come. Of course he was a man, but the sex part of it did not enter into this friendship, for he was so far superior to me in every way. That he really was fond of me, I knew—he wasn't "interested," either. He no doubt has not thought of me often, but I need no reminders to think of him. Don't you think one feels instinctively how people feel about them? I can remember when you first wrote, and I was under such a strain, and everybody laid everything I said or did to the effect of the "cure"—when I had just as much good sense as I have ever had. I read the letter and then threw it from me as though it was poison—for I saw visions of the winter after the order of a Miss Christopher who is a soothsayer and not entirely sincere. I wanted to ignore the letter, but somehow I couldn't, for I felt the sincerity in spite of my convictions. Then later when I did write, again I felt drawn to do it for no particular reason—It was about a year ago at this time and I have always been mighty glad of the impulse that made me write to you.

How I did laugh at your letter! It seemed a pity that the "sketch" couldn't be one that I would like, for I'd love to own one that I could enjoy. I happen to know something about...Mr. Welsh's sketches, for, as you will remember, I stayed at his studio, and I have a very lively recollection of some of them....What do you suppose I wish? That is for an idea what your husband looks like. The reason I would like to know is so I can picture you better in your home. I wonder if you have any Kodak pictures of him that I could look at and send back, as I sent you Caroline and the baby? If you think this request unusual and imprudent, just ignore it. I also do not know how to place you on Brimmer St., but I have it all fixed in my mind's eye for next summer. I will be with you many times in imagination. . . .

I must tell you I went to see my mother. I went most unexpectedly. I wrote you of how kind Mr. Welsh has been to me since my return from N.Y. and how he has helped me. I want to mention now, before I forget, that Mr. Welsh knows why I returned from N.Y. just as you do, for I wrote him as frankly as I did you, but think he wanted to be kind to me when he said he thought it was due to my better impulses asserting themselves that I left the life in N.Y. To return: As I said, I was so grateful for Mr. Welsh's help— not only because of the help, but because of the way he offered it— and I wanted in some way to show him how I appreciated it. I could think of nothing [other] than to do the things he asked of me from time to time, some of which I did not do because I did not want to. I was reading over some of his letters; and again and again he said he wished he could make me feel more kindly to my mother. Without a word to anyone in the house here, I dressed and went to her house. I told her why I came.

It would seem that a meeting between a mother and daughter who hadn't spoken to each other or seen each other for eleven years would be a very sentimental thing to describe, but I am sorry to say my mother never was given to any kind of sentiment—the real or the cheap kind. It was most prosaic, and not at all like anything you can imagine. I tried my level best to awaken in her some of the feeling that I read about, that exists between parents and their children, but it was useless. It is bewildering to me sometimes when I think deeply. It is the same old *why? Why* this and *why* that? For truly, why do I crave all these things—when I am the same flesh and blood as these people, who are as phlegmatic as an oyster? I can ask questions in regard to myself and my feelings for hours, if I permit myself. But I know better than to begin it, for I wind up by being bitter at the whole scheme of life. Anyway, we have "made-up," and she comes here—and if she sees me, she speaks to me just as I'd speak to any one of a thousand people I know. My brother said I was silly to go to her; in fact, he was downright cross, for he said she did me harm—not I, her—and it should have been her to come to me. I feel, though, that I could afford to go to her regardless of how she has treated me in years gone by; for now I bear her no ill feeling. She is perhaps right, as far as she sees it.

I must stop now and go to bed, as I am very sleepy—I will finish in the morning. Goodnight, my good friend; I can think of being cheated of a mother's affection with less bitterness when I think of how you are fond of me. Maimie

Several days have elapsed since I wrote the foregoing, and now I am so tired that I don't feel I can write intelligently—yet if I don't get this letter written, you will think I have quit writing for all time.

I don't know whether I've told you anything about my being able to study stenography, after all. It came about in this way.

Mr. Welsh was very anxious that I go to Dr. Chance's again on the same old errand—that is, to make it possible for me to have a glass eye and thus remove the "handicap," so that I could find remunerative employment. While on an errand to Mr. Suiffen's office, I mentioned how futile I thought having anything done to my eye socket would be, and I asked Mr. Suiffen if he wouldn't mention it to Mr. Welsh, the next time the subject came up, that I wished he would use the money it would cost for the eye to give me a training of some sort, so that I could be fitted for work even with the "handicap"—which my intelligence permits me to see can never be removed in this world. I hesitated about writing this to Mr. Welsh because I thought he knew how anxious I was to learn stenography, and I disliked to say any more about it—though I have been so anxious for the opportunity since I have been in the East and have been living a regular life. Then I heard later from Mr. Suiffen that it was all arranged. The strange part of it is that Mr. Welsh is not supplying the cost of the lessons, but a "Miss Lea." In a letter from Mr. Welsh, he mentioned that "Miss Lea" had consented to pay for the lessons; and then when I was in his office this week, he asked Mr. Suiffen, before me, if the money had come from "Miss Lea" for the lessons. Of course I didn't ask who "Miss Lea" was—but it does strike me peculiar that a person should do this thing for me and I don't know anything about her, and it isn't thought necessary to tell me. In a sense, it makes me feel very small to think Mr. Welsh would say nothing about it to me. It makes the accepting of it hard—but to be frank about it, for this one purpose I'd accept the money if it was kicked to me. Still, I do wish it was done differently. I think you will understand how I feel. I feel differently, though, about this than anything that has heretofore been done for me. I know when I will have finished this course, I will without question or doubt, regardless of anything—except my health, of course—be self-supporting. Prior to this, when I have accepted kindnesses from Mr. Welsh or others, I was always uncomfortable because I knew there was nothing sure about the next day or week. I might then be in the same fix and need the same assistance. But with this help it is entirely different. I will never again need work, as long as I have my usual good health, and if I desire to work. When I see these silly girls with their overdressed appearance get positions that pay $10.00 and $12.00, I know I will have no trouble doing the same or better—for in the right kind of places, the appearance of the stenographer is of small moment as long as she is neat. I really feel people were justified in refusing me positions in department stores, etc., to sell, for my appearance is really not an advantage. But as a stenographer I think I will have no more difficulties. I start Monday, and it is likely that I will be finished by April or May, which is not so long.

I am still at my brother's, and no doubt shall remain here until I get through, though it is very hard at times. Again we have no girl, and I am "it." We had a nice little white girl, but she stayed only a week. I guess it is not only me that finds it hard here, for he never can keep a girl in the house over a week, and he changes the boys in the store quite as often. I am paying my board here—the entire $5.00 that Mr. Welsh gives me (that now includes laundry and meat for Poke)—and yet I have to keep busy all my waking hours. I was to start at the school today, but there being no girl, I didn't go. I hope they get one by Monday. You have no idea what hardships I have to endure here—the insults and the taunts are almost beyond human endurance. Yet what can I do? Last night, for the first time in the six weeks I've been here, I went out alone. I went to my uncle's (the one who has seven orphaned children). Caroline wanted to go, but James wouldn't let her. I went because I heard one of the children broke her leg in the schoolyard. I left after eight o'clock (as of course I had to clean up after dinner), and as I was going out I asked Bro how I would get in, and whether he would give me a key. He said I should come in before he closed. As he closes around 10:30 now, I showed him where that was impossible, as it takes an hour to get to town and then twenty minutes to Uncle's from town. To get back by 10:30 was impossible. He offered no way for me to get in, until finally Caroline offered to get up if I rang. Which I did—at twenty minutes of twelve, when I got back. It was ten minutes of ten when I got to Uncle's and I left about half past ten. By the time I made connections and then rode out there, it was, as I said, twenty minutes of twelve. I began to ring—and did ring and bang on the door, and tried every way to awaken them, but did not get in until four o'clock. The policeman firing a gun in the rear brought them out. I should have gone downtown to a hotel, but I didn't have a cent for carfare even. I sat on the steps most of the time, crying. Now this seems awful to say, but I think my brother knew I was out there. My reasons for thinking this are because Caroline's eyes were very red and swollen, as though she had been crying, and she did not say one word to me. And then, because of my brother's attitude. He said little or nothing, but scolded me frightfully for kicking on the door and scruffing it. He said, "Why didn't you go to a hotel when you couldn't make us hear?"—yet he knows full well I didn't have a nickel. I asked him today to lend me the carfare to go to school with, until such time as I can repay, and he blankly refused it—and added if I went out again at nights, to please see that I return before closing time or stay downtown. You can see how terrible it is for me to swallow all this when I wouldn't talk to a dog that way. He only talks that way because he knows he has me just where he can do this and not be in danger of having me come back at him. I can scarcely refrain from speaking my mind, and don't only because Mr. Welsh asked me not to. I never say one word to him other than what is agreeable—and he never says an agreeable word to me. And he continually taunts me about my "millionaire friends," and calls me "Miss Jesus Christ," and says as a great joke that I believe in Jesus for $5.00 a week, and tells me I am "cheap." Can you realize what I have to bear? My only hope is that it won't be so hard to bear when I go to school and pass the greater part of my time away from here, and that in the spring it will be all over.

I am so anxious to start Monday—or rather, as soon as I can make arrangements about the small expenses, etc. I wish this "Miss

Lea" was a person—by that, I mean someone I knew, so that I could work hard with my studies and thus show my gratitude. I really need no incentive, though, for I have many. I want to get independent as soon as possible, and I want to show Mr. Welsh that he was justified in thinking I would eventually do right. And then you, too, will be glad when I have a good position. And I am going to have it, too, by summer—and I'll never again be in a position anything like I am now. I'll look back and wonder why I didn't get "busy" long ago.

I wrote to Ira what I intended doing, and he is glad for me. You have no idea how much of a man he is—and I think I made him so. He is again getting along fairly well—as well as before I joined him, but not quite as well as when I was in New York with him. He of course understands that I will not return now, and though he has offered to send me a small amount, I told him I didn't need it; for I feel it is enough that he has that hungry-for-money crowd at home to feed, without my taxing him. He is going to go to a night school starting Jan. 2, to take up English and German, or perhaps French. I will keep up my friendship for him—I don't see where there is any harm in it. Do you think there is? Sometimes I think perhaps I should not.

I almost forgot to tell you about Albert. He was in Newark and I asked Bro to let me invite him here for Thanksgiving dinner, as I felt sorry for him in that little town, without friends, on that day in particular. . . . James sanctioned the invitation . . . and Albert came. He was very much touched because I remembered him, and we had indeed a fine dinner. I was—for the first time in eleven years— in the midst of my family, for my mother was there, and some cousins and an aunt. Albert and I talked over his situation, and I planned with him, and the outcome of it all was that he went to Memphis, Tenn., to join my oldest brother. He has been working a little, but with winter already here it means a hard time to procure work. As he had a little money—in fact, just to get there—I suggested he go, as he had always been able to earn a good living working for my brother and didn't have to do "carpenter's work." He left Friday morning of last week. . . .

I will say "goodnight" again—and "goodbye" this time. I do hope you are well, and that your kiddies are, too. Christmas is so near that they no doubt have lots to think about. I am making an embroidered pillow sham for the baby, and that will be my

Christmas. I love the baby best in the whole world. If you could see her, you would understand. I will close, and want to thank you again for the present. I will wear the neckpiece Sunday to church. You are very good to me.

In School   *Chester Avenue, Philadelphia*
My Dear Friend,   *December 13, 1911*
I MUST TELL YOU FIRST HOW HAPPY I AM. I WANT TO WRITE YOU ABOUT   **43** ‽
something else and then tell you about the school, but I am so enthusiastic that I will tell you first about the school. It is the biggest thing of my life, this opportunity to go to school. Since I realized what I missed by not having any childhood and necessarily no education, I have wished it was possible for me to take up something—in fact, most anything—but now I feel this is the beginning of a new era. For I am not only being educated, in a sense (for we take English here, and now I will know about moods and tenses, etc.), but it will be the means of my being above living questionably or accepting favors. When I walk around town now I am a different person, for my future looms up large. It is a question with me why I did not do this long ago, for certainly at various times I have had large sums of money that would have amply paid for the lessons. But my life being such an irregular one, my desires were not the same as now. I had ambitious thoughts, but they would come and go—for I had no one to help me. I did not have anyone that cared whether I earned my living one way or the other, and I lacked sufficient backbone to want to do things just for myself. It's all different now, though, and I no more think of doing wrong than you do. That may sound strong, but it's so, nevertheless. And I never feel weak. It is just the last thing I'd think of. For instance, even in New York, or prior to going there, when I was in actual want, the thought of doing anything wrong never occurred to me; and sometimes I would wonder why I didn't think of that. Now, when I have business in town, I go; but it is always a hardship. And even now that I go each day to attend school, as I said before, I think no more of anything connected with wrong-doing than you do. Therefore, I don't think anyone could scoff at what I say—that when I get thru with this school I will indeed begin a new life.

Did I tell you that I once attended Peurce's Business College for a period of three weeks? It was when I was about fourteen years old. I was employed in a store and earned $5.00 a week. I was home then, but my mother wanted the $5.00; and because I paid out $2.00 of it for the night school, to learn bookkeeping, and some for carfare, etc., she made me go elsewhere to live. And as I had to pay $3.50 for board and room, you see, I had to stop the school. And somehow, now, it seems as though I was starting where I left off. Isn't it ridiculous, when all these years have passed, it seems but yesterday? The girls here are from sixteen to twenty, and I feel just as young as they do. When I think of silly big-pompadoured girls like the average here, getting positions easily, and the most stupid beginner won't accept less than $8.00—I feel as though I can scarcely wait to get out to work, for certainly I can expect more. In the three days I have been here I can already write most anything in shorthand—of course, not readily, but still I can do it. Everything is so different now. It isn't any question in my mind as to whether I will go regularly, etc., etc., as it would have been four or five years ago, or even not so long ago as that, but the question is how soon I can get thru to go out to work. I am so happy over this that I have written Mr. Welsh every day, almost, for the past two weeks, to tell him of my feelings. It is very ugly now at my brother's, but I am not letting him or his attitude disturb me. You see, now that I am not there at his beck and call, he misses me; but rather than forget it and make the most of it, he just tries to worry me. But I am oblivious to it all, for my heart is singing, and I can't hear his bickerings. He insists that I am not going to school. Goodness knows, but I think he thinks that Mr. Welsh and Mr. Suiffen aid and abet me to deceive him and to do wrong. He doesn't really think so; he knows quite as well as you do, all about it; but he hates to give me credit for anything. . . .

My dear Friend,   *Philadelphia, December 30, 1911*

ભ 44   THERE HAS BEEN SO MUCH CHRISTMAS, FOR BOTH OURSELVES AND FOR the store, that this is my first opportunity to write you since receiving your letter. . . .

I hope your Christmas was all that you expected. Do the little ones still believe in Santa? I mean Helen and Mark. I should judge not, as no doubt you would not deceive them. . . or do you think that innocent deception? Caroline always consults me about what she shall do when the time comes about what the baby shall be taught in regard to certain things. She asked me about whether she should, next year, tell her that fable about Santa, and I was in a quandry—for, in everything, I remember your advice about being "true to oneself," etc. So I told Caroline I would ask you. Do you know, when one makes up their mind not to practice deceit, after a little bit it is very easy to avoid it, and there is no necessity for it? I can truthfully say that I never tell to anyone anything that isn't exactly so—sometimes, to be polite, I avoid the issue. I do this because you showed me why it was not necessary to do or say anything unless I can feel easy about it. And nothing is so restful and calm as living away from fooling anyone. . . .

I have no thought of leaving here to live elsewhere, for while at times it is unbearable, still it is "home." And really, you have no idea what little one can get for $5.00 in strange homes. I looked about when I first learned I could attend school, and the "fair" place is exceptional—and they want $7.50 to $8.50 a week, and that doesn't include laundry. The places where they would give me a room alone and board for $5.00 are retreats for laboring men where they eat off tables covered with red tablecloths. As I wrote you before, I don't think I feel as hurt at Bro's insults now as formerly, for I know it is ignorance more than a desire to wound me. Today a check came from Mr. Welsh for $5.00, and he ridiculed it until I was so hurt I could not speak. But I feel cross at myself, now, more than at him, for paying any attention to him. Whatever I do that attracts his attention, he asks: "Do you do that because Mrs. Howe said you should?" That always makes him laugh. And it doesn't amount to a row of pins, but he says it so incessantly—and only when it is about ridiculously unimportant things that you don't know anything about. He will adopt the new things I show him—but not before he belittles me and ridicules me. I can't tell you how I despise to hear him say your or Mr. Welsh's name. He uses one or the other in every sentence that he addresses to me. I will be glad when I start in again to go to school Tuesday, for not only am I anxious to resume my studies, but I want to get away from having to be in the store.

When I start again at school I will be truly happy, for it is so interesting and promises so much in the end. I have no fear of losing my enthusiasm. For the idea of learning something is, and has always been, the uppermost thought for years—If not, how could I have gone ahead, even as little as I have—for I had no school training to speak of. . . .

I will not be able to write more, as it is time for what we call the "supper rush," so will close wishing that the New Year be a happy one and that you and your children and husband remain well. Yours affectionately, Maimie

Your little note just came. It will be lovely in the country, but I wonder why you only take Quincy, and not Helen and Mark. You see, I am very inquisitive. But how will I know your ways if I don't ask?

Philadelphia, January 13, 1912

45   AT LAST I HAVE TAKEN THE TIME TO WRITE. IT SEEMS RIDICULOUS THAT one hasn't five minutes in a day to stop, but I really have not, and it is because I am trying to go on with my studies. My greatest trouble is the getting up each morning—oh, how I hate it! It never seemed to me that I cared much about lying abed, until recently. I never did sleep in a cold room though, before, and that has something to do with it. And too, I sleep on a cot that has no spring, and the mattress is only about an inch thick, and the whole cot is only two feet and two inches wide—and it is nothing to be wondered at that I am just as tired at six o'clock as I am when I retire, no matter how early it is. It seems so hard to get to school on time; and as I have from 3:30 to 5:30 that I can stay to practice on the typewriter, I do it. And at night I have my homework; and if I don't get to bed by 10:00, I can count on being late to school the next day. Saturdays there is the store; and the last few Sundays it seems I haven't had a chance to write, for it is given over to bathing and getting my clothing in shape for the entire week. I had a letter started to you and must have left it in one of my schoolbooks, for I can't find it now. So I will start afresh.

When I began at school, Mr. Suiffen told me it takes three or four months to complete the course, ordinarily, and I did think that was rather a short while—because those that I knew who had taken the course and have succeeded, it seemed to me, were at it longer than that. I made inquiries then, and learned that it was impossible to do it in less than eight months according to the method taught at this school. And the reason for Mr. Suiffen's error was that when he went to school, it was possible to make it in that time. But since then, the course is much improved; and the pupils must be able to pass tests in English as well as stenography before they can go on with the lessons, and half the time of the day is given over to that. . . .

I have not seen Mr. Welsh recently, but am anticipating a great pleasure, for Mr. Welsh promised to visit us Tuesday. . . .

I did want to ask you what to do about this! About two weeks ago, I received a letter from Ira, who is now at home. He wrote just a pleasant, newsy sort of a letter. I did not answer, for more than one reason. I really didn't get a chance and, too, I thought since I know he is truly fond of me, and I don't care much about him, I would rather he sort of forget about me. And then, since the letter, he has written two postals asking me to write him. I somehow feel I shouldn't, and for that reason, I don't. Then again, the thought came to me—why shouldn't I keep up the friendship with him? For you know how distasteful it is to me to have to live with Albert; and though Ira is but a boy, he might some day be in good financial circumstances—for he is a very earnest and hard worker and can earn from $50.00 to $75.00 a week, and Albert does well to earn $20.00. And, too, I like Ira much better than Albert. Of course, I have no idea of any plans for years yet; but other people divorce and marry again—and I might do that, if it is even years and years from now. I have only thought a little about this and don't know whether I'd care to marry Ira even if I could; but with this in mind, I might write to him and keep up a sort of friendly correspondence. Will you write me what you think about this? . . .

Our Babis is so sweet, and is beginning to stand, and understands what we tell her. I love her so much that it is so hard to be away from her all day. She's so heavy now that it leaves me all worn out to frolic with her, and yet I can't resist her. I am wondering if you and your children and husband are all well. The days have so far been quite severe, and most everyone has a cold, although fortunately right now I haven't any. I will be glad to hear from you again, for it seems like an age since I've heard from you. But I know it is my own fault because I did not write sooner. With much love. . . .

Philadelphia, February 16, 1912

YESTERDAY I RECEIVED A LETTER FROM MRS. [GRABAU] AND TODAY YOUR   **46** ✣
letter, in reference to her.[20] It is all a bit confusing, yet why it should be I don't exactly know. I don't resent her wishing to know

more of me or Ira or his family; still, I feel much as I did when you wrote me the first time. Instinctively, I feel like sending her about her business. Doesn't that prove what a sweet disposition mine is? I must explain, though, that I wouldn't do such a thing, and only admit it to you so you will know me as I am and not think I am as amenable as I should be. The fact that she is of my own race and from as humble origin should make me feel she is really the sort I ought to like—but I am afraid that she is not like "Mrs. Howe." Still, I don't know—for I felt as I do now when you wrote, and since I was wrong in my estimate of you, I may be of her—so will profit by my experience and not send her "packing," as I might have done. When I write her—which I shall do tonight—I will write of Ira, as her letter was mainly in reference to him and his family; but when you write her, you may write that which you choose.... On second thought, I will make this suggestion: You know her only from her writings; and while one's writings are generally supposed to reflect oneself, one's character, etc., that would not always prove correct, as some are very clever with the pen and would trick one. So until such time as either you or I meet her—if either of us ever do—suppose you do not tell her *all* about me—leaving out the ugly part, until you feel sure she would not condemn me. Although I will tell you, from my knowledge of Jewesses—or Hebrews of both sexes—they are very unforgiving, in fact much more so than the most conventional Gentile. Not that I would want to sail under fake colors, but if I thought she could not accept me as you do, then I wouldn't want to know her....

Do you know, I have wanted to ask you for quite some time how that puppy is thriving? You know I am somewhat of an authority, and should it develop any "symptoms," you must be sure to let me know....

James has just made an oyster stew and invites me to join him, so I will bring this letter to a close and say "Good night."

Philadelphia, February, 1912

CƷ 47 I WAS MUCH INTERESTED IN—AND AMUSED, TOO—AT YOUR REASONS FOR the cognomen (?) *Brownie*. But as I once was very well acquainted with a little cocker spaniel whose name was Brownie, then I feel that your Brownie and I were friends during one of Brownie's earlier lives. The Brownie I knew met with a tragic death and when I get through writing some little things I wanted to tell you I'll tell you about the Brownie I knew so well. . . .

Sunday we celebrate "Purim," which is in commemoration of the time that Esther and Mordecai had the edict set aside that was to destroy all the Jews on a certain date. You no doubt remember the story in the Old Testament, and the Jews hold a holiday of feasting and rejoicing on that day. It is the custom for the Jews who are able to send small sums as gifts to the poor, and in lieu of that they bake cakes called *hamantashen* that are rolled in the shape of an old-fashioned pocketbook and filled with a seed called in Jewish *mun*, but C. says it is "poppy seed"—in English. . . . We sent boxes of them to our brothers who are away and to some Hebrew friends. . . .

I will now write you about Brownie. Perhaps you could tell the children about this little Brownie.

When I arrived in Memphis, Tenn. (leaving Albert in Texas when the climate was so damp, I was afraid of malaria). . . I went to the Peabody Hotel the first night, as I wanted to select a boarding house where they do not, alone, *not object* to a dog—but I wanted to get in one where they *liked* dogs—On all hands, I was rebuffed—when it occurred to me to hunt a place that not only had *Boarding* on the door, but where there was a dog in sight. In the South there are few laws, and only a few of them are paid attention to, so dogs are on the streets at all times—as even the winters are very mild, and they can be turned out all the time. In walking up to the main thoroughfare, which is called Main Street, I passed a street which looked very nice; and as there were no car tracks (less chance for Poke to be run over), I strolled down there. And almost the first thing I saw was a cocker spaniel whose color was such that one would instinctively call it *Brownie*, as you would call some dog *Rags* or *Sport*. It was on the step of a house a little nicer than the average, and it barked saucily at Poke. But I rang the door-bell and asked if they took "guests"—which is the proper word in Memphis. They did; and when Mrs. Frey came to the parlor, she at once made a fuss over Poke and would be glad to have her. Her dog's name was Brownie, and another guest had a fox terrier which was making itself heard, having got wind of Poke's presence, and its name was Buster. I moved in; and long before we womenfolk got so we exchanged confidences, the three dogs were fast friends, romping all the time together. For some reason the ringleader was Miss Poke—whether that was because she was the one female between two males and sort of led them a merry chase, or whether it was because I had made more of a human of her than they had with their dogs, and she necessarily had more sense and was superior to them. It was so much fun to watch them. The two males would lie quietly on either side of the step; and as Poke was only allowed out after the sun went down, they began to know when to expect her. As her head is snow-white, I bathed her every day to show her off, for she had to be perfectly clean to be able to win the honors from Brownie. After tea the ladies would bring their chairs out on the gallery (porch); and the moment Poke and I appeared, the two dogs would be up and ready for a romp. It was easy to be seen that Poke was the ring-leader, as it was she who had to start the play. For instance, if it was tugging at a rope or rag, it was Poke who got the article; if it was just rough tumbling, it was Poke who started by giving Brownie or Buster a jolt that would knock them right over; if it was ball, it was Poke to come to me to beg for a ball. . . . At that time I affected wearing white, winter and summer (white linen from head to toe, heavier linen in the winter than summer), and she never once dirtied me by jumping up—to ask for the ball, or anything—

I will digress a bit to tell you something of our neighbors. Directly opposite was a large tract of very disreputable land on which was a small hut—no windows, just a central door—in which lived a Negro family; and on this door was a sign reading *Jones' Restaurant*—which of course was a standing joke on me. A more disreputable place would be hard to imagine, although it was not at all vicious—just dirty and run-down. This condition would hardly be possible except in the South. The reason for the condition—such a place on the same street with elegant homes—is because the South is so poor, and not progressive, and generally land-poor. Property is left to them—but not being able to sell it, it gets into such condition, and they can't sell it and are too poor to improve it. Next door to us, on the corner, was a maiden lady who ran a "bo'din house"—but for men only—and ran a very exclusive place. She was the sort that was entirely unlovable, and did not love anyone—dog or human. Instinctively, our dogs did not go near her grounds, but ran wild and had a good time on the premises of the Jones Restaurant. For like all Negroes, they were good to the dogs, and in fact would give them gunnysacks to use to tug at. And not only did our dogs like to go over there, but every mongrel for miles visited Jones' as a last resort—for while one didn't get bones with meat on them, one would get something. And in time our street began to look like the vicinity of a dog pound. As summer came along, we remarked more than once that it would not be a bad idea to quit giving these stray dogs food, and to tell the colored folks across the road to quit—as, what with fleas and mange, we might ourselves have a mad dog to contend with. For our dogs sometimes played with the curs, and might get bitten—although I did not permit Poke this pleasure often.

To return to our own dogs. This dog Buster had no training whatever, and was as badly spoilt a dog as one could see. Barked without, and with, the slightest provocation, and did everything that dogs who are raised properly do not do. In that, he took after his owners. They knew no restraint—neither did he. So I really liked the dog but little, though I fully realized it was not the dog's fault. Brownie, on the other hand, also had little training, but was naturally a gentle creature, so grateful for the least kindness shown him. Buster was fed in fits and starts, whenever his people felt like it. And Buster did not seem to mind it, for he was given four or five times what he should have had, and ate gluttonously, to last until the next time. As for Brownie, he was fed only when there was anything left—and when there was little left, Brownie was left. In fact, the Freys visited and went to dinners and card parties a great deal, and no meals were prepared. (I only roomed there, and ate an occasional meal, paying for each single meal.) You can see then, that Brownie was hardly pampered and, if anything, I think was neglected, although Mrs. Frey pretended to care a great deal about him. After I came and they saw how regularly at 5:30 to six o'clock, Poke had her one daily meal—never twice the same sort of food, alternating between meat, liver, "lights," corn bread and gravy, and dog cakes, etc.—they were a bit better to their dogs. But as the time went along, they drifted back to the same habits. At first when I would get ready to feed Poke, I'd give to the others too, knowing they had nothing all day. But as time went on, I cut out feeding Buster, for many reasons—some of which were that he ate so ravenously I could not afford it (for no matter how slight the expense, it counts up); and, too, his people began to let me feed him entirely; and too, because I really did not like him. As for Mrs. Frey, she too drifted into letting me feed Brownie all he got—but I loved

Brownie. And he ate as Poke did—just enough—and was *refined* about it; and too, he seemed to love me so much. Anyway, months went by, and the feeding and caretaking went on as before—only Brownie and Poke. Then, when they played, Buster joined—but you could see Poke was really fond of Brownie; and then, Brownie being the smallest, even Buster seemed to give him a little less rough time of it. Finally Brownie became as much my pet as Poke, because I gave them the same care: they both slept on my floor; and they went with me on our long walks along the Mississippi River front, where there was lots of running-space.

Then it came about that the lady next door came to see Mrs. Frey to tell her to keep our dogs in for a few days—that she and some of her new boarders were placing around on the ground "buttons" (poisoned bits of meat that will kill a dog instantly) in hopes of killing the many mongrels that were drawn to the neighborhood by Jones' Restaurant. Mrs. Frey thought it was a hint to us, also, for she said her reason in wanting to kill them was because they disturbed their rest at night howling about the place—and a few other ridiculous reasons. When Mrs. Frey told me, I was speechless. I was miserable, for I had begun to like some of the mongrels, and couldn't bear to think of their coming to our place because I had been kind to them, only to find their death. I knew Poke could not possibly be hurt by a "button," as she will eat nothing that is not on a plate—perhaps she would if she was terribly hungry, but she is never terribly—or even a little—hungry. I feared for Buster and Brownie, and was very careful not to let them out. Then, it troubled me so much that I'd wait until I heard no one about next door, and I'd take off my shoes and crawl about, hunting the meat. And for a week or more, I found two or three pieces. And every morning would find a dog or two dead on the street. I never saw them, because I wouldn't look, but I was always told. Mrs. Frey remonstrated with this lady, but could not move her. I did not go to her—for I feared I'd want to hurt her. I began to get an idea in my mind that she was after my Poke, because some nights I'd find the buttons on a plate, instead of on the ground, as before. And it preyed on my mind so badly, one day, that without a word to anyone, I went on a search for other quarters—and found them, in a few days. The day I left, I found Brownie crouched against my bags in the hall, and he seemed to know. I felt so attached to him that I offered to take care of him until such time as this woman would cease her murderous attacks. But Mrs. Frey said she thought when I left, it would be all over—that she, too, thought it was to get at Poke, for no other reason than because I tried to stop her by law from killing these mongrels. And it seemed I could not, as long as she placed these buttons on her own premises. I left, moving about eight blocks from there. Poke and I walked to the place; and I had to carry Brownie back, as she followed us for more than a block.

The next morning Poke awakened early, and no doubt wanted to see what sort of a place it was, so began to worry me to let her out. As I did not wish to rise then, I rang for a bellboy, and he took her to the door. And with the instructions to Poke that she should not go off, I went back to sleep. I awakened at nine o'clock and rang for the boy to bring Poke in, which he did. And pretty soon he knocked on my door, wanting to know if I had only one dog—for Poke had been playing with a small brown dog, and the dog was now outside the door, crying piteously. I knew it was Brownie, and I had him bring the little scamp in; and after lots of welcome, I began to consider what to do. For no doubt he had wandered off hunting us in the direction he saw us go, and was successful in finding Poke—and would do it every day, the moment he was let out. After feeding him, I phoned Mrs. Frey and then took him home. She said she would stop it by not letting him out for a while, until he forgot us. The next day, then, was Sunday—and long before I was ready to rise, the boy came to tell me the little brown dog was out there with his nose pressed against the glass, crying to get in. There was nothing to do but let him in. But I was no little provoked, as I saw where it was going to be a nuisance, this taking him back each day. I began to suspect Mrs. Frey had a hand in letting him out, for then he would be fed, with no trouble to her—and what with her card parties, she had no time to feed Brownie. There was something about the dog so appealing—more so even than Poke—and instead of putting him out, I phoned Mrs. Frey and told her I would not take Brownie back, and for her to send for him. She said she had no one, and said I should put him out and he would come back. Evidently she didn't care. I hated to do it, for I was truly fond of him. But on the other hand, I just could not have him there, as the landlord objected; and, too, I did

119

not relish the walk each day in the intense heat of a Memphis summer day. After due reflection, I did put him out, telling him to go home—and in fact leading him to the street that led home. He came back, of course, and finally I gave it up and went in, telling the bellboys just to let him stay there until he grew tired. It was almost six o'clock before he must have given up and gone home. And a little later, Mrs. Frey called up asking me what I did with him. I called the bellboy, who explained he had left only a short while ago. She must have then gone to hunt for him. For she phoned again about half an hour later, saying she had found him lying near their kitchen door, cold in death! He had gotten one of the buttons, of course. And I was for a long time very miserable, because I put him out—and to this day have never forgiven myself that I did not feed him, before sending him home.

That is all. We buried him in Jones' Restaurant yard, which was very large. And Mrs. Frey did a lot of crying, and of course placed the blame on me. . . . And to this day, at the mention of Brownie's name, Poke will run around in a circle, and bark, and seem to remember that he was her playmate.

I hope I haven't bored you with this tale about Brownie. I feel you and the children might sometimes think of your Brownie as our Brownie on earth again for another lease of life. That is how I felt from the first when you wrote me about him. I will be glad of a snapshot of Brownie.

March, 1912

✂ 48   SINCE WRITING THE ENCLOSED, SEVERAL DAYS HAVE ELAPSED, AND NOW before sealing this I will add a bit more to this already "young book"—Mr. Welsh, . . . when I first began to correspond with him, would send back my letters if there were any grammatical errors in them: he made just three corrections altogether, and then ceased. I never forgot the corrections, and never made the mistake again. So lately, in a recent letter, I asked him if he would not do as he did in the beginning—that is, tell me of my errors. And he answered that he certainly should have corrected errors had there been any, but there had not been *one.* But—he would suggest that I adopt "brevity of style"! I think that was it, but perhaps don't quote him accurately; still, I caught the drift. And it rather amused me, since I write him only one-third part as much as I write you, I wonder now, frankly, if you don't think I might be a trifle more brief! Perhaps the fact that I write more carefully to Mr. Welsh, using my very best penmanship, explains why there are no errors.

I have nothing of any import to tell you, except that I am so terribly lonesome. I feel I would be almost as good as actually being in good company, should I write you.

I don't quite understand why it is, but for the past few weeks I have been filled with a great unrest. Nothing seems to satisfy me and...I am frightfully depressed....Today after leaving the dentist's, I decided not to return home but thought I'd go to a theatre and perhaps then feel better, because I thought it was want of amusement and recreation that is getting on my nerves. I decided to make a night of it by going to dinner in a restaurant and then to the theatre. As I have less than a dollar each week for spending money, you can see it was going to be a plunge....As I walked along the street, debating whether to go home and "forget it," I saw a vaudeville and moving picture house—"10-20-30 cents"—and while I never relished anything of that sort, it occurred to me perhaps even that sort of a show, with the music of a sort, might relieve me. I looked about for a place to get a ticket, and saw first a boy selling some very fair-looking daffodils. And as they were only 25 cents for a very nice bunch, I decided to forego the meal and buy the flowers for Caroline for a Purim gift—*Shalakmones*, as we call it. As the show only lasts an hour and a-half, or two at the most, it was not much of a sacrifice, for I could eat as soon as I arrived home. I paid 10 cents for a seat and went in. I never knew before how low this form of amusement is. It was horrible. A very silly-looking man sang some silly songs with a nasal intonation, and the gist of all of them was just a bit vulgar—and how it did amuse my neighbors! I sat thru three acts of this sort, fairly holding myself in the seat, for I thought each time perhaps the next act would be a girl, pretty and young, with a sweet voice—as I had once seen when I went with Mr. Suiffen, and another time with Ira. But no such luck, and I was about to go, when the moving pictures were on. I stayed to see them, and was agreeably surprised to find they were not these cheaply sentimental affairs, but pictures of actual happenings of unusual interest throughout the world. I have learned since coming home that this has been going on for some time—that is, the depicting of current events to be shown in the moving pictures. One event pictured was the return of the Boston cardinal and the parade in his honor, and the inside of Father Hoff's (I think that was the name) church.... In the picture of the parade, I recognized some familiar landmarks of Boston, and Tremont Street was very plain. It was the one thing of the whole evening that pleased me very much, as I felt as though I had been near you—for I pictured you on the street among those people. I do hope you have a change of clothes, but I always see you exactly as you looked in what you wore the Sunday you called on me. I left when the "current events" were over, and before a reel called *The Creole's Revenge* was shown.

This, then, was the extent of my dissipation—and I am home now, and not feeling one bit better mentally. I wished after I returned that I had gone to a show, and yet I know I couldn't afford it—and perhaps it wouldn't have helped any. Somehow I feel if I could get away from here I'd be able to take a good long breath, and yet perhaps I'd be worse off. Somehow, while before I only troubled when Bro hurt me, now I feel wretched at everything they do which I don't like—even Caroline annoys me. Bro has a way of speaking small of all his customers—and that only what he has is the best—and Caroline seems to be getting much that way. It is very tiresome....

I am afraid I am not easily suited. I know I almost hate this place, and yet it is all the home I have.

Philadelphia, March 14, 1912

℮ 49   YOUR NICE LONG LETTER CAME. YOU ARE VERY KIND TO ME—TOO KIND. I must thank you for the Purim present but also feel I should tell you that it embarrasses me a little, for while I shall accept it in the spirit it was given, still it is a sort of warning that I must not tell you all my fancied troubles, for you to take so seriously. By a strange coincidence, in the same mail which brought your letter and gift came a letter and a box of salted almonds as a Purim present from Ira. A regular windfall. Contrary to what I wrote you, there was no Purim present for me from Caroline—in fact, from no one—and I felt a bit left out until I received the gifts from you and Ira. I will do as you asked me to—that is, use the money for amusement—but as I have grown into such a miser I hate to break the brand new $5.00 bill. Too, I don't feel keen about anything playing this week. I feel I want the best I can get when I spend this. I have told Caroline she can count on going with me when I go, but James said she would not be able to accept. I asked nothing further but I think he was aching for me to say "Why?" so he could say something insulting about accepting charity. He has such a *sweet* mind—but if it wasn't that I find it is a terrific grind for me, I could laugh at a large part of it. Sunday I am going to my sister in the asylum and shall take her the salted almonds and will then break the $5.00 bill.

I have been experimenting in the past week—a change in regard to my stenography course—and now that I am determined to go ahead with it, I shall write you all about it. It may also be the means of relieving my condition, for it will take away some of the things which I found so depressing and wearying on my nerves.

You may recall when I started I wrote you that Mr. Suiffen thought by close application to my work I had a chance to get through in four months—and to graduate a finished typewriter and stenographer. After attending about three weeks, this began to worry me, for I could see there was little chance of my finishing in four months at the way I was going. I began to ask questions. The girls about me—one was in her ninth month, another her fourteenth month, and so on. And while they were younger than I—still there wasn't so much of a difference to make me think I could get thru in four months.... The whole object of that school—and no doubt the largest percent of other business schools—is to keep you there as long as possible; and no thing is left undone to eat up time that should be used by the scholar in practising....

When I began my stenography I was given a small red textbook. And right from the beginning, all the teaching I got there was out of that book, going from lesson to lesson in which was one exercise after another for practice. Had I known it, I could have purchased a book of this sort and gone on with the lessons without a teacher. The same with the typewriting. Anyway I went to work [at home], and though I had no typewriter, in my stenography lessons I got thru with exactly five times as much work as I did in a like number of [hours] going to school. That settled it with me—for I took my notebook and went to Mr. Suiffen and put the matter before him.... Mr. Suiffen asked me then what I wanted to do, and I told him: to eliminate this long trip back and forth each day, and to study at home, and not waste my time. With the money I have for carfare, I could rent a typewriter to use any and all the time. Then, when I did my exercises, I could take them to be examined to a Miss Thress who lives in the same block with Mother and who is a graduate of that school; and, too, when I came across anything that was hard, she could explain—and at 25 cents a lesson. . . . Mr. S. suggested I try it for one week more at home and then come to him. I did (that was last week) and, more determined than ever, I went to him Fri. eve, and he thought I had indeed progressed. He saw Mr. Fry and he said he would give back the difference in money between that which I had used in attending school and the amount paid in. . . .

So this week I have had my room kept warm with a gas stove, and I have a table in it and I study unmolested—and it is all a delightful change all around. It eliminates lots that was terribly unpleasant. Such as getting my own breakfast and eating a poor lunch and having to be associated with a class of hoydens I wouldn't ordinarily be thrown with in a thousand years. Next week I shall have a typewriter, and I hope to finish in even less time. . . . You see, most of those people struggle along to get the diploma—but that offers no attraction to me. Neither does the idea of graduating. When I think I am able to hold a position I will go out and get one. . . .

I already took several lessons from Miss Thress and find I can understand her much more than I did the teacher who explained the hard passages there. . . . Oh, it is all so much better that I don't understand why I didn't see it before. I hope you see the advantage of it, because I don't want you to think I gave up the going to school on a mere whim. I feel the fact that I wasn't making much headway had something to do with the horribly depressed feeling I've had all this while. I am still somewhat nervous and depressed, but nothing as bad as I felt before quitting the school. The girls were all so rough and coarse that they kept me in a constant friction with myself. . . . You cannot know the petty persecutions that I suffered. . . . Even finding a crude picture of a face on the board with a patch on its eye and my initials under, during lunch hour. Oh! I am very glad to get away from it. . . .

I have written you about all that I know. Except that we have a Polish girl instead of the Negro woman we have had, and this one knows no English besides Yes and No—and I am the *interpreter!*

My parents were originally from Poland Russia; and when my father lived, we always had one in the kitchen and one as a nursery maid for the children. At that time we spoke and understood it as well as English, but of course forgot all about it—or I thought I had. To my astonishment, when this girl was brought to us, I found I not only understood her well, but words and even sentences came from my lips that mean things connected with the duties of housework. And just think, I never knew I knew it, because I hadn't talked to one for so long. I rather like the idea that it has come back to me so well.

I will close now as my hand is cramped. You have no idea what a hardship it is to write longhand when one can write in shorthand.

That reads—"I trust that you and the family are well and that I shall soon see the picture of Brownie. Poke is getting some taken too."

Philadelphia, April 26, 1912

I AM REALLY ASHAMED...FOR HAVING PUT OFF WRITING FOR SO   50 ଔ
long, especially since receiving the gloves. I have no excuse except that I hated to write to complain—and I have wanted to do nothing else. It is unbelievable how discontented I am. I go about as though I had all the troubles of the world, when my only trouble is that I hate to stay at home. I am with Mother now and have fallen into the habit of spending much time here, but I have to go back and that is what makes me miserable. If you knew what I have to contend with, you would scarcely blame me, for my brother's attitude toward me now is plainly contemptible....We average now two violent rows a day, with grouchy, ugly attitude all the rest of the time. If I have no money, I am derided and my "millionaire friends" are mocked; and if I have money: Why do I accept charity, and why don't I "fling it back at them"? Do you see now why I despise to write, when I have to write such "beefing" letters? I grew so desperate on Sunday of last week that I packed my belongings— decided to pull out Monday, and did not go only because I feel I ought to make more definite plans before moving. On Sunday my brother struck me, which is the worst that has happened as

yet—and that, because I said his daughter was as much Gentile as Jewish, therefore he should think of that, and speak more moderately when he was berating the Gentiles. Oh! he is unbearable.

I must thank you for the gloves.... I love white gloves, and have worn them twice, but expect to wear them oftener when I get to working and can go places. Here, I can only go to Mother's—and then, under protest. Mother realizes how awful it must be for me to live there, but she cannot ask me to live at her house, for it would cause an open breach between her and her present husband.

Last Tuesday week, I took Mother to see a Jewish play (using the last of the $5.00 you sent me). We saw some really clever Jewish performers, and the evening was spent very happily—though the show was rather dramatic and thrilling, as I think most Jewish plays are. At any rate, I know they play on the emotions much more than do English dramatists, and I couldn't stand to see a play oftener than once or twice a year of the sort we saw. It was about a Jewish girl who had been betrayed and who was not forgiven by her parents until her death. It affected Mother very much, although I shook if off immediately we left the theatre. We went to a neighboring Jewish café, and Mother and I had some Jewish wine that sells for 35 cents a bottle and Jewish cake. We met some old friends of my father, and mother had a really good time, reminiscing. I stayed with Mother that night. But the whole evening was spoiled when I got back to James's house in the morning. He thought I should have invited Caroline to go along, and I couldn't see it that way, as Mother wouldn't have enjoyed an English play, and Caroline would not have understood a word of the Yiddish play. I feel I did right, since I had taken Caroline once before—out of the $5.00 you sent—and too, I couldn't make the money stretch over a third ticket....

You know that next week I am to go to work for $5.00, copying letters for speed practice. Of course, with the coming of May 1, the four months are up, and Mr. Welsh will no longer pay my board, which is right. But with just $5.00 I can't go very far. And yet, even if it was more, I don't see how I could go to work, and live here. I am just a little short of being all-around servant—and even if I had to go to work eleven times, there would still be the duties to attend to, and I don't see how I could possibly live here and not attend to them. The one who would suffer most would be the Babis, because she is almost entirely my charge, except when she is eating—and when she is in a very playful humor, then her father takes her. The thought of going to work from here seems awful, and yet I couldn't live anywhere else on so little money. That is, I mean any fairly decent place. Will you be terribly shocked if I tell you I am thinking of going back to New York City? My reason is this: If I lived in Phila., I couldn't very well live anywhere but with my brother—I don't like to tell everyone why it is so unbearable to live there. Then, too, in New York I have a position which I could start with—as assistant stenographer and typewriter, in an office where I'd take dictation part of the time, from seven different men and two women. Which is all very good practice, and the pay would be $8.00 to start. I knew of this place, and wrote Ira Benjamin to go see about it. He did. And then, en route to his home to spend the Passover holidays, he stopped over here and told me what Mr. Silverman said—which was that he'd be glad to have me, and while I was with him, I could be on the lookout for a better position. Of course, Ira knows all about my disgust at having to live here—I told him, and he saw it, for James takes no trouble to disguise it. Ira, of course, is one of the reasons why N.Y. seems more desirable than here; for he is the only one I know who cares a fig about me—that is, I mean, in that way—and he would make it much pleasanter for me than it would be in Phila. True, it would cost me all of the $8.00 to live. But Ira will help me, and I can't see why I shouldn't take his help. For he offers it without condition, and I have put up with so much here that I don't know but I would be justified in accepting the prospect of a pleasant life this summer. Of course, I haven't finally decided, and probably I won't go— I can't bear to think of telling Mr. Welsh. . . .

I cannot tell you how the disaster on the *Titanic* affected me. It seemed so wholly unnecessary—and so many people, who had so much to live for. I cannot think but some of the men who were fathers should have been saved. It is so pitiful, and too much for me to conceive. I was in an accident on the Fall River Line, going from Boston to N.Y. in 1900, on July 4, when the *Priscilla* bumped into its sister boat. It made a terrible hole in our boat and killed a great many of the stokers—and not a few passengers who were panic-stricken jumped overboard. It was, in a small way, much like the *Titanic* disaster. We were helped to Newport at 4:30 A.M., and the collision happened at 10:25 P.M. And even in those waters (for it was off Point Judith), it had an element of danger in it—sufficiently for me to have an idea as to what they experienced on the *Titanic*. . . .

I heard again from Mary Antin, and intend to answer soon. It was not very interesting; in fact, she is insistent about wanting to know Ira's mother. I will be on the look out for the *Atlantic.*

I feel like an ingrate because I didn't acknowledge the gloves until you wrote again. You will believe me that I was not careless—only that I couldn't bring myself to write this miserable letter.

General Delivery, White Plains, New York
May 21, 1912

℃ 51   I SET MY ALARM AN HOUR AHEAD, SO THAT I COULD WRITE YOU AT length this morning. It is the wee sma' hours, but I feel very alert, and could chop wood—I feel that strong. You know something, I suppose, about this section, and that it is very hilly. For that reason, one gets plenty of exercise, good clean air, and naturally one wants to sleep much. That is my whole trouble: I can't get enough sleep, and everything—letters and many another duty— awaits the time when I won't be sleepy, which as yet has never arrived. I am going to ask a favor of you again in this letter. I hope you won't think I am taking advantage of your kindness. But first I shall tell you lots of things. . . .

Now—I shall go back to Port Chester, and tell you that I worked there. . . . In Port Chester I lived with a Hebrew family who are related to my mother's present husband. . . . It was thru them I got the position or rather that I heard of it. I was engaged for general stenographic work and typewriting, and the salary is $12.00 a week. Oh! I am not an underpaid hireling, as the novels say, by any means. But I am truly an overworked one, for no matter how much one is paid, they can't do but so much work and no more—unless they work when they should be resting. I was influenced into coming to the White Plains office by the fact that Mrs. Silverman's sister lives here, and I could live with her. . . .

I shall tell you about the office. It is a branch of a large meat concern dealing mostly in undressed beef. There is a manager, a bookkeeper and a stenographer, and me. I came there to do most of the "hack" work. You know, in an office of that sort, when they send out one letter to a customer, they generally send it to all; and when an inquiry comes in, it is one that they have dozens of in each mail, so they have "form letters" that answer various inquiries. They used to open the mail, and the unimportant letters were marked 1 to 7, according to the form letter which was to be used in answering it. I was not familiar with the letters, but after one is there awhile, one must know them verbatim. Of course, that would give one good practice on the typewriter, but one would soon lose their speed in taking dictation. At any rate, when I saw these form letters they struck me as being very poor. The style was stilted, the English faulty (even as I know it), and much that was superfluous in them is a sign of illiteracy (using set forms as one is recommended to do by the "Ready Letter Writing" books). I don't know who originally wrote them—but the stenographer over me had been there since 1898, and they were in use when she came! When I thought it over, I copied them; and that night I wrote three of them entirely anew, and the other four I patched up and cut away from. Then, the next day when I saw the manager idle, I handed them to him with a note explanatory. Up until I went home that night, he said nothing—and I laid awake the best part of the night worrying, thinking I had presumed and would lose my place. The next day as we got ready for work, he pulled out some paper and announced before us all that we would use new form letters. He gave what he had in his hand to the stenographer and she made four copies of each. I looked at what she was copying from—and though the wording was exactly what I had given him, he had copied it in his own handwriting. That gave me my cue, for I judged then that he wanted it to appear as though he wrote it. You can imagine how hard it was for me not to be able to crow a little. He said not a word to me—then, nor since. He himself is very illiterate. The stenographer said at luncheon that she wished she could earn each week what he had to pay some expert letter-writer in New York City to write those letters, and I had to keep "mum." At any rate, I thought I did wonderfully well in writing those letters—but instead, I fixed up trouble for myself. He changed our work so that the other girl does the form work and I do the general letters. The aggravating part of it is that he thinks better of my "longhand" than he does of the typewriter, with the result that I write all the important letters and all his personal letters. I used this hand

My Dear Mr. Dixon

—and he likes it, because I think he wants people to think he wrote it. I sign his name, and no "per" after it either. Sat., he got my "goat," for sure—if I may use that word—by handing me a stack of fancy stationery, and I had to write invitations for a reception his wife is giving June 1st. Those I had to write like this, with a fine point—

*White Plains
New York "*

and after writing backhand with an easy flow for so long, it was very tiresome. I demurred faintly, but it had no effect. The hard part is that when doing form letters, which I was engaged to do—when 5:30 comes, you cover up your machine and depart; but this work is different, for if letters come in the 5:10 (last) mail and they are at all important, they must be answered before leaving. And so far, there has not been one night there was [not] around ten letters, with the result it is 7:10 and 7:15 before I start for home. Too, by doing that work I don't get practice on my typewriting and stenography, and I may lose it, which is really deplorable. With the exception of a very little work, I could have done what I am doing now, before I learned my course. The thing is that it is hard to get into an office to prove oneself, unless you do know typewriting, etc. Still, with it all, it is so good to be earning one's living independently, and to get $12.00 to start, when beginners are generally willing to get experience and $6.00 a week.

Now I shall tell you about my home. As I said, the family is poor, and their home not what I should like; but as they were scrupulously clean, I was satisfied. They had no furnished room for me, so I bought the furniture for the room. Of course, it took a few days to learn what I know now, but here it is: There is a father, mother, and daughter, and she is a hunchback. They married, I think, late in life; for the daughter, Ida, is I judge about nineteen or twenty, and they are past sixty, and she is their first and only child. Mr. Arons was at one time a man of position, teaching in a school in Russia that prepared men for the Church. He reads and speaks the real Hebrew, Greek, Latin, French, German and English. For quite some time, though, he has been a cigar maker. But recently (about two years to be exact), he broke down in health—has spinal trouble (no doubt where the daughter gets the hunchback), and though he still works at cigars, he earns from $5.00 to $6.00 a week, and is sick in bed every second or third week. The mother, of course, does nothing. She is quite feeble, but can do the house-work, and everything is immaculate. The daughter commutes every day, working in a New York office, and only gets $9.00 a week, out of which (I think her ticket for the month is $7.00 or $8.00) she pays railroad fare to N.Y. and one streetcar fare each way in New York—and I think keeps continually paying doctor bills, as they are very proud, ridiculously so. The father has taught the daughter all the languages he knows, except Greek and Hebrew, and she uses her knowledge of them in the office [where] she works, as it is an importing office, but only gets $9.00 for it. I judge, in actual money, they get an average of $10.00 a week, for all three to eat and live on. Naturally, they live poorly. Of course, one knows there is much misery in the world, but if one doesn't see it, they are not troubled. I rather wish I hadn't come to them, for I am taking their troubles to myself; and I am afraid I could not lay away money to save it, and see these two poor old souls hungry and in pain for want of medicine, etc. But it is too late now. Even if I should move from them, I'd feel I ought to help them. They have wealthy relatives who, on Purim, send them $25.00—and that is all for the rest of the year. The first night I was there, they sat down to three slices of bread—one for each—a small saucer of sour rhu-barb, and weak tea without sugar or milk. I was to get my own food then; and I had two chops, and new potatoes, and a whole loaf of bread, and what seems like a king's luxuries compared to their fare. I couldn't enjoy my meal, seeing them starving them-selves. They are very proud, and Ida was telling me how they had poor digestive organs and they only ate meagerly at the doctors' orders. I finally prevailed on the old folks to eat—only when I showed them I'd have to throw it out—but Ida was obdurate. In two days time, though, I had them "eating out of my hand." The old lady can cook some delicious things very economically. I'm afraid I won't be able to save much, but then I'm young and—considering Ida's deformity—I'm perfect. Sunday Ira brought a basketful of good things from New York, and that will help. We sure had a feast Sunday—two chickens! Mr. Arons told me he hadn't tasted chicken since January, 1910!—and that was in a hospital. Goodness knows since when Ida or Mrs. Arons had any. I bought him a bottle of brandy, and for Mrs. Arons a bottle of port. It cost me $1.60, but really the brandy has helped Mr. Arons so much. He works piecework; and as he felt better yesterday—the food, no doubt with the brandy, helping him—he earned $2.00, against $1.00 last week.

Now, as for the house we live in—it isn't so bad, but it has no bath, and that is a terrible hardship for me, and the toilet is in the yard. It is next door to a blacksmith shop—so you can see it is not what it should be. They pay their rent by the week, $4.00, which amounts to about $18.00 a month. Now, there are lots of nice houses around here to be had for $25.00; and with me living with them, they could afford it. It costs them more to live as they do because of its lack of modern conveniences. But the reason they couldn't take an $18.00-a-month house is because they would have to pay a whole month's rent in advance, and they haven't the money all at one time. Sunday, Ira, Ida and I looked at the houses and picked one out at $25.00 which is almost perfect. It is a new house, never been tenanted, and sits on a small elevation all by itself, with yard enough to grow vegetables—not alone for our table, but really to sell—and maybe Mr. Arons could earn a living at that. Now, Ira gave me $10.00 which will help with the moving, and I am going to ask you to lend me the $25.00 to pay the month's rent in advance. And I will give it back in full, inside of two weeks. Of course, I will have a salary Saturday, and so will Ida. And besides that, I am to get another $10.00 payment on the ring [I recently sold], on the first. The reason we can not wait until we have the money, is because on Thursday we want to move in to the house. Tomorrow (Wednesday) and Thursday are Jewish holidays, *Shevuoth*—it is a holiday handed down since the time of the Jews in Egypt. It means that they must not go to their regular labors, but those two days must pray to God asking that their crops prosper the coming summer. It is not considered a sin to do that sort of work—that is, moving. In a way, it is for that purpose—because the Jews in the cities moved out to the country to work on the farms, so Mr. Arons tells me. Of course, they were reluctant about preparing to move (we talked it over last night), as they had no money and they know I have little. But I promised them I should have it to pay down by Thursday morning. Ida and her father will get everything ready while her mother scrubs and cleans up the house—for they will not leave it except that it is in perfect order—then, Thursday, I told them, we would move. I hope you won't think I am too ready to ask you, especially since I have not paid back in full for [your previous loan], but that will all be cleared up by June 15th—the $25.00 sent back in not more than one or two days over the week—two weeks at the most. If we don't move Thursday, we can't move for a week, as we pay here starting Thursday. And this particular house may be gone, as it has only been completed and ready for occupancy since last Thursday. I have the option on it until Thursday. It is up a hill and is just great. It has a brand-new porcelain bath and toilet and washbasin, which is the greatest boon to me. . . .

[Ira] is coming up tomorrow to spend *Shevuoth*—Wednesday and Thursday—here, and of course will help with the moving. . . . [Mr. Arons] does not seem to like Ira over-well, and I think it is because he got the impression that Ira has no finer feelings and is worldly, from his *dudish* appearance. Ira noticed it, and so did I. . . . Eventually [Mr. Arons will like Ira], for he is really very likable—only he gave out a false impression, for he thought these people I was living with were wealthy. . . . Had he known how humble and poor they are, he wouldn't have come done up in that fashion, I know. Goodbye—I will have to rush now to get to work, so will close. I hope you and the kiddies and Mr. Howe are well.

White Plains, May or June, 1912

I KNOW YOU THINK I AM NOT THE SAME "MAIMIE" SINCE I DON'T WRITE   52 ❧ you as I did. I am though, and I am just as much in love with you and want you to like me just as much as I ever did. But when I have other things to do, I think I can let you wait—because you will understand, whereas my employer and others won't understand. Too, I was determined to return to you the $25.00 I borrowed. And maybe I didn't have to struggle to manage it, even when I did. I said "two weeks," but I never dreamed so many things could happen to prevent that. I did manage it by the end of the month, as I was determined that it be paid by then, if I had to go hungry, because I am tired of being irresponsible. . . .

I will have to tell you all that has happened since I wrote you last. Before all else, I will say I have not seen Mary Antin as yet. It may appear that I am not anxious to see her—I really am, but so many things have prevented it, so far. I had a second engagement with her for a Sunday visit, but broke it myself—and only because I had nothing to wear. I really mean *nothing to wear*—not like Miss McFlinsey's "nothing to wear." (Is that the right name of that famous lady? I think it is.) But at any rate, I am still expecting to call; and unless something again unforseen occurs, I will see her within the course of a few days.

Well, we moved— But the day we moved, Mrs. Arons fell down the rickety old steps, and though her injuries were not serious, they were painful enough to be bad. It was not due to the moving. I foresaw this would happen, as I am not so sure of myself on stairs, and the ones in the old house made me dizzy—they were steep, and so old they were unsafe. At any rate, I thought either Mr. Arons or I would fall down them—as he is so feeble, and I am not so sure of my eyesight—but as it happened, it was Mrs. Arons, and she was all alone. We were all over at the new house, and I had just taken Bennie to the train and come back for Mrs. Arons and Poke—when I discovered her in an unconscious state at the foot of the stairs, and Poke calmly lying with her head in her lap. Of course that meant doctor and medicine, and also Ida's and Mr. Aron's time at home to get things in shape and to take care of the mother. When I came here, I really felt like bolting, because I saw so much distress, and I wanted to selfishly get ahead. But somehow I did not have the heart to do it; and I feel perhaps it was meant for me to help these people as I was helped. Of course, at first I helped a bit; but gradually I shared my money with them as though they were my own family. In fact, when the question of meeting the expense of the larger house came up (I insisted on the change), I reassured them by saying that after their money was exhausted, I would pay the rest. Ida's pay is always the same—except when she gets less, thru staying away—but Mr. Aron's pay is according to the work he gets and can do. So they lived: some weeks having enough to eat comfortably, and some weeks eating bread and weak tea. Of course, when Mrs. Arons got hurt, I had to meet that expense because they tried to do without a doctor, and I couldn't bear to hear her moaning. So I called the doctor, and of course went into debt for that, and medicine. The doctor came three times, $2.00 a visit. Then of course, the fact that Ida and Mr. Arons were not working would mean added expense for me to pay. Well, I thought I could bear that—if I had to remain in debt for a week longer.

Saturday morning about 8:30 I had to go out to the stationers. So I asked for my mail, and found a letter from my mother—or, rather, written by a neighbor—saying that she had been ill all week—heart trouble—and that Thursday she became so ill that the doctor said she must go away at once to Atlantic City, if she wished to live. And then the neighbor wrote a note for herself to me, saying she thought it was a serious stroke, and if I could manage it, to come. This seemed like the last straw, but I just had to go. I had no money, but just enough to get to New York. I stopped work at once and found Bennie in New York, and he borrowed the money for me to go. I got there Sat. night, hoping to see my mother before she went to Atlantic City, as she said in the letter she didn't want to go alone and would wait to go Sunday, when she could close shop and go with her husband. When I arrived I found she had to go Friday night—as the attack was so bad, she was very low. When I asked who took her, I was told she went alone. I thought that strange, if she was so sick. But her husband explained he couldn't go, so he phoned James. And he said he would go, or he would send his wife—only that they had tickets for a show! That ought to show you what a family I have. I didn't know what to do, because I felt I really ought to see her before going back—but as usual, I had no money. I did not *want* to ask money of James, because I really did not think he would give it to me. I went to his house, though, to see them—and you haven't an idea what a baby Potsy-girl has become. I am so fond of her. But because of James being so ugly toward me, I am forced to drive the baby out of my thoughts and heart; otherwise, I should be very miserable when I think of her. They seemed glad to see me—though James acted as though he had seen me every day, and when I offered to kiss him, he seemed angry and annoyed. I told them I was going in the morning (Sunday) to see Mother. James laughed at me and said that Mother was not sick—she was only feigning illness. Why she should do that, I don't know, but that was the way he reasoned it, anyway. I then went

135

into the real estate office on the corner—the proprietor I did some writing for when I was home—and explained the situation freely to him; and he loaned me $5.00. I hope this doesn't sound like one long tale of borrowing—but it is just what I had to do, and I don't know even now how else I could do. And that isn't all the borrowing I did—as you will see. Sunday morning, after sleeping at James's house, I left on an early train for Atlantic City. Mother had sent her address Friday night, as soon as she was located, and I went to the address she sent. Such a time as I had to find it! I was about ready to go away, for I couldn't believe my mother would sleep in such a neighborhood. It was the vilest Italian and Jewish section. Almost ready to give up, I saw my mother. Words fail me to describe the sort of place she was in. . . . It was the worst thing you can imagine, and even worse. I remonstrated with my mother, and she said she wouldn't go to a Gentile place, and the only other Jewish place was $3.00 a day. I could not bear to leave her there (the bed she slept on looked as though it could walk off, and had no linen, only blankets), and I had no money. I thought then of a plan. So I asked Mother how much she was paying in this awful place, and she said $7.00 a week. So I packed her up and took her to the $21.00-a-week hotel. I explained she could pay the $7.00 she expected to pay; and I would send her $7.00 for each week she remained; and I felt sure James would give the other $7.00 to make the $21.00. How I expected to pay $7.00 more each week—beside my expense here—I don't quite know, except that I thought I'd ask for an advance from the manager, to be paid off so much a week from my salary. Of course, this was a supposition on my part. Well, I took my Mother to this hotel-sanitarium; and she had a lovely room overlooking the ocean, with red rugs on the floor, and a box-spring bed with fresh linen-changed every day—a telephone in the room, electric lights, and a private bath that was worth the $3.00 a day alone, for it had double faucets with hot and cold, fresh and salt water. The elevator carried her to the seventh floor, on which was her room, and it looked to me as though she could scarcely want for more.

As I wanted to be at work Monday morning on time, and yet didn't want to leave Mother any sooner than I had to, I stayed until the last train from Atlantic City to Phila. (for I had a return ticket to N.Y. from there), which left at 12:00 (it was an electric train, being the cheapest way to get there), and I arrived in Phila. at 1:30 A.M. I debated at the depot whether to go to James's house, or take a train and go right on to N.Y. I decided to go to James's house, thinking it would be the better plan—since there would be no train to White Plains, and I'd have to go to a hotel in N.Y. to spend the time until morning. Too, I thought I'd have an opportunity to speak with James about helping to pay for Mother's vacation. By the time a Chester Avenue car came, it was 2:30—and exactly 3:15 in the morning when I rang James's bell. When he heard it—which was at once, for he now has an electric bell by his ear—he opened the window and angrily demanded, "Who is there?" When I spoke, he began to berate me for coming at such an hour. I told him to come to the door and not entertain the neighbors. He took his time about coming. And when he came, he opened the door and still growled: Why did I come? I started to explain—but it made me so heartsick to think this was my brother, that I simply told him I was on my way back to N.Y. but stopped to ask him about the money for Mother. He told me he wouldn't give a penny toward it, that if he wanted to distribute his money, he didn't need me to act as his agent; and if Mother wanted to stay at $3.00-a-day hotels, she could ably afford to do so. I told him I knew that well enough; but since she wouldn't spend her money, and as we never had to do for her before, it wasn't too much for her to expect us to do it this once. He answered sarcastically that as I had left her to manage the best she could for eleven years, probably she could manage a bit longer. To finish, I said: "Well James, I thought as a brother you would want me to come to your house, rather than go to a strange hotel— especially since I am not able to afford a very good one—but I see I was wrong. And rather than stay if you don't want me, I'll go." He was mounting the steps to return to his bed, and as I said that, I picked up my bags as though to depart. And he cooly turned around and walked out to the store and opened the door for me. And without another word I walked out.

It was then 3:30 in the morning and raining very hard. It may seem like weakness on my part to tell this—but I walked to the corner to a doorstep and cried for perhaps half an hour. I don't think I was ever so miserable. An officer came by, and I asked him when there was a car to town. And he said not until 4:30, they ran every hour, starting from 12:30. He suggested a taxi, but as I only had 45 cents in my pocketbook, I had to walk it. It took me until 4:30 to get to the West Philadelphia station. I was drenched to the skin, and my hat—which was new—was gone beyond hopes of repair, as the straw was cheap. The car which I should have taken at Chester Avenue whizzed by just as I got to the West Philadelphia depot. I had thirty minutes to wait for a train to New York, and no place to wait in, as the regular waiting room closes until 7 A.M. I was so sleepy, and I went out in the street hunting a restaurant. There was none in sight, but a saloon looked very cheerful; and a Side Entrance sign was the most welcome thing I saw that night. I went in, and as the night was raw, I asked the man to make a hot whiskey for me. He did, and I drank it; and as I was sitting there, I saw a door that led to a lavatory. I went in, leaving my grip by the chair I had occupied. I was in the lavatory five minutes. When I came out, my bag was gone! It was a very nice bag—pigskin, hand-sewed—left over from days of plenty. And in it was all my little articles of toilet, and a change of underclothes, and no end of little things that I will never be able to buy again, and the 45 cents I had—but, fortunately, not the ticket. I realized at once what had happened, and I took it as part of the luck I had been having. The contents of that bag were my most personal belongings and contained my few luxuries: the white gloves you sent me; the good hankerchiefs you sent me at Christmas; the green bow (fortunately I had the flannel waist on); my one pair of silk stockings; the fountain pen Mr. Welsh gave me; a pretty night wrapper; my brush and comb—in fact, everything. Did you ever hear of such luck? Of course the bartender said he knew nothing, and accused me of being *drunk*, and said I didn't have any bag when I came in. He also said I had to pay for what I had, or he would call an officer—and, in fact, grew so abusive and profane, I was glad to get out. I went then to the police station, and was so wretched, I couldn't tell my story, for crying. The man in charge sent a policeman with me to the saloon, and of course the bartender told the same story he told me. No doubt the officer was in league with him, because in a minute's time the officer was threatening me with arrest for not paying the man. I saw that I had nothing to gain, for I could not get the bag without applying to someone to help me, and the only one whom I would apply to would be to Mr. Welsh—and he and others would question how I happened in a saloon at 4:30 in the morning, or at any time at all. (I can truthfully say that it has been a year since I tasted liquor, and never before in my life went into a place of that sort.) I saw I could gain nothing, and as there was a train due in a few minutes (the six o'clock train), I went on to N.Y. —a very sad passenger, believe me—and then on to White Plains. As soon as I washed up a bit, I went to work—not more than an hour late—and I surely had to struggle to keep awake. I did not think much of my troubles, as I was too tired and sleepy.

The next day, though, I began to worry dreadfully—and that was, as to how I was to get the $14.00 a week to send to my mother for a period of goodness knows how many weeks. I asked my employer—and immediately afterwards I'd have given anything not to have done it. He was nice, but told me it was unprecedented in that office. I had asked for the advance and told him I'd pay it back so much off my wages each week. All day I was so cross at myself for asking him. And then when I went to get my hat to go home, he handed me the check I [had] asked him for—$14.00. I wish, though, that I hadn't asked him. I sent it to my mother; and I hoped, then, for a week, that all would be well.

I was kept busy with getting the house in shape, as Mrs. Arons was disabled and Ida...[is] not over-strong, and Mr. Arons is very feeble. I worried dreadfully how to catch up financially—and my expense here was looming up so large, as both Ida and Mr. Arons were not earning up to their regular amounts. Then I had an opportunity of earning 50 cents for an hour's work, in a small business place here. And I had been doing it every few nights, from the time I am thru at the office (at around 7:00); and then when I was thru, the man gave me the 50 cents. As the money didn't seem to stick by me in such small amounts—just dribbled away somehow or other—I suggested to the man for whom I did the work, that he pay me every so often when I asked him for it, thinking in that way to get together a small sum to pay off a debt. I started the account the day after I returned from Atlantic City. In the meantime, for my salary, all I received was $7.00, the rest being kept out to pay off my debt—and I needed $14.00 again, to pay my mother's hotel bill for the second week, besides the expenses here. I can't tell you then how I worried—for though my mother fortunately only stayed there two weeks, I didn't know, then, how many weeks she might have to stay. I was certainly in a rut, and I had to borrow $25.00

again. And this time, from a regular money lender—although not one that charges enormous rates of interest like the "sharks" the newspapers write of. Then things went along fairly smooth; and I was working hard, because I went to do the tailor's books every night; and I was hoping to catch up. When I had worked for him ten nights, knowing it would be $5.00, and it would pay the debt to the real estate man in Phila., I asked for it. And then a few things happened. This man had always been (apparently) interested only in my work there, and I hadn't the least idea that he might become "fresh"—and then I wasn't sure, because what he said might have been only meant in kindness. He once said, when I remarked that it was very close and asked him to switch off the electric lights (all but one) that were directly over my head—"I'll bring you in some ice cream—that will keep you cool." He knew I hadn't had supper. I pretended not to hear him and didn't answer—though really I would have been glad of the refreshment, and could not afford the 10 cents it would cost. Then, as I was leaving, he said, "How about that ice cream?" and I told him I didn't want any, and if I did, I'd buy it myself. I was nice to him because I couldn't in fairness say that he was trying to get friendly—it may have been just kindness. That was all that ever occurred between us that was at all personal. Then, the night I wanted the $5.00, I worked a bit longer than the hour; and he came in from the front of his store and said I had better quit, as no doubt I was hungry. I remarked that I was, and that I'd like him to pay me. He came over then to the desk, and he point-blank—without a word of introduction—made a proposal to me that I go up to the city with him and he would give me "a couple of five-spots." I was so surprised I couldn't think quick enough to say something, and I think now that he took my silence for a sort of consent. And before I could say Jack Robinson, he had me tight in his arms. Of course, I struggled and screamed—and in a few seconds was out on the street, leaving behind several things. Seemingly no one heard me, because next door several men were standing listlessly. They saw my excited exit, but I said nothing to them, just flew home. When I told the folks, Mr. Arons advised that I should say nothing to anyone else about it, because he is a very coarse man, and to justify himself, might say bad things about me that would make me leave town—as this is a very small village. The next evening, Mr. Arons stopped into his store to get my sun umbrella and little handbag, and also the $5.00—and he refused *point-blank* to give them to him, and said he would give them to me if I called. And somehow, to date, I have not had the courage to go for them. This man is a Hebrew, and a very coarse one, and I really think he would make life here impossible for me if I troubled him. He has been in business here for eighteen years, and I feel his word would have some weight. As usual—after all this happened, I learned that some years ago this same man received a horse-whipping from the husband of a respected lady here whom he insulted and *assaulted*, perhaps as he did me. Really, what with this experience, I feel as though I had been thru a fire. I am almost stripped of everything, and I can't see how I could have helped it. I did not tell Bennie about the loss of the grip in Phila. because, frankly, I didn't like him to know I would go into a saloon of that sort, for he thinks I am above that. And, too, I didn't tell him about the tailor, for he might either go there to fight him, or think it strange that this man should attack me without provocation of some sort.

I think now that I have told you all of my ill luck, except perhaps. . .that I have to take a two-weeks vacation, starting July 14th—my birthday—and no pay for the two weeks. That's cheerful, isn't it? I'd like to avoid it, but I can't. Everyone takes the vacation; and starting June 17th, they have had a professional substitute up from New York, who takes each one's place for two weeks and stays under contract for two months. So if I worked or not, she would get the pay. The manager knows how badly I need the money, and said he wished he could avoid making me take the two weeks, but this was arranged from the main office and was out of his hands. A firm in N.Y. supplies these substitutes, and they receive the pay. Hadn't I had this run of trouble, I might not have cared much, and in fact would have welcomed it. I might have gone to my mother's for a stay, or remained here. I heard of a place in the mountains where working girls are taken care of for a nominal sum, and I thought I might go. But on second thought, perhaps I wouldn't care to mingle with the girls there and, too, I would object to the "rules and regulations." My trouble is that I am a "working girl" who has lived like a "lady"—and it's hard to curb my desires and live as the working girl should. Believe me, since losing my bag, I am more like a working *man*, not alone a girl—for all I invested was 50 cents for toilet articles. I really must stop telling you my troubles. The reason they were not told you before this, was because I did not want to write you and tell you what a "Jonah" I am until I could enclose the $28.00....

My mother...really seemed touched by my kindness to her. In fact, when I took her up to her room in the hotel in Atlantic City, after I had made all the arrangements for her, she sobbed like a baby. She said that not any of her children had ever done anything for her before—which is true. But as I explained to her, neither had she ever done anything for them, except bring them into the world—and threw us out as soon as our father died. She was really very much touched, and all her letters to me were deeply grateful....

I have the picture of the place at Cotuit that you sent last summer, and I looked at it only a moment ago and I am glad I have it. It looks as though it might be ideal for the hot weather....

It has been very hot here the past few days—so much so that I get terribly discontented at my work, whereas up to now I have been intensely interested. I keep thinking how cool and comfortable I was the latter part of the past summer, when I lived at the hotel in New York City and had nothing to do except take care of my person—and I surely did that. Of course, there is a lovely bath here, but no hot water; and while I bathe every morning, it is a hurried, shivery bath, and every night, the bird-bath is all I can keep awake for. Too, now that I have nothing but a tooth brush and cake of soap, it is different from when I had everything that goes to make one feel well-groomed. I haven't time for much "fussing" either, and think of that when I am in the office, and feel discontented. You know I won't give up—so don't get a bit alarmed. At least at the present writing, I feel I have great strength. But I must admit it isn't out of a sense of moral or any other sort of right, entirely. It is just because I want to get a place for myself where I really belong, and I know a person like me can only get it by working like a nigger against all sorts of odds. Do you know, it isn't a bit hard to stay "good"? I used to admire the women I saw who stuck to the "path," and wonder how they had the courage, etc. But I found out it is all humbug. It's really only the way one gets started. The girls who have the right sort of parents—no matter how poor, or even ignorant they are—have no difficulty in staying "good," because it is just how they get started. The men don't bother them, except in rare cases, unless they are already bad—provided, of course, the girls have people who care a whit for them. I found that out since living here with the Arons, who are known as my "cousins." I see the men whom I know [like] a book; and if they met me "boarding" or "visiting," they'd start to hunt me down—whereas [now] they are just as polite as though they knew me from childhood as being thoroughly respectable. I know men pretty well, and know it never occurs to the ones I meet thru my work to ask me to go out—whereas if they knew the truth, they would beseige me. So you see, I am not having much trouble in being "good." And yet I'm not entirely contented—but I think I will get over that.

I am wondering what you think of my long silence. You know, I think, how I hated to write unless I could return that money. And really, when I came from Phila. and had such a terrible loss, and so much heartache over what transpired there, I felt as though I should like to write you all that happened.

Did I tell you we had a garden? We planted radishes, onions, cucumbers, peppers, beans, corn, sunflowers, pansies and nasturtium. And we have had onions and radishes, and soon the beans and cucumbers will be ready for the table. The flowers are pretty— the pansies are so vivid. . . .I get up at five now so that I can do the watering, and it is really my greatest pleasure. Of course, when Bennie comes I have pleasure—not because of anything half so much, as it is pleasant to know someone cares for me. He is really very nice. He keeps himself looking like a magazine ad man, and he is really spotlessly clean. It is refreshing, too, for the men in the office positively have a stench. He wanted me to come to N.Y. for my two-weeks vacation—and he would take a vacation, and we would have boat rides, and go to the parks, etc. But I happen to know that his sisters also want vacations—and I know he will try to manage it for them and me, with the result of perhaps having to borrow from those sharks. For he sends them money each week, and never less than $25.00—and I owe him money now, and I intend to pay it. I spoke to him when I came here about our relations, and he has stuck close to what we agreed on. The people here don't know about his affairs, nor do they know that Albert is in the land of the living; and they continually ask me why I don't marry him. And I wish I could.

I went to church today (I go every Sunday—Mr. Welsh asked me to, and I really get great comfort from it), and on my return, passed the tailor I worked for; and he was with two other men. They saw me coming and they really made sport of me. One of them stuck a silver dollar in his eye, I suppose to mock my patch. So you can see what I have to expect of a man of his calibre, if I should go for my money to him.

Before I forget, I wish to ask you for the *Atlantic*. True, I haven't a bit of time for reading, but I am anxious to read Mary Antin's story; and, too, I like the magazine, and was reading the continued story—the name escapes me, but I recall it was about the peer who wanted to marry the actress. I thought the style the story was written in rather odd—freakish, as it were—and yet it makes for entertainment when something better seems too heavy. I must close now or you will surely get weary. I hope your children are enjoying the best of health and you and your husband are well. When you write, will you tell me if Cotuit has a village—I mean, with stores in it—and if it is a resort, or not?

July 10, 1912

℞ 53   WOULD YOU MIND IF I THROW MYSELF—OR, RATHER, MY AFFAIRS—ON your shoulders for a minute, and ask you to tell me what to do? I realize this is evidence of a weak character; but it is so hot and uncomfortable, I am excusing myself for being weak. If one asks to be told what to do, the chances are they are evading—for everyone knows when right is right. But, truly, I am not sure in this case.

You sent this check and told me plainly what to use it for, and I would like to do just as you say. Then comes the thought of responsibilities, etc.—and, also, a recent letter of Mr. Welsh, in which he quotes Scripture to the effect that it is deadly sin to be in debt. And I am troubled by that old question: whether right is really always right. You see, I owe a debt to a moneylender, and this money would just clear me of it—whereas if I don't pay it, my spending of the money will cost me $4.00, the interest of an entire month, in which time I could pay it. And yet you said it must be spent on pleasures! Too, I need clothes—really need them, for the skirts of all my clothes have given out. Why they should, I haven't been able to learn—except that I wear them to death. I should like to get a dark-blue or dark-brown lightweight summer silk dress, all in one piece, that only requires buttoning to be entirely dressed—one that is not too out of style, and yet not a fussy one. I had a dark-blue foulard that lasted over two summers, out of which I got more comfort than anything else, for I could look well and yet not have to fuss up. Now, to buy one of these would cost $15.00 or so—and I don't know whether that would be pleasure, or even right, in the face of my debt to the People's Loan Company. And yet I truly could not get a bit of pleasure out of my vacation unless I get a dress of some sort in which I could look well and [which would] be large enough to be comfortable in, and which I could wear to go to parks and boat rides, and not be worried as to my dress getting soiled. I need a hat, too, but I can dispose of that by investing a couple of dollars when I go to the city. I don't own a hat of any description at present. It seems strange that you should say in your letter exactly what Mr. Welsh said in the letter in which he sent me that $10.00. He said, "Use this for your own benefits—do not spend it for the Arons." And yet they are truly more deserving than I am, for they are old; and Poor Ida is one of the handicapped. Just think, it is so hot I can scarcely breathe—and yet Ida has to put on an arrangement under her clothes that looks like a harness and weighs eight-and-a-half pounds!—

I must tell you something. Do you recall Mrs. Gregory, the old lady who was a seamstress and whom I knew for so long [in N.Y.]? Sunday night, about eight o'clock, I went to church—open-air song service—and there she was, sitting three chairs from me! When she realized it was I (should that be *me* or *I*? I think it should be *I*), she was so taken back, I thought she would faint. She was in White Plains only by accident. It seems she is still employed by the same firm, and they had a dress that had to be in White Plains for Sunday; and she asked for the privilege of bringing it here, and thus get a day away from the hot city. While walking along, she saw the chairs being prepared for service. And she sat down and had her supper (it was in a parcel brought from New York) and stayed for service, expecting to go home on the ten o'clock train. Just think of a poor old soul like her wandering about alone like that! She reports that her son Gilbert has not been seen or heard of since early spring—and she worries as though he was of some use to her, although he is only a worthless scamp. Ira was not here Sunday night (he was home), but he came last night, and he said I should have asked her here to stay, for starting next Monday she will be out of work until September 15th. I admitted we had the room, but no bed. He said he would give $6.50 that it would cost for a bed. Then I reminded him that even as little as she might eat, it meant another mouth to feed—and I am really doing more now than I ought, for in this frightfully hot weather Mr. Arons cannot work, and that means that much more for me. I told him it would cost at least $3.00—or perhaps only $2.50—a week, for her to stay here. And for two months, that would be $25.00 or so; and I knew he was in no position to spend that. You remember what sort of sisters he has. Now, one of them is to be married, and Ira is supposed to have $200.00 to give her by September 1st, for *nadan*—which is either Russian or Jewish, and means a sort of dowry. I would give her "nuttin"—which is American slang for what she really deserves. Every time he is short of money and cannot send the required amount, this particular sister writes that they cannot take care of his baby a minute longer, and threatens to bring it to him on the next train if the money is not forthcoming. You can see, then, that he has no licence to worry about poor Mrs. Gregory, who is obliged to live in a hall bedroom. . . . Just think, . . . to her, White Plains is a heaven. . . .

To return to my own affairs: True, I am selfish enough—but how can I use that $25.00 without helping these poor ones, who are so old, and to be pitied in this hot weather? I want you to tell me: would it be right not to pay my debt, and not to help Mr. Arons or Mrs. Gregory—and go off every day for jaunts with Bennie? Even though I really need the vacation and wish to goodness I had the dress, I wouldn't ask whether it was right or not. As it is: it's easy enough for me to appear unselfish, as before I could enjoy myself, I'd have to buy a dress—and I guess I'll have to buy it anyway, vacation or no vacation. If I had the dress now, I'd call on Mary Antin, for I really cannot go as I am. You remember your little polka dotted dress that was my "quick-dresser"—and it looked fine on me, but it is in rags. They all go first in the skirts. I am wearing to work now the blue gingham you gave me, and that is a rag at the bottom, though it has been fixed no end of times.

I was pleased with Mark's picture and amused at the ejaculations of everyone I showed it to: "Why he's barefooted!" He looks so sweet. I have his picture and Helen's (in which their heads are together and they look so affectionate) on my wall in a *passepartout* frame. How he has grown! He appears to resemble you, and so does Helen. Do they?. . . .

Mr. Welsh reports that it is delightfully cool where he is, and it makes one wish they could be fortunate to escape the heat. I hope you, too, are comfortable. It appears you must be, from what you write of Cotuit. I imagined Cotuit was as you wrote, but feared it might be a haven for the society people—and I didn't think you would care for that. . . . .

This picture is of Ira, taken the Sunday I wrote you about, when he first came here. Does he look anything like you imagined? I had it in a little frame, and will ask you to return it. Do you see Poke in the picture? I was wondering where Brownie was when Mark's picture was snapped.

July 25, 1912

I AM TO LEAVE TOMORROW FOR MY VACATION, AND AS I SHALL BE GOING   **54** ✑
about most of the time, I may not get an opportunity to write you—and if I am long silent you may think I was done to death this time.

I was glad to get your reply to my letter, and of course I did as you wished. You no doubt knew that was what I wanted to do, but I hated to be selfish and not have any excuse for it. I really was ashamed to, but I threw the whole responsibility over onto your shoulders. And hypocrite that I am, I let everyone see the part of your letter which says I—*me, May Jones*—must be the sole beneficiary: and what else could I do? Clothes are strewn about my quarters like autumn leaves—and I am to go "broadin' " as the darkies in the South say.

My dear friend—it makes me happy, doubly happy, to be so nicely equipped for this trip after my many troubles, and to know you made it possible because you care for me.

I became dreadfully weary after my shopping trip to New York Friday—it seems it is not my forte to do what other women seem to do with so much ease. I am indefatigable at writing, and yet any other work tires me very quickly. I dropped from a $15.00 foulard to a $2.75 gingham! How are the mighty fallen! I had to pay as much as that for a neckpiece in the palmy days of yore. I do not regret it, though, and do not even dislike these straits. Though the feeling of rebellion does assert itself when I am close to some "fine lady" in silks and satins on the train or in the street. I am afraid I bore you with this perpetual talk about my small affairs—but you see, it is all of my small life. I managed well, I think, for I was able to buy the many things to complete my wardrobe. What with a dress, a hat, pair of shoes, and furbelows, I had enough left to buy a grip, and sunshade, and a birthday present for Ira on the 18th.

It is arranged that while I am gone Mrs. Gregory is to occupy my bed, and in that way she, too, will have a bit of a vacation. I am leaving $3.00 for her two week's board. I will go to my Mother's but as there is no room for me in her house, I shall rent a room nearby, but board with her. We will go to see my sister and take her some things. Too, we will go to a thirty-second cousin's farm in Haverford, Pa. Mother writes he has an automobile, therefore "must be rich." I hope he is rich in tolerance—for Mother has ignored him up to the advent of the automobile, and now we are to swoop down on him for over Sunday. I shall suggest taking along lunch to eat by the wayside, should he choose to kick us out.

And too, I will call on James (with the sweet disposition). I really did not think I should ever enter his place again, but when I think it over, it seems to make me as small as he is, to take everything so seriously. The 14th was my birthday. To my surprise, I received a package from Caroline containing a pair of drawers that she made herself, and which were really lovely; also a little package of the Babis's hair, explaining that it was bobbed for comfort, and the clippings saved for me. It was wrapped in *toilet paper*—Caroline *is* bright. She suggested that I make a small pincushion with it, but that does not appeal to me. It pleased me better to turn a drinking glass over it and place it on my window sill, where the sun plays on it in the morning while I am dressing. And as I look at it, I can see the head of that precious Baby bobbing about me. It is such a pretty red, with blonde glints on it. It is not just like your hair, but it resembles it, in that it has that wavy appearance. There was also two cards—birthday cards, sickly-sentimental—I don't believe Caroline chose them because of their sentiment, but because they are ornate. Now, while the gift was from Caroline, I appreciate that it was sent at James's instigation, for Caroline does not breathe until James gives the signal. Knowing this, I feel as though James is really troubled at my silence; and I hastened to write, assuring him of my love and that I would be in Phila. and would be to see him. I was really surprised that they remembered the 14th was my birthday. I have a slight suspicion that Mother told them. You know—after all, he is my brother; and if he is coarse, it is not his fault. It is really my fault that I have a little knowledge of nice things; for as you know, it is a "dangerous thing" and causes much unhappiness of the heart. I could remain with him, I suppose, thru my visit; but even if he was not so grouchy, I'd rather not, I think: I find, when I give it thought, that I am a creature of extremes. I would rather have the highest or the lowest in every thing. I find that instinctively I avoid being where I have to mix and mingle with the half-bred, the half-souled and the half-educated. They seem to offend my spirit. James and Caroline pretend so much; and it moves me to furious scorn. All said and done, I prefer realities, at any cost. The frank bare boards of our kitchen table here, I don't mind—but what I loathe and abominate in James's house is the white oilcloth table-covering in lieu of the white linen. This is a fair example of the difference in the home I have here, and the one I had in James's house. Here we clean our plates to a high polish with bits of bread. At James's house, one has to be overcareful, not because they eat according to Hoyle, but any little thing that they *do* know about does not escape James's attention.[21] At any rate, I shall go there, and if I do eat, I shall be very careful not to offend.

I wish you could see my dress—it is really very nice. Of course it had no end of "fashionable" trash on it. I removed every last bit of it. I am wondering whether I couldn't have bought the dress for 25 cents, had the manufacturer left off the trimmings. . . .

In the *New York Sun*, which our manager takes every day, I noticed an article—which I think is published weekly—giving the name of the books most called-for at the various libraries; and Mary Antin's name "led all the rest." *The Promised Land* was the book desired by perhaps many of our co-religionists—who, I understand, are the largest readers of the New York public libraries.

Goodbye— My very dear Friend, I thank you again, and your kind sister, that I am able to go on this trip and to feel comfortably equipped. You may address me here, as I will not be gone long and they will forward my mail as soon as it comes. I hope your family are all well.

August 24, 1912

∞ 55   I HAVE LIGHTED MY LAMP, AND IT IS JUST 2:30 A.M.—AND ALL BECAUSE I am worried. Nothing serious, but I want to tell you about it. . . . When I am worried, then I feel most that I want to write to you.

In the office here I was given carte blanche as to revising certain form letters, and I felt very proud when the main office wrote our manager congratulating him. Our manager took all the praise, and I was satisfied, because it was just enough for me that I did really do them. After awhile I was given the pleasure of revising as many as three and four letters every couple of days. They all were sent from different branch offices whose managers are friends of our manager, telling him to "do them over." No doubt he offered to do them, either in letter or by word of mouth. When I left for my vacation he *only* gave me six letters to revise—and sent me four more while I was home. And while they didn't take up such a lot of time, still, they interfered with my vacation considerably, as they were to be done and returned post haste. When I returned, I found a bunch more stacked up—and all besides my regular work. And mind you, he had never said one word in explanation of this extra work—just piled it up on me.

Now, the past week, the New York office had some extra work, and all our force went there twice, and worked it out. Just prior to starting out, he called me aside and gave me to understand that I must not let them see that I am the author of the letters that are being done in the White Plains office. Of course, he didn't say so outright, but he gave me it to understand. I let him understand I was "wise," as he calls it, and we went in a body to the New York office. While there, I was not comfortable, because I was in a room with perhaps fifteen men—all bright, city men—and they disturbed me so that I was ill at ease. Explain it I cannot. But I feel free to say that I don't think that the matter of sex had anything to do with it. Of course, I may be wrong, but I feel had they been women of the keen sort these men were, I'd feel the same way. At any rate, here in the office I am cock of the walk, and there I felt like a sore

150

thumb. Too, for a while they were so busy "looking me over," that that may have been why I felt so wretched. At any rate, as I was sitting in the place assigned to me, I felt myself growing cold and trembling all over. I began to cry as though I had been struck. I cried and cried, until I grew hysterical. The two girls from our office and several from the New York office tried to help me, but it was of no avail—until I cried it out, and then I grew quiet. They had no divan in the office, so one of the girls was sent with me to Wanamakers (which is close by) to lie down in their rest room. She left me there; and after I felt better, but very foolish, I went back to get my lunch and things—not thinking they would want me to work. When I came in, I was the cynosure of all eyes, and how I did wish there was a kindly face in all that lot. Our manager came over with a scowl on his face, and asked why I didn't return to my work. And when I told him the atmosphere of the place was unbearable to me, he grew abusive, and said something after this sort: that the sight of a man got me crazy; and that I wanted to attract attention to myself. Up to this, while he was always just a shade from being grouchy, he never was ugly to me. While I was trying to explain, the manager of the N.Y. office came up; and our manager said—in a sarcastic manner, after the inquiry was made as to what had been wrong—"Oh! Miss Jones"—as he calls me—"is a temperamental stenographer. The office does not harmonize with her, so she says." I couldn't and did not speak. But I saw that the New York man was in sympathy with me. And he said, "Come over here." And he showed me into his private (very elegant) office, and asked me if I could work in there; and I said yes. Could I help it if I just couldn't work in that larger office? So I went in there, and he left me there, except for coming in about three times to get some papers out of his desk. About fifteen after five, just as everyone was no doubt preparing to go home, this man walked in and said I had better begin to put up work, as it was 5:15. I was writing in longhand and, as I was in the middle of a page, I did not stop at once. So he came over and looked over my shoulder, and said, "How long have you been *pushing a pen?*" (to quote him). I said about five months. He said, "Oh! no—impossible. Where did you get that commercial hand?" Without stopping, I told him briefly of my little experience, and said I thought, considering my little education, it was a "gift," after a sort. Then, he seemed amazed more than ever that I could keep on writing and talking at the same time. He asked me if I had a "bowing acquaintance" (still to quote him) with English as she is *spoke* and written by New York City business people. I then explained that I was not a White Plains product, but hailed from Phila.—and I was writing all the time. When I got ready to go, he asked to look at what I had been writing while I was talking—a matter of ten minutes—and he seemed to marvel because I made no errors, and all the punctuation complete. He seemed to like the writing, which was like this:

Your order was filled and will send you

But all through the conversation, not one word was said as to my ability as a letter-writer, or was any reference to anything made that might give a hint as to my writing the letters our manager is supposed to write. On our return to White Plains, not a word did he say to me—though he also said nothing to anyone.

The next day, after two hours work in our own office, we went again to New York. On the train, I was told that if I valued my job, I'd reject the "private office" this time. And I answered that, as now I felt more acquainted, I didn't think I'd feel at all uncomfortable with the rest. When we came in, I took the place originally assigned to me, and I worked until luncheon time. . . . About two o'clock I saw the N.Y. man coming my way; and pretty soon I heard him say, "I want you to do a few letters for me." As I was his employee for the day, I could not but obey. As I got up, collecting some loose sheets, something made me look up, and I saw our man glaring at me; and I grew cold, for I saw I was going to get into trouble. I walked directly over to him and told him. And he shrugged his shoulders as though it was one to him, no matter what I did. In the private office, I took three letters for reply, and one to quote some prices to a prospective customer. Of course, the three letters were form letters—but the other one had to be personal; and I said, "Hadn't you better dictate this, as I am not acquainted with this exact style of work." He said, "Quit stalling, now. I knew all the time that 'Beef' "—as he calls our man—"was working someone to death out there—and when I saw the collapse, I knew it was you." I was not able to speak, for I knew he knew; and to lie would be silly. And yet I saw trouble ahead. I went to work there—and frankly, I wrote the letter in question in my best

152

style. Will you be sure to tell me this: Should I have pretended, and written it poorly? I don't feel I should, but perhaps I don't see it in the proper light. On the return, not a word was spoken to me; and I slept little that night. Two days more elapsed before any reference to it was made; and during that time conditions were about the same in the office, only that I was not spoken to except directly in reference to my work.

Then today came the climax. I worked hard—harder than usual, having had a new idea as to filing references for new business, and was trying it out. Just as we were finishing up the day's work, the last mail came; and as usual, I opened the letters, expecting to answer any that required immediate answer. Of the eleven letters and three postals, two needed answering, as I thought; and it is always left to my judgment. I only answered two. Everyone but the manager had gone when I got up to go. He asked me if I had answered necessary letters, and I said yes. He said, "Wait until I look them over." As he did, I saw him making two piles, and I knew he was going to say I had to answer one of them. I felt myself getting hot and then cold—because it was not just. I was very tired and hungry, and it was 6:30. And I felt I was going to cry, so I walked to the door. And he sprang up, and said, "You'll finish this work or you needn't come back." Surely I could not afford to lose my position—but oh you can't understand how terrible it is to feel you just have to take such treatment. He grabbed me by the arm and jerked me back. And I just couldn't control myself—and I picked up a heavy letter file and went after him. I believe I could have killed him, I became so furious and strong. Of course, it was all over in a minute. He took hold of me, and instantaneously I lost my temper and dropped the file. But I could see he was pretty well scared. I then cried—and sat on a chair, while he went over to the washbasin, preparing to go. When I began to think calmly, I saw what I had done was going to cost me my position. And the terror of being in the position I was in last spring frightened me so. I began to explain to him how tired I was, and how the extra work was wearing on my nerves. And as I talked, he said nothing. Finally I became quiet. And then he started in to say how I had tried to impress the New York office and finally "worked my way into the manager's attention"—and then he said he supposed I'd kept a few "dates" with him, and that I only made an ass of myself, etc., etc. He heaped abuse on me; and when I could stand it no longer, I told him that he had no right to accuse me of being friendly with the N.Y. manager, as I gave him no reason to believe I was the sort. And he laughed insinuatingly and said he could have made a "hit" with me too, had he cared to, but he didn't go in for "one-eyed women"—And I didn't wait to hear any more, but came home.

I have written it all out as I know it, and if I seem to spare myself, it is not because I am lying. I worked hard and faithfully, and I don't know what to do. I am so tired mentally as well as physically, and I am so hurt, that I don't feel I ever could possibly go back to that office again. Of course, it may appear that he would not let me work there further, but I know better. As long as I want to, I can work there—provided, of course, I can stand for his tricky, dastardly character. Probably when morning comes, I will see light, and act accordingly. I told no one in the house; and as I couldn't eat any supper, I have a frightful headache. I wish I could ask you right now what to do. You see, by the time you could possibly answer, I will have to go back to work, or make up my mind to quit there; and yet as I see winter approaching I get frightened. For under no conditions will I ever go to my brother's to live; and I have no other place.

I am going to close, and before I go back to bed I am going to ask God to show me what to do in the morning. I am all shaken up; and probably when I get calm, I will know what to do.

New York City
August or September, 1912

C⋑ 56   I AM SETTLED AFTER A FASHION, AND NOW WILL TELL YOU ALL ABOUT IT. You will remember that I wrote you of my return to my work, even though it was very ugly to be in the same office with the manager. . . .I decided. . .to write to the Chicago office—the home office of our firm—and explain the situation and ask if they couldn't locate me in some other of their nearby branch offices, since I understood their business—and referred them to the New York manager, who knew what I could do. To my surprise, I received a reply from the N.Y. manager, in which he wrote that the Chicago office had asked him if he could use me—and he told me to come prepared for work as soon as I could. I gave up then at the White

Plains office that very night—and it was no small satisfaction to be able to show the New York letter, in which I was also told not to bother about the salary due me in White Plains, as it would be arranged from the Chicago office.

The next day I presented myself here and started right in to work. The salary is the same; and though I commuted at first, I found it very [difficult], as the trains made me ill and I was not at my best in the office for the rest of the day.

Getting room and board in the city is not the easiest thing in the world—and it proved a frightful ordeal to me. Mr. Welsh suggested the YWCA and I went there to please him. Fortunately for me, they were filled up and could not accommodate me. The atmosphere in such a place would make me want to do something hideously wicked, just to see what it was like. Then I began a wary hunt, using the ads in the newspapers as a guide. It was dreadful. The ads that appeared most encouraging were the worst possible. Then when I found a room I liked, the price was terrible. And so, almost entirely discouraged, I gave up looking and began asking people. And then, thru a young woman who has a public stenographic office, I found and rented this place—and I have as much right to live here as I would have living at the Waldorf. It is 'way above my means, but it is so ideal, and the places that I could afford so sordid, I couldn't resist the temptation. I have a room and bath and little kitchenette. The house has only one-room-and-bath apartments, and all women; and though gentlemen visitors are permitted, they must all be out by 11:30. There isn't anything of the YWCA about it, but it is thoroughly respectable; and the women are all businesswomen, and the air about the place is so thoroughly clean morally, and refined; and I can't say as much of the other places I saw . . . .

I want to write Mr. Welsh too, tonight . . . . Is he not a wonder, though? He is walking home from Sunapee to Phila. You know, he is sixty years old but I don't think he feels over forty— He is very well preserved. When I had nothing else to do but look after my person, I was, too, much younger than my years. Ira asked me the other night why I had pimples on my chin, and I was astonished to find I had quite a cluster. There was a time a pimple on my face was a tragedy, but now I haven't time to even look at my face.

I must tell you that Saturday I expect to have a talk with our manager and ask him to see if he can arrange to have me taken on at one of the offices in a small town, nearby to here or Phila. While I should like it here immensely, I feel a gnawing discontent all the time, because I see so much that I desire; and I envy the women I see on the streets; and I haven't even the courage to work in the office with the clerks there, who all are so well dressed. I am very happy in this dear little apartment, but I haven't the means to keep it up; and I get so grumpy about it. I don't think many women in New York who earn $12.00 live as good as this—unless they get help from their "new friends," and from what I can understand, it is not considered a terrible thing here. Ira offered to pay my rent, and then offered to move into this apartment with me. He is a man, and by no means a straight-laced one, and he gets on my nerves dreadfully since I've been here—so much so, that I have not allowed him up here since Friday, when he came up and refused to go at 11:30, telling me they'd never know in the office. I see I'm getting to where I'm beefing again, so I'll have to cease. . . .

Since writing this last night, I was talking with my employer; and he told me he might arrange to get me in the Wilmington, Del. office, although he said he thought I ought to stick it out here. He was very kind, but I am a wee bit afraid that after all it is not as entirely impersonal as I thought. . . . He tried to take me to dinner at night to help me with my expenses. . .but I won't start that; so you needn't be alarmed, as I will get out of New York before I do that. . . .

New York City, September 23, 1912

౭ 57 I HOPE YOU ARE NOT AS TIRED OF HEARING ME ASK FOR FAVORS OF YOU as I am of asking them? I am obliged to ask you this time, although I should write to Mr. Welsh ordinarily—except that he is on a walking trip somewhere between Albany and Phila. just now, and I could not catch up with him in time to do any good.

This is the trouble this time. Ira and I were to White Plains today to visit the Arons—I had left some things down there and Bennie went with me to bring them back. I don't know whether I told you that I left my furniture (for the furnishings of my bedroom were mine) with them as a present so that they could rent a furnished room, and thus make them able to stay in that house and not oblige them to return to their miserable rooms. . . .

As we left the depot this morning, we learned that the Italian who owned and ran the newstore and cigar store right by the depot was killed in an automobile accident early last week. I stopped in to talk with his wife, as I knew her well. I used to stop every day to speak to her little girl and boy (twin) babies that were always so clean and sweet. In talking with her, she said she was not going to keep the place, as she expects to have another baby in two-and-a-half months and wanted to go to live with her mother in Paterson, N.J. Ira immediately thought of her place as a good one for Mr. and Mrs. Arons, as Mr. A. makes the cigars, and this store is really a well patronized cigar store. This Italian (Mr. Ambrogi) was able to take care of four children and drink a lot of liquor out of what the store brought in.

Bennie found out she wanted $200.00 for the store, but afterwards agreed on $160.00, and she could have the stock of cigars that were on hand. Bennie knew Mr. Arons had a few dollars saved up that he said he was saving to be buried with; and whatever was lacking, Bennie would put to it, and Mr. Arons pay back so much a week or month. We went to the house, and they were all elated—Ida and Mr. Arons and Mrs. Arons—at the prospect of having a little business that would make it unnecessary for Mr. Arons to go out much this winter, and at which they could all help. Pretty soon it developed that Mr. Arons did not have quite as much as Ira thought he had, for he had invested some money in a lodge or society of some kind that would bury him. It then worked out this way: Mr. Arons had $30.00, and Ida said she could draw $10.00 at her office. That leaves a balance of $120.00. Ira could and would pay it in full, only that he has just gotten thru marrying off a sister and it had cost him considerable. As things were, they stood $40.00 short to get the place. None of them have any way of getting it, except as they earn it (or thru money lenders) —except me. And I thought I would send to Mr. Welsh and explain; and he would, I felt sure, help the Arons to get this small business. . . . For although he never did anything for them, he always was willing to help Mr. Arons—but we all pulled thru the summer without needing it.

Ira is here waiting to take this to mail. I told him that since Mr. Welsh couldn't be located (or even if I did, I couldn't expect to hear from him by the 26th, which is the day Ira is to go back to White

157

Plains to close with Mrs. Ambrogi, to whom he paid a deposit of $25.00), I would write you and ask if you would care to lend us the money. I thought at first that if you did, I would write as soon as I got in touch with Mr. Welsh, and he would return the amount to you, and then Mr. Arons could pay him at leisure. I told Ira (who is here) that I could not get in touch with Mr. Welsh until October 4th or 5th, when he is expected back in Phila. So he said then, you tell Mrs. Howe that you won't have to bother to ask Mr. Welsh, for by that time, I will take over the debt, for on the first I will be able to pay it back.

I hope you will understand this, for I am writing under pressure, as it is nearing 11:30, and it is the rule that the men who are visiting must leave the building—but Ira thinks it is a fast and loose rule, to be broken at will. And as I am anxious that Ira is able to get the news and cigar store for Mr. Arons, I let him come up when we got home until I wrote you—but I can't write as clearly as I would if I wasn't worried. I should die of mortification if they ever ask me to tell Ira to go. He makes sport of my nervousness about it, but I can't help it.

I will close abruptly, although I have other things I wanted to write you. I have a letter started to you before I had the trouble in White Plains, telling you about my visit to Mrs. Grabau. I will mail it as soon as I hear from you—finishing it first, of course.

Do you think I am too ready to ask for favors? I wish I didn't have to ask them.

Ca. September 28, 1912

℞ 58   I HOPE YOU DON'T MIND MY USING A PENCIL (MR. WELSH DOES). I'M sure if you knew how restful a pencil is after holding a pen all day, you wouldn't mind.

I had a letter to you started, written while I still lived in White Plains, and I had thought to continue it; but, as has happened before, when I read it over, it did not read in harmony with my present mood, and to continue it would be impossible. So I've destroyed it and will write it all fresh and stick to it until I've finished—for fear this may also never reach you.

I have other things I wish to write you, but I'm going to let them go to the last, and write you now of my visit to Mary Antin. As you know, I had an intuition about what she was like, but I

158

resented my own feelings in the matter; and pressed on by your advice and Ira's desire that I make friends with someone in White Plains who would spur me on (for he insists that I am capable of greater things), I made ready to go one Saturday when White Plains was enjoying a holiday, due to a new railroad being opened up there.

I phoned Mary Antin, and though I did not tell her, I let her think I was just in White Plains on a visit—intending to tell her the truth when I saw her, provided I wanted to continue the visits to her home. It took me two days to get myself into shape so I would look as I thought was my best. As I had the new "fixings" that you and your sister made it possible for me to have, I looked quite presentable. I always wear clothes (provided I buy them) that are absolutely plain; in fact, I like the "tailor-made" idea, and I think my summer appearance after I received your gift was as neat and orderly as possible. At any rate, I attended to the last detail, just as I should had I been expecting to visit you or Mr. Welsh. I also warned Ira through the mail not to wear a gay tie, and he came looking very nicely. We phoned again, and Mrs. Grabau said she would be at home at four o'clock. When she described just how we should find her house, it developed that it was next door to a house that Ira and I had noted on several walks thru that section. It is a large house, built with straight up-and-down lines like a box, but painted pure white, and everything set out on it like a picture book house. It seems it is kept in battleship order, and it is always a gleaming white, as though freshly painted. Ira...had been in rhapsodies about the place; and though it is not what I should care for as a house—still, it is the home of refined, nice people (as I afterwards learned), and quite nice because of its cleanliness and order. I tell you about this house to show you later a phase of Mrs. Grabau's character.

We alighted before her house. There was a man cutting the grass that I thought was Mr. Grabau, but later she said it was her brother. He was a rather handsome man and smiled very pleasantly when we asked if it was Mrs. Grabau's home. He did not offer to show us in, so we rang the door bell and waited a few seconds, when it was opened by a person who proved to be Mary Antin. But I did not dream it was she, but thought, rather, it was a maid of the governess variety—for I noticed a few child's playthings scattered on the porch. She opened the door, and without a smile or a word, ushered us in; and as the parlor, or living room, or whatever it is, is just off the hall, she showed us in. And as we were about to be seated, I turned with a smile [intending] to ask if Mrs. Grabau was in—when she said, "I will return in a moment—I was just attending to my little daughter's supper." And I was never more relieved in my life that I hadn't asked. But then and there, I knew my intuition had not failed me.

While I am sitting there awaiting her return, I will tell you what she is like, both from my first impression caught at the door, and later, thru my visit. Until you see her head, she looks like a fifteen year old girl—very little, very thin—in fact, a tiny woman— dressed in a very frowsy looking white pair of shoes or slippers, that might have been tennis shoes. Her skirt, too, was white linen and the only thing that saved it—and the waist, which was a white linen drawn-work affair—was its superior quality of linen; but otherwise they were both mussed and quite soiled, and looked at least three wearings overdue in the laundry bag. Now her face—As I said, it might have been a very youthful person's, except for the many lines in it, and the extreme hardness of the eyes, that seem absolutely unsympathetic—and, as I learned afterwards, shifty, thru not being entirely sincere. Her hair is very much curled; in fact, it has a kink like the Negro head, and as is sometimes seen among Jewish children of the lowest order, except where the exception proves the rule. I've always had a failing for curly or wavy hair, and my most vivid impression of you is the color and wave of your hair. (Once Ira asked me, "Hasn't Mrs. Howe any other nice things about her but her pretty hair, that you always lay stress on?") Mrs. Grabau's hair did not please me—in fact, I disliked it. It didn't seem as though it curled because it wanted to, but because it had to. So much for her general appearance.

Now, the hall had no furniture, or even a rug in it; so that was nice, and promised much. But when we got seated in the room, and while awaiting her, I seemed choked up with furniture. This room seemed to represent the various changes in Mrs. Graubau's fortune and taste . . . . [In a recent play titled *Milestones*], the three acts depict the three stages of one person's life—youth, middle, and old age: and so with Mary Antin's furniture. I'm sure some of it was bought when she thought plush furniture was the "fashionable" thing. Then came the intensely simple mission—that suggests the installment house—and, if you will excuse this, I will say that I'd have to be built square-in-the-seat to enjoy the hour spent on the chair I selected to sit my visit out in. Then there was some few things that were added last-and-least, since she became famous. But furniture and hangings there were in plenty, with lots that should have been given to the Salvation Army long ago. Little, fancy things, that I can not name, were scattered about, too; and plenty of dust, to give it all a "comfortable" appearance.

On a square library table were some books; and under it, on the shelf part, were more books; but as far as I could see, there were not any other books in the room. One book—the most exquisite binding I ever saw—Goldsmith, I think, or it may have been Longfellow—had written on the fly leaf: "To M.A.G. from her brother—the binder of this book." And if it was the brother who was cutting the grass, he certainly is an artist—and the book redeemed the room and its furnishings. Other books (about four in all) were beautifully bound (but not like the aforementioned one); and it may have been the brother's work, but did not have any writing to indicate it. The books were all standard copies of all the best-known writers—among which were some seven or eight copies written by Mary Antin.

Twice, she came thru the hall while we were seated there (that is, in the room directly off the hall, but opened so widely that it seemed part of the hall), running up the stairs and then down, making four times in all. And though I expected her to look in, with perhaps a remark that she would join us shortly, she kept her head averted. And nary a look did we get, until she came to the door, and then in—with the first smile of a sort-of welcome that we had as yet received, though we had been there nearly fifteen minutes! While she was gone I did not speak one word to Ira, for I feared that if I did, I'd say something that might prejudice him against her. And I thought I'd rather wait until after our visit, when perhaps I'd find I felt differently about her. Naturally, then, when she entered I had become quite solemn and so had Ira.

Her air was ridiculous. She said, "Mrs. *Jones*—and is this Mr. Benjamin?" Her smile seemed to break her face all up, and did not seem real—and one felt instinctively that the smile would not just fade away naturally, but that as soon as she released the string, her features would snap back to the same sharp look we saw at the door. And sure enough, it did.

She led off by asking if we had any trouble finding the place—and then said, before we could answer, that she didn't see how we could, though, since she had told us it was next door to "the white house"— And almost in the same breath, she went off showering abuse on "the white house—and apparently it was the only annoyance in her perfectly ideal life. It seemed the grotesqueness of its architecture attracted attention to her home, that she despised. And when Ira said he liked it, I only wish I could describe the look she gave him. I then suggested that certain traits in the Hebrew race made me think our natures made us like the bizarre, until we had been trained differently. And I said I thought some day, when Ira was likely to build his own home, he would never select anything that looked unusual. Still no remark from Mrs. G. I ventured further (thinking this topic—our Race—was her pet one, judging from a letter or two that she wrote me, and also from her stories), that I recalled when I was a little girl, how I had been given permission to pick some roses [one Sunday afternoon] in a well-filled garden belonging to a fine Christian gentleman who was friendly with me...I picked about ten red roses—as much as I could then hold (I was seven or eight years old). And after about four or five such Sundays, he went with me into the garden, and asked me why I did not take a white rose or a pink one? And I told him I didn't want to pick them until they were *ripe.* For I no doubt thought they started white, became pink, and then red. I heard this story told by him to many visitors at his home after that; and in every case I heard comment which, even as a child, I remember, had great bearing on the fact that I was a Hebrew, and the brighter colors naturally appealed to me. Oh, yes: it seems—though Mr. Webb explained, and I understood—I never wanted a rose other than a red one. And once—when the red were about gone—I refused any, rather than take the paler ones. I thought this might interest her. But she only commented that one's tastes were most likely the result of environment—and as I glanced about the room, I thought she had better have left it to the Race.

As she seemed anything but talkative after going off on that long tirade about "the white house" (I think that is her pet grievance), I subsided, thinking probably she would broach whatever subject she was interested in. The silence became painful. And I then spoke about the celebrations in White Plains. She returned the remark that she never went there, except when she was obliged to do some shopping and couldn't go to the city—but her visits were very few, because White Plains is such a *common place!* Now, what do you think of *that*? I could have shrieked. Bennie then and there began to see into her, and as he told me afterwards, led her on by agreeing with her about the horribly coarse people there, and all that sort of thing. As it is—White Plains prides itself on being quite exclusive. Trying to keep up a standard, they prohibit everything there—short of breathing, and paying excessive rents. As in every place—where there must be shops, and business houses—an element made up of the working people, like myself, creep in; and then persons like Mary Antin become annoyed. I wonder whether the town she was reared in as a child in Russia was exclusive enough to suit her? Naturally, Phila. was alluded to. And as I raved about it, she explained that she'd never been there, and somehow had no desire to see it, for she had never been impressed by anything she had ever heard of it as a city. I spoke of its features that I thought were nice. But she was not interested, as she told me again—so I dried up! Boston, then: Bennie had been there one night and a day, and knew quite a little of it. Was she better informed about Boston? Not a bit of it. She had been there a great many years of her life—but, too, she had been away a great many years, so only remembered a few things of Boston! I told her I had lived there too, and remembered quite a bit about Boston. I mentioned this: That I knew the stores of Boston well—and then, not being there for a long time, I forgot a great deal. One day, Mrs. Howe sent me some dresses and fixings that were hers before she went into mourning—and several shops' names were on the packages—and it all seemed so clear to me. That is—Washington Street, Boylston Street, Tremont Street, Sumner Street; Jordan Marsh's, R.H. White's, Filene's, Oppenheim's, on the corner (I think) of Boylston and Tremont, opposite the subway entrance—and lots of other places. No interest whatever. I was silent again; and it again became painful.

Ira ventured—did Mrs. G. ever meet Mrs. Howe? Hurrah! She was interested! No, she hadn't, because on her visits to Boston she hadn't the time; but she hoped to some day try to spare the time.

For some reason, this made me furious. It sounded as though she was patronizing you— I forgot to tell you: In the early part of our visit, I said I had thought to come the Sunday before; and she spoke up that it was well I hadn't, because she was entertaining and couldn't have seen me. Perhaps this may have been socially correct—to say she couldn't have seen me—but it cut me, and I felt small. As though, had I come all the way—as she thought, from New York—she would not have seen me, because she was "entertaining." I don't believe you'd say that to anyone! To return to what she answered Ira: I felt mad all through; so I said, "Did Mrs. Howe say she could see you whenever you could come?" I meant it as a call-down; and I'm glad to say, it "took." She returned that she did not think you wrote much, now, and that did I know you well? And I said, "Yes, very well: she is my best friend, and came to Phila. to see me 'round Christmas." I know that was a bit of a lie—but I really couldn't help it, and I let her think it was last Christmas. And then she abruptly said—"How did you become acquainted with her?" I said, "Through a mutual friend, Mr. Welsh." With that, she perked up: "Who is Mr. Welsh?" And I told her. And if she thought she was so important—when I got through, she wasn't quite so cocked up about herself; for she did not know this Mr. Welsh; and I did.

At about this time a child came in the room—perhaps three or four years old—a sweet little girl. And though she had a little of her mother's features, she looked too pretty and sweet to be any kin to Mrs. Grabau. She, too, had on a very soiled dress. Not a good, healthy soil from playing outdoors, but a soil that was plainly two or three days old; and not very dirty, but just mussed and dank looking. It seems her mother has instructed a maid to take her to bed, and she would not go. I was very much surprised at what followed. It took all the persuasion and coaxing and promises the Mother could think up, to get her to go to bed—and only when her mother would take her, would she go.

It seems the two maids she has are the two girls she expected from Russia—the time I was to visit her, but she had to go after them. She told me, then, they were her cousins, but no doubt [they] are being trained into maids. It may be they have no back staircase, for while we were all in the room, they came down the stairs en route to the kitchen—to prepare the evening meal, I think. I noticed they were large, robust, girls of a very cheerful appearance (as they were coming down the stairs), about eighteen and twenty,—but as they passed her, they actually slunk by trying to make themselves as little as possible. Their shoes creaked horribly. And with the perpetual frown on her face, she turned to look at them—Ira told me later (which I noticed myself), they became so frightened, they could not stir; and when she turned back to us, they almost fell trying to get out of sight.

Before she took the child up herself, she extracted a promise that she would go up with Rosa, one of the maids.... Returning in an instant, [the child] said, "Mother, I told her what you said, and asked her if she'd take me to bed—and I can't understand her when she says yes." I thought that very dear, and asked if I could hold her a moment. She came willingly, and her mother told her to kiss me goodnight on the cheek. I was quite taken with her—and before I could say Jack Robinson, she had lifted my patch up, loosing it at one end, and hurting me dreadfully. It seems she was curious about the patch. And then Mrs. G. tried to get her to go to bed—and had she been mine, she'd have been whisked off without a lot of promises. I thought she would be a firm mother, but it seemed the child is the proprietor of that house.

When she spoke of not understanding the girls, I said, "Do they speak Russian?" and she said, "No, Yiddish." I asked "Doesn't the child understand any Yiddish?" and she seemed shocked I should intimate such a thing. "Oh! no—not a word." Ira said that was the straw that broke his back. Of course, there was nothing to do but await her return. She wasn't gone long—and reported that "she" was already in bed, and as she slept readily, would be asleep in a few minutes. It then occurred to me that she must have been put to bed without washing her face and hands—and no doubt she does not insist on the tooth brush....

Up to now, not one personal word had crept into the entire visit—and if she was interested, as she wrote, in knowing more about Mr. Benjamin's mother, etc.....not a word did she say. While she was up with the *Babis*, I thought to suggest to Bennie that he say something to her in Russian—which he speaks well—and they speak about his birthplace, which was in the very same village she was born in, and of people she should know—and then we'd go. He did; and she retorted that she did not understand, having only a slight recollection of the language. While they were talking of this village in Russia (and though she thawed out some, it was still with that same important reference to the fact that she had so many new interests, that the older ones were quite vague), a bell rang out, and it seemed to me it was a supper bell. I interrupted to remark that we must be going, that we must not keep her from her supper. She said oh, that was the first bell, she still had ten minutes before the next bell that was the actual supper bell—and then: wouldn't we stop for supper? I hastened to explain we had a *dinner* engagement—for I wanted to be sweller than she, who was only having supper! She insisted a little—but only a very little—and all the time, I thought Ira would tear my skirt off: he was trying to let me know he didn't want to stop for supper.

As we were standing there, I thought to leave a pleasant taste in her mouth at our leaving. So I told her I had noticed in the *New York Sun* an article saying that it was a slack season at the public libraries of New York; then, it gave the books in greatest demand—and I noticed one of Mary Antin's was named. (It then was during the season that most everyone is away but the people that are likely to want to read Mary Antin, I think.) At any rate, I told her this, honeying it up—and she answered "Oh, yes, there are a great many comments, but as there are a great many newspapers, I don't see everything. My clipping bureau sends me many, but I don't have time to read them." Just then, Bennie heard a car coming, and we started for it. But it was only an auto, so we stood in the road. And she strolled down...and she began again about the terrible disgrace of living next to such an atrocious thing. She was still ranting about it, explaining they were not going to remain long, when the car really came, and I hurried off.

I think I've told you, word for word, of our visit; and I hope it did not bore you. I intended to tell you just generally, without giving my opinions, for I feared you might think it was ugly of me to tell just what I thought, and might think I was not a fair judge. But when I received your letter, and you said some ladies whom you knew thought she was conceited when she was a child, I felt then you would not think me unfair to criticize her. And I must say I never saw such conceit, especially in a person of her intelligence. She is cocked up about Mary Antin to such a degree that she is sickening. Ira thinks she is bright and intelligent, but not unusually so—that is, not more so than a great many Jewish girls of her own sort—but that her face is so mortally ugly that she has been left entirely to her own devices, and thus worked out her own salvation. That is Ira's version. According to him, I am just as capable as she—only that because I was pretty, I was not permitted to think and work in solitude, and thus become a Mary Antin. . . . Not because I want to appear modest, but because I am sincere, I say he is wrong. She is really a genius—for a genius anyone must be, to write as she does, and yet be a person quite different from anything her writings would indicate. I don't think it would prove her as clever if she was, in reality, the sort of person one would judge her to be.

During our visit she made no comment about her husband, but the little girl spoke of him as though he was away on a trip. And Ira said he got the impression there was no master of that household—but of course he may be wrong. Oh! how he guyed me, on the car coming back, about how I attached so much importance to her wanting to know us. He said he understood her thoroughly. Had we been greasy-looking, and after the order of the conditions of life we had both been born into, she would have been more gracious—in a sort of patronizing way—but as we both are clean, and look as though we stay that way, and have clothes that did not suggest imitation of elegance, she was taken back, and wanted to be natural, but couldn't. The funny part of it was that somehow, the day we went, I kept you in mind and sort of expected her to be of your sort; and I felt so downcast on my return, as though you had failed me. I could not be rude to Bennie, but I did wish he could have gone home, as I wanted to be alone. I was terribly crestfallen, and he guyed me so much until I could stand it no longer; so I dug up a reason to get cross. . .and got rid of him. It was perhaps the only time since I've known you that I felt troubled and wanted to write you, but did not think I ought, since I wanted to tell you about Mary Antin and how she disappointed me. . . .

Almost another week has elapsed since I wrote the foregoing. I was deterred from finishing by another busy session of which I shall tell you as I go on in this letter.

First I wish to acknowledge and thank you for the check. The amount was correct—I surely wouldn't try to help them if I had to borrow the full amount as you at first thought. . . . About the place for Mr. Arons: you must understand it isn't really a full-fledged store. It is more like an enclosed stand, but sound and warm for the winter. The thing that the $120.00 paid for is fixtures and "good will," as it is called. That means the trade it has—and it really has a good one, especially for newspapers, magazines and cigars. It is right at the depot, and also at the termination of a trolley line and the place where the autos wait that do business between White Plains and neighboring towns. Did I ever tell you that Ida Arons is a hunchback?—and like most of the cripples of that sort, sews beautifully and, too, has indefatigable patience. She expects to exhibit and perhaps get orders in the same store. . . . Now I think you will see why we thought this place so good for them. . . .

I wanted to ask you if you did send me a book recently. You spoke of it, and I have since lost trace of two letters Mr. Welsh sent me (one containing a dollar bill with which I was to buy woolen stockings for him to wear on his walking trip), and I wrote the White Plains post office (as they were closed Sunday when I was there)—and they answered they had not received a letter, but if I would send 16 cents in postage, they would forward some fourth class mail. . . . I don't want to risk the 16 cents if it is not from you. I don't remember the name, but it was by Phillpots, I think. . . .

Right now I am reading *The Widow Le Rouge* by Gaboriau. I am reading it to please Bennie, who got it at the library and liked it so much. I do not care so much for mystery and detective stories.[22] I remember in one of your recent letters that you referred to Thomas Hardy, and that his descriptions were so long—yet I liked them; and do you recall, when I lived in New York last fall and summer, I read everything almost that Thomas Hardy wrote. And that took some time, as all his books are "fat" ones, as Bennie says. I liked him; and now I like William Dean Howells—and am only reading this one by Gaboriau to please Bennie.[23]

I will now tell you about the change that has kept me busy. I have a roommate who shares my expenses, and it all came about so providentially. I must tell you, though, that before I did take this place I went to any number of places whose *addresses I got at the YWCA*. At several places I was asked on sight: "Aren't you a *Jew*?" and when I said yes, I might as well have confessed to being a thief. All signs of welcome were hauled in, and the rooms were "spoken for"—a choice term among the *genteel* places in N.Y., when they mean you don't look good to them....At any rate, last Wed. I did not go to work, but went out to hunt for a room. (For heretofore, I went in the evenings, when it was dark, and everyplace looked so treacherous; and on the side streets where most of these places are, men accosted me either to go and get a drink or to give them money for a drink.)....After searching around four or five hours, I came home thoroughly tired out, but at least had arranged for a room and left a dollar for a deposit to "show good faith"...when a knock came at my door. It was then about 5:30. I opened it to find a fine-looking woman of perhaps forty. After a lot of apologies and explanations, it developed that she is a "forelady," in charge of a lot of young women who do auditing in Wanamakers. She had seen me in front of the building; therefore, in behalf of a friend, Miss McCoy, who is an assistant cashier in Bloomingdale's store (formerly she worked in Wanamakers), she wanted to know where the little white shields I wear on my eye could be purchased. Miss McCoy, too, has but one eye; and she too has been wearing a shield, two years. She never saw any but the ordinary black silk ones with the rubber bands, or a pink celluloid kind that no one could wear longer than an hour for—the heat it gives is powerful. This woman was attracted by my patch, and told Miss McCoy— who made inquiries, and couldn't buy them. I gave this woman a couple of them, and explained how to make them. As I make hundreds at a time, I have learned the easiest way to go about it. I have taught quite a few people how to make them, and besides have made thousands of them for the Wills Eye Hospital in Phila., who use them instead of the black ones with the unsightly rubber band—which is hard for a woman to wear—when they dress the eyes of the women in the clinic.

The next night at the same hour, when I was just going to eat, in came Miss McCoy. It seems the shields are for the left eye—and as it is her right eye that is gone, she couldn't use the same patch. I invited her to eat with me, and then drew the shield for the right eye, and made a dozen for her. It altered her appearance, and she was so grateful that I was embarrassed. Too, I have devised another scheme which makes the patch almost unnoticeable; but this is a recent idea, and everyone congratulated me on it when I was on my holiday in Phila. I cut my front hair so that the hair on my left side is just a bit longer than my patch, whereas on the other side it is shorter. As I finish dressing my hair, I curl these "bangs," and though I pin them back slightly, the ones on my patch side seem to have fallen down—and almost entirely cover the patch. Of course, it doesn't cover the patch entirely; and anyone talking to me, or looking directly at me, can see it; but it is very effectual—especially here in N.Y. For if I go out to the store with my bangs pinned back, I invariably have a lot of children following me or trying to get ahead of me—and all sorts of things that I don't like are asked me. Whereas, the other way, the nuisance is greatly abated. The moment I showed Miss McCoy, she wanted to go home to cut hers. But she took her hair down here, and we managed it together. And she is now wearing her hair "artistically careless"—which, as it happens, she hates almost as much as I do. Prior to this summer, I always wore my hair as close as possible—and a stray hair never was seen, once I was dressed for the street; for my hair was of even lengths, and a net and brilliantine made it ruly—though it is naturally so. Fortunately for Miss McCoy, her hair has a slight curl, so that on "off" mornings, if she doesn't care to, she doesn't have to curl it—though I have to, .every morning (now, though, as winter comes, the curl stays in a week or more).

I spoke to Miss McCoy of what was uppermost in my mind; and she thought it such a pity that I would have to give up here, since it is so nice. I told her frankly my predicament—and it was she who asked to come live with me. She only earns $10.00 a week, but as she works in the restaurant department, she gets breakfast and luncheon and, two nights (Friday and Saturday), supper. We are each paying half now, so that it is really cheaper than living with the lady who has my dollar, for she wanted $4.50 for the room—gas extra, meals extra, and no place for Poke, which would make it necessary to send her away; and I would like to keep her. . . . I don't think you would want me to send her off, when she is always so glad to see me when I get back at night. I now keep a towel—in the hallway, behind a radiator—which I pin on before I open the door, because try as I will, I cannot keep her from jumping all over my skirt as soon as I enter; and it usually takes thirty minutes to brush off her hairs. I am prepared for her now, and let her jump at will.

About Miss McCoy: She moved in Sunday. Ira helped us to get comfortable. He didn't like her coming, at first, but is reconciled now. And as she only lived a few blocks off (seven blocks one way, and two blocks north—that is a "few blocks" in N.Y.), he carried over most of her things. As our place is small, I suggested she leave behind all but essentials—as where she lived is a place of this sort, run by girls who work, who rent the building and then all pitch in for expenses. They call it the "Irish Legation," and though it is not a rule, it seems no one but the Irish or of Irish descent lives there. Miss McCoy tells me the idea was furnished by a recent story of George Barr McCutcheon,...Robert Chambers, or some one of those gushy writers—which I am sorry to say is what she likes. I may be able to show her what is better. The Legation is not nearly as nice a place as this, so Miss McCoy was glad to be here. Though as I only expect to remain until I get a position in a smaller town, she left her things and may move back at any time. Bennie made *only* four trips there and back. And finally we are very comfortable.

Miss McCoy is perhaps twenty-five—or twenty-six or twenty-seven—short and dark, with a pretty grey eye. It seems a pity to lose such a pretty eye! Other than her hair, which is pretty and black and inclined to curliness, and her one eye, she is not pretty. As far as I can see, though, she is clean; and though she only took weekly baths, that is (I think) because she never had her own baths. She will take morning and night baths now—for I would hesitate about sleeping in the same bed with an entire stranger, unless I saw for myself that she is clean. As it happens, mine is the greater will, and while I wouldn't care to be domineering—still, I think she will not refuse to do my bidding. She did not tell me how she lost her eye, and of course I did not ask her. I told her how I became so afflicted; but as she did not volunteer any information, I don't know. But I think there was a tragedy. For she did tell me that she is really a *Mrs.*, but has not had the support of her husband for two years; therefore, though not legally (for she had no money for a divorce), she took her maiden name again. As the loss of her eye is only two years old, too, I think there is some sort of a tragedy. She was born in Ireland and has a mother there, but lived in Boston since being in America—except the two years...that she has been in N.Y. She is a Catholic, and a devout one, apparently—for on my way to church Sunday morning, I stopped at her room and found that she, too, had gone to mass: as had every woman in the Legation, but the one in charge.

Doesn't it seem strange for a Jewess and a Catholic to live

together? Although I do not attend the Hebrew synagogue, I still call myself a Hebrew, for somehow I feel that I am. And though I started to go to the Episcopalian church only to please Mr. Welsh, I go now because I find lots of comfort in regular attendance there—and while there are things I do not really care for there, I find plenty that helps me thru the week.

I asked Miss McCoy about *The Opal* tonight. Then I shall tell her about you, and show her my pictures of you and your family, so that she can get acquainted with you....

I was trying to think if this isn't the first letter of any length that I ever wrote you that wasn't full of trouble. I will tell you a secret. I have other things besides trouble, but when I do have trouble, I aways make haste to tell you about it as you are always so kindly sympathetic—except this [recent] time when you were cross at me for being so unbusinesslike and spending more than I could afford. I know you were right—but I could also not have told you about it, and then worked it out as best I could. If I tell you my troubles in every letter, it's because I never tell anyone else; and that is why, as you wrote, I seem to get into so many scrapes—for I tell you them. When I write home, I am sure they think me a genius for getting along so fine. And of course, to Mr. Welsh, my only other correspondent—I write only things that will not worry him. On second thought, so that you may feel entirely sure this letter is from me, I'll tell you that I broke a bridge lately installed: that leaves me no teeth that hit, so that chewing is impossible. The bridge cost $30.00, and the dentists tell me the remnants have no value—and it means another $30.00 before I can chew at all. Now, isn't that just like me? And, too, it is nearing winter, getting cold at nights, and I am worrying what I am going to do in between now and fur coat time. Miss McCoy wears a sweater—but I despise them. Still, I may have to wear one....

I will close now, as I am sleepy. I wish you would write what you think of my taking Miss McCoy in.

Mrs. Mark Howe   *West Street, Wilmington, Delaware*
Brimmer Street, Boston   *November 14, 1912*

✖ 61   I HAVE STARTED WORK IN REAL EARNEST. THE CALL TO COME TO WILMINGton was sudden, and I left Monday night. Since then, what with getting located and getting down to business, I have not had a moment for myself—and I don't know what you must be thinking of me. . . . As you can imagine, there is lots I could write. But every waking moment is truly precious, for the reason that Frances and I are the office force, and folding and stamping and addressing of envelopes is our work at night. We do this to save the office the $20.00 a month that a boy would receive. The idea is that we advance as the office does—and naturally when the expense is cut down, it shows better for us.

The weather has been lovely until today—it is raining, and Frances has got along without a coat. We are still hoping that your friends have a coat they can spare. If not, we will arrange to buy one of a credit house, and use Frances's salary as security for the amount. It is a waste of money to buy a cheap one—so if she has to buy one at all, it is better to get one that will last three or four winters. Don't you think so?

Wilmington, November 22, 1912

OUR OFFICE IS WELL ON ITS WAY TO REGULAR WORK. I AM THE "BIG   62 ❧ smoke." (I hope you know what that means, although I don't like to have you think I use this class of language. I don't.) Our manager is spending much time between the Phila. and New York office. . . . So far, I have run things; and I have no doubt that I will be in general charge of the office affairs, while the manager will conduct the business from the outside. He is a very able business-man, but not overly clever in the use of English—and he thinks I am in a position to teach the men who teach English. His only fault is his impatience with Frances—who is not as quick as he thinks she might be, to grasp things. When she has to take any orders from him, I generally coach her; for she cannot seem to grasp it, and he won't go into details more than once. She is quite sullen today because he wrote in a letter of instructions (to me, about some business), on the margin: "Do this yourself, as I want to feel sure it will be letter-perfect." And Frances saw it, as she opened the mail before I returned from lunch—which we go to separately—and she is furious. I felt sorry for her, as I should not like it myself; so I tried to comfort her by running him down. But she was very curt to me, so I am leaving her to fight it out alone. She is not angry at me, but one would think she was. I know that she feels it, because she really has no confidence in her work, and this notation makes her

173

estimation of herself correct—so she is good and provoked at herself. I hope I have not bored you with the recital of all of our small woes. You must know that this is all of my life now, so it is just this that I can write about. From eight in the morning until nine and ten at night, I keep hard at it—and yet I am perfectly contented, and in fact as happy as I've ever been in my whole life. Are you not glad? Sunday we are hoping to walk part of the way or perhaps the whole way to Phila.—but I guess it will be "part of the way"—and Miss Poke is to go along. . . .

The weather continues beautiful—clear, and not too cold—and I hope it is the same in Boston. Next week, Thursday brings Thanksgiving Day. It will be the same as any other day to us, unless it is clear—then we shall go into the country for a walk. The people at our house are going en-family to Phila. to an aunt's, and we are asked to go to a restaurant for our dinner, which we shall do. Of course, it won't be very cheerful—but as my folks don't think they have anything to be thankful for, they don't have a Thanksgiving Day. Personally, I have much to be thankful for. I am feeling better than ever before, and am at peace mentally; and I am happier than ever; and I have you and Mr. Welsh, and I love you both. Yours lovingly, Maimie

I suppose I should say that I am glad that I have Frances's company, as I used to be very lonesome at times, and cry a great deal.

Ca. December, 1912

∞ 63   MISS MC COY WROTE THIS TO ONE OF THE NEWSPAPERS UPON READING something that made her very indignant. . . . As she had two copies of it, I asked for this one to send you, thinking it may give you an idea of the sort of girl she is.

WORKING-GIRLS' HOMES
To the Editor of *The World*:
As a working-girl I read with interest the plea in your morning paper for another working-girls' home where a "helping hand" and "elevating influences" may rescue her from degradation. Without wishing to appear cynical of any good effort, I should like to say that I have lived in two of these places where "helping hands" are held out, and where they always put you to sleep with four or sometimes eight others in a room, so that rest is impossible, giving

you the poorest of food, making you feel like a pauper generally, and rounding out all material deficiencies with very long prayers and useless restrictions.

Isn't it time that a little sense and less sentiment be used in reference to this "overworked" working-girl? We are not an abnormal product. If we can't earn livable salaries we do retain enough human nature to want three good meals, a comfortable bed with decent privacy, and the right to think ourselves as individuals instead of an institution. The woman or women who will recognize this fact and open a plain, unvarnished boarding-house for women on small salaries will not have to use any "helping hands" to save girls from immorality.

It is worth while noting that if immorality exists among working-women, particularly in department stores, it is among women who draw salaries of from fifteen to twenty-five dollars weekly and not among the six-dollars-a-week girls. —*Working Girl*

Wilmington, January 14, 1913

TONIGHT, I AM TO GO TO THE CITY; AND AS I AM READY TO GO, AND 66 ❧ must await my train, I will write you.

I have so much news to tell you that I don't know where to start. As for myself, I have been getting along very well; and perhaps because I am kept so busy, I cannot take time to have troubles of my own. [Since her illness], Frances's place in the office is taken up by a Miss Baldwin, who is really very proficient; and as there is nothing personal in her employment here, I can get twice as much work out of her than I could out of France—although if France was physically able to return to the office, I'd take her back at once. But as she is not, and won't be, for some time, I am very glad to have Miss Baldwin—who, while yet a "Miss," is a woman of perhaps thirty-five or thirty-eight, and an able stenographer.

I was to get a raise on the first, and in fact, the raise came—in this wise. The Chicago office allows us so much for operating expenses and since the first, they sent $3.00 more each week, which was to be my raise. But for awhile I won't take it, for this reason: To be able to get the very able services of such a person as Miss Baldwin, I had to pay $3.00 more per week than I paid Frances McCoy. This may sound as though I was posing as being cheated out of $3.00 a week for the benefit of the firm, but it is not what it seems. The idea is, that by getting a better worker, the office will turn out more business; and as the business improves, the status of the office improves correspondingly. With that in mind, I know it will not be long before our office will receive mention; and as it does, my position is more assured. Too, they allow an office expense-money, pro rata to the amount of business they do—and as I aspire to the managership of this office, I have an object in my madness when I take on a stenographer of Miss Baldwin's sort.

Now I shall tell you about France. She left the hospital today and is at Mother's house by now. My sister-in-law Caroline took her home in a taxicab—that is, if everything turned out as we planned it should. I was with France over Sunday all day in the hospital, and there were new developments which, unless something new happened, will be very good for her.

First, I must tell you that my mother didn't want France...for no particular reason, except that I think she had some qualms about the fact that Frances had so many things with her incidental to her religion—such as prayerbeads and little fancy pictures and figures of Christ—and the thought of any thing relating to Jesus Christ is very hard for my mother, who is an Orthodox Jewess, to digest. But when I was up Sunday, I won my mother over—in fact, she saw that I was hard-put to know what to do with her. So she gave in, although it was only after I promised it should be only for a few days, at the most.

Before I started up to the city Saturday night, Mrs. Bauman, where I live, gave me orders that she didn't want France back until she could take care of herself. I am very much disgusted with her, for I think—though she may have suffered much inconvenience— she might have been willing to help me a little by having France for the ten days or so until she would be around again. But I can't explain the attitude of such people, so must accept it. It may be because she is the sort that she is which accounts for the fact that she is always crying about not having any friends. Be that as it may: I am no longer a friend of hers; and though I live in her house, and expect to remain there, *I do not* feel kindly disposed toward her. She was in the city one day while France was in the hospital, and though she could have very readily stopped in to see France, she didn't—and in explanation said, she was not in that part of town. When we took France to Phila., she carried on and cried as tho France was her own child, and said so many times. I've no doubt that the tears were cheap, and she didn't have any trouble shedding them. For on Sat., she spoke very plainly, saying that she couldn't afford to have France there and only get the small pay she did—and then have to wait on her, besides. She intimated that I should pay her money for the time she did wait on France—but I didn't care to understand. It is quite a blow to me that she should have turned out this way, when she was so kind in the beginning of our life there. At any rate, when I went to the city with the knowledge that Frances couldn't come back to Mrs. B.'s here, I was hit mighty hard when my mother acted stubborn about taking her back there—and I knew arrangements must be made for France to leave the hospital on Tuesday. As I said, I finally persuaded my mother, much against her will, as soon as I arrived in the city.

Then, when I went to the hospital, I made up my mind to tell France how mean Mrs. B. had become; but evidently she knows people better than I do, for as soon as we began to talk about it, she guessed what had happened—and I couldn't help but admit it, of course. She felt badly, and cried a little; but I explained to her that the world was not entirely peopled with such as her, and I did not think we should take it seriously that she turned out to be a person of that sort. To go on, then—Frances began to tell me of something which proves, more than ever to me, that the darkest cloud has a silver lining. Here I was almost frantic, wondering what I could do with her for awhile, and not let her see the difficulties I was in—and then, presto!—she told me of something that clears the horizon; and all seems very fair again. It seems in the next bed to France was a woman—quite aged, I believe (for when I saw her the first few times I was there, she looked about seventy-eight or eighty, but France says she is not over sixty; and she and France struck up a friendship, as they both originate from the same places in Ireland and know people who are there yet. She, it seems, is not a rich woman—nor yet a poor one—and since she left the hospital, has sent France several things (besides priests, which seems to be the biggest boon of all).

Now this old lady became ill while visiting a daughter in Phila. who—she braggingly told me—supports almost entirely a Catholic church in her vicinity. She herself lives in Greenville, Kentucky, and offered to take Frances with her. She has two sons and two daughters still there, and they run a bakery, I think—or it may be a dairy—and she offered to take France with her, with the understanding that France can have work there in her place. France seems willing to go—although she seems a bit reluctant about leaving the vicinity because of a certain priest in Phila. to whom she confesses, and who I think has really got her almost daffy on the subject of religion. Personally, I would be glad if France went, for many reasons—and one is that she tends to make me irritable with her religious mania. I have not tried to persuade her, for I would not want her to think I am trying to get rid of her—which I surely am not—but she really is the source of a great deal of trouble to me, which I think was perhaps because she was sick. But at any rate, while I'd be lonesome for awhile, I'd not mind that—if she went there to better her condition. I am going up to talk about it tonight. If she had let me tell Mr. Welsh about her illness (which he doesn't even know about, because I wouldn't tell him and then have him offer to do for her, only to have to explain that she wouldn't accept help from him—and all because he once expressed some views of the Catholic religion that didn't suit her), I could have gotten a place thru him where she could have been cared for—for a while, at any rate. As it is, I am nearly desperate, and if anything happens that this plan of going with Mrs. Fitzgerald falls down—then I can only suggest that she take a room in one of the boarding houses in the city near the Church, until she is able to work. For I couldn't possibly bring her here, as Mrs. Bauman just won't have her. Isn't it a pity that the Catholic Church, with all the help they receive, couldn't provide some such place for just such an emergency? But though I talked with the Sister Superior, there isn't any that would be the place for France at this time.

I have written pretty nearly all I had to tell you. But now that it is nearing time for me to go, I can't concentrate my thoughts, and guess I'd better terminate this and write you tomorrow—or rather, I should say, at my earliest opportunity. For, as I don't expect to be in the office until noon, I'll be so busy that I don't think I will be able to write, even if the developments are that she is to go. I may send a postal, though. On second thought—will you write *at once*, that you think it would be a good plan for France to go there, where she will practically be in the country, which she loves so much—provided, of course, that you *do* think it would be a good plan for her? I think, since I have had her with me, that no issue ever came up that she didn't say that she would do this or that, if you thought so—even in opposition to the priest. And though I do not want her to go against her will: if I see that she is inclined to go, yet cannot decide, I'd know a letter from you would settle it.

Goodnight— I have not written this nicely, but you will pardon me, I know, when I tell you I did not eat any supper so that I could write you.

Box 583, Wilmington
March 1, 1913

THIS WEATHER MAKES ME FEEL AS THOUGH I WISH I HAD BEEN ABLE TO   67 ✉ accomplish something through the winter—and when I view my condition after the way I struggled all thru the winter, I feel I'm not as capable as I had deceived myself into thinking I was. True, I have kept my position—and I really have a good one, in which much trust is put in me. But try as I will, I can't seem to make any headway, so that small necessities won't trouble me so much. When the seasons change, as they are doing now, I feel the smallness of my life, and I get terribly discouraged. For need of many things makes me wonder if, after all, it is worthwhile to struggle as I do. I just have nothing to look forward to. . . . Mr. Welsh is going to Europe in a few weeks—though that can't make a big difference, for I rarely see him. . . .

I did not hear from Frances—but the bill she left reminds me of her almost every day, as the firm it is owed to has been pestering me about it. I wrote Frances and sent her the letters they sent me; and in reply she sent me a card, saying she would pay it at her earliest opportunity. So far, she hasn't done so; and knowing her very well, I have not dunned her. I just wrote a pleasant letter, for I know had she it—or a chance of getting it—she would send it. And rather than dun her and perhaps make her want to come back to work it out, I shall not ask her further. . . . I have kept myself entirely free from debt and have paid up a few that I incurred when I lived with Albert on Walnut Street.

I do not know whether you know that I haven't Poke—although I wrote you at length about it, in the letter you did not receive, I believe. When I left Mrs. Bauman's, I couldn't get a place in a clean house of the kind that would not get on my nerves—for I did not have a lot of time to hunt for it. I advertised and mentioned about Poke; and though the ad cost me 25 cents a day, and I ran it a week, costing me $1.75, I did not get but two replies—and they were from places which were out of the question—smelly, horrible places. So in desperation, I took Poke to James my brother, and then moved here. James was very fond of her, but because of his store, he couldn't keep her, as she could not be tied up....I then advised James to talk with any women who seemed to fancy her. The following Sunday, I came up and gave her to a woman who lives in a nice home and had a little girl; and I went back to work Monday, pretty miserable. But since then I am a little reconciled, although some nights I am so lonesome, and I can't sleep for thinking she may be hungry or want water. I have not trusted myself to go to see her as yet, but I hope to Sunday, for perhaps it will relieve this frightful depression. I must go to work now, so I will close abruptly.

Wilmington, May 7, 1913

68   I AM TERRIBLY LONESOME LATELY. I CAN'T EXPLAIN WHY, EXCEPT OF course that I was never so entirely alone in my private life as I am now, for even when I did not have human companions I always had Poke, who was always so understanding and, too, so exacting and selfish that she at least was someone to quarrel with....

[Our firm's] business is suspended here...either for good or at least a good long while. You may know that the new laws make many businesses appear to be trusts, and so our firm would be, except that they get around it thru a technicality....But to play safe, they are suspending all operations here, and that ends all possible trouble, for they are making the business that was un-lawful—lawful, thru some legal methods of which I am not familiar....[24]

The matters at the office, then, are all at sea. And I am too, in a measure—except that the firm will take care of me, until they place me in another position. They are almost insistent that I come to the Chicago office, for they want me as correspondence clerk—which would be over about forty stenographers. But I can't see why I could go; for I frankly am afraid that if I am away, I'd be as lonesome as I am here—only worse, not having the many visits to Mother's and James's to look forward to. And too, I am not in a position to take a position over so many girls for I feel that my appearance would make me more sensitive than I should feel in a small office....I am to get $8.00 a week until they make room for me in some nearby office, and that will no doubt be New York— and I hate to think of it.

Now that I have told you—don't you think I am truly the original "Jonah"? I might fill a few pages with the story of how this has shocked me—and how I spent three days in despair, thinking of ditching it all and taking up again the life of the least resistance. But, instead, I will tell you that I have come to the frame of mind the little yellow dog was in, who got so tired of running away from wicked boys who wanted to kick him, that he backed up to every little boy whom he saw with his foot raised ready to kick.

Your interesting letter deserves a better answer but I'm sure you will understand when I say right now I can't think of anything except that it is up to me again to get together my little things and go on—and on....

"Philadelphia stands for the old life—
and Canada for the place where
I was, for the only time in my life, free."

PART TWO: 1913-1922

Mrs. M. Jones
Apartment 8, Sherbrooke West
Mrs. Mark Howe   Montreal, Quebec
Cotuit, Massachusetts   August 21, 1913

I ARRIVED HERE BY RAIL WITHOUT MISHAP, AND WAS MET BY MY   69 ⊠
employer and his daughter. I took breakfast with them and then
went to our office. As I told you, I was to have a contract, and I
signed up for one year, as did Mr. Kaufmann. And I thought I was
doing well, to be assured of $50.00 a month.

It was only a few hours later that I found the joker in the
contract. This is the most expensive place in North America to live.
It used to be the cheapest and now is acceded to be the most
expensive. It is claimed that the land boom made the change. At
any rate, I find that the most miserable stenographer starts at
$50.00, fresh from the schools, and that $75.00 to $100.00 a
month is the average wage for girls who would get $40.00 in Phila.,
or $50.00 in New York. The first thing, Saturday, I went to find
quarters—and room and board is entirely out of the question. For
the sort of place I would live in wouldn't consider less than $50.00 a
month—or my salary in full. A room and getting one's meals out,
was better; but the room I have, I am paying $22.00 a month
for—and that is mild, in a place where there is a modern bathroom.

Then, when I went about to get my meals, I found my $50.00 would just keep me. So I (on Tuesday) had it out with my employer. I told him that I would not abide by my contract, since I found he had tricked me, knowing I was in ignorance of the prices that prevail here and what the services of a stenographer are worth. He denied all this at first; but when I confronted him with facts, and he saw I was sincere in my statement that I would at once go back to the States, he agreed to give me $60.00 to start. And with that I was satisfied. For though positions of the sort I hold pay much more here, I must not forget the fact that my appearance might make getting a position hard. And too, a working knowledge of French is *absolutely* essential before one can get any position: in our office I have the assistance of two underclerks who are born "pea soups," as they are called here (either in derision or jestingly, I don't know which)—and I get assistance from them when I have to send out a letter to a French correspondent. . . .

In the place where I have this room is a young woman (when I say "young woman," I mean, "unmarried") who has a large room with housekeeping privileges; and she is a teacher—originally from Massachusetts—but a typical old maid. She has had me in for tea on Sunday; and now I have made her to like me, because I take her dog out at night, and bathe, and feed it (when I have something). And too, she likes it because I like to read her books— which are, in the main, classics. Now, starting on Monday last, she is doing some private teaching, and will for two months and longer, if she gets more pupils. I came up there Tuesday night, and she was out; but outside her door, the boy had left her chops, etc. . . . . I saw on her door a note saying she wouldn't be home until 7:30—almost an hour away. I went down to the janitor and had him to open the door; and I took the things in. . . . And I prepared her little table and had the chops done just so—so that when she came in, we sat down to as cosy and nice a dinner as one could want. . . . Miss Brown was elated. In fact, she was so grateful, she cried a little—and then told me she had not had a meal prepared for her—except in boarding houses—since she was nineteen, when her mother died in Springfield, Mass. I take it she is about forty-two or forty-five. Since then, I gave her—or rather, insisted that she take—13 cents more from me, as my share, making my dinner 25 cents: which is cheaper by 25 cents than the modest meal I could buy. Since then, we have come to this apartment: I am home by six o'clock, and she, not until 7:30. I am to pay 25 cents for each meal, and prepare it in her place for both of us. And on Sundays I am her guest for breakfast, tea and supper—as a sort of return for my preparing the food the rest of the week—and on Sunday she does the cooking.

Don't you think that I was lucky to be able to make such an arrangement? But here's the rub: I don't know a thing about cooking, other than just guessing. Even when I fry or broil a chop, I have to take if off the oven and taste it to see if it's done—I can't judge by looking at it. Frances McCoy spoiled me when we were in N.Y., for she can cook by guessing as well as any professional chef. Yesterday I tried to get a cookbook. . . . If you have one and it is not being used, I should like to borrow it, or have it to keep, if you don't ever really use it. You will understand that I don't want you to buy one for me, for I should feel like a beggar then. Miss Brown said she would buy one if you hadn't an old one; but I won't let her, for I don't know what she earns, or a thing about her conditions. But I do know the school teachers are not overly well paid here in the Protestant schools, as the government is Catholic. I do know that she said her hat she wears to her work is eight years old. I don't know whether that is eccentricity or inability to buy another one.

The hills here are terrible and make walking out far from a pleasure after working hard all day. I don't seem to mind them as much as I did in the beginning, so I have hopes that eventually I won't mind them at all. I will, when I can afford it, buy a pair of walking shoes—the kind that lace almost to the knee. . . .

Do you know that to bring Poke here costs $50.00? I had it firmly fixed in my mind that I would try to bring her with my second month's salary—but when I learned this on Saturday last, I was completely knocked out. Of course, I spent a terrrible night Saturday. I don't know how I will ever bear to think that I can't ever have her—or even, perhaps, never see her again.

I will have to close now, for this subject makes me very miserable and my head is aching. I did want to tell you only the nice things—and now I have told you the misery I am in, too, about my little Poke. I will be able to think of it calmly after a while, but now it hurts dreadfully.

I trust your family is well. I think often of you, and it seems ages since I had a letter from you—but know it was my fault for not writing sooner.

ℭ 70   I AM IN RECEIPT OF YOUR LETTER AND SNAPSHOT ENCLOSED, ALSO THE cookbook, which came last week. I really did not like your having bought the book, but since it is just what I wanted, (even better than I ever thought it could be), I haven't the nerve to story and say I am not pleased. . . .

I haven't heard a word from Mr. Welsh since I have been here, which is more than a month now. . . . I have an idea [Ira Benjamin] may come here—that is, I mean to Canada—sometime. He seems to think there is much to be had for the young man here. In fact, long before I came here, he always spoke of Canada as a desirable place—though he always meant Western Canada.

Mrs. Mark Howe
Brimmer Street, Boston   *Montreal, October 5, 1913*

ℭ 71   I AM ATTENDING TO THE USUAL SUNDAY THINGS—WASHING MY HEAD, fixing my nails, feet and hands, massaging my face, etc. I am telling you all this so that you will know how I am spending the day. In fact I spend every Sunday like this, except usually I break the day up to go to church in the morning and then to meals. Today I have not been out yet. . . .

Miss Brown and I have been having our food together as before, and I do the cooking of it. Only that soon after the dishes are done, I go down to my own room rather than stay up there until bedtime. Not that I find it more agreeable to do so—but somehow I like to be entirely alone sometimes. By being too much with her, I found, I was falling into her old-lady ways. Goodness knows, I am old enough—but I do like to think I have some youth left and with her it is impossible. For she condemns everything that has anything to do with life and the joy of living. She starts to talk—and it gives me a pain in the ear. Such platitudes and rot! As though any people can be classed off and nicely packeted away, according to a system. I know *every one* individual is different from any other person that has ever existed, for they have a different combination of things in their get-up. The same as so many musical selections have the same notes, only arranged so differently that every piece is a thing apart from any other, though some may be classed along the same lines. According to Miss Brown, all stenographers are subject to the same desires and whims, etc., as are all teachers. She says, being a successful stenographer, I have proven I couldn't ever be anything else successfully. I like to tease her; so I say I expect some day to write short stories successfully—though to date I have never tried to write one single word. It gets her goat (to use the vernacular) when I say that—and I enjoy seeing her getting enraged at my impudence. . . .

How the time does fly! Here it is October 5th again. Last year this time, I was preparing to go to the Wilmington office. How profitless the year has been for me! All I've done is to eat and sleep—and I am not as well off, for being way off here without Poke. I am not making any progress. But wait. As I tell Miss B: as soon as I get to be thirty years old, I will get the quota of wisdom due me—and will then begin to do something toward making my life other than a humdrum, drab existence.

October 28, 1913

I WAS QUITE WORRIED BECAUSE I HAD NO WORD FROM MR. WELSH IN 72 ✂
five or six days—and I felt afraid the visit was off, and I was very disappointed. Then today came a letter, and it has several pleasant things in it. He is coming—and coming directly, and purposely, to Montreal—to see me. . . .

I will get a vacation around the holidays—two weeks. I'd love to see Babis—so much so, that I may put up with the other things I don't like at James's house, to spend a while with her. The idea is this: if I can leave my room here and not have to *pay rent*, I could go, railroad fare and all, for the amount it would cost to stay here—and perhaps just a few extra dollars. I feel if I went, I could bring Poke back—and perhaps save much on her entry, for with a person it doesn't cost as much as sending her alone. But the fact is, I feel so good at the thought of seeing Potsy that I think I will have to go. . . .

I still get books at the library, but after this one, expect to discontinue doing so, because it is such a long walk to the library, and many times I sit up later than I should to finish a book, so that I can return it in time. It isn't exactly the few pennies for the fine that I think of, but because of the fact that someone may be waiting for the book. I know, many times, I have wanted books and get so provoked because someone kept them out so unnecessarily long. What I intend to do about reading is to read some history. Miss Brown has some of the French Revolution and some American

187

history. They are really reference books, but quite entertaining, too, as I found and, too, instructive—and I am so woefully ignorant about history. Napoleon and Columbus seem to me to have been in some controversy or other—that's what I know about dates. And as for such things as Miss Brown knows—God grant that I never know it! She knows just how many shells were used in the Battle of Bunker Hill and, too, in any other scrimmage, in any other war, with any country. . . .

I did not eat lunch today to write this, but to write you is like a good meal, especially when I get fat letters—they make me so happy, and are so satisfying.

November 10, 1913

☙ 73   I SHALL TELL YOU OF MR. WELSH'S VISIT. . . . I WAS NOT ABLE TO MEET HIS train, because it came in just when I had to be at work. But I arranged to be off Thursday after lunch; and I wrote that in a note, and left it at the Windsor, to where Mr. Welsh was going. So at twelve, I hurried home and cleaned up, and put on the white waist you sent me, then went to the hotel and found Mr. Welsh awaiting me, seated in the lobby. He thought I looked remarkably well; and after he gave me the little gifts and note, we walked out. It was a bright day, but the coldest we have had so far. In fact, it snowed just a tiny bit. . .As he expressed a desire to see my room, I took him there. I live on a very fine street, the widest in the city, and the main "walking" thoroughfare, as it is only two blocks from the main business street. We walked along, and Mr. Welsh asked me what this building was, and that building. Then he spied a building which has a very good-looking exterior and looks much like a school, with the name *John Ruskin* on it. He stopped, and said: what is this? and I said, "This is where I live." He looked at me, incredulous—but it was so. For while this is an apartment house, its exterior is built along simple and quite odd lines—and no doubt the owner of it knew what he started out to make it appear like, for the idea is carried out all thru the place. Mr. Welsh was delighted. It has a wide lawn in front, and a very old-fashioned rustic gate on the side, and two very old and twisted trees on each side of it. We came in, and Mr. Welsh said he was never more pleased than to see my room—which, while simple, is so clean, and the furnishings sufficient to be comfortable and restful. We then went into the living room and sat there until it was time for Mr. Welsh to start back to his hotel, to get ready for his train to Ottawa....

I was deeply touched at the sight of him in the hotel, when I first saw him, but do not think he has aged, even a little bit, since I saw him in May. He does not, I think, look anywhere near his years, and he is so good-and-healthy....I was quite blue and melancholy all the next day, for I did feel like someone that amounted to something when I saw Mr. Welsh—but after he left, I felt so alone and useless in this big world. Miss Brown was at work, and Mr. Welsh left before she was thru, so she didn't see him. But she has friends of her own that she goes to visit, and I didn't want to share Mr. Welsh with her, anyway. Somehow, now, with Mr. Welsh come and gone, it doesn't seem as though he was here. It was all over so soon. I don't know why, but I have felt more alone and lonesome, since he was here, than before.

I have some hopes of going to the States for the holidays, but I don't know whether I will go or not. I will see later. Just now, it doesn't seem as though I ought to go—although I would love to see Potsy, and sleep with her again, and feel her hold onto me. She did really love me—for even yet, when she is scolded and spanked a bit, she cries for me, and threatens to tell me of how mean they are to her, when I come. Too, I thought I might bring Poke back with me. But as I am so undecided, I won't think too much about it.

I believe I have told you everything in this and my other long letter. I am enclosing a picture published in a Montreal daily, of Mary Antin. Close to here is a small fruit and grocery store; and occasionally I go there for apples to bake. The wife of the proprietor is a living likeness of Mary Antin, and is also a Russian Jewess. Of course, I noted it the first time I was there. But only the other day, I spoke to her. She was reading while waiting for trade. I asked her what she was reading; and when she told me the name of the book—by Herbert Spencer, which I have since forgotten—I thought: surely she is another Mary Antin. This week, then, I cut out the picture, and I showed it to her without the name or reading showing, and asked her if she knew anyone that looked like her. And she said: "She looks very much like my youngest sister." So I felt I was not so far off. Then I told her who she was—and really, the woman became excited. She couldn't believe that she was really talking to someone who had seen the wonderful Mary Antin. She told me she had read her books and stories—and, to my surprise, had more knowledge of "Mary Antin" than I had, only had never seen her portrait. I took over to her several of my *Atlantics*, and she promised to keep them clean (the store is none too clean), and she loaned me several books which I had never read, relating to Judaism. She is very poor, and yet has about two- or three-hundred bound volumes of every description and sort. Poorly bound, most of them, and as she said, "bought off a junk dealer," who finds them in the refuse. I asked her if she took any measures to rid them of infectious diseases, and she pooh-poohed the thought—but when I brought her two books home, I put them into the hot oven and left them there overnight. Miss Brown won't sanction my reading them when I tell her of their origin, but I think they are all right after sterilizing them. This Mrs. Goldstein gets her clothing from the same source! and yet reads books that would be Greek to me. I feel great sympathy for her, as I believe she is a genius who has never had a chance. Her husband is a gentleman—if being kind to her, and being well-informed, makes one. He is quite well-mannered, and told me he had studied and mastered French since coming here, but is not robust, and his health interferes with his work. Mrs. Goldstein told me confidentially he had heart trouble, but was not tubercular.

I will close now and go upstairs to prepare tea. This is Miss Brown's day to cook, but she has a raging headache. I went out yesterday, with the idea of buying a luncheon cloth and some doilies, to embroider a bit and give to Miss Brown for a Christmas present; but when I contemplated the work to be done on them, I lost heart—for I know neither my eyes nor my time would make it possible by Christmas. Miss Brown has an occasional visitor—one of the teachers, in for supper—so as we both like to show off a little, I thought to make her one of the luncheon sets which are too expensive, all embroidered, for my purse. I will have to think up something else. I hope when you write you will tell me of Mr. Welsh's visit to you. I hope you and your family are well, and that you will write when you have a chance. Yours lovingly, Maimie

I received a letter from my mother, written in Jewish. I have had Mrs. Goldstein to read it, and though it was nothing of much import, still it was quite touching. It is in answer to my letter saying they had nothing to expect of me. She says she does not want it for her use, but to save for me. I will give her the benefit of the doubt, but will not send any money—for the simple reason that I haven't any to send. As it is, I am only right now $8.00 ahead of my expenses, and I really ought to spend a part of that for a nose atomizer and some cold cream.

November 27, 1913

IT IS A BIT COLD IN MY ROOM, AND MY FINGERS ARE STIFF, BUT I WILL 75 ✂ write in spite of all this, for I feel in the mood. And perhaps at such times when the room is warm, I will be drowsy—and that accounts for some of the long waits between letters.

I received the booklets. Thank you again. The cookbooks had the first attention, for I am beginning to really like "domestic labor"; and hints as to cooking, etc., seem quite interesting—where, before, I used to look on one who found interest in such things as an "old hen," and one who would be likely to have all sorts of time for reading rot of the sort the Sunday papers print on their magazine pages. Possibly, my predeliction is due to the fact that I am sometime going to have a home of my own. (I think I will have to consult one of the clairvoyants of which Montreal boasts many. If so, I may at least have what pleasure I can derive from anticipation.)

The Ballad of Reading Gaol is certainly gruesome. I had a copy—of part of it—that was printed as a prospectus by some publisher who sold Oscar Wilde's complete works, I think. At the time I read it, I felt it was a wonderful poem of its kind, but I couldn't grasp the meaning of but snatches of it. At the time, I excused myself, and (though I did think it a bit over my head) because the poem was incomplete. I felt reasonably sure, had I had it *all* to read, I would have understood it better. Since reading the copy you sent, I find I am still very much at sea. Much of it is Greek to me. Some of it is brutally plain; but when he writes: "Yet each man kills the thing he loves,/ Etc., etc., etc.,/ The coward does it with a kiss,/ The brave man with a sword!"—then, speaking of the man who was hanged, he says: "He had but killed a thing that lived,/ Whilst they had killed the dead"—I would like to understand both of these more than the occasional thing or two in the poem that is beyond my powers of comprehension. If you know, and it is not too much of an explanation, I'd like it immensely if you'd explain it to me, when you write again. I read the entire ballad to Miss Brown, and she seems to understand it even less than I—for I had much to explain to her.

191

I do wish, too, you would tell me what the story is about Oscar Wilde. Miss Brown says she knows his writings are not permitted in the school library. And though she had never read anything about him, or any of his writings, still, she thinks he was supposed to have been very clever—and that is all we know. Further than that, a recent article in a Chicago paper which I see in our office occasionally, had a reprint from one of the London papers to the effect that the story of Mr. Wilde's death was "greatly exaggerated," as Mark Twain said, and that near friends of his were very positive that he was alive. This, of course, makes me feel there is a "story" of some sort about him, which should be quite interesting. Surely, he must have spent no little time in jail to be able to write so bitterly of it.[25]

I do not recall whether I wrote you that I had, among my many experiences, spent some time in the Phila. prison. Perhaps I told you, but I know I've told no one else but Mr. Welsh. And of course my immediate family know it—for it was they who were the cause of my being sent there. I don't think I did tell you; and since I feel in the mood tonight, I will tell you what I remember of it. It was such a terrible experience, and I was only past thirteen years old! It was the regular prison, and not the place of detention that they use now to send juvenile offenders to. I think of it but seldom. Tonight I thought of it due to re-reading *The Ballad of Reading Gaol* and talking about prisons to Miss Brown.

I had left school directly after my father's death, and was put to work in the house, doing the sort of work I despised, because I had never been taught how—and, too, because I loved school and books and the things that school meant. I was thirteen in July, and in September—my second term at the Phila. high school—I was not permitted to go back to school. Prior to my father's death, we had a general servant in the house, and a laundress and scrubwoman who came, each two days in the week. After his death, I was given it all to do but the laundress's work—and I did it very poorly, and always only after receiving severe whippings. In October, or perhaps November, I told a young girl who was librarian in a city library close to my home, of the reason that I did not come for books any more—which was, that my mother wouldn't permit me to read them, and a book for which the librarian wanted to collect 80 cents had been thrown into the fire when I had been found reading it. Of course, I had no 80 cents to pay her, and I was very much ashamed of it. I think this was my original reason for getting work in a neighborhood store, to work at night for a small weekly sum, as a "saleslady." After this—and after a violent scene with my mother, who told me if I didn't like my life at home, that I should get out—I went to the city, and there got a regular job in a department store, at $5.00 a week, though I was only past thirteen years old. I was a "saleslady"—and this store, to this day, is quite the place for men to come during the afternoon hours to make "dates" for the eve. I found I could stay away from dinner, and go along with some boys, and come home and tell some sort of story—and that it was accepted, due to the $5.00 I was bringing home! Once, there was some kind of a fuss again—and when I threatened to leave home, my mother said she hoped it was soon.

Of course, the inevitable thing happened. Some young chap took me to his room; and I stayed three or four days before I put in an appearance in the neighborhood of my home. As I neared our house, a man spoke to me by name, and told me he was a "special officer" and that he had a warrant for my arrest. He took me to the Central Station, which is in the City Hall—the large building which is in the center of the city of Phila. Of course I was terribly frightened—but imagine my horror when I was placed in a cell! It was a horribly filthy, vile-smelling hole. I cried and begged they should send for my mother—and though they did, after awhile, she refused to come. It was nighttime, and there was no light; and I could hear the rats, which I feared more than death. I was terrified, and pleaded to be taken out of there. It was only after I permitted one of the men, who seemed to be in charge at the time, to take all sorts of liberties with me, that I was permitted to come out of the cell; and I sat up for the rest of the night in the room where he, too, sat all night. The man was perhaps fifty, or even older.

In the morning, there was a hearing. My mother was present; and I recall my uncle was with her—and he was acting with her to persuade the "Commonwealth" that I should be sent to some house of refuge as being incorrigible. This uncle is the same one who did me the first wrong, when I was a tiny girl, and any number of times since then. It seemed that in order to prove me immoral, so that I should become a public charge (without excuse to my mother), it would have to be proven that I had committed a crime, and the man produced. A further hearing was demanded for this—as, in my terror, I had told the name and address of the chap, and of course they were going to arrest him. I was led away to the same cell, pleading to my mother, in shrieks, to take me home. It was morning, and not so bad as at night; but as I had nothing to read, and the terrible fear of spending another night there seemed imminent, the hours seemed years. There was only a bench and an exposed toilet in the cell, and it was, as I thought, terrible.

At noon, there were footsteps and the jangling of keys, and the cell was opened. I thought for sure my mother had relented, and I was so grateful. I put on my hat and coat, and came out to the large room—and though I did not see anyone I knew, I was laboring under the delusion that I was being taken home. I saw some men in line, and I was told to get behind the last one. Still, I had no suspicion of what was coming. The line moved, as did I. And oh! what a lot they were! There were perhaps eight men (three Negroes), and they were the dregs and scum of the earth. I looked on them with alarm, and was dismayed that I had to walk with them, though I did not even guess at my destination. We filed down the stairs, and the line in front got outside; and as I was last, I saw them filing into a prison van—the kind called "Black Maria." They are usually painted quite dark, and resemble a closed box with air- or peep- holes on top. It was just at noon; and there were thousands going thru the courtyard, enroute to their lunches. Quite a crowd had gathered to watch the prisoners; and as I saw that, I became so mortified that I could not move—though, due to the imprecations of the guard behind me, I really wanted to. Of course, little ceremony was wasted on me. I was fairly dragged to the van, and thrown in. When I recovered my senses, I found the wagon was moving. The men were each in a compartment. Though there was no door between, there were sheets of iron that made semi-walls, permitting only one person between each wall. Yet they all seemed to disregard this, and sat out on their seats, talking and laughing. The ride lasted perhaps an hour. Time can never efface my impressions thru that ride. Their humor was shocking—such obscenity and scurrility! One of them told me to cheer up, and said he would look out for me after he got out—for he would only get thirty days, whereas no doubt I'd be sent away for a number of years, until I was of age. I then knew for sure I was going to prison—and oh! how I feared it! The ride was probably the worst of the whole harrowing experience.

In the prison, which was the Moyamensing Prison, I was led away by a woman to a room where a man sat before a large book—no doubt to enter the names, etc., of the prisoners. It was to this same prison that my father had given a library of two-hundred books, printed in the Yiddish language, for the benefit of the few Jewish prisoners who were kept there and who could not read English. I recalled, as I stood there, hearing my father speak of the place, and the pity of sending Hebrews there—who generally committed an offense only because they were not familiar with the laws. I was overcome with the thought of what my father would think of my being there; and I don't remember what happened, exactly, only that later, I found myself in a little bed, in what seemed to be another cell. As there was a woman sitting beside me, I did not seem to mind it so much, for I only cried quietly. Presently, the man who had sat by the books came in with a notebook in hand, and asked me many questions, which I recall I answered freely. I know now, that he knew from my name—which was not a common one—that it was my father who had given books and money to help Jewish lawbreakers, and that he communicated with my uncle; but no step was taken by him to have me released from there. I recall hearing him and the woman who sat by me, comment on the fact that I was sent there; and they both didn't seem to understand it. After the man left, the woman brought me some very coarse, rough-looking clothes and took away my own, though I cried dreadfully to not have to put them on. Then they took me to another room, and before I knew what they were going to do, they had combed my hair out—it was cut off to the ears. I was taken back to the cell, which was similar to the one I had occupied in the Central Station, only larger, and had a pallet of straw on a black iron frame bed. Besides, there was a chair and a lamp and a stone floor, and one tiny window, with bars, that faced a courtyard; and on the other side—perhaps three or four yards away—was another wall with the same window, at which I could see faces that were pressed against the bars and fingers clutching them. The woman left me after awhile, and brought me a Bible—for which I was grateful enough. She said the books were all taken that day, but tomorrow she might get me a real book. I entreated her to remain with me—for she was indeed kind, and had much commiseration for me. She assured me she would return as soon as she could. When she left, I went to the window. And immediately I was seen, the persons began to call to me, asking what I was put there for. They were women and, I take

195

it, saturated with the spirit of prison life. I don't think they could see me any plainer than I could them, so they took it I was a woman. From what they said, they could scarcely think me a little girl. There was food brought me. All I can recall of it was that it was given to me in a metal dish that closely resembled a pie plate. I believe I tried to eat it, but couldn't. I had gotten quiet by night, and then the lady returned. And though I had to put the light out, she sat by me until I fell asleep.

I awakened in the night, and then it was that I became panic stricken. I beat on the bars of the cell and cried until someone came. This time, it was a woman and a man. The woman was of the grim-visaged sort, entirely without compassion, and threatened me with all sorts of dire things unless I was quiet. I cannot remember how I passed the remainder of the night, though I do know I did not get back into bed.

The next day, the kind lady came, and I recall she gave me two chocolates that were very stale, and a book which I think was *Robinson Crusoe* or *Pilgrim's Progress*. I found when reading, it did not seem so terrible to be there. I recall I was ashamed of the fact that I didn't seem to mind it so much, and that I rather enjoyed the privilege of reading undisturbed. I was all right until night (or, rather, evening) came, when I became unnerved again. And I must have gotten some privilege thru this lady, for at eight o'clock at night, she took me to another place, where I slept in a bed, with other women in the room. I think it might have been the prison infirmary. Before daybreak she took me back to the cell; and I was given a book, closely printed, of Shakespeare. Some time around twelve, they brought me my clothes, and I was taken back to the Central Police Station. This time, I am glad to say, it was in [a car], accompanied by a maid who belonged to the court.

It seems there was some sort of talk, of which I remember little, but my mother and uncle were there—and then this man took me to the Magdalen Home, where I stayed a year.[26] It is a mild sort of reform school for girls who have gone astray. Though I was the youngest girl there by four years, still, I taught the ones who had little or no schooling, during our school hours. I received absolutely no school training there whatever—except what I derived from teaching girls of seventeen and eighteen their alphabets and the simple sums.

I did not think to tell you this story so thoroughly; but I felt, when I began, I just wanted you to know: then, as I wrote, it seemed to be as though I was writing the story of that particularly ugly part of my life as though it was a narrative. Somehow, I feel now as though perhaps I wrote you this before. If I did, I wish you'd tell me. I want to have a more retentive memory than I seem to have. Perhaps, though, it was to Mr. Welsh I wrote it. I know I wrote it once before.

There are so many things I wanted to write you about. Pertaining to the subject of prison: Miss Brown (who, by the way is Nina Brown...) expressed herself very strongly on this point and some others. She seems very strong in her convictions about things of that order. Her views of a girl who has gone astray are of such a nature that I feel like a thief in the night when I hear her talk. Tonight, particularly, she was very vehement, and I just had to come away. Somehow, I feel I want to tell her, and not sail under false colours. I have a feeling that perhaps she guesses some things about me and expects me to tell her; but, somehow, she has never inspired me to confidences. I haven't even explained to her how it is that I am not with Mr. Jones; and though generally she is well bred, she asks pointed and leading questions. Last week—Thursday, Friday, Saturday and Sunday—I was laid up with an intense headache. Fortunately for me, it came so that Sunday was one of the sick days, so I only lost three days' pay, and not four. Miss Brown came down each night with some hot soup for me. I just could not eat; and naturally it must have made her peevish after all her trouble. Sunday she was down with me the best part of the day; and Sunday night, I gave way to my feelings and cried a lot. She was very kind, but in an impatient way. When I got quiet, she began quite a homily, which she prefaced with the remark that she had wanted to tell me this for some time. It was that she thought I ought to go home (no doubt she thinks I could live home without work), for I was not qualified to be out in the world with others, and that the intense headaches were the result of trying to do with one eye what it requires two to do with—and a whole lot more. The general trend of her remarks makes me think she does not realize the real position I am in. She said, tonight, that tomorrow being Thanksgiving in the States, no doubt I'd get a box from home. She has the wild idea that my people would be likely to send me something. I know this was said with an idea of drawing me out; but I said, "Perhaps." Now, from all these little things, I feel that in a measure I am perhaps not doing right, and it worries me; for I wouldn't want to be eating at her table every night and partaking of her friendship, if the conditions are such that, if she knew, she would not have been willing. Shall I tell her? She doesn't seem to have very much charity where things of that sort are concerned; and I am afraid. . . . I am really sorry for her—or, in fact, anyone who cannot open up their hearts enough to be charitable toward girls who have gone wrong. Otherwise, Miss B. is really a fine woman. She has a fine character and is as honest as a die. I was thinking about a Christmas gift for her, and she settled the whole question by telling me just what she wanted me to make for her. Doesn't that show a sound mind? And yet I hate to deceive her further.

I must not forget to tell you that I did not get the October *Atlantic* though I have received the November number you sent today.

I saw Mrs. Goldstein, the little fruit woman, last night, and she seems to have a frightful cold, and so does 'most every person one meets. Thank Fortune I have so far escaped this. I bought some aspirin tablets, and gave her some. She seemed in much misery and had nothing to take; and though she said she would buy some, when I recommended aspirin, I felt sure she wouldn't. She had the book which I found her reading the first time I engaged in conversation with her. It is some treatise on sociology I believe. Too, she had a book called *The Age of Fable.* She told me, too, that she liked Dickens, but so far had been unable to find anything (meaning in the junk) but a copy of *The Old Curiosity Shop*— which happens to be the only Dickens I own myself. It seems she likes lighter reading than Spencer, but only likes standard books— and it seems as though the junk heap only gets very deep stuff or the sort of light reading which she would disdain. She told me she had read much Swinburne—and had memorized "Excelsior" and "A Psalm of Life" when she first learned to speak English.

As yet, I have not fully decided not to go to Phila. for the holidays, yet I don't really think I will make it. I seem to lose time thru headaches, and of course, I don't want to go unless I can bring Poke back with me. . . .

I had wanted to write about the possibity of writing my autobiography, as you suggested, but as I couldn't seem to feel sure of my own opinions on the subject, I didn't write. There seems so many reasons why I could not do it. For instance, the little time—even if it only took fifteen minutes a day—is so hard to spare. There are so many tasks—stockings always to be darned, letters to write, sometimes work for the office—that I don't feel I could accomplish much, if I did start. I really feel I could write it—if I could write it a bit at a time. And maybe I will try it; and, if it goes easy, keep on with it.

My dear friend,   *December, 1913*
I WILL WRITE YOU, THOUGH IT WILL COST ME A NICKEL. AM I NOT   76 ❧
reckless! By writing now, I will be obliged to ride to my work.

I have a most interesting tale to tell you, but as I should want to tell it to you in its entirety, I will not have time this morning—so will just give you an idea what it is about. The girl who is maid-of-all-work in the apartment here—seventeen years old, just from England since August—and I have found out she is to be a *mother.* It is a very sad thing. The girl is not the "Biddy" type of a servant. In fact, she speaks better English than I. She is very tiny and quite pretty. I have tried, even before this, to be kind to her, for her story is quite sad. I discovered her condition by chance; and though she expects the child during December, no one in the house knew it—though now Miss B. and I know it, for we are going to help her. It will mean no trip, and no Christmas, to speak of, for we are going to spend our money for materials (in fact yesterday we each spent $5.00) and necessaries. Oh, I should like to tell you it all, but I haven't the time. I couldn't go to Phila., as I would like to; for, due to loss of time at work, the amount of my savings is small—so that now, this trouble of Ethel will use up the amount, and I will stay here. I am so tickled that I have money to help her, that I don't mind not going so much—although I do feel bad about poor Poke, for I had planned to have her here. I will try not to think of it too much.

Poor Oscar Wilde! I don't care how degenerate he was, I don't think he should have been sent to prison for it. His writings, if they were all you say, proved his calibre was good, but he was unfortunate. I have always contended that about such people.

They are born deformed (a sort of moral twist), and should be pitied as much as a body that is born with a twisted back. I knew a girl once who had a brother with such tendencies. He was a most refined person—in fact, he was the quintessence of everything gentlemanly. Yet his poor sister had many times to go to Sing Sing to visit him, at various times that he spent terms there. He was so mild that the tales told of him were incredible. I know he was a true gentleman, but he was born with this mental or moral disease. His mother committed suicide because of this in his nature, which she recognized from the time he was perhaps fifteen years. I knew these people intimately and it brought to me a thorough knowledge of the son's troubles—and he was positively deserving of pity, and only inhuman people could censure him.

I am acting on your advice about refraining from telling Miss Brown of my past. Since this new happening about Ethel, I have found that she is not altogether without charity about such things. She did say she thought unless we took Ethel in hand at once, she would perhaps become a bad girl, for—"once a girl does such a thing she has no fibre, and will naturally drop, and nothing on Heaven or Earth can lift her unless she is helped in the very beginning". . . .

I find I have now only a few more minutes, so I will make ready to close. Miss B. walks with me to the car this morning. She is a bit cross with me because I had Mrs. Goldstein in here last night. She said there is a possibility that my eye became inflamed the other night thru my associations with the crowd from the fruit store— and last night when Mrs. Goldstein came here, Miss B. was furious. . . .

I will run on now, though Miss Brown hasn't come down yet. Do you know, she never lets me see her with even her collar off? And I can't understand it. I told her once I wouldn't care if she came in while I was bathing, and she looked at me as though I was saying something to be excruciatingly funny. We are going to have a machine sent home for Miss B. to run up the slips for Ethel's baby. It will cost us $3.00 for the month. Miss B. was going to make me a present of some drawers, but now we are using the money for the baby. I will tell you about it in a letter soon, and also tell you about losing my eye, as you asked me to. Yours lovingly, Maimie

It is a long time since I have written such a harum-scarum letter.

My dear Friend,   *December 5, 1913*

I AM IN RECEIPT OF YOUR POST CARD AND LETTER. I HAVE WANTED SO
much to write you every day, for I have much of real interest to tell
you. But it doesn't seem possible to make the waking hours stretch
out more. I find unless I get my full eight hours sleep, I am not able
to do anything the next day, and the time skipped from my sleep
does not profit me much.

I do not want to tell you about Ethel until I can tell you
everything about her, from the first that she came here to work.
And I am sure I can find time to do it soon, but so far, I haven't
been able—for since last Wednesday, I have been clerk thru the
day, and from six on, servant girl—and in-between times, almost
everything else. . . .

As for Ethel, she is in bed at Dr. Ronayne's hospital, awaiting
the birth of her child, which is due every day. She is a sweet-faced
little English girl, and the man is in England, living near her home
in Essex. He is now in his last year at a big English university. Her
story is not the usual kind, except in the one respect. I will write
you fully before the week is out about her. Her story is one of the
saddest in many details. My sympathies are all with her, and I am
doing the housework at night so that the position stays open for
her. I could use some money for her, although we are getting along
first-rate. I would like, though, to make some Christmas for her,
and for that, there is no money. Miss B. is working with me in our
plans for Ethel, but there is a coldness between us. And I hope to
make it all up for tonight; for I've thought about it all forenoon, and
life is too short to stop to quarrel about little things. And as she is
older and more "sot" in her ways, I will "golopize" tonight. Her
crossness started some time ago, about Mrs. Goldstein, and since
then she has found innumerable small things to keep her cross.
Among other things, she is now harboring an idea that my
conversation is not "elevating"—this, she told me, because I want
to find out about what Ethel has to go thru, and all the whyfores.
She thinks this immodest. I had a real interesting conversation
along these lines with a young intern at the hospital on Wed.
night—and Miss B. had to take some whiskey to steady her nerves
when we got home! If I had time, I could write you for hours.

My dear Friend,   *December 20, 1913*

I HAVEN'T BUT TWENTY MINUTES, BUT I WANT TO TELL YOU OF THE VERY newest happenings here. Mrs. Goldstein's store burnt out. Not entirely, but almost so. It happened Sunday night, but I didn't hear of it until last night, which was the first time I had a chance to go over there. My first thought was perhaps Mr. Goldstein had made the fire himself. I know this thought will shock you, but...I know among the Jews this is a frequently done thing, especially if there is sufficient insurance carried, and if business is bad. I knew their business was very bad; in fact, the story goes that Montreal is having a great slump, due to a boom recently that had no real foundation. At any rate, I went over there thinking it was a small conflagration that would net them a little insurance money and that they would resume their business exactly as before. But when I came there, I found the place boarded up and in a really horrible condition. The inside of the store is burnt completely, and will not be any further good—stock and fixtures. Of course, it wasn't much at its best—but it is entirely gone. No one was on the premises, so I looked about, and found Mrs. Goldstein in a neighbor's house. She was dry-eyed, but she is suffering much mental anxiety as to their future. She knew, no doubt, that I would think it was a "made fire," so she hastened to show me their policy—which only called for $150.00 in case of a total loss; and I could see that the small amount of the face of the policy would not have been sufficient incentive for them to "make" a fire. She said they closed the store Sunday night, about 9:30, and went to a nearby coffee house to have a hot cup of tea and talk with the people who congregate there—mostly socialists and deep thinkers. They were only there fifteen minutes, when a boy came running to tell them breathlessly that their place was burning. By the time they got there, the engines were there; and though the fire did enough damage, the gutting of the place with water finished it up completely. Since then, an inspector has called from the insurance company, and has offered them $100.00 in full settlement; and since the insurance company doesn't call it a "total loss," she will have to take it. Mr. Goldstein was in bed, having become quite sick over it. The Jewish people in her neighborhood are good to her, but it is indeed pitiful. She told me that two weeks ago, a man came asking them to buy further insurance, but as she had a payment to make on a loan with which the business was originally bought, she told him to call after

New Year's again. I could not, of course, do much for her; but I sat down at a table there and wrote about fifteen letters to various creditors, explaining conditions and asking whether they would extend them further credit, if they used the $100.00 the insurance company will give them to rebuild the store. Poor Mrs. Goldstein! Her only good clothes were all burned—for, she said, she had on her working clothes. I took over the green waist you sent me, and the suit. I did not like to, but I really felt I should. She said she would return it, and wouldn't hear of it as a permanent gift, but just as a loan, until she can make something—but I don't think I'd care to wear it after her. I would rather have given her other things I had—but as that was the warmest, outside of my heavy coat, I couldn't do anything else. Miss Brown is too small to give any apparel, but she sent two pairs stockings and a black woolen under-skirt and a canton flannel nightgown. Oh, yes—I gave her an old pair of shoes. She does not cry, but it is indeed sad. I told her she had much to be thankful for, that *they* were not burned—and she said she wishes she had been, if only a little, so that they would take her to the hospital to rest out.

Well, I haven't time to read this over and I really don't like to tell you especially now for I think it will make you feel badly. It surely did me. I cannot seem to get time to write you about Ethel—but, so far, no baby has come; and all night, for three nights, she has suffered intense pains. Dr. Ronayne said it may require instruments and delivery by force. Yours lovingly, in haste—Maimie

Please don't let this letter full of bad news depress you. Just think how good it is that my eye is perfectly sound; and Dr. Byers said he wished he had as good eyesight as mine—and he also said I was in perfect physical condition, and he gave me a pair of dumbbells to exercise with.

Saturday afternoon, December 20, 1913

THE OBJECT OF THIS LETTER IS TO ASK A LOAN OF MONEY, IF YOU CAN 80 &
spare it, for Mr. and Mrs. Goldstein; and I will stand sponsor for it—that is, I will collect it and see that it is sent you, as I get it. The amount is $50.00, to be repaid out of the cash taken in thru the week, and to be paid out at the rate of $5.00 a week, for ten weeks. This I ask only because I don't recall ever knowing of a case more

worthy—and since immediate action must be taken, I can only apply to you. For to write Mr. Welsh would take a host of explanations, since I have never told him of my friendship with Mrs. Goldstein.

I will write you briefly what their plans are. In the most part, I have made this plan possible:

They are abandoning their old place that was burned up almost completely, and will start out afresh and in a different line—although somewhat similar to their other business. They will take (or, rather, today Mr. G. is seeing the landlord, whom I have already written to) a small store, situated right next door to a little coffee or tea house patronized entirely by Jewish people with socialistic tendencies, and who also are given to reading of the better sort of books—English, and Jewish translations. The store is tiny, but the rent is quite large, as the neighborhood is quite alive with Jewish people and, of course, rents are large because of it. Now, it is my plan that they sell newspapers; English and American magazines of the popular sort, as well as Jewish versions of them. Then, they will carry a stack of Jewish translations of various books—and, as they buy more, run a sort of circulating library, charging five cents a book.

In the store they will have some of the fruits, candies, etc., of the sort they had in the other store—but not so much—and tobacco (for that class of Jews are inveterate smokers), and post cards. And as the *pièce de résistance*, Mrs. Goldstein will have a place arranged so the persons who pay 25 cents a month can get their mail—and sell stationery, etc.—and have a table where they can have the free use of pen and ink to answer [letters]. Then, in conjunction with that, Mrs. Goldstein will let it be known that she will write English letters for 5 cents apiece, provided the stationery is furnished, and Jewish letters, too—although she will perhaps not have much trade for that, except that she writes one occasionally for me to my mother.

The insurance company sent a check for $100.00, out of which they had to pay a broker $15.00 for some service he rendered the day after the fire, before I arrived on the scene, to help them thru by seeing people for them.

Now then, the store is to be taken with a view to fitting it up, starting Monday morning. There will be rent, deposit for gas and electricity—and the few fixtures they will have to have to start with, and the few things they cannot get on credit. This will take all of the cash they have on hand and, besides, a few dollars they are borrowing from a young man who lives in the house where they are being sheltered. (He had $25.00 saved with an idea of using it to bring a brother over from Russia, but he is loaning it to them, and he will let the brother wait until the money can be gathered again. There is no time limit on his loan.)

I have no money to lend, for my money for my trip home went for Ethel—who hasn't yet had her child. (But Miss B. is there now, and the latest report from Dr. Ronayne was that he thinks it will positively be here by Christmas.) Instead of the money, though—I have written and written, for the past three days, and already have arranged for the daily papers (six Montreal English papers and two Montreal French papers, two Montreal Jewish papers, and two New York Jewish Papers), *Saturday Evening Post*, and a host of magazines that are worked on the "return" system. I have had an extension of credit made possible at the fruit place, but the rest takes cash.

Here is what the $50.00 is for. In Canada, two weeks starting the Monday before Christmas [a vacation] is given to a vast number of people. There seems to be many reasons for this, but I think the fact that there are some Catholic holidays in-between Christmas and New Year makes this plausible. During those two weeks, a great many of the Jews are without employment—without and mostly with pay...and as they have much time and their regular pay, it is quite the harvest time for those who have anything for them to buy.

Mrs. G.'s store is right in the heart of the neighborhood where they spend their time—St. Lawrence Boulevard—and yet, as the holiday starts so soon, to get any of this festivity money, she will have to get the place in immediate shape. With $50.00 they could make several payments for bills outstanding, and get three times the $50.00 worth of stock, from the jobbers in the immediate neighborhood.

Needless to say, I was not asked to raise this; but when I volunteered to, and told Mrs. Goldstein from whom, she was quite happy again—though I told her there was a possibility that, due to Christmas, you could not get it for her.

This, then, is how the matter stands. If you can help her and will, I will—as I said in the early part of the letter—attend personally to the collections and sending it back. I might mention that a bank draft or an express money order would be better than a check, if the money is to be sent at all. For, in the case of a check, there is no one I could take it to except Mr. Kaufmann (my employer), and that would give him a wrong impression—for no matter how I explained, he might think I had all that money for a Christmas gift. And as for the Goldsteins: if they tried to cash a check for over $5.00 or $10.00, they would have to wait until it was sent to the bank for collection—and the means would defeat the end, for to get some of the holiday money, they would need the stock at once.

I am home, and my vacation starts from today, so I hope to get the long letter off to you about other things. I am going to act as servant in Ethel's place for the two weeks. I don't mean just off and on, but in full reality, as Mrs. Noakes would get another maid if I didn't. And yet I don't think I will mind it, for it will be sort of playing house—especially since it is only a five room apartment, with no fol-de-rols to make for extra work. It is very simply furnished, but in very good taste. I will await your answer with some anxiety. Mrs. G. will be here at six to get dinner, as Mrs. Noakes asked her.

January, 1914

CR 81   IT IS NOW 3:00 A.M., AND AS I AM RATHER SLEEPLESS—THE FIRST TIME in ages—I got out of bed to write, rather than waste the time "just thinking.". . .

Mrs. Goldstein is doing quite well in her store. This week she borrowed (through a loan agency that, unfortunately, makes her pay 16 2/3 per cent per month) some money, and is sending Mr. Goldstein to California. He will find something to do there, and if he gets well, will return. The doctors claim he has no tuberculosis, but a form of sciatica, and that California climate will help him. I saw him, and it is my belief he will not live long. Her business has paid since the first day she opened, though she has had scarcely any stock, but, the weather becoming so cold, there is much gathering at her place to read and write, for she has a big stove in the middle of the store which is cheery and inviting. I very foolishly (since I have so much else to do) promised to help her with any special work for which I am adapted, and now I find it takes a large slice of my time.

I spent two hours there, three times last week, ordering stock (by mail), selecting her Valentine stock and post cards, looking over bills and arranging her cashbook. Besides, while I am there, how can I refuse to write such letters as the poor souls ask me? One wants knowledge of a brother who went (two years ago) to a mining camp of the Canadian Pacific Railroad, and I wrote to them and to the town where she believed he went. Another (a young boy) asked that I write a lawyer about a settlement of $30.00 due him from the City Traction Company for injuries that have crippled him, but for which he was only given $50.00 damages— $20.00 of which is the lawyer's, and $30.00 his—which he hasn't been able to collect from the lawyer since August, though the Traction Company paid said lawyer. It doesn't seem much to do for them, [yet] how it does rob me of time!

Then I want to tell you of Ethel. And while I am at it, I will go into her story, which I remember now I only promised to write you. She is a tiny little thing, doesn't look over fourteen or fifteen years, except that she insists she is older. She came here to work as housemaid in August, just about the same time I came from the States. She was not inclined to be talkative—so I knew little about her until I knew all about her. She did not like Miss Brown, so for that reason I saw little of her, except on Sat. afternoon and Sundays, when I was at home more. Occasionally, thru the milder weather, she went to Sunday night service with me; and we often talked of Poke, for she had a dog, too, in the "old country."

Then, right after Thanksgiving Day, on a Sunday, I heard from the lady here that Ethel had been ill. About four o'clock, I passed her in the hall, and she looked very sad. I was struck by her appearance, and was very cross with myself for not having sought her out. For though she was general maid here, she was not a "Biddy"; and as she was young, I should have tried to make it pleasant for her.

I went to her door and knocked; and when she came to the door, I could see she had been crying—and bitterly, too. I came in and told her I was lonesome, and pretended not to see her swollen eyes. I insisted that she come to my room and I would ask Miss B. if I could bring down some tea; and she came. I got the tea, and she was making an attempt to be pleasant, but it was a poor one. I knew the girl was very unhappy, and I determined to try to help her if I could—but first I'd have to find out what was wrong. I talked generally without appearing too personal (for she is a person with the finer instincts) and I [still] didn't have an idea what was wrong [by the time she had] to go to get tea for the family—agreeing to return at seven and go to church with me. She got up and started out of the door—and it came to me with a start that Ethel was pregnant. For it was then as plain as day, though I hadn't a suspicion that anything of that sort was wrong. I was shocked—in fact, stymied. And when she returned a moment later for something she'd forgotten, I was as though ill, and I couldn't speak. It truly seemed incredible—the girl never was away from the house for a second. At any rate, when I regained my composure I decided to, in some way, get her to confide in me, and if possible help her. She evidently knew what was wrong, and perhaps might do herself an injury.

When she returned at seven—she looked infantile, really. I couldn't credit my eyes; and with a red wooly tam o'shanter and a short sweater-coat, she looked not over nine or ten years. She is tiny and blonde, without being really fair. Her spirits picked up en route to church; and in church she sang the hymns with some vim. On our return, as we neared the house, I noticed she again became anxious and was quite another person. Try as I would, I couldn't seem to make the right move and get one personal word out of her. We came in; and at the door in the apartment, I said, "Oh, Ethel, come in a minute, it seems so lonesome in here." She came in. I turned on the electric light and turned around, and happened to look square in her eyes. She quailed, and lowered her eyes—and I saw her tremble. I put the light out directly, and turned around and took her in my arms—and of course it was just the right thing. She cried quietly, sobbing a little, at first quite loud. I let her cry for a while, and could not help but cry myself. It was such a pity! The worst of it was, I couldn't account for her condition . . . . The only man here, Mr. Noakes, . . . would not be guilty of so heinous a crime.

Still in the dark, I led Ethel to the bed. And we sat down on it; and in some way I let her know I understood what was wrong, but that I was her friend and would serve her to the utmost. She did not speak for awhile, sobbing gently and hiding her face in my lap.

Finally, by being patient and drawing her out, I got the story. She came from England in that condition—and it was the real reason she came. She is one of a large family of children—the oldest, in fact—the father, quite worthless, and the mother about a bed-ridden invalid, from abuse and hard work raising the family. Where they lived, they were thought much of, Ethel's grandparents on both sides having been of the better class. So when Ethel had to go to work to help keep the family, one of the wealthy families took her in, to make of her a maid. Not a servant: I mean the sort that attends to the personal wants of the lady of the house, or some such thing.

While there, a nephew of these people, whom they had adopted for a son—due to having no children of their own—became very friendly with Ethel. In fact, she went to school with him as a little girl, and he was then her "boy," as she says it. He, it seems, was serious in his intentions; and when he openly declared himself, his people immediately asked Ethel to go. The town is very small, and the chap was only nineteen and a second year student at a college. So Ethel decided to come to Canada with some other girls of the same town who were to go under surveillance of some Christian lady and her husband. They were to go with an idea of getting work. This boy promised her he would come as soon as he graduated. In the meantime, she was to get a position and help her mother by sending back the money. As developments would have it, the party wasn't ready to leave; and Ethel still being about, she and the boy saw much of each other. His people, fearing he might entangle himself with her, sent him off to finish his studies in a far-off and much larger university. This was in early spring; and for some reason, the leaving of the party was postponed, and Ethel did not go. Again, the plans were made to go; and this time she did go. Now, it seems in the first instance, when she thought she was surely going, he was preparing to go, too; so they went for a walk to spend their last evening together. And during that walk out in the country roads, she says, they committed the one indiscretion (and subsequent investigating by Dr. R. proved this true). In between the time this happened and her departure, she wrote him, and he wrote—but not the loverlike letters she expected. Then, when she found out the pitiful condition she was in, she wrote him; and he never answered. Though since coming here—when she wrote once imploring he should write her—he wrote a cold, curt note that I saw, asking her to please not trouble him, as he was engaged to marry; and as he had never, as he understood it, given her any reason to think herself anything but a friend, he did not wish to be troubled. He should really be made to suffer for this, but she will not have it. And, too, she says it would kill her mother, who is sick and has been getting worse since I took Ethel's affairs in hand—for her letters to E. are written by the nurses that come to take care of her daily.

Now after I learned all this, I cautioned Ethel not to do anything further; for she told me she had been contemplating suicide that very night. She surely arranged it—as to whether she would have had the courage, or not, I don't know. I talked and talked, and then took her to her own room to put her to bed—but later felt uneasy, and went in and brought her back to sleep the night out with me.

She somehow did not want Miss Brown to know. . . . The baby was due in one month's time, and yet, except you knew, you'd never guess she was in that condition. At any rate, I went straight ahead, and mostly on my own nerve. And now Ethel is ready in about two or three days to leave the hospital, and has a baby boy.

The only help in money I got was from Mr. Welsh, who sent $70.00, $30.00 of which went to England, to Ethel's mother—representing two months money that Ethel was want to send her. The room cost $15.00 a week and $15.00 for the delivery; and she has been there since a week before Christmas.

The other help was from Miss Brown, who has aided me untiringly. And now Ethel is devoted to Miss B. And Miss B. has "bagged" school on pleas of headache, to wait on Ethel during the water famine, and now is just Ethel's slave. And she used to call Ethel *that chit* downstairs" because Ethel refused once to go [on] an errand for Miss B.

So that Mrs. Noakes will take Ethel back, and so that she get no other girl—I have helped with the housework. And thru the vacation I had I did all that I know how to do and could do, without water, in cleaning house. The boy was a fine youngster when he was born; but during the water famine, he took convulsions and has never been quite the same. He was born Christmas Day; and as Ethel would not have him named after his father or her own, and as she asked that I name him, I called him after Mr. Welsh—George Herbert Holmes (Holmes is Ethel's name)—and if he lives to be a man, he has a splendid man to pattern after. Dr. Ronayne, at whose sanitarium Ethel is staying, said if the baby pulls thru the next month it will be fine. But it is having a hard time, and this is due to the lack of water. One day Dr. Ronayne informed me I had to take Ethel and the baby home—and if it wasn't that I cried so hard, he would have made me do it. For on three days in succession, all the water in the sanitarium, for thirty-five people, was less than four gallons—and water at 80 cents a gallon when you could get it—[27]

February, 1914

IN GOING THRU MY PAPERS, I FIND THE LETTER WHICH I PROMISED YOU 82 ☉ about Ethel. And since it is almost complete, I'll send it enclosed without attempting to finish it—as so much has happened that it would take years to write it all out in such full detail.

Directly after writing the enclosed pages, George Herbert, Ethel's boy, died. Perhaps it was for the best, as he was in convulsions most of the time, and as Ethel could not nurse him and hadn't money enough to keep him with her. Ethel was terribly stunned, for he died after she had received much encouragement on that day, from Dr. R., that he would pull through.

We bought a [cemetery] plot; Miss B. and I and Ethel followed the coffin, and all three of us caught terrible colds. As I am very strong and not susceptible to colds (since I never take any care of myself), I shed mine in a few days. But Ethel and Miss B. became very ill—so much so, that Ethel was thought to be unable to recover. I did not stay away from work, but nursed them all the time I was home.

We all three ran up some frightful bills, what with the water famine trouble, the birth and death of little George Herbert, and then Ethel's severe sickness; and, truly, I pretty nearly lost my nerve, if you know what that means. I mean by that, I got to the stage where I didn't think I could ever come up straight with the world, so didn't care a hang.

Now then, all this time I was working, and working very hard. Our Mr. Kaufmann opened the Quebec office on January 1. You may recall that when I came here, we had a difference of opinion regarding pay; and he only offered me a very small wage with the understanding that when he opened the Quebec office—which would be around the first of the year—he would give me an advance in salary, besides giving me the managership of this office when he was opening up in Quebec.

He certainly did give me the managership—but not one word did he say about a raise in salary. He was in Quebec, so I thought to wait until I could speak with him (rather than write it) about the promised raise. He wrote every few days that "soon" he would return; and I waited.

In the meantime, our bookkeeper, Miss Lynn, quit; as she gave the customary two weeks notice, I wrote Mr. K. whether I should get another girl; and he advised my waiting until he came, which would be "soon."

I thought Miss Lynn quit because the position was a trying one, which it surely was, for we had to send everything of any import to Quebec to be O.K.'d before we could act on it. I learned later why she left. In the meanwhile, I did the bookkeeping. As I know little about bookkeeping except what my common sense teaches me, the books didn't look any too well. One Saturday, when I wrote Mr. K. that I wanted to see him and, too, that he must get a bookkeeper, I received a wire saying that he would be in Monday.

As I wanted to have the office in apple-pie order, and as I stayed late, Nina phoned; and when I explained the situation, she offered to assist me. As she has expert knowledge about bookkeeping, she began on my books to balance them. We stayed until long after tea time. And when I left, I was convinced that what Miss B. told me was true, and that is: that our books showed a discrepancy of about $4,560.00! At first, I discredited it; but I saw it could not be otherwise. In a flash, I saw why Miss Lynn had quit. No doubt she, too, knew of this, and got out from under before the crash came. Mr. K. was a habitué of the bucket shops here. He is a stock gambler, in a picayune fashion. You see, this office, while not affiliated in the running of its business with the Chicago office, is financed by it; and every cent taken in here has to be sent to the Chicago office, and they send money back for disbursements. In some fashion, somehow, Mr. K. had held out in one year's time over $4,500.00! I was quite excited about it over Sunday, and wired Mr. K. to be sure to come; and he did. When I confronted him with the fact about the books, he fell right to tearing me out for daring to call a stranger in to go over his books. Later his anger subsided, but he said nothing further about the discrepancy. He engaged another girl for bookkeeper; and everything went along as though nothing had happened. On Wednesday A.M., he called me into his office and told me he was returning to Quebec that night, and hoped all would go along well—and not one word about the discrepancy, nor about the promised raise of salary. I finally asked him what he intended to do about the discrepancy, and explained that unless he could show me quite to my satisfaction that everything was all right, that I wouldn't stay. He thundered and fumed again, and told me it was none of my business. And then I intimated that if he didn't explain, I'd write about it to the Chicago office and ask them to explain.

The upshot of it all was that he offered me the position in charge of the Quebec office, and made it appear as though he had expected to give it to me all along, with a salary of $25.00 a week—$100.00 a month. All this, and not one word about my demand for an explanation about the shortage Miss B. discovered in his books.

I could not seem to pin him down. He would not treat the matter as though it was of any importance or any of my business.

Thursday night he was still here, and still nothing did I know. I hadn't accepted the Quebec position because he would not satisfy my mind that all was well in his dealings with the Chicago office. As it happens, I know he is under bond with the home office, so they would not be affected by any dishonesty on his part. Yet since almost everything was in my charge, I feared it might be that I'd get entangled in this mess; and since I had knowledge of it, I couldn't go ahead without being absolutely sure I was right.

On Thursday night I sent a night letter to Mr. Lucey. It was he who secured this position for me here and, as it happens, this phase of the business would come directly under his department. He was on a trip, but the wire reached him in New York on Friday. He wired he would be here Sat. morning.

After I explained the situation and showed him some figures which I had surreptitiously taken from the books, he said Mr. K. had positively spent that money, no doubt in the bucket shops, hoping to repay it, and only getting deeper in debt. He told me I must hand in my resignation at once, and he would give Mr. K. ten days in which to do something before sending the chief auditor down, or rather up, here. After that, the bonding company would have to see why Mr. K. fixed the accounts as he had been doing.

You can imagine how dazed I was all thru this. Frankly, I didn't quite realize what all this meant to me for several days. Mr. Lucey instructed me to return and quit at once. I did so. Mr. K. was at first inclined to be frightened, I think, at what he thought I proposed doing; but he said something that gave me the cue, and I led him to believe that my reason for "picking the quarrel," as he called it, was just as he suspected—so I could break my contract with him. This contract I had with him was a sorry affair. It gave him (as do most of the laws here), the employer, the right to discharge me at will; but I was supposed to give him a month's notice, or forfeit a recommendation and, besides, any salary he might have held out from me.

At any rate, I came home. So far, it never occurred to me what to do about the fact that I was again without work, and I hadn't a whole dollar—for I owed 'most all Mr. K. paid me, in the store near here, for groceries. When I entered my room, though, it struck me very forcibly that I would have to do something, for I was taking care of Ethel and things generally. . . . When I told Ethel of what had transpired, I could see that she, too, was struck with the thought of what would become of us now.

Mr. Lucey said I should not think of leaving the company's employ, and that in a very short time he would find a vacancy for me—but it would be in another city, and that he thought, most likely, Boston. I told him I preferred staying in Montreal and would try getting a position here, though (of course) I'd be glad for him to get me a post, provided I failed in my quest here.

Afterwards, we went upstairs to get Nina's dinner (and our own, of course) ready. I will digress here a bit to tell you what I think I forgot, and that was, that all my trouble to save Ethel's position in the house here until after she left the hospital was in vain; for since the birth of George Herbert, she has never regained her strength, and she is very frail and nervous, especially since the little chap's death, and could not do housework. When Nina came in and she heard the bad news, she felt worse even than Ethel, I think. She is a dear good soul and . . . she was afraid—for she was thinking this might mean my leaving Montreal to find work elsewhere.

We had a talk on the matter, and it was decided that E. stay with Nina until I get work or, if I didn't get work at once, I should too give up my room and come up there. This I was loathe to do, for you know how fussy I am about having everything in my own way, and I am really quite attached to my little place here.

I started out to find a place; and it was quite a dreary day, and before I was out an hour, I knew the outlook was dreary too. It was the old story, where they did need a "secretary" (for that is what they call a person here who is fitted for the work I have always done). I was asked what was wrong with my eyesight—and advised to return when my eye was "well." In despair, I decided to give it up and try only writing for the positions advertised.

I stopped in the chocolate shop to have a cup of tea, and there met Jean Holland, whom I have known since before the Christmas holidays.

Now then, I will tell you all about Jean, for it is with her now that I have cast my lot. Isn't is strange how things will happen that convince me (anyway) that every little mood is predestined?

Jean is about my age. Born in Dublin, Ireland; has two brothers in Canada, but no parents living. She has an unusually good education and has a university degree. Since coming to Canada, she took up newspaper work. First she was with *The Star*, an evening paper, in the capacity of reporter, but later became interested in the advertising end of the paper and was on the advertising staff for one-and-a-half years. She left there to join the advertising staff of Henry Morgan and Company, as she was offered better pay. She was there for more than two years, and only left because she had a better offer with the Consolidated Rubber Company. She is very clever in fixing up the layouts for ads, and is really quite an artist in a small way. When with the Consolidated Rubber only two months, she found that being a girl—and a rather nice-looking one—was making her position there unbearable. The man she was directly under made advances to her; and whether he meant well or not, it was entirely repulsive to Jean, for he is a man of perhaps fifty or sixty, and a big, redfaced, fat, coarse type. (I've seen him.) Jean had to resign, she couldn't stand him. It was about that time I met her. She had tried to get a post; and in the advertising field, she seemed to have lost all chance. For women are not regarded here in the same light as in the States, and such firms as might have considered her application—the departmental stores, for instance—felt she had not given Morgan's a square deal when she quit, and did not care to engage her.

She had decided there was nothing much to hope for in the advertising field; and as she has to work to live, she took up "public stenography," coupled with French translation. This is something that is well-paid-for here; for while most people can speak and write both languages, few have Jean's ability for translation. She is thoroughly versed in French grammar as well as English.

She hired a desk, in an office with use of the phone, etc., and then went about among her friends asking that they give her any work they may have of that sort.

That is how I met her. I needed some form letters of ours translated into French for the benefit of our trade thru the Province of Quebec, which is entirely French. Since then, I have seen quite a lot of Jean. In fact, in the beginning I helped her with her business, for while she has much ability, she has absolutely no business acumen; and she found she did not conduct her business—small as it was—along paying lines. After keeping her around a bit, I found I had much in common with her. Therefore, when we met in the chocolate shop, it was only a few minutes before we determined to go into business together. Originally, it was our idea to go in for stenographing, translation, etc.; but since then we have sort of gotten away from our original plans and now are in a sure-enough business. It is too long a story, to tell you all about how we got around to this, but [later] I will tell you just what we are doing. This part of the letter I have written on four or five occasions, but I am determined to finish it tonight!

I am still living in my own room and still have Ethel with me—and besides she *works for me*, and I pay her a salary of $4.50 a week.

> Business Aid Bureau
> Eastern Townships and Bank Building
> Montreal, Quebec
> March or April, 1914

⊂ৈ **83** WE ARE IN THE "BUSINESS AID BUREAU"—JEAN HOLLAND AND I. WE HAVE working for us: Ethel, at a salary of $4.50 per week; Louis, errand boy, and assists generally, at $5.00 per week; John Farrell, multigraph operator and typewriter, at $10.00 a week.

Doesn't this all sound as though we were "some punkins" now?

The "Business Aid Bureau" as a name was my inspiration, and we have since registered the name at a cost of $10.00.

The various things listed above explained in this wise:

Multigraph letters: We have one motor multigraph, put in by the Multigraph Company, and being paid for by the month.

"Circularizing": Whatever it means, we haven't had any of it yet to do; therefore, on our next order of paper, we will leave that out.

Printing: Many of the orders for multigraph letters give us the order to have the stationery for the letter printed; and I have an arrangement with the Keystone Press, by which we get 20 per cent of the amount of the order; therefore, it pays us to try to get the printing to do.

Distribution by hand: Like circularizing, it is not done here. These things are done much in Phila., but not here, where apartment and flat houses are the usual order of things.

Mailing lists: We have an arrangement with "Might's Directories of Toronto," as their agents here, and get 20 per cent of the amount asked for any mailing list in Canada.

The rest of the things—filling in, signing, folding, enclosing, addressing, sealing and stamping—all go with the multigraph work, and it is this which we do most of.

I know you will understand now why I have not had time to write you. While Jean shares the business with me, she has absolutely nothing to do with the management of it. She has absolutely no knowledge of how to make money.

We took an office: installed partitions, put in the multigraph machine, two typewriters, a telephone—and began business. We hadn't a sign of a desk. We have one now, but Jean sits at it most all the day, for I give her work; and since I give out all the other work and go after any business there is—i.e., by asking for it over the phone—I don't get a chance to sit down, even if I had a desk. But some day, I hope to have a second desk. I give Jean all the correspondence to do. She is an excellent stenographer and typist. We are not making a bid for any more stenographic work, though we do not turn away any of Jean's old customers. Our idea in doing this is that we were advised to, by a kindly disposed customer. He explained that where girls were young, and not dreadfully plain-looking, there would creep up into the minds of people possible doubts—when men are seen coming into the office and staying any length of time—as to whether we are really *all business*. On top of this, we find that the time consumed taking a letter pays much more when used in our other work. The same goes for translation; and we don't take that unless it is sent in by someone Jean has been doing it for ever since she has been in Canada.

217

Of course, the multigraphing and mailing out of letters keeps us busy; but I must not neglect to tell you what we have hit on which, in time, is going to be the big thing for me. . . . In fact, the first day I hit on something which has proved a sure winner. Mr. Buchanan, Montreal representation for the Sweepervac, a fool kind of vacuum cleaner, (I believe), came in to dictate a letter which he wanted us to multigraph for him. The letter was not one intended to sell the Sweepervac—rather, it was one intended to gain for their demonstrator an interview in the houses of the best people here. This letter, he dictated and left. After it was "set up," I read it. It was, as I thought, a "frost." It was an appeal to a woman of another sort—one looking for something for nothing.

We had to send [Mr. Buchanan] a proof to be O.K.'d before we ran it off. Ethel was "errand boy" then, and when I sent her with the copy, I sent along another letter that I really dashed off without any preparation, and told Ethel to tell him to give thought to the fact that my letter was written to interest the better-class housewives.

He came back with Ethel and went into ecstasies about the letter. He asked me what my charge was for my letter. I said $2.00. He said it was worth $5.00—or five times that, if I [wanted to charge that much]. We billed it at $5.00. And since then, I have had quite a few other letters to write: that is, if the letter sent us to be multigraphed is a poor one, we send along with the proof a letter which I write; and sometimes they accept mine, for which we charge $5.00, as they are made aware of on their bill. . . .

Now then, if you are a "businesswoman," you are thinking what a pile of money we are making; but I will have to explain that.

In the first place, we had almost nothing to start with. In the vernacular of the street, it was a "shoe string" that we started with. And yet we had a fully equipped business; and the secret was that I secured almost everything on credit—that is, with an arrangement that some of the things be paid for in monthly payments until paid out, and some of it in thirty or sixty days. With the result that almost each day something is due, whether it be a time-payment or the goods returned. Our furniture is very scant—only that which was absolutely necessary—but we truly have a well-equipped shop. We had to install three typewriters; of course, they are reconstructed Underwoods but, at that, are worth $75.00 apiece here—

$50.00 in the States. Then, I have one small sealing machine, and the multigraph, for which we have three parts: two composition types and one motor-driven multigraph machine. This represents about $800.00, and we pay for this in monthly installments. Besides this, there was any number of expenses—telephone, rent, lettering window; printing of letterheads, bill heads, envelopes, and the paper for same; registering of business; and other incidentals. Now then: the salaries *have* to be met, very first thing. That is the most important and first thing we arrange for; and what's left gets doled out to the various creditors.

I might say that right from the start we seemed to fill a long-felt want here. There are many small places that do this work in conjunction with other work, but none that specializes in it, and none that are so painstaking in their effort to turn out nothing but 100 per cent perfect work. In the start, we had Jean's small following, supplemented by some business I was able to sway thru my connections here in the meat packing business. There, right off, we sent out a letter (I wrote it) and multigraphed 500 copies, asking for business and explaining very simply our capabilities. We got some replies and many inquiries over the phone. We sent out then a second letter, this time going into our business in detail (I haven't any copies here, or I should send you some). This, too, brought inquiries and requests that we send a representative over to talk with them about some work. Here we were stumped, for in our letters we gave the impression, without saying so, that we were a "man's business." We got around that by connecting up with a printing house, The Keystone Press; and when a representative is asked to call, we phone them, and [they] send their own salesman, to whom we pay 20 per cent of the job for his services.

It seems all the forces of the business world in Montreal are arranged against a woman developing a real business. In spite of that, I am going to work up a real business that will be a big money-maker—

Again, two days have elapsed since I wrote the foregoing, and there have been several developments.

In the first place, when we took our shop, it was from a man who had leased it by the year and had given up his business; so the place was idle, as he had not been able to sublet it. We took over his lease and, as the new leases run here from May to May, almost

219

as soon as we signed the sub-lease, we had to sign—as the real tenants—the lease for the whole of the coming year, beginning May 1. When we appeared at the shop this morning, a young chap from the real estate firm from whom we rent asked that we see the manager some time before twelve. I went—and, imagine! we have to get out of our present premises! I am being terribly brave about it, but I have certainly received a blow. We have been to a large expense putting this place in shape to be convenient for us—we spent $40.00 for partitions. Besides, we have 2000 sheets of paper and envelopes printed with this number. And worst of all, there is only one week left to find another place; and as good places with reasonable rent are scarce, we feel we will have to pay more rent than we would like to, in order to find a suitable place. Our rent here was $35.00 a month—electricity, phone and janitor service extra. It amounts to $40.00 a month.

Oh, I forgot to tell you why we have to move. In our lease there is a clause saying a lot of rot about not having machines in the office, or more than two typewriters for the amount of floor space we occupy, and any violation of this means the breaking of the lease. This is a standard clause here, and generally no attention is paid to it. In fact, the real estate agent knew the nature of the business when he rented us the place. But, on the same floor with us, is a large advertising agency—and as large as they are, they are picking on the Business Aid Bureau because we get some work which they might have gotten. We were told frankly that they objected on the grounds that the noise from our office interfered with the men who write the copy. These men are no less than six doors off—and yet the men on each side of us, who are kindly disposed yet quite honest, say it was only in the very beginning, before they were used to it, that they noticed any discomfort from the noise.

Now we sure are in a fine predicament. We have to move by next Wednesday. The thought frightens me. We haven't the remotest idea where to go, for now we will have to be sure to pick out a place where there will be no one to want to see us put out, or any crank who might object to the noise—for there must be some noise. (Getting sleepy again.) This time, before we move, we will consult a lawyer and be sure we are right before we move in. We saw one ($5.00 expense) to make sure we were obliged to vacate;

and we sure do have to. Fortunately, the $5.00 will cover the expense of looking into the new lease when we find a place.

Just think, we put up $40.00 [for] partitions, and alterations and repair. True, much of it we can lug away with us—but what if we don't need it? This really is a staggering blow—for we owe $20.00 yet of that $40.00; and we will have to pay, by the first, the balance.

Frankly, though we are "businesswomen," we are poor as church mice. Though we pay salaries to everyone else, our salaries are generally scraped together. Poor Jean—she has little perspicacity where business is concerned; and today, when talking over this new twist in our affairs, she seemed so at sea. As it is, I take only enough each week to pay for room rent and "eats," and not a sou besides. I walk both ways now to work. This is essential now, for a short while, but I have trouble showing Jean why. She pays regular board, $8.00 a week, and she thinks it terrible that I don't let her have $10.00 each week—whereas, so far, I haven't had over $6.00 any week since we are in business. Of course, there is that much more to my credit in the business. It is hard for Jean to see that while we are always terribly strapped for funds, still, we are making the foundation for a business—for each time we meet a payment, we own that much more in valuable machinery. She doesn't worry a rap about the fact that the payments are due and we aren't ready to meet them—for she is Irish, and I am Jewish. Jean thinks everyone will be as easily convinced they don't need the money as she is when I speak to her. It sort of throws all the real responsibility on me. But on the other hand, her absolute knowledge of things I am only guessing at half the time is invaluable. She is kind enough to say my English is good—yet when I finish some work she always finds a *was* where a *were* should have been, or vice versa. . . .

I must retire to face tomorrow, a hard problem—we are so totally unprepared for it. Besides, on the first of May so many jobs have been promised, and— Well, I shall try to make it go. . . .

The *Atlantic* comes regularly, and I thank you—I am intensely interested in several writers who appear regularly. . . .

Mr. Welsh sails for Europe this coming week, I believe. I think he is away from Phila. even now.

Goodnight, my dear friend. Write me truly, frankly—do you

think I made a good move? I was afraid to ask before I went into it—for I was so determined to go in it, if I could, especially as I really believe this particular line of work is my forte.

May, 1914

☞ 84   I WANT TO LET YOU KNOW OF THE CONDITIONS AS THEY EXIST HERE, AND then get your advice and help, if possible.

I have already written you of my difficulty in having had complaints made against our business, as a "manufacturing plant." We were ordered to move. . . . I then lost no time in hunting a place. . . . I went into one of the best real estate offices here, and I was in consultation with a gentleman who. . . understood the situation thoroughly; and in view of the fact that we must be in the wholesale and financial district, he told me I was in a very fine way of not getting any place at all. You see, they are a bit *savage* here yet. Multigraphing to them comes under the same head as printing; and printing is specifically tabooed on the bases of any place that is even possible for us to do business—[except where] rent is prohibitive.

It really looked as though we would have to give up as we started, and I was in desperation. . . . I think I aroused a sort of sympathy for us and our undertaking. . . and he took me to a bank here that also rents offices; and this satisfactory arrangement was made:

. . . I was given the use of the back of [a] store that has an entrance on a very good cross-town street. It is perfect for me; and yet due to the low rent of $30.00 a month which I am to have it for, and due to a lot of red tape it would involve (and maybe deprive me of the chance of getting it), I have to take it without a lease: just an agreement in writing, for me to use the office part of the store (light and power extra) for $30.00, and notice of one month, if necessary (that is, if there is a tenant for the store)—and then the use of any one of their other offices that may be vacant, at the same rent, for $30.00 (for if an office is vacant after May 1st, they make no attempt to rent it). . . .

Now then, as soon as I had this all definitely settled, I went over to the Multigraph Company to tell them, for they, too, were exerting every effort to find the Business Aid Bureau a haven. Imagine my disappointment when I found I had struck another snag: my original arrangements with the Multigraph Sales Company are such that this move changes the entire plan of payment on our machines.

This did not frighten me, for I saw a way out of it—and I immediately set about getting things straightened out. First, I will tell you what the trouble with the Multigraph Company is, and then I will tell you how I proceeded to overcome it.

The Multigraph Company has heretofore encouraged "jobbers" —as they call people like us, who buy the machines and "job" the work. When I got my outfit, this was still in force. But since then, from their main office came a letter saying they were discontinuing their former method of helping jobbers into business by furnishing the machines on installments; all the supplies; and O.K.'ing any accounts for paper, etc. I was lucky to have started before this went into force, for if I had not, I shouldn't have been able to get along as I have. Therefore, this edict had no effect on me, except that in buying what multi ribbons, etc. now that I need, I have them billed thirty days, and pay cash for them at the end of that time.

Now when I explained to Mr. Shakey *re* the removal, he told me plainly that "the office" would not permit me to move [the machines] from my present address, where they are protected against the lease or by the lease, to this place where I could show no lease.

I forgot to tell you why the Multigraph Company discontinued their jobbers accounts. They explained that it conflicted with their business for big firms here, who should buy a Multigraph machine, but prefer to send it out, because there are enough public stenographers with machines to always get their work on a minute's notice. This, then, conflicted with their business of selling many multigraphs. I think he said these conditions do not exist in Montreal, but it has been found to be poor policy in other cities, so they are discontinuing it all over the world.

This makes my business better than under the old conditions, for competitors cannot spring up all around me—and, as yet, my business is in a class all by itself in Montreal.

The Multigraph Sales Company told me that they would not ordinarily let so much stuff stand out without the protection of a lease—for it could be seized for personal debt, and I have over a thousand dollars worth of their goods. . . . Now since I started, I have paid them $400.00....It is $400.00 toward owning our plant.

Mr. Shakey said he would put it up to...the man in the Toronto (head Canadian office) office, and ask for leniency, explaining my predicament *re* not being able to get in anywhere on such short notice.

The result was that if the B.A.B. reduced their account to one-half the original amount, the Multigraph Company would not be insistent about the lease, and take a note for the balance, to be paid as before—$100.00 a month, or $25.00 a week. This, they explained, even in spite of the fact that this would not be done under ordinary conditions. This did not seem to me to be very hard. I felt sure I could manage it, and I will tell you how I went about it.

I could do nothing about collections, for though there was a goodly sum due, it was all waited for by bills due on the first (today).

Last week, or two weeks ago, Mr. Welsh wrote me that he was going to Europe, sailing on the 27th or 29th (the numerals were indistinct), and explained that he hoped my business would succeed, and—as he was to be gone for two months—he would leave with Mrs. Edwards, a woman who does some work for him, some money in case I should find myself in some business trouble that required speedy aid. Doesn't that seem wonderful—for him to think of that, though he knows so little of business, and especially when all this did happen so suddenly? I knew of this need in time to reach Mr. Welsh, but as I knew of another way to get it, I was reluctant to trouble him with my affairs on the eve of his journey. It was my intention to get it from another source and then write Mr. Welsh and ask him to return it—for I did not relish writing this Mrs. Edwards, who is a total stranger to me, so intimate a story as this is.

My brother Sam, the chemist, was in Memphis, and had gone there to my oldest brother. He had that week written me that he was in Chicago, having left my brother in Memphis, and that he hoped to go into something there. He said, further, that he was delighted that I had gone into business, thought I was plucky, etc., etc., and that if I needed help *financially*, he would be glad to make me a loan.

Do you wonder, then, that the trouble I encountered with the Multigraph Sales Company, did not frighten me, since he *offered* to help me—and I had never asked any one of them for a cent to help me struggle into this business? Immediately upon hearing what I had to do from the Multigraph Sales Company to retain my business, I wired him (a night letter) and accompanied it with a letter, in which I explained the situation and appealed to him to only lend me the money until I could communicate with Mr. Welsh, who would be glad to relieve him of carrying my debt. The next morning I got an answer wired (a night letter): "Leaving tonight for Phila. Your letter reached me in time. Will send money so that you receive it on the first. Hope you understand must have it returned in case I wish to go into business. Sam." I was quite satisfied, and showed the wire to Mr. Shakey and went on with my preparations about moving.

The day after the first wire, I received a second one reading: "Sorry to have disappointed you. Can't let you have money. Mother has used it for a purpose of her own and can't draw it out. Hope you get help elsewhere. Sam." This knocked me out. I knew at once the trouble was that as soon as he arrived in Phila., my mother and James jumped on him. For though Sam is the least liberal of them all, somehow he must have felt some sympathy for me to offer and then promise so readily. The withdrawal was absolutely prompted by them. (Incidentally I enclosed the letter from Mr. Welsh saying he would leave money with Mrs. Edwards to relieve me in case of sudden business emergency, and he has not returned the letter.)

I wrote at once, at length, in fine detail, and explained how they *must* come to my rescue; that aside from being my brothers, it wasn't human for them to see me floundering about in the sea and, knowing that I have the first start I ever had in my life, to let me go under—when between them, they surely can raise the $200.00 necessary to keep me up, especially since the assurance of return was absolute (Mr. Welsh's letter *re* the money in Mrs. Edwards' care being the assurance) and the loan was in reality only a favor. Too, I asked that the letter referred to above be returned, for it has in it Mrs. Edwards' address, which I don't know offhand, since I never heard of her before this letter. I explained to Sam that I did not like to trouble Mr. Welsh on the eve of his departure, nor did I fancy writing to Mrs. Edwards before Mr. Welsh had gone—and yet, if he would not see fit to help me, to return at once the letter and I would write to Mrs. Edwards.

I am sorry to say that since the second wire of refusal they have not sent me a word—though my second letter was a general appeal to my mother and brothers. They ignored me entirely. I am dreadfully hurt. At this time, I am too much concerned about the business to think of the personal part of the affair—but I know they have forfeited any right to think of them as persons I am related to, and I will never communicate with them, and I hope never to see one of them. I am very bitter about this. Had they let me know what to expect after my second letter, or sent me the letter I asked for, I should not feel so bitter.

I must return, then, to my position now. It is as it was: the Multigraph Sales Company will not permit me to move the things—unless back into their place—and if I did, it would mean the end of the business—for I couldn't get them again except I paid for them in full. The rear of the store is ready for me to enter—and I haven't the money to give the Multigraph Company. And I haven't even the address of Mrs. Edwards, who had the money for just such an emergency from Mr. Welsh.

My office here is not rented. Due to my not getting notice to go until so close to the first, all renters had signed up, and there is no immediate tenant. But the rent being low, they will soon have a tenant. Because of the place not having an incoming tenant and because I explained all this foregoing to the agent, he has given me permission to remain until next week, meaning for me to do something not later than Monday or Tuesday, so he can make good his promise of eviction to the complaining tenants.

Now I have stated the difficulties, the conditions; and I ask—can you help me? I would need at once $150.00, for though I have to pay the Multigraph Company $200.00, I will have collections that will cover all urgent bills and payroll, and leave me $50.00. Then, as soon as I can ascertain Mrs. Edward's address (I can find out from Miss Mateer in Mr. Welsh's office—Mr. Suiffen has gone to Alaska), I will ask for the money left, and will repay with it the loan. If the amount she has does not cover the $150.00, I will explain it to Mr. Welsh in a letter to his Rome address and ask him to repay the balance—and I know very well he will....I hope you will understand my coming to you; I only did it as a last recourse....

I am so tired I can scarcely think or write coherently. I walked all day hunting a place where I would get a lease, but met with no success. Yours affectionately, Maimie

I am writing Mr. Welsh explaining my reason for having to appeal to you, and also about not having Mrs. Edward's address; and I will ask him that he write at once whether Mrs. Edwards can repay you or whether he will personally attend to it.

May 3, 1914

I AM JUST NOW IN RECEIPT OF YOUR WIRE. I NEED NOT TELL YOU HOW **85** ❦ relieved I am. My nerves have almost given out thru the strain of the few days, and the worst of it is that I haven't a bit of help from Jean in deciding what and how to do.

It is a beautiful day (Sunday), and I persuaded Jean to take Ethel and go for a country walk. I stayed in to wash my head and incidentally hoped to have a wire from you.

They will be glad to know of your assisting me. I knew you would if you could, and I thank you from the bottom of my heart for helping me to keep my business. I haven't the ability to express to you in words what this business means to me. . . . Again, I thank you. I will write tomorrow.

May 5, 1914

YOUR WIRE CAME; AND THEN YOUR LETTER I FOUND ON MY RETURN FROM **85A** ❦ work last night. I can only say that I have never worked as hard as I will work now, to prove you were right. I might say that I never go to bed except that I am "dog tired"; yet now I will work even harder and, for awhile, a little selfishly, giving to my business every second that it requires. . . .

I received an answer from Sam enclosing Mrs. Edward's address. His letter was so absolutely impersonal that it might have been written to a stranger. He acts entirely under the advice of my mother; and her advice would be never to give anyone help that requires money. There is something so empty in their relationship with me that I think it folly for me to force it any longer. This condition exists not only with me, but between themselves. Their love for each other (if it could be called that) is absolutely hollow. It was only to please Mr. Welsh that I resumed relationship with them; for my memory of my life between the ages of ten to fifteen were such, that never of my own accord would I have troubled to become one of them again. It sure was a rank failure; and now I will use my better or more mature judgment and leave them to their own devices. Do you know, when Frances McCoy stayed at my mother's house, I paid for everything she had there, with my own earnings and some help you gave (Mr. Welsh did not contribute anything, for he never knew much of her)—and lately when I wrote my mother that I was getting on very well, she answered that I should try and send her some money to repay what she expended on Frances? In a word—they look on me as though I was very much of a fool; and I know if they were questioned they would say: "She hasn't any idea of the value of a dollar, and we might as well get it from her, for when she is old we will have to support her." Isn't that a cheerful thought? (Their reason for believing me so incapable of the knowledge of handling money, is because I would give my earnings for Frances or to my mother in the shape of a gift.) Anyway, it will be my aim to make of this business a safeguard against the possibility of ever having to appeal to them; and from today on, any news they ever receive from me will be through other persons, if they are to ask. For I will not ever write them or go to them. I still write to Ira Benjamin, and occasionally he sees them; so that will possibly be how I will hear of little Potsy—the one of the whole outfit that I love so much that I could never make anyone understand.

I wrote to Mrs. Edwards last night, and though your letter made me think she perhaps would not have that much money there, I asked her to send what she can, explaining everything fully.

I want to tell you what happened yesterday. We had several very good jobs, all set up on the "drums," as they are called. But we were not able to "run" them (though they were proofed and O.K.'d), for I had given the agent my word that the multi would not be operated again in that building—for it was only through his kindness that I am permitted to remain until I go into my other quarters. Just the same, all day Monday and until noon, we were beseiged with phone messages from McKenna (florists), McNeil Company (brokers), and Williamson Company (typewriter agents) for their work. Especially McNeil Company—for their work is quotations which change and must be gotten out at once. (I might mention in passing that 98 per cent of our business is always marked "rush" orders—I hope to build a reputation on our ability to cope with "rush.") I was at my wit's ends. Of course, the others simply say (over the phone), "I will take it up with Miss Jones as soon as she returns."

To send out this work to some other multigraph house wouldn't do. There isn't that feeling here, with the French, that they wouldn't try to get these accounts; and to explain would give our business that feeling that "girls run it and they are so unreliable." So I took myself into the chocolate shop and had a cup of tea and thought the situation over. And this is what I did.

I went to see the agent; and after explanations, he let me see the letter from the complainants *re* the noise of the multi. Our neighboring advertising agency lead all the rest. There were seven, in all. I went in to see all of them, leaving the advertising agency last.... They all seemed absolutely indifferent as to the running of [the multi], explaining frankly that they signed their names because of the fact that the man who brought the letter was the "Big Man" of that floor, and with or without their names, he could have me evicted on the strength of my lease—which does not countenance "manufacturing, etc."

It took a lot of courage, but I walked into the lion's den—asked to see Mr. Stephens. He evidently had never seen me, for he did not recognize me as "*Miss* Jones of the B.A.B." It was really quite uncomfortable at the start; but once I got started, I was all right. What helped me was that he was a gentleman. The strange part of it is that he is of the sort of people you and Mr. Welsh are of; and because of that, I looked at him, but talked as though addressing your husband, or a man I seemed to know.

I cannot describe to you how badly he felt, though he said little. Just signed a note I had typewritten, to our agent, giving me permission to run the machine for the next few days until our place is ready (it had to have extensive fixing of small things. Mr. Martin is doing it out of my first month's rent), only between the hours of 5:00 A.M. to 8:00 A.M.; 12:00 noon to 1:00 P.M.; and from 6:00 to 11:00 P.M.

I know for sure that he is president of that concern. Yet he said he would "sign it for Mr. McKim." I think he was ashamed of his part in it all. Too, I think perhaps in business—men are all the same—but I think when he saw me, and saw that I have handicap enough without big rich concerns trying to handicap me further, he felt how pitifully small their part in the affair was.

The only thing personal he said was, "Have one of your men come in to see me." I said: we are all women, and I am the oldest and the owner of B.A.B.—can I serve you? He looked discomforted—then said, "No, I haven't anything now, but occasionally we need some addressing, and I will phone you." I then told him our new address. He puzzled a minute and said, "That is the old Tooke store." And I said, "Yes, we are to occupy the back," and I saw he wondered where I was going to get such money for rent on St. James Street.

When I started out—in trying to be polite, I sort of backed out. It was only a short space to the door, and I didn't like turning my back square to him, so I sort of stepped without looking—and ran straight into a clothes tree. He jumped up—and by that time I laughed that I was stupid, and got out of the door. When I got into our office, I found that my nose was bleeding; for I had run into it on my blind side, and the slightest jar on my nose (where the bone was removed) causes it to bleed. The bang was slight, yet my nose bled copiously; in fact, it bled all last evening at intervals.

We went ahead with the three "rush" jobs and got them delivered without any explanations.

I had a talk with Jean Holland last night. I had never had any real understanding with her as to her share in our enterprise, especially since she has dropped any intention of sharing the responsibilities. She says I can do all that better and she won't cudgel her brains about anything. She says—"I will take that up with Miss Holland when she comes in"—that is, if some one directly asks her to quote prices, etc. She means when I come in. When I remonstrated with her about letting the others hear her tell a deliberate lie, she fixed it all by calling me "Miss Holland" at our luncheon, or during any moment when we are humans together. This makes everyone laugh, but it makes me think: if I am destined to be Miss Holland, Miss Jones, and the manager, when someone wants to talk with "him"—then why should Jean share fifty-fifty with me? The absolutely aggravating part of it all is, when I talk with her about it, she will say someting like this: "You are right again—certainly I don't deserve half, or in fact anything more than you think I am worth. Just let me have $10.00 this week, and after that, just my room and board and oh! Maimie, leave me a little for an occasional concert and a car ticket." This, every week, though I only take $5.00—up to $7.00—at the most. Now isn't that terribly provoking? She has absolutely no business sense, but is absolutely a wonder for good humor, breeding and ability; and that is a combination seldom found when employing girls. I can't seem to arrange what to do with her interests here. In the first place, her valuation of money is so poor that when a check comes in for $75.00, she dances around me— "Lets you and I and Ethel go down to the country over Sunday—and oh, Maimie, do take Esther"— whispering, "she needs it." And Esther and Ethel look at me like the slave driver of the concern and Jean—"just lovely."—But Jean says, "Oh! that's so!" when I remind her that Mr. Goodwin will want that as his payment for the paper used on that job, and the printer (Keystone Press) for their work on the letterheads and envelopes— and by that time, we will have $25.00 left: and what about the salaries?

I will have to close, as it is time to dress. You see, Ethel does the getting of our meals now and looks after me a bit, for my time is too taken up with correcting proof and writing copy to do the little jobs I used to do for all of us. And besides, now I have always ten or twelve tasks a day more than I can fit into the day, no matter how hard I work.

I thank you for your interest—your kindness, I was sure of. The girls do not know you loaned me the money. You will understand, I know, when I tell you why. Not that they are not conscientious; they are that. But...it is something like teaching a child to walk: and I want them to understand our business *must* walk, and that there aren't any hands to reach out, in case of a stumble....I explained it this way: that I got a loan on the business. Their business ideas are so vague that they are quite ready to believe we have something tangible to borrow money on. Ethel, wishing to prove she has some idea of business (for I am always reproving them for their lack of it), said, "How much interest do you have to pay?" I was stumped. For I thought I was not telling the lie, since you really did loan it on the business, as you value it from the standpoint that I will make the business pay. But the interest! So I answered: "I won't tell you—you won't believe me." And that seemed to satisfy all of them, for they immediately began talking about how we would join the women's suffrage movement here, and thus get their business—for they send out many letters. Oh, they are the busy little schemers! You can judge from that how fitted they are to help me in the management of the B.A.B.

Mrs. Mark Howe
Cotuit, Massachusetts   *June 8, 1914*

✂ 87   JUST CAN'T FIND A MINUTE TO WRITE YOU....I NEVER QUIT THE OFFICE
until 12:00 midnight and 1:00, and was up and out by eight o'clock.
I work like that right along—I have to, for I am taking in more
work and have *less* help, thus getting more money out of this. I
keep paying out, and as yet have never had a cent left more than to
just pay for my room and board. I get regular board now, as I
haven't time to share the pleasant arrangements with Nina Brown.

Today, Monday, I am obliged to stay home a few hours—I am
not well, but it is not serious—I will be fit as a fiddle by noon. I
didn't think any person could work as hard as I do, and yet I never
felt better than I do now.

Last week the Alaska Feather and Down Company that makes
the Canadian Ostemoor mattress gave me a contract (the first I've
had) which makes them send me every bit of work that goes out of
their place for multigraphing, translations, addressing, filling in,
mailing, etc. This is worth in profit to me about $7.00 a week,
$30.00 a month, and it will take care of my board. I did not ask for
this contract. It was given because Mr. Findley felt he could depend
on me, and as he goes on trips three and four times a year, of a
month's or so duration, he wanted to be sure "graft" would not get
the jobs sent elsewhere.

I think Jean will go this or next week. She does not want to, but I
advocate it. She could earn a salary of at least $25.00 a week as
straight stenographer—or more, in an advertising department—but
it would take years before this business could pay her any such
returns as it is mostly hack work; and what brains are required, I
thank the good Lord I can supply.

Entre nous, she worries me to death. Her views are very childish
and absolutely unbusinesslike, and I just ride over them ruthlessly
—and she immediately digs up a few more, a bit more silly. Your
correction of my *it's* was timely, because a man refused to pay
$8.50 for a job because it contained that error—yet Jean O.K.'d the
proof. Her excuse is: she thinks I am *cute*, the way I persist in using
apostrophes promiscuously. She is an idealist and a very charming
girl, but an absolute drawback in my shop.

Though she protested, I sent out (multigraphed) 500 letters to
large concerns here and in Toronto, asking for a place for her on
their advertising staff.

232

I must make this business stick. I will, too, given no handicaps —and everything and everybody must lend themselves to this plan, or get out of my road. . . . One thing though, I will ask you—or, rather, tell you of—and I'd like your unbiased opinion.

In corresponding with Ira Benjamin, I write very irregularly—in fact, once or twice to his eight or ten letters. Of course, he knows of my business venture; he thinks it fine, etc. In a recent letter he stated his child was very ill—since then, I heard nothing. Yesterday—or rather Sat.—I heard from my brother Sam (who has written twice since the episode about the loan—but I do not answer). He said he heard that Ira Benjamin had had much trouble; his child had been very ill and had died. I suppose soon I will hear from him telling me all about it. It was threatened with pulmonary troubles; therefore, perhaps it is best that it was taken away, for it was always sick.

Now then—this leaves Bennie free to go at will, and I could readily bring him here and, in some way—as salesman, perhaps— fit him into my business. I will say this, and I know you will believe me: *I would only be interested absolutely* as far as he can help me in my business. I find this business has vast opportunities, and I have only one body and one day's time for each day's work; and I can't do it all alone. And so far I haven't found any one to help me, outside of the real physical work. He is a very clever salesman and almost crafty in his knowledge of business principles—and dealing with the French Catholics here, one needs that trait.

I of course only suggest it. Do you mind telling me frankly if you think the plan feasible?

If I had a man like him, I'd cut out all the small practices of a female-controlled business and make it a real cold-blooded business proposition. Now—in many cases—I get work out of sympathy; and I don't want it: I abhor it. I am fully able to cope with the best of them and I don't want anything I am not entitled to. If I was never seen, I could sway the business with the same absolutely-best-in-me manner and get the respect of a firm without a lot of slushy sympathy—for which I pay dear, since big jobs escape me because of it, and in big jobs only is there big money.

Imagine: [At a recent meeting of] the Montreal Publicity Association (its members are the biggest men here—mostly English, though) new business enterprises were discussed. One man, to give an example of stick-to-itiveness, told of my being ejected on the first of May, etc., etc., and how I succeeded in staying above the water, etc. I saw a verbatim report of this—brought to me by a customer who thought I'd be proud to know of it. In the body of it is: "...and just think, this girl is still doing business, though buffeted at each turn by the enemy 'Competition,' and this girl has only one eye, making her achievement really marvelous in this hidebound city of ours, where the odds are so great for the newcomer." This is what I'd give anything to avoid. Another thing: One of the elevator boys towed in a kid with a job of multigraphing to be done. The kid didn't speak English. Jean was out. I called the elevator boy back to interpret. What I could make out was that the man said he was to turn the work over *personally* to the lady with the bad eye—for I heard the *mal d'yeux* and understood it.

If I could get away from that I could build up a big business, and I sort of look to I. Benjamin as the one to help me. But I'd want your opinion about this first.

July 30, 1914

೮8 88   AS FOR YOUR QUESTION AS TO HOW I MANAGE HERE WITHOUT NINA B....Since Nina left I get my breakfast of a glass of milk and one roll of Mrs. Noakes whom I rent from, so you can see I am but slightly inconvenienced.

Did I tell you that Jean has gone to Nina, and Ethel is in Battle Creek?...Nina got wind of an opening in her school for an ad writer and got the faculty to communicate with Jean. This school is going in for a campaign to have Canadians of means keep their girls in school here rather than send them to the States and the Old Country. Jean looks after this and answers all the letters of inquiry, and besides has other minor duties that have to do with the bookkeeping (I believe).

Ethel: I had her with me; and she lived with me, sleeping in my bed. I came to regard it as a losing game on my side— I'll explain. After she came from the hospital, she came to my room and, without any comment, took up her life with me, sharing every-thing—food, bed, clothes, and anything of the very few conveni-ences I had. Mrs. Noakes made me pay $1.50 a week extra for her after she had been here the second or third week, which I suppose was fair, after a fashion, but I never told Ethel. Then, when I opened my business, I took her in. Of course she had absolutely no experience in any branch of it, but I instructed her as we went along, and I paid her, at the start, $2.50. She really wasn't worth that—and don't forget I was teaching her a trade at the same time: multigraphy and general office work, including typewriting. As she sent that $2.50 home to her mother and never left herself a cent, I added another $1.00 a week to that, so that she could have a penny for herself. And don't forget I paid every cent of her keep—no matter how little it was, it deprived me of many necessaries. After the $1.00 raise, she asked me to try to pay her a bit more so that she could send her mother $4.00 a week, as the mother was really very ill. I did that; and by working a little later, she made up the difference. Now, that $4.50, with her keep, was by the biggest stretch of the imagination all she was worth, and lots more than I'd pay a cold stranger for the same work.

All thru this time, she plagued me to death about wanting to return to England, and I always was non-committal about that, for I knew there she'd be a darned sight worse off.

Jean Holland and I parted the best of friends—although I am still indebted to her, for I was not able to pay her in full toward the last, as collections have been horrible. Then Jean wrote me and, among other things, advised that I do not keep Ethel any longer than it would take for me to get her another post. Jean asked me not to question her reason for giving me this advice but to rely on her friendship and love—to let Ethel out. . . .

Now then, I gave Jean's advice much thought one day, and decided to act about it as I would want someone whose friendship and love I wanted (as, for instance, yourself) to act if I was in the same position Ethel was in. Do you understand? I called Ethel in and read her Jean's letter from beginning to end. She was smiling just before I came to the part about her; and when I read that, her face became serious—and that is every sign she made that she understood.

When I finished the letter, I asked her had she anything to say—and she didn't answer me, and I questioned her no further. Her attitude accused her of some treachery which I don't want to know anything about (it hurts me to think about it). So I asked her to tell me if she had any plans for a change, and she said no. So I thought it all out, and went about getting her a post in this fashion:

What she can do best is nursing and caretaking, as a sort of companion. I wrote a letter to that effect, then multigraphed 100 copies and sent them to as many doctors in Montreal and Quebec City. They were of a list for which I paid the Mights' Directories $3.00—doctors who conduct private sanitariums and who have patients convalescing who are about to go on a trip. Inside of a week, Ethel had the position and left. The lady is old and very wealthy, but does not live up to her means, and will not pay for a trained nurse. They went to Battle Creek, where they stay at a sanitarium for two months, then go to Europe—which of course suits Ethel. I feel I did my duty—getting her the post cost me nearly $10.50. I would like you to comment on this. Do you think I acted wisely in taking Jean's advice—especially since Ethel would not declare herself? . . . Ira said it was best, as Ethel was tubercular, and the sanitarium life will help her (they will sleep in the open); and she might have given it to me.

Now to go back a bit. . . .

I had the office all ready to move into. The day I was ready to move, the McKim Agency, thru Mr. Stephens made me a proposition to amalgamate with them; in this wise: throw over my outfit, and contract my time for five years at a salary and shares in the stock of their company. This offer was considered such a good one and such an unusual one, that it was talked about all over the town by the people in kindred businesses. Yet I refused it.

I want my independence, and I would not sell the B.A.B. and thus cause it to lose its identity. I want to get away from this "having a job."

I went ahead with my plans to move, and then had another proposition put to me by Mr. Stephens, who is the nominal head of the Canadian advertising world. You know it was this agency who brought about the necessity for my move. I was assured that whether I took up their proposition or not, they would arrange it so that I could remain in the building with a lease.

It was not necessary for me to get advice on this subject, but I did, and I was told on all sides that if I could remain—and though I would lose the money paid in fixing the other place and in the getting of the new stationery, and though I had paid a month's rent —that I should stay. And I did. . . . I brought over the fixtures I made for the new place and installed them here and, besides, signed a year's lease with my former landlord, Euing and Euing. They said not one word about the machines; and I took the hint and said nothing, too. This proves, then, the power of "pull" and "influence."

Now this is my arrangement with McKim.

They have no multigraphs, of course, but have much use for them at times. They formerly gave their work to the "Advertising Letters" and got a trade discount. They have accounts with big firms which for so much per year, they handle all their work incidental to advertising. Very often their advertising for their clients takes the form of letters sent out by the thousands—and of course that's where the multigraph comes in. As it stands now—I do all their multigraphing. They invoice it thru their own books and give me 75 per cent of the amount, and they take 25 per cent. Of course, all their accounts are with nationally known firms—and yet since May 25th, when I did the first job, not one firm has paid in one cent; and of course I only get mine after they get theirs. They handle the C.P.R. account, and I've done about $150.00 (as my share) of work for them so far, which I won't get until December 25th— They pay advertising bills once a year!

Besides this arrangement, I write letters for them when the subjects treated are "ladies'" subjects. They pay me 40 per cent of what they charge for a letter—for unlike me, they have no fixed charge. I wrote a letter for them for a ladies outfitting store, which they charged $20.00 for, and I got $8.00. I know this firm wouldn't have accepted the same letter of me for $5.00, but went into rhapsodies over it at $20.00 from the McKim Agency. Such is prestige!

Now then, when I get work which I can't handle (and I occasionally get it, and used to send it away, explaining it is out of our line), I take it, and the McKim Agency does it, and on the same 40 per cent basis. In that way we work together, only I retain the identity of my business and they have the benefit of my equipment—which, with the various other help which we give (since we do all their addressing, etc.), they could not install without an outlay of two to three thousand dollars; and that outlay would not pay them as well as the arrangement they have with me.

I think I did well to affiliate myself with them. But frankly, none of the credit is mine—for this all came about, I think, thru Mr. Stephens' regret at having put a couple of girls to a world of trouble thru their desire to do a weeney bit more business.

Now about Ira Benjamin.

He was in the city about three or four days when he hit on a plan in which he can run a business in conjunction with mine where he could benefit by my beginning, and yet would not be limited by the small possibilities of my particular business.

As he explained it, his earning in the business couldn't be worth $50.00 a week to me, and unless he was worth that to me, he would be throwing away his time. His reason for coming here was mainly as a holiday trip; but since he has been here, and I asked him to, he is going to try to go into business—not with me but using my business for our mutual advantage.

He will trade under the name of the B.A.B. for obvious reasons. Saves registration fee, rent, phone, and at the same time, should it later prove itself worthwhile, he will give it an individual name. He is going to try selling thru the mail—mail-order business. He starts with six silk waists of a fair quality. He sells them 20 per cent cheaper than the women in the small towns could buy them in the small towns, and with each purchase gives a gift of some jewelry. . . .I wrote the description matter, and we (the B.A.B.) send it all out. . . .My only connection with the business is that I will do all the work and charge my regular rates. Besides, he pays me rent, telephone, stenographic services—and just as a dead cold stranger would. Only that, of course, he sets the prices, and in all cases I get a little the best of it. . . .

About our personal arrangements— Frankly, Ira has been too busy getting together his waist proposition to think of anything else. But strangely (last night), for the first time, something was said on the subject.

I had a bad headache, and we were working at the office. I finally couldn't stand it, so said I was coming home. He began to get his things together, and I said it wasn't necessary, and that I'd always managed it alone, and it was only ten o'clock, etc., and that I knew he had lots to do. And, besides, I wanted him to feel on the same footing with me as he would with a male partner. He listened, and then began for the first time since he has been here, and entered into our personal arrangements.

He said he had no trouble in treating me as he does his sisters. He said his respect for me in my desire to live right was so enormous that it drove out any other thought he might otherwise have had, but in view of the fact that we had been so close in our relationship, he couldn't help but feel a personal interest in my life—but that he would never let it intrude on me. And he assured me that he would go on like this until he had plenty of money, if it took until he was fifty—and I would never be subjected to anything I didn't want or invite. But he insisted I must not expect nor ask him to stifle the gentlemanly instincts which I brought out in him and which he has tried to retain. And such a thing as seeing me home when it is late or I am ill, or at any time doing any of the things a man should perform for a woman, he expected me to tolerate—or he would have to go away. For he would refuse to be with me and not show me the courtesy he would any woman, no matter what her position. I thought probably he was right on the subject and we went home together. I always ask him in, and he always refuses—and I think always will, even though he knows I could see him in Mrs. Noakes' living room.

I will have to close now—and my very, very dear friend, do excuse the terrible scribbling. I must keep up with the work—which, by the way, is very slack now, and has been all month, except for the advertising we are doing for Mr. Benjamin. Yet I don't want to lose my friendship with you.

I hope sincerely you and your family are well and happy. Yours lovingly, Maimie

Isn't this "war talk" too terrible?

September 8, 1914

THE SILK WAIST PROPOSITION...HAS HAD VERY LITTLE RETURNS. OF   **90 🙰** course this was gotten up without any idea of a war of such magnitude appearing on the horizon.... The people here are so scared, that flour is all that can be sold. Had the Allies been having most of the victories, no doubt the populace here would breathe freer and the money be spent easier. But all we hear, even though the news is strictly censored, is that the German Army is advancing right and left into the strongholds of the Allies, and everyone is scared, and justly so....

Nina Brown, my companion, the school teacher...is very ill, and dying. You perhaps know, for I think I wrote you, or perhaps it was to Mr. Welsh, that she was or is tubercular.... Jean, who is with her, wrote—or rather, I received it today—that Nina's life is despaired of, and I am being brave about it, for I worked hard all day, but I can't help but be a bit dejected, for I'd so much like to be able to serve her. I did not think to tell you, and I feel better now that I've told you. For you know, she was a fine girl. Perhaps she is gone now. Jean said the doctor said she would only last while she had a bit more strength to fight, and Jean said in one week's time she has become very weak. She was good—good as gold—never did a knowing wrong, and besides she was *moral*. Please believe this, for although she was my friend, she never did an immoral thing; and I wish (now) I had told her (for I never did), and she would perhaps not have cared to live with me in such intimacy. Jean is also a virtuous girl, and I'd stake my life on it, so I am some day soon going to write her of myself and let her know. For I know Nina will know when she is before God, and I wish I had told her. I will tell Jean, though, in a very little while. She is also very much in misery over Nina, but I don't think she feels it as I do, for Jean has many many friends, and I have few. But such fine ones! Mr. Welsh, Mr. Suiffen, Miss Outerbridge, Caroline, Jean, Ira, Poke, Nina and Mrs. Howe. I wrote them out so as to see how they look. I have not cried today, but I feel as though I shall soon. For Nina is so far away and I am such a wretched manager, otherwise I could go to her, though I know in my heart it is too late for she has gone.

Ca. December, 1914

◘ 92   MUCH OF THE "STARCH" HAS BEEN TAKEN OUT OF MY SYSTEM BY THE change in my affairs since "before the war," but in order to keep from feeling too sorry for myself, I think of the poor sufferers in other ways than lack of money brings—and I feel perhaps I should be grateful it isn't worse. The thought that arises always is—"and this was my one big chance"—and that conditions over which I have no control have deprived me of my "chance"; but perhaps if I was strong, I'd feel I can make it yet, for I am fairly young. I'm a bit stunned now, but when the clouds lift, I feel sure I'll go at it harder and better than before, don't you?

Shall I write you a sort of table of the things that have happened since October? Perhaps that will be the best way, and then you can see just how I stand.

I had a very hard time of it in Phila.—I couldn't possibly have picked out a worse time for a visit. But anyway I enjoyed seeing them all—the baby (who is a young lady), the most. I don't think she knew me, exactly, but from the very first accepted me just as though we had not left off seeing each other ever. . . .

I saw my sister. She was a wee bit better mentally, but physically very poor—a condition we always notice and which doesn't give one much to hope for, since these changes come frequently. She knew me and commented that I looked older and better than when she saw me last.

As for Poke—I know you will be disappointed when I say I didn't bring her back!. . .I thought it best not to. . . .I will tell you of my meeting with Poke in detail.

I came there on Sunday. I rang the bell. An old, old lady, quite feeble, came to the door—and before I opened my mouth to speak, I spied Poke, poking her nose past the old lady's skirt to see who was there. And she knew me instantly. Either her sense of sight or smell told her, because she bounded by the old lady and past me and down the stairs, so fast that she skidded and fell down—recovered herself; bounded away for an instant, and back up the stairs—so quickly that I didn't see her coming—and then hurled herself up against me with such force that I fell over onto a porch chair. Then she was up in my lap, licking and sort of snapping at my veil, tearing it with her paws. I finally held her and tried to talk to her—but couldn't for her violent shrieks of pleasure, which no one could mistake. She mauled me so that I was a disgraceful-looking sight and finally rolled herself up in my lap and, to all outward appearances, was fast, tight asleep. But if I even moved a finger she'd open her eye and give me a critical look to ascertain whether I really intended going—and as soon as she was satisfied that I wasn't, was to all intents fast asleep. . . .

I will tell you now why I let her stay. The old lady was home alone. The other occupants of the home are her young son and his wife. It seems Poke is the old lady's special charge—or vice versa—and they are inseparable. Before the addition of Poke to the household, the young couple never went out without leaving someone to stay with the old mother. But now she feels quite safe with Poke, and they go out not only for the day, but for weekends, and Poke seems all the company the old lady wants. She spoke in German, and to Poke in German—and she understood her as well as I did. The upshot of it all was that I hadn't the heart to take Poke away from her. Being an old lady, her eyes were watery all the time, but as she described Poke's life and her own, the tears flowed over—and Poke, seeing it on one occasion, moaned. And she told me that Poke always moaned when she cried—so I take it she cries a lot. And though I, too, have cried when I have been lonesome—and especially at times when I fall or hurt myself—still, I couldn't take Poke from her. She tried to assure me that she wanted Poke not so much for herself but to make it easier for the "Kinder." It seems she felt that the daughter-in-law, being a young girl, would eventually become provoked with the mother because the son would never go anywhere unless the mother was looked after. But with Poke there, they never considered her, except to ask if she wanted to go—when, she assured me, Poke went too, or she wouldn't go.

Now then—could I take her?...

I sat there awhile after deciding to give her up; and then I decided to think it over and return the next day. But I never returned. I couldn't muster up the courage, for Poke was really hard to leave. I have given her up now entirely; and I think the past month—or, rather, the month after my return—was given over to being moody. For I was really very fond of her, even if she was a dog.

I saw Dr. Chance—the man who did the work on my eye—and he said I ought not to do any work that necessitated using my eyesight. Not knowing how in thunder I could earn a living any other way, I have to disregard his advice.

Too, I saw Mr. Wistar Brown III, a lawyer and one of the directors of the Indian Rights Association (that Mr. Welsh is associated with) in reference to procuring a divorce from Albert. Though Mr. Brown is a close friend of Mr. Welsh,...I did not know of this when I went to see him. I was directed to him by the "Legal Aid for the Poor Society," and he consented to securing the divorce after I gave him all the facts in the case. The divorce will cost about $150.00—$25.00 of which I gave him at the start. He is to be paid in installments, and perhaps I won't have to appear at all to get it.

I took this step more to please my mother than anything else. She knows Ira Benjamin is here—and so does everyone else in Phila. (my family and his)—and she thinks if I had a divorce I'd marry him. Which fact I'm not so sure of—but I think if I had the divorce and

242

the right to marry, I could tell my own mind better. And, too, I think if I was divorced and had the right to marry, I could enjoy life better. For I could know the right sort of men, who are not so willing to see a woman that is married to another man. I think perhaps if my business hadn't suffered, I shouldn't have bothered—another thing the war is responsible for!...

Since I've returned...what work I got in was *chance* work—and generally notices terminating business and breaking contracts, etc.—all of which promised no follow-up work. I was despondent and, too, I was doing the work for nothing, almost. And yet I did hate to give up, though I was generally advised to. For not only was I not earning enough for current expenses, but I was going into debt of the sort that one has to pay—for wages, etc. Too, so much of the work that I might have gotten was being done gratis by the Multigraph Company—this, in the way of government, regimental, and fund announcements.

Finally, one day Mr. Benjamin and my friend who is with the McKim Advertising Agency came to see me, and they told me my attitude was suicidal and that I'd have to give up. I fell all to pieces, and I cried openly—I just couldn't help it. Later, when I was cooler, I talked it over with them. They admitted it was hard, but pointed out how other houses had suffered—because right and left one large and supposedly firm house was failing, after another—and they showed me a course where I could save myself....Their idea was that I should call in any money due me, and with that pay all debts for things consumed—such as paper, electricity, etc.—and for which I had nothing to give back. This I did—but due to W.H. Scraggie's failure (the biggest departmental store here—of a low order, something like Siegel Cooper's in New York), I was not able to collect all owed me. I had two other failures, but was paid 50 cents on the dollar, which about covered my investment—but for the Scraggie account, there had been an outlay of over $100.00 for paper alone! But by hook and crook, I paid all the debts (except $75.00 worth) of which I was advised to pay.

Now, then, we went to my landlord—or, rather, his agent—and we made the proposition to him like this. My lease runs out May 1, 1915. If the war is over by then, or before then, of course I will immediately resume business, and all is well. If not, I will try to resume it anyway on May first—and perhaps due to people adjusting themselves to the new conditions, it will be possible to find enough work to keep my shop busy. I paid him up to December 1st, leaving six months unpaid for.... For the six months, he is to accept 50 per cent of six months rent, payable in six payments—and if I don't open May 1st, he of course owns what is in the office....

I finished all the jobs, then closed the office. And it will stay that way, until either the war is over—or [until] May 1st, 1915, even if it isn't over....

In the meantime I'm without work—

Salary is now out of the question—hordes and hordes of girls work for a pittance, but most of these girls have homes, and when they get there have good, warm suppers—so they don't demand much. But I have to earn a fairly decent wage as everything is high...and frankly I'm hungry half the time.

Mr. Benjamin affiliated himself with a large real estate company here and is doing good—for the fact remains that Americans can do much more in business than Canadians.

When I closed my shop, you may know I was rather despondent—in fact, I was downright heartbroken. I asked for work in places where I am well known; and in almost every instance, though they would be glad to have me, they were ashamed to offer me the miserable pay they are now giving competent help. In lots of cases, there is not real need for this shaving of salaries, but greed makes them do it—since the girls in sheer desperation are willing to accept it. I tried going to the places I wasn't known—and immediately the question of my sight came up, and I was told to come back when my eye was well. Mr. Benjamin got me a position in the office he was in—$8.00, and that's considered a lot now—but I gave it up at the end of two days. For there were other girls and men clerks, and I knew they had it that Mr. B. was my sweetheart. And they are a vulgar lot, and their humor drove me frantic; and I knew it was only a matter of time before Mr. Benjamin would know of it and perhaps interfere in some way—and then perhaps lose his connection there, which is good. And I'm selfish enough to want him to do well, because he buys me an occasional really good dinner. Truly, I can't seem to think of much else now but good things to eat, and I think it's because the last month I've lived on such plain fare.

Then I worked two weeks for a firm that I owed $30.00 to. Or, rather, I went for them to Hamilton, Ontario (and was there five days—which, together with the work before I went and when I returned, took almost two weeks)—and by it I discharged my debt. The work was closing up their agency there. They paid my expenses while in Ontario, of $2.00 a day; and I saved enough out of that to live here a week.

I haven't a job in sight, even. Do you wonder I don't like to write? It seems so humiliating. I'm offered all sorts of work in the headquarters where work is being done for the soldiers—but as it is done for charity, I can't take it, as I must have money for food and room.

I hope to see a Mrs. MacKenzie today—to see about getting up a new fund for girls who were in offices, to make it unnecessary for them to go *on the streets*, which seems the only resource in these horrible times. Really—I know, perhaps better than others, how hard it is to keep from doing that. And I think if the rich people here could see it—that looking out for these girls is as important as sending Christmas boxes to the soldiers. . . .

Recently two girls have been sleeping with me—they just really had no places, as they had no work and were asked out of their boarding places. So I shared my bed for almost a week—to Mr. Benjamin's great displeasure, who said they were in the habit of going places with men and [that] I didn't know what they might do; and perhaps Mrs. Noakes wouldn't keep me. At any rate, I felt satisfied that they could get some sort of a man if they wanted to be bad—and the fact that they preferred to be with me proved they were all right. They were both handsome girls—one, the younger, being really beautiful. One was Scotch-Irish and the other French Canadian. Lulu, the French girl, met a man—thru another girl— who took her to luncheon. And after luncheon the girls went to his apartment; and there they found that he had sleeping accommodations for twelve people. And every night as much as eight or ten girls sleep there—and he told them about it as though he was the Good Samaritan. His apartment is in one of the finest and newest apartments here, and he is a member of one of the oldest and richest families here. Lulu, it appears, told him of me and Margaret, and he invited the three of us to dinner in a very fine restaurant,; and I went—mainly because I was hungry for decent food and, too, because I wanted to see into this thing. For according to Lulu he has intercourse with any or all of these girls as he fancies them and runs a regular harem there.

245

I found him a most suave person—but a gentleman, apparently to the fingertips. He seemed a little annoyed, at first, because he said I looked at him critically. But after he had some cocktails he forgot that and was very affable. Not any of us drank anything but coffee. The dinner cost him $12.00—and we could have lived on that for a week! After the dinner, he asked if we would go to his apartment, and I went gladly, for I wanted to see the place.

It is fitted out almost sumptuosly, but evidently for a bachelor's apartment—and yet there were *five Baldwin couches,* on which two or three can sleep quite comfortably, besides his own bed. He has a Chinese man who is the housekeeper. Food and a bed, any girl can get there, provided she is pretty. And if, after they've slept one night and eaten, and won't have his attentions, the Chinese servant is told they can't remain or return.

We found four girls there, and one of them a Jewess—who was really beautiful and who, it seems, is his favorite and occupies the bedroom. The talk was not vulgar—and really the conditions were so odd and remarkable that my head hurt trying to figure out how this man came to start such a thing. He asked me to play the piano. I said I couldn't. He said, "I'll bet you can play, though—you look like a musician." I smiled—I thought it was sarcasm. Presently, he went out of the room and then called "Oh, Mrs. Jones, look here a moment," and as I neared the door, he said, "Here is an instrument you can play fine—all Jewesses are very adept on this." And when I looked, he had naked himself and it was disgusting. As I had not removed my wraps—nor did the girls—we lost no time getting out. I hope you don't mind my telling you this exactly as it happened.

With this in mind, I thought: If two large houses, with beds such as institutions or hospitals have, were thrown open for girls who are out of work, and a small sum set aside for the maintenance of it, girls could come in as they need a haven, and would find a bed and some sustenance. In return for which, they could sew, or knit, or do something for the soldiers. I know the expense couldn't be very much—because empty houses in the heart of the city are plentiful; and the equipment could be very meagre, and yet be comfortable; and the girls could and would do the work themselves. If I could get Mrs. Mackenzie to start this thing, I'd run the place and collect funds for it—just for my room and board, until May 1st. They seem mad here about providing delicacies for the soldiers for Christmas—whereas girls like Margaret, Lulu, Stella and myself (and I could mention twenty-five more that I know) will not have even food for Christmas. For everyone is busy with the soldiers and can't stop for anything else. If I can secure Mrs. MacKenzie's help, I will go also to Lady Allen. I am not myself desperate, for I know very well that I can ask for and get some assistance. But many of these girls have no one to apply to, for up to now they always contributed to someone's support in the country towns from where they came—and the easiest thing is to accept things and a bed from some "Good Samaritan" like Mr. Vance.

If I cannot get any encouragement from Mrs. MacKenzie, I am going to the owners of two houses, quite near here, that are enormous and have been empty for years—and see if we can occupy them until May 1st. And if we secure the houses, I will personally *beg*—for coal first, then beds and chairs; and if we can't get food, at least we can manage beds for the office girls out of work....

Is it not terrible that this war must go on this winter? While my sympathies are of course for the Allies, I feel so dreadfully sorry for the Germans who are fighting in the East, for it is very cold there now. Mrs. Noakes has two brothers who were reservists and who are now at war—one in Belgium and one in France. He sent several snapshots home of German soldiers who are prisoners; and for some reason, I'm feeling so sorry for the Germans—who are really the underdogs, since it is now so certain they can't win.

I will write oftener now. You can understand, I know, how I hated to tell you of my real conditions. For I was so proud all last spring and summer!

March 26, 1915

MY MOTHER IS HERE. IT CAME ABOUT IN THIS FASHION. MR. BENJAMIN   93 ⊠
wrote her (some time ago, I believe) that she ought to come. Of late, I have written very seldom to my family—but in consequence they seem to have been writing more than usual. In one of the letters, someone writing for my mother said that she wanted to come, but right now hadn't or couldn't afford the money, but perhaps she would come in the summer. Then my brother James wrote, saying that he was not able to give Mother the money necessary for her to take a trip, but couldn't I send it?

You can scarcely understand what this made me feel. Though I had never asked them for money—for their letters are always written to forestall that—still, I made no attempt to conceal the fact that I am long without work and that I have had a very hard road to travel thru this winter.

At first I wanted to write him and end forever any attempt at friendliness. I was infuriated. It was such an insult—it proved that he either did not believe me, or, receiving my letters, does not give them an intelligent reading and hasn't known anything about my difficulties. I didn't answer his letter at all. But then another circumstance brought about a condition which resulted in my mother's coming, Mr. Welsh giving her the ticket.

Mrs. Noakes, my landlady, has near relations, all people of large means, living not far off. She receives no benefits from them—but derives much happiness from the fact that an uncle has a Japanese cook! One of these [relations], an aunt, wrote her recently to come to her home, the aunt being left alone. The male members of her family received commissions and are enroute to the front; and the aunt needed her comfort and company. Mr. Noakes was anxious to have his wife go because, as he told me confidentially, if she went now, he would not be obliged to send her off this summer to some high priced summer resort—which he can ill afford, as his salary has been reduced 50 per cent. But she isn't the kind to take that in consideration, and would perhaps insist on going somewhere.

All this was satisfactory, except that Mrs. N. was not satisfied about leaving me to take care of the place as she had done before, unless I'd promise faithfully not to allow one girl across the threshhold. A very pleasant outlook to be sure! She isn't as bad as that makes her appear, but she has her notions; and recently her pet theory is that I am the victim of my own good intentions, and that she isn't going to be a party to the crime of finishing me. She has taken a fearful dislike to Stella Phillips, a beautiful red-haired girl that I am trying to keep out of the gutter. (Mrs. N. doesn't mean to be, and she doesn't know that she is, fearfully "catty" about Stella; and the real reason is because Stella is the handsomest girl I've ever seen.) Since Mrs. N. wouldn't leave me to take charge, and I had nowhere else to go, I wrote to Mr. Welsh. In the same letter, I wrote of James's impudence in asking if Mother could take a trip at my expense. Mr. Welsh sent a railroad ticket for her to James; and as it was only good for two days, I believe, she came away at once; and I never knew she was near here until she walked in.

This changed the aspect of things here. Mrs. N. felt she could go and leave Mother in charge. I suppose she could see in Mother's eyes that there would be no "nonsense," as she calls it—for, of the two, Mrs. N.'s is really the more charitable and kindly-intentioned. Mrs. N. is mostly "bark." If a girl asks for me when I am in, she shows them in and scowls at me behind their backs, and does everything to make me uncomfortable. If I am not in and they call, she will ask them in and assure them I won't be long—and gives them a magazine, and generally entertains them with long accounts about my good qualities: which I can scarcely credit when they tell me; but hearing it from so many, I am sure it must be so. Now, isn't she a queer person? Her fear is that I will bring some girl in off the street who will wake up in the night and kill us all off for the forty or fifty cents there is generally in the exchequer.

Now, my mother is quite a different sort of person. She smiles and fawns upon the world at large, and it is my belief that she was never sincere about anything in her life.

The day after she came, Mrs. N. went on her visit—to return the "very" day Mother leaves. So she says, but she won't. This she says so that I won't think that after Mother goes I can run an asylum here for "blind cats," as she calls my friends, and [so that] by thinking she may return any minute, I am not likely to have anyone overnight. Thus, Mother was installed. She also prepares breakfast, and dinner at night for Mr. Noakes, and though she doesn't like it, Stella is here the most of the time.

I want to write you of my mother, my feelings toward her, etc. For though I know it isn't of the greatest interest to you, still I feel I want to write it; and you will understand.

That I don't feel the attitude or relationship that should exist between mother and daughter you know. And though I account for much of this by bearing in mind that I've seen so little of her, there is an aloofness that I am sure is not because we don't know each other well. In the first place, she isn't honest and above-board in her dealings with me; even her thoughts aren't sincere to herself—if you can understand that.

According to the books I've read and some of the nice people I've come in contact with, a mother and daughter is perhaps the closest relationship. And when I look on this woman, and I force myself to keep in mind that I was born of her, that I lay in her arms as a baby, nursed of her breast and was at one time, her chief interest, I listen for a cry in my heart for her—and there isn't any. I look at her and feel toward her only coldness. This I am sure is unnatural, and I feel sure I am to blame. Don't think that I bear her any ill will for wrongs, fancied or real—I don't. I want so hard to love her—or even like her—and I can't. I can't explain what prevents me; but spontaneously, when commenting on her to Mr. Benjamin the other night, I said, "That woman is the nearest thing to nothing that I ever knew." Fine thing to say of one's mother, but I said it—and regretted it immediately afterwards.

Sometimes, I pick up a girl—weak in character, morals, health, everything—and I find a certain amount of pleasure in using my strength in all these things to better the weakling's status; and no matter how many times they fail me, I lay it to the weakness entirely, and keep right on. Generally, I hang on to prove that someone's theory is incorrect about this person; and even though I may not be altogether successful, I call it worthwhile if I have made the girl learn to keep her teeth clean, or wear brassieres to confine large busts, or trifles of this sort, which all lead to better things. Too, I'll pick up a girl who is strong—in her vices. Never did a thing except to further her own interests; and her interests are generally vicious ones. This kind of girl I like to have find her own strength and learn to appreciate it and use it in the proper channels. Generally, this is easier than to make a weakling strong—and the result, if not always entirely satisfactory, is encouraging, for at least I've shown them how they can utilize their strength; and the time comes when this girl remembers that she can use this strength for clean things as readily as she can for undesirable things—

I tell you all this to show you then, [while] I feel so indifferent to my mother...I have the capacity to feel for and do for persons unknown to me and who are "bad" in so many ways—as "bad" is considered by the general public.

My mother is a woman of fifty-four years of age; smaller than I am, but a bit stout—though not ungainly. While not a smart dresser, still she doesn't look like a frump, nor is she one who overdresses. Her appearance is quite creditable. She is clean in her general habits, and though not versed in all the little things that are considered good form at, or away from, table, still she doesn't annoy me with mannerisms as do so many other members of my family.

Now then—why can't I like her? It must be because of the woman which is under the skin.

She is generally very affable, quiet-spoken and not critical. But she never seems to be anything but froth; she only hits the bare outside of things. All these things I felt...ever since the time I saw her again after our separation of eleven years; and though I vaguely reasoned all this out, before I was of the opinion that environments had much to do with it, and if I once got her away from her little clique, I would soon learn if she had any depth of feeling toward me. But I don't know now any more than I did before. She is always kindly but never sincere. All bubbles and froth—and yet she wants to give the impression of solidity. From the first night she arrived, until tonight, I've thought to talk to her along lines that would bring out her true self but I haven't been able to. She evades everything and [falls] back on that melodramatic "mother role."

We get along most serenely because we never scratch thru the veneer.

She wasn't in the place five minutes before she told how she had expected to tip the porter on the train and found that she had lost or forgotten her pocketbook. How embarassing—not to have a nickel! I gave this no serious thought, but slept little that night and was quite bitter. For this speech wearied me: it shows the trend of her mind. I gave her the surprise of her life the next day when I told her that I hadn't a cent and did not know where I could get one. I saw the way the wind was blowing when she said, "Call Ira up and tell him to come here." I told her I knew he hadn't any money; and she was quite sad for a moment. Then she told me that on going thru her effects she found she had brought along $10.00 in another purse. Do you wonder this sort of thing makes it hard for me...?

All week, the slightest thing brings the "mother role" to the front—but frankly, I don't believe she feels it any more than I do, and I wish it was not necessary to keep up the bluff. When she talks to anyone in my absence or when she thinks I am out of earshot, she is quite voluble; but when I am around, she assumes a meek attitude, and mumbles and shifts her eyes. She never addresses me and looks me straight in the eye. At the slightest mention of anything praiseworthy, she calls to mind my brothers and sister in their youth or present life—and her manner of telling it makes of me an outsider. She speaks of herself and my brothers and sister as "we," and I am "you."

Can you judge from this what is wrong in our relationship?

I hope I haven't bored you with this—I wanted to get this off my chest. Even Mr. Benjamin, who knows all this, is not the person to tell it to—for he keeps the "mother" idea safely to the front (for he has a very dear mother who is all sincerity and love), and he can't understand why I don't love her, and how I can manage to see anything undesirable in her. He blames me entirely. And I feel guilty and wish I could accept her. Of course, I am as fine to her as I know how to be. I am, as nearly as I can be, like a daughter who loves her mother.

Her stay will be until after Easter. She can do nothing to better my condition. Only, while she is here, I am more cheerful, for it is being a bit more like other folks who have kin.

As I believe I told you, she has a little money saved up. How much, of course, I don't know. I always thought it was a tidy sum, but I may be wrong. Now, her story is that when she married her present husband, she pooled her interests with his and, as he grows older, he has become miserly to the extreme and refuses to part with a cent, except for actual necessities. So, to quote her, she isn't "able to lay aside even a little, with which to assist her unfortunate daughter." Of course, this may be true—and I believe it is, for I know her husband and can well believe this. So you see it isn't because she doesn't help me that I bear her this feeling that I am ashamed of. Since she has been here she spent what she had, but no more is forthcoming. I hope it is true that she is not able to help. If I find this is not so—I will cease trying to care for her entirely....

I have received the two numbers of the *Atlantic*. I thank you. I read both articles of Mr. Sedgwick. He is a wonderful writer. It must be fine to have such an education, to be sure what one writes is grammatically correct and, too, to have such a vocabulary!...[28]

I am answering your letters—each thought as I come to it. Therefore you will understand why I jump from one thing to the next, apparently without reason. This I do to cover each point touched upon in your two letters. Your idea of my being able to find work helping girls who have [gone astray] has been suggested to me both by Mr. Welsh and Mr. Benjamin—and as I think of it, I recall that a probation officer here also suggested it. It is a splendid idea and it is work I would find congenial, if not very lucrative. But

I must have some pay to live on—and there's the rub! I would prefer not to write this, for it sounds ridiculously egotistical, but I believe I am correct that I can do more, given the time, with a girl who is on the street, toward getting her to go to work, than any ten ladies whose method of procedure is along the lines laid down by "rescue workers." Yet I don't think I could convince them of that. In Phila. I made an attempt to do this; in Wilmington; and here—and have never received any encouragement. Too, I would be a failure in this work if I was bound by the rules and regulations that I remember from my own experience, and come across now, that are used by the so-called rescue people. Suppose I did want to help, I could not do it except in my own way—I mean, I could only do it sincerely in my own way. Yet if I was paid a salary, no matter how tiny, I'd feel bound to work along lines such as they advocate; and they'd perhaps raise their hands in horror at my methods. Personally, I think 95 per cent of this "rescue work" is all bosh. . . . The girl is a down-and-outer—but she hasn't had a permanent change of ideas about her mode of living; it is only that she hasn't a bed or food, and is willing, for the time, to fold her hands and sing hymns. But they think they are smarter than those in whose charge they are, and only await the opportunity to get back again—and the next time (they think) they will better their conditions. Of course, there are exceptions—but I believe it is only when the exception is older and really is tired of the catch-as-catch-can method of living.

A probation officer here advised me to try to get work here along these lines, but cautioned me not to mention that I had ever lived a "fast" life, for she knew I would not be given the place. When I said I hadn't the desire to apply to do work for God and begin by cheating, she capitulated by saying that I should either say I am five years older or, if I did admit living in sin, not to make mention of how long, and to say that no one in Canada knows it. I'm not so hidebound that I couldn't or wouldn't do this to get a good place—but I don't fancy the idea of living in an institution; and the pay is almost nothing. So I never applied, and Miss Girouard feels sure I didn't want work very much.

Of course, I'd be glad—more than that, I'd be happy—to do this work for pay that would keep one above want. But who will pay it to me? The people who are organized to do this work wouldn't approve of my style of "rescue"—I am positive of that;—and immediately I'd be obliged to do my work along lines laid down by others, I'd be a rank failure. For I'm really not a successful hypocrite, and I wouldn't keep the bluff up for long, I know. I might say that though I am not paid, and should be doing things to earn my living, yet I never pass a day that some move isn't made in the interests of some girl or other. . . .

I do not think I shall go back to Phila., for many reasons. . . . I could not expect to live at James's. They do not live over the store now, but have a tiny home near it. Sarah (Potsy) is four years old and, another baby will be along shortly. For this reason, the mother of Caroline stays there all the time, and they have a maid— making it impossible for me to live there. And [even] if they had a place, it would be living in hell to be there. James won't let me touch Potsy. He calls me "blind"—and you may know it doesn't make me comfortable. He loves Potsy, and I sometimes dropped her—or rather bumped into things and we both fell—this only when she would wiggle and twist out of my hands. And now, at my last visit, several times he reminded me not to pick her up—"for you know you are blind on one side, and why risk her life?" Isn't that ridiculous, when she is four years old? He won't let me walk out with her. In fact, I can only touch her when he isn't around. And she is so sweet. She has grown into a fine child. Not very pretty, but sturdy, and has the fine character and sweet disposition of her mother. She talks like a Bostonian, with broad a's; and we don't know how that is, since no one else in the family does. They all joke about it—but I love to hear it.

As for living with my mother, that is out of the question, as she has no home now. She sold her place last May, and since then [they] have boarded with relatives.

Now, as for any material help that I can get from them—it is practically nil. I will tell you why. I am not sure, but I think they don't really believe that I receive no benefits from men generally— nor that I don't give any. I haven't any real proof of this except their attitude. They've never relaxed. They've never let me become one of them. I am an outsider. In my presence nothing personal is discussed. This may also be because of the fact that I don't believe in (and say so freely) their hypocritical attitude toward their religion. As far as they are concerned, they are not troubled much by religion, but they think they are quite all right as long as they at least have no religion. But because I go to church on Sunday and because I have Episcopalian prayer books and hymnals, I have committed a heinous sin toward Judaism and, I believe, toward our entire family.

Too, in Phila.,...I am always haunted...by the fear that some one will know me—either the man I apply to for the position, or someone who calls there. And many firms there—hundreds of them—I wouldn't try to work for, because of that, or because they may be some kin to me. I have many kin in Phila.—all Hebrews, of course, and all in business—whom I always shun.

When I worked for the *North American* in Phila., I had made good friends among the girls there—all girls who hoped someday to do something real in the newspaper field. One girl had a fiance, and she asked me to theatre with them—seats in the gallery. I went and enjoyed myself thoroughly. The next day I noticed a coldness, and each day it grew worse. I couldn't stand it any longer—and asked this girl point-blank. What she told she had heard was the truth; and I didn't attempt to deny it. Someone recognized me while with them in the gallery.

Now do you see why, if I could, I would rather not return to Phila., as long as the chances there are as bad as they appear to be? According to Mr. Welsh, there is even more distress there than there is here; and taking it all in consideration, and not forgetting that I had some prestige here in business, and that I have yet the fringe of a business to hang onto, I don't think I would be bettering myself to go to Phila.

Of course, I am hopeful. If I wasn't, I'd long ago have given up trying to hang on here. People generally say that by summer, negotiations for peace will be underway; and everyone thinks (including Mr. Benjamin, who stays here for that reason) that next winter will find Montreal very busy.

The immediate outlook is very bad for me. There isn't a thing in sight—but I do feel something will turn up. I can't explain it—or perhaps I can, by saying that I feel, my troubles being due to the war, I expect will depart with signs of peace. And I have that "waiting" feeling. I can't shake it off entirely—even though each day looks more hopeless than the last—that I will be all right if I can only hang on and start here again, after the war....

I would rather stay here for many reasons, all things being

equal; and my reasons are all due to the fact that Philadelphia stands for the old life—and Canada for the place where I was, for the only time in my life, free.

When a person determines to do a thing that requires strength, it is of course harder when everyone about is offering to break down this determination; and following the lines of least resistance is most natural.

Since last summer, I have spent many days seeking work, directly or indirectly, by going about in the business districts where I am known; and on some of these days, I was downright hungry. I have gone for hours without food, and could have gotten it by simply phoning to Mr. Benjamin. But I was ashamed to, and couldn't...make up any scheme to bring him out that wouldn't immediately let him know that I was hungry. Mind you, I don't think I care a rap about being more or less poverty-stricken all the time; but it makes me feel like a miserable rat not to have enough food—and I can't stand it.

Now why I tell you this is to show you the difference between living here and in Phila. If the same thing happened in Phila., I would be asked thru one day, many times, to "have a drink"; and a luncheon engagement is readily managed. And yet I prefer to stay here, where no man ever asked me to have a drink, and I don't have to exert any great effort to refrain from doing so, when I am cold or hungry.

Will you say whether you agree with me and Mr. Benjamin, and Mr. Welsh's opinion, that it is as well for me to remain?

The $5.00 you sent, I used to pay for what was most urgent at the time. I owed $4.00 in a little shop for groceries. I paid $2.00 of it. I had borrowed in cash $1.50—50 cents at a time, from Mr. Noakes, in the last ten days. I repaid that. I bought some things in the drugstore:

a package of R & G. Rice Powder	.19
1 Tube of Pebeco Paste	.39
1 toothbrush	.35
1 bottle of Droxygen	.19
2 cakes of soap (Ivory and scrubbing)	.10
1 pkge. of absorbent cotton	.10
1 roll of adhesive for my patches	.49
	$1.81

I hope you won't think I was silly to buy these things all at once. You see, I've needed a new supply for so long—one thing gave out after another, but I hadn't the money to spare. The $5.00, and $2.00 from Mr. Benjamin paid for this and my laundry, owed for two weeks back.

Do you see, I did spend it all for myself? But in order to show you I am really not altogether selfish, I'll admit that all the 50-cent pieces borrowed from Mr. Noakes were for Stella Phillips' mother, who promised to return them and didn't. She may yet, some day, but it is doubtful, and one can hardly blame her. I live in affluence and luxury compared to those people, and they are more willing than I am. The only thing that gets one's nerve is that the 50-cent pieces are borrowed to take to the priest as offerings! I wouldn't have given them to her, had I known it—I thought it was to buy food for Stella and her two sisters, brother, father and mother. Stella told me how her mother used the money—after she had gotten 50 cents three times.

I have read frequently of late of Mr. Osborne and the great reforms he is instituting at Sing Sing. I should like very much to read his book—if you have it—and will send it back...I will be very careful of it.[29] If you haven't it and would have to buy it, I don't think I'd like you to spend money for me for that purpose.

I sure would like work among unfortunates, but I'll confess to you that I have a perfect horror—or terror, rather—of institutions. Please try to understand this. I don't mean I wouldn't work in an institution, if I could not get other work; but frankly, I recoil from it just the same as though I anticipated being an inmate.

Sometimes, when I undertake to help a girl find work and she offers objections to work of this nature or that, I immediately label her as a shirker and instinctively I dislike her. Don't feel this way about me, please, for I am sincere about trying to forge ahead. But don't put me in an institution. I've formed such a picture in my mind of my life there, since reading your letter, that I've cried several times in self-pity. I've been in so many of them, and I dread them. Roughly, I count eight—for disorders moral and physical— and even as an attendant, I should suffer if confined in one. I feel sure I'd want to and would liberate those I'd feel sorry for. It's so terrible, especially when those confined have bright minds and are eager for better things. It is terrible—and prisons and institutions for reform should not be tolerated by Christian people.

I am very grateful for Mr. Sedgwick's help. I have thought much, since receiving your letter, about his offer to help me; and I can't tell you how it pleases me. I know, knowing me through you, you haven't represented me as a whining pauper, and that he hasn't given the money to me because I am such a woebegone creature. I don't ever want to get in the class that in Jewish is called a *schnorrer*—i.e., a professional beggar, of the sort who permits all sorts of help to be given and who pretends that it is done out of friendliness, when in reality it is pity....Will you thank him for me?....As for how I will spend it, I cannot say—only that I can't realize ever needing it more than I do now....I have had every class of ad in the paper in the last six months; I've had all sorts of replies; but somehow, as Mrs. Noakes says, I can get the jobs, but don't keep them—for she thinks it is getting the situation when I am asked to call....

My mother has fretted me to death about this letter. She can't understand what on earth anyone can write so much about.... This week is the Hebrew Passover— We had a clash over the necessity for doing some things she considered indispensable in order to properly welcome in this feast. I find my sympathies are not in favor of these customs, which seem to me all hypocrisy and cant, especially when it means doing things that are positively barbarous.

Mr. Herbert Welsh
Baynton Street, Philadelphia
My dear Father,   *April 27, 1915*

⁖ 96   I AM ACTING ON YOUR ADVICE ABOUT WRITING, THOUGH LAST WEEK I did almost no writing whatever, due to having had to stay several days in bed. I was ill, but am quite well today. I doctored myself, but was able to buy medicine with some of the money out of that which you sent for Alice. My illness was due to having taken cold, no doubt, for I had earache, headache, and backache. You see, I am still wearing the same clothes I wore all winter; and as it has been very warm, I had to take the coat off at times, when coming up the hill which leads to my house—and due to this, my mother thinks, I caught cold.

Stella is also ill, but I've had her under the doctor's care (for which there is no charge) since Monday. This doctor is a fine

Christian gentleman. I only found him out the past fortnight. He said he would give me advice at any time I ask it, for any of my girls; and he is an able physician. I have been to no less than twenty-five doctors, since I have been in Montreal, for one girl or another, and this is the only doctor who has interested himself in my attempt to help the girls. This will be a great help and a saving of money. Of course, I will have to pay for medicine at the drugstore, but not when it is a small dose of something that he can administer.

Stella's trouble was diagnosed by other doctors as weakness due to various troubles, but it is positive now that she has an advanced case of leukorrhea, which the doctor says is similar to gonorrhea.[30]

The doctor assured me it did not come from any contact with a man but, due to her being so weak, the disease was natural in a girl who had so young been with men. She has dizzy spells. I wrote you before that when her mother beats her, she is, for a week or more, very morose and, I thought, acted a little stupid or unbalanced. It develops—according to what the doctor says—that this is caused by loss of blood which she can ill spare.

My heart aches and the tears come as I write, for I love this girl more than any other; and I try so hard to do for her, and I am so handicapped. But I pray earnestly, unceasingly, and I know I will conquer. Yesterday, at tea, she was talking; and as I watched her—her face is so beautiful and so delicate—I saw how transparent her skin is, due to lack of blood. Truly, with the light properly placed, one could see straight through her nose. She goes daily, now, to the doctor, who gives· her treatment—douches, etc.—and in five days she feels almost miraculously better. I have much hope from this. It was trying to me, as you can imagine, for I spare no efforts to do everything to better her health, which I considered of paramount importance. But now I've gotten to the root of it; and once this discharge is controlled—which causes the weakness, dizziness and backaches—I think she will grow steadily better. We always see to it that Stella gets the best food of all, and that which is most strengthening, and it was so discouraging to see it all go for nothing. The gymnasium classes had to be stopped, for the doctor thought she was too weak. But he advocates long walks; and this morning we go on our first walk together. The doctor asked that she have chicken broth twice a day, but I told him frankly I couldn't afford that—and he said we could try beef. Fact is, we have little meat because it is so expensive; and then, Mother is a vegetarian and hasn't tasted meat in twenty years—so it is hard to get meat, when she so strongly objects to it. The doctor thought oatmeal gruel good for Stella, with real cream; and I get that, even though it is expensive. But as for chicken broth—it would take two chickens a week, and at the rate of $1.25 to $1.50 a chicken (for I'd only buy it at good places), I can't do it. For the money gives out too soon as it is.

Now, my dear father, I will tell you of the changes that will take place. May 1st, Stella's mother moves, as I told you, to one room in a married sister's house, and of course, Stella has to vacate. Now, Mrs. Noakes is still gone (though she was home last Tuesday for the day, and expressed herself as being very pleased with the condition she found her house in—for she came unexpectedly) and she will stay away all summer; and as soon [as] Mother is ready to go back, Stella will come here to live with me. Mother is here more than two months; and as Caroline—my brother's wife—is to give birth to a child in May, my mother is fretting to get back to attend her. By good fortune, when Mrs. Noakes came on Tuesday, we discussed it freely; and I have made an admirable arrangement, for she is willing to let me take charge alone. It is a case of Hobson's choice, for she doesn't want to come back and stay in the city all summer—and as I take such good care of her flat and pay her, besides, she couldn't help but give in to my arrangements. Mother will go as soon as she can, and I will have to ask you to send the ticket again. She evidently took it for granted that you made the trip possible and—though I had not considered that part of it—she no doubt expected from the start that you would see to her returning, as you did her coming. She takes this for granted...I judge this from her conversation. So I am obliged to tell you, though I don't like it. I will say for her that she is sincere in her gratitude toward you for having made the trip possible. She said (to quote her exact words to Mrs. Phillips), "Stella is a good girl. When Maimie was her age, I'd have been happy if she was only half as good and obedient as Stella is to you. But then, what's the difference? The 'bad' girls have the best hearts, and you will some day have much pleasure from seeing Stella married and settled down. Look at this—of all my children, it is Maimie who was able to give me the only trip I ever had in thirty-five years, and I am sure Stella will give you a like pleasure some day."

To return to our arrangements. Stella is obliged to come here May 1st—or go to the House of Good Shepherd, which I pray God nightly that she be delivered from doing—and Mother will go as soon as you send a ticket.

Now, then, Alice is still here, but goes May 1st to work again. I got her a job to do general housework in a small flat; but as it is a job where she will have to "sleep out," I agreed that she can stay here until a job to "sleep in" can be procured. It is my aim to get her a job to go to the country for the summer—thus killing two birds with one stone, for she will be away from her old associates and, too, regain her health. But now this isn't possible, because I am obliged to tell the truth about her career before seeking this employment. And to take a girl whose character is unsettled to the country, at an expense—I am afraid I won't be able to find anyone just now willing to do so. But after this position, I will seek one for her in the country. But for the present, she will sleep in the couch in the living room, except Friday, Saturday and Sunday nights of each week, when she can occupy the bed of Mrs. and Mr. Noakes—for each weekend he will join his wife, starting May 1st. (They can buy weekend tickets from May to September, and this he will do.) In that way, I can offer a bed over Sunday to any girl or girls—and oh, if you knew what a world of things are running through my head to do this summer, because of this rare privilege! This isn't an ordinary flat; it is a bit extraordinary to be able to have for this purpose. It is furnished in such good taste and simplicity—

Goodness! how I run on—I forgot entirely that you were here and know for yourself how the waifs I pick up will look upon the possibility of having weekends here—to bathe and learn to keep clean— I am so enthusiastic. Do you remember how I wanted to have a place like this in Wilmington? Well, I have it, all furnished, and so sweet and clean, with two double beds—Of course, from Tuesday to Friday, I can only use one bed and a couch; but weekends I can house five girls—six on a stretch—and I am going to do it. Stella is as enthusiastic as I am. Of course, she is very young; and that she said, "Oh! Maimie—and now when Mr. Noakes is gone, we can have some fellows in, too," you understand, is because she can't gather in my exact plans. But that is good enough. I said, "Yes, we can have fellows, too—if you have any that are of our class." Stella knows but few boys of this kind. Her former acquaintances were "club men" who own powerful motor cars, etc.—and they certainly will never get in here, if I know it.

Well, do you think I am right in being enthusiastic about this rare chance? The expense for rent will be as it has been for the two months that Mother is here—$6.00 a week, or $25.00 a month—which gives us beds, use of a dining room and kitchen, with light, and gas for cooking, and a fully equipped house for living. When Mother goes, I shall have the girls that come prepare the meals—both because they all love to, and fight for the chance and, too, because I am not fit for it. (At present I have a cut finger that is two weeks healing—I went to cut a lemon and, not gauging correctly, bore down directly on my thumb and cut almost ¼ inches deep.) My nervous temperament makes me unfit for the small business of cooking our tiny meals—and, too, when there are six potatoes to peel, it takes ten minutes to quell the riot, if Alice and Stella are not permitted to peel them together. These two do not "hit" it together, but their differences are not serious. It is always brought about because Stella won't let me share my love for her, without protest. If I meet a new girl, Stella worries me constantly as to whether I like the girl better than I do her. So you can see how easy it is for them to quarrel, since just now I favor Alice more, for she is on thin ice. She is now two months away from her former bad life, and of course this is a dangerous time—this I know from my own experience. For she no doubt feels a longing once in a while to return; and she never goes out for a minute, that I am not nervous as to whether she will return. She has the suit of Miss Outerbridge's, and I fashioned a hat out of some little ribbons Miss O. sent; so she looks real sweet—and that, too, sometimes makes them want to see some of their former associates, so as to "show off."

Now then, if you think my plan as good as I do—it will be done like this:

Mother will leave as soon as she has the ticket.

Stella will come and occupy my room with me in Mother's place. She will go to the doctor's daily, and I will be on the lookout to get her an apprentice's position in a hairdresser's shop. Everyone thinks this would be the best thing for Stella, inasmuch as the work is light, and her glorious hair and face would make her an asset in a shop where women come to have their persons attended to. Do you like this idea? It will be subject to your approval. Of course, as an apprentice she would get no pay, but in time she would be worth $8.00 or $10.00 a week, if she is proficient.

Alice will stay for a while, sleeping on the couch, eating her meals at her work—and, as she progresses, I will try to get her a place in the country.

Now I have a new girl, Hazel Lowe. Canadian born; seventeen years old; one of three sisters, all of whom are fast, and Hazel is the only one who wants to come here. She is very affectionate—and pretty. Flashing brown eyes—long, narrow face—good teeth, and a small mouth. Dimple in her chin; high color; and masses of brown hair with a wave in it. She is tall and thin. Her education is nil. I believe she is entirely illiterate, though she says she can write—I doubt it. She confessed to Alice that she wishes Maimie would teach her to write, too; but she told Stella she could—no doubt she was ashamed, for she knows Stella well. This girl has a mother and father who live on what these girls bring in and the earnings of one boy, who is a cab driver, gambler—and altogether worthless.

Too, I've seen Georgette Mayfield twice this week. I heard she was in a house of ill fame and went there Monday and saw her. She looked very well, but complained of her lot. I went again Tuesday and took her a book in French, which belonged to Jean Holland— and would have gone again since then, but I was ill, as I told you. And of course I wouldn't send Stella there. Stella is very good for such errands, as she praises her life since obeying me, and—she being the *prettiest girl in Montreal*—they all take her word far more than some girl's whom they think might stick to me as the next-best thing to starving. I wouldn't think, though, of sending her to a place like that; it would bring her in contact with the life I strive to make her forget.

There is a bit of bad news yet to tell—it is about a sister of Stella's. Her name is Sharon. It is barely possible that I have never mentioned her to you before, the reason being that she has always been out in domestic service—and I only heard of her myself. She is twenty years old, and since fourteen has been "sleeping out," doing housework—in the city, of course—but I never saw her until last week, though of late Stella mentioned her occasionally, because she was ill. This girl, while "red-headed," hasn't any of Stella's pulchritude, and her temperament is decidedly different. She is a plain, stupid-looking girl, with all the earmarks of the kitchen. Phlegmatic and entirely uninteresting. Illiterate, of course—but very religious. For according to Stella's mother, this daughter was the only one that gave the respect to the Catholic Church that Mrs. Phillips thought right. Well, this girl, came home very ill last week; and as they hadn't money to take her to a doctor, I did. I took her to my new friend, and he told me she has been pregnant for nearly six months. It was the most surprising thing I ever heard. For this girl lacks everything that one associates with girls who lose their heads. The facts are these: She has some girl friends—three sisters, all devout Catholics—whose father is a night watchman in a factory directly back of this house; and they (the daughters) and their father (without a mother) live there. Sharon was there always on her nights off. She said [that] in December a chap who came there freely had intercourse with her. I am quite ready to believe it happened only once, and never before or since. Anyone would believe it readily who saw and talked to the girl. To prove to you that she is a silly, unsophisticated girl, I will tell you what she said in explanation—"He did it to all of us—and the three Thompson girls aren't sick."

The fellow's name is Carey, and he is an all-around good-for-nothing. He has no father, and isn't twenty-one. His mother is a tailoress, and I went to see her. She said it would be folly for him to marry the girl, and she wouldn't lend herself to ruining any girl by insisting on his marriage. She said he hadn't worked since he was twelve, and she only supported him to prevent his doing worse than he does. She earns $8.50 a week—and after seeing Father Cotter, we arranged to send Sharon to a convent where the pay is $8.00 a month. The mother of the boy agreed to pay this out of her wages. After the baby is born, she can take it or leave it. Of course, this remains to be seen. I will take Sharon there tomorrow at 9 A.M. . . .

If it was done in passion or to earn money, it would be bad enough—but I know positively that it wasn't. It was done just as she might make him a cup of tea. . . . Of course, all this is too bad for all of them, but Mrs. Phillips is tirading and ranting more than ever, and poor Stella is having a very hard time of it, in consequence. Her mother struck her, causing violent nosebleed— on Wed. of last week—when Stella insisted that she stop calling Sharon a "whore" in the presence of Joan, the youngest sister. . . .

I will close now, as I must go out to see Father Cotter by appointment about Sharon's trip tomorrow to the convent. I assured Sharon of my cooperation—and I shall try to have her take the baby out. For after all, it is her baby, and it seems a pity she shouldn't have it.

I will have to write some letters for my mother, and my hand is tired already. Your loving daughter, Maimie

My dear friend,   *Ca. May 1, 1915*

I HAVE A LETTER IN THE WRITING TO MISS HUNTINGTON BUT WILL SET IT   **97** ⊗

aside to answer your letter. . . .

I am quite well again—it was as you surmised a bad cold, and very troublesome until I checked it. It was an inexpensive sickness. Fortunately, only the week before I had—for the first time in the one year and nine months that I live here—found a doctor who showed any desire to help me, help a girl when she is ill. I went to him with Alice—she burned her hands dreadfully—and though I have been to at least fifteen doctors here with girls, beginning with Ethel when she was pregnant, I never had one ask me why I came with the girls, nor any questions as to the whys-and-wherefores of my existence. This doctor, a Frenchman, did; and I was only too glad when he showed this interest to tell him truly everything. I always tell now that I once lived an immoral life (my uneasiness because I never told Nina Brown taught me the lesson)—and he was perfectly lovely. He speaks only a broken English; but he said at any time, I could come as often as I pleased and bring any case, and he would be happy to attend them. Of course, I have to provide the medicines; but he said at any time when the medicine or application was trivial, he had the means to supply it in his office and would be glad to. You don't know what a piece of good luck that was, to find him, for every girl I know now needs medical attention. And when I found I was ill, and it was possible to have a doctor without an outlay of $2.00, for the visit, I had the doctor—and was soon on the road to recovery. I feel as usual today, though strangely, in the past month, I've lost considerable weight. This doesn't trouble me, because I prefer being thin—if, of course, I am well. But it does seem strange that during the winter, when I went for days with so little food that it seems incredible, I kept getting heavier; and in the last month, when I have had regular meals (since Mother has been here), I am steadily losing weight. One thing may account for it. During the winter, when I had much to contend with—due to owing for everything I had—I had little money to buy food. . . . Well, one night, I discovered that hot water, sipped as hot as one can stand it, will stop that gnawing and continual demand for food, so that one can sleep. I began then to take it and, finding it helped, I got into the habit of drinking it very often. I don't mean that I was always hungry and couldn't buy food. But if I had 25 cents and had a meal at noon—if I felt hungry before seven—and would wait to see if Ira would ask me to come to eat, rather than spend my 25 cents, I'd begin drinking hot water, and read. And it gradually got to the stage where I drank ten or fifteen cups of hot water thru the day and night. When Mother came, she insisted it was not good and, too, she didn't like me to get up in the middle of the night. (She "stews" about my eyesight, and no doubt she's right—though it is five minutes of four in the morning now, I can't sleep, and I am wide awake! I was out all day—didn't rest a minute—and went to bed at 7:45 P.M. So you see I've had my quota of rest—eight hours.) For she complained that this prowling around, reading and writing at night, makes me nervous. I gave up drinking the hot water, and now only drink one cup every morning—instead of breakfast. Speaking to the doctor about this—he said the hot water had undoubtedly added to my weight; hence the loss of it now. I am now about normal—135 pounds, I think. I am five feet six inches tall, and 135 pounds is considered normal.

You ask me what I think of your plan to assist me until I am able to find something to keep me. I can't think anything except that it is mighty good of you and Miss Huntington and Miss Payson. And since, as I wrote to Mr. Welsh, the burden will not fall on any one person, I do not feel as I would if I thought I had made a dead weight of myself for someone to carry....

Now, then, I pay $4.50 for my room. Less than this would mean carfare, for downtown the rate starts at $5.00...and of course if I lived out of the beaten path, I would not be able to get the girls to drop in. The street I live on is the best in town, but I live on the lower end of it. And yet it is lovely here. The trees are very close and the lawns large, and altogether—winter with the snows, or summer and grass—the aspect is so peaceful....

For laundry—this apartment house permits no washing to be done on the premises...therefore, we send all...to the laundry (meaning washwoman), and we pay her $1.00 a week....

Now when Mother first started to cook for us, she made it expensive, because she never touches meat (has been vegetarian for

266

years), and yet prepared meat for us. Later, when I found our food was costing too much, I arranged that we ate her style (vegetarian), thus having less expense (though Stella got broths and stews, etc.). In this way, Mother prepared a light breakfast for herself and Alice and Stella (I don't eat until luncheon), then luncheon for the four of us; and generally some is left over; and thru the day, if any girl "blows in," as they call it, . . . Mother heats it for the girl if she is hungry. And they are always hungry, growing girls generally are. Then at 6:30 we have dinner. Mother only takes tea and toast, but I have my one regular meal then; and we (Alice, Stella and I) have coffee with it. . . .Mother makes enough at dinner so that there is some left to warm for the next day's luncheon, provided no one comes in hungry. It's a peculiar thing, but when these girls come here, no matter how much they need food, they manage never to come at meal hours, but just after it. This, I think, so as not to be asked to sit down at table with us—they prefer to eat a quick bite in the kitchen. . . .

For the upkeep of this, which has existed only for the last three weeks, $1.00 a day is required, and I think it marvelous that Mother could do it. She managed well—but that was for bare food. It took extra money to buy stationery, stamps, car tickets, occasional other expenses (such as I wrote before), and half-soling of shoes. And for Alice, Stella and Mother, movies—they went on Saturday nights. I don't go; I suffer dreadfully the entire night if I do. . . .

Starting Monday all is to be changed. Mother goes home. She is fretting to go now because of the "visitor" expected at "Jimmie's" house. She states frankly that she abhors the duties attending such things but she is concerned about "Jimmie's" business when Caroline will be obliged to stay away. And she is expecting to "take cash" for James—though I know he won't have her. Poor Caroline is still cutting cheese, etc., and expects the baby in a week at the outmost. So for Caroline's sake, I'm glad Mother will help in the store. She expects to go Monday.

Alice's people (where she works) go away to the country on the seventh of May; so in one week's time, Alice will be gone—though now she sleeps here, occupying the couch in the living room. Mr. Noakes knows it, but Mrs. Noakes would have my life if she knew it. She wouldn't care, only that she would want money for it—whereas Mr. Noakes told Alice, when she offered to owe it to him, to "forget it"; and promptly gave her his pillows. He is generous to a fault.

That will leave Stella to share my room. Her mother gives up her place today (everyone is moving and the excitement is intense all over town, because Sat. is moving day), and she is not taking another. She is selling the few sticks of furniture that she had, and goes (taking one bed) to Emily's (her daughter) house where there are four babies, and Mrs. Phillips will have plenty to do. The father—who is a drunken sot—goes to Hotel Dieu, where he will be taken care of for the work he will do. I got him the place and they will try to effect a cure for his drunkenness. Father Cotter—my Catholic priest friend—is helping with this. Mrs. Phillips takes Joan (nine years) with her, but Stella is now without a home—and as long as I have a bed, I will share it with her. I love this girl.

Now then, there is Stella alone to be considered other than myself.

For my room rent, the price is the same for one or as many as I care to take in it—and you won't mind if I keep Stella with me....

Oh!...I have been crying. I am all unstrung— My mother must have taken out some of the sheets of this letter to someone to read. She can't read, and Alice is not able to read "writing," and Stella wouldn't read it to her, and couldn't read much either. So I can only think she took it out while I was over to Gabrielle's. For she knows I am writing a detailed account of my expenses, and she is sarcastic and hints about things I know she could only read here. She is crying now too—and I can't bear it. I didn't write one word in this that is any of her business—but she came in just now and told me to count up what she ate, and she would send the money for it when she gets home. I shouldn't mind—though we have never had a break before since she is here—but it upsets one. Stella is rubbing her head, for she became almost hysterical. I did not answer her—only to say, "Please, Mother, be calm. I don't know what you are excited about." And, she replied, "Oh! yes, you do! You think to fool me, but you spend your days and nights writing to people that I was bad to you years ago, and that now you are feeding me." So how could she get such an idea, unless she read this letter—rather, had it read to her? Though I am sure I did not write that.

When she began to insult me, I walked out of the room; and she called me a *momzer* meaning "bastard" in Jewish; and I said, "You probably know better whether I am or not." And then she began to cry and is crying yet. I cried, too, but only from mortification—for I abhor rows, they are in such bad taste. And to give her credit, this is the first semblance of one we've had since I was twelve years old and she put me out.

I stopped and went to her—and all is well again. She did not read this letter, but I am sure had your letter read. Not that I am positive, but I think so. For when I explained that I am obliged to write in fine detail my expenses—inasmuch as my correspondents pay them—she said she didn't object to what I wrote to Mr. Welsh, as he had real love for her, as much as he had for me, but when it comes to those "women in Boston"—So you see, she must have taken out one of your recent letters—though she must have brought them back, as they are all here. I never lock them up.

I want to tell you about Stella—why I love her more than any other girl, and why I seem to favor her. I will go into it thoroughly. First, let me say she is Poke and Potsy to me. I cannot say it any better than that. After that: she is (I hope) to be the one perfect specimen of a girl who has been beaten down as I have been and who will come out on top. Her disposition is rare. She never shows me any affection—nor I her—but I feel when she is about as I did when Poke was with me—

I find I can't write this letter any more. I am going thru great stress of mind today. You will get a letter from me when I am able to write telling you more of the above. Today I can't write.

My mother is going home today—tonight, rather. She wired James for money—and she goes tonight. She was to wait until Monday, but she won't; and as I know I can't write, I won't try to. But I will answer more of your letter when I write again—and I will write Miss Huntington. Tell her I got the box. Everything in it fits me, and no one else—except the white skirt fits Stella. My mother was going to fix them up for all of us to wear. The light-blue dress (fancy one) I sold. The lady in the front apartment offered $4.00 for it, and I took it. So tell Miss Huntington not to send $4.00 this week. I'll use this. Was that all right?

I am very unhappy—I've had lots of trouble today. My brother from Memphis wrote me and said I was unspeakable things, to take my mother where there are girls of this sort. He said lots of things. I

269

believe she wrote him something in Jewish—otherwise, he couldn't know. I wish Mr. Welsh wouldn't insist on them—any of them—and I'd never see any of them again.

I am so miserable today that I feel I will never look in her face again. And yet, I think: after all, she is my mother—and what is wrong with me, that they all hate me? I know I must be somehow at fault—or why doesn't one of them like me? I've got three brothers, a mother, and many uncles and aunts—and I can't turn to one of them. And my brother said he'd consider I'd done the family a kindness if I would get off the earth. He said I lost my eye from disease, so need no pity—but I didn't, so help me God—and I didn't ask him for pity. But Mother must have written that I criticize him for not helping me. He was always so kind to me when I was a child—he used to keep her from beating me. And now I don't know what got into him. It was his letter that made her start the tirade this morning, though I thought it was the reading of your letter or some of Miss Huntington's. In his letter, he said that she must not eat another meal here—and come to him at once. This isn't James, but Sy, my oldest brother, who used to love me. When I was about ten or twelve he would be very kind to me. And I never wrote him *one word* of my needs. He knows it from James, perhaps, but I never did him any harm. And he said I have made him trouble enough, and if I want to oblige the family I ought to destroy myself. These are his very words, I am copying them:

"She has made it impossible for me to communicate with you if you stay there. She is only doing you harm, and you can't do her any good. Get away from her at once—and if she has good sense, and wants to do you and the family the best turn she has ever served them, she'll get off the earth as soon as possible."

He knew I had to read it to her—she can't read English. So you see, he means for me to feel this, and I do. He never would have written this if she didn't tell him something—and I hope I won't have trouble with Mr. Welsh about it, for I won't bother them any more. I will be off the Earth to them, for sure.

I am sorry to write you all this, but I have no one else to tell. Mr. Welsh would not understand, and I am ashamed to tell Ira—Stella knows why she is going; and I've had to go to bed, so won't be able to see her off, so Ira will do it.

You will remember that I did not finish my letter. But I will; and

I'm mailing this, so you won't think I've been negligent—and I want it to reach you before Monday.

My mother has shut herself up in the kitchen and only spoke to me thru the door—and as I am ashamed to talk so that Stella understands, I pleaded with her in Yiddish to let me in, and I'd only ask her to explain why she has turned on me. But she answers that her sons are her natural children; I am an unnatural child; and she will do as they bid; so if I will put up with her presence until eight o'clock, she will go.

Please believe that I never *once* answered her impudently since she started this morning—in fact, I am too astonished to know what to say. Yet it does take two to start a quarrel—but how I started it, I don't know, unless she mailed away something in Jewish that I don't know of. I am very troubled, I don't know what to do, and I can't tell anyone else—so do you care that I told you?

May, 1915

WILL YOU JUST FORGET THAT I WROTE THE LAST TWO OR THREE PAGES OF the letter you received the other day?

I feel they were written under conditions that made me overdraw the conditions. I've no doubt they made me appear a martyr—and occasionally I am not above playing that role, even though there is only a tiny excuse for it.

It is true my mother was most exasperating on that day, but I think my description of the annoyance was a bit overdrawn. You know the old adage about it taking "two to make a quarrel"—it still holds good. Unconsciously, I did make this quarrel. And had my mother, during a great stress of mind, written to a sympathetic friend, her views of the situation—I've no doubt, I should appear to be the terrible one.

I don't really know what "riled" her—only that I am sure I am as much to blame as she. She left that night. I was not able to go to the depot to see her off, as my head and eye ached. I cried myself into this condition. She was seen off by Mr. B. and five girls—Gabrielle, Stella, Alice, Lou and Margaret.

She told Mr. Benjamin (who knew of the "rift in the lute," but not of the conditions) that I lost sight of the fact that her "boys" were very dear to her—hence, our quarrel. But to save my life, I don't know how this applies. For I've no recollection of their names being mentioned in anything unusual, until my brother wrote a very trying letter—insulting, inasmuch as he knew that I, or some friend of mine, must read it to her. Even when the letter came, I said nothing. But I confess I cried a great deal, for I was hurt—because I always counted on this brother's love, and hoped sometime to go to see him. That he lived in comparative ease and luxury, I never commented upon, nor asked him for any assistance. I always thought that he must know my condition. And he knows, too, that I have been trying to live clean; and as he did not send me at any time a penny or a gift, no matter how slight, I thought probably he did not credit the fact that I had been living the life where one receives nothing except that which they earn—and gave it no more thought.

Enough of this. I hope they all have plenty—and I will hope some day to have them all feel downright sorry for their neglect. For I am a sister—and they throw away daily what I suffer for lack of.

My mother left, having made peace with me, for which I was duly grateful—for it would have been a pity to have her go in anger, when she stopped here through two months of continual harmony.

I wish to write you a little about Stella—for I recall I left off directly in the part where I expected to tell you of her.

This girl is no different than thousands of girls, except in appearance—she is "different" in that she is far more beautiful than most girls.

She is a type, and I know the type well.

When I act in anything for her, I see a composite picture of Stellas, Maimies, etc.—their number is legion. I know so well her every thought and action. And even better than she does, I know her hopes. You will hardly be able to grasp this, not ever having lived thru it, but my recollections of the same thing when I was seventeen are very fresh, and very readily brought to mind.

Stella and her type are innately refined. Perhaps not in the sense that some might call refined, but that word suffices to explain that she is the opposite of "bourgeois." That her parents and environments are sordid is an accepted fact; and that [they] have refused to drop into the same rut and have had an idea to outgrow the conditions they were born into, makes them "different." And this difference is frowned upon, and only bad can be seen in it.

272

If she and the rest of her type were ugly in face or form, they would have no trouble, no matter how different their views. But there's the rub. Stella, being pretty, is the subject of petty jealousies. When the mother is a natural one and has the love of God in her heart, she takes pride in her daughter's pretty face and pretty ways. But Stella's mother and my mother, and many mothers of this type, prefer their children to run along in the same groove that they've made, and any indication of anything else is sensed as immoral, and done to lure men.

I can recall one incident in my life that will furnish proof that this is so.

When I was sixteen, I was home for a week or two—and a man who delivered crackers to our store spoke to me at the door, then went in; and I heard him say to my mother, "Who is that girl?" and, my mother telling him, he went off on a long string of compliments. I could hear them, and see their faces in a reflection from the showcase mirror. Among other things, I heard him say, "Are they her own teeth?" And my mother answered she *thought* so. All the time, the expression on my mother's face never changed; and the expression was plainly that she experienced great agony of mind when I was discussed. I was young, and though I had always been conscious that I had wonderfully regular teeth and that they were generally thought false because their formation was so perfectly even—still, this man's compliments seemed to stay with me.

I had a little money—for I was posing then, in the nude, for the art classes—and that evening I asked a drug clerk, showing him my teeth, what I should buy to preserve them. For everyone, directly after admiring them, would say, "You should take every precaution to preserve them"—and yet I did nothing except rub them with a rough towel to make them shine.

He advised Listerine and toothbrush and prepared chalk. I bought the outfit and, taking it home, placed it on my table, after having used it. The next day when I returned, I knew something had happened by Mother's threatening face and by the scared attitude of my brother and sis.

Nothing daunted, I went upstairs to clean up—for at that time Mr. Benjamin was my "beau," and I was home so as to see him. He lived directly across the road. I found my Listerine, chalk and powder gone! I called downstairs and learned that Mom had them.

I came downstairs, and when I asked her for them, she turned on me and before my brother and sister. She attacked me after this fashion: "You have no shame to bring those kind of things in to a decent home! Your poor sister—everyone will damn her along with you. You disgraceful hussy—to put such things on a table!" etc. All this in Yiddish.

I wasn't surprised, because this wasn't anything unusual. Anything I introduced was frowned upon. But I couldn't understand the "disgraceful" part of it until when I met Mr. Benjamin...and he knew of it too; for my mother always liked to parade her troubles in order to win sympathy, and she had confided the whole affair to Mr. Benjamin's father.

It developed that she went to a drugstore conducted by a Hebrew and asked what these things were for—the Listerine and the white lumps. The man no doubt told her it was used to keep the mouth in condition, the Listerine being a wash prepared to keep the mouth free from disease. That was enough. Of course, I only surmise this explanation—for how could a druggist say otherwise? She had it (and told Bernard Benjamin) that I was doing unnatural things with my mouth and that the druggist told her the solution was used only to prevent disease from such practices—and that explained why I didn't become pregnant. And I had to live in that neighborhood and know for certain everyone who would listen had been told this.

Now then: this one circumstance is repeated daily by thousands of mothers whose daughters, naturally, living in a new age and learning the newer things, want them, and are continually hounded because they want to live different. I could write everlastingly of experiences such as I wrote in the above, one surprising you more than the other. But they wouldn't surprise Stella—or her type, whatever her name—for they are living thru the same thing with variations.

And somehow—Stella is Maimie. Do you get the idea?

I am afraid I am not able enough to describe how I mean this. But I know every heartache and longing "Maimie" had. And instead of running true to form—which is, that being older and not desiring the same pleasures, one must condemn them in a younger person—I foresee what will make this girl's lot easier and relieve that terrible pressure that everyone condemns her—and love her instead.

274

Do you know, it is a bit selfish? For I never think of her as Stella, but as Maimie at seventeen—and any kindness shown her is really shown to the Maimie of about ten years ago.

Last night, we were returning home at a little before tea time. Stella said, looking in the window of a very fine shop, "Gee! I could eat one of those cucumbers." I said, "I like them too, but they are too expensive yet," and we walked on. As we passed other grocer shops, I could see her eyes hunting down the cucumbers, but she said no more. As we neared St. Lawrence Main (where there are tiny shops and things are cheaper), I said, "Stella, you run along the Main and buy a cucumber, while I go in and get tea ready." I figured in my mind how to make up for this extravagence. (The cucumber was 15 cents—and we could get a half-dozen eggs for that.) I got tea ready, and though Stella should have been back in five minutes, there was no Stella. I was very hungry. I walked to the door several times, but no Stella in sight. Then I telephoned to nearby grocers, asking if the "red-haired girl" [was there] (or, rather, as I really said, *"Est La tete rouge elle la?"*) [sic], but no one had seen Stella. Finally, when three-fourths of an hour had elapsed, I decided to eat alone, for I was certain she had run into her mother or drunken father and was obliged to go home with them. I ate with a heavy heart—for Stella had on a new suit that Mr. Welsh sent her and a hat newly retrimmed (it was my last summer's one), and I knew her mother would tear if off her back. She has had the suit a month or more, but does not wear it home, as her mother would say she had only gotten it one way, and perhaps destroy it. Imagine my surprise, then, when the bell rang and in walked Stella...frisky, and she danced around for several seconds before she saw the displeasure on my face. She immediately become serious, and got her broth off the stove and brought it out and began eating it. But it seemed every mouthful was choking her. Still, I said nothing—only about our food and the necessity that she eat bread with her broth (she has broth twice a day but I live on vegetables, cereals, eggs, etc.)

Had I soundly berated her and demanded to know where she had been, I would have done as her mother and Maimie's mother would do—and I wanted to do as Helen Howe's mother would do. For I know girls of seventeen years can't have perfect understanding of things. When she finished her tea, the tears were falling, though she made no sound. I cleared the table while she washed and dried the few dishes. After that, I got a book that we are reading. It is a little girl's book, but I read it for Stella's sake, and I like it myself. It is called *Little Women*—you surely know it. As I settled down to read it, she walked over and put her head in my lap while she sat on the floor. And she cried steadily while I patted her head. (Such wonderful hair as she has—I believe I will enclose a lock to show you the colour and texture, which is like wire.) As she got quieter, I began reading, and she stayed on the floor. Still I didn't ask her where she had been.

We undressed and retired. And after I put the light out, she asked me if she might tell me. It was that she had met a chap, and he was going to meet a girl whom Stella knew from her church. And she wanted the girl to see her suit, and she didn't think it would take so long—etc., etc. Now, what an unusual thing! Doesn't this happen almost every day with young girls—and what of it? But Stella's mother (or mine, for that matter) would beat her and tirade for hours.

I will guarantee that this girl will never do that particular thing again—though tomorrow she may do something equally exasperating.

I hope I have been able to make you understand about Stella. I never permit myself to feel anything toward her but the love "Maimie" never got any in her youth, except from men, for short periods—and she was always hungry for a woman's love. And when, as I wrote you, Mr. Welsh shows her more attention than he does to me—I confess, I feel hurt; but she never knows it (nor does he). And I never permit jealousy to hurt Stella thru the other girls—for this was the bane of "Maimie's" existence in her youth.

I don't recall whether I wrote you before of her parents, home, etc. . . . . Her mother is a sober, industrious woman, but a horrible shrew. This she isn't altogether to blame for, as her husband (Stella's father) is a common drunk, having helped to support their six children only in fits and starts. The mother was before her marriage a domestic, and since then has done "day work." The father is a street laborer. Their home is typical; but poverty has made it even more squalid than the usual home of this sort of people.

From such a place this Stella came—and it is hardly to be believed. She is absolutely beautiful. Just now, due to the ravages of the disease, of which (I believe) I wrote you, she is painfully thin.

Last night, I bathed and massaged her, and the thought came to me...that to describe the physical condition of this girl, I couldn't say anything better than that she looks when naked as do the pictures of people depicting famine in India, or some such place. This isn't a bit overdrawn. But this will be changed, now that we have the disease in check.

When Stella was eight years old, she was already with men. Now, the phenomenal part of it all is, that she could meet people who have had experience with girls of her sort, and they would never detect that she was anything but a nice girl out of a home where there is harmony and contentment.

I can recall distinctly that I was ever on the alert as a girl to learn the things that distinguished "nice" people from the other kind. I don't know just why I thought this desirable, inasmuch as I didn't show any desire to live as "nice" people did. But I can recall hundreds of times when I would meet a man, son of "nice" people; and he, thinking to come down to the level of a girl of my sort, would either express himself coarsely or in language that would not be considered good English by "nice" people; and I would take great pleasure in correcting him, thinking to show that it wasn't necessary to come down—I would come up. In this way, I learned much. Often it wasn't their speech, sometimes their mannerisms at or away from table. But I knew all this because I wanted to know, and nothing ever escaped me. If I was with a man in a restaurant and I knew he was of plebeian people, I never troubled to study him, but kept my eyes glued on someone at a nearby table whose appearance stamped them as of "nice" people; and if I saw once that people of this sort did not bite bread but broke it, I never bit bread again in my life—etc. I had no trouble to learn, because I wanted to so much. But with Stella it is all different. She isn't as keen witted as I was; and she never has a "purpose" for anything— and I was full of them. She isn't observing. Apparently when she did associate promiscuously with men, they were of various sorts. And while she knew some...sons of nice people—I refused to know any other kind. Yet in spite of all this, she has the earmarks of a lady bred and born. When it is necessary for her to act on her initiative, she will instinctively do what a lady would do. Isn't this surprising, for a girl from a home of that sort, who had no experience in any other home until she came here?

As for cleanliness—though perhaps I had to teach her a few

things, she is wonderfully cleanly in her habits. All this appeals to me. I am anxious to see what she will be, if I am permitted to do for her as I should have been done by as a child.

Last month I advertised for work, offering my services as a worker in a home for my keep. The night the ad appeared, Stella perused the paper indifferently, but noticed this ad. She asked if I meant the place for myself. And when I said I did, I noticed she was very white, and her eyes a bit staring. All of a sudden she keeled over into a dead faint, without another word. I was alone. (Mother had gone to see Alice, who didn't stay here then and who was ill.) I tried simple means to revive her. But as I became frightened, I started to shriek, and my front neighbor came in and then brought a doctor from two doors above. The doctor said, after reviving her, she had a shock, and her heart isn't very strong.

When Mother came, I had Stella in bed and resting, though she wasn't asleep and her eyes still staring....I got into bed and soothed her. She put her mouth to my ear and repeated, over and over, "Maimie don't go away"—but softly, so that Mother couldn't hear. I assured her I wouldn't. And I won't—now that you and Miss Huntington have made it possible for me to stay.

Will you let me know whether you think I am right—or rather, whether it is foolish of me to live over Maimie's youth in Stella?

June, 1915

CB 99   I HAVE A FEAR THAT YOU ARE IMPATIENT WITH ME THAT I HAVE NOT AS yet answered your letter and thanked you for the check you sent me.

I am not able now to write you what I have gone through with Stella. I wrote it in part to Miss Huntington and mailed it today, after it had been all but completed for more than a week.[31] But I hoped to be able to write some good news to finish it, but couldn't. I asked her to send it to you....

I attempted to do for Stella Phillips, in the first place, just because she was such an unusually beautiful girl, with a rare disposition. But I've stirred up a hornets' nest, and now I am sick trying to figure out what to do.

She was in the hospital. She is back here now. She has every imaginable thing wrong with her. I only learned the whole truth a few days ago. Gonorrhea, syphilis and tuberculosis—all this

278

vouched for by the specialist whose word is the last in the medical profession here.... Yet here is a problem: I have done so much and gone so far—can I let go? I didn't bargain for all this. But it's as bad as it can be.

She sits here sad-eyed; and I love her deeply and I am almost helpless. The hospitals are overcrowded with soldiers—to go, and returning from the front—and I was told in all three hospitals here that there was *no money* that could buy her a bed in the hospital. Only the Notre Dame hospital offers her a bed, in the pest house or isolation ward.

I have prayed unceasingly all day. I hope to see the light.

I cannot answer your letter as I should like, but one point I wish to touch upon:

You ask that I try to find employment. I felt a little hurt at that—for I thought you would believe that I would not relax one moment in my efforts to find something. I accept the help because I have to, and I understand the spirit it is given in. If I was returning to my onetime life, which excluded work, I would find my old associates, etc. I don't think you meant I wasn't trying to find work, though your letter at the first reading made me think so....

I've never stopped looking for work. I never answered many in person, ever. I knew I stood no chance when in competition with other girls, when the prospective employer saw me. But by letter I have never stopped; and when I get a favorable reply, I go in person. Only once was I given a chance; and then, because I had to have a light swung over my machine, Mr. McLaughlin thought I'd better not try, because he said he had a very dark office—which was only an excuse to get rid of me.

I am not very optimistic, but I think that is due to my frame of mind concerning Stella. Still I promise that I will find work soon—very soon, if I am obliged to go out to Ste. Anne De Bellevue, to the tuberculosis colony, to work for my keep and a semi-yearly bonus, which is open to me starting July 15th.

I am not very nice to read today, and you will be provoked with me; so I will close. I will go tonight to walk alone on the mountain; when I return, I will be better. I sent for Mr. Benjamin to come to tell me what to do with Stella. Yours lovingly, Maimie

I read with interest about the Bach festival, and I hope you and your family are well.

☜ **100** I AM GOING OUT TO FIND A PLACE FOR STELLA—AND I INTEND TO FIND something this week. What or where it shall be, I don't know; but I'll not stop until I find some place. . . .

There isn't a free hospital in Montreal that will take this disease—the worst one, syphilis—to cure. Ordinarily, there is *one* free hospital in each city that will tackle it—and we have one here. But at present, what with the soldiers preparing for and returning from the front, Stella can't get into it. Also, the drug that is now used successfully in the treatment of this disease, called "salvarsan," or "606," is not to be had *at any price* here. The government called in every bit of it for treatment of the soldiers. I believe it is a German drug. Mr. Benjamin learned that it is still to be had in the States, but was also very expensive. It is given by injection, and is a *sure* cure and a speedy one.[32] The other trouble, gonorrhea, is a local one—disgusting enough, but not considered dangerous. And then there is the tubercular trouble, which you probably know can be taken care of by right living.

Of course, it all sounds terrible, but she can't be allowed to die. I will hang on with my last breath and trust to the Lord that I will not suffer for it. It doesn't seem possible to some, but I venture to say I can take care not to become affected—but expect to and *positively will* have her out of my place by Saturday of this week. I feel as strong as a lion, and someone will give way to my pleadings and take her over to be cured. Of course, I am very careful that everything is thoroughly disinfected. I use disinfectants very freely— I keep [bichloride of mercury] solution in a bottle close by— and everything is watched. You know I am careful about generally unclean things, so I can assure you I am far more careful in this case.

My plans for today are to see the heads of all institutions where pay is taken, and beg admittance for her, just for humanity's sake. If this is not possible, I will go to see people—men and women whose names I have—and ask for help to pay one of these hospitals. Failing this, I shall go to see Mr. Nash, one of the vice presidents of the C.P.R., . . . whom I intend to ask, cajole, and threaten into sending me and Stella into the States—and as a last resort, I shall take her to Phila. and leave her in Blockley, the city hospital that I know takes care of this disease successfully.[33]

I hope all this doesn't frighten you to thinking I've become desperate—but it is only because I am *determined* to do something, and at once, and I am through with red tape. In a hospital she goes, this week, and you will see that I will manage it. . . .

Will you think it strange that I ask that you send this letter to Miss Huntington? This, to save time. For I am busier than ever this week, as I am also writing a series of advertisements for Mr. Benjamin, to be used to sell stock in a moving-picture house. It is entirely his business, so there is no pay in actual money—but he helps me a lot. Yesterday he ordered things from a drugstore for our protection which, when I saw the receipted bill, astonished me—it was $7.86. I have everything now for Stella or any other girl that needs little home remedies. This also includes two dozen cakes Life Buoy soap. . . .

I will not write more, as I see Ira is looking at his watch.

I wrote Mr. Welsh all this, and am now awaiting word from him as to his views. . . .

My dear friend,   *Philadelphia, July 13, 1915*
I AM IN RECEIPT OF A LETTER TODAY FROM MISS HUNTINGTON, AND SHE   103 ⬩
tells me I did not give my Phila. address. This was stupid, and unusual for me to be careless on this point, but I hope to be excused by reason of my being so upset with such a quick change in my affairs. I expect to return to Montreal the last of this week—to be there for Sunday, unless developments in Stella's case require my attention further. I have found it very trying to be here for I have not had one moment of rest.

As I believe I wrote you, I had Stella placed in the Jefferson Hospital, and all seemed most satisfactory; and I called there frequently for the first five days. The sixth day, on my arrival, I found Stella all dressed in street attire—and she informed me she was discharged and was most happy. I investigated and found it was true, and I was never more surprised and helpless in all my life. I asked—and was told that the doctors, having gone over her case thoroughly, found her in such condition that they considered her a menace and could not keep her. That their hospital was an active one, and their rules were such that her case could not possibly be taken care of there. When I reminded them that they were told of her condition, they agreed that they had been over-indulgent in taking her at all, but did it to oblige. Yet on serious consideration, they couldn't keep her—not if we paid $10.00 a day! They said she should be in a hospital for venereal cases, and the only one here was the Philadelphia Hospital—which, being a city hospital, wouldn't admit her—a Canadian. Or so they thought.

It was not a pleasant outlook, and I was never so discouraged. I was careful not to let Stella know, for I know if it was I who was in her plight, I would only want to destroy myself.

I begged for, and was given permission to leave her there for one more day. When I walked out, I didn't know which way to turn, but began all over again, appealing to various doctors whose names Mr. Welsh gave me. They all agreed, after telephoning Jefferson, that she could not be accepted in any of the hospitals— with the possible exception of Philadelphia Hospital where, it was thought, she would be taken in and all danger of being deported removed, if the head man in the Board of Health be appealed to. This man, Dr. Zeigler, I saw. And two days later Stella was admitted to the Philadelphia Hospital, which is almost solely used for the treatment of just such cases as hers, at an expense of $4.00 a week. Medicine extra.

She is very unhappy there. Of course, it isn't a bed of roses, but I am sure it must be endured if she is to get well. As I told her, the Bible says "the wages of sin are death"; and if, by some providential clemency, we who sin escape death, we must expect to suffer a little, or a lot. One thing certain: she will get well there. For they waste no time in getting their patients pronounced cured, and off the premises.

As for other news from here—there has been nothing of event except the circumcision of the new infant, which was celebrated like an Irish wake, I believe.

I do not wish to distress you with the details of another rupture with those whom I am obliged to call my family. But in passing, I will say I have taken the last bad dose of this medicine; and if I am obliged to go to the poorhouse in my old age, I will go gladly rather than ever again be in their midst.

Until yesterday at noon, I was as friendly as one can be with such a loveless, selfish outfit. But since then I had to undergo one of James's insults, that was more than I could stand; and after crying for hours, I grew calm and prepared for sleep. And this morning, coldly and calmly, I have decided that I must forego forever what pleasure I derived from being one of them—for there is no profit in it for me, and apparently they are not interested. Mr. Welsh has always asked that I be friendly with them; and I have been, against great odds; but I see now the folly of it. I have felt this way before, but Mr. Welsh has insisted that it was my duty to be forgiving and forgetful. But now—today—I have written him of my decision, and I've told him no power on earth can make me change it.

I have been so belittled by James's treatment of me in the fortnight that I've been here that I feel as though "Maimie" in Montreal is one person, and this "Maimie" here another one, who is of the lowest sort. I mustn't go into this, it is all too distressing. James does not consider what my feelings must be. He speaks as though I were a physical wreck (due to my sight) and a moral one, and for that reason, I can't take his child out of the sight of its mother. He treats me as one does an irresponsible person, and it is more than I can stand. If a man is in the store, and I smile or appear friendly, he orders me as one could a child of ten to "go back home"—in such a manner as to convey at once to anyone that if I were to remain, I might try to arrange a meeting with the man. Oh! it is more than I can stand! Therefore, I will return and never again write to any of them, thus dropping out again from their lives—as they have no real interest in me, not as much as they (this includes my mother) have in a plant they own.

I saw Poke yesterday, and she knew me. She was on the street. As I came along and whistled, she looked up—her ears went back, and she flattened herself and sort of crawled along until I came close to her. This, without looking up. And as I reached down, she looked up—and then bounded off, to rush around in circles like mad, and coming only close enough after each revolution to have me touch her back. Then away she'd go again. Finally, she became calm and I went to the porch. She sort of acted queer—kept her body flat, and slinked along. But once I sat down, she jumped up and began her old tricks of reaching up to my ears to kiss them. And I know she knew me, because she never once attempted to kiss my mouth—and later, when some of her new family came out, I saw that she kissed them full in the mouth, and without end.

I stayed an hour with her. Most of the time she was lying in my lap, apparently asleep, but keeping an eye on my every movement. I had the family there to call her; and she did her old trick of looking at me to see if I thought she should go. Whereas when they held her, and I called, she bounded off to me with a glance in their direction. Later, when I had to go, I had her taken indoors—but she went unwillingly and I heard her protesting until I got in the car.

I will not go again.

I hope you and your family are well. I will perhaps leave Saturday for Montreal, but if I don't, I shall let you know. Yours lovingly, Maimie

As I will not go to James's house any more, my address until I return to Montreal, will be c/o Mrs. Daniels, Walnut St., Apt. 3B, Phila., Pa.

Montreal, July or August, 1915

CR 104   I AM SO GLAD TO BE BACK. I LEFT ALL UNPLEASANTNESS IN PHILA., AND feel now that I must have a chance. I feel so ready. My poor Stella will get well, I know it. I can't tell you what a horrible place it is that she is in—but what else could I do? It seemed the only place for her. She was dissatisfied in the beginning, but is resigned now. For I have made it a point that each complaint is a reflection on me, and she will never complain.

Do you think it silly for me to feel so much satisfaction in the fact that she loves me? When Miss Christopher (one of the ladies connected with the Door of Hope) said she didn't like Stella because she was stubborn, I knew that Stella only appeared so because she wanted to be loyal to me. I know the workings of her mind. She has little to say at any time, but I understand her every act. When she is well, she will be a wonderful girl. You know it is proverbial that young girls such as Stella are ungrateful and selfish. She isn't; and she is long-suffering. She has never expressed her gratitude, but it is wonderful how she loves me.

I told her how to make her enforced stay in such unpleasant surroundings seem less unpleasant. (You know, it is the country poorhouse, and is indescribably horrible.) I told her: Had a person the knowledge that he could steal millions of dollars, ensuring comforts for a lifetime—and all the punishment meted out to him would be imprisonment in a frightfully squalid place, for six months—if he were regardless of any moral principles, most anyone would say they would stand the six months enforced imprisonment. Now that is just what she is doing—stealing life. For

284

that hospital—even though it is a horrible place, she has no moral right to it, for it is maintained by taxpayers for Phila. people. And she being not of Philadelphia, and not even an American, is just stealing a chance to live, since it is the only place that would take her in and where she had a chance to fight for life. Now, isn't it worth living for six months with horrible Negro women, all cut up in debauches and eaten up with diseases, if, at the end of that time, one has a chance for life among beautiful things; and Stella will have that chance?

I believe you will understand what I am driving at though I think I have written around in circles. This due to the fact that I am writing while two girls are talking. One is Augustine (the young woman I left here to use my room and take care of my place and keep Mr. Noakes' room clean), the other is a new girl who I find has been waiting for me to get back. She was sent to me by Father Cotter because she has had a good education in newspaper work (country weekly), and he thought I could find her a place. She is a pretty girl, but her teeth and breath so horrible that I become ill when talking to her. You know, no more do I sleep with a girl; this, I am determined in. So Augustine is talking about taking her to a lady's house where she can get a room, and pay for it when she finds work. She has been until today at the Friendly Mission, but they only keep a girl one week—and she has been there a week tonight. I gave her tea, and think by Tuesday I will have found a place for her, though it will only be housework. No other jobs are available just now. . . .

I wonder if you know Miss Mary Kelsey of Chestnut Hill, Phila.? Some time ago, she wrote to Stella, saying she had heard of her through Mr. Welsh; and the letter was very sympathetic. Stella didn't answer it; and as it was not addressed to me, nor was I mentioned, I did not feel I had to acknowledge it—especially as I have such a horror of writing to persons that I feel are not specially interested in me as a person, but in me as a *question* (if you know what that means.) Then Mr. Welsh wrote saying I should have written acknowledging her letter to Stella; and much as I disliked to, I did. Since then I heard nothing, until yesterday—when I received a letter postmarked Portland, Oregon, saying she was enroute from the Fair, and is to be in Canada, so will stop over in Montreal and be here a whole day. And she will see me, for I'm to meet her at the train in the morning and be with her until evening!

And now I am spending all my thinking time wondering what she is like, whether she will be like you, or Miss Outerbridge—or what she will be like. . . . I must tell you that I was thinking about what I would wear when I met her; and when I slept, I dreamed that when she came, I went to meet her—and found myself at the depot in a nightgown and a horrible red kimono (which I never owned), and which was so tight that I couldn't put my arms out to greet Miss Kelsey. It is *Miss* Kelsey; . . . but I don't think she will turn out to be a young woman. I have no reason for thinking this, for her letter is a general one and the handwriting firm. But I don't think I can expect too much—and that someone is coming to see me is good enough, without expecting someone dressed fashionably, and sweet eyes and beautiful form, and all that.

Now I have told you some cheerful news, I will tell you something which is disturbing.

When I came home, I telephoned to see if Mr. Benjamin was in town; and he was, but was out. I left my name. He didn't telephone, but sent a note saying he would see me in a day or two—that he was very busy.

Then Saturday night he came; and after some persuasion, he told me what the trouble is. I saw he was haggard-looking and seemed dreadfully worried; and questioning him closely, I find he did not escape infection from Stella. This seems incredible, inasmuch as I was thrown with her constantly, slept and ate with her—and all except the last few weeks, made no effort to avoid contagion except the ordinary ones of cleanliness and order. Mr. Benjamin, at my request, went to Dr. Lauterman the day after we left; and Dr. Lauterman was out of the city. He went again on Dr. L.'s return, at my constant request thru the mail; and Dr. L. examined him—also Mr. Noakes and Augustine. And of all, only Mr. Benjamin was found to have contracted some infection— though Mr. Benjamin (and Dr. L., since then) assured me it was only a local trouble, was absolutely *not* in the blood, and was not really anything to be frightened about—only that Mr. Benjamin had worried himself into fevers which kept the place from healing. He cried like a little boy of four years. He seemed to hate to tell me and thus worry me. I assured him I would not worry—but my heart is as heavy as lead. To think he was only three days around her. Dr. L. told me today that Mr. Benjamin had evidently not been in perfect physical condition. This I knew—because he was in small country towns eating questionable food, and was perhaps more susceptible than we, who had plenty of nourishing foods.

When I was in Phila., I was thoroughly examined and a blood test made. I was told by Dr. Clerf that I was in wonderfully good health and that my blood showed I ate the best foods for me. I never eat meat, and due to having to stretch my money that you sent as far as possible, I have always seen that I got the most nutrition for the money; and Dr. Clerf said my blood showed this plainly. I've no doubt, had Stella been living with me and her diseases so acute during the winter when I was most of the time hungry, I would have contracted something. I do not lose sight of the fact that this is something more I have to be grateful to you for. I must tell you that to contract the worst of the dread diseases that Stella had—syphilis—one has to have a broken place on the skin, and only so can it enter the system; and I always knew that, and I've always been very careful of infection when such conditions prevailed. But the other and minor trouble—gonorrhea—is contracted in a dreadfully innocent and easy manner sometimes. By the use of a towel it can be gotten. The germ seeks a mucous membrane; and a little sore place is noticed, and then matter. And yet it is easily cured and does not enter the blood, especially if properly and intelligently cared for. (I am becoming expert on these things, and was criminally ignorant before.) The disease is a local one, and can be cured at its inception and goes no further. Dr. L. is treating Mr. Benjamin, and he charges enormous fees. But Mr. Benjamin thought it more economical to go to the best doctor, as having such a thing affects his mental condition and hinders his work. Therefore, by getting cured quickly he is able to earn money quickly. As it is, he has not been able to do anything, as he can't go away, and his business is "on the road." Dr. L. said Mr. Benjamin told him he believed he contracted it through the use of our toilet; and Dr. L. said, considering the place where the disease manifested itself he is sure this is so. I have been quite miserable about this, though he is practically cured now. For he did not write me, and yet I knew something was wrong. He said I had nothing to chide myself about—that he probably would have been taken with some illness, as Dr. L. said (and he knew) that he was in a terribly low physical condition and was very susceptible. (I forgot to tell you that when people are well and properly nourished, the disease finds it hard to get into the mucous membrane, which has a protective covering. But when the system is in poor shape, it is readily infected.) Be that as it may, I feel dreadfully guilty, for no doubt he suffers physically (though he insists not), and just to look at him, one can see he is mentally almost frantic. He has to keep well fed and rested to fight the disease, and is earning no money. He said he doesn't worry about that, as he has a drawing account with his firm of $10.00 a week, and that keeps him nicely; and then Dr. L. said he would be quite cured by a fortnight and is practically rid of the disease now. I have felt badly all day, but easier since talking to Dr. L. And now that I have written it all out, it seems I feel better. For it isn't so bad, after all, and all has its purpose. I was determined never to house a girl without having her examined—yet since I escaped so miraculously, I might have taken a chance, if the girl seemed in great straits. But with Mr. B's experience in mind, I feel sure I will never subject myself to such a menace.[34]

Now you know the worst. I had to tell you, and though I know you will feel sorry for Ira, I don't want you to worry; and I shall not either. I asked him to come for me Monday evening to go to Lafontaine Square, and I will talk about things that are away from all this rotten business; and I know I can take the horror out of his eyes. He seems as though crushed entirely. But I will take my book *What Men Live By*, and read extracts from it. He has read the book in its entirety, but I have marked places to read to him tonight that will drive away the grief that I can [tell] has engulfed him.

I left the house in Augustine's care. She is a French Canadian, no better nor worse than the mass of them, but certainly not as I should like her to be in her ideas of cleanliness. The result is that since I have returned, I have cleaned and rubbed and polished until my shoulders ache. The average French Canadian, when asked how he feels, says, "Not too bad," or "Not too good," but never "Good" or "Bad"—and so with Augustine: the house is not too clean nor not too dirty. When I called her attention to the skillets, which were not what I call clean, she said she thought they were not too dirty. Imagine eating from them. Mr. Noakes is long-suffering; if Mrs. Noakes were home, she would know soon that they were not too clean! At any rate, I pitched in and worked ever since my return, night and day, until last night—when a bottle of oil (quart size) broke in my hand. I bumped into an open closet door which, being on my left side, I couldn't see—and it smashed into tiny bits, cutting my hand in seven places; and of course I can't do much for a day or so. The worst of the work is done, but I wanted to go thru the closets etc., airing and straightening things, for I feel it in my veins that Mrs. Noakes will come in for a look around. She wasn't here in my absence—in fact, doesn't know I was away, I think—and she's about due now. Of course, it isn't my business to look after the entire place as I do—but I'm glad to do it, if it will keep her away.

Now, while I did not intend to write of the following in this letter, I shall do so, though only touching it generally.

Mr. Welsh thought he saw a chance for me to conduct a place along the lines of the Door of Hope—though without many of its features, and not so large to start with—and make it my life work. It has many features that are interesting, and I'd love to have the chance to follow my ideas of how girls should be shown the actual misery of wrong living, thus removing the glamour and leading them into right living. Mr. Suiffen talked with me along these lines; and he said he thought the money could be procured to start it and to maintain it, giving me a living wage. I expect to go into it in detail thru the mail during this week, with Mr. Welsh. Mr. Suiffen is a practical businessman and has many ideas that are only possible of a practical mind. For instance: He said that my appearance and my impaired sight were a great disadvantage in the business world, and overshadowed what ability I had. Whereas many, many women are engaged in welfare work and social problems—who earn a living wage and who are not as well fitted as I am. And these disadvantages, as seen from a business standpoint, would be a distinct advantage in work of the sort I have been doing in a general way. That I can always get an audience and a position for some other girl of perfect physical condition is often just because of my appearance; and Mr. Suiffen said it was another way of making the best of a disadvantage or handicap. Too, I can handle girls due to having been one of them, and yet—I believe— am so far removed as to be able to command their respect.

I will close now, as I must get to work. The pain in my hand is practically gone, but to move it starts a great flow of blood from the many cuts; so I must work slowly. And when I am finished, I will be able to say with Augustine that the place is not too dirty.

I do hope you and your family are well. I wonder if you will tell me how you feel about me now. I mean—do you care for me; or have I, by my repeated failures to accomplish something, made you feel I am something of an incompetent?

I tried to see Miss Wald in N.Y., but she was in Washington calling on the President with Jane Addams.

Miss Huntington wrote you were going to visit with her soon. Will it be very soon? Yours lovingly, Maimie.

...I saw at least twenty or twenty-five [children in Blockley] in the venereal ward, all suffering with contracted syphilis. I talked to several...a girl of eleven or twelve; [a girl who] can't be over three and-a-half years old....It is all too horrible, but as Dr. May Mayson in Phila. said, it must be faced—and then made a subject to be discussed openly and, in that way, less dangerous....

When you write, I will be happy.

August 20, 1915

ᙅ 105   I REC'D THE ATLANTIC MONTHLIES, AND FIND MISS WALD'S ARTICLES especially interesting. I do wish I could have seen her while I was in New York. Did I write you that I just missed her because she had gone with Miss Jane Addams to confer with the President on matters pertaining to the war? I could have seen her had I waited several days, but I hadn't money enough to put up there anywhere, and they didn't ask me to stay at the Henry Street House, where I called....[35]

The latest news of Stella is that there was a Wasserman test made, and her blood found to be "negative." This doesn't mean she is entirely cured, but means that she is not dangerous to associate with and is well on the way to recovery. If it were not for developments in which the Immigration Office of the U.S. figures, she would be here now. About the above interference by the immigration authorities I wish to tell you.

The immigration authorities learned of Stella's being in the hospital and sent their agents, who decided she was to be deported. Of course, she was discharged from the hospital as cured—as far as she needs their help—so it didn't matter much that she was ordered deported. At present, she is there at the hospital awaiting the return of the agent, who in turn has to await the necessary papers from Washington. When we came away from here, we had passports. This isn't considered necessary, but I got them to avoid just such complications—for I feared they would act as they did, if they learned of her presence in the Phila. Hospital. In her last letter she writes that the head nurse, Miss Evans, thinks it is fortunate that she was not taken away as soon as discharged, because now she is getting further treatment, which is all beneficial. Though she no longer receives Salvarsan, because even in the States now this drug is priced at unbelievable figures—because Germany sends none, and they are fast exhausting what they have. It just happens that I have the letter in which she tells me that she is as good as cured and I am sending it along so that you can judge how she took the news.

Really, you can't conceive of how much I feel for this girl. I know I couldn't worry more for her, were she my own sister. I don't know how she will act when she is well and doesn't need me any more—people so soon forget what is done for them. Her birthday was August 1st; and Mr. Benjamin gave me the chocolates I sent her, which she never received—which was trying, because besides the 60 cents he paid for them, I paid 18 cents in stamps and tax on them. It is expected that she will return every day; and if she is not well enough, she will go to a place I have in mind in the country for the remaining weeks of the summer—and then she will have to get work. It may be difficult to get her the work I'd like for her; but I know with her appearance, she'd be taken on in a nice ladies lunchroom as a waitress, or perhaps to usher in a theatre—neither position requiring physical or vast mental strength. Her mother at my instigation has just had an eye operation on her eye, at the Royal Victoria Hospital, where she remained a week. I was able to get it done and her bed in the hospital, without any pay whatsoever; and now she will have to get to work again. [Many of the "goodies" Mr. Howe sent me] were taken to her during the week she was in the hospital. She goes out "by the day" because the father is a horrible person who is intoxicated all the time. Truly, Mrs. Phillips deserves better than she has had, and I pity her. She does my washing now, but it has come to where I can't send it any more with any pleasure. Because in the last batch (though it was beautifully done) I discovered some bedbugs. And I couldn't take any chances like that again—for if they got in the beds here, Mrs. Noakes would hold me to a strict accountability.

Before I forget, I must tell you that Mr. Benjamin is quite all right again. I did not think anything about it when I wrote you, but when I mentioned that I did, he seemed terribly put out. He actually cried. It seems he values your good opinion and thinks that you will think of him as a horribly diseased person. I assured him you weren't that sort, and yet it didn't seem to comfort him. He thinks of you as the quintessence of all that is desirable in a woman, and I suppose it does make a difference that you knew of his trouble. As far as it is concerned, it has entirely vanished. I saw and spoke with the doctor who was treating him, who said that the main trouble had been his condition of mind. . . . Never before had he any trouble of a like or in fact any nature (for he was seldom ill), and he felt this was a terrible thing. The worst of it has been that he was obliged to stay here under the doctor's care, whereas his business took him on the road; and he hadn't earned a penny in six weeks, besides having had a doctor bill of $40.00, besides nearly $10.00 spent for medicine. I did not tell Stella of this—rather, I didn't write it (for I didn't know it myself until I returned)—for it would cause her much disquietude. And yet, on her return, and when she is well, I will tell her, for I think it is well for her to know what a menace she was.

I recall in the spring when you sent that box of lovely things— that I wanted to tell you that, after all, the dress and the biscuit-silk bodice did get separated. I retained the latter. . . . I had an old black silk waist which I took the sleeves out of, and sewed on a brassiere Miss Huntington sent, and I am using this combination for my "best." And it looks well—for the basque just fits me, and I appear quite modish. Just this week, I noticed it is beginning to crack in the front a little.

I know you are worrying as to how I intend to manage this winter. And though I will tell you not to let it worry you, I know that isn't easy. You will probably think I've thought it all out as to how I will do—but really, I haven't, because I just can't. . . . Conditions are bad enough—couldn't be worse—but if any person knew that they were going to exist for a given period, they would act, knowing there was no recourse. But as it is, "hope springs eternal." And in my case, hardly a day—two at the most—but something seems to clear the way for a change in the near future, but unfortunately so far hasn't materialized. Here, as everywhere, I've no doubt, everyone hangs on to the hopes that at the end of each season, the war will be over, and with it the hard times.

In my letter to Mr. Welsh, I wrote that according to what I see and read, no one should expect or even accept, in these days, more than their mere keep. There is so much suffering and misery from need and other causes that I don't expect, and wouldn't accept, more than just enough to keep alive. Yet even that seems difficult to accomplish.

Attempting to think it all out clearly seems impossible; all sorts of thoughts crowd in, chasing out the original problem of how I intend to manage. But by putting it all down, I can see it, even if I cannot arrive at any solution. So if you don't mind, I will write it all out here, and you, too, can see where I stand—for I know you do think for me and worry not a little. I can't help but feel sure of this. Your kindness to me makes it very evident.

If these were normal times, and after considering everything, I should make an attempt to interest people in starting a mission of some sort, for friendless girls, with me at the head; and for my labors I should expect my keep and a tiny sum over it to put away so that I could feel I had some sort of an assurance that I wouldn't end my days in a poorhouse or old ladies home.

In order to do this, I'd want to—and feel sure I could—interest Montreal people who could give something toward its support. Just now that is out of the question.

My own intelligence, aside from several experiences I've had, tells me that it is not possible to enlist the sympathies of Canadians in any enterprise that doesn't in some way affect the soldiers or, missing that, their families. Truly I don't blame them. Not that I think they should be so anxious for the soldier above every other consideration, but because they are beseiged on all sides for money to aid all sorts of causes that are military, I don't blame them for feeling no other consideration counts. As an instance: nearly every building that has heretofore been used for charitable purposes, of various natures, has been taken over for military purposes—barracks, recruiting offices, this or that league—but all for military purposes. What of those who benefited thru these other and original lines? They must manage as I will have to. Miss Rothwell, a probation officer, had some interest in Stella Phillips—due to her mother's having reported her to the police courts and she having been placed under Miss Rothwell's eyes. On my return from Phila., I called up Miss Rothwell to ask for an appointment to tell her what had been done for Stella Phillips. She informed me that her services (at the city's cost) had been turned over to the Patriotic Society and she had no time for Stella Phillips, her business being now with *Tommy Atkins*. I asked her what woman had been put in her place—and she said all were now working for the Patriotic Society. What of the many girls she looked after—for I knew personally at least eight—whom she encouraged, watched over in a measure, gave little lifts to when they were without food, etc.? These girls still exist—and more of them, due to conditions worse than existed formerly—but they are not connected with this war, so must shift for themselves.

I tell you all this to show you my opinion of what chances there are for raising money thru Montreal people for a new mission. . . . It is accepted then that I couldn't expect a livelihood—not now anyway—thru conducting a mission.

It is an old story, that the way is blocked for me to take up many of the situations that I am mentally fitted for—and which now also there are few of. Aside from these where mental ability is necessary, it is absolutely impossible for me to get those of the other sort. Salesperson, waitress, worker (physical) of any sort in a shop (due to insurance which prevents their employing anyone who has defective eyesight)—and sifted down, there is nothing else but housework. Which, since living here, I am fitted for—but can you think of any house that is fairly well kept that would have me? . . . Figured down, and logically, there doesn't seem much chance for me unless I happen on the proper place and I have no doubt there is such a place, provided I could wait long enough for it.

In the various agencies where I have applied, that are maintained by the city or otherwise to cope with this "unemployed problem," I was given a blank to fill out, and that I never heard from them is because they no doubt find others whose plight is worse, and leave me to find help elsewhere. You think (perhaps) how could anything I wrote make my plight seem less pitiful than others? Well I'll tell you. One question was: "Should you not find work, would you starve unless you resorted to unlawful acts." (I suppose they meant stealing, or adultery, etc.) I answered in the negative, for could I say truthfully that I would starve when I know that you, Miss Huntington, Miss Payson, Mr. Welsh, Miss Outerbridge and one or two more, would not let me do that?[36] Now bear in mind that I do not keep in mind that I can depend on any of these friends, and were these not abnormal times, I am sure I'd not have to put them to the test. But just the same, when a point-blank question of that sort is put before me, how else can I answer it and stick to my determination to be above deceit?

Other questions, such as, "Have you received an education? (which no doubt is asked to determine one's ability) made me appear less needy than others; for though in the strict sense of the word I did not recieve [sic] an education, yet I am not to be classed as "uneducated":

"How many languages can you speak?"

"How many languages can you read?"

"How many languages can you write?"

And I answered "five" to the first (German, French, English, Yiddish and Russian); "four" to the second question, and "two" to the last. All this, I am sure, made me seem less hopeless than some of the others who, at the most (French Canadians), are only bi-lingual.

I bring all this out to show you, then, why I can expect no help from such sources. Though I did write in the proper classification that I was unable to cope with conditions mainly because of my impaired sight, and even more defective appearance, I received not a word from them—though Stella (who also registered) did. Though in her case she was referred to the Catholic Church—who recommended that she leave all worldly cares and enter the Sacred Heart Convent as a penitent. Sweet outlook! That means for life. So, you see—here I am, right where I started and no nearer to the solution than when I started.

Suppose I had not these friends,—that's the thought that comes next—what should I do? That's the worst of it—one can't really know what they would do unless they just had to do it. And always the thought comes back—"But you have those friends." You see, I am writing to you as I would *think*, and I hope you will understand that I am not so brutally frank to make my case seem better: it is just because it is all *so*, as far as I can see.

I picture myself in another girl's place, and I eliminate friends who can, or do, help. Then comes the thought "Well, she could sew (perhaps), or nurse, do housework—or even go in a factory of some sort." Yet all that is closed to me. So I can't really and fairly, do what another girl would do.

When every other consideration fails, there comes a thought which I can't eliminate any more than I can that I have friends who will not let me starve—and that is Mr. Benjamin. We have never discussed this phase of the situation—but I know he realizes it as I do, that if I have no means, and work of some sort isn't available, I will have to return to live with him.

Just now he hasn't a dollar in the world. I mean just that. On Tuesday, he bought me a strip of war tax stamps; and when he got his change, he said, "This is my all," (and it was 20 cents) "until I put something over"—meaning selling some stock. The only reason that the plan of living with him comes to my mind is because, for the same rent he pays, I could live; and though food for two costs more than food for one—eaten together, and with care, I could live on what his food costs him in the restaurants (for he eats only in absolutely clean places, and they are always expensive). I haven't discussed this probability with him; and I believe—if it were necessary—I'd have to suggest it, because he never has in any way referred to this possibility ever occurring again. . . .

When I think about the possibility of returning to that life again, I feel more puzzled at what the girls would think of me, and the fact that my brother James's prophecy would come true (for he says I am a prostitute at heart—he didn't tell me that, but I saw it in writing to my oldest brother, who scarcely knows me, and whom I wouldn't know if I met him) than I do about the actual wrong I should be committing. For I have the knowledge that I don't want to be bad. But I don't see what else I shall do, if I don't soon find some way of earning my keep. When writing to Mr. Welsh several days ago, I didn't mention this possibility. I hope you won't consider this deceit. I couldn't do it—it would pain him, and I hadn't the courage to inflict it on him. I know too that you won't welcome the thought; so I say, don't let it fret you, for perhaps it may not come to that.

I cast about in my mind for excuses for myself, and I can think of many. So a new thought comes to me: "Suppose this was some other girls' plight. Not a young girl who, just because she came to you," (I am addressing myself) "would make you want to shield her, but some girl you heard of. And as you are always able to criticise girls generally—except those whom you interest yourself in—what would you say she should do?" I'd say, first off—"Oh! she can't tell me she can't find work—I'd find work for her!" But really I am not lazy. There isn't a moment I'm not active. I'm too much so, if anything—so I won't admit laziness as a fault. Then I'd say, "If she isn't lazy, perhaps she's super-sensitive and imagines she wouldn't be desirable." There may be some truth in that. But I can offset that, by saying I always answer the ads by letter, and almost invariably get an audience—because I do know how to answer ads to command attention—and then when I go in answer to them, I am let down hard by the first or second question. Further I might say: "Well, she surely could sell something from door to door." Yet in my case, that is not possible. Here (and in Phila., and perhaps everywhere) any person who thru any affliction goes from door to door, to canvass, is liable to fine, imprisonment, or both. . . .

"Then what do girls do, who not only haven't a good appearance, thru a like affliction, and who aren't able to see as well as others, yet who haven't been gifted with intelligence enough to pick up an education sufficiently good to get positions such as you have had?" I don't know exactly what they do, unless they resort to living as I did formerly; or perhaps marry; or if they do work, are laundresses, potato peelers, scrubwomen. And perhaps, instead of feeling any pride because I have been able to pick up a little knowledge, I should regard it as "a dangerous thing," since it takes me out of the class that I've every reason to believe I should be in.

When I was in Phila., I saw an ad in the paper; the party advertising wanted a woman to do some research work. I didn't understand clearly what was wanted, but I wrote, and received an answer telling me to call. When I did, almost the first words were that having impaired eyesight would make it impossible for me to do the work they required of me—for I told in my letter that I had no experience in the work, but was willing and most anxious to find work such as the ad made me believe they had to offer. On top of that: in Phila., my doctor who cared for my eye during my trouble, said, again, I must do little reading or writing. Proving conclusively that I should have remained in the scrubwoman class mentally, so that reading or writing would not be the things I love to do most. Every so often, a clot of blood gathers on my eye—bloodshot, as it is familiarly called—and gives me almost no trouble, hardly any pain, but just has a stiff, dry feeling; and I suppose that is why Dr. Chance—and Dr. Byers, here—think I must not read or write much.

I did not go into all this, in this fashion, with Mr. Welsh in my letter; so this is really the first time I have summed the situation up as it is here. And I must admit it frightens me. It can't be that this can last long; and yet on this point many authorities differ. Some think the war may last many years. That would be too cruel. I hope it is not so. Yet today the boys were calling "Extras!" about the fact that President Wilson has sent for our American Ambassador to Berlin to return. But as this is a Boston—American—extra, I hope it isn't authentic. It makes it even worse, if that is possible. Then again, if the American people are drawn into the war, it may bring the war to an end more rapidly. But again—what if there are German-American uprisings in the Middle West, where there are so many? Really, my head is bursting with pain. It is all so confusing. . . .

I hope you haven't grown weary reading of my trials and tribulations. As I said before, I would wish that you do not worry about what I shall do. As I write, it occurs to me that writing you this is similar to when some girl (one I like especially well) tells me she has not her room rent and the landlady won't let her in; and when I haven't any money to help with, I am told not to worry, that she will manage—and somehow they do! But I do worry; and inasmuch as I can't always provide a bed or help with the room rent, I know what they have to resort to, but I can't help it. So you must do. I am sure you cannot take care of me indefinitely, and it seems so now. So if I must "manage somehow," I suppose now is as good as any other time to start.

I've no doubt Mr. Welsh will help me—though he too writes he has many calls and cannot do much—but if I must, I shall manage somehow. But tonight I am as much at sea as to what that "somehow" will be as I can be. Of course, there is still that hope that something will give and I will find the very opening for me. Before I do anything now, I pray God for guidance, and somehow I feel He won't let me get terribly adrift, as I was at Christmastime last winter.

Good night. I find I end up by feeling sad, when in the start, I was just calm. It is not out of a sense of self-pity—believe me, it is not that—but because I haven't made good, when you, and the rest who are so good, have no doubt expected so much of me.

August 30, 1915

ℂ 106   DID I WRITE YOU THAT I HAD HAD MY HAIR CUT OFF, AND NOW IT IS LIKE a boy's who wears it "bobbed"? When I saw various doctors about the incessant headaches that I suffer so intensely with, they told me it was due to the fact that the scalp on the left side had been raised and operated on, and would always be tender—and what I call a "headache" is really only due to the tearing of the hair at the scalp when I coil it (the hair) and pin it up. I found there must be some truth in this, because when I come in and let my hair down I feel such wonderful relief; and, too, the head was only sore on the left side, and never until I had been out for hours—for in the house, I always wore it in a braid down my back. I asked Dr. Lauterman's advice, and he said he could see no reason why I shouldn't wear the hanging braid on the street—but I feared that this would make me still more conspicuous. And then I had it cut off; and under my hat, it is scarcely noticeable. It is such a relief that I would not care if I looked a scarecrow. But strangely it doesn't look badly—in fact, is sort of becoming, for my hair is thick and bushy. And it is great, for I wash it now frequently and it keeps fluffy.

I received your card and I found much comfort in it. I was quite unhappy Fri. and Sat., but was able to lose my terror by Sunday; and by Monday, I was comfortable. You see, when I wrote you the long letter, I had for the first time written out the situation here; and it surely looked discouraging.

I will tell you of Stella. She arrived Wednesday A.M.—and even I could have been convinced that it wasn't Stella at all, but an older sister. She is looking remarkably well. Has put on twenty pounds, and I look at her and I can scarcely believe it is the same girl. When I took her to Dr. Lauterman, who originally examined her, he said it was almost incredible—the improvement in her. He praised again and again the treatment she received, and said, had he not examined her himself, he would not believe it possible that any person could so quickly get in her condition. She has become stouter—her skirt does not button—and, her face being fuller and color high, she looks older and more like a woman. The doctor said she was quite well, but must guard against the return of the disease. There is a test called "Wasserman," which people who have had that dread disease must take at least once every three months for ten years—some doctors say—or, better still, all during their lives. These tests cost from $10.00 to $15.00. They are done with guineau pigs' and sheep's blood, and the blood of the person being tested.

Stella eats all her meals with me, but sleeps at home. She eats with me because her mother hasn't a morsel of food she can spare;

and she sleeps at home because I took oath to Mr. Benjamin, when he helped me to get Stella to the States, that I'd never take such a chance again—and while Dr. Lauterman said it was perfectly safe, Mr. Benjamin actually cried at the thought of my sleeping with her. His own experience has made him overcareful; but I had to keep my word. He gave Stella's mother $1.00 Sat., so that she would not be nasty. I think he feels if she were, I'd take Stella back in spite of all my promises.

For the present, Stella must have a little more time to get stronger, and I wrote Mr. Welsh asking if it were possible to send her down to some "habitants'" house in Quebec, where—for about $10.00 the month—she could in one month's time get fit for returning to normal living and work. There was some money collected for Stella's case in Phila., and I feel reasonably certain it wasn't exhausted; and I'd be glad if about $15.00 could be used to send her to the country—$10.00 board for a month and $5.00 fare both ways, and incidentals.

True I could get her a position now. I am pretty sure of it. She is so pretty—just blooming—and could, I know, get into a confectioner's shop or a milliner's. But it isn't exactly fair, for if she fell down, it would be a toss-up as to whether it was her fault or due to her still-weakened condition; whereas if she has one month on a farm, with plain but plenty food and some light work to help the farmer's wife, I am almost positive she will on her return be able to get and hold down a pretty good job. Really she is beautiful; and I will—if she is able to go off to the country—get her a good position in some fine store where appearance counts.

Though her appearance has changed considerably, her general mental condition has changed more. I mean by that, that she asserts herself. Prior to this, since the time I first knew her, she was absolutely without opinion or desire, and it would be hard to imagine any one more acquiescent and "ductile" (I just learned this word) about everything. While she is not aggressive now, nor disputatious, still there is a change; and it is one for the better. For the first two days of her return, I spoke to her of the conditions that prevailed in the hospital. I asked these questions, I think, because I wanted to learn about such things. And yet, no doubt I had a morbid curiosity to learn what creatures such as I saw there, do and say. On the second day, when I was washing her head, I began talking again about the hospital; and though I asked unguardedly of things she saw there, still I was careful not to hurt her. And then, to my surprise, I saw she was crying. While I soothed her, she told me that I couldn't imagine how horrible it all was, the things those women (sometimes only ten to fifteen years old) did and said, and what physical condition they were in (you know Blockley, where she was, is the almshouse; and the venereal ward is the worst place you can imagine), and she wished we could arrange never to speak of it again, as it was so bad that she hoped soon to forget it. And wouldn't I make a compact with her, never to speak of it again? I felt it was a just rebuke, and I was only too glad to agree never to mention the place. For it has served its purpose, and we could not make things better there by talking about them.

One of the things she said I must tell you. Sobbingly, and without meaning to be impudent, she said, "You are not like my old Maimie, you are getting like those terrible social workers." This, because I asked so many questions. I wonder how some of the well-meaning social workers would feel, could they hear that? I know several who nearly drove me to distraction when I was in the Orthopedic Hospital.

So now, Stella and I are playing a game. I said not only would we forget the horrors of the Philadelphia Hospital, but all the painful experiences of her life in the past—and in fact, "make fun" that she was just born again. When she was with me before being cured, I was always tolerant, I never set her to tasks that required much care; and if she did it incorrectly, I was lenient and seldom made her do it over—and generally she did things shipshod. Her job was to set the table and go on messages and wash my hairbrush and comb—but nothing more of any account. Now, because she was just born, I give her tasks simple enough, but show her every step of it as carefully as you would Helen—and you see, that's the game. And we laugh all the time. I showed her how to undress this afternoon—and made her take everything off about fifteen times, until she did it properly. I directed her, for instance, "Don't roll up anything, spread it out, to get air." I told her why the air was necessary and beneficial. Then she'd ask, "What is the air?" And though we laughed, it is just like a little girl who is learning all over again.

Until now, she never made any show of wanting to learn anything. Her business was getting well. And though she couldn't help getting a little learning about various things while with me, she didn't show any special desire to learn. Now, though she hasn't said so, I think her desire is to gain as much in information and experience as she possibly can.

After luncheon, I was paring potatoes and carrots and grating cheese, to have it all ready for tea. So I had Stella read a chapter of Jane Austen's *Pride and Prejudice* that your cousin sent me. Before this, she read to me, also. Because when the work to be done was of such a nature as to rest the eye, I always did it, and let her read to me, no matter how poorly. When she used to come to an unfamiliar word, she'd pronounce it the best she could or, failing that, she would spell it out; then I'd pronounce it correctly, and she'd go straight ahead.

But today, she asked what they meant. *Ostentatious, synonymous, nuances, ubiquitous*—I was all right, so far. But she found *ductility*—and I was stumped. I had to admit I didn't know; . . . I just looked it up. Of course, I could have bluffed it out and said it related to ducks—and now I wish I had, because I see that Stella has lost much respect for my erudition. She thought, she said, that I shouldn't have come a cropper on so small a word, when I knew bigger ones!

Yesterday, I passed on the buff silk basque which formed the nucleus of my "Sunday" outfit. This, because it split in several places; and the girl I gave it to, being very flat across the chest, was able to hide the worn places. This girl, Margaret Barker, was a stenographer. Immediately after the war, there was a panic among the stenographers; and Margaret was one who had really gotten very low. She claims she never really was bad—i.e., that she did not cohabit—but aside from that, she was going very fast; and I am not sure whether she tells the truth about that. Anyway, I took her and another girl in for awhile; and though Lou (the other girl) was a nuisance in many ways, Margaret was very nice, under the conditions. As matters grew worse, and she could not get a real *position,* she took a *job.* You see, there is a difference. The latter means hard work. I got the place for her; and though the pay is poor and the madam a poor befuddled snob—still, Marge at least was independent. Before I went to Phila., she came here every time she was permitted out; and then, when I was gone, she had to cast about for some other way to kill time—and the result is, Margaret has a beau. And a man—a real man, no miserable apology for one—who is in business, and employs about ten clerks! Isn't that fine? When I returned, I was told about it immediately by all the girls, Marge included—and everyone waited breathlessly for my verdict.

On Sunday, two weeks ago, he came with Margaret; and I call it a wonderful piece of good fortune. I don't wonder he likes Marge, as she is clean, comely, sincere and not lazy, and will make him an excellent wife. His name is Brook—Donald. Has a grocery in a fashionable suburb here, and employs ten or more people; has delivery wagons; three telephones—and though Robertson's is larger, "Brook's" is every bit as fine a store. He is about forty-five (Marge is twenty-four or twenty-five), and if he isn't an Apollo Belvidere, at least he is clean looking and devoid of nonsense. He lived with and supports a mother and a sister; and Marge has been taken there; and all is regular and respectable. I would have liked the credit of having arranged this all, but I must confess that I had nothing to do with it. Except (and you see, I do want a little credit) that I took Margaret to the lady's house where she met Mr. Brook, and had this lady to promise to look after Margaret in my absence—as Margaret never went anywhere but here, and I knew she would be lonesome.

Of course, Margaret, who is generous to a fault, claims I am the one most responsible for her happiness. Though he is as bald as a billiard ball, and wears thick glasses, and has quite a stomach, yet he is not at all bad looking. His redeeming features are his expansive smile, showing good teeth that show care, and a florid but clean-looking skin. Mr. Benjamin asked around for me, and the report is that he is a gentleman; never had any scandal connected with his name; and is generally reputed to be rich—and Bennie thinks that means forty or fifty thousand dollars! What do you think of Miss Margaret Barker? They are to be married before Christmas, and he is going to take her to his mother's home, and then will build a home. This he told me; and he looks like Albert Jones when he says something—meaning, that it is without any attempt to brag.

I'll confess that I cried a great deal the night they were here—after they left, of course—but I cried out of sheer joy. She deserves it because—not being as quick witted as Lou Fletcher or as I am—Marge would have gotten left in the race.

☎ 107 YOUR IDEA ABOUT THE DIVORCE, I WELCOME BUT HESITATED ABOUT telling you. I saw a lawyer in Phila.—not this trip, but the last one, in 1914; and though I went to this man sent by the Legal Aid Society, it developed afterwards that he is a close friend of Mr. Welsh and a director of his Indian Rights Committee. I told the lawyer of knowing Mr. Welsh, and though I told in Mr. Welsh's office of having seen this lawyer, I did not mention it to Mr. Welsh. I should have, had the proceedings gone on, but I reasoned it was not right to worry him since I wasn't able financially to manage it anyhow.

The entire divorce would cost $125.00 at the most; but Mr. Brown said it might only be $85.00, and I already gave him $25.00 of that amount to start the case. He said I should have no trouble getting the divorce, as I told him what was true, and that is: Mr. Jones never supported me and did desert me. Then, in February, 1915, Mr. Brown wrote that I must send $50.00 for the next step; and after that, it would only be a matter of a few months before the decree would be granted. But neither Ira [nor I] have had the $50.00 to send; and here the matter rests. (Ira gave me the $25.00 in the first place, so you can see had he been able to manage the $50.00, he would have.) Then when I wrote Mr. Brown that I could not send the $50.00, as I was without funds, he answered that it would not be necessary to send it in a hurry—that the $25.00 would stand until I had the rest. Here, enclosed, is the receipt for the $25.00.

☎ 109 EARLIER THIS EVENING, I WAS IN THE STATION (CANADIAN PACIFIC Railroad), and what I saw there I want to tell you.

Mr. Benjamin and I...went through the CPR station....We heard music—it was so fine that we thought it must be the Grenadier Guards. (Since the war a band of music is likely to be heard any minute, anywhere. The recruiting tents stationed on many corners have bands—of a sort—and "God Save the King" can be expected at any time; and it is funny to see them all pop up in the streetcars as they pass while it is playing.)

...We only supposed it was the Grenadier Guards—and that, because the music was excellent. They were playing the "Soldiers' March" from *William Tell*—or so Mr. Benjamin said (he knows many of the better-known operas, having worked as a "super" in New York in grand opera; and, as he says it, "sung with the best artists," such as Jean de Reszke, Schumann Heink, etc.).

Imagine our surprise—for instead of the gaily uniformed Grenadiers, we found it was a small company of Italian reservists leaving for the front. The company—about sixty-five men—were the shabbiest lot I ever saw, and looked as though they had just dropped their picks and shovels in some close-by excavation to join their colors. But it seems instead, they had traveled many miles and were brought along to embark from here.

The wonder of it was the music—for we have grown accustomed to seeing fine men go off to slaughter. Their instruments were such as you'd see on the vaudeville stage in the hands of comedians trying to burlesque a band, but they played beautifully. As they were all plainly laborers, I was amazed at their ability, but Mr. B. said it was not ability so much as inspiration.

They stood at attention in the station and played the *Italian National Air* and the *Marseillaise*—and such a demonstration as there was, for the music was wonderful. It was a small band, and one might have imagined himself in a concert hall.

Aside from their music, . . . there was something else noteworthy about them.

We are accustomed, as I said, to seeing the troops leave; and though there is always the catch at the throat to see such fine lads go off to such an unholy business, still your Canadian Soldier goes to war more as a lark than as a business. When the first contingent left, it was the consensus of opinion that they'd never see the "front," so their going wasn't taken so seriously. Since the killing off of so many of them...the various companies leaving for Valartier to await their full contingents are less hilarious. But still, being young and more or less irresponsible, they go quite flippantly. . . . It was not so with these Italians; and it was this fact that brought the catch at the throat, and then made one cry openly, unreservedly. They too were young, but had the weight of years of toil on their bodies and faces; and though their faces were devoid of expression, their eyes burned right thru one. With them it was no lark. They were going to attend to their business.

While the band played they were only interested in it. And when it ceased and the demonstrations began, such as passing out of cigarettes, chocolates, etc. (the regular order of things when the troops leave), they took shyly what was almost put in their hands—a contrast to what the Canadians do, for they grab it out of the donors' hands. And they smiled tired and heavy, with the whispered *gratsi* (I am not sure of the spelling), making one feel these were men to be pitied truly. They looked—in repose—hard and coarse and lacking everything that should make one interested in them personally; but when the favors were received, and they smiled, one knew they were full of the romance and sentiment that is generally associated with their race; and all the hardness was gone.

We stood very close; and when the band ceased, one of them pushed closer to the edge we were on and said to Bennie—in Italian—"Will you come around to this other side?"

I thought it remarkable that he singled Bennie out, although because he speaks Italian well, many people have said he resembles one. When we were children, we lived in the heart of the Italian district, and though I remember but little, I am told I could speak it fluently at eight or nine years. But Mr. Benjamin speaks it as well as he does Yiddish.

We went over to the other side; and he talked a little and gave Bennie some pieces of dirty paper which were written upon. I saw, too, that he wanted to pay for what he asked Bennie to do, but Bennie refused to accept it.

When this fellow took out his purse—to get out the coppers which he offered Bennie for stamps—I noted first that it was of a most primitive design. Long and narrow, with a tin rim at the top, and a wire clasp, and dangling from it a tin medal of the Jesus. In persuading Bennie to take the coppers, he caught the medal in the cord he had wrapped around his belongings...and the medal dropped. I saw it, and before either he or Bennie could stoop to recover it, I did; and handing it back to him, he looked straight up at me, and I will never forget his eyes. Then almost unconsciously he crossed himself...and opening his coat, he took out a very dirty, worn, flat cardcase, and placed his medal carefully therein.

Mr. B. had no cigarettes (and I think he had no money to buy any), so he took out his tobacco pouch (he smokes a pipe) and attempted to drop its contents in this fellow's pockets. But he wouldn't have it, and instead took out a pack of cigarettes—no doubt given to him just a few moments before—and as they were all smoking. . .he offered Bennie one and took one himself. And then Bennie got his little silver matchbox out that has Poke's picture on it—he had it done several years ago—and after they both took a light, Bennie gave it to this lad, who took it without argument. For he seemed to fancy the little picture on it. To our surprise, he emptied the matches in his pocket, and out came the flat wallet. Taking out his Jesus medal, he placed it in the matchbox, and grinning at us, he placed it back in the wallet.

We stayed there about ten minutes more, and Bennie chatted with this fellow, who said they were reservists, and some—he, for one—didn't know of the war until Italy became embroiled; and then thru their agents he was notified to join some fellow-reservists at Calgary. Just think how loyal they are! He said he had spent $65.00 so far to get this far. This, for fare and board (no doubt) while waiting for the others. He was working in the mines, and has been from Italy four years, but can speak no word of English.

The letters that he gave to Bennie to mail and enclose pictures of him (taken in Calgary) were addressed to women. Two had names similar to his—Bruchesi. But the third one must have been the sweetheart; for this one—Miss Dini—was written to on "sure enough" letter paper, and the others on torn pieces of white wrapping paper. Bennie bought the stamps, and I have just readressed them, for the envelopes of each had to be opened to enclose the pictures.

When they began to march again—the band playing—he looked at us as though we were truly friends; and though he had relaxed while chatting, he became shy again. And when Bennie gave him his hand in parting, the tears gathered in his eyes, and he squeezed Bennie's hands, both of them, and I patted him on the back, and they were off. He was Salvatore Bruchesi—twenty-six years old— from near Milan. I will never forget him.

. . .I was surprised to learn that Miss Wald is a Jewess—though now that I think of it, I should have guessed it, as her name is quite "Yiddish." The *Lillian* is a quite popular translation of *Lilke*, meaning a lily, and *Wald* is German for forest and is a familiar Jewish name. I knew several families by that name when I was a child and lived among the Jews. Generally the Wald is accompanied by something to distinguish it, such as *Blumenwald* (flower-forest), *Rosenwald* (rose), *Greenwald, Waldman, Waldheim* (home), etc. I do wish I had seen her when I was in New York.

I will now answer your questions, and assure you that I feel no reserve in writing to you on the subject.

You write, would Mr. Benjamin be eager to marry me? I am sure he would. We talk very little of the subject. Tho' once in awhile we find people take us to be "engaged," and we talk about it—but generally, before others. When Mr. Benjamin came here to Montreal, you will recall that he told me he proposed to stay near me. When I said that all I was interested in was to make the B.A.B. a success, he said he was willing to help, and assured me would not ever force his presence upon one. In the beginning, he annoyed me greatly; for when I would want to stay at the office to work, I couldn't be comfortable, for I'd know—someone would tell me or I'd see him—that he was waiting outside. And instead of being able to work, I'd be fretted about the fact that he was mooning outside. Then I finally spoke about it—for he'd meet me outside just as though it were quite accidental. He insisted that I shouldn't work late—and aside from that, I must know that sooner or later some man would take it upon himself to see me home—and he'd decided he'd do it every night. I stormed and raged—but every night, he was there. Several times he talked about getting a divorce for me. But I was only interested in the B.A.B., and wouldn't give it serious consideration. Then, one night we met, and I was provoked because I had been to see a girl (didn't tell him or anyone where I was going), and coming out of her house—there he was. When I started to harangue, he said I might as well get resigned to it, for he would always be there, until I was thru prowling around at night. I was terribly provoked, so I said many things—among others, that I thought he was at fault, because he only worried me. And that seemed to take root. And the next day, he wrote me a letter and said that he'd not worry me with his presence, but I must know that he'd still be there at night at a distance, and that unless I invited him, he'd not address me, nor ever worry me with his advances. But that he was ready and anxious to marry me, provided I'd let him get the divorce for me; but I'd have to let him know when I was ready, for he'd never say another word on the subject. And he really never has. He never smiles when I refer to this, so I am sure he must have meant it. . . . [When I was in Phila.] I went of my own volition to see about the divorce, with nothing else in mind then to marry Ira; so when the lawyer said it was quite simple, I wrote it all to Ira—who took it as though I had gone there to get the divorce in order to marry him, and sent the $75.00.

Since then, while he was always able to make a living, he has not been able to earn as much as he was accustomed to earning before the war; and with each sister needing clothing, etc., he hasn't had any money to spare. (When I think about it now, I recall that there never was a month that he hasn't spent from $10.00 to $25.00 to help my girls, even though the help comes 10 to 15 cents at a time, usually—though he has given lump sums of $5.00 and $10.00. So even though he talks freely of the need for the divorce money, he talks nothing of the possibility of my marrying him. Sometimes when we discuss his mother, he will say, "when I bring her to Canada;" and once my mother asked him when he expected to bring her. He said, "When Maimie and I are married. She will cook for us. She loves to cook." What he expects to do with the two sisters who are at home is, I know, to make them do more for themselves or shift some of the responsibilities on the married sisters. As I understand it, someone would have to stay with his mother anyway, so he permits the two sisters to stay. But should the mother come here (and he says he intends to remain in Canada), then the girls will go to live with Lina or Elaine, who are comfortably fixed financially, and who help the girls now by paying for some finery occasionally.

I think I can say safely that had I a divorce, Ira and I would marry at once. And as for his means, I am sure that with the money he sends to keep up the home in Jersey, what his living costs here, and what he spends in running back and forth on the trains to see me, we could live on comfortably—provided his mother came here (and she wrote my mother that she would like the change). His mother is not against his marrying me. She rather favors me, because she sees that he has only advanced since he has gone about with me. For he has sent more money each year since the time of our meeting again in New York. His sisters object—but they are selfish and their objection doesn't count.

I feel I can say that I am very fond of Mr. Benjamin. This I am sure of now, more than before I went away to Phila. I was so terribly hurt by my people, and didn't know but I might be super-sensitive—or, being used to such kindness and consideration from my friends with whom I correspond, that I might be unfair in expecting people of lesser intellect and breeding to treat me in the same fashion. But on my return, once I was again with Mr. Benjamin, I saw mainly where the trouble was. He credits me with more than ordinary intelligence, kindness of heart and purpose—and by his regard, I am inclined to judge myself. When they—in Phila.—acted about as they used to when I was fourteen or fifteen years, I felt so belittled that I craved to get back to Mr. Benjamin's valuation of me. And that I think of marriage with him as being a pleasant situation is but natural.

When I was with him in New York, I used to regard each violation of what I had learned to be "good taste," or "good form," as serious—and though they were things I had formerly done, I looked down on him for committing them. All that has changed now. He has learned to handle the Queen's English with more dexterity; and as for other things, he is observant and remembers. Though now I do not regard it such a catastrophe, should he drape his forefinger around the spoon in his tea cup and allow it to remain while sipping the tea. This particular offense has ceased, but new ones always pop up; and now I regard them as jokes. Perhaps I have developed a sense of humor—which I was always accused of being without.

Yes, I am very sure were I able, I should marry him. I know I would be even better able to do things for the girls. As it is, very often, my word for a girl is questioned—but were I a householder and had standing, I could demand that my reference for a girl be taken.

While Mr. Benjamin isn't quite as ready to believe good of every girl as am I—still, he can be persuaded. In almost every case, where a new girl comes under my care, he pronounces them unworthy. And then when I remind him that I was always rated likewise, he capitulates by letting me know what he can find about the girl. His word about what a girl has been is better than her own. He asks some of the fellows about town. If the girl is generally known, that means she has been in the game long; and Mr. Benjamin thinks it better to try to help those who are young in the life. Yesterday, he told me of a girl whom I had found a place for—that she was in the Palm Garden Saturday night. This girl, Hazel Lowe, I saw Monday, and she denied it—but later admitted it. So you see, Mr. Benjamin does find out things I wouldn't be likely to know. Hazel owes me $3.00; and when I saw her Monday, she gave me 50 cents and said she was tempted to go into the Palm Garden because she was hungry for something good to eat. So I told her if she was ever that way again, to come to me—and I'd save the 50 cents to spend with her on something good to eat.

I have said nothing to Mr. Benjamin since receiving your letter— and this, because he has such strong feelings about my telling everything that he may think I shouldn't have let you know that he was not able to pay up for the divorce. He is in almost first-rate condition—though he goes nightly to the doctor—and he thinks he will be earning money again by the 15th. Tonight, he went to church. They are having service in the Episcopalian Church for some of the soldiers who are gone, and he is friendly with one of the men interested in the church, so never misses a service—though I believe he goes because he likes to be with his friend, and doesn't give any heed to the service.

As I wrote you before, Mr. Welsh does not think one should apply for divorce, though I believe he hasn't any real fixed principles against it. I think he believes in divorce as the lesser evil, in my case or any girl's, should she contemplate living with another man. I had thought to tell him I was determined to get a divorce, but this was when I thought I should be free of the need for small money. I wrote him on the subject and told him how my mother urged this, for she wishes me to be free so that I may marry Ira. And if I recollect correctly, he told me he didn't believe in it but if I had decided on it, I must be sure to pray unceasingly for the Divine Guidance. If you think I should write him of it, I will. But I do dislike to—for I know he would be pained, and I do hate to worry him. I thought I would wait to tell him again when I should make the next move to get the divorce. And of course, that was to be "after the war."

As I usually do, I am keeping for the last some very good news. I shall tell you about it from the beginning. . . .

My landlord, Mr. Noakes, is a senior clerk in an insurance office—a British house—and since the war began, he has had his salary reduced twice, and was given notice that unless peace is declared by Jan. 1, 1916, the firm would close down their Canadian office, and he must be prepared to find work elsewhere. As it is almost universally accepted that the war will not cease by January,

1916, Mr. Noakes knows he will be obliged to lose his place—and of course, another place is almost out of the question for a man such as he is. He is English, in the extreme. Conservative (without push), and has a game leg that prevents him from being aggressive—though he isn't that way naturally. I always knew that he enjoyed some sort of remittance monthly; and he assured me he could manage with it, but he couldn't keep up this establishment, and Mrs. Noakes remaining with her aunt is the logical thing—for he couldn't afford to live nearly as well as they had, and Mrs. Noakes is not a woman who enjoys retrenching and would "beef" for ever, had she to do her own housework. Remaining at her aunt's—who really is much in need of her company thru her bereavement, occasioned by the loss of her sons and husband—he was relieved of her keep. The expense of keeping up this place and the luxuries enjoyed by Mrs. Noakes are just what she likes, and he abhors. Recently, my brother Sam advised my reading *Pride and Prejudice* by Austen; and later, Miss Huntington sent it. I read it, and wonder if you ever did. The father of the girls in the story is Mr. Noakes in so many ways that I could scarcely believe it was so well drawn, and thought I might have imagined it—until I gave it to Mr. Benjamin to read, who said, after reading only several chapters: "Mr. Noakes is surely a Mr. Bennett, and Mrs. Noakes the same silly sort of wife, minus the daughters."

I was obliged to agree with Mr. Noakes that it was foolish for him to keep up this place. And he said he was fully determined to break up housekeeping for good and all, as he was of the opinion that, if he kept the furniture in storage, after a few winter months Mrs. Noakes would grow tired of the country and insist on his taking up an apartment which he couldn't afford. But by actually selling their belongings—which she was then and is now quite willing to do (assuring him that should they decide to take up housekeeping after the war, she'd prefer to pick out all new things!)—he could feel some security that she'd stay with her aunt indefinitely; and he was going to stay while in town at his club. He is a Boer War veteran—was "Captain Noakes," but didn't care to be called that until the war broke out. And now he does a great deal of flaunting of said title and has much to interest him in the various *mil'try* (the English say this invariably) organizations and clubs.

When Mr. Noakes spoke of selling out, he said he hoped I

would...advise him what was best to do, and he was going to ask Mr. Benjamin's advice also. (Like the average Englishman, Mr. Noakes thinks Americans have wonderful commercial ability, and he cordially hates anything that has to do with the exchange of values.) We talked it over then with Mr. Benjamin, who advised that the stuff be put in storage, because at the present time so many are breaking up their homes—going to the war—that secondhand furniture is really not to be sold at all....Too, knowing as we do that all Mr. Noakes' things are good, strong and in perfect condition and good taste, we thought he had a right to expect a good price, but were sure he wouldn't get it. In fact it could not be sold at all; but by selling them piecemeal, he could dispose of the bulkier things. This Mr. Noakes objected to doing, because he said if he had one chair in storage, Mrs. Noakes would insist on adding to it and starting housekeeping—the very thing he wanted to avoid—and he was in hopes that he could dispose of it lock, stock and barrel, even if for a tiny sum.

Matters were in this shape when I went away.

In talking to Mr. Welsh, I told him of the circumstances that I could not remain here longer than Oct. 1st [when Mr. Noakes' lease is up]. And later, he asked me to talk with Mr. Suiffen re the expense, etc. of keeping up a sort of mission—in a single room perhaps—but to put it all plainly on paper as to costs, etc., so that he could put it before a few friends, with an idea of sending me a regular amount and have me make it my work. And if I had the means for a mission, I *would* put it above every other considera-tion—and make it my lifework.

I think I wrote you of what Mr. Suiffen had to say on the subject. His clear-headedness made it seem much easier, and especially when he pointed out—as I wrote you—that there must be a certain amount of social reform and welfare work; that women in the main must engage in it; that thousands are in it, who receive a living wage for their services, and who are not better fitted for the work than I am; and that considering all the circumstances of my life—and my appearance, which would be an asset rather than a liability in such work—he thought I should try to make it my life-work. But when finances were talked of, I told him there was little or nothing to be expected from Montreal or Canadian people, aside from their help to further the war; and that I couldn't in fairness to

Americans ask them to further a mission here; but I would hold the thought to use it when the war is over—when, I feel sure, many ladies here could be interested.

Mr. Suiffen said he'd do something about it. And the next thing I heard, he was sent off by the Indian affairs work to Montana or California. And while I felt disappointed I thought it could be taken up on his return, and probably conditions would be better for it.

On my return, almost at once, Mr. Noakes began throwing the responsibility of disposing of his place on my shoulders. . . . Almost at the start, it was up to me to suggest the best way for him to do. Inquiries proved that auctioneers wouldn't even bother with it—for they find it impossible now to sell furniture, and everyone wants to sell. Then there was nothing else but for him to call in a secondhand dealer and sell it for a lump sum, which would be so little it would be hardly worth talking about, or to advertise it and sell it a piece here and there to persons needing same. The last promised the most money, but it meant torture to Mr. Noakes to contemplate "bargaining," as he called it. . . . Mr. Noakes asked would I take over the selling of it; and if I did, he would give me the furnishings such as one can not dispose of without giving them away—such as pictures, books, etc.

I wrote of this to Mr. Welsh and told him of the entire business. I forgot to say that Mr. Noakes and I (with Mr. B.) made an inventory of the place. Counting everything at only about 70 per cent of its value, it came to $965.00. This did not include many of the little things which were to be mine. I thought by having the entire month of September to dispose of it, I could get around $500.00 or $600.00 for it, at any rate, for him.

When Mr. Welsh answered my letter, he wrote that he wished it could be taken over for a place for me to conduct a mission for friendless girls; and between then and October 1st, he was going to see if he could raise a thousand dollars to buy it over. You see, Mr. Welsh thought Mr. Noakes wanted the $965.00 he counted was 70 per cent of the cost. As a matter of fact, I knew Mr. Noakes would be willing to take very much less. . . . I told him Mr. Welsh was going to try to raise the money to buy his things for me and wanted to know what sum he considered the very least he would accept. Of course, he turned to me: "Mymie, how much shall I say?" I told him it wasn't fair to put it up to me, for I was interested party, and

I'd rather that he would figure it out himself, without either Mr. B's or my help. He decided that since the dealer offered only $300.00, and he was going to give me the odds and ends anyway, he'd accept $300.00...for, as he said, he hadn't any certainty that he could sell piecemeal; and he would rather sell it even to a dealer than be obliged on October 1st to store it.

I thought $300.00 really too little. But he insisted that he would accept from Mr. Welsh—since it would be used for charitable purposes—the same amount the dealer offered: $300.00.

I felt pretty sure Mr. Welsh could and would raise the amount, but I wanted to be sure Mr. Noakes would understand; so I asked could the payments be made easier than $300.00 at once. And he agreed to take $200.00 in a lump sum, and $25.00 for four months—but later decided that if Mr. Welsh could send him $275.00 at once (rather by November 1st), he would accept it instead of $300.00 in installments. He explained this by the fact that if it is a contract (and it would be, unless it were an outright sale) he would have to have Mrs. Noakes' signature to the sale—and if she knew the amount he accepted...she would never stop ranting about it....

I wrote this, then, to Mr. Welsh—who, it seems, had a rare piece of good fortune by having $175.00 sent him by two friends for him to devote to some of his charities. Mr. Welsh wrote asking me to state plainly in a letter just what money would be necessary to acquire the furnishings—the entire expense—and how much I would require to maintain it for my own living and the help to the occasional girl who would stop with me, and those that come and go; and to outline what I thought I could do in the way of help toward the girls, provided I had this place. This I did; and I will write you, as nearly as I can remember, about what I wrote him.

There are three rooms here, and kitchen and bath. Everything is complete in the slightest detail and though not sumptuously furnished, still in very good taste, and just a bit better than just well furnished. All the furniture is fumed oak, very heavy, old English style, and not nailed or screwed, but pinned. There are no fancy things, everything has a reason or purpose in being in the place. In every detail it is furnished very comfortably, and has many conveniences such as one does not see ordinarily in Canada. There is an electric vacuum (a good one), electric fan, [electric] heating irons, two electric percolators for coffee. . . . In Mrs. Noakes' room, the dresser and bureau have plate glass fitted tops, and in my room there is one on a library table. I tell you this to show that it isn't a poorly gotten together place. . . . Now it would cost $275.00 to acquire it, and there isn't a penny's debt against it. . . .

Now then, it would be impossible to remain here. The rent is prohibitive and the landlord isn't willing to reduce, though everyone else in town has. An apartment, heated, such as they [used to get] $40.00 and $50.00 for, can now be had for $25.00 to $35.00; and I'd hope to find a place for $25.00—for I'd have to be centrally located, and too, it would have to be a heated place, for having no man to care for the furnace, I'd be cold oftener than warm. So I would and could find a place for $25.00. To move the furniture would cost from $15.00 to $20.00—so Mr. Noakes thinks; and in order to start the mission I'd have to have:

275.00 for furnishings
25.00 for rent—in advance
20.00 for moving
320.00 to start with

Then it would require, for every month, from $65.00 to $70.00 a month to keep up. This would pay rent, gas, electricity (heat with the rent), water, telephone and food—for me and one other person.

Mr. Welsh's idea was to call it the *Montreal Mission for Friendless Girls*; and it would be my plan to keep only one girl on the premises, and not allow that one girl to stay more than three months. I would only keep her, at all, if she had had no training or needed careful watching, and in that time teach her, so that she could command a fair salary—for I'd find out what a girl is fitted for, and I think I could train her. If a girl showed aptitude for stenography, I'd teach her that; but for the most part, it would be "general housework," or "table maid"—or even "cook: general"— or mending and patching in linen rooms of hotels or institutions. If, at the end of three months, a girl isn't ready enough to go out to work (steady, I mean, morally) and able to do something I've taught her, then I think she should be let go, to make way for another girl, who is probably very anxious for a chance. At the Door of Hope (in Phila.) they keep girls two or three years; and as they have only room for seven or eight girls, I don't think that is fair—for their girls are all big and fat. And if they aren't ready to mix with the world, they should be sent out anyway, to give a few more girls a chance—especially when they've been fed and cared for a year or more. Really, I know that 20 per cent of the young girls are only immoral because they never had a chance; and I believe—unless Mr. Welsh or you or others think differently—that no girl could expect (if she is well physically) to be looked after for food etc., for more than three months, in my place.

Aside from the one girl that I will care for entirely—if I get the place—I will arrange to have the girls around town use my place as much as they wish, whether they're still living in sin or not. There would be three rooms, kitchen and bath. One of the rooms would be my bedroom. And unless I know a girl well, and am sure of her, I will try to sleep alone. Of the other two rooms, I would make one the living and dining room, and the other, just as my room here. But instead of using this bed, I'd exchange it for a davenport, so that thru the day, the room could be sort of a living room, too. And it would be in this room I'd let the girls come at will, as they do now. In that way, the other living and dining room could be semi-private. And I'd have the telephone in the hall.

Now then, I'd be able to do so much more for the girls.

I'd have plenty of books such as they like, though no trashy stuff. Every girl that has ever come here more than two or three times has read *The Opal*, and *Linda*, and *Elsie Venner*, *Old Curiosity Shop*, *Daniel Deronda*, the lives of Pelleas and Ettarre—and now *Pride and Prejudice* is a new favorite—and they love every one.[37] And I believe I can say, without exaggeration, that not one girl ever read a good book until she came here.

Then I'd beg around for the issues of the various magazines, as they get out of date. Then there is the phonograph, with a large number of good records, supplemented by the ones I bought with the more popular airs—for the girls insist on lively ones. I don't buy trash—but when I could afford them, bought the *Sari Waltzes*, *Pink Lady*, etc.; and the girls dance to them. Some of the girls come here mainly because of the phonograph; and one girl, Annie Radovitch, brought some records—old ones, but the kind the girls like—

Then there are two writing desks; and I would permit them to write and receive their mail here, furnishing plain stationery, if possible; and I'd try to confine this to the writing of letters to girls and home. And if to beaus, then only to respectable ones—if I can manage it.

The telephone they could use; and I'd receive messages for them only, of course, if they were legitimate ones.

If any girl wants to learn to write or wants to improve her writing, I'd teach her at her convenience.

Then, they could come—as they do now, in Mrs. Noakes' absence—for baths or to have their hair washed. Generally, one girl washes the other's head; but I show them how to bathe properly and quickly. As a rule, the girls bathe infrequently and like to take several hours at it, but I insist a bath should not take over fifteen minutes.

I wrote to Mr. Welsh, that if it is possible, I should like to be able to offer any girl a cup of tea and a biscuit. In fact, there is a little tea machine here that will make five cups of tea. And here in Canada, a cup of tea is often preferred to liquor by the same class of girls who drink beer in the States—and any girl, especially in the winter, will go a long way for a good cup of tea. I'd like to have it so that a girl could have a cup of tea just as readily as a glass of water—and I could buy inexpensive tea.

For the same amount, almost, that it costs for my food, I could feed one girl—and that would be all. For if I attempted to feed more, the cost would be excessive; and besides, the place would become less what I'd like it to be and be more like a "hang-out" for shiftless girls.

Because I'd always keep it up, as this place is [kept up], the girls would respect me and the privilege of coming here. But I would like to be able to offer any girl a cup of tea.

Then, above everything else, I'd always volunteer to find places for them. If a girl is still "in the life," as they call it, I can—by being friendly with her—slowly but surely change her views and get her to consider going to work.

This, then, is what I should do, if the mission were possible. Mr. Welsh thinks it is, because he has $175.00—contributed when there was no thought of buying the place—and thinks he can raise the rest. As the place must be taken over by the first of October (for Mr. Noakes must get out of this place), I will write Mr. Welsh that we must make arrangements before then. . . .

I wonder if you will approve of all this? Of course, it isn't as though I had managed anything by my own efforts. But I do think it would be wonderful if I had a place, to run a sort of home, for the girls to come at will; and I'd do everything in my power to help them. I'd keep a book account of my affairs and expenses, which would also include all the girls names, etc.; and I'd try to have only the English Protestant girls to come (or Jewish), because what help is extended to girls at all here is thru the Catholic Church, and of course they are only interested in girls of their own religion.

I will let you know just how I do, but I feel pretty certain Mr. Welsh will raise the balance of the money for it, since he has more than half the amount already.

Since I told Mr. Benjamin of the fact that Mr. Welsh will take the place over for me, he has been crestfallen. . . .It seems he fears that if I have the place and go into the mission work entirely, I will not want to marry. [But I] read to him what you wrote—and when he saw that you thought even were I to get married, I could still engage in the work, he was easier. He said if he had the ability he would write to you, but he hasn't the courage to attempt it. He wants to tell you that if you can arrange for a divorce for me, so that I may marry him, he would assume the debt for the cost and repay it. . . .

I received a lovely letter from [your cousin] Saturday, and she enclosed a check for $8.10 again. I also received one with check enclosed from Mr. Welsh, on the same day. So I will write Miss Huntington not to send any money this coming week.

Before I close—and I am ready to, now—I want to tell you that I went yesterday to look for a place for Mary Henderson (American, but in Canada ten years) in general housework—and for the first time, ran into a place where a man advertised for the one purpose of having the applicants to cohabit with. His ad read—"Young girl, experience not necessary, for light housework. Will pay well. Must have smart appearance and not over twenty-one years."

I went with Mary Henderson. She is pretty, and quite fresh and rosy in her appearance. She has worked a little, but has "done the streets," as she calls it, since 1913—two years—and now is willing to work.

The man who advertised is a Frenchman, so when I went to Recorder Lauctot, I got scant satisfaction, for he said I must not imagine men are always seeking to harm. He not only wouldn't listen, but was a bit insulting.

The advertiser, when he saw us, was as willing to have me as he was to have Mary Henderson, and offered us money. I listened to him, to see just what the game is. At any rate, he can't place any more ads. For I went to *The Star* office and wrote out my statement—which Mary Henderson also signed. And should he ever attempt to place an ad, they would refuse to accept, and use my signed statement to prevent his ever doing such a trick again....

I wish you would send Miss Huntington part of this letter—or all of it that has to do with the possibility of my taking over the furnishings of this place for the mission.

September 13-15, 1915

∞ 110   I RECEIVED A LETTER FROM THE BARON DE HIRSCH INSTITUTE ASKING IF I would call on their secretary Tues. A.M.[38] It may be in reference to a position, but I doubt it, as I am considered a proselyte and, as such, do not come under their care. It may be they have a girl who has been arrested "on the streets" who knows me, and they want to ask about her.

September 17, 1915

∞ 111   I AM IN RECEIPT OF YOUR LETTER AND VERY HAPPY THAT YOU THINK well of the project which I outlined to you, and I thank you very much for your kind offer of the tea and magazines. Isn't it strange that whenever I thought of the mission, I pictured girls coming in and making tea (without having to ask me)—and when the cost of the tea came to mind, I figured that you perhaps would arrange with some ladies who would like the thought of keeping up the table!

I will go into this to show you my thoughts on the subject.

When it is cold here, it is so frightfully cold that the one thought uppermost in each one's mind is to get something to make them warmer, naturally.

Once when I pitied some fellows in the Bonsecours Market who were knee-deep in ice while unpacking frozen beef, one of them, who spoke broken English, said: "It is not too bad. We have much spirits"—and with that, showed me a fair-sized keg of whiskey, with a measure under the tap the size of a tumbler. And I saw this man—a lad, really, of about eighteen years—draw this full and

320

drink it off as I would cold water on a hot day. He offered me the same amount; and when I thanked him and told him I was a "tee-totaler" (that's what the English here call any one who doesn't drink liquor), he said, "Oh! well, I give you to this faller, and he give you to the tea." I followed, out of curiosity, and was taken behind a door where there was a huge stove, and on it, a huge—black, and very dirty—water kettle. On a packing box stood the teapot and cups (huge ones); and the men were drinking. I can't explain to you how different they looked than the men around the whiskey keg. Not that they were cleaner or gentler, but their faces were human. They all gave me welcome; and when I said, "Comment ça va?" they laughed at the fact that I spoke French, for they could see I was "la belle Americaine" (as they call all American girls)—something the French can distinguish almost immediately. I drank the tea, after a fellow clumsily made a cup clean by washing it with the hot boiling water and drying it by rubbing it into clean sawdust. The tea was bitter, but hot, and it sure filled me with good cheer—for I was most frozen. My escort—who couldn't speak a word of English— then took me to the front of the little shack where the men were tea drinking and showed me a brass plate which read something to the effect: "Canadian Ladies' Relief. Tea Station No. 6." And I learned later that this association has been discontinued thru the death of several of the ladies interested, and it is now kept up by voluntary contribution. I was working then, so I put my 50 cents in the box, and several times since then have dropped dimes at two other stations where I occasionally.go for tea—where they keep the places cleaner.

Now then: people before me saw the advantage of giving tea without price or question, for the natural inference [is that if the men had] to pay, they would buy liquor, for the most part. [But what about] the young girls who wear scant clothing (this for the sake of vanity generally) and who roam the streets? (for there they satisfy the cravings for companionship of the other sex). Mind you—I don't mean the regular "streetwalker," but the young girl who finds, at sixteen, or fourteen sometimes, that she has a pretty face and the boys are attracted to her almost without effort. The street walker has a lot of friends who have "joints" where she can go in to get warm, or buy a drink. But the young girl—the flapper—she has only the street, the moving picture show, or go home (the last place, of course).[39]

Now then: suppose [this girl] knew of my place—and I am to be right in the proper place to get the flappers, as I will explain later—and she hasn't to walk out of her beaten path, and can come in to find Maimie (no *Mrs. Jones*), who will let them all know that, "I have lived as you have lived, and I understand." And they won't have a long-faced woman, whose years would make them say—as I have said—"Oh yes, when I am as old as she is, I won't run around either!" I won't put on airs, but be one of them—letting them, at any time, use the toilet, take a bath, wash their heads—curl the hair, if they choose (for you can't change them without conceding a little to their views, especially if they are harmless ones)—use the telephone, read or write. And—more than anything else—have a cup of tea.

If there is any thought that, given carte blanche at this, they may prove greedy, I think that can be quieted by the thought that no one can drink more than two or three cups of tea. And were it candy, or fruit, or sweets of any kind, they might be gluttonous. But in the case of tea: when a girl comes in off the street, I'd see to it that she had the feeling that she can make a fresh cup of tea whenever she wants—and I miss my bet if they don't soon make it a regular thing of coming up in pairs to have a cup of tea. For where else have they this privilege.

At present, I get to know them well. And each girl, no matter how poorly gifted she is, thinks she could do so-and-so, had she the chance. Therefore, I'd harp on these things, but show them that only thru one avenue can they arrive at their heart's desire—and that is thru effort. As I often say—"You can't wish yourself into this or that situation." Unfortunately, just now, every girl—*not* excepting those who are as ugly as sin and as graceful as elephants—thinks she'd like to act in "the movies." Thank goodness, "movies" are not made in Canada. So that can easily be disposed of.

I can recall, in my youth, when I would want to get shelter or warmth of any sort ("movies" were not as prevalent then as now), I had only a fellow's apartment or rooms to go to. And of course, when there were refreshments, it was beer or whiskey. I can recall one fellow's place where I went often, to stay for two or three days and nights—just because he had all the magazines. And girls who are less desirous of gaining an education even than I was, will go a long way to see magazines—provided it isn't a public library, where they would have to be quiet, or a church charity....

On Tuesday, while I was hunting an apartment, I saw a girl coming. She appeared smartly dressed, but unmistakably fast. She was about sixteen or seventeen. I saw her directly in front of the place where I have since signed a lease to take over the apartment on the first. As she neared me, I saw that she recognized me, though I didn't know her. There was a little change in her gait, the agitated swinging of her handbag proving she knew she was being observed. As we passed, she smiled slightly; so I said, "Hello, Girlie, isn't it warm?" She stopped and made a face, but said nothing. I know her type as well as I do my name. So I leaned toward her and said, "I'm about faint with the heat, can't we go somewhere to cool off?" So she said she hadn't an idea where, unless we went to the Imperial (around the corner—and the mecca for the flappers—and at the crossing of the two most frequented streets). The Imperial is the movies. So I said it was too hot for that. So she advised going in to "Hoffman's" apartment in the Brindeau—outside of which we were standing, and from where she had just come—and didn't I know Hoffman? He is a good fellow and never locks his door, even when he isn't there; and the girls go there to cool off, or to get warm. That suited me down to the ground—especially now that I am right over "Hoffman's" head. My apartment is over his. So we went in.

First, I will tell you of the girl—that what appeared "smart" in her attire, on closer inspection lost all that—although she, along with the other girls like her, catch something of the air of smartness, and in her cheap, flimsy get-up, can, at a distance, give the impression of being expensively and smartly gowned. Her hat—a fall model—was of blue satin that, close-to, looked like paper, and yet with two quills sitting pertly at cross angles. She looked chic in it. The dress: I could only see the skirt, for she had a mangy white wooly article, which was supposed to look like a fur, strung around her shoulders. Her neck and part of her shoulders were bare, as a décolleté gown should make them. The entire girl being tiny, the "fur" covered all but the skirt—which was also blue satiny silk, but close-to was plainly made by herself by hand, and ripped here and there in the seams. It was spotted and flecked, though one could see she had tried to clean it—but being such cheap goods, she had only succeeded in pulling the goods into bare places, with hairy hangings. The slippers were the piece de resistance. They were once white—or perhaps brown—but had been bronzed at home, and in the sun, looked mottled; and where the shoes rubbed, the bronze glistened like brass. Her stockings were silk, of course, and flesh-colored. Then she swung a white (dirty) kid bag. And that completed her costume. The *tout ensemble* looked smart from a distance, I must admit.

Now for the girl herself; her hands were knobby and ugly beyond words, with the nails worn down into the quick from scraping pots—and the scrapings still under them. Remember this was only a flapper still living at home. But just on the verge—for she was accepting money, plainly evident from her clothing. Her face, coarse-skinned; and where the powder had stayed on, it looked scabby. She had no other "make up," probably because she hadn't any. Aside from all this—she was beautiful. You never saw such eyes and teeth. Her mouth was perfectly formed, as were her nose and ears; and her eyelashes perhaps the most noteworthy. I didn't see much of her hair, but it was dead black. I am sure her eyes would attract anyone.

So we went into Hoffman's flat. And Hoffman, though German-sounding, was quite plainly a Frenchman; and he was there. He was elated that she had brought me in. He didn't lock his doors, and I saw at a glance why. For had any one intended to steal anything, they'd have had to bring a dray—for there was nothing in sight except the big pieces of furniture. Hoffman—an oily individual of perhaps fifty-five or sixty, undersized and most non-descriptive—at once admired my form. I uttered no word from the time we entered, which I knew wouldn't strike him as strange, because the girls are always shy at first, and the ones that are most shy become the boldest as they become better acquainted. Too, he spoke in French, and I could pretend not to understand. He brought out some whiskey, and when the little girl said we wanted something cool, he was most profuse in his apologies for not having ice, explaining that he stopped his ice supply September 1st.

I looked at the magazines—all in French, and mostly with pictures of *la Guerre*. And around the room, stuck up with pins, pictures out of fashion-plates, showing women in undergarments. The idea was so ridiculous that I could have slapped the dirty little beast's mouth, when—as I looked at them—he said he thought I had a better form than any there. I think had I smiled even once, I'd have had him to deal with; but I didn't. I asked him re the heating of the place and the hot water and such things; and finally it dawned on him that I was going to take an apartment there. So he thought we would be good friends. I assured him we would; and the little girl (who, I learned afterwards, knew of my work to keep girls out of such places) burst out laughing.

We left there and went up to the empty apartment which I have taken; and we sat on the windowsills and talked.

She thought she should tell me that "most" of the tenants of the Brindeau are bachelors, who make of their places rendezvous for girls such as she. I knew this—and just for that reason, I am going to live there. It is a very large place—in two sections—and has forty or fifty (I think) apartments. I know you've got to go where there are fish, to catch fish. Hence, I will keep my place in the Brindeau, though I would like it better, of course, if I could live in the west end of the city.

This little girl—her first name was May, and I've forgotten the last name—I have since gotten a position for, after tracking around all day . . . .

Yesterday, in hunting a place for May, I came across a man who was interested in mission work, and he told me of a Rev. Dr. Tucker who conducts the City Mission here and whom I will go to see as soon as I am settled. This man assured me that Dr. Tucker did wonderful work, and that every girl he gets work for is "respectable." I couldn't help smiling at this smug little Christian. So I said, "What about those who, through ignorance or youth, are not respectable?" "Oh," he answered, "Dr. Tucker is a particular man, he wouldn't house a girl a minute if she wasn't respectable." I think Dr. Tucker is a good man for me to see. Not that I will try to convert him into my way of thinking, but I will tell him that whenever he finds a girl is not respectable and therefore does not [qualify] for his help, to let me know.

Mr. Welsh sent me $175.00 which has been given to him by other people, and I opened an account in the Royal Bank of Canada, giving Mr. Noakes a check for $100.00. This, to assure him that we would surely take the things and not oblige him to store them at the last minute. There is $145.00 necessary before we can start. This I feel sure Mr. Welsh can raise.

I have a lease on a place in the Brindeau Apartments. There are five rooms, exactly as here, though a bit larger—except the kitchen, which is tiny. The apartment—No. 9—is one flight up, with two rooms, of two windows each, facing on the street. The others are back rooms. I am quite elated at the prospect of fixing them up, for I feel as though I was fixing up a home—my first home in my life.

The agent is painting it up and making it more habitable. And starting next week, everyone is going to lend a hand at night and Sunday, to hang pictures, put up curtains. . . . It is admirably laid out for my needs. The living room opens up from the hall, and the dining and bedroom (which I will try to keep private) is away from the rest.

Mr. Noakes has been just fine. On Monday, he brought up four big thick *woolen* blankets that Mrs. Noakes had taken to the country, and he said, "This goes with the stuff, Mymie, so I brought them back." I don't know all Mrs. Noakes thinks, but I know she is having a fine time thinking how she is going to select an entirely new and up-to-date home this winter. And Mr. N. says she will jolly well stay with her aunt and enjoy the "lee*mouse*ine," as Mr. N. delights in calling the little coupe the aunt has—and which Mrs. N. is always talking about. . . .

I wish you would write Mr. Welsh that you approve of the mission. For I know he would be encouraged by your opinion, feeling that you know me and could judge whether I am capable of conducting the mission.

Again I thank you in the matter of the divorce. Do you not think it would be well for you to write the lawyer and explain you are helping me to secure a divorce? As I wrote you, this man is a fine person of your class of people, and though I knew he did not expect to profit much by my divorce, still if he knew that you were doing this for me and that I am absolutely without means, it might be possible that he could get the divorce at less expense, or more quickly than along the regular route. If you think this advisable, I will wait to hear from you before I write him. You might ask him how far the divorce has progressed and how much—rather, how little—money would be required to consummate the proceedings. And if he knew that I was without work or funds, I think he could do better than he originally told me.

I have read your letter to Mr. Benjamin (I had lunch with him today), and he takes very seriously your letters. He said, "Don't ever destroy that. I'd want to read that every time I got the blues, if it were mine." So I gave it to him. . . .

I received a letter from Caroline—the first communication from any of them excepting Sam since I left Phila.—and she started off the one-page letter by telling me the very glad tidings that James is leaving Sunday, Sept. 19th, to visit the Exposition in California, and will make many stops while traveling. She is such a good soul, but her stupidity annoys me so that I am desirous of shaking her. The idea of James traveling for pleasure, and she will have to assume the burdens—she with a two months old infant, and a child of four. She has a servant—who also has to prepare foods for the store, so Caroline has the bulk of the housework, besides the store to look after. I wouldn't care if they were rich, but I know he barely makes ends meet, and this tour is to show off to those he will visit. You know he weighs 240 or 250 lbs.—and he surely does love himself. There wasn't one word in the letter about the dear little Potsy girl or the baby—just James, who is king. She told me all about his trip, then concluded by saying that if he could arrange it he might stop to see me—but I know how much chance there would be for that, because he knows how much impressed I am by his swenking.

You are indeed right: Sam isn't at all like James, and my father wasn't at all like my mother. And Sam is exactly in views and appearance as was my father at his age. My father helped everyone. My father was a great man, and he is remembered by every Russian Jew who was in Phila. prior to his death. Even here, among the Jews, I find regularly men who knew, or knew of, my father.

I will close now, thanking you again for your offers of help. And I feel everything will come out all right, because I want it to, so much, and I have such wonderful friends.

September 21, 1915

MR. WELSH ASKED ME TO WRITE TWO FRIENDS OF HIS, BOTH MEN I DON'T 113 ❧ know, but warm friends of his. In each case the request was, "Write him of your plans in regard to conducting the new mission, also of your work in the past—in fact, anything that you choose, to have him know more of you."

Somehow I find it very awkward to write under such circumstances. Not because I don't know them, but because I can't feel their understanding and sympathy. I find I can write reams to you or to one or two others, without effort, apparently; but when I try to write to these others, my fingers become stiff and my brain paralyzed. I always write them eventually; and on Sunday past, after hours of painful attempt, I wrote the two men, as Mr. Welsh asked me to. I know it is not unreasonable for him to ask me to write these people, for he knows I have the ability—after a fashion—so I think it must be stage fright, or self consciousness.

Therefore, Sunday night when these two letters, written and re-written, were finally in the mail, I drew a deep sigh of relief and went to my bed feeling that I had indeed "earned a night's repose."

Imagine then my agitation on Monday morning, to receive a letter from Mr. Welsh, asking me to write to a lady, telling her of the new mission, etc.—this lady also a stranger. I always feel nervous when the letter is to a man, but collapse entirely when it is to a lady. This because, in my early life, all ladies of respectability took the form of "cats" to me—in the sense that they would purr around me, only to get close enough to attack me. While I feel quite different now, the approach of a new lady—I use the term "lady" in its real sense—makes me unconciously guard myself. And a letter to one becomes torture. Do you recall when you first wrote to me, how terrified I was? Well, I feel that all over again, with each letter that Mr. Welsh asks me to write. . . .

I began the letter. . .on scratch paper, intending to copy it—though I write to you, Miss Huntington, Mr. Welsh, Harry, etc., directly on the paper I send—as you can readily see! The writing became more and more labored, and finally came to a direct halt. Apparently I had written myself out the day before. I stopped to commune with myself. For I was provoked to find myself as self-concious as a schoolgirl, and flayed myself by reminding myself that I could "write like a streak to Mrs. Howe or Miss Huntington."

All of a sudden the *brilliantest* idea came to me—and I truly believe it will be the means of making my life easier. For these "write a letter to Mr. Blank" requests have almost driven me to distraction.

Instead of telling you of the idea, I will tell you just how I followed it.

I cleared away all the scratch paper, took out this pad, began my letter, "Dear Mrs. Howe," keeping in mind about telling you of the new mission particularly—and away I went, just like greased lightning. Sheet after sheet, with never a stop. And if once in a while, the fact of the true conditions asserted itself, I brushed it aside by telling myself that Mr. Welsh's friend may read it, if she likes, but I am writing it to Mrs. Howe.

And I was well along to the sixth sheet (both sides), when I was interrupted by an old woman who comes weekly to worry me to death about her granddaughter, who works in a laundry and is quite good—but young and full of spirits. And the grandmother wants me to make her live at home, rather than with her married sister. I've investigated the affair, and find she is quite all right where she is—and the grandmother is a well-known miser, who wants the girl's earnings and will allow her no pleasures. The old woman had me fooled for a long time, but Mr. Benjamin found she owns "lots," for which she has paid $300.00 apiece, and is still making payments on more.

Instead of being glad of an excuse to stop, as I generally am when writing "duty" letters, I really resented the intrusion—so you see my "idea" is a successful one. I soon got back to it, finishing my letter with two sheets more; and now I don't care how many letters Mr. Welsh asks me to write—though I wonder if my "idea" will hold good when the letter is to a man. I hope you don't think I am silly to try to fool myself, but since I really found it easier, it can't be criticised.

After the letter was finished, I copied and corrected the sheets, changing the heading, and it was quite all right. Not alone did the ideas come freely, but I didn't have to stop every few minutes to find out if I was correct in thinking a word "looked wrong," after I had written it. When I write to strangers, I fear their criticism—whereas I feel you will think it quite enough that I know the word at all, without expecting me to know how to spell it perfectly!

After I got my letter finished, I decided to send you the original for various reasons. First, because I really wrote it to you; then, because I think I have the plans for the mission more concise and regular (and I'd like your criticism of anything in connection with it) in this letter than in the one I wrote you. Then too, I've got still another idea, in connection with this letter, and want your advice before I carry it out.

Mr. Welsh will, I am sure, from time to time ask me to write others that I am not acquainted with, to tell them of the mission, its proposed work, etc. This, at least until the mission is in working order. Now in this letter—which you will find enclosed—I've covered every point, and, as I think, made it very plain. And since his requests are to "tell them in a letter" of the very thing that this letter describes as well as I am capable of putting it—would it not be all right for me to copy this letter, changing the beginning and ending to suit the individual it is written to? I would want to be sure I was doing right. I mean, I would want to be sure it wasn't deceitful. But as I reason it out, it doesn't seem so. For Mr. Welsh writes, "Tell them of the mission." He doesn't say, write them a personal letter. It is the mission and its work that is the issue; therefore, I couldn't possibly tell them better of the mission than I have in this letter.

If you think it quite all right for me to copy the main facts of this letter, to be sent to others, I would want to know, would it be all right for one to send the letter to Miss Huntington to correct for me? On second thought, I think I had better not have her correct it, for that, in a slight degree, is deceit, for I'd be giving out the impression that I am a well-informed person.

You will find the letter enclosed, and I will not send a copy— should Mr. Welsh request another letter—until I hear from you that it is all right. You need not send it back, as I have taken a rough draft of it. I would like you to read the enclosed letter . . . before you go on with the rest of this letter.

Now I have a piece of good news that I have been keeping for the last.

I got yesterday a short (typewritten) letter from Miss Wald, and she enclosed a money order for $30.00. I sent the letter to Mr. Welsh yesterday, so can only tell you about what she wrote. That she was sorry to have missed my visit; that she received a letter from you telling her of some help that I've been to the girls who are worse off than I; that she wished she could be of "real value," to me but asks to be permitted to contribute the $30.00 to such expenses as are incident in such work; and that she hopes some time we will meet.

This money coming at this time was especially timely, as I will explain as I go on. I have not answered her yet, I want to write a really fine letter; and I will do it after several days of no letter writing, when I will feel fresher. And just now I have a miserable watering of the eye, which apparently is there for no reason at all, except to blur my vision or make it hard for me to write pretty. I haven't a pain or ache—no cold, no headache—and yet my eye waters in the corner. And Dr. Byers said I need no glasses, but—"don't use your eye." And that makes my blood boil, for I'd truly go mad if I couldn't read and write; and I think if he'd give me glasses, I could do so without worrying about bloodspots and water in the eye. But he is the doctor, and the best eye specialist in Canada. He treats my eye gratuitously, but loves to give me prescriptions which cost from $1.00 to $2.00 to fill. He says, when he sees me, "Here is the only patient I have that wants glasses; all the rest claw at me when I mention the word." Goodness knows, I dislike them enough, but I want to use my eye. And think if I had glasses, I wouldn't be pestered by everyone (even to the youngest girls who come here) to "look out for your eyesight," when I am seen reading or writing.

To return to Miss Wald's contribution of the $30.00.

I am very enthusiastic about taking over this place, and have planned it all, as you will see by my letter enclosed. To do this, to start with, will cost $320.00—$275.00 for the place; $25.00 for one month's rent in the new place; and about $20.00 for moving. To maintain the place as I would like to, and being very careful of expenses, would mean from $65.00 to $75.00 a month.

Toward this, so far, I received from Mr. Welsh the $175.00 I wrote you of—I believe—and which I've already paid to Mr. Noakes; and your promise of ten pounds of tea and magazines. (I will acknowledge and thank you now for those received Saturday. I enjoyed reading the story of Osborne's work, and about books in general, in the *Transcript*.) Besides this, Mr. Welsh promised his support, out of his own pocket, of $40.00 a month, leaving $145.00 to get yet for the beginning of the mission, and $25.00 (at least) a month for the regular maintenance of the mission.

There is a sum of money in Phila., held by Miss Mateer in Mr. Welsh's office, which was collected for Stella's case, and which wasn't entirely exhausted, and which Mr. Welsh has written to have forwarded to me to be used for the mission. I haven't any clear idea what the amount is, but it must be around $25.00 to $50.00— It was originally $160.00, and I think $100.00—more or less—was spent for her case.

Therefore, that will reduce the $145.00 required to start with.

Now Mr. Welsh, thru his friends—to whom he is writing and to whom I am asked to write—hopes to raise the amount needed, both in outright contributions and in promises of sums regularly.

In a letter I received from Mr. Welsh yesterday morning, he seemed a little discouraged (though I feel sure it was due to another cause—the death of a lady, a dear friend), and wrote he hoped the mission was possible, but it depended now on contributions—unsolicited, always.

Then Miss Wald's letter came, and the $30.00. She stated plainly that she wanted to contribute it "to such expenses as are incident and inevitable in the kind of service you are giving." That doesn't mean that she wants me to use it for myself, but for the girls, doesn't it? So I wrote Mr. Welsh of it, and told him the $30.00 was plainly a God-sent gift, to make it possible for me to have the mission to conduct. With the $30.00, it reduces the amount needed to $115.00—and Miss Mateer still to be heard from, and Mr. Welsh's friends that he wrote he is sure will help to a certain extent.

Though I am sure (almost) that the amount can be raised, to maintain the mission along the lines, as outlined, yet I am looking further and have a plan to save the day, should the amount not be gotten. This plan has to do with the maintenance of the mission, not the buying of the place, which I feel reasonably sure can be accomplished.

Should the $65.00 to $75.00 not be forthcoming, and I will have the $40.00 as promised by Mr. Welsh, I will go ahead as I've outlined with these changes. Instead of keeping a girl or any girls on the premises, I would rent the *best* bedroom, with the *furnishings that are in Mrs. Noakes' bedchamber* now (which are very good); and I would get $20.00 a month ($5.00 a week) for it, for a couple—man and wife—or two women, or a woman alone, provided any woman alone could afford it. This $20.00, with Mr. Welsh's $40.00, would make the place possible. And Mr. Benjamin said, if he earns it, he will give $10.00 in a lump sum (monthly) toward the place; if not, $5.00 (monthly), surely. And thus, even though I would hate to give up my plans of making my place a practical mission, I'd be able to do as I do now, only with more freedom. . . .

Stella is working at learning to make cigars. She hates discipline and regular hours, but she's getting fatter and handsomer each day, so needs the discipline to keep her in form. She's a beautiful girl and of a wonderful disposition. I hated to send her into the vile-smelling tobacco factory, but it couldn't be avoided....

Perhaps Miss Huntington would like to see the "brilliant idea" letter. Will you send this, and the [enclosed] letter to her, so she won't feel neglected?

Mrs. M.A. De Wolfe Howe has asked me to write to you about the mission to be conducted in Montreal....It is Mr. Welsh's idea to call our mission "The Montreal Mission for Friendless Girls."

I know the girls very well. Their ambitions, hopes, lives, etc., and when I try to do anything to better their condition, I bring to mind my own experiences and try to supply—as much as possible —that which the girls lack to make their lives (away from sin) interesting and happy.

In my own life, I am sure I lacked love.

When Mr. Welsh came into it, I knew for the first time what love of the clean, unselfish sort is.

Many girls, before they give themselves over to the sinful life, have the love of their parents, but people of the sort they spring from—as were my people—are singularily [sic] undemonstrative and often it isn't for lack of love, that the girls go astray, as much as for some evidence of it, which in the sinful life, they get in abundance—of a sort of course....While there are many places in the larger cities where a girl would be treated kindly by people who are as unselfish and kindly as is Mr. Welsh, yet the average girl of any mental power shuns them. This I know from my own experiences and from what girls have told me. I was many times sorely in need of a friend and knew they were to be had in "missions" and "settlements," but I was never the sort that belonged to the "beggar" class and I believed that places of the above sort were conducted to help any self confessed incompetents, who applied for help.

If I had ever—through some circumstance—come in contact with any of the fine women, that I realize, now, work so unselfishly and hard in the "missions" and "settlements," I am sure I should have been spared worlds of misery and some awful experiences. This then is what I hope to do. Supply the love—i.e.—really show love for every foolish little girl that I find on the downward path....

My attitude toward the girls has always been that of a comrade. I let them know right at the start that I have lived their lives and understand. Because I am not much older than they are, they know I can enter into their plans, plays, etc., without taking an old lady's viewpoint and frowning upon everything which it is natural for youth to enjoy....

You know that Mr. Welsh met me through having passed me on the street, and was attracted to me by the patch I wore over my eye and because I looked plainly in need of a friend.

Just so, I meet girls almost every day, sometimes in the most unconventional manner.

I will tell you of a meeting with a little girl last Friday at noon. I tell you this to show how I meet the girls sometimes—and they are generally the girls that would scorn to go into a "mission."

I was passing a corner, where the cars leave for the races—which are now in session. It was a busy corner, but I noticed one young girl walking to and fro apparently awaiting someone who was tardy. She was quite young—about sixteen years—rather pretty, and from her general manner and appearance I recognized that she was one of the girls who had already sinned.

I watched her for a few seconds and the message that Mr. Welsh told me he obeyed when he first saw me, came to me also, "Go after that girl and give her the message of Christ."

As I walked up to her I noted that she wore a simple "wash dress," freshly and stiffly laundered. The dress and its laundering betokened that the wearer was not "gone" altogether for the dress was made and laundered at home as one could see at a glance.

She saw me advancing and turned away guiltily, for she didn't like being noticed standing on a corner waiting for a "date."

I stood by her side several moments before she looked up and when I remarked that it was fearfully hot, she barely spoke in reply, but looked away nervously.

I said, "I'm flat hunting and I hate to go about alone. Don't you want to come along with me for company?"

She answered that she couldn't because she was waiting for a man who was to take her to the races. I said, "Girlie, really you are too nice to go out there. You look as sweet and clean as an angel and the races is no place for you. Don't go out there. Come with me, and we will have lots of fun poking around in other people's flats." And she came.

As we walked I complimented her appearance which was indeed noteworthy for she was minus all the tawdry furbelows that such girls affect, but then this girl is a bit better grade than those whom I generally meet. She can read and write and though of "factory people," her face shows refinement and care on the parents' parts.

I complimented and spoke of her other attractive features, her good and cleanly teeth and skin, and pretty eyes. She liked that and I don't see why a girl shouldn't be complimentary to those poor little things that thrive on it, and who usually get it only from men.

She was quite happy with me all afternoon and soon lost the air of a young lady who made "dates" and became a little girl.

Later I took her to my room. After we had some rice pudding and tea, I played several tunes on the phonograph and she looked at my picutres and I told her who everyone is and she liked the story about Helen Howe's red fox and told me she has the torso of a doll that she had as a child which she finds great comfort in holding if any one "hollers on me."

Before she left she said she would come next week to help me move. This offer was entirely unsolicited, so you see, she is just a little girl willing to do anything to get the love and attention her youthful heart desires.

She is without work and I know just where I can get her a place to work making braids. The work would just suit her I know, and I think I can nip her career on the streets in the bud. She was quite frank in telling me of herself. I learned that she has been a "bad girl" only since May, yet since then she has been "bad," frequently and promiscuously. Her name is Clara Young. She was in need of shoes—having had on canvas, flat, white, slippers in a dilapidated condition—and told me the man who was to take her to the races was to have brought her a pair on their return provided he won. You can judge by this how surely Clara is headed for the downward path. I will try to have her take a position and hold it.

I have taken a flat right in the beaten path frequented by these girls who are just starting out.

One bedroom will be my own and I hope to be able to occupy it alone but if the bed space is needed, I will be glad to share it with another girl.

In the other room, I will always keep a girl—or two, if later that is financially possible. . . .

It is a theory of mine that anything done to help or better a girl has its value even if not perceptible at the time. In the case of these girls, even though they are but children—for I find it is with the younger ones that I am most successful—their experiences in the evil life makes them wiser than their years, and one must bear this in mind to cope successfully with their various problems.

If at the end of three months in my care, with love and every kindness shown her, a girl will not try to live by her own efforts honestly and decently, I am of the opinion that she had better make way for the next girl, who is also a victim of circumstances and needs the lift I can give her.

In selecting this one girl, to stay with me, from the many who will come to visit thru the day, I will take the one who seems most in need of that help which I can give her. Love, attentions of all sorts, training, etc., and I feel reasonably sure that in three months time, this girl will have benefitted and will be willing to go out to work and keep the good work up by giving her place up to the next girl.

Should she fail me and return to the evil life, I will hope by prayer and constant evidence of my interest to eventually bring her around to see the horror and terrors of a life of sin (in contrast to the wonderful peace and joy of an honorable life.)

I will hope to do the greatest good to the greatest number, and will try to emulate Mr. Welsh who never gives a girl up, no matter how obstinate her case proves to be.

Aside from this one girl—who will stay with me for the period of three months—I will take in for a night or two any girl in need of a bed. I could put to bed three more girls besides myself and my "three months" girl—i.e.—each of us take a girl in our beds and one other could occupy the couch.

This business of being "locked out" is a serious one and is often the beginning of a girl's career in brothels.

Living at home a girl's parents lose patience with her and after repeated threats to "lock you out," if she persists in coming home later than the prescribed hour, she is finally "locked out." The girl is not prepared to go anywhere and the hour being late, she casts about in her mind as to the place where she would be welcome at such an hour, and the only place she can think of is a brothel.

Often when I hear from a girl's mother that she "stopped out all night," and I speak to the girl she tells me she either was "locked out" or being in company and the hour growing late before she realized it, knew if she went home, she'd only find herself "locked out," so she stayed with the "fellows" all night.

It is at such times that I would want her to feel at home and come to me for the night, no matter how late and I would put her to bed somewhere. In the morning I would hope to effect a reconciliation between the girl and her parent. This I have been able to do several times already.

So much for my place as a refuge.

Aside from the sleeping at my mission I will keep the living room open to the girls who care to come. They will find attractions which I know they will enjoy and which I hope will tempt them to come to me rather than to the places where they went formerly.

I have for their entertainment, a phonograph, with some good records and some lively ones to suit their tastes. Also some books such as they can enjoy to read. . . . They prefer the racy stories found in the 10 cent magazines but if several chapters of a good book are read to them, they will actually fight among themselves for the privilege of finishing it first. In this way, many of the girls, read good books here for the time. . . . I hope also to be able to offer the girls a cup of tea at any time when they come in. . . .

Above all else, I will urge every girl to agree to work, if I find her a place and that I am sure I can do. I am fairly well acquainted now in all the larger factories and in a few of them—though I tell them frankly about the girls—they are willing to give them a chance. At housework it is not so easy, for "madam" is generally most decided in her desire to secure a "respectable girl." Their chances are slim at housework though occasionally I find a woman willing to give a girl a chance to prove herself.

Aside from the material help, I will hope to direct them spiritually, as far as my ability permits me. . . .

If you, or any friends are interested in helping on the "mission" I have planned, Mr. Welsh, Mrs. Howe and I will be most grateful for even the smallest assistance. Yours sincerely

Please don't criticize this terrible handwriting. It was never meant to reach your eyes. I shudder at the thought of what Miss Huntington will find wrong with the grammar. I've no doubt, I've got moods, tenses, subjunctive verbs and plural adverbs all deliciously shaken into a froth. M.

October 6, 1915

∞ 115   I GOT MOVED ALL RIGHT AND EVERYTHING WENT FINE. . . . THE NEW
address is Ontario Street *West*, Apt 9. . . .

Ontario Street West, Montreal
October 16, 1915

∞ 115A   I AM WRITING JUST A FEW LINES TO LET YOU KNOW THAT MRS. YERKES
(who is here now) will be in Boston, Tuesday A.M. (traveling from
Montreal, Monday, all night) and hopes to see you.

Mrs. Yerkes is the head lady in the Door of Hope in Phila., and
came here on an errand for Mr. Welsh in regard to me and the
mission. She will, I think, tell you about it.

She is going to see you, I believe, as Mr. Welsh's friend; but I am
asking her to go as my friend—that is, see you for me. I am sending
with her a letter to you. I hope you will be in the city to see her.

She knows of you thru Mr. Welsh, but has heard of you thru me
(I believe) much more—at this time and on previous occasions
when we met in Phila.

October 19, 1915

∞ 117   I AM AGAIN ONLY WRITING A NOTE, FOR I AM SO ANXIOUS TO KNOW IF
you saw Mrs. Yerkes and got my note, and how you liked her. I
didn't relish (or fancy) the entire affair, but I suppose it could not
be helped.

Shall I write Miss Huntington all about it, or will you tell her
according to what you learned from Mrs. Yerkes? I don't mean that
I am ashamed to write her, but I am really weary of making
explanations. This past week has been so trying that I'd like to
emulate the wild ass of the desert and run off to shriek in the
solitary vastnesses of some far-off desert.

Don't think I am discouraged for *I'm not*, but I am a bit weary of
what I feel sure is the work of a hypocrite.

Some day I will write you who is at the back of all this. I know
positively; and it isn't anyone whom you'd suspect from the
conditions. But for the present, I'll tell you it is a woman (an old
lady), and one who cloaks herself with a deep religious mantle. . . .

Montreal, November 3, 1915

∞ 118B   BEFORE ANYTHING ELSE, I WANT TO SAY THAT UNLESS YOU HAVE ALREADY
subscribed for the magazines, I think it would be well not to,

because a friend of Mr. Welsh—Mrs. John Dewey—wrote that she would do so. I wrote her that I receive the *Atlantic* every month, *Scribners* occasionally, and the *Literary Digest* (from Miss H.) several times a month, and that any other magazine would be welcome, especially those with pictures.[40]

You will find enclosed a letter from Mr. Brown—the lawyer— and my answer to him, which I will ask you to mail. As you will see, I am taking it for granted that you will meet the $25.00 he asks for.

I hope he does not think it absolutely necessary that I come to Phila. to stay for any time; but if he does, I presume it can be managed. I talked it over with Mr. Benjamin, who thinks I should not let that condition stand in my way, even if the mission would close down for a month or so. He said he would see to it that the fare was forthcoming. . . .

I have a whole list of thanks to tender to you.

For the tea, which is all stacked up in my closet, in my room—for it is best to have things like that out of the way, so that the girls won't get careless, thinking we have lots of it. When I saw the ten pounds stacked up, I thought it looked like it would last thru several winters; yet in less than a month since we've started cooking, one pound is gone and inroads made into the second pound.

I will admit that I am one of the best customers the teapot has. When in doubt, I suggest a cup of tea, and somehow everyone is willing. When Mrs. Yerkes was here she expressed surprise at the fact that even the morning people stop at three for a cup of tea; and yet I think it's a pleasant habit, for it encourages congeniality.

The books were delivered and I thank you. The *White Company* I am reading—rather, just started—and find it very interesting.[41] Anything connected with the Catholic Church interests me, more now than ever, for this being such a strong Catholic city, one has an opportunity of learning the various phases of the religion. And while it is condemned wholesale, I am led to believe it has its very good points—as much as any religion has, if it is accepted as it is intended by those who teach it.

Did you ever read the life of St. Francis of Assisi? I have lately read much of him, and think Mr. Welsh is as near like him as it is possible for a person to be. . . .

[Mr. Welsh] writes he can see no reason why I shouldn't get the divorce; and as Mrs. Yerkes was so enthusiastic about Mr. Benjamin, he was happy that marriage with him seems possible. But he wants to see Mr. Benjamin to talk with him first.

I was made happy by this last condition. It makes me feel less like a stray cat. I was quite proud to show this letter to Ira; and he told me I looked quite cocky because Mr. Welsh has to be consulted. I think I have reason to be, because not one of my own family would turn a hair—Sam excluded—if I married a Chinaman!

Mr. Welsh sent me eighteen multigraphed copies of the letter, re the Mission. So far I have sent none out, other than to the four people whose names you gave me. This, because I want Mr. Welsh to write just to whom I should send one, for I want to be very sure that it reaches only understanding people. I shall write Miss Huntington, too, to ask if she would like me to send one to her friend in New Haven (I believe), whose name is Johnson, and perhaps to Miss Evans.[42]

I must tell you that when the copy as you revised it, went to Mr. Welsh, he wrote back saying I had left out what he thought were most salient points; i.e., the references to religious matters that were contained in my first letter. I thought he wouldn't notice it, but he did.

Often since the idea of the mission was born, I have written saying that I wish it were possible to keep the religious references out of the Mission, and if possible to call it—if it must have a name, though this, too, I advised against—"The Montreal Mission for Friendless Girls." The whole idea of the name is wrong. I will explain.

I thank God you are not friendless; but if you were—and were eighteen years old—you would no more admit it than any girl does. The kind of girl—the human jellyfish—that is willing to be classed as "friendless," I haven't much time for. Do you not agree with me that I should spend my time to help the kind of girl I can do most with? There are various kinds of "bad girls," and I couldn't possibly lend a helping hand to all. And as I can work best with the kind that I believe I was most like—as a young girl—is it not likely to do the "greater good" to devote my time to them? And I'd like to see the place I'd have walked into, when I was a young girl, that was known to be a haven for "friendless girls"!

Were I able to carry out my idea in this mission, there would be no name of any kind—in other words, the Mission would be sugar-coated and easier to swallow. And there would be no "Mrs. Jones" (which Mrs. Yerkes insisted upon); and it would be "Maimie," as always. And even though she insisted upon, and I agreed to it—there is no "dignified" eating alone, in state. We set the table as nicely as our housekeeping arrangements make it possible—clean cloths, serviettes, bread-and-butter plates, extra butter knives, individual salt and pepper shakers, serving spoons, etc.—but I eat with anyone who is here.

I don't intend to use the mission's name any more than I can help—and few, if any, of the girls will know the mission *has* a name, if I can help it. And certainly I won't use the name as Mr. Welsh calls it—"The *Christ* Mission for Friendless Girls." The moment the girls would know they were dealing with a church mission, it would call out hypocrisy instead of sincerity. For they would think I was more interested in giving them spiritual help, rather than material help—and the girls are always quite willing to oblige, even to the extent of telling a raft of lies!

Any "self-respecting" errant girl—if such a term is permissible—might be willing to admit that she is "friendless" (though they really don't think so, for they can and do reel off dozens of "friends' " names)—yet she wouldn't want any other girlfriend to know she was going to a mission for "friendless girls." Isn't that admitting defeat? For every man they know is a friend: and it is inborn in our sex to want to be thought of, as much admired and desired by the opposite sex. Therefore, if the "friendless girls" has to be used, the mission will defeat its own end.

I will cite an imaginary case to show you how that works out.

First, let me say that it is a known fact that errant girls generally travel in pairs. As a rule, a girl goes wrong alone, but soon she picks up with a girlfriend. And their men friends generally travel in pairs.

Suppose I were able to know Mary Jones. If Mary is a stupid girl who has been "bad," I am not particularly interested. She generally works out all right. By that, I mean she soon finds one has to be clever and up-and-doing to be successful even at living in sin—and she falls back on a job as the easiest thing she knows to do.

But if Mary Jones is a pert little miss, pretty, and clever in deceit, etc., and whether or not she is successful in her life in sin, I can reach her, given a fair chance. I find a way of appealing to each girl differently; but in the end, it is the same. For I appeal to their conceit. Being young and over-flattered, conceit is the biggest part of them.

Now, Mary is pretty cocksure of herself. Her attitude toward me at first is that I am pretty much of a fool. But soon the same girl will defend me, if anyone else says (as she herself thought) that "Maimie is a soft head."

Suppose, right off, Mary learns she is in a mission. Miss Mary is quite a different person right off. For mission purposes she has quite another story: Her parents were cruel; she has worked hard—and above all, she "adores" going to Sunday school!

When they met me—or, rather, sticking to Mary Jones—when she met me before the mission had a name, she was bent on showing me how she had had a good home; and what she likes best in the fellows; and all about the girls she "runs" with; and how "soft" she's had it, for she never worked, etc., etc. You see, I get at the root of the mischief—for Mary knows she has admitted all this. And I can suggest to her, since she is clever, that she use her cleverness to further her own interests. For they all admit there is no future in being "on the town."

First off, and without an invitation, Mary brings her friend in to see me. This second girl has been fed up, by Mary, about "Maimie." This, to show on what terms of familiarity she is with me:

"Maimie is a *raving* beauty who has lost her eye and has been a 'bad girl' and is now devoting herself to giving other girls a start" —So far, it isn't so bad. But some of them have it: Maimie writes books (and perhaps they will figure in them), and can speak eighteen or forty-eight languages, and you can always get a loan out of her, etc., etc.

This second girl generally comes in knowing more about me and my affairs than you do—really.

Then Mary marches right over to the phonograph, and without a by-your-leave, puts on her favorite record. It is generally "Who paid the rent for Mrs. Rip van Winkle when Rip van Winkle went away," or "Don't never trust no traveling man," sung by Irene Franklin. These records are the favorites. Then the friend is asked to listen to Maimie's favorite record, "The Herd Girl's Dream." And they invariably—Stella included—call it "The Hired Girl's Dream" (it is a perfectly beautiful thing played on the piano, violin, and harp), and wonder what the "words" are like.

Then—and this in my presence—Mary shows the girlfriend anything of interest.

"This is Maimie's niece, and she is 'Potsy,' and she can't remember the words of any tunes, so she sings 'Rummy Dummy Deedle'; and when Maimie wants to think of her she sings, 'Rummy Dummy Deedle' at her work."

"And this next one is the picture of two kiddies in Boston. And here's another picture of them taken when they were babies, almost." And then comes the story of Helen's red fox as told me by Miss Huntington. Then you are described as being just my size, and—"Maimie gets all her clothes."

Next is Mr. Welsh, and the description of him is generally sugared for my benefit, for I am sitting by and generally appealed to, to corroborate anything that seems a bit farfetched. Truly, their minds cannot grasp anything so absolutely pure as is Mr. Welsh; so I think they don't believe it all, or perhaps don't know how to believe it.

Then comes Mr. Benjamin's picture. . . . They never forget to say that he is a Jew and a relative of mine.

From then on, it is about the prints. The cats in a basket were painted from one real cat, whose photograph is below; but Maimie likes dogs better. Then comes all about Poke. And when little Alice Evans was telling of Poke once, she said "he" could talk—and I was brought out of the kitchen to prove it! How Poke came by her name; how I was not able to bring her here; etc., etc.

Then comes a little watercolor by Mr. Welsh; and again the criticism is sugared. "You can see—if you hold it off, and shut one eye—that it is meant to be houses." (Poor little watercolor! what a time I've had to make the "houses" really show. It looks most like a smear, and could readily pass for a futurist impression of anything.)

Finally, the books: "Really *Elsie Vernier*—if you skip the first part—is as good as a novel; and *Linda* is just grand—" Etc., etc.

And so it goes on. And the friend is anxious to join our little circle, so that when the telephone bell rings, she too can talk to the girl at the other end, and be one of us.

Naturally, if they both like to come, it is surer that I'll see them often, but if it is only one that likes to, the other one can draw her away.

But if the conditions as they now exist are known.

What girl is going to bring her friend to my place? Rather, I mean she couldn't drag her, unless it will be a cold day and they can get a cup of tea. And when they come: if, as Mrs. Yerkes suggested, all "personal" pictures were replaced with good prints of appropriate religious subjects—I can just see the deceitful little minxes pretending to be interested just long enough to grab the cup of tea, empty it and—"Have to be home."

What do you think? Am I not right in thinking it isn't fair to make a girl class herself as "friendless"? It is all right to use it between ourselves—i.e., when I write to Mr. Noakes or you or any friends the mission had made—but to use it with the girls strikes me as being illogical.

When—to come back to where I started from—Mr. Welsh criticised my leaving out the religious references in my letter, I wrote him that you had revised the letter to be sent out to your friends and had thought it better not to have the religious note sounded. You see, I blamed it all on you. Mr. Welsh promptly responded that he thinks you far more capable of knowing what is better than he does, and that in this matter *and in all matters*, I should follow any advice you'd be kind enough to give. Therefore I ask you what you think of making this mission a "different kind" in more ways than one—as, for instance, leaving it nameless?

Did I tell you about the lady who called to solicit funds for the Red Cross? I think I wrote it only to Mr. Welsh.

The collection day had been announced for some time, and I had 25 cents ready as my share. (I won't in any way help the war along, but I do think the Red Cross should be helped by everyone.) [As the Red Cross lady] was leaving, she said, "May I ask where is the mission that you conduct?" I said, "Of course. Right here."

"Right here! A mission here! I never saw a mission like this."

...Now—Since my Red Cross lady thinks this is a different mission than she ever saw, wouldn't it be as well as for us to drop the "Friendless" title? And be "different" in more ways than one?...

Change of subject. (You see, I am getting the trick of writing like one writes a treatise.)

You recall that I wrote you that I thought "one person" was responsible for the accusations about me and told them to Mr. Welsh....I hope this interests you, and I will tell you of it, even though in my own mind I scorn petty quarrels and bickerings; and once I've written it out to you, I shall promptly forget it and pity this person. My main object in explaining this to you is to square myself for hinting at dark doings on the part of a rival (doesn't this read like the doings of a movie heroine?) and not have you think I am one of those persons who go about harboring suspicious ideas that she has a rival or enemy. I warn you this will be a long story, for I've got a whole pack of clues, evidences, etc. to drag forth....

When, in 1910, Mr. Welsh had me come from Oklahoma...to go to the Orthopedic Hospital to be cured of the morphia habit, this person first appeared on the scene....She is a typical missionary. No matter where you'd see her, you wouldn't mistake her calling....She cannot look one right in the eyes, and quotes from the Bible at every second word. I did not fancy her when I first saw her, though I judged her harmless. Later, when I was ill in the Orthopedic Hospital and in none too pleasant a frame of mind, she came several times a week. She was a bore, but due to her years, white hair, and errand—for Mr. Welsh—I tolerated her....I have seen her but seldom since, avoiding such meetings as much as possible.

I have known—rather, guessed, for several years—that Mr. Welsh pays her a salary, which is all she has, as I understand it; and I think she thinks, now, that if "Maimie" were to be deposed, she would come in for a full-fledged mission, to run along her own lines.

Just imagine this: She is well past sixty, but never married, and I think she still has "hopes." She wears a wig (which scandal I learned from Stella and afterwards had corroborated by Mrs. Yerkes) and fusses up and dresses to kill. She never speaks above a whisper, and never speaks ten words without religious references. And this woman Mr. Welsh pays a salary, to go to the houses of prostitution (the fullblown ones), and she is to try to lead the girls right! She carries tracts and dispenses them freely. It is a sin and a shame to spend money on them, for they never are looked at except to ridicule.

Now I know for an absolute fact that few people from the

Tenderloin know her name, but every girl in the Tenderloin knows her by the name of "Creeping Jesus." I knew this five years ago; and when Stella came back, she asked me if I knew that the girls who were in the same ward she was in, for the same trouble, call her by the above name?

I've always known that she did absolutely no good, yet thought her harmless until. . . .I knew she had stirred up this scandal. . . .I do not intend to let her worry me further, but I did write Mrs. Yerkes and Mr. Welsh that while I am quite satisfied that no one meant to harm me, yet in order to be as fair to them as I'd want them to be to me, I must tell them what is on my mind; and for one thing, I think Mrs. Yerkes' being here three days before I knew it, and spying on me, was a "small" piece of business, and hardly what I should have expected from those who give their lives over to teaching others to play the game in the open. Further than that, I wrote (to Mrs. Yerkes) that I knew Mr. Welsh was not capable of suggesting such a method of procedure, so I must lay the blame on the "Rescue Band" at the Door of Hope. Also that I believe while the entire thing was born out of malice and uncharitable beginnings, it may do a lot of good for the mission, since a woman of Mrs. Yerkes' sort can vouch for what she saw.

Bless my soul, if—on top of all that—I don't get a note from her saying that she found all in the Rescue Band elated to hear about how I was doing—but one person (not naming the person), and that person, knowing Mrs. Yerkes loves me, wants more proof from a disinterested person, so Mrs. Yerkes suggests that I have Father Cotter (a Jesuit priest of big standing here, and who is always sending errant girls to me, to meet me) write a letter.

The letter was *writ* and dispatched; and it was a wonder. I don't know what my suspicious friend is going to do now, for Father Cotter praised me and my work to the skies—far more than I ever dreamed he would—and said things about me, which, if they are true, makes me a very superior person! He sent the letter here unsealed, and I sent it to the Door of Hope.

But with it, I landed on the whole outfit with both feet.

I wrote that I did not ever again propose to go thru such an experience.

That I questioned the authority of the Rescue Band to want proof of my sincerity, fitness, etc., and that I wouldn't be party to such a petty lot of bickerings, etc. That while I felt Mr. Welsh and those who lend support to any work I do have that right—I have their word for it that they wouldn't exercise that right, feeling sure I need no surveillance. And that I now give them (the Band) notice to withdraw their interest in my affairs, for I will not countenance it. (Doesn't that sound cocky?)

I went further to say that I had always heard or read that in various undertakings where women predominate, they spend so much time quarreling among themselves that they lose sight of the work they started to do when they started their combination.

Just so in this case. If I must spend hours and hours writing and talking, first to satisfy this one, and then that one, nothing would get done; and frankly I don't see how the Rescue Band can do much, for they are always having trouble in their own midst.

Just think! Mrs. Yerkes' visit to learn of my treachery, Mr. Welsh paid out of his private purse for. Judging the cost, without extravagance, it was nearly $50.00—and since it was for the cause, wouldn't that $50.00 spent on an icebox, bed, couch, hall carpet, etc., have done more good?

In closing I told Mrs. Yerkes that while she, as a private person and a friend, was welcome, and is welcome, to write me asking any question, bidding me to do anything, I refuse further to deal with her as a unit in the Rescue Band—and if Mr. Welsh becomes submerged by that Band, I shall cease to do his bidding. For, I said, I need encouragement and sympathy, not discouragement and suspicion; and from what I can judge, I can expect the latter only from the Band. . . .

It would take a man like Dickens to aptly describe this Band and its doings. Aside from Mrs. Yerkes and Mr. Welsh and a Mr. Watters, the members are the funniest lot; and I attended several of their meetings lately [in Philadelphia], and really stared in astonishment at some of it.

The Door of Hope has some very good features—though its name is its best one, I think. They can house eight girls—having eight beds. But if one extra girl is brought in, as I brought in Stella—my, what a rumpus! This committee has to be consulted, that committee must be notified; and believe me, it shows the scope of their minds. Were it my mission, I'd make a pallet under the sink and stick the girl on that, before I'd do all that fussing.

In Stella's presence, my friend (?) called up Mrs. Yerkes (the nominal, but not resident head of the Door of Hope) and told her all about our coming and said—in Stella's presence—"She has disorders of a very bad sort, so I can't put her with another girl, and it won't do to put her on the couch here...and really I think Maimie had better try to keep her somewhere until we can meet to decide what to do"!

Of the eight girls, four have been there nearly four years! When, in a conversation with Miss—, I said I thought one of them, particularly—Nettie—was a most respectable, quiet and apparently efficient girl (for she does all the cooking), and wondered why she wasn't put out to take her place in the world and allow some other girl to come in, I was told in a whisper, "Oh! you don't know. It is true Nettie looks capable, but she isn't mentally 100 per cent, and the moment she was sent out into the world, she'd go right into evil life."

Did you ever hear such a thing? If she is mentally unbalanced, she should be sent where such people are kept, and perhaps treated—for she surely gets no treatment in the Door of Hope. And then, are they going to keep her there for life because she might go with a man? I never heard anything so ridiculous. But Stella threw some light on the affair. Nettie is kept because she cooks well. Another one who has been there as long, or longer, sews well. And so on. So, you see, they are, in a word, the active workers, and the "ladies" stand around and spout from the Bible.

May they rest in peace for after this, I shall never disturb them nor will I let them disturb me.

I must say right here that I thank you from the bottom of my heart for saying that you believe in me. I know you do, and it is extremely gratifying. Miss Huntington expressed the same sentiments. Do you wonder I rebel against such friends (?) as they are at the Door of Hope, when I have such friends as you and Miss Payson and Miss Huntington?

Did you know that Miss Evans—she who has the school in Boston and is a friend of Miss Huntington—sent me a big box of apparel? Such a time as we had!....When the box came, I sorted out so that each girl got what she needed most...I didn't give them away indiscriminately, as I explained to Miss Evans when I wrote her in thanks. I only gave to those girls who were trying to stay decent and need the help the clothing means. For with small wages as are paid now, a girl can't possibly buy clothing—and that's where the trouble is. She soon gets them by foul means since she can't get them by fair means. . . .

I wondered if you ever read *The Paths of Judgment* by Anne Douglas Sedgwick? Isn't it funny, though I've read the book and made mental note of it, I am not sure I remember correctly either name or author? It is by the same lady who wrote the story in the *Atlantic* that I liked so well—about the mother of the young soldier, who took in the little actress that he married because of her condition. The book was in the janitor's rooms, and he said it wasn't much good because "the people threw it in the garbage who owned it". . . .I borrowed it and it was a fine story. It reminds me somewhat of *The Opal,* except the weakest character is a man.

The enclosed clipping you may not have seen; and as I know you are interested in this work of Mr. Osborne's, I send it. I saw somewhere that Mr. Osborne has a married sister living near Boston, so I wonder if you know her and, perchance, her brother, Mr. Osborne. I think he is wonderful, and I'd hate it dreadfully if he wasn't allowed to go on with his [prison reform] work. . . .

Will you mind sending this letter on to Miss Huntington? Several matters touched on in this letter I'd like her to know, and it would save me writing it again.

Nellie. . .is the girl who has helped set up the mission. . .I believe she likes you best of all those she hears me speak about. You see, Miss Huntington forfeited Nellie's admiration because in a recent letter, she wrote she was doing her own housework and, of course, is no "lady" now—for you know the English do love to bow down to someone. You have all her admiration because I told her you wear a black trailing gown and earrings—and don't, for goodness sake, ever let Nellie know you go into the kitchen!

November 17, 1915

I MUST TELL YOU THAT I THINK IT SO STRANGE, THAT WHEN HELEN WAS   120 &
fixing up a gift to send me, I must have—about the same time— been fixing up my gift for her, and our letters crossed! I have not received the package yet but will write her, as she asks me to, when I do.

349

I can't express to you my pleasure on receiving Helen's little letter. I have already read it to three girls who know of her, and they all seem impressed with the fact that she *lined* her paper. You can't know how we love Helen. She and Potsy are the pets here, but since I never hear a word of or from Potsy—don't know even if she lives—Helen is the favorite topic of conversation. For, like me, all the girls I know like to love something that is little and cunning, and Helen is so sweet in all her pictures. Her hair, and the expression in the eyes, are most remarkable. As I told you, when Helen is spoken of by my girl friends, one would think they knew her since she was an infant. You see, the thought comes from my collection of pictures of her at various stages in her brief life. . . .

I am enclosing some snapshots I thought you might be interested in. Mr. Benjamin and me, you will of course recognize—and my dress, also, which is the blue serge one you sent a long while ago. These pictures were taken in the summer, before Stella and I went to the States for treatment for her. She is, of course, very much stouter now, and truly the most beautiful thing you ever saw. . . . Lately she has shown a most selfish disposition, but don't hold this against her. It has been my fault, I petted her too much. But she was so sick, I couldn't help it; and now Mr. Benjamin claims she is selfish and unappreciative. But that's not important—she's not that way with others, and I brought it on myself. Do you know, I enjoy seeing her take advantage of me? Don't mention this when you answer, for sometimes I read your letters to Bennie and to Stella and others—and they'd all pounce down on me for saying I like to see Stella selfish. There's something peculiar in it, though. I feel a warm sense of gratification when Stella acts that way with me, and resent it, if she does it to others. For instance, if we have some "goodies" and I lay mine aside for later consumption, Stella roots around and eats it but never does that with other people's things. . . .

The old gentleman in the picture is Mr. Girouard, a French Indian whose summer place we visited. He was a customer of mine when I conducted the B.A.B., and has been friendly ever since. I like him, but lately have discouraged his attentions when I learned he means them to be taken like sweethearts. It is the French in him. He makes love to everything, I think, that is feminine. But he is a fine man, at that. The other lad in the picture is Bob Faubourg, also a Frenchman (Canadian), and he is Stella's "Cavalier." He's as big as a minute—about five feet tall—and Stella is five feet six inches, and yet she thinks him fine. No accounting for tastes!

The report enclosed, you will understand, is Mrs. Yerkes'.

I received an acknowledgment from Mr. Brown for the $25.00 you sent. He mentions again the necessity for my being in Phila. for a while in the spring. I hate dreadfully that I'll have to, but it seems unavoidable, and the part I dislike most is telling Mr. Welsh that I'll have to come there.

I hope he will see the reasonableness of it. Of course, I will be glad of the divorce so I can marry again. Yet even were there no Mr. Benjamin, I should like to drop this Mrs. Jones business, which requires so much explaining. And you don't know girls as I do. They figure the Jones part out with varying degrees of scandal. I have heard of at least fifty versions of it. No two are alike, and in all of them Mr. Jones figures as the man who put my eye out. Aside from the girls there is so much explaining to do that I'd welcome dropping the Jones in my name as being one thing less to "explain"; and if it does interfere with my plans for a month or more, just think of the good that will come of it for the rest of my years.

Anent the name of the mission. I have decided, for the present, to say nothing about it to Mr. Welsh, but not use it at all with the girls—for of course he never said I should. The place is taken in my name; and when I ask a girl to come to see me, I'll say, "Come to my rooms," as I did formerly. Perhaps, later, when there is less "explaining" to do, I'll bring up this issue and say that you agree with me that "friendless" is a stigma that any girl would balk at. . . . I hope your cold is better—and poor Helen! I hope the beads get there so she can play with them while her cold makes her stay indoors.

Isn't it fine that you have the French girl? *Je suis bien aise. Je vous souhaite une bonne nuit. Votre amie,* Maimie

The Montreal Christ's Mission for Friendless Girls
[*November or December, 1915*]

DURING THE EARLY PART OF OCTOBER OF THIS PRESENT YEAR (1915) IT WAS 121 ✣ my privilege to visit Montreal and at the request of Mr. Herbert Welsh I visited and spent a large part of my time with Mrs. M. Jones of The Montreal Christ's Mission for Friendless Girls. Mrs.

Jones rejoices in the fact that through Mr. Welsh she herself has come into a purer life with a larger vision of her responsibility toward the rest of the world; and wants all the world to know that if in her life she achieves anything it is only because Mr. Welsh has made it possible.

When I called at Ontario St., West, a large apartment house, I asked direction from a small boy in the courtyard, and almost while I waited for his answer a voice came from a window on the second floor, "Mrs. Yerkes, Mrs. Yerkes!" I at once found my way to Mrs. Jones's door. I found Mrs. Jones and "Nellie" waiting at the door and from both received a most cordial welcome. Nellie is an English girl who has recently come under Mrs. Jones's influence, and been persuaded to give up a sinful life. They were both busy putting the new apartment, which is to be used as the mission, to rights, and showed me their work with much pleasure.

The apartment has five rooms which the two had cleaned; they had repainted all the woodwork and repapered some of the rooms and were justly proud of their work.

The living-room, cheerful and cozy is to be used by the girls whom Mrs. Jones hopes to have visit her. The pictures on the wall are to be a help as they will suggest topics of conversation; the Victrola will offer entertainment and through the kindness of Mrs. Howe it will be possible to serve a cup of tea to all callers. A Bible on the centre table will be used as occasion offers to warn the girls of danger and point to a way of escape. The few days I spent with Mrs. Jones convinced me that she was deeply in earnest in her desire to reach the girls who so sadly need such help, convinced me also that she understood the girls very fully and knew how to approach them. While with her she arranged for a meeting with Stella Phillips and her friend Bob Faubourg. I found Stella looking much stronger and better than when I had seen her in Philadelphia, and from all the evidence I was able to gather, she is continuing to do well. Bob was in appearance a manly young fellow who assured me that as soon as he obtained employment he wanted to marry Stella. We spent several hours together and I was much pleased with them both . . . .

Upon my last afternoon in Montreal, which I spent with Mrs. Jones and "Nellie" we held just before I left a little dedication service. I read the beautiful Fifth Chapter of St. John with its story of the healing power of the Lord Jesus, and then kneeling together we gave the little apartment over to Him to be used as He would in the healing of the sin sick souls of the girls who may be reached by Mrs. Jones.

It was good to visit the Montreal Mission for Friendless Girls, and it will always have a warm place in the hearts of those who are especially interested in work for girls.—*Christine G. Yerkes*

December 11, 1915

I'VE BEEN BUSIER THAN USUAL WITH THE WORK FOR THE GIRLS.... FIND- **122** ✂ ing that the stores were putting on extra help for Christmas, I lost no time corralling my girls—who have always asserted that they would work could they find it—and I've got five on the job. These are not my regular crowd, but some girls I know well, who try to "kid" me. And I called their bluff.

It isn't enough to get them the jobs, the trick is to make them keep them. And strangely, these girls are keen about saleslady jobs, and will do anything to keep the job (they like the excitement and crowds)—except rise early in the morning. So I've appointed myself the Rising Bell for those who have the most difficulty in getting up. Those girls are all "roomers," and live in the same neighborhood—close to here, for the girls who "room" won't go very far from the city proper. So I get up at 5:30 these mornings—and believe me, it's no picnic—and I go the rounds, getting the girls up. It's not the easiest thing I do, because here, too, the heat is not turned on until 7:30; and it takes quite a little coaxing on the part of my alarm for me to put my feet out on the icy boards. But once I'm up and bathed, I feel like a two-year-old, and I am glad that I have to get up.

When I get on the street, it's as dark as night and cold as Iceland. But as I hurry along, I pass the scrubwomen who have been up and at it for hours, and I feel ashamed of my laziness! The first morning, as I passed, I called, *"Bonjour!"* And for a moment, they look to see if it's a friend. And then they recognize that I'm just trying to be friendly, and they smile, and some of them call back it's *tres froid*. And I feel as though I really did some good to make their worn faces break into smiles. The scrubwomen are the old French-women—and smiling isn't an accomplishment of theirs.

One old woman—seventy-two, she told me—who goes my way, cleans in the post office. And she's had this "government job" (so she called it) since 1883—thirty-two years! She said: You are *La belle Americaine*; and when I asked how she knew, she said because *les Anglaise* do not speak to old people without formal introductions. This old woman was born in Malone, New York State, and can't speak a word of English!

Besides this getting-out-early job that keeps me busy, I drop in on the girls regularly—they are mostly in Almy's, the cheap store—and see that they haven't forgotten to return from lunch. This takes up considerable time.

Then I've had one hard case, which I was called on to take care of by the local Charity Organization. The girl—Lillian Terrebonne —is the most abandoned creature you can imagine, and it's an awful tax on my love to include her. The Organization, I am sorry to say, isn't all it's cracked up to be; for, as someone said recently, "They do not relieve those in need, but make those who apply for help confess that they have no right to demand help." And where they can, they shift the responsibility. Of course, I receive no help from the city, and they do. But I feel that I must consider the girl and not the conditions under which she came to my notice.

When Lillian came under their notice, they telephoned me, saying she is a "bad girl," and knowing of my work for them— would I be interested in seeing what could be done toward reclaiming her from the evil life? They told me their district visitor had called on her that day and found her sick in bed, without friends or food. They said, "Tomorrow we will send her a day's rations." I asked what she was doing for *today*; and I was told that the district visitor said she saw some bread and milk there, so she "supposed" she was all right overnight. They suggested my going the next day, but I went at once. It was about 5:30. I took some soup in a tin, and some other things, and was off.

It was in the worst section of the city, and in a lodginghouse where everything goes. There was no bell, so I walked in and sought room 9. There was no light; and in the pitch dark, I crawled to the top floor . . . and seeing a light under the door, I knocked and asked, "Is this Miss Terrebonne's room?" A voice said "Yes, come in." And in I went, but I couldn't see what I went into. The room—an attic one, with slanting ceiling—was that dimly lighted that I could barely distinguish the bed. (This is a familiar arrangement in rooming houses of puttying the gap in the gas jet, allowing only a small aperture for gas to escape and thus saving gas. In my rooming house days, being an omnivorous reader, I always purchased an extra tip and replaced it to read by, carefully changing it in the morning before I went out.) And the air in that room! It was so thick, it could be cut with a knife. Of course, the window has not been opened since cold weather came—for though we may preach about fresh air, fresh air is cold air and stale air is warm; and warmth is the thing most desired by the Canadian populace. I could distinguish cigarette smoke, the odor of escaping gas, and something else that puzzled me, besides stale air. Of course, I just couldn't stay in that room, so almost the first words I said were "Lillian have you enough covers, for I want to open up this window to change the air. For you can't get well unless I do." She answered thru the haze that it was all right, and I opened the windows—with some effort, for they'd been closed since September.

I took off my things, cleared a chair, and came with it to Lillian's side. She is fair, small-featured; hair cut short like mine; and very sick and feeble looking. She was regarding me very intently, and as I had said that Mrs. St. John had sent me, she knew I was a "social worker."

"Come now, Lillian, tell me what are you thinking? Well you needn't tell me. I know. You are thinking that I am going to pull a long face and ask a million questions—and then read you a tract and preach a little, leave my card and tell you that I'll come again tomorrow. But you're all wrong. I'm going to do nothing of the sort. In the first place I am Maimie Jones. I don't own a card. I'm not connected with the Charity Organization. I don't pull long faces and I hate tracts and lectures myself, though goodness knows I've had enough of them. Besides, I laugh at everything and chatter everyone to death. I don't ask questions, either, because I know more than you do why you are sick, alone, etc., because I've been all that myself."

Then Lillian laughed, and we were both at ease. Pretty soon I told her about myself—as I tell all the girls—and it wasn't unusual, then, for her to tell me. (Don't think we sat there freezing all this time, for I had closed the window.)

She has no parents, and no kin on this side. She is twenty years old, though she looks younger—her fair short hair makes her look youthful. She is from Wales; one-and-a-half years in Canada, and a "bad girl" only three months.

When she arrived she went to work in a cigarette factory and roomed in a respectable family. The husband—a Frenchman—

seduced her. After that she took service in a place in Verdun, and her employer was a woman who was herself employed during the day. In her absence, Lillian was frequently "bad" with the various men who delivered supplies, thus augmenting a meagre salary.

After a year of this, her employer removed to the States and Lillian, not finding a place that suited her, answered an ad for stage work and was taken on at the Maple Leaf—a horrible dive. She admitted she could neither sing or dance; and when I asked why they took her for the work, she answered because they thought she'd look well in tights. At the Maple Leaf she worked for four weeks, receiving no pay. When she remonstrated with the employer, he said she should do as the others do, make "dates" from the front—and he told her he had women offering him pay to allow them to work on his stage so they could get the men for "dates."

Lillian was soon at this, and she explained to me that she was never "very bad." She was never like some of the other girls who worked there and who have twenty-five to thirty men in a day: she never had more than ten! (Of course, you appreciate that Lillian is not the sort of girl I work with. For I work better with my own kind, and truly I never knew a girl like her. But still, she is a human, isn't she?)

I fixed her some supper; and to show you what the Charity Organization does for the desititute, the "milk" Mrs. St. John saw was acreoline and water, and the "bread"—or what appeared to be bread—was the end of a corset box protruding from a cupboard. I went out and bought a gas jet and a newspaper, and fixed her light so she could read, and I left her for the night.

I wrote out a report to the Charity Organization, and the next day bundled Lillian up and took her to the General Hospital, where they infomed me she has gonorrhea (they called it "acute gon"), and that she had been there before, and they had prescribed certain dressings. And the odor in her room that had puzzled me was some "paper and hair and orange peel that I had burned tc kill that smell of the medicine they gave [me], so that everyone wouldn't know at once what was the matter." . . .

The next thing was to get her cured. She is in an awful condition, broken out entirely, the disease having made such headway. The hospital point-blank refused to take her in. She requires two or three months of treatment, and they couldn't begin to take in all such cases that come to them. The House of Good Shepherd refused her because of the disease. The Charity Organization said they have no place to suggest for her except that she be arrested and sent to prison for six months.

Poor wretch, I just couldn't stand for that, since her only sin had been one I have committed, and I shouldn't like being driven off to jail. True she isn't clean and nice, nor of the sort I was, but that isn't her fault. God didn't give her the same amount of brains He gave me; and surely she is a human being, and originally from far better people than I originated from.

The Charity Organization washed their hands of her. Said if I was going to be sentimental about such things, they'd leave it to me.

I should have brought her right here to stop, but Mr. Benjamin —to whom I told of the case—got on his "high horse" and said, if I did, he would wire you and Mr. Welsh and ask that someone with more sense than I have be sent here to take over the rooms. And I believe I'd have let him do it, only I was afraid Mr. Welsh would send Miss Christopher—and as long as I have a breath left, she won't get my pretty place away from me. So there I was and there I am.

I took Lillian back to that frightful room. And I provide her with thirty cents a day, besides have her here for dinner at night; and so she will have to stay until over Sunday, when I shall get busy again. Last week was a holy one for the Catholics and I couldn't do much toward finding a haven for her.

Now do you see why I bundled Stella off to the U.S., where such things seem as nothing?

Don't worry. I won't attempt this with Lillian, but I will move all Montreal's Heaven and Earth to get Lillian into some place where she can be sure of a shelter for several months.

I want to thank you for the books and Helen for *Pollyanna* and the little towel.

I don't think Helen realized how good a book *Pollyanna* is to send to us but if you read it, you will understand. It is so easy to understand, and *Pollyanna* isn't such a goody-goody to be tiresome. And as for her game! Everyone we know is playing it, Nellie being the teacher. I have read it aloud, several chapters at a time after luncheon; then I read it the same way to another set of girls in the afternoons. And Nellie read it alone, and now she reads it—especially the part that tells how to play the "glad" game—to every new visitor.

I am sure we never received a book at once entertaining, and so full of things we can practice to make our lives happier. As for being "glad," well, we have many reasons without much trouble in finding them—not the least of which is that Helen sent *Pollyanna* and not another book less likable.[43]

The little towel hangs in the bathroom, and everyone knows its business is to be looked at and not used.

The other books— I have read the Barrie book and the book by Mr. Howe, so far. The latter I find much pleasure in, especially because I am learning something worth knowing. I knew a little about each author, but I could not have said whether they were Americans or not. It is so interesting, too. It is like taking medicine without knowing it. Mr. Benjamin has read it too, and he thinks perhaps Mr. Howe could tell him the names of other books written of authors—American or otherwise—that he could read and understand so readily. I suppose people who are educated, even, are hazy about things in the lines of authors, and it is fine to know. And I think Mr. Howe's book makes one feel that an author is a human like oneself; and when I shall read anything now by Poe or Irving, I can understand better their viewpoints....[44] I thank you for the magazines. The theatre magazine made a great hit here, naturally, but I like the *Scribners* and *Atlantic* better. But of course I am a "highbrow," or so Rae Rabinowitz used to call me. Did you notice in the *Metropolitan* the article about Osborne, and the Sing Sing man's work?...[45] I am mailing a box today, with a gift for you, Helen, and Mark (Mr. Howe and Quincy will have to wait until next year, for by then I will have something perhaps appropriate for men!) The lace for Helen's undergarment was started by me and made by every girl—a little at a time—who could be trusted to keep the work clean.

There is another gift coming to you that I think you will like. It is a photograph of me. They are to be ready December 21st. Not snapshots, but sure-enough posed photographs. Mr. Benjamin is paying for them—$8.00 for a dozen—and I am to give them to my friends, reserving one for him and one for his mother. The photograph decided upon makes me look a very serious person, and I seem to have lost that "something" that made the nurse in the Phila. Hospital say to Stella, that I look like "a woman with a past." I look very mild and might be taken for a school teacher! But you shall see for yourself.

I must tell you that Miss Wald sent me a signed—or autographed (isn't that the word?)—copy of her book, *The House on Henry Street*. I believe I am getting to be a snob, for I feel great pride at having books signed by their authors, and pretty soon will scorn any other kind.

I am sorry to say that Mrs. Dewey—Mr. Welsh's friend who offered the magazines—has not written again or been heard from since last September. And yet, I don't think you should send for magazines until we see what the New Year may bring, for she or someone else . . . might send a year's subscription.

Do you think *Vanity Fair* has anything in it that could injure our "delicate" minds?[46] I got four old copies last summer and the girls go wild over them. I failed to see anything in them that is harmful. In fact, I saw much that is beautiful; and even an occasional nude figure doesn't strike me as being suggestive. And the girls—they go thru *Vanity Fair* dozens of times, and my four old copies are in tatters. The styles or modes get much attention; and I wonder what you think of this magazine, as covering the many things the girls like to look at? Of course, they never read them, they only love the pictures. (Mrs. Yerkes, when she was here, said she never looked into a copy, but the name was enough!) I see it advertised at $1.00 for six months, and if you don't see any objection to it, I'd like it.

I wonder if you've heard that we are to have a Christmas tree supplied by Miss Evans? This is the first Chrismas tree I've had in my life, and I'm as elated as though I were five years old! All the girls are excited about it, and I am hoping to make a pleasant day of it. Mr. Benjamin offers to pay for the "goodies" for the day as my Christmas present, instead of a little puppy originally agreed upon—and now I am torn between a desire to make our little crowd happy for one day, or to make myself happy for many days. I did want that puppy, though, and lately it has become an obsession, to have a little puppy who will be lots of fun for all of us.

Isn't it strange that all girls love puppies—I mean, the girls I know? And yet it would be nice to have a spread to go with the tree. I am not deciding quickly; and I told Mr. B. I'd say for sure by Saturday, so he can get what I want.

Since writing the foregoing, several days have elapsed. I have still got Lillian Terrebonne on my hands. No one wants to take her in and I am at my wits end what to do with her. Oh! if this were only the United States! Lillian is Protestant, so the Catholics say, what will you of them; and the Protestants say, all institutions for girls of Lillian's sort are kept up by the city, and *they* should take her in— and all city institutions are Catholic; and we are right back again to where we started. And in the meantime, I have Lillian hanging on my neck. The girls who know of her are all up in the air because I have her here—but that gives me a pain in the ear, for they might all have been in Lillian's condition if they were left on the road they were headed for when I met them. And Lillian has some rights. She is a human being.

It's a fine business when right here in my own home (for it is my own home) I can't do as I please. Last night I came in at 5:30 with Lillian; and Nellie, Berthe and Gladys Carter, were all stewing because Lillian was to stop here several nights. So I had to take her out again—for I didn't want her to hear the rumpus—and I put her back in that vile room. I know your heart would ache if you saw how she follows me about, relying on me to do the square thing—and everybody, Mr. B. included, wants me to have her "sent up" for six months. I just can't do it, and so near Christmas. I can't help but cry, I feel so bad that no one feels as I do. I know Miss Huntington will. And I hope you won't say she ought to go to the Fullum St. jail. Lovingly yours, Maimie

Will you let Miss Huntington read about Lillian Terrebonne, please?

Report of
The Montreal Mission for Friendless Girls
January 1, 1916

CB 124   TWENTY-THREE YOUNG GIRLS HAVE VISITED THE ROOMS SINCE I MADE MY last report.

Ordinarily there are not so many, in fact six or seven girls visit regularly. As I reported last month I am not having the girls come in as promiscuously as formerly. This being only my second month of actual work, I feel sure, as the months go by, the number of girls who are sincere in their desire to do better will increase.

Due to the kindness of friends in Boston and Philadelphia I was able to extend Christmas cheer to the girls who are regular visitors and to some others who are still following a life of sin.

It was my original intention to make Christmas only for those whom I knew to be sincerely interested in the efforts being made for them, but later when unexpected Christmas money was sent, I thought the donors would be glad to know that I included some of those who are not yet ready to give up the sinful life, but whom I consider "hopeful." Most of the girls of the latter class "room" (meaning they rent their sleeping place only, and have nothing in common with those under whose roof they are), and Christmas means a season of lonesomeness and remorse. "Home" and its ties are dearer on that day. Therefore, for that one day, Christmas, I asked no questions, making each girl happy by including her in the festivities.

Several days before Christmas I distributed about fifty cards, in French and English, on which I had written the following:

One side	Other side
For Christmas and Sunday	Please Come
Day and Evening	A Christmas Tree
Maimie D. Jones	Refreshments
Ontario St. West	Companionship
(near cor. of Blenry)	Welcome
Brindeau Apts. No. 9	and
City	Love
(over)	are what you will find here.
	(over)

Unfortunately on Christmas Day the weather proved to be most inclement, but Sunday made up for it by being fine, and during the two days that I held "open house" twenty-three girls called.

Nellie C.	Augustine G. and
Berthe C.	1 yr. old baby
Virgin C. (Berthe's sister)	Stella C.

Lillian T.	Esther B. and 2 children
Gabrielle S.	Marie R.
and son	Corona D.
Annie S.	Bernadette D.
Alice E.	Marie Jeanne D.
Stella P.	(three sisters)
Edith S.	Evangeline B.
Mary B. (Edith's sister)	Lilly W.
Margaret McD.	Dora M.

I am not giving the last names of the girls as several of them disliked my having done so in a recent letter to a Boston friend, and as I wish to treat all alike I will not write any of them.

Of the twenty-three who were here, eleven sat at table to a regular Christmas feast, though as the girls came in they were given food, substantial and light.

There was a large Christmas tree at the door of the living room. It was attractively decorated with bright sparkling ornaments and tinsel, while suspended from its lowest branches and on its base were gifts for each girl and candies boxed. The room was almost entirely covered with green and "Christmasy" things.

Two gentlemen (one a friend of Mr. Herbert Welsh's), who called Christmas Day, expressed much pleasure and surprise at finding the place so pretty.

As there was a constant coming and going there was no regular order of entertainment, and the girls spent much of the time commenting on each other's gifts, examining and exchanging theirs for others that for the moment pleased their fancy better. We played the phonograph, sang and danced, and I read aloud some letters that were sent by some young girls who attend a school in Boston to some of the girls here. These letters were very popular and I was asked to read them for each girl as she came in.

Later, when the crowd thinned out and order reigned, I asked if the girls would like to join me in the Lord's Prayer, and while on our bended knees I asked our Heavenly Father to bless us all and to speak to the hearts of these girls (as He has spoken to mine), to make them want to love and serve Him.

As to the regular affairs here: Due to the taking on of extra help for the holidays, I was able to put five girls in positions in the department stores, and in each case the girl had never worked before.

During the past month the Charity Organization of this city telephoned to tell me of a girl who had come under their notice and whose case, in their opinion, might be better understood by me. This girl, Lillian Terrebonne, I found in a most pitiful condition, physically and every other way. I have befriended her and seen her regularly. She is from Wales and though apparently from respectable people, has fallen lower in the evil life than most of us can imagine. Lillian does not respond as readily to my friendly advances as do most of the girls, but I hope to reach her heart and understanding eventually by prayer and constant care.

Another girl was called to my attention by the Social Service Department of the General Hospital, Lilly Weiner, a Roumanian Jewess, blonde and slight, and just recovering from an attack of the disease from which many of the girls are affected. The disease is located in Lilly's eye, and in consequence for the present she must not attempt work. While Lilly was in the hospital Mrs. Fowles (who is in charge of the S.S. Dept.), in talking with her, thought she could be helped and called my attention to her. Lilly cannot read nor write; in fact, she doesn't even recognize numerals for what they are, but can speak four languages indifferently, Roumanian (similar to Italian), Yiddish, English and French. Unlike most Jewish girls who are in the evil life, Lilly is a meek, unassuming girl, lacking ambition and without trickery and cupidity. One can scarcely credit that she has been living the life she confesses to have lived since coming to this country. She is so backward about taking advantage of kindnesses offered her that I am constantly obliged to go after her and haven't made much material headway. She goes daily to the hospital for treatment and I hope, when she is well, to place her at work where she can live the tranquil life she seems best fitted for.

In cases such as the two just mentioned, I experience much difficulty, because the girls generally that come here have not fallen so low as have these girls, and they refuse to mix with them; therefore, it is painfully embarrassing to my girl friends to meet them here. They don't want to anger me, yet they draw back from mingling with them. As I explained recently, there is as much class distinction among "fallen girls" as among any other set of people, and to force them to mingle gains nothing for either side.

Of the other girls, the regular visitors:

Nellie C. still goes to the dentist regularly and does largely the housework of the rooms. She will go out to domestic service very soon, as the dental work is about completed. She has not once broken faith with me in any respect, and this is an unusual record.

Berthe C. still continues in the home of the druggist who gave her work after I took her off the streets. She is anxious to take up stenography (in French, of course) and I hope to be able to teach her later.

Augustine G. and her baby (Hubert Sidney) are doing fine. She was "laid off" Christmas Eve, but the manager of the store assured me he was satisfied with her work and would take her back as soon as trade picked up again, which will be January 15th. After an absence of a year and a half, Augustine will go for a visit to her home in St. Ceasare. I have hopes that there will be a reconciliation and she and her baby boy be taken into her mother's home and love. I constantly pray for this and I ask our friends to pray also that this may come about.

Stella P. is still working. She continues in the best of health; she has grown stout and is beautiful. She seems to have lost all desire for evil associations. She is always with Bob Faubourg in her leisure hours, and they will be married, but not before the war is over. This, because Bob cannot secure wages enough to keep a wife at present, and too, may go to the "front." She was here Christmas Day and was made very happy by the cards and remembrances from friends made through me, especially the several she met while in Philadelphia last summer.

Gabrielle S. and son remain at the aunt's house, and are very comfortable. Gabrielle is becoming restless and recently confessed a desire to meet men, but we hope to overcome this by prayer.

Annie S. is working steadily. Just now is the "season" for the "tailoring" which she can do. She contemplates marriage with a steady young man who is saving his earnings for this purpose.

Gladys M. is not working but has returned to her mother's home. I consider this a partial victory, that at least she has given up her "room" and lives under her mother's roof and returns there each night.

Alice E. is working in the glassworks. Her mother is kinder to her than before, and Alice comes here instead of to the dance halls that she frequented formerly.

Stella C., who is of a fine family and who have large means, has returned to her home in Quebec. This I feel sure was the result of my earnest prayers and those of my friends. She decided to return on the spur of the moment and though she did not promise to remain, she did give me her word that if she returned to the city she would let me know where she is.

Margaret McD. has a position that is the envy of all the girls, for it falls right in line with their craving for adventure. When I took her to the store that promised to find an opening for her, the manager was baffled for a moment as to what use they could make of her. Margaret stutters, so of course could not be a "saleslady"; she is "left-handed" and clumsy with it, so would not do for a "wrapper"; she has had no schooling, so could not be used in the auditing department. Finally an opening was found. Margaret was detailed to stand around and watch the Christmas shoppers to see that they did not pilfer. In other words, Margaret is an embryo detective, and the girls feel she has captured the prize situation. This post has had an astonishing effect on Margaret's sense of right and wrong. Heretofore she trod, roughshod, over every law or rule, but now upholds the dignity of the law with her last breath, and is never so happy as when moralizing about what is right and vice-versa.

Esther B. is still serving in the *salle à manger*, in the French section. The pay is poor, the work hard, and Esther is discontented. As she has been at home in her mother's house with her two boys (of different fathers, and to neither of whom Esther was married) for more than six weeks, I am sure she will remain, when I find her a place where the pay is better and the work less rough.

The other girls mentioned in my list, I am sorry to say are not working, nor have they done anything noteworthy toward living a cleaner life, but as these are my "hopeful" ones, I hope to be able to give a better account of them in my next Report.

In conclusion I wish to thank our friends for their generosity in keeping up this work. The funds until now have been enough to meet the demands. Sometime, when a large contribution has been made, I hope to set aside a little to have on hand in case of a sudden and urgent need.

Finally I wish to thank my friends for their kindness to me personally. This has been the happiest Christmas of my life. May God bless you all. Maimie Jones

Oxford Hotel and Grill, Montreal

Haintie—
                                                    January 1, 1916

125 I AM SORRY THAT THE "BOY" DIDN'T THINK TO SEND YOU A NEW YEAR'S card, this isn't because I love you any the less but merely because I just didn't think, however dear I take solace in the fact that the first use I am making of this pen. . . you gave me, is to write you as near as I can a fitting response to your kind new year's letter which I received this morning. Popoo I read and reread your letter a dozen times and each time I read it I felt more sorry for my negligence in not doing likewise. Dear but I am happy very happy to be able to say to you with some feeling of security that I am today in a position to make a fresh start in the right direction or perhaps I should better say in the light direction for there is a light, a bright light shining and dear I will from this moment on do all and every thing toward keeping that light aflame. Please popoo help me to have done with the small ways of people who live in the depth; I will rise with you and now on this day the first day of the New Year, I feel clean and strong and full of love for you, my most *proshaus,* and again I say from this moment on I will do all to stay clean and strong and full of love for you.[47] With the help of the great God that gave you to me to have and to hold and to love and to cherish, I will do all that and more I will help him to help you in all your undertakings. I will help him to make you happy and popoo I am strong, full of the strength born of the knowledge of doing the proper thing in the proper fashion.

Popoo—I have mentioned to you briefly that I have given much thought recently to circumstances in general and I have decided with the beginning of this new year to begin life anew—to strive more for the spiritual happiness than for the material—true the material is essential. But I am sure that this is only secondary. I am convinced that if I seek only the spiritual happiness, that the material must follow naturally.

Dear I join with you in a most earnest prayer that the great good God give us health and strength and I swear to obey his law of living now and for ever more and having done this, we will be happy—having done this well we will be very happy. Our happiness will be in proportion to the service we render. Be sure that I will not be lax nor lazy— I will serve! serve! serve, that you may be happy, that you may be content. Yours Every bit, Your Own Boy

My dear friend Helen,   *January 11, 1916*

I WAS VERY HAPPY TO GET YOUR LETTER THIS MORNING BECAUSE OF THAT   **126** 🔊
dear little poem.

Now Helen, you must not say it is bad. I think it is wonderful
that you could write it. I never tried to write a poem and know I
couldn't if I tried. . . .

Perhaps it will interest you to know an experience of mine,
when I was about your age. Your poem made me think of it.

I knew a little girl about my own age whose name was Annie
Moore.

Annie was blonde and pretty and her mother kept her "dressed
up" all the time, in fussy clothing which was then the style even
among nicer people—for Annie had a lovely mother and her father
was very fine. The Moores lived close to our home but I and the
other girls—my playmates—lived in smaller houses. Annie's father
had a large jewelry store and they were known to be rich.
Ordinarily poor people envy the rich but I don't think poor
children envy the rich children. At any rate, none of us envied
Annie. We shouldn't like to have to do the many things Annie had
to do and moreover we abhorred a lot of "fixin's" and Annie
always was smothered in them.

Annie's mother didn't "allow" her to do this or that and we
were "allowed" to do anything we chose. The only thing we
stopped to consider was the hours we had to be in school.

Annie was as gentle and sweet as she looked but she was not
popular with the children in the neighborhood.

Her shy manner made them say she "put on airs" and Annie was
the last one in the world to do this. She longed for nothing in the
world so much as to be with "our crowd" and be free with us, but
she was not of us and just couldn't mingle even when circumstances
threw her in our company.

I was the ringleader of this set of girls. Perhaps I was just a bit
more harum-scarum than the rest, and perhaps for that reason, I
gave Annie less consideration than even the others did. And I
always knew that Annie was keen to be an associate of mine but I
regarded her with contempt—a rank outsider, with her blonde
curls and dainty ribbons.

I had been in Annie's house several times, when her mother—
who knew, no doubt, of Annie's longing to be with us—brought
several of us in for some sweets. And we always sat stiff and

awkward, regarding her mother's advances as though they were going to injure us, and only too glad to be liberated.

But one day, something happened that made me feel sorry for Annie, and of course my entire attitude changed toward her.

The back gate of Annie's house came out to the street on which I lived, and often I would notice Annie at the gate—inside of it—and when I went by I never glanced at her, though I knew she was watching for me and hoping I'd speak to her.

This day—that the change in my attitude took place—I had in my hands several cubes of sugar. We always had the lump sugar for our tea and I had taken several pieces to feed to the horses in the fire station, as I passed on to school. This day, I passed on the same side as Annie was on and she said, "Hello, Maimie," and just then a piece of sugar rolled out of my hand right in front of where Annie stood, but it was just outside of the gate. I answered "Hello, Annie!" and didn't even stop to pick up the piece of sugar. As I walked on, I turned and looked back unconsciously and I saw Annie with a stick trying to reach the sugar. She wasn't paying any attention to me so I stood there until she had the sugar within her reach and I was amazed to see that she put it in her mouth! I was never more surprised in my life. Annie Moore, rich Annie Moore, picking something up from the street and putting it in her mouth, and of all things just plain sugar—for which I had only contempt, because we always had it in quantitites on the table, to be used at will.

As I walked I thought of Annie. My entire attitude had changed. Instead of my former feeling that she was unbearable, I thought of how sad it was that Annie had to pick up dirty sugar from the streets. And I retraced my steps, and when I got alongside of her, I shoved into the gate the rest of the sugar, which had by this time become sticky and a bit soiled from my hand.

Annie ate greedily of the sugar, jamming her mouth so full there was no chance for conversation. And not until the last piece had disappeared into Annie's mouth did I say a word, and when I did, it was on the basis that I spoke to my other girlfriends—for by eating that dirty, sticky sugar Annie had qualified and was one of us.

I am sure I did not ask her, but before long I learned that Annie's mother didn't allow her to have sweets—and even sugar, because it was in blocks, served Annie for candy.

I have a faint suspicion, now that I think about it, that Annie ate the huge packets of it that I brought to her every day, in order to keep my friendship for I can't believe that she really craved so much sugar.

So it went along for a week or so. Annie stood at the gate every day, and on my way to the school, I handed her as much as a pound of sugar, which she chewed and swallowed rapidly, getting down most of it in my presence, for I liked to see her eat it, and I chatted.

Then one day—when there was no school—and I came to her gate with the daily supply of sugar, Annie suggested shyly that I come into their yard. From there she enticed me into the house—which I was reluctant to enter until she told me her mother was not at home—and in the house, Annie led me to a room which she called her "playroom."

I remember distinctly that room, large and shadowy; and since Annie had no little brother or sister to play with, I imagine it was lonely play.

Annie showed me her "things"—with which I was impressed but not interested, until by the window we came to a shelf which held books. Fat books with fascinating covers that promised wonderful stories and pictures!

I remember as well as if it were yesterday, that the first heavy book that I pulled down was covered with shiny paper and pictures on it and was *The Chatterbox*. I didn't know what the word meant; but I remember after a casual glance at the inside that I thought I couldn't possibly look through them all—for she had lots of books —that afternoon, and I was worrying about it.

Pretty soon, I was stretched out full length on the floor, with Annie beside me, apparently having forgotten about her pretty clothing—and we turned the leaves and Annie was explaining the pictures and short stories. These things had all been made plain to her by her parents, no doubt; but as I listened, I thought what a "silly" she was. For stories about fairies and giants and pirates, I didn't believe; and I thought then that Annie meant for me to take her explanation of the stories literally.

This was the beginning of many pleasant hours spent in Annie's playroom—though I would never consent to going in except when Annie assured me her mother was out—and besides Annie permitted me to carry off any of the books, and I surely loved them, and had not one book of my own.

When in company with the girls, I made much of Annie, as much as a hoyden such as I was could make of a dainty little thing like Annie, and Annie was very happy in being of our crowd. And even though there was still a sort of reserve between us when Annie was around, it was nothing like it had been, and Annie was satisfied.

One day, I was called in from my play, my brother said Mother wanted me. When I came in, I found Mr. Moore—Annie's father—with my mother. My mother said Annie was sick and her father wanted me to go with him to Annie, who—he thought—would be cheered up by having a little girl visit her.

My mother made me ready; and in Annie's room, after the grownups left us alone, I had a good time, for I played with the many dolls and toy blackboard, and all Annie did was watch me. I don't think I spoke to her once. She seemed so out of the world, lying there so blonde and pretty in the dainty white bed.

After that, for awhile, every afternoon someone came after me and took me to Annie's house to play. After the novelty of it wore off, I included Annie in as much of the play as she could enter into while in bed.

Steadily we became companionable; and I called her "Anne" though she always said "Maimie" in a sort of timid way, as though she was afraid I'd resent such familiarity.

Often Annie's parents came in when I was there; but their presence always made me painfully shy, and they must have observed this, and did not come in frequently. One day, Annie's mother said—as I was leaving, and out of Annie's earshot— "Maimie, did Annie read to you the poem she has written to you?" I don't recall whether I answered but I remembered the question: A poem? Whoever heard of little girl's writing a poem? By the time I joined several girls, I forgot all about it. . . . The next day, as Annie's mother showed me into Annie's room, she said "Now Annie, I think you should read to Maimie the poem." And Annie began to read.

After the first line or two, I couldn't follow her. For such things as "my love for you" and other unfamiliar things in which I was the central figure, apparently, had taken me completely off my feet— and when she was through I was divided between a desire to run, or strike Annie.

What I couldn't make out was why she blamed it all on me—for in my life at that time, to figure in anything meant having done something that was not allowed; and though I was dimly conscious that Annie was frightened and her mother quite pleased about the affair, I was downright mad about being tricked into being put into what Mrs. Moore pleased to call a "poem."

My visit that day was not a success. Annie—who knew me well, I am sure—must have known I wouldn't take this honor as her mother expected I would. And when, after a much shorter visit than usual, I made ready to go and Annie's mother—still mindful of the pretty verse in which Annie told of her love for me—suggested that Annie give me a copy of the poem, Annie hastened to assure me that she only had one copy and was going to tear that one up.

I didn't much care what she did with it. All I wanted was to get out of that "queer" house where girls wrote poetry! Who ever heard of such a thing? And besides the whole business struck me as being unusual, and I made up my mind I'd keep away from them all: Annie and her peculiar mother, who made such a fuss over a poem!

I am sorry to say, Helen, that I never saw Annie again. As I learned later, she had lung trouble and soon passed off into the world where I am sure she belonged. At the time I knew her, and since then, I've always thought that Annie was exactly like the pictures we see of angels—and I am sure she is one now. Her disposition was angelic too, as I believe you can see from the way she treated me.

Often I have thought of Annie and wished I could have understood her better. . . . I also think of that poem . . . Annie wrote almost on the eve of her death. Would it not be wonderful to read that now? After all these years, to read of the love of a sweet little girl who loved me for some reason which I could not understand then, and I still find it a mystery. . . .

With much love to you and Mark, I am, Sincerely yours, Maimie

My dear friend,   *Winter, 1916*

I HAVE JUST FINISHED READING THE LETTERS AND POEMS OF THE   **126A** 🖂
convict X107.

As I suppose you know, they have made a great impression on me. I'll have to read them again—perhaps twice more—to really know whether she has my sympathy, pity or blame.

It's a wonderful magazine, this—the *Harpers Monthly*—I have often looked thru one on the newsstands, but never had one. The illustrations are wonderful, and it certainly seems a pity to treat it like an ordinary magazine—I shall keep this one, you can be sure.

Having just finished X107's letters, I'd have to think a great deal of myself to believe I can criticize her or her writings. But I have some impressions which I am afraid I won't dissipate, no matter how often I read them.

Her ability to write, I believe, is unquestionable; and her poetry has charm and realness not always noticeable in poems when signed by those whose names are well known (though lately I have noticed that poems written because of the war have real feeling in them, and they often sadden me for days).

Now I'd like to tell you that where conditions are known about girls like us, and it isn't conditions that the girls have created in their usually very active brains, we condemn outright the girl who goes to the limit who has a mother and a home. If I told the story of X107 to some few girls whom I know, who have mental worth they'd immediately condemn her. Her story, as one can get it from her letters, does not tell whether her ability to write comes from having had some schooling or otherwise; and I can't judge because, from my own experience, I believe it is possible to do much without ever having had one's feet under a desk, as Ira says. On the other hand, her references to the lovely clean place which she abandoned at times to go to the "joints" proves she had a home—that they ate regularly—and schooling goes with that.

I haven't lost sight of the fact that she speaks of another personality that existed within her own, that dragged her to the other life—but I am afraid I haven't a great deal of patience with that. It seems as though it were used as a means to heap the blame on someone else. When I was associated with Frank in Boston, in 1904, I remember that he, being older, always tried to excuse me for my wrong doings—such as staying away for weeks at a time—by saying that "Mimi" had taken me away. And "Mimi" was supposed to be another personality of mine. And I got so that I found it quite convenient to heap on "Mimi" all the *dirty*, contemptible things that Maimie did. I found this growing on me; and I remember that when, coming out on the street on a bright sunny day, after having spent the night in debauch, I'd feel so degraded—

especially if I saw children playing or was near where there were flowers and green—and to still the ache in my heart, I'd look up in the sky and ask something of somebody. I suppose it was sort of a prayer—that was meant to be an appeal to deliver me from the bad influence of "Mimi." And now I realize that was all bally rot. "Mimi" never did a thing that Maimie didn't want her to do. And as I never did anything weakly—even did my evil in strength—I decided that "Mimi" was a sloppy excuse for a weak-kneed individual. And I've never stood for another one of those silly excuses for doing wrong. Not long [ago] I caught Ira bringing to life another "Mimi,"—and I soon put a stop to that, by letting him know that I wanted to feel that I alone was to blame for anything I did. And he saw my viewpoint.

As for X107, I wish she were in Montreal, and could come here. Not that I could help her, for I presume she is older than I; but I could like her, I know. I know we'd have much in common, and I know she wouldn't be lonesome.

God, how lonesome one can be in a big city! I went thru it when I worked in New York, just after I knew you. I congratulate myself now that I came thru it without having gone back—for it was awful.

I don't share her viewpoint. (I don't like to even think that "X107," so I've got her fixed as Ruth Ramsey, and that because she reminds me of Ruth who was an associate of mine at one time, and who wasn't unlike X107 in her utterances—so X107 is now Ruth Ramsey to me.) The viewpoint about people knowing about her past and the prison term, etc. . . . .I'd have liked her to be original enough to want to live now in the open. *I am what I am.* It sticks in one's throat at first to admit it, but it gets easier. And when, as people sometimes say, "Oh but you're different," I get so tired, and I say I am not—it was just that I was given a chance and I took it; and any girl will, given the same amount of brains by God. Failing having received that, one must be more lenient—but above everything be kind. . . .

I am afraid you will think I take a great deal on myself to criticise anything which has so much in it to excite pity and not criticism. But this is the result of a quick reading—and type is, after all, a cold affair! Perhaps were she here, I could see only the pity of it all. Though I warn you that I am practicing a code now that admits of no cheap sentimentality, for I find that is as bad—perhaps worse—than cold indifference. Perhaps I'll even be institutional!

Thanks for the story. After Ira has read it, I'll read it to the girls. And I'll always keep it, and I'll always wish I could meet her; and when I go on my trip [to Philadelphia], I'll catch myself wishing I could stop off in Boston to get Ruth and bring her here to work with me. Wouldn't she be a wonderful help to the girls here!

Pine Street, Philadelphia
March 3, 1916

𝕮 127   IT SEEMS SUCH A LONG TIME SINCE I WROTE YOU. I HAVE WRITTEN VERY little to anyone, and I thought I should write so much, being that I had a few duties here. I don't know exactly what was wrong, unless the sudden change in my mode of life explains why I have felt so dazed all the while. Truly, I have been quite lost, although within the past week seem to have caught up with myself.

You know how much I loved having the girls around me, busying myself with their affairs; and here, really, days go by and I don't address a word to a human being. I still take the French lessons, and though I do not slight them, I do not feel until now that they did me much good. The things I have been learning were more or less parrot fashion. Though the teacher tried to make me understand the whys and wherefores of tenses, gender, etc., I seemed stupid—but notice that the explanations seem to reach me better this week. What brought about the change I don't know, unless it is the fact that I know—or think I know—that I am nearing the end of my stay. Even if the lessons were not studied as they should have been, I did study (that is all I do)—but I was not wholly awake, it seems. I can gather the benefits when I return to Montreal and am normal again. You will understand better when I tell you that being in Phila. I am constantly reminded of things which are not pleasant, and I am always expecting that I will be embarrassed and I don't do things that I'd do elsewhere. Were I in New York City, for instance—I would know that I have no one there, . . . and I'd go about making the best of it. But here, when I feel so dreadfully alone and grow to have my own company so much, I am forced to think of those who [might] be expected to want me. And instead of blaming them, I am sure that it is I who am all wrong, and in consequence I like myself less, and grow

374

morbid. Too, I don't feel natural here. I don't do things I'd do elsewhere; I feel instinctively that someone seeing me will misjudge my very acts. Oh! it is just that I do not belong here, and I will be so heartily glad when I can get away!

Especially to get back to the work of having the girls come for the readings, which I miss so much. When I prepare my tea here, I feel the tears gather—for I feel so lonesome, and it is such a contrast. Always at tea time the girls were freer in their talk, etc., and it grew to be such a pleasant custom to have any or all come for tea—and often the thought comes that perhaps they, too, feel lost around 4:30, when we used to be so merry.

I hear from some of the girls—mainly, they are poor correspondents—and Mr. Benjamin has seen everyone from time to time. He writes that one evening last week he went into a restaurant where he goes frequently, and was surprised to hear the man at the desk say over the telephone, "I'll ask the waiters for him, but I don't know any Mr. Benjamin." He went to the telephone to find it was a woman calling from Verdun (suburban) and wanting to know whether he could come to Verdun, to see a girl who is sick and who has a message she wants to send to "Maimie." Of course, he went at once, and found Edith Sanford (who—as do most of the girls—knew Mr. Benjamin ate in that restaurant). Edith was sick, had been so for two weeks, and wanted my address. Mr. Benjamin tried to have her tell him what she wanted of me, saying perhaps he could help her, but she wouldn't tell him. Finally he left her, and going downstairs, he met the landlady, who said that Edith is pregnant—discovered it since I've left—and that she said she intended to write it to Maimie and await Maimie's letter as to what she should do. Mr. Benjamin went back and told Edith she must not do anything, and that he knew I would advise that the baby be born. But Edith said she would write anyway. . . .

And this circumstance has given me so much courage today: to feel that way off in that desolate village, one girl is waiting for my advice on an important—vital—matter. Do you wonder that I want to get back to it? It is just things like that, that make me feel I am some use in the world—and, on the contrary, here I am assailed right and left with things that make me feel I am worthless.

In a store, close by, where I buy stamps, newspapers, etc., the clerk attends college at night, twice a week—some sort of banking course at Temple University—and being that I am generally so lonesome, I have taken to talking to him. He is about twenty-five, but appears older, and is really interesting—his mind being above the small things of the small business he is in. Several times I have eaten (armchair lunch rooms) with him, each paying his own check; and I felt that besides being someone to talk to, I was really doing some good, because we talked of the man's responsibilities in this question of the "fallen woman.". . . This chap admitted that he had attached no importance to his own responsibility in such cases, but I am sure he was impressed. Then Tuesday—last night—when I stopped for my paper, he said he would be through at 10:30 and wanted to speak to me. I didn't want to come back, but I agreed to, when he asked that I do it because it was important that he speak to me. When I returned, we walked to the restaurant for coffee. And he told me that Dr. Ashcraft (whose very existence I had forgotten) had seen him with me and had warned him that I was other than I purported to be. And he asked me outright whether I was Mrs. Jones of the work I had said I was in—or the woman Dr. Ashcraft said I was?

Do you wonder I hate to remain?

The month being up, I wrote to Mr. Brown, saying I hoped the affairs of the divorce were working in the order he expected they would, and that I'd be glad for any information he could give me as to when I would be free to go. But he has not replied as yet. Monday I saw Mr. Welsh for the first time in some little while. He was very glad to see that I looked well, and he kissed me on the cheek, and it is the first time he had done so since before I went to the hospital to be cured of the M——. And I take it he was moved to do so because he was pleased with me. I tell you this because I know you will know that I had much happiness from this.

Several nights ago, I had a dream in which you figured, and I tell it because it has impressed me so.

It appears you were in a carriage—Oh! I must not forget that I was watching this in a moving picture. And in the carriage was Mr. Howe and Mr. Welsh. The carriage drove up to a curb, and many people came to the curb to greet you; and there were flowers thrown at you. And when you stood up to get out of the carriage, I saw that you were dressed as a bride and Mr. Howe, a bridegroom. Mr. Welsh's presence was not clear. And the place where you drove to was a church. And it seems in my dream I watched this in a moving picture; and then the picture showed other "important happenings." No doubt this wedding was one of them!...

I do wish I knew whether I can go soon, for I am almost frantic every night to find some way to be interested. Reading or writing at night still brings on the bloodshot eye the next day; and to avoid this, I don't try to study at night. And having nowhere to visit at night, you can imagine how dreadfully long the nights are. It is more or less amusing that Mrs. Smith, who is paying for my French lessons, said that it was strange that I don't go to the "very fine picture shows." That these shows cost 25 cents, and thus equal to a meal, never occurred to her—and is parallel with the story of the fashionable woman who said, when she heard of a woman dying of cold, that it was strange that those people who haven't the means for fires, don't go South for the winters.

I long so much to talk to Potsy, and at times it becomes an obsession. Several times I've watched her play, but, knowing she would mention it at home, I haven't addressed her. I walked by there three times, and each time I saw her. And once she saw me, but I suppose had been told not to go to me—for she only stood on the corner with her finger in her mouth and watched me.

I received Helen's dear little Valentine, and I will write to her. It is wonderful that she can master the French she has, with only the few years she has had of mental training.

Mr. Benjamin reports that the outlook for the business is good. He has had lots of encouragement, but has so much trouble with the entries at the customs. He has had to actually bribe some of them to make them hurry. For he needs the shipments; and they are accustomed to the bribes and wait for them. Last week he spent $15.00 to get his goods thru, which is decidedly illegal, but it is the custom. For some time yet his earnings will be small—so that $15.00 out of his own pocket makes quite a difference.

Did you hear that there is a possibility that I may come to Boston en route to Montreal? Lovingly yours, Maimie.

I am deeply interested in the "Black Sheep" letters in the *Atlantic*.

Walnut Street, Philadelphia
May 18, 1916

THOUGH IT IS ONE O'CLOCK, I HAVE A DESIRE TO WRITE TO YOU AND WILL 129 ❧
write until I grow sleepy.

I will tell you right off what has upset me, and it is that I will not have the divorce until September. . . . It is enough to make me want to go to Mr. Brown and say what I think. You see, since the Master's meeting (which was, by all the laws, nearly two months late), the court has had various days for the hearing of divorce cases; and had Mr. Brown bestirred himself the case would have, at the very latest, been in the courts at this meeting—which is on the 22nd of May. But it isn't. This I learned from the court register. And since he hasn't it in the court yet, it is no longer possible for this term of court, which breaks up for the summer session and opens in Sept. Before which date, I hope to write and insist that he sees that it is in the courts in due time. I feel more than sorry because it is simply impossible for me to stay here any longer.

I haven't been idle, for Mr. Welsh has kept me busy on the various works—all for the good of humanity—which he is interested in. This past ten days, I helped to move his studio; and it was no mean task. In spite of the fact that I have, during the last part of my stay, been happy—for I am with Sarah all the time—still I fairly ache to get back, and find I can't sleep nights thinking of it. . . .

Needless to tell you how disappointed I am that I cannot carry out my earlier plans. But evidently God knows best; and I can only remember that, after all, everything works out for the best. I can write that easier than feel it, especially when, on the face of things, it is apparent that Mr. Brown might have done better. I had been so happy in my plans. And when today, I learned positively that my case was not on the record for May, and that I surely will have to wait over the summer—I felt I had better just hurry back and get interested in the work for the girls.

By the way—and just now this occurred to me—when you are packing to go to the country, I hope you will find something for us, either for the rooms or girls. This thought came as I thought of my return. I'd like to take the girls back each a present. Had I marrried, I should have, for I suspect persons would have sent me some presents and then I would have shared them. As it is, I expect to find the girls sort of scattered, both as to residence and clothes; and I will be glad if I can have some things to fit them out a little. Now that I've written that, it occurs to me that I shouldn't have, because it has always been your custom to send without being asked. But I know you won't think I'm bold. . . . Miss Huntington sent me some clothing. Most serviceable, and beautiful. The garments fit me perfectly. One suit—a dark one—I said I expected I would be married in. . . .

I received the *Atlantic* and as usual am reading it from "kiver to kiver." I enjoyed the sketch which poked fun at the archeologists. . . .

Goodbye, my dear friend, I am sorry that things haven't turned out as I had planned, because I think it would have been as you wished also. Having really made the divorce possible, I know it will be trying for you to know of this delay, which is all obviously unnecessary.

Give my kindest regards to Helen.

Walnut Street, Philadelphia
May 20, 1916

I AM SORRY, HELEN DEAR, THAT CONDITIONS HAVE ARISEN THAT MAKE **129A** ✉
my coming thru Boston impossible. I should have liked to have seen you more than you can know. My disappointment has been so great that I can scarcely think kindly of fate for the fact that all my plans have gone for nothing.

Ontario Street West, Montreal
December 7, 1916

YOUR LETTER, WITH HELEN'S ENCLOSED FOR JOANIE, I RECEIVED AND I **130** ✉
am happy for both. Joanie has not had her letter yet—though Stella saw it and told Joanie yesterday. So I've no doubt after school, Joanie will be here, and she surely will be happy to know she has a letter—the first she's ever had. The school system here is such a confusing one, due to the fact that there must be Catholic and Protestant ones—and both public schools—and each has an entirely different system, and each charges something. But there are exceptions; and in order to go to school where Joanie attends (which she says is an "Academy," plainly to be seen because it has high steps), she has to register herself under a different name. And I just hate to see poor little Joanie's eyes twinkle with the cunning that must of a necessity now be part of her nature when she tells how she happens to go to this school and how they avoid payment. Her mother is tricky and a demon, and yet both she and Stella are the sweetest children—with refinement unbelievable. Joanie is only

a child, but I car enjoy an hour with her far better than with girls three times her age, as far as intelligent conversation is concerned. While they are Irish to the backbone, Joanie talks English with a French accent, having been (all her life) thrown with the French children. She knows French equally as well as English.

Stella was delighted because you took an interest in Joanie, and we will be glad for anything—even discarded things—to give to Joanie. Mr. Benjamin said that when we come back, he thought he'd take up the matter of Joanie going to school under another name....Mr. Benjamin thinks if the case was taken up by the proper authorities, Joanie could go to school just the same; or if it did cost—the cost is only $2.50 a year—he'd pay it.

I think the difference in the fact that Mr. Benjamin is here will hardly be felt. To begin with, there isn't a girl here who doesn't like him; and several—Augustine, particularly—go to him for everything; and he understands the girls who have babies even better than I. And he wouldn't like me to give up the work.

As he goes to the YMCA every morning for a swim, exercises and breakfast, he will continue to do so, and I will not see him until 6:30. Twice a week he goes to the gym, where he gives physical exhibits, and he will not be here for dinner—that is, Monday and Thursday—and after the gym he takes a French lesson at the YMCA....On Sundays I will continue as heretofore—and Mr. Benjamin has come and gone at will, and I cannot see where it will make a big difference....

I can't help but smile at your cynical reference to the fact that you don't want me to have an "institutional" [wedding] present— whatever that may be—but I have visions of certain things seen in the Door of Hope....I hope you haven't an idea there is anything institutional about this place. I am always amused, when "social workers" call, when they ask, "But where do the girls come?"—expecting me to lead them thru my nice comfortable rooms to a dreary naked place. But it affords me much satisfaction to say that *this* is the place. And in the absence of the institutional signs, they regard me incredulously. The fact that often we have to eat in relays proves we are not institutional, for, like in any home, we have just enough cups for the family. Whereas in institutions they have them by the gross. You see, I am a bit peeved at your referring to anything institutional here! You know, I have a sense of order that sometimes bears me down; and I hate to let it beat me, for I know all institutions are orderly. So once in awhile I have a great time allowing things to get well messed up, and allowing the girls to eat peanuts and drop the shells right straight on the floor.

As for the present, I don't like to say that I need anything, because for ordinary occasions I have plenty—and who wants to keep a stock of linens on hand for occasional parties where there are thirty?

It is so funny, how well Miss Huntington knows me. I couldn't help but smile when I read her letter. When I got yours I thought to immediately answer that I'd be glad if you'd make your wedding present a money present, so I could make it a Christmas present by way of a feast for the girls; then Miss H.'s letter put cold water on that, for she says I mustn't ask for money. I thought to ask you and Miss Huntington and Miss Payson to let your wedding presents be my Christmas for the girls. Failing that—though I'd like it immensely, and much more than to have "things"—we do need a carving knife and fork (the one we use is good still, but it is a kitchen knife), and Miss H. sent me six community forks; and I could use the knives and tablespoons, or even only more forks. Then we need cups, to match our set, purchasable here for 40 cents a cup and saucer. It is a good set that came with the furnishings.

Any of the above we could use—but truly I'd rather have the money, to be sure that we had a real Christmas here, like we had last year. It's been pretty poor "pickings" for the girls here, since my return in June; the tea parties were discontinued, except on Sundays; and with the anticipation of so much pleasure for me in the near future, I can't help but wish I could give the girls a rousing good Christmas. . . .

I forgot to mention that I'd like a pair of white gloves to be used on my *honeymoon*. [When this] occurred to me, I thought, I won't buy any, because Mrs. Howe is sure to send me some for Christmas—and I never have any, except when you send them, so I always associate white gloves with you. The size is 6¼ to 6½.

Now I think you have as frank a statement as I am capable of making. I hope you won't find it too confusing to understand.

Montreal, December, 1916

BETWEEN MOMENTS OF THE GREATEST EXCITEMENT, I AM HOPING TO 131 &
write to you, so that after tomorrow I will feel free to go on with my Christmas arrangements and then go right off to Phila.—and I

know that letter writing will be out of the question after tomorrow. Unfortunately, Miss Huntington's bag containing the presents for the girls has not come yet, and I am as nervous as a cat that they won't come at all in time for our first Christmas doings, which will be Saturday. . . .

Now I want to go back a bit and thank you for your check, which was the first one that came to make me feel Christmas festivities were assured. . . . We are having a slam bang time. Mr. Benjamin is up to his eyelashes in the preparations. . . . I bought two fowl, and they will be steamed before roasting and will be quite as nice as turkey. I've done this before. The geese are not so sensible a buy, but the French girls do love greasy things—and would just as soon have a hunk of salt pork as anything. Perhaps the cold here makes the need for greasy foods; and they are brought up with it. Wasn't it in one of Mark Twain's stories that I read that the Eskimos, when they go to court their sweethearts, they carry boxes of candles as our men do candies?

The box with my fussy things came and I can only say "thank you" again, for you know how much I love these things. I put the box near me on the bed last night when I was trying to get some rest about seven o'clock, and I felt soothed just by touching the gloves and smoothing them. I never own a pair of white gloves except as you give them to me, and then I am very careful of them. And no one "gets a lend of them," as we say here—not even Stella—until they are nearly gone. (In the opera *Pinafore*, when the man sings, "I am the Captain of the *Pinafore*," he also sings, "And I'm *never, never* sick at sea!" The underscoring marks the emphasis on the "never." Then the chorus sings, "What, *never*?" and he responds, "Yes, *never*." [sic] Then the chorus sings again, "What, never?" and the captain replies with a softened voice "Hardly ever." I tell you this because we use this all the time when anyone deviates from the exact truth. Mr. B., who just read this page, whistled the tune when he read that I do not lend my white gloves!)

I have some minor [things], on a slip of paper, that I want to write you about before I get too busy.

First item: Mr. Brown came to life, sending me a copy of my divorce decree and an *unreceipted* bill for $25.00. . . . No itemized bill came, and no reason for the $25.00—only a "pay it." What do you advise? Don't forget that he took this case over from one of the associations that operates in the name of "charity."

Second item. . . . Recently in the hospital where Nellie was confined. . . I was obliged to register a violent kick against existing conditions which were called to my attention thru Nellie's stay. The hospital is an exceptionally good one but "girls" of our sort have no privacy, for their affairs are discussed freely by the doctors within earshot of other patients. The wrong was partially righted, but one nurse—a superior sort of person—said to Nellie "Oh! the doctors don't bother much when *she* reports anything, because she's a well-known morphine fiend and is not responsible." Nellie told me this. . . . I could not say anything, because it is my conviction that one convicts herself by remonstrating. . . . what can I do but bear it?

Please forgive blots. Poucet got frightened and shot by the well, and I made a grab and tipped it. I'd write it over except for the mad rush I am in.

I have something on my mind, and I am going to ask you to advise me what to do. . . .

There are in Phila. some ladies interested in me and my girls here. They are for the main part a new group. . . . The mainspring of this group is a friend of Mr. Welsh and Miss Outerbridge; and she I have known for two-and-a-half years. . . . We will call her Miss A.

Miss A: a young woman of about thirty-three, and sincere and altogether fine.

Through Miss A., I met Mrs. B.

Mrs. B. is a woman with family—a widow—and as well-bred and fine as Miss A., but very much of a *poseuse*, and I don't believe entirely sincere. She talks a great deal; and I believe "Maimie and the girls" give her food for conversation.

I believe Miss A. and Mrs. B. to be very wealthy, but neither have ever done a thing for us—not even a tiny bit.

Now thru Mrs. B. I met Mrs. C.

Mrs. C. is without family, and though husband is alive, is minus his company for reasons not uncomplimentary to her. . . .

Mrs. C. is very, very rich. She is neither well-bred, nor has she acquired the polish that money brings. . . .

Miss A. and Mrs. B. trouble me but little. Mrs. C. does—considerably.

When I was in Phila. she gave me some things for the apartment and $10.00 as a wedding gift. Since then, thru writing to Mr. Welsh about hoping to have a "shack" in the country, she has taken a hand (for Mr. W. knows her now thru me, and I believe turns over to her his troubles) and raised thru some of her family the amount to make the country shack possible—and also offers to pay for a party on the first day the place is opened, designating a certain day because it happens to be her birthday. Certainly no one could have a quarrel with such generosity, and you may be sure I haven't. But oh, the misery of writing to her. I don't write sincerely, so I don't write at all. It's a terrible thing to have to admit, but since she wrote the offer as outlined above, I haven't answered her—and it is three weeks or more!

I am writing today, though, at length, so it isn't about that, that I write you this. It is to ask you to point out to me how to accept Mrs. C. so she doesn't upset my theories about being sincere....

While lunching with Mrs. B—at her home—she (Mrs. B.), who talks a great deal, told me of Mrs. C.—i.e., her origin, family, etc., and her troubles with her husband, who is a monster. During this edifying conversation, I said "Oh, I knew that Mrs. C. wasn't real"—meaning really of the sort that Mr. Welsh or Miss Outerbridge or you are—"I could have known it if only from her voice." And Mrs. B. said, "Oh, isn't that funny—Miss A. said that you'd know as soon as you were introduced to her that she isn't one of us, but that you'd understand that she can do worlds of good with her money."

Since then I saw quite a little of Mrs. C. By keeping silent and yet openly showing my astonishment at the wealth that makes huge limousines, etc. possible, I made quite a hit with her, I think; and she—Mrs. C.—was in her glory because she was into something with the "swells" of Chestnut Hill....She doesn't dream that she is being exploited by Miss A. and Mrs. B.—and here Mrs. Maimie finds that in order to keep Mrs. C's interest, she will have to adopt the attitude of Miss A. and Mrs. B. And how can I, when I want to be sincere with the world and stop pretending?

I think Mrs. C. is of the belief that the girls here are all like me. The following will make you believe I am open for membership in the "I Hate Myself Society" which the girls here talk about all the time. She found me clean and intelligent and able to appreciate in her that which she prides herself on—her stylish appearance, etc. (I wish she'd send us her clothing, but she doesn't)—and I've no doubt when she writes she keeps me in mind and thinks the girls are all of my sort. With the exception of Stella and Rae Rabinowitz, the intelligence is away below par, and...I think she has them pictured above their worth.

Shall I disillusion her and lose the possible benefits?

Shall I write as if to compel her attention, and thus reap the benefits?...

I am capable of doing either but is it sincere?

What shall I do? I hate to write knowing it isn't sincere. I hate to accept her benefits knowing they are given under false pretenses. And yet, aren't most charitable things fostered under the same conditions—and should I set down my personal feelings and be insincere for the girls, who are at present in greater need than ever, because of the fact that they must have money to get along, as everything costs terribly, and what they have to sell is the only thing they can get enough money for, to live...?

Blanche Hurley. French Canadienne and...is nineteen. She lived in Quebec with father—a house painter—and stepmother, and some five sisters and brothers, all tots. She is engaged to marry a young soldier who went away with the first lot and who has won honors, but at present is in a convalescent home in France. Blanche's relations with her *soldat* were always honorable.

Blanche's father—not a drunkard nor lazy, but in ill health—cannot earn much. He has tried to enlist six times and wears the "offered my services" badge. He brought the family here with money loaned by his doctor, the idea being that he could probably do better. I've no doubt the folks in Quebec wanted to be rid of their support.

Coming here they found rooms on St. Catherine St. East, almost in the "bad district."

Blanche isn't over-pretty, but has a clean, intelligent appearance; is tiny and very much underfed. She got a place in a florist's. This is three months ago. The pay was $5.00 a week. The father found no work, and the $5.00 fed the family, no clothing being needed; and the rent was left to accumulate.

But the landlord threatened to put them out on the street, and when Blanche came home on a Friday night and heard this, she couldn't suggest anything. But when she returned to her work—for all shops are open here Fri. and Sat. night—and a man asked her to go out, having asked her before, she asked him if he'd give her $12.00, and he said he would.

That he didn't give her the $12.00 is another matter; but he did spend the best part of the night with her.

The landlord didn't put them out that week; and the money was gotten by Blanche $2.00 at a time the following week, in one of the houses back of St. Catherine St. East.

The father has a job now, working on the harbor, painting, secured thru influence by Mr. Benjamin.

Blanche comes here and is doing a large part of the housework, for which we feed her and give her $3.00—though she isn't worth it. And the stepmother and the children were packed back to Quebec, where they have some kin who aren't poor—and they must take care of them.

Now I only tell you of Blanche to show you that I have hopes to take her out to this shack this summer, to put some gaiety in her—for she is as sad as a funeral; and I feel that I might have to write Mrs. C. in spite of my dislike, so that I can be sure to have for Blanche what I have promised to her.

I hope you make out from all this what it is that I have been worried about—and will write me what you think I should feel in the relations with Mrs. C?

I have lots to write you but can't now, for must get dinner and then write Mrs. C. . . .

I am hoping that when you pack up to go to Cotuit that you can find something for us and, if possible, a dress—even a very old one—for Joanie

Miss Annie O. Huntington   *Letterhead of James Pinzer*
My dear friend,   *Walnut Street, Philadelphia*
      Ca. January, 1917

132 SUNDAY MORNING—NOON—AND AT 3:30, I AM TO BE MARRIED! AND everything was all arranged before my coming by Ira's sisters, who have been truly wonderfully good.

I have not found time—from the time the Christmas activities started and until I had to go—to write even a word of thanks or acknowledgment to you or Mrs. Howe for your gifts and fine letters. I have a letter to her in the writing, but try as I did, I could not close it.

I was fifteen hours late in getting here. Ira left before me and got in on time. I have never been so happy. Everybody has been lovely—except my mother, who landed on me with both feet, five minutes after I arrived, to tell me that when she saw Mr. Welsh she was going to give him a piece of her mind and "spit in his face," because he has proselytized her children. This, because Sam has just—within the past two months—made his religious position known to her, and she found it easiest to look for the cause in my direction. I assured her of what is perfectly true, that Mr. Welsh never in his entire life wrote *one word* to my brother Sam. And as for my influence—if two letters a year could do it, then perhaps I am to blame, but that I am strictly opposed to his views. That did little or no good, for she kept her face frowned all evening. It hurt me a little, because I can't conceive of anyone uttering such words as wanting to "spit at Mr. Welsh"—and especially from her, who should feel so grateful to him. I found I could not sleep, but don't think it was that. But it helped. I could see her face as she said it. I am waiting for her to come now, and I intend to tell her that if she says one word to Mr. Welsh on the subject, that she'd never know that I exist—as far as any communications, that she'd never hear from me. Apparently—though I took oath, much against my desire, that Sam never had a letter in his life from Mr. Welsh—she did not believe it. I could have been sarcastic and reminded her that had she been so anxious that we retain our Judaism, she might have shown us what it meant—for we were like heathens—and that putting Sam in Girard College was the easiest way to be rid of him—and did she expect him to learn Judaism there?[48]

Enough of that—but I had to tell someone. I did not get a chance to tell about it to Ira last night before he went to his sister's—and I won't tell him at all, now that I've told you.

But I have lots to feel happy about.

The rabbi of the church here refused to marry me because I could not answer truthfully the questions that a girl must, before she marries, anent religion. They ask outright your religious attitude. And Ira knew that I wouldn't lie, so he arranged to have Dr. Dorfmann perform the ceremony—he being a very broad Hebrew and a personal friend of Mr. Welsh—and we will be married at his home, at 3:30 today.

I am to be all fussed up—with the dress Mrs. Toulon sent, a *new* coat that Ira bought me in Montreal; and Miss Payson's hat, *new* shoes, and the gloves, veil and handkerchief Mrs. Howe sent me; and the lilies-of-the-valley that came in your suitcase.

Now won't I just be fine?

I will write you at length, before I leave, and tell you all about our Christmas. The suitcase filled our needs fine, and we had a wonderful time.

Will you send this to Mrs. Howe so that she will know that I had her and you in mind at this moment?

Wouldn't it have been fine if you and she could have been present? I am very happy, but a little bit sad, too. I think much of my sister today and reproach myself that I didn't get here in time to see her the first thing. I would have, if the train hadn't been fifteen hours late. Lovingly, Maimie

P.S. I would be glad if you had any books to send, if you sent them here. I will stay a week or more.

Mrs. Mark Howe   *Montreal, April 23, 1917*

℃ 133A   I AM GOING TO CHURCH THIS MORNING, THOUGH ONLY BECAUSE IRA wants to hear Mr. Case (a returned officer and director of the company that employs Ira) speak after the sermon. I've given up the regular churchgoing. This, because of the fact that I do not feel the sincerity of the churches that preach militarism—and they all do, and it is so tiresome, their humbug. You know I am one of those pacifist rotters, though I am ashamed of it—but what shall I do? I can't believe that God who is omnipotent sent men on earth to be killed by us—for no matter what cause. And I can't follow the clergy who have the congregation sing: "Peace on earth, good will to man"—and then conclude the performance with sermons intended to incite men to kill. . . . So why should I keep up the farce that I believe these places the houses of my God?

Miss A.O. Huntington
Jamaica Plain, Massachusetts   *Montreal, May 4, 1917*

℃ 134   I HAVE HAD A "HAPPENING." I THINK YOU'D CALL IT A SERIOUS ONE. I poured boiling water all over my left hand, and I guess I'm in for it—i.e., the hand is tied up to my chest. And though it burns, I feel a teeny bit glad, because the right hand is free and you see I can write about it. The right hand got a little of it—rather, the arm did—but not enough to disable me. But I can't do much else than write, at least today.

Blanche Hurley—a French girl with an Irish name—had been staying here. She just went off to a good situation. I mean by that, that the situation is good, but she is *punk*—but I'm hoping the person who engaged her won't find it out. The use of the word "punk" is rare with me. I sometimes use slangy words, but never that one—but in Blanche's case, it isn't slang, it is purely descriptive.

She stayed here nearly three months, and that I am still sane is proof-positive that I'll never go mad. She was the worst I ever had, and the place was filthy. You know, I believe, that I take the girls now as I always did, only that Mr. Benjamin pays a small salary—so that I can be forgiven for feeling angry once in a while. Anyway, Blanche was the laziest and the most impudent girl that ever stayed here, but I never once lost my temper. And I lived thru it, though I worked harder than ever to find her a place—and she went Sat. Today being Monday, I went after the dirt with a determination backed up by lye, soda, hot water, etc., etc. I worked through to the kitchen by four o'clock. I don't ever—when I go on one of the cleaning rampages—clean the accustomed places, for that is always quite all right. But you know every house has "snooky" dirty places that I just delight in getting after—such places as behind the stove, the inside of the stove, behind the pipes, under the sinks, etc. I took all the pieces of the gas stove apart, put them in a dishpan and, with a kettle full of boiling lye water in my right hand, I poured into the dishpan—or I thought I did. I soon found out I missed my aim—for I was pouring it on the rim of the dishpan and all over my left hand. The shock made me drop the kettle, and in that way, the splash of the water burned my two arms.

Since I wrote all this, I feel a bit silly. No doubt this has happened often—but you see, it never happened to me. So as soon as the fire in my hand let up a little, I rushed here to tell you about it. I know you will feel sorry. It was dreadfully painful. I had presence of mind to pour baking soda and then oil on the burns, and though the smarting made me cry for about an hour, I am all right again. I told Ira, over the telephone, that the pot was too heavy and my wrist gave out. I always invent fables so as not to call his attention to my lack of sight. This I do mainly because he persists in treating me like a cripple. If he knew the truth about this, I'd have him pouring my tea and coffee—and while I wouldn't mind that, it annoys me to have him do it as if I were not capable of doing it myself. Sometimes we have fearful rows because he wants me to play "sweet old lady"—and I don't fancy the role. You know, we are on the second floor, and there is a fire escape out of our salon window to the . . . roof. And I was on it several weeks ago, and I saw that up and down the length of it were cigarette boxes, hair, etc., thrown out on the snow all winter. And now that there is no snow and spring is here, I thought it a pity. So as I happened to have a long-handled dust brush out there with me, I cleaned as far as I could reach, and then I mounted [the stairs]; and before I knew it, I had stepped up on the roof. Looking out, I saw that the firemen had assembled at their door and were watching me; and one of them shouted that I mustn't start down, but I didn't let that trouble me. He flew across and started to mount, but I started to descend. And I was about two storys down before he caught up to me, when he helped me down. And then when I reached here, he said I was breaking the law and could be arrested for being on the escaliers. I thought this strange—since unless one tried it occasionally, how would he know that he could use it in case of a fire? At the foot of the fire steps—*escalier* seems a better word—were a number of people, and they thought there was a scandal on foot. Now when Ira came home, he actually stalked in and told me he heard of my—"promenade," he called it—and he said he was of the opinion that I was trying to "show off." I wasn't, for I hadn't thought anything about it until I saw the tin caps of beer bottles and the cigarette ends decorating the front of the house. . . . So when the battle was at its fiercest, he threw at me—"You can't see well enough to walk on a level, and yet you mount to the roof." Just for that, he'll never have the truth out of me—for I certainly won't let him make a cripple of me when I managed all these years without being mistaken for one.

You know I got so agitated when writing the foregoing that I had to stop, because I found instead of writing you of my happening I was writing you bad words about Ira, who isn't bad at all.

There was no one here when I burned my hands, but fortunately Geraldine came in almost directly after it, and then Gabrielle, Stella and another Blanche—not Blanche Hurley. I am in fairly good shape, although the left arm will be useless for a while.

I am reading one of the French books you sent me, *Sans Famille*, and it's a wonderful book. I wonder if you read it when you were taking French at school. It is in two parts, and I am just about thru the first book. This burn will give me time to finish it.

I must tell you that I had a nice letter from Albert Jones. I wrote him Sunday of last week. Not for any reason, except that I just felt sort of sorry for what this war will mean to him. The Colonel—or Captain, or Something—Jones who won so much fame in the last war was a close relative. At any rate, the Jones family—mother, sisters, etc.—are "Daughters" of this-that-and-the-other patriotic thing, while Albert and his brothers are always identified with the military life of Dayton. I knew he couldn't go because of his glass eye, but he has two brothers—or had, for he wrote me one died of tuberculosis. Charles, he writes, will not be able to go, because of some special work he does in the making of aeroplanes. Both Albert and Charles have been intimates of the——(I forget the name of the man who makes aeroplanes near Dayton.)

Albert was very grateful for my interest, and I wrote as nice a letter as I am capable of. I touched very lightly on the fact that Ira and I were married. I feel very glad that I wrote, because in his letter he seems so sincerely grateful for the attention. He even wrote he wants to be remembered to Ira. He said, too, that Sy, my oldest brother, still helps him. You know, Sy is a socialist, and he doesn't know anyone who will listen to his theories as well as Albert—for Albert never talks.

Too, my brother Sy sent me a photograph of himself with his wife and *her* son. I don't know if he sent it, there was no letter. It may be that Sophie wanted me to see that she had a diamond brooch, and sent the picture. I haven't had a word from this brother in more than ten years. What prompted the sending of the picture may have been that I sent mine. But recently, although I frequently write him, he never answers. Ira told me that if, when the war is over, he can afford it, he will send me there to make friends with my brother. Because often I cry for the best part of the night because I dream of being with him. This brother is almost blind. I believe I wrote you this. He accidently shot himself—in the face—when about twenty years; and though the powder entered both eyes, he sees a little—through the chinks, as it were. He is a fine man—just as fine as Sam—but allows himself to be led by his wife, who is Catholic, and very very coarse.

You don't seem a bit interested in the fact that we are to take a place this summer. I thought you would be, and I have been planning about it so much; and yet you never figure in the plans. The place is secured—i.e., I have found the place and am now awaiting to make the payment, which is collected, but is yet in Phila. (Since writing this, it has come and is paid, and the place is ours.)

I am going to write you all about the place, in spite of the fact that I feel lately that you aren't bubbling over with it as you would have been last year. It may be I "imagine" all this—but I feel so vicious about this war, especially since Mrs. Howe wrote, "I can't think of anything but the war." Perhaps if I persist in writing both you and her, I may make you forget the war a little. I wish this arm didn't rub when I write. I think that's what is making me write these catty things.

The arm hurts, I'll wait and write tomorrow.

I had been answering ads, and had even placed an ad, and so had quite a list of places to look at, as the possible retreat for us during the summer.

There were so many conditions that in order to make it worthwhile to go to the various places, I had to sift thru—down to the tiniest particle:

must be on the waterfront
no objectionable neighbors
not near any "resort"
not near any roadhouse
within 15 or 20 cents R.R. fare of Montreal
within the limit of $200.00
entirely furnished

Must have: electric lights—on account of my sight (gas isn't to be had at all, but electric light is prevalent); bath (inside toilet, I mean); garden.

So the first Sunday, Ira, Hilda and I started out to find this ideal place.

We took the cars to Lachine, intending to walk along the lake shore, as all our answers were in that vicinity, this being the only waterfront that is within commuting distance. Arriving in Lachine, we discovered that the lists had been left behind! That was my especial work. I had them within my leather bag (that you sent me), and the last minute decided not to carry a bag.

Being there, we had to make the best of it. I tried every possible way to put the blame on Ira for forgetting the lists, but somehow it couldn't be done, since I had to admit they were in my bag. (But really, shouldn't he have said at the door, "Now, have we everything?")

Several days have elapsed since the above was written; and being that I am now Madame of a Chalet, I am very busy, and really will have to write less in order to do more. . . . We found our house in this wise.

I saw it and I said it was ideal, being the only house but one that actually sits on the water's edge and isn't separated from the water by a road. Besides, it has grounds, and no houses built up [around it]. But as it was a winter-and-summer house, I thought it useless to even inquire about it, though it had a *To Let* sign up. That is to say, to all appearances the price would be out of my reach. I spoke of it to the man at the station, who said: "That house belongs to Miss Glen who writes for the newspapers and magazines. She's an "old maid" and owns all the property around there. She is a crank and no one can rent that place except it just suits her—and believe me, she isn't suited easily. She could have rented the place dozens of times but she will only rent as she takes a notion."

Instead of discouraging me, it somehow emboldened me.

To me, "old maid," when expressed generally, means a person who isn't married, and who is sweet and kind, and I like them. Especially the "she writes for magazines" made me think she would be nice, and not of the sort who would object to having us.

I was right in my surmise.

I don't believe I could have found another such place in Canada.

The house is not big and blowsy, as most country houses are apt to be, but small and yet roomy—compactly laid out. It is painted white, is wooden, but has a concrete foundation. It is entirely covered by a grapevine. It has much shade, and even some apple trees.

Ringing the front bell brought an old lady to the door, who was in gingham and looked the part of a poor relation doing service for her keep. (Later this proved to be so.)

She showed us in, and we went through a tiny hall that had a grandfather's clock that is so old and worn looking that one feels it can't possibly still be keeping time—but a second glance proves it is still on the job. Suspended from it, at a corner, hangs a big shotgun. I don't know yet if this is purely ornamental or can do its bit, if called upon.

In the living room, where we awaited the owner, was a big square old-fashioned piano, but not the conventional dark wood. Rather, it looked like Circassian walnut does these days, without its high polish. Some cretonne-covered chairs and cretonne curtains made this room bright—but everything in it is as old as Methuselah. Not the kind of old that jars one because it looks as though it were never used—but old and *worn*. I could see into the dining room, and saw a telephone and electric lights. All very encouraging, in one way, but dreadfully discouraging when I thought of the price she would want.

In the room where we sat were full-length French windows that opened onto the porch and in full view of the river. And the possibilities of the place fairly made me sick—i.e., the thought that maybe she wouldn't consider us.

When she came, she looked not unlike Miss Payson, though very blonde. Straight as a reed, and as active as a boy. And though her face looked severe—when she smiled, I felt I could have her house. I stopped being a critical person looking to rent a house under such and such conditions, but I fell into the role of Maimie asking Miss Payson for a place she had to rent. And it worked like magic!

I told her not only what we wanted, but what I had met with on the part of the agents who wanted me to sign leases that I knew I couldn't live up to, to the letter. And I believe this appealed to her.

She showed me her price as listed on the books of the agent who handles her property. It was $700.00 for the season. The season means six months.

I told her, then, how we were fixed; and I also told her of my girls. And she asked for names and addresses of persons that knew me, and told me she would write me. I never slept that night. The place fairly bewitched me.

The next day at four o'clock, I received a note from her saying that she wanted to see me. I went to meet her at a local newspaper office, and she said if I could raise $350.00—that is, half the sum—I could have the place. Her price is $700.00 but she agreed to take $350.00 from me.

The amount we had allotted for this was (and is) $250.00. But I couldn't see any way to do than to take it, trusting to raise the other hundred by asking everyone to give me a little extra to meet it. Truly, I could think of no one who would let us have their place, knowing about the girls, for they'd think we would use the place badly. I think Miss Glen felt otherwise from the reports she had from Mr. Noakes and others that know how I keep this place. I told Miss Glen of the conditions; and she agreed to take the money, $250.00 in one sum, and the other in small amounts, as I had it, up to the time we vacate.

Do you see in this an appeal for you to help me raise a portion of this amount? I feel I ought to write you and ask you to do this, because the Phila. friends thru Mr. Welsh made the largest amount possible—though I shall write Mr. Welsh to see if he can raise the difference in small amounts. Of course, I only ask this if you can do it without interfering with what you are busy with. We hope to have it for Miss Glen by the end of the season, but I think if we are a little short, she will wait. And Bennie tells me not to worry, for if I don't manage it through the friends of the work, he will pay it—if Miss Glen will accept small monthly payments of $5.00 or so.

I will tell you further about the place.

There is a kitchen and a cellar, all in the condition that I know you or Miss Payson would keep the place in Maine. Upstairs are three large bedrooms, but any amount could sleep in each room. The beds are all old-fashioned four-post beds. And a bath. And hot water (and cold running water) from the fire in the kitchen. Then there is another small room—bedroom, downstairs—that I suppose would be called the "maid's room."

Miss Glen is a chicken fancier, and has a white, very modern chicken house and some hundred chickens, pure white Leghorns. She takes them along, of course; but if Bennie can manage it, he is going to get us some chickens for eggs. This is "maybe." He'd like to do lots and lots, but of course he can't do more than his money permits. (Oh! yes! Libbie, his sister, is engaged. We don't know whether the war made this possible—but just the same, she is engaged to be married in September. Ira has to furnish the means for the wedding. It strikes terror to our hearts—but after all, it will be one less for him to keep; and perhaps Libbie can do something for Sonya and Roseanne after she is married.)

To go on about the house: Between the porch and the water is a little kiosk sort of thing, that is actually in the water and is reached by a walk of boards. In it one may sit, or from it bathe. One side of it holds a rowboat and a canoe for our use.

We are within thirty minutes of Montreal. Ira will pay for all transportation. This was agreed on from the beginning. By buying tickets in quantities, it will cost twenty cents the trip. "Over Sundays" will be our regular arrangements, but when any girl has a holiday or conditions make it possible, we will have a "working outfit" to stay there all the time.

Fortunately, at our right is a small house, almost like a bungalow as we have them in the States, that belongs to the same property and is rented by a man, his wife, and an elderly maiden sister who shows *deep interest* and who will look after us. She is a lady and the girls will respect her.

Do you not think our conditions ideal?

Now: can we have some seeds and some slight general information how to plant and care for them? While several of the girls claim to know how, Ira and I are absolutely ignorant on the subject, and he thinks it would be wiser to ask for a general plan how to go about it. Jeannie Faulk, who professes to know, clashes with Nellie's views, and I hesitate to let either do anything; and when you send us seeds, I will go along to superintend the planting.

If you find I am bold in this letter, please excuse me. I was never so excited in all my life over anything. Do you know, I've never [lived] in the country and never had a piece of ground (except in New York State) that wasn't sidewalked, to fuss with?

There are all sorts of implements in the place for gardening; and I will be so happy if we can really have some flowers and vegetables though Ira thinks I am hoping for too much.

If you or Miss Payson have a flag—an American flag—I'd like it. I mean one to fly from the house or window. I priced one and I find I can't buy it. So thought I'd tell you of my desire, and perhaps old flags are to be found in an attic, and I can have one.

Mary O'Brien marched in here at 9:30 last night, with her baby in one hand and a suitcase in the other. I had a fright, thinking she had quit Mrs. Winter's place at Ste. Anne de Bellevue. But I was delighted to find she was only on a holiday—though it was rather an unexpected one, and to come at that hour. Of course, we made her comfortable by having the baby and Mary sleep with me—for Jeannie Faulk occupies the couch—and Ira slept in the dining room on the floor. Don't say "poor Ira," for he not only suggested it, but likes it. I think he comforts himself by thinking that at least, if he isn't in the trenches, he is having hardships! He actually begs each girl to stay, and volunteers to sleep on the floor, and he won't take anything but a sheet above and under him. The baby is beautiful. It was so sick and puny before it went to Mrs. Winter's in the country. It is black and hardy and is in wonderful condition. So is Mary. Jeanne Faulk is a tiny girl—as big as an eight-year-old child—and has a boy of three years—and was until last week living the irresponsible life. She's with us now and is everything that Blanche wasn't. Ira likes her, and perhaps we will be able to take her and her boy to the country.

(Ira is preparing dinner because my hand still keeps me a bit of an invalid.)

I am hoping to get some things from Miss Evans when her school closes.

For the time being, I am busy arranging about the place, where we hope to start our first "over Sundays" for next Sunday. If the American flag is possible, can we have it soon? Or any cushion tops or old sweaters? Don't lose sight of the fact that I am supposed to be an invalid—so I must be humored, and I think I can ask for things. But the flag most of all, because I want every one to know that we are there as Americans.

My kindest regards to all, Miss Payson especially. Lovingly yours, Maimie

General Joffre was here yesterday, and Ira and the different girls saw him.[49] I couldn't go out in the crowds, on account of my hands being tied up.

Lachine, Quebec
June, 1917

Miss Payson and Miss Huntington

SINCE I WROTE YOU, MY MOTHER HAS BEEN HERE AND GONE. . . . YOU **135** ✎
will want to know the whys and wherefores of her visit, so I shall go right into it.

Directly on our installation here, I wrote James that if he had any intention of giving Caroline a vacation, with or without the children, that I thought he ought to take advantage of this lovely place and send her here. He didn't answer—then, or yet. Fact is, she never had a vacation; and unless a miracle happens, she never will have; and the question was never agitated—though I wrote once before that (after he took his lovely trip of several months across the continent, visiting the San Francisco Fair) that he should endeavor to give Caroline a change and a rest. My hint as to Caroline's needs shot over the mark; and a letter came back from Caroline saying that Mother is so happy that I will have the benefit of a place in the country, etc.; and the letter was written so that I understood that my mother wanted to come. My heart went out in pity for her—for after all, she is an old woman, and the prospect of spending the summer behind James's counter selling smelly cheeses wasn't over-alluring. But I was helpless. For entre nous, I am having a terrible hard time to make ends meet, and every cent of Ira's money has gone into the pot since we came out here. Don't think it is because I manage poorly. Really, I do manage well, but the appetites of young girls who have been half-starved is something to contend with; and it really requires a person who has a heart of stone to do the portioning out of the food. (I can only use the paper on one side while out here, due to the dampness for it becomes like blotting paper. This to explain, so you won't think I've become careless.)

To return to my mother. I felt keenly my inability to send for her. In fact, as I enjoyed this place, my heart was heavy and my conscience smote me that my own mother was in the warm, smelly store. Besides, she really had been quite ill all summer, the doctor claiming she had tonsilitis. (But that doesn't seem possible, for a person to have that so long. I believe it is quite a fad these days to blame everything on the tonsils, as it used to be everything was blamed on the appendix.) The more I thought about [it], the more positive I was that it was my duty to bring her here to enjoy what there is here to enjoy. The fact that I didn't enjoy the prospect of her coming made me feel more certain than ever that it was my duty to bring her here. It's no trick to do your duty when your duty falls in line with your pleasures. I soon dug up a reason why she should come. Knowing her, I thought she would make an excellent

Food Dictator; and in that way control the outgoing of the food—which in its quantity ate up every penny of Mr. Benjamin's salary, even making him lapse in the money due to be sent to his family. Finally I was inspired. I wrote James a personal note telling him that I *needed* Mother here, but that we weren't able to send the money for her. I then asked if he would advance me the amount necessary, knowing as I did that a sum like that is of no moment to him, and yet to a man of my husband's small salary it is a great deal, etc. James loves that role, and it worked like magic. He didn't condescend to reply. He did it on the grandiose manner that I am sure Mr. Rockefeller bestows his benefits. He gave Mother her fare, expenses, etc.; put her on the train; and as in the stock companies, the wire announcing her coming arrived at the same time Mother did. I know the money was given, not advanced—for I know James. As long as I am willing to play pauper and *mendiant*, (this is correct in French, but I believe it is *mendicant* in English), James will always play the role of the Grand Marquis.

My plan about Mother being Food Dictator fell down flat. The girls did not accept her as such. When she refused, I was appealed to in this way—"Maimie, give us each a banana and a slice of bread. Then we will eat less at supper. We are starved." And I always thought—and think yet—it can be done. But at suppertime they are twice as hungry. And I always remember when I was in the Magdalen Home and often ate the banana skins out of the waste-baskets that I emptied in doing the teachers' bedrooms. I have caught Adelina eating banana skins here—but not if I know it will any girl do it more than once!

Well, my mother's stay was short. The place is damp, for we are as if on a houseboat—directly on the water—and she suffered with a stiff joint in the knee. The knee has always been a source of trouble to her, but here she was almost lame and finally had to leave. During her stay, I found that she caught the idea that the girls owned the place as much as I do, and gave them that deference. And, in all honesty, she really gave me very little trouble. Of course, she sang eternally James's praises, and spoke of those whom we had known at home who had once lived wrong, and then married, as *fardorben* (which is German and Yiddish and means, frankly, "rotten" or "degenerate," when applied to humans), and she made these allusions too frequently for me not to know that she has *views* on certain subjects. But all in all, she was a "good fellow" with the girls, and everyone was sorry to hear that she wasn't staying.

Of course we had to dig up her return fare, and that came out of Ira's salary yesterday; and today I feel crippled. In fact, I am stunned. Because it leaves me with nothing; and I don't know, even if I wanted it, whether I could get a few groceries on credit. I never do charge things. But like anything else, one never does it until they do.

As the girls have come in to clean this room, I will cease for a while. I started this Sunday A.M., but it is now Monday, and the rooms are in a frightful condition (as they always were over Sunday).

You would laugh to see the attitude of the girls this morning. There are two factions. One is on a strike with existing conditions, and the other side is of the opinion that what I want is right. Stella with the opposing faction. And as she is my right hand bower and knows I don't take anything like that seriously, she is acting as if it were all in dead earnest. She stays until the 9:45; and she just said, "Hilda, you pull down all the curtains, because we must get these rooms clean." And she's waiting for me to answer, "Oh! I didn't mean that even the *curtains* must come down"—but I am saying nothing. But I will have to stop writing—or Hilda will take Stella seriously and I'll have to put those curtains up again!

Lachine, Quebec
July, 1917

Mrs. Mark Howe

℞ **136**   STELLA WAS DUE HERE YESTERDAY AT NOON, TO BRING JOANIE FOR A short stay. Ordinarily I do not have time to meet the girls on the road or at the station, but yesterday I was upset about Joanie's coming (for she's here under false pretenses), and I walked along, thinking I might tell Stella to take her back even before she actually got here.

But long before I got to the avenue that leads to the station I saw Joanie coming, with her arms out, and shouting. I made out finally that she was saying "I have a letter from Mrs. Howe!" Stella [had picked up] your letter when she asked for the mail at the station. I opened it *tout suite*. And when the check appeared, I simply tucked it away without comment—but Stella had seen it. When Mr.

Benjamin got home Stella told him that "Mrs. Howe had gotten there first"—i.e., you had given me the first birthday present. As Ira seemed quite pleased, and Stella, too, I didn't tell them otherwise.

My birthday is Saturday, and the chicken is all picked out—though not one of ours, but one belonging to Mrs. Edmonson—for I will not be able to eat ours. The girls are working it out: that is, it is taking fifteen hours of helping Mrs. Edmonson. And we only have four hours worked out. No one here to spare now, strong enough for the work. My idea of the girls working is a good one for the girls that I have had under my wing for a year or more—but the others are too irresponsible and, in most cases, too weak physically to stand up under such work. Joanie says she will pick berries, but I only learned since last night that she is being treated for curvature of the spine. I think that is what it is, because Joanie says the doctor says she has an *S* curve—or it may be a *C* curve, Joanie doesn't know which. But she goes twice a week to the dispensary and they do things on her back. I took a look at her back when I was putting her to bed, and it is quite pitiful. The shoulder blades almost knock at each other. They curve in like this ⟩ ⟨_____. And besides, she is thin almost to emaciation. I wish I could do more for her. But having to do even the little I can and *do* accomplish, with packs of lies and deceit on Joanie's part makes the doing very difficult. She slept last night with Adelina, who, though sixteen, is no taller than Joanie and Joanie thinks Lina is a child like herself. I asked that no one tell her otherwise, for in that way, she plays as a child should. Well, Lina said this morning that Joanie told her that when she goes home she will say she was in the country with the poor children who go thru the Summer Outing Fund, but she wouldn't mention my name. And when Lina asked why, she said that her Mother beat her until she fainted, for the last time. This was news to me, and I haven't questioned her. But Mr. Benjamin, to whom I told this, and who had breakfast with her this morning (he doesn't eat with us, but takes breakfast earlier on a tray on the porch), said that Joanie said she knew she'd get a beating for this vacation, but she didn't mind. Doesn't it make your blood boil? It does mine, and I feel enraged enough to go to town and have her arrested for cruelty. But I know in the end Joanie would suffer, as Stella has, when I protested before. The little pictures of Stell and

Joanie will give you a better idea of what they are like than even the larger one of Stella has. Except that Joanie, by closing her lips, hides the beautiful straight white teeth; and in both, one misses the colorings that they both have a lot of—though Joanie hasn't the red hair.

I have the *Monthly*. Thank you, and for the seeds enclosed, which are now being planted by Hilda.

Thanks very much for the check. I am going to have an extra sort of Sunday this week, for my birthday—and this $10.00 will pay for it. I know this would be as you'd wish if you were here to advise. Because every girl wishes to do something, and I am letting them know that the $10.00 relieves everyone of the responsibility of getting something toward the birthday party.

I must tell you of a real party that we had. A Mrs. Hoopes, who is a friend of Mr. Welsh, wrote that she wanted to give us a birthday party. . . . Mrs. Hoopes had a birthday June 2nd, and she wanted us to have the benefit. And believe me, it was a party to be remembered. I went on with the plans, for she insisted that it be an ice-cream-and-cake party, with fixings like the richest girls would have; and she insisted that I mustn't play any tricks of economy— that the girls must have the most—and [that I invite] as many as I wanted. Well, it cost *$50.00*.

But you know me—I did scrape off a little to pay for essentials. Since it was at the very outset of our stay here, I made the $50.00 go toward paying for some of our installation, in this wise: I got two small tot chairs; one high chair; necessaries on the porch; and a much needed acquisition for Ontario West. Then, as it was a Japanese party (it being my idea that we all wear kimonos, thus avoiding that dreadful condition where one girl refuses to come because the other girl will wear finer dress than she), the kimonos are doing service here as house or morning dresses, with aprons around to tie them down. Augustin made them all—and, really, they are smart, and made after the smock fashion rather than kimono, and only reach to the knees. We wore skirts with them. A friend of Mrs. Hoopes made us place cards. They were so pretty that I didn't put the names on them, but used them to decorate the table. These cards are Japanese girls carrying parasols that work on a pivot, and I kept them in place with a piece of clay under each—for we had our party outdoors. At present, they parade on the piano with their parasols at various angles, there being thirty-five cards—though only twenty-five were at the party, which includes Ira and me. . . . Besides the party, the money gave us the three chairs afore-mentioned; some lanterns; kimonos, and last but not least, a very good ice cream freezer.

By the way, in a recent letter, this lady—Mrs. Hoopes—asked your address, saying she will pass thru Boston this fall and will see you. She is spending the summer in Camden, Maine, and I think is interested in knowing you through what she has heard of you as being good to me—though I may be mistaken. In any event, she has asked your address, and she shall have it. And I shall hope that she calls to see you.

Montreal, December 19, 1917

WHAT EXPLANATION CAN I OFFER? MY SILENCE PUZZLES ME EQUALLY AS IT **137** does you. In trying to understand it, I've reached some of these conclusions.

I used to love to write, and when I had spare time, or even when I should be sleeping, I rushed to ink. Now I despise to; and I even feel annoyed when I am asked to "do" letters for Yiddish, Russian, Polish, or French people. Of course, I do them, but I hate to. And I gave up writing for. . . families of men in German prisons—though with this work I used to earn money.

My only reason, as I can make it out, is because I am always so troubled. And if I thought I'd always remain so, I'd write anyway; but it always seems as if I were to find it better "shortly." And I always hope to write "shortly"; for in writing to you and to Miss Huntington, I would have to write everything—troubles and all—as I felt we were so intimate. But when the "shortly" did come, I was head and ears in trouble again, and I did hate to admit it.

You recall I used to write you when I was troubled. I think this was because when I had these troubles, I'd find on going to bed that I couldn't sleep. I'd feel so outraged; and when I wrote to you, I got relief. And I believe now I tell it to Ira, and he always advises that I wait, and, I'll see, everything works out right. And in that way I hesitate to write, and I wait for what Ira calls "shortly."

I know I could and should write short letters or postals, to let my friends know I am all right. Poor Mr. Welsh, I treated him to a siege of silence, and he writes—advising me as if I were ten years old—that I should learn to write short letters, often. As if I didn't know this! Of course I do. And don't think I don't suffer—I do. For

Miss Huntington's picture hangs directly *en face* the chair in which I sit when I am in my room, and I always see her eyes reproaching me. Though your picture is there, too, it is not so large, nor so distinct; and it is she who reproaches me daily. But I just shift my eye and feel uncomfortable.

I suppose by this time you imagine all sorts of dire things have happened. Perhaps they weren't so bad—but, to me, seemed terrible. And I feel I have been a failure.

Suppose I tell you starting from last summer in July why I had so much to contend with.

The money for the upkeep of the place kept getting less and less; and Mr. Welsh would forget to send the $12.00 which he used to always contribute. When I stewed about it, Ira always came to the rescue with the needed amount. But as his salary is not elastic, he had to deprive his people of their regular amounts. This naturally brought protests, and they were always addressed directly to me. I worried and worried—not so much on their account as on Ira's. Because I could read his thoughts; and in the evenings I could see, as he sat on the porch, that he was worried. When we talked of marriage, I had insisted that by the upkeep of the work, he would have very little expense and could still take care of his people. Instead, he was head and ears into debt, and they were receiving practically nothing. They had arranged to take a stipulated amount, but they never stuck to it—for Sonya or Roseanne would need something, and write to Ira; and he never refuses, if he has the price. And that money was never deducted from the sum originally planned. You know how much I care about money. I just don't care; and I'd send them our last five cents—but I had this country house. Which was such a big fine place, had I even the support I had on Ontario Street. But it all fell away. Often, I think that some of my friends, when they sent money for the work with the girls, actually thought most of me—and when I once married and they knew I was being taken care of—just didn't think much about the girls. But I—what could one expect of me? Once I had a roof over my head and a bed to call my own, could I shoo the girls off? No indeed, they clung to me, and I just had to carry them. These are the "old girls"—and without wanting it, "new girls" were always coming into our circle.

Well, being into the "country house," there was nothing to do but stick it out. Ira threw every dollar into the pot; and I even got thousands and thousands of envelopes to do, and did them at all times and hours, to keep the place going. What the girls earned by working helped but little. For when they received money, I just couldn't take it away to pay for general expenses, when each girl has her needs—room rent, or shoes, or something. Of course, when they worked for food or vegetables it helped—only, the girls ate more. Anyway, it was nip and tuck; and I saw Ira being weighted down; and I was always using boracic acid to keep my eye open, to earn a little extra with the envelopes for the Patriotic. And so the summer wore on.

I must tell you that my mother, on going home, told Mrs. Benjamin of the fact that Bennie was keeping up the place—for I had told my mother, in a moment of unguarded intimacy, of our conditions and that little or no money reached us, except what we both worked for. And poor Mrs. Benjamin told the girls; and Libbie treated me with a series of letters in which I was accused of using their holy brother to maintain a refuge for prostitutes—and she wasn't careful enough to call them that Ira wrote her. And then, he broke down and had weeks of crying spells—for he loves them beyond any reason—when they didn't write; and he went into debt for $150.00 to send Libbie in Sept., when she finally got a man and was married. Now—this summer business kept me in such a frenzied condition that I couldn't write unless I told it; and Ira has worked up a lot of false pride in not wanting me to have it known that we are not just getting along. He has had two advances in salary of $5.00—but as everything advances accordingly, it didn't help much. (This is all as it was in the summer, but is better now, as I will write you. . . .)

Did I tell you that I had poison ivy almost all summer? I had Miss Huntington's book, and cured myself always quickly. But it was fresh every time I went into the garden. I made a paste of kitchen soap and soda, and I bathed two and three times a day in it, for I always had a fresh attack of it—for poison ivy was in abundance at Lakeside. And though several of the girls got it, I arrested it immediately with Miss H.'s cure, as in the book—but as I was there all the time, and must be susceptible, I was hardly without it all during July and August. And in Aug., I couldn't address many envelopes, because my fingers were always sore from handling the strong soap and soda solution.

Now while I endured much mental pain because of what I wrote you in the foregoing, I felt I would be relieved when the summer was over—for I had decided to take drastic measures to see that Ira was not made to carry on the work for the girls, and, too, to insure a regular kind of living for him.

Then, one day Mrs. Lizzie Cohen, (whom you may recall, for it was for her that I once went to New York, to take Hazel to), Miss Cohen's wealthy sister, called up to say that she wanted to send Hazel to Baltimore—i.e., to New York, to her sister, who was sending Hazel to a fine girls' school near Baltimore; and that though she had advertised, hoping to get someone to take Hazel, she had had no replies from reliable persons; and now she was prepared to ask me and to pay my way. Her intention was to only pay half my expenses, and Ira was so anxious for me to have the change that he agreed to pay the return fare. But I refused to budge under those conditions; and Mrs. Cohen—being so anxious that Hazel get there by the 15th—finally bought the return ticket and gave me $10.00 for expenses.

Of course, I didn't know for certain I was going until the night before. But before that, I had written to my mother and to Sarah that I was coming. And I was so elated at seeing Potsy (Sarah), that when I got on the train here, I sent a wire—unbeknownst to Ira—to James, and told him I'd arrive West Phila. Sunday, at 11 A.M., and whether he'd try to have Sarah with someone at the station to meet me.

I arrived with Hazel in New York at 7:30; and her aunt was there, and took her over. The aunt gave me $5.00. She said I should use it to have a "good time" in New York before I returned, inasmuch as she couldn't entertain me—as she was leaving in the afternoon for Baltimore with Hazel. I told her I was going on to Phila. to stay a week; and as I wanted to make the nine o'clock train, she let her chauffeur take me (while she waited at the New York Central, with Hazel) to the Pennsy. I just about made the train, and you may know I was happy.

I suppose you can guess already that no one was there to meet me.

Let me digress to tell you that...Sam (my brother)...had finally written to my mother in full his views; and I believe she learned for the first time about his being so religious. And he told her he had given up his very good place to work for his keep in the YMCA, there to provide recreation for soldiers and sailors stationed in Honolulu. . . .He wrote only of Jesus Christ and his life being given over to work for Him—and of course the name *Jesus Christ* is like a red rag to a bull, when said to my mother—and it appears she immediately laid it all at my doors. . . .

Arriving at West Phila. at eleven o'clock, I went to James's; and it was 11:15 when I rang his bell. He answered the door. I smiled and lifted my bag to enter—and he held the door open only with his body and said, "Oh, no! You can't come in here. Not so fast. You go further. We have peace here and we don't want an agitator. Etc., etc." All the time he looked over my head, smiling, as much as to say he had beaten my game. As usual, I was dumbfounded; and though I usually cry, I didn't this time—I asked what he meant. And he said, "Never mind. I don't want your explanations and I'll not give you mine. Just gather your truck together and clear out." And he banged the door shut. I stood there for several minutes, hoping to see Caroline or Potsy, but I didn't.

Crying as hard as I could, I walked to [52nd, to the house] where my mother is—and I received the same reception. She didn't even open the door; and she said she didn't want me there, and she didn't want my explanations, either. She had a sort of crying voice; so I appealed to her to let me see Sarah just once, and I'd go right back. This, she said, was impossible because James knew that on my last trip I had gone to church with Caroline and Sarah. (This is a lie. I never go to church in Phila.—and haven't gone in Montreal for two years.) She said Caroline had admitted to James that I had talked to her about raising her children as Christians. This, too, was a lie. Caroline never told James that. But James probably told it to my mother, to make my case a worse one. I might say that aside from writing Sam sisterly letters, *never mentioning* religion, I also had nothing to do with his conversion—much less had Mr. Welsh, who had never written Sam one word. Of course, Mr. Welsh was roundly abused, and so was Miss Huntington—for Sam must have written mentioning her name. I told my mother that Miss Huntington couldn't possibly persuade Sam to accept Christ, when it was my belief that she doesn't go in for that version of religion. But my mother was relentless; and though she didn't open the door, she cursed me roundly.

When I walked away from there I was so heartsick that, in spite of my promises to Ira to see his mother, I walked back to the station, caught a train just going out to N.Y. Arriving in New York at about 5:00, I went into the rest room, and laid on the couch, and got the 7:45 to Montreal, and was back there Monday morning. I was at Ira's office before he got there. You can imagine his surprise. He didn't scold me, he was too sorry for me.

He took me out to Lakeside. I was sick there in bed for ten days. I forgot to tell you that when I left Montreal Sat. night I had dinner with Hazel on the train—and I ate my next bite of food in Montreal again, Monday, at eleven o'clock at Lakeside.

Now, do you wonder I hadn't any heart left when I returned?

By that time it was cold, and the girls didn't want to come out [to Lakeside] because it was really disagreeable. During those days I was in bed, Ira and I talked over and planned our work or future. We decided that I'd have to give up the rooms. I knew if I told Mr. Welsh that we hadn't the means to run them, he'd dig up some money. But that would only be temporary relief, and it would be that Ira's salary would be jeopardized. Too, I was determined that I'd have to plan so that Ira would positively have three square meals a day. When I only had myself to consider, and when I alone had to suffer, I didn't care if it were always "feast or famine." But I knew I must not permit this to go on, for Ira does require man's food.

Then, just at that time, the French riots were going on; and as we lived just at the intersection between the French end and English end of the city, it was right there that the riots took place.[50] Too, our place was on the edge of the Tenderloin, and the police were very aggressive—to the extent of stopping every girl who attempted to cross a certain boundary line.[51]

Everything considered, we decided to store our things, sublet the flat, and board. This we thought we could try, and though I would keep up my interest in my girls, it would be done entirely thru a regular visiting arrangement. Mr. Welsh was reluctant about having us close down, but he agreed that I was obliged to think of Mr. Benjamin's interests. So everything considered, we set about these plans.

You see, when we were in the country I made a practice of visiting girls who couldn't come out—and found in that way I reached things I couldn't possibly have, if I waited for the girls to come to me. I found I could keep in actual close touch with the girls who were *trying*—eliminating, to a certain extent, those who came to my rooms to benefit and make little or no effort. You see, I could—and am, really—looking after only a few, in comparison; but I have these very, very close. When I told this to my girls, my own special little crowd, a great hullabaloo went up, especially from certain ones. Ways and means were thought of; and while all good enough, thru the responsibility upon me, there would always be the same "feast-or" condition for Bennie. The girls agreed, then, that we "shut up shop," for the winter, anyway. Which we did. I furnished one room partly, for a young French girl, Germaine, and her mother; and it was to be sort of a meeting place; and we meet $5.00 a month of the rent.

Right here I must stop to tell you that the night of the morning of the Halifax disaster, the city here was nearly frantic. Telegrams came that the people were freezing on the streets. It was twelve degrees below here, and report had it that a gale was blowing there and a terrific snowstorm (which has since proven to be true). Everyone was nearly frantic. Some men got up a train (at their expense) and made it known by telephone to each number in the book that flat cars would be at the tracks of the C.P.R. all the day until six o'clock to receive any kind of coverings, to be sent direct at seven o'clock to Halifax. And I couldn't resist paying $2.00 and backing a wagon up to the storage house door, putting on it all our blankets, covers, bath rugs—and even two carpet-rugs and some chenille curtains. You see, these things didn't really belong to me, but I felt I couldn't permit them to stay there idle, when there was such a need for them—especially as our need was not definite for them. I did pray for guidance, and talked with Ira, and acted—feeling I was doing what was right. I have since written to Mr. Welsh. If he considers this right or not, I don't know yet. He hasn't answered. And when I left the storage house, seated in the front with the driver, I drove along to the C.P.R. tracks; and by giving the man an extra 25 cents he allowed me to get down and ring doorbells; and I asked for things. I didn't get more than a bunch of rags, practically. Except in one place, a woman gave me a huge feather bed (a Jewish old woman), and another woman gave me *seven* odd pairs of pants, and *four* coats.[52]

When we gave up the flat, I secured a nice room in a boarding-house. I explained to the girls that they couldn't come there. For you know what boardinghouses are; and you can imagine how

409

much they'd tolerate strings of "queer" looking girls coming there—especially since, even if I only permitted a few to come, they'd all come. (Of course, Stella was the exception.) And I had to even prevent the calling up by telephone—for after our third day, there were just seventeen calls for me; and of the seventeen, eleven were from one girl who had been arrested. The food was good; and I thought my scheme excellent—when, upon my offering to pay the board the third week, the Madame suddenly discovered that she needed the room. I understood what was wrong. Although the girls were forbidden to come, they did. Though not in numbers, still they came. And though the Madame knew I was interested in "social welfare" work, she had no sympathy with their coming to her door—to perhaps chase away her respectable roomers.

Bennie and I were disconsolate, for we knew that no matter where we went, the same thing would happen again. One can't shake off such a responsibility with a shrug. We thought then to go to a hotel. While more expensive, still, we felt we'd be likely to remain. In a hotel, incoming telephone calls trouble them not at all, and messages at midnight, just a little. So, like it or not, we'd have to make up our mind to pay more and live where they'd keep us—or go in hiding, and you may be sure I wouldn't do that.

Fortunately, I had known that the Windsor Hotel, the second best hotel here, has an "old side"—i.e., the section that has not been renovated. And when Gertie Turner worked here, I called; and she and other chambermaids had rooms on the "old side"—regular guest rooms—but the explanation was that, being without modern conveniences, they were rarely rented. Ira came to see Mr. Wilson, the second manager. He explained our predicament—i.e., about my work, and my inability to keep the girls from telephoning at all hours, and even coming when they were in trouble—and our certainty that no boardinghouse would keep us for long. And apparently Mr. Wilson was interested. For we are regularly installed, and have had almost no trouble.

I stop here to go out—and knowing my trick of perhaps not finishing this, I am going to mail this. And hope tonight to bring my letter up to the present, for there are about ten more items I wish to write about.

I will acknowledge also your check and Miss H.'s, for our feast to be held in Germaine's room Sunday. But more of that tonight. And something else that will more than surprise you.

While this letter will arrive before Christmas, I wrote it with the idea of its being my Christmas letter to you and Miss Payson and Miss Huntington. And now I will close—and send the finish, positively, in the next mail. For my pen seems willing to write, and my heart is easier—though only because I have really gotten a letter off to you. Will you telephone Miss Huntington tonight— i.e., the night of the day you receive this—and tell her I have written, and tell her I have some great news in the following letter?[53]

While we live at the Windsor Hotel—still, because of our position (for we pay little, and we eat in the department with the managers, bookkeepers, etc.), I don't like running to the desk for mail as if I were really a guest—for they do have a big hotel. So we have a postoffice box: Mrs. Ira Benjamin, Station *B*, P.O. Box 255, Montreal. . . .

Mr. Welsh wrote you had some *Atlantics* for me, and I am *very* anxious for them.

The Christmas letter follows. Lovingly yours, Maimie

I do hope Helen hasn't forgotten all about me. I thought of her this past week, for I bought a pair of warm mitts for Joanie, out of your $5.00, and I wrote on the card: "From Helen Howe's mother."

My dear Mrs. Howe, *Philadelphia, December, 1918*

AS THE CHRISTMAS SEASON APPROACHES, I THINK CONSTANTLY OF YOU **138** and Miss Huntington, for you and she were always responsible for the most part of any Christmases I have had.

Since I have been here, I've tried to write you what I have been doing, but just could not do it. In fact, I don't write Mr. Benjamin—not even postals. I can't find time.

I have only seen Mr. Welsh once, so do not know whether he wrote you about what I have gone thru. I will take it that he hasn't written, for I believe I should have heard from you if you knew.

Caroline, James's wife, whom I loved so much, was a victim of the influenza epidemic.[54] She died October 10th. I can't tell you what that means to me. I have to tell you all about it. I have never written it yet. Surely God's ways are mysterious, for everyone in this family—the two children, James, Caroline's sister Adele, my mother and even the maid—were ill with influenza; and of them all, God took the one who was an angel. Sarah nearly died. She was in danger for three days. I nursed her through.

411

I used to say that were it possible to end the war, I would make any sacrifice asked of me. I said this so frequently, that I believe God took me at my word. My idea of a sacrifice was the giving of my life, or the giving up of any comforts. I had never thought it would mean the giving up of one I loved so dearly. When the news came that peace was declared, I was glad—so glad—but not jubilant. For I felt that Caroline paid the price, and it is hard to believe it is fair.

She was only taken ill on Monday—this, during the height of the epidemic—and Thursday, 4 P.M., she died. I was not here, of course. The entire family were flat in bed, and not a servant nor nurse on the premises. She had absolutely no attention—it could not be had for love nor money—and was seen only twice by a doctor. Poor Caroline, whose service to the world should have earned her attention! A telegram was sent me by a member of the Benjamin family, who knew of their predicament. I received the wire Friday night, and was in Phila. Sat. at 9 A.M., having made a special that was bringing doctors and nurses to the East for the epidemic. Traveled to Harrisburg on a train, but came from Harrisburg on a freight car.

Arriving, I found the door open—that is, unlocked. And opening the door, I smelled the stench of mortification, so I knew the body was still on the premises. In a small room which they call the parlour, James was stretched on a cot; and against the other wall, on a couch, was my mother. In the hall under the stairs is a box seat, and on it was Mr. Gross, my mother's husband. In the back bedroom were Sarah and David and a servant (Negress), Sarah being very far gone. In the next room lay Adele, Caroline's sister—and in the front bedroom, Caroline was dead, her body lying there with no more attention than is given a cat.

Such wailing and crying as was set up when I came in. I thought James had lost his reason and that my mother would never survive. I did not cry. I didn't dare to. I saw what I had to do and I wish to report that I did it.

I tended the living first. Sarah got my attention, to begin with. Words cannot describe the chaotic condition of that house. Though Caroline had been sick but four days and, in all, the housework had ceased but a week, the place was filthy. Everything that was handled was left where it dropped.

Though I did not get burial for Caroline for more than a week, I was able to get the body to an undertaker's by night. I had to wash and dress the body at home, and I even opened her arteries, my assistant being a boy of eighteen years whose only knowledge of the undertaking business was learned in driving one of the auto carriages for the undertakers. The body was taken away in a grocery truck loaned by the wholesaler where James buys his merchandise, and I had to put her in a clothesbasket. The boy and I carried her out, and I left her at the undertaker's at 7:30. I came back in the truck; and I had all sorts of fumigation things, and antiseptics. All that night I labored to remove that terrible stench. And then for three days and nights I never stopped treating Sarah. It was seven days after my arrival that I took off my shoes and outer clothing even. Though Ira wished to come with me, I didn't permit it, and even kept him in ignorance of the condition of affairs—for I didn't want him to take the risk. However, when I was able to think more lucidly, I called him by long distance telephone, for I realized that Caroline would have given her all, were conditions reversed. On Ira's arrival, he went at once to a relative of ours who is a cornice maker; and between them, they made the casket. Then Ira dug the grave next to my father's in Har Nebo Cemetery; and the next day I went to the undertakers, and Bennie and I had the sad duty of placing Caroline in her coffin. I dressed her in my wedding dress. Needless to say, she was no longer our beautiful blonde Caroline—but oh, how I loved her. I could be sure she is happier. Only, it stays in my mind how terrible death made her look.

We had a hearse and one carriage. Bennie and I and James went—though he was so terribly sick. Mr. Welsh sent a beautiful wreath of white roses. And I watched the roses all the way to the cemetery as the hearse kept in front of us; and I kept up the thought that the roses were Caroline, and not what we put in the casket.

All is well here now. Sarah goes to school, James goes to business. Ira is in Toronto. David is fine, but needs constant attention. I take care of the home and the children. I have a woman to help, but she is the common Negro type and is little help. I should have written you long ago, but I never can. I have made such a mess of things. I seem so useless when it comes to housework, but I keep it up. I go to bed so tired every night, how can I possibly write.

When I lost my baby last year, Caroline, who wrote to me

secretly (for James had forbidden it), said she felt so badly for me, that if she were able, she'd send Sarah to me to stay awhile to comfort me. I can recall now that I thought that I'd rather have Potsy than even my own baby. And now I have her, and I love her, but how it hurts me; for she loved her mother, and it is so sad for her. Even David who is three-and-a-half years, is inconsolable.

Last July, Ira got into some trouble about his registration papers, for he reported his age as thirty-two, born in Russia, and when his father's citizen papers were examined the dates made it appear that Ira was not telling the truth. He was in no end of trouble, and the affair was only straightened out when I came to Phila. in August— while Ira was being held—and found an uncle of Ira who was able to explain the trouble. It was due to the fact that Ira's father was in this country but four weeks, when he was made a citizen (so that he could vote at a presidential election), and the papers were made to read six years. You may be sure that he knew nothing about it, for he was not able to speak English nor write it; and this was all worked out by the scheming politicians. . . .

I haven't the remotest idea as to plans for the future. Mr. Welsh, whom I saw once, advised my returning—but how can I leave the babies, who love me so? Ira will come at Christmas to talk over and decide what is to be done. He wants me to do that which I want to do. The reason for the difficulty in arriving at a decision is due to the fact that my mother is still reigning supreme. Even as she ruled Caroline's every move, she does thru James manage even the smallest detail of this household. And all of Caroline's pretty ways and beautiful ideas that she filled the children with are being thrown right and left, and the habits and ideas that existed in Russia are being installed. I rebel to a certain extent, but wishing to avoid friction, I go on as though I don't see it. But it is just breaking me all up. I hate confusion and dirt; and my mother, whose love for money is her first and last thought, thinks that order and cleanliness cost money. And she is the cook—and you can just imagine my living where herring (raw) and butter are put on the same plate, and where cooked meats are put away wrapped in newspapers. However, the children are wonderful. Sarah goes to school; and when I go over her lessons with her, I find her very bright. She is seven-and-a-half years old. She is learning French from me, and sings—with very good accent—four French songs, including three verses of *La Marseillaise*. Even brother David already understands the ordinary commands, such as one uses at table, etc.

I hope you or Miss Huntington will find time to write me a letter and tell me how you all fared during the epidemic. I never forgot you for one minute; and when I was working so hard that week, I thought that if Miss Huntington knew what I was living thru, she'd come to help me. I hope no ill befell any of you—and will you write to me? I hope your children are well. Will you tell me how everyone is—Miss Payson, and her nieces? And I will be so glad of a letter, because it is so near the Christmas season, and I know you always think of me—but do not buy anything for me, as I go nowhere. And I always loved the gloves you sent me, but I don't ever go out anywhere; and everything, I have—even more than I need. If you can, write me soon. Lovingly to you and Miss Huntington, Maimie

My address is James Pinzer, c/o Walnut St. Letters must be sealed.

My brother Sam may come home for a visit. He is at Camp Grant, Illinois, but expects his discharge soon, as he was a volunteer, and they are being let out first. I sent him a Christmas box yesterday.

Hotel Somerset, Chicago

March 6, 1922

My dear friend,

IS IT POSSIBLE THAT YOU WROTE ME TO SEGUIN, TEXAS AND YOUR LETTER 140 ⊠ was returned? I have just had a communication from the postmaster at Seguin that leads me to believe this. When I left Seguin, I told them to hold any mail until I sent them an address. I wrote my cousin several days after my return, and as far as I knew she had attended to the forwarding of my mail. This past week I learned from a young girl who had written me that my letter was returned to her, stamped to the effect that I had no forwarding address. I wrote Mr. Draeger, the Postmaster, and today I received his reply that he had never received a forwarding address, and that he had returned three letters to the writers—two to Chicago, and one to Boston. Can that have been yours? I did not hear from you after I wrote explaining the mysterious boxes. And while you have the same privilege that I took—i.e., of waiting one year to respond to my letter...I am inclined to believe that you won't.

We are in a hotel, but it is one of those that have full arrangements for cooking and housekeeping. Bennie had selected this place before I came. It is desirable, inasmuch as it is new and spotlessly clean, but it is patronized almost entirely by big, fat, Jewish ladies and their thin nervous husbands. However, I use the downstairs attractions very sparingly, so avoid contact. I have not met anyone here, so take it that they do not find me any more worthwhile than I find them.

I have two little canaries—a gift from the Texas cousin—who are busy preparing a nest for some expected young ones. This and two private, as well as a class on Thursday nights of pupils to whom I am teaching French, keeps me very busy.

I have read my *Atlantics* (may I have some more if you have them?), and so has Ira, and now they are being read by a young man who is studying law and working as a porter in this hotel at the same time. He is a day student at the Northwestern University. He is a Filipino. He comes to me to get assistance in English. Does this astound you?—

I am obliged now to bring this sketchy letter to a close, as I am due to meet a girl at 10:30 in a dispensary—and it is a case of first come, first served.

You haven't any idea of what I am thinking of these days. I want to write you fully and ask your advice as well as that of Miss Huntington, but just now I can't go into it, except to give you a hint and ask you to think about it.

I want to go to school—i.e., I want to take up the study of something. I am fearful lest my equipment is inadequate. I haven't any idea of what I should aim for, and above it all, I am so afraid that I overestimate the worthwhileness of it. I haven't discussed this with Ira, mainly because in his estimation I know now more than anyone alive! However, I know what I have yet to know.

My love to you all.

Maimie

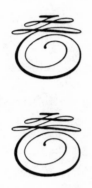

ANNOTATIONS

1. Maimie married Albert Jones, a man she described as considerably older than herself, in 1906.

It is interesting that Maimie mentioned only once, in the entire course of the correspondence, that Albert, too, was sightless in one eye. See Letter 134, p. 391.

2. The Miss Outerbridge described by Maimie, in this and succeeding letters, does not herself appear in biographical dictionaries. Her family, however, does. She had a brother, Albert Outerbridge, who was born in 1841, graduated in law from the University of Pennsylvania in 1862, and became a trust officer of the Land Title and Trust Company of Philadelphia. Another brother, Alexander Ewing, Jr., was a well-known metallurgist. It appears from Maimie's letters that Miss Outerbridge was a philanthropist associated with the "social gospel" of good works of the period. Most likely, she made her home in Philadelphia, where the rest of her family lived.

3. Mrs. Howe's early, and only, novel, *The Opal*, was published in 1905 by Houghton Mifflin and Company, Boston and New York. Mrs. Howe published the book anonymously, a not uncommon practice among female writers who were "Gentle Americans." See *Introduction*, p. xvii.

4. "M——" is Maimie's designation for "morphine addiction." She also referred to her addiction as "the morphine habit" and "the morphia."

5. Maimie does not explain this lapse.

6. Letters 21 and 22, separated in the Schlesinger typescript, are actually a single letter written over a two-week period.

7. Keith theaters, named for Benjamin Franklin Keith (1846-1914), were a nationwide chain of popular-priced vaudeville theaters. Keith was the originator of the "continuous performance" vaudeville theater; he attempted to raise the standard and conditions of vaudeville by paying good salaries to talented performers.

8. The celebrated French actor, Sarah Bernhardt (1844-1923).

9. The *Philistine* was a *bibelot* ("side pocket" periodical) of the period. Calling itself a periodical of protest, it attacked literary leaders, established publishing houses and magazines, colleges, doctors, lawyers, and preachers.

Fra Elbert Hubbard, editor of the *Philistine*, used the magazine to voice his resentment against magazine editors and book publishers who had turned down his novels and essays. He alternated between socialist and big business stands. By 1915, the *Philistine*'s circulation had peaked at 110,000, and it was being widely imitated. When Hubbard died, on the ill-fated *Lusitania*, the periodical was discontinued.

The *Fra*, a periodical begun by Hubbard and named for him, lasted two years with a peak monthly circulation of 50,000.

10. The *Cigarrthist*, a pamphlet published by Hubbard, appeared in 1906, 1908, and 1909, with the subtitle *Being a Preachment for the Young Person and Others*. It advocated a strong stand against smoking.

11. Israel Zangwill (1864-1926), a prominent member of English literary society, was also a fervent Zionist. His best-known novel is *Children of the Ghetto* (1892).

12. The *Pall Mall Gazette* was a periodical which combined a newspaper format with literary features. Like many of the writings and authors Maimie referrred to in her letters, the *Gazette* was British and aimed at an educated, elite audience.

13. Frank Stockton (1834-1902), a Philadelphia short-story writer and novelist, wrote first for children. Later, for adults, he wrote such popular works as *The Casting Away of Mrs. Lecks and Mrs. Aleshine* (1886). His short story "The Lady or the Tiger" (1884) became a popular classic.

14. *The House of Mirth* is a novel published in 1905 by Edith Wharton (1862-1937). The hero, Lily Bart, is shown to leave a true-love relationship, in her ambitious search for wealth and position.

15. There appears to be no book bearing this exact title. Maimie may have been referring to a differently titled biography of Stanley.

16. Dr. Silas Weir Mitchell was not only an author; he was also a physician specifically concerned with female neurological disorders, who gained fame for his "rest cures" for upper- and middle-class women suffering from "hysterics" and "nerves."

In an unpublished passage of Letter 37, Maimie said that Mitchell's books were "even more interesting" to her because she had for a time been a patient of "his son, Dr. John Mitchell," who "helped me get rid of that terrible M——."

17. George Meredith, 1828-1909. Maimie went on to say that she found Meredith's poetry so depressing that she had given up reading him.

18. Thomas Hardy, 1840-1928. *Tess of the d'Ubervilles* was first published serially in 1891.

19. The *Atlantic Monthly* became a leitmotif in Maimie's letters to Mrs. Howe. From its inception, in 1856, the *Atlantic* was addressed to a highly literate reading audience. Fanny Howe was a contributor to the *Atlantic*; her husband served briefly as assistant editor (1893-1895) and as a vice-president of the Atlantic Monthly Company (1911-1929).

20. Mrs. Amadeus W. Grabau, known to her large reading audience as Mary Antin (1881-1949), was a first generation Russian-Polish Jewish immigrant, who arrived in Boston in 1894. In 1912, she expanded a childhood book *Plotsk to Boston*, an impressionistic description of her family's life in Poland and their journey to America, into her renowned autobiographical novel, *The Promised Land*. In it, she portrayed the difficulties faced by Old World Jews, and contrasted them with the choices and opportunities available to Jewish immigrants in the United States. The book was first serialized in the *Atlantic Monthly*; subsequently issued as a complete book, it sold 85,000 copies and went through thirty-four printings.

21. Edmond Hoyle (1672-1769), English authority on games. The expression "according to Hoyle," still current, is not ordinarily applied to rules of etiquette.

22. Emile Gaboriau (1835-1873), a French writer of detective stories, created in his works two characters who became well known, Monsieur Lecoq and Pere Tabaret. Gaboriau was the author of *L'Affaire Lerouge* (1886); Maimie may be referring to an English translation of that book.

23. William Dean Howells (1837-1920), the American novelist,

champion of realism in fiction, was editor-in-chief of the *Atlantic Monthly* from 1871-1881.

24. Maimie is referring to the complex anti-trust laws initiated by Progressive reformers of the period to dissolve monopolies.

25. Oscar Fingal O'Flahertie Wills Wilde (1894-1900), the Irish aesthete and writer whose works included *The Picture of Dorian Gray* (1891) and such witty comedies as *The Importance of Being Earnest* (1895).

Convicted of homosexual practices, Wilde spent two years in prison at Reading. His poem *The Ballad of Reading Gaol*, growing out of that experience, protests the lack of compassion and understanding inherent in society's punishment of lawbreakers. The refrain that Maimie quoted ("each man kills the thing he loves") is the central thesis of the poem—sufficiently far-fetched, perhaps, to justify her bewilderment.

26. "Magdalen" refers to a reformed prostitute, taking its derivation from Mary Magdalen's repentance of her life as a prostitute and her discipleship under Christ. In the nineteenth century, Magdalen Homes for "wayward" girls were begun in the United States, with the purpose of reforming prostitutes. Some of the Magdalen Homes were sponsored by the Catholic Church, some by other churches, by female reform societies, and even by non-church groups.

27. Maimie several times referred to the "water famine" in Montreal, in this letter and in the letter that follows, but without further explanation.

28. Ellery Sedgwick (1872-1960) was a well-known literary figure who became both the editor and president of the *Atlantic Monthly* from 1908-1938. It was Sedgwick who admired but refused to publish Maimie's letters after the Howes sent them to him.

29. Thomas Mott Osborne (1859-1929) was mayor of Auburn, New York, from 1903 to 1905. In order to investigate prison conditions, he assumed the fictitious name of Tom Brown and entered Auburn Prison. Later, as a famous penologist, he became a warden for Sing Sing Prison in Ossining, New York, where he initiated liberalizing prison reforms. His ideas are set forth in his books *Prison Walls* (1914), *Society and Prisons* (1916), and *Prisons and Common Sense* (1924).

30. Leukorrhea is a common infection of the lower tract of the vagina which results from infection of the cervix. The cure involves

douching, or in severe cases, cauterization of the cervix. The ailment is not related to venereal disease.

31. Annie O. Huntington, probably a cousin of Mrs. Howe. She became a benefactor of Maimie and a frequent correspondent.

32. Salvarsan, an arsenic compound, was introduced by a German scientist, Paul Ehrlich. It was not a certain cure for syphilis except when used in combination with bismuth—discovered later, in 1931.

33. In an unpublished passage of "The Maimie Letters," Maimie described Mr. Nash's relationship with a young Montreal prostitute. Her remarks suggest that she considered threatening to expose the respectable Mr. Nash, should he refuse to assist her in getting Stella and herself across the Canadian border.

34. It is not clear from the text how Maimie understood Ira's affliction with syphilis. From popular evidence of the period, one might assume that Maimie actually believed that syphilis could be transmitted by the indirect means she describes. On the other hand, Maimie may have suspected a sexual encounter between Ira and her favorite, Stella. In that case, she might have been unable to admit the possibility of betrayal even to herself, and hence, unable to communicate that possibility to Mrs. Howe.

35. Lillian D. Wald (1867-1940), well-known social welfare worker and reformer who established the pioneering Henry Street settlement house in New York City's lower East Side as a neighborhood center for civic, educational, and philanthropic work among poor immigrants. By 1913, it occupied seven houses and two uptown branches. In 1912, Wald became President of the American Union against Militarism.

Jane Addams (1860-1935) was one of the earliest and certainly the best known among workers in the field of urban reform and in the settlement house movement. Establishing the famous Hull House settlement in the slums of Chicago in 1893, Addams created a model for other efforts to help immigrants in the urban slums. In addition, Addams offered educated, middle-class women like herself a socially acceptable way of working outside the home for the good of society. Addams tried to use her immense popularity to gain support for her anti-war views during World War I. In 1919, she became the first President of the Women's International League for Peace and Freedom. President Wilson consulted with WILPF leaders regarding their mutual dreams and plans for a League of

Nations. The Washington visit which deprived Maimie of meeting Lillian Wald was one such occasion.

Wald's and Addams' pacificism and concern for the poor and deprived coincided with Maimie's own expressed pacifism and with her efforts to assist the unfortunate.

36. Miss Payson, either a friend or relative of Mrs. Howe, was also a benefactor and correspondent of Maimie.

37. *Linda*, a novel Maimie repeatedly referred to as a favorite of her reading "girls." Elsewhere, Maimie gave the author's name as Margaret Prescott Montague. Neither the book's title nor the author's name appears in standard references.

Elsie Venner: A Romance of Destiny (1861), novel by Oliver Wendell Holmes (1809-1894). The novel focuses on the doctrine of original sin and the concept of human responsibility.

Dickens' *Old Curiosity Shop* features an innocent, Little Nell, fleeing from the wickedness of the city and finding refuge in death.

Daniel Deronda (1876), novel by George Eliot (1819-1880). Its principal character, a Jew, is an exemplar of moral virtues.

"Pelleas and Ettare." Pelleas is a legendary figure, a knight of Arthur's court, who loved in vain the heartless lady Ettare. The legend is the subject of a poem in Alfred Lord Tennyson's *Idylls of the King* (1869). Maimie may be referring to the legend or to Tennyson's poem. It is also possible that she refers here to *The Loves of Pelleas and Ettarre*, a novel by Zona Gale (1874-1938), published in 1907, whose main actors are an elderly couple. Gale was active in many progressive and radical causes, including feminism and pacifism; it is interesting to speculate that Maimie's ideas may have been influenced by Gale's books.

38. At the end of the nineteenth century, the immensely wealthy Baron Maurice de Hirsch, a German Jew, began to assist in the re-settlement and welfare of Eastern European Jews through a great variety of philanthropic enterprises, of which the Baron de Hirsch Institute was one.

39. Although the term "flapper" is commonly associated with the nineteen-twenties, flappers were a small but recognizable group during the early years of the twentieth century. They were usually single adolescent girls, characterized by a cynical and rebellious attitude toward Victorian sexual standards, the use of cosmetics and cigarettes, and provocative and seductive clothing.

40. Like the *Atlantic, Scribners* and the *Literary Digest* were highly reputable literary periodicals of the day.

41. The White Company was a group of English mercenaries led into Italy about 1360-1390, to fight against Florence for Pisa. Sir Arthur Conan Doyle published in 1891 a spirited story with this title, about a similar company. This may be the title to which Maimie refers.

42. Miss Evans, a friend of Miss Huntington and director of a school in Boston, became Maimie's benefactor and correspondent.

43. Pollyanna, a character in a novel of the same name by Eleanor Porter (1868-1920), published in 1913, was a "glad child" with an unshakeable "everything will go well" attitude. The word has come to be used, often derisively, for anyone having such attitudes.

44. Maimie is probably referring here to Mark Anthony De Wolfe Howe's work entitled *American Bookmen: Sketches chiefly biographical of certain writers in the nineteenth century* (Dodd, Mead and Co., 1898). The books included biographical accounts of the lives and works of such writers as James Fenimore Cooper, Ralph Waldo Emerson, Nathaniel Hawthorne, Washington Irving, and Edgar Allan Poe.

45. The *Metropolitan.* When the magazine began to appear, in 1895, its chief attraction was pictures of artists' nude models. After 1898, the publication became more respectable and began to include the work of serious writers such as Theodore Dreiser. Articles tended to focus on notable persons and institutions.

46. Begun in 1899, *Vanity Fair* was at first known for its "naughty" pictures. In 1913 it became a fashion magazine, merging in 1936 with *Vogue.*

47. *Proshaus* was evidently a private endearment, probably a corruption of *precious.*

48. In his will, Steven Girard (1750-1831), a nonbeliever, established Girard College, a non-sectarian institution which emphasized "a love of union, sobriety and industry," as well as a disdain for religious sectarianism. Located in Philadelphia, the school (grades 1-12) was available without tuition to fatherless boys such as Maimie's brother.

49. Maimie is undoubtedly referring to General Joseph Jacque Césaire Joffre (1852-1931), commander in chief of the French army

during World War I from 1914-1916. He would have been heartily welcomed by French Canadians on his mission to North America.

50. The riots to which Maimie refers may have been over the controversy between French and English citizens concerning which language was to be taught in the province's schools. In 1912, the Department of Education limited the teaching of French to two hours a day. In 1916, two teachers were dismissed over the bilingual controversy. Riots resulted in Ontario, where Maimie was living. The riots Maimie mentioned, however, may have resulted from the August 28, 1917, conscription law, which was bitterly opposed by labor and French Canadians. Anti-draft riots occurred. The latter cause is more likely, given the date of the letter. Whatever the cause, it is important to recognize that the Canada of Maimie's period, as in present times, was continually torn by English and French hostilities.

51. During the first twenty years of the twentieth century, vice commissions were created in nearly every major city in the United States and in Canada to study and survey the proliferating but openly tolerated redlight districts which existed in a state of de facto legalization. The outcome of this anti-prostitution crusade was the legal closing of the former tenderloin districts and the illegalization of prostitution. In addition, because brothels were closed, there was a massive increase in the amount of streetwalking, as well as a rise in pimps and in criminal syndicates which "protected" prostitutes from the newly created police vice squads and customers. Very few efforts at rehabilitation were attempted. Rather, citizens simply wished to erase the "social evil," as it was then called.

52. On December 6, 1917, the capital of Nova Scotia, Halifax, was nearly destroyed by a collision between the Norwegian ship *Imo* and the ammunition vessel *Mont Blanc*. The event was treated in the novel *Barometer Rising* by Hugh Maclennan.

53. It seems clear that Maimie intended to announce that she and Ira were expecting a child. Whether or not she wrote that letter, we do not know; however, the next letter in the collection, Letter 138, written December, 1918, approximately a year later, refers to the loss of "my baby last year" (p. 413).

54. Between September, 1918, and June, 1919, a pandemic of influenza swept the United States, killing 548,000 persons, with the highest mortality rate among those under five and between the ages of twenty and forty years of age.

AFTERWORD
Searching for Maimie

I have never stopped searching for Maimie Pinzer. When her letters were published in 1978, so many questions remained unanswered. Why had she stopped writing to Fanny Quincy Howe after 1922? How had she spent the second half of her adult life? Had she returned to school "to take up the study of something"—a desire she expressed in her last letter to Howe? Had she perhaps become a social worker and continued her work with young troubled women like herself? Since she had married and taken responsibility for her brother's two young children, what kind of family life had she and Ira created? And had she ever fulfilled her dream of writing short stories?

Patricia King, then the director of the Schlesinger library at Radcliffe College, had conducted a broad search for Maimie's relatives. In 1978, I took up the search, and called and wrote many potential informants. I became an amateur detective, slightly obsessed, in search of the rest of Maimie's story.

Some of what I have learned cannot be confirmed independently by archival sources. The rest of Maimie's story, moreover, is so astonishing that it now raises even more questions—more, it seems, than anyone can hope to answer. Searching for Maimie, I have finally realized, is a process, one that may go on for the rest of my life, and will, I hope, be taken up by other literary and historical scholars. I share the sentiment Maimie expressed in her last letter to Fanny Quincy Howe: "I know how much I have yet to know."

I now feel certain that Maimie stopped writing to Fanny Quincy

Howe after 1922 because the circumstances of her life dramatically changed after her marriage to Ira Benjamin in 1917. No longer alone and worried about her future, Maimie seems to have lost her desperate need to confide in a woman who had provided so much emotional and financial support for twelve years. Her needs for intimacy and security were now met by her husband and their two adopted children. I am not suggesting that Maimie "used" Mrs. Howe for twelve years and then cast her aside; rather, I think Mrs. Howe helped her grow into a mature woman who could put her past behind her, marry, and use her formidable intelligence to make her way in the world.

Between 1922 and 1927, Maimie and Ira lived with their two adopted children in the Admiral Hotel in Chicago, the last city from which she wrote Fanny Quincy Howe. One of Maimie's cousins, who was astonished to learn about the "hardships" (her term for Maimie's work as a prostitute) Maimie had suffered during her youth, visited the Benjamin family in Chicago during these years. Maimie, she wrote, "appeared to be quite successful,"[1] and worked for a time as an interior decorator for a department store. Her apartment, she recalled, "was truly luxurious. Maimie loved to find old antiques and would get up around 4 in the morning and clean them up. I was under the impression that she sold many of these things and also that her apartment was so unusual that it was used as a showplace. I also thought that she was connected with one of the large stores as a decorator."[2]

Maimie apparently cut an elegant figure during the twenties. According to a sister-in-law, Maimie no longer wore the dress of a working girl or that of a social worker. Instead she "wore a patch over her eye of a different color to match the dress she was wearing."[3] None of Maimie's relatives, however, had any idea whether Ira was working, what he ever did for a living, or how they afforded their luxurious apartment and elegant clothes.

Based on her cousin's description, Maimie and Ira had temporarily joined the middle class. The growing consumer culture of the 1920s had opened up all kinds of new occupations for women, including the kind of work Maimie apparently took up, as a decorator. At last, Maimie was able to surround herself with the elegance and beauty she had envied in other people's lives. As a working woman Maimie almost certainly knew that Americans were bitterly debating whether married women should work

428

outside of the home. But Maimie, it appears, did so. Her income probably anchored the family's security, as was the case in so many working-class families. With so little information about Maimie and Ira's finances, we can only speculate that they, like so many others, had somehow found a way to thrive in the speculative prosperity of the 1920s.

It is quite possible that Maimie realized her dreams and became a published writer during this decade. According to her sister-in-law, Maimie was "then writing stories for magazines, which were republished in the Reader's Digest," the first clue that Maimie may actually have become a published author.[4] Endless searches, however, have turned up no published material under any of the family surnames that Maimie might have used. Her sister-in-law, however, was quite specific and wrote that "none [of Maimie's short stories] were ever returned but the checks did not take care of her."[5]

Did Maimie publish under another name? I think it is quite likely. In one her letters, Maimie recalls that Fanny Quincy Howe published her essays, short stories and even her novel, *The Opal*, under a variety of different pseudonyms. From this, Maimie probably learned that ladies, as a matter of modesty, avoid publicity and publish their written work under other names. Though I cannot find "the smoking story," I am convinced that Maimie did in fact publish some short stories, perhaps in small literary journals that have not survived and that are not listed in guides to periodical literature.

As her letters reveal, Maimie was a highly talented writer, an artful and skilled storyteller who knew how to shape real-life events into captivating plots, and how to create suspense. Even more, she had an uncanny ability to create lively characters, whose revealing gestures and dialogue made them thoroughly convincing individuals. In 1915, the editor of the *Atlantic* had praised her writing, but declined to publish her letters, for fear of tarnishing the reputation of the magazine. It is quite plausible, therefore, that Maimie published short stories in literary magazines that were later reprinted in either the *Literary Digest* or the *Reader's Digest*.

By the roaring twenties, editors of mass magazines had liberalized their publishing practices and would probably have welcomed Maimie's stories. Fueled by Hollywood's new image of the sexy young seductress, and the mushrooming cosmetics industry, American advertisers began publishing stories about the flapper, a modern young woman who drank, smoked, danced, and petted. As young women cut their hair and shortened their skirts, they created a youth culture that rejected anything that smacked of Victorian primness. Married women, too, felt the changing mores. Advice books began to idealize a new "companionate marriage" that required husbands to be faithful and wives to behave as sexual playmates. The strict Victorian divide between "good" and "bad" women was fast vanishing. Given her hatred of sexual hypocrisy, Maimie would almost certainly have felt far more comfortable in the post-Victorian world of the twenties. She most likely looked different as well. As a young woman, Maimie dressed as a working-class version of the Gibson girl. In Chicago, however, we should perhaps imagine the fashionable Maimie with bobbed hair, and matching short skirt and eye patch.[6]

Sometime around September 1927, the Benjamin family apparently visited Maimie's relatives in Philadelphia. It was here that Maimie informed her cousin that she and her family intended to drive to California. Maimie asked her cousin to join them. After gaining her father's approval, the cousin decided to join May (her family's nickname for Maimie) on her westward adventure.[7] Shortly afterwards, Maimie, Ira, their two adopted children, Sarah and David, and Maimie's cousin, drove to California. The journey west, according to Maimie's cousin, "was a marvelous and educational trip."[8]

I am not sure why they decided to go to California.[9] One of Maimie's brothers lived in California, but they had never been close. Perhaps the Benjamin family was facing financial troubles. According to her cousin, Maimie and Ira had come up with the rather surprising idea of trying to see "what success Sarah and David could make in the moving picture industry." Maimie's cousin wrote that "they were truly beautiful children, but unfortunately they couldn't control their weight, and this was a great problem. . . . and I remember how vexed Maimie became."[10] Apparently, Maimie and Ira thought they could enhance their income if Sarah and David entered the film industry as child actors.

Whatever the reason, Maimie and Ira were not alone in their decision to journey westward. California in the oil-crazed 1920s drew thousands of other Americans. Ruled by a fourth-generation "Downtown Establishment" that prohibited unions, Los Angeles actively wooed Midwesterners, as well as foreign immigrants, to join one of the greatest internal migrations in the nation's history. By 1930, the sunny land of freedom had created 50,000 new manufacturing jobs in Los Angeles county alone.[11] In addition to manufacturing, Hollywood—another industry that generated enormous wealth and countless jobs—began to develop into a booming business. Mythic land of sunshine, opportunity, and glamour, Los Angeles beckoned to those who wanted to create a new life and enter a transient society in which one's past was left behind. For Maimie and Ira, such an adventure must have seemed extremely appealing.

One strange series of events that unfolded in Southern California in the 1920s would oddly intersect with Maimie Pinzer's life. The subject of the controversy was Aimee Semple McPherson, the fiery radio evangelist who had embarked in 1917 upon a religious and divine healing career that quickly brought her international fame. In 1923, McPherson settled in Los Angeles and built the five-thousand-seat Angelus Temple. A master at combining traditional religion with the techniques of vaudeville and the theater, McPherson used costumes, scenery, props (including live animals), huge choirs, and an orchestra to turn her sermons into major spectacles.

McPherson's message found a ready audience among the many transient newcomers in Los Angeles. She became so popular that the city routinely dispatched special trolleys and extra police on the evenings she preached. (By her death in 1944, her Foursquare Gospel Church had grown to four hundred congregations and boasted a worldwide membership of twenty-two thousand.)

About six months before Maimie and her family arrived in Southern California in late 1927, McPherson became embroiled in an international scandal, widely publicized by a media circus that daily reported anything she said or did. Rumors began to circulate that the religious leader was having a love affair with a married man—Kenneth Ormiston, a technician hired to manage her religious radio station. On at least one occasion, McPherson and Ormiston chatted and flirted while talking over an intercom, without realizing that the congregation could hear their banter; some members became angry at his less-than-reverential attitude toward the service in particular, and her religion in general.

On May 18, 1926, Aimee Semple McPherson suddenly

431

disappeared while swimming in the ocean and was assumed to have drowned. Twenty-five thousand people congregated near the beach on Memorial Day as police formulated contingency plans in case her body were discovered. Meanwhile, Ormiston had also disappeared. Reporters from the *Los Angeles Times* told the district attorney that they believed McPherson was hiding out with her lover. Then, on June 19, a letter from the so-called Avengers arrived in Los Angeles, demanding $500,000 ransom for McPherson. On June 23, McPherson surfaced in northern Mexico, claiming that she had been kidnapped and held captive in a shack, and had escaped.

To this day, no one is quite sure what actually happened. The public, however, along with some members of her congregation, became deeply suspicious. Doubts arose about the plausibility of her story. The district attorney decided to file charges against her for perjury, but then dismissed all accusations when a witness changed his story. Rumors flew, and some of her detractors believed that Aimee Semple McPherson had not only bribed the judge, but the D.A. and the witness as well.[12]

With charges dropped, Aimee Semple McPherson embarked on what she called a major "vindication tour" in January 1927. Since no written evidence proved that she had lied about being kidnapped or having an affair, she was determined to repair her reputation and regain the loyalty of her faithful following. About six months after McPherson began this "vindication tour," Maimie Pinzer somehow rented a "mansion" (her cousin's word) in Hollywood from the famous evangelist. When McPherson embarked on the tour, she took her daughter with her and sent her son to stay on a farm in northern California. Both of McPherson's children were therefore out of southern California when Maimie arrived in Los Angeles, and neither of them remembers meeting Maimie Pinzer, whose eye patch might have made an impression on young children. Both of them, however, recall that a constant stream of strangers passed through their home. Roberta Salter, McPherson's daughter, recalls that her mother frequently rented other houses, for herself, as well as for others.[13]

Whatever the case, in late 1927 or early 1928, the Benjamin family apparently settled into a home that Aimee Semple McPherson had once occupied.[14] According to Maimie's cousin,

432

"we never met Aimee Semple McPherson, but Maimie and Ira rented her beautiful house on Foot Hill Drive, Hollywood." A narrow street without sidewalks, Foot Hill Drive sits at the foot of the wealthy Hollywood Hills. In the 1920s, it did not have mansions, but rather single-story craftsman-style bungalows, vintage stucco cottages, and some large two-story homes. Some of the houses, however, sat high on the uphill side of the street, offering views of the valley below. To Maimie's cousin, such a home, surrounded by palm trees, may well have seemed a "mansion."[15]

While there, Maimie and her cousin made a surprising discovery: They found letters that Aimee Semple McPherson had written, apparently to a "boyfriend." In the most casual manner (so casual, in fact, that it has the unmistakable ring of truth), Maimie's cousin wrote me that she "and May discovered Aimee's letters to her boyfriend. What May did about them I do not know." The letters, she wrote, were discovered in Aimee Semple McPherson's "former bedroom."[16] Since McPherson mainly lived in the parsonage of the Foursquare Gospel Church, I can only speculate that this was one of the houses she rented to escape reporters, or perhaps for romantic retreats.

Did Maimie find love letters to Ormiston—the written evidence that journalists and scholars have sought ever since 1926? I can't be sure. Since her cousin did describe the recipient as a boyfriend, the letters probably contained some kind of incriminating evidence. But as a former prostitute, Maimie would not have judged McPherson for having had a lover. Maimie always held rather cynical views about sexual respectability. Moreover, as her letters reveal, Maimie always rushed to protect, rather than tarnish, another person's reputation. So it is not surprising that the content of these found letters never reached the public.

In California, again, Maimie's cousin had no idea what Ira did for a living, if anything, but money never seemed to be a problem, nor was it ever discussed in her presence. "I traveled a great deal while in California, and only saw splendor and exciting people visiting her whenever I was around."[17] While at Aimee Semple McPherson's "mansion," moreover, Maimie apparently developed an entirely new network of friends and acquaintances connected to the film industry. Her cousin remembers quite a number of extravagant parties that Maimie threw for her family members, as well as for her new friends. "I recall a birthday party May gave

433

for me, and she had these new friends who were mostly of the moving picture industry there. May was truly one of the most charming and exciting women I had ever met and was truly brilliant and well organized."[18]

Maimie's cousin stayed in California for two years and then returned to Philadelphia. She next encountered Maimie and Ira when they returned to Philadelphia from California. What year that was, she could not remember. Busy with her own children and her own career as the owner of a fashionable women's clothing shop, Maimie's cousin lost all contact with Maimie and her family. But she said of Maimie, "I always felt that she would be successful in anything she would tackle and especially in the writing field."

Another tantalizing clue. Perhaps her cousin knew that Maimie had published short stories in the twenties and therefore expected that Maimie would have continued writing during the thirties. Again, no evidence substantiates the existence of any stories published under her actual surnames.

The last years of Maimie's life are particularly shrouded in mystery. Her adopted children apparently lived with her for nearly ten years. Maimie reportedly died at age fifty-five in 1940 in Germantown, Pennsylvania.[19] Her husband survived her for another five years. According to her sister-in-law, Maimie "died a pauper."[20] Since the Great Depression had not yet ended, this is not entirely surprising. However Maimie and Ira had survived during the 1920s, they, like so many millions, may have found themselves unemployed and newly impoverished. Neither I nor the attorneys engaged by the Schlesinger Library, however, have ever been able to locate a death certificate. Since we have no evidence that she remarried, it remains puzzling that no one can find a death certificate under any of her known surnames.

Another great mystery is what her children know, if they can be found. Both of her adopted children survived into adulthood. Her son became a successful sales representative for a clothing manufacturer and her daughter married and lived in Philadelphia. As of 1978, both were alive but could not be tracked down by any relative, lawyer or myself.[21]

What Maimie did in Germantown when the family returned to Philadelphia is not known. By returning to Philadelphia, however, Maimie had returned to her roots and the ghosts from her troubled past. There she had other relatives, including friends

434

from her youth. There, too, she returned to the greatest secret of her life—the fact that she had been a victim of incest during her girlhood.

Maimie did in fact reveal this terrible secret to Fanny Quincy Howe. In one of her letters Maimie described how at age thirteen, her mother and her uncle had brought her to court and had her declared an incorrigible child and sent to a girls reformatory and then to a Magdalen Home for Wayward Girls. With justifiable bitterness, Maimie wrote that this uncle "was the same one who did me the first wrong when I was a tiny girl and any number of times since then."

In the mid-1970s, when I first found and edited these letters, most Americans had not fully grasped the extent or the consequences of incest. As a result, I believed what I read about the uncle, but did not adequately comment on its significance. I also assumed that few scholars or readers would agree with my interpretation. Incest in a Jewish home? An uncle who molested Maimie? In a note, I wrote, "One can assume from this statement that Maimie was in some way sexually assaulted by this uncle." I believed Maimie, but did not yet know how to discuss this carefully hidden secret.[22]

This is a superb example of how revelations excavated by feminist activists have educated scholars to the hidden injuries women have suffered in the past. In 1976, when I wrote my introduction, few of us knew how many women had experienced incest, and few of us thought about how deeply damaging such an experience could be. Today, Maimie's words practically leap off the page. Of course she was molested. Of course this uncle repeatedly abused her. Now, after years of open discussion by feminists, it is perfectly clear.

The sexual abuse Maimie suffered, moreover, helps explain much of her troubled adolescence, as well as her relationship with her family. Scholars of prostitution, for example, know that girls who have been sexually abused frequently regard themselves with shame. In their own eyes they are already ruined and tainted, and sometimes begin to act the whore they believe themselves to be. Many teenage runaways who became prostitutes during the 1960s and 1970s, for instance, had run away from incest or sexually abusive relationships in the home.[23]

Viewed from this perspective, Maimie's personality and life

take on new meaning. Maimie frequently wavered between self-hatred and self-acceptance. On the one hand, Maimie blamed herself for these early sexual assaults. She became sexually promiscuous and gradually slid into working as a prostitute. She felt socially unacceptable.

Yet at times Maimie also realized that she was the victim of her uncle's abuse. Then she would fight for respectability and especially for forgiveness. This, unfortunately, her mother would not confer upon her. Maimie's antagonistic relationship with her mother, whom she constantly described as hollow and unforgiving, is now more understandable. Like many victims of incest, Maimie must have raged against her mother for failing to protect her from her uncle. To add to the initial injury, her mother then assigned Maimie the permanent status of moral misfit within the family.

What is most astonishing is that Maimie actually told Fanny Howe this dark secret from her past. Perhaps Fanny Howe also did not grasp the significance of Maimie's words. In any case, Maimie raised the subject just once; she never discussed it in her letters again. (Whether she told her cousin, her sister-in-law, or her husband, we do not know.)

Part of searching for Maimie, then, has meant not only discovering information about her later years, but also reinterpreting her life. I consider it a privilege to have known Maimie so long and so well. She was a remarkable individual, a talented, brilliant, and sensitive woman. After two decades, I still consider her one of the most fascinating individuals who have accompanied me on my journey through life.

My search for Maimie never ends.

Ruth Rosen
Berkeley, California
October, 1996

1. Letter from Maimie's cousin to Patricia King, Schlesinger Library, June 21, 1978. In deference to the wishes of Maimie's family, expressed upon the book's original publication, names of family members have been omitted from this afterword.

2. Letter from Maimie's cousin to Ruth Rosen, October 8, 1978.

3. Letter (dictated) from Maimie's sister-in-law to Patricia King, Schlesinger Library, July 18, 1978.

4. A letter from Maimie's sister-in-law to Patricia King, Schlesinger Library, July 18, 1978, mentions that Maimie was writing for magazines. In her letter to me dated October 11, 1978, Maimie's sister-in-law says that Maimie wrote for the *Reader's Digest*. However, I have examined guides to periodical literature, as well as all the years of the *Reader's Digest* from 1922 to 1940, but I have found no entry under anyone with the first name Maimie, and none under her original or married surnames. I thank my research assistant Cliff Hawkins for helping me with this arduous search, which included a page-by-page search of all issues of the *Reader's Digest* and the *Literary Digest*, as well as all guides to periodical literature. Both of us spent untold hours hoping we might turn up the "smoking story," but alas, our work has only created another agenda for scholars who are inspired by Maimie's probable literary publications.

5. Letter from Maimie's sister-in-law to Rosen, October 11, 1978.

6. For a general overview of American women in the 1920s, see Dorothy Brown, *Setting a Course* (Boston: Twayne, 1987).

7. Letter from Maimie's sister-in-law to Rosen, October 11, 1978.

8. *Ibid.*

9. Regrettably, the informants I questioned in the late 1970s had already died before the decision was made to reprint *The Maimie Papers*, with this new afterword, in 1996. In the late 1970s I asked all kinds of questions of her relatives, but none of them was clear about her motives. None knew about her former life until the book was published. They simply told me what they were certain they *did* know. In all cases, I have been as conservative as possible in retelling what facts appear to be true or plausible.

10. Letter from Maimie's cousin to Rosen, October 8, 1978.

11. Mike Davis, *City of Quartz: Excavating the Future in Los Angeles* (New York: Vintage, 1992), p. 118. Davis's work is one of the best critical studies of the development of Los Angeles culture and society.

12. The story of Aimee Semple McPherson's religious charisma, and her disappearance, is best told by Edith Blumhofer, *Aimee Semple McPherson: Everybody's Sister* (Grand Rapids, Michigan: William Eerdman, 1993). I am also grateful to Edith Blumhofer for providing me with information that allowed me to contact the children of Aimee Semple McPherson, and for discussing which scenarios seemed plausible to her.

Other biographies I used in summarizing the career of McPherson include: Lately Thomas, pseud. Robert Steele, *Storming Heaven,* (New York: William Morrow, 1970); Daniel Mark Epstein, *Sister Aimee: The Life of Aimee Semple McPherson,* (New York: Harcourt Brace Jovanovich, 1993); and Lately Thomas, *The Vanishing Evangelist: The Aimee Semple McPherson Kidnapping Affair,* (New York: Viking, 1959).

13. Telephone interviews with Roberta Salter in New York and Rolf McPherson in Los Angeles, February 29, 1996. I want to thank Roberta Salter for her patience and good humor in answering my endless questions.

14. In numerous conversations with the archivist of the Aimee Semple McPherson collection, I have tried to figure out how Maimie came to rent a home from Aimee Semple McPherson. The cousin turned out to be right about the address. Foothill Drive is a small street in an exclusive area of Hollywood, with large homes that can certainly be characterized by a young Jewish woman as mansion. This is an expensive and lovely area of the Hollywood Hills. It does not appear that the church owned the property or that Aimee Semple McPherson did either. The most likely explanation is that someone attached to the church had rented it to Aimee Semple McPherson at one time, perhaps so that she could avoid the media circus, and that someone connected with the church rented it to Maimie and her family. There is no record that either Maimie, her husband or her cousin were members of the congregation or adherents of the church. I want to thank Lida Mae Stuart, archivist of the Foursquare Gospel Heritage Center, for helping me with all the daily inquiries that I made, even after I promised I had asked the last question.

15. I thank Lil Taiz, a former student and now a professor of history at California State University at Los Angeles, for researching how the neighborhood looked during the 1920s.

16. Letter from Maimie's cousin to Rosen, October 8, 1978.

17. Letter from Maimie's cousin to King, June 21, 1978.

18. *Ibid.*

19. The date of Maimie's death was part of the information given to the Schlesinger Library when the papers were donated and lawyers contacted relatives who had known Maimie of her family.

20. Letter from Maimie's sister-in-law to Rosen, October 11, 1978. By this time Maimie's sister-in-law was too ill to talk to me and needed to dictate her letter. She was unavailable for follow-up questions.

21. With great frustration, I have tried to find the children of Maimie's brother, who lived with her and Ira for over ten years. I tried writing and calling every address and phone number anyone had for them, and even tried calling everyone with their actual last names. Patricia King had already scoured the country for clues, as had attorneys for the Schlesinger Library. But all leads proved unsuccessful. In 1996, I again tried finding

the adopted children, but again could find no leads. None of Maimie's relatives knew where they were, even in 1978. Information on the children comes from Memo from Patricia King to Raya Dreban, attorney, May 1978. If these children are still alive, they would be able to fill in the many gaps and answer the many questions that I and readers will always have about the life of Maimie Pinzer.

22. Many colleagues, scholars, and editors, including those engaged in this project at the Schlesinger Library and The Feminist Press, also read my introduction and similarly failed to see the importance of this secret in Maimie's life.

23. See Ronald Simmonds and Leg Whitbeck, "Sexual abuse as a precursor to prostitution and victimization among adolescents and adult homeless women," *Journal of Family Issues* 12:3 (September 1991): pp. 361–80. Also see California Senate, Select Committee on Children and Youth, *Runaway youth and resulting prostitution and drugs,* senate hearing, Sacramento, CA, April 13, 1994.

LITERARY AFTERWORD
Document, History, Art[1]

When *The Maimie Papers* appeared in England, Doris Lessing issued the following statement: "To be a woman, poor, and alone, in America during the early part of this century was not easy. To survive at all was difficult. Maimie survived—and more, helped others. She was remarkable. She was admirable. But above all, she was lovable. You think how much you would have liked her vitality. I really do recommend the book."[2] Lessing's comment is useful as a beginning: I want to talk about Maimie as woman and as survivor. I find her consciousness "remarkable" and if not always "admirable," then, in the main, "lovable." I would have liked her as a friend, mainly because of her fidelity, her honesty. I feel, perhaps as Lessing herself does, an affinity to this woman and to her book; I have had the same feeling only about Agnes Smedley's *Daughter of Earth*—that I know these experiences as though they were my own; that I recognize sentences as though I had thought them.

I say this not only because I think a critic needs to clarify, even at the start, her biases, whether they are preferences or objections. I say this also because I should like to explain why I think this book is a "literary" work, why Lessing "recommend[s]" it, though she does not catalogue it as document, history, letters, autobiography, or epistolary novel.

I am also sensitive to questions about the making of this book, and I will begin there. But I want to use the occasion as an exercise in literary definition: what makes *The Maimie Papers*, in literary terms, "more than" document or social history—a work of art? I will anticipate my point a bit by noting that at least one of

441

Maimie's important qualities as a writer was her ability to be a reliable social consciousness or, in other words, social historian. To put it another way, and I will return to this later, the writer of fiction who is not adequate to the social history of the period portrayed in the fiction (or in the autobiography or biography, for that matter) cannot write "good" literature. What is wrong with *The Blithedale Romance* or *The Bostonians*, or for that matter, with *The Great Gatsby* and with *A Farewell to Arms* has to do not with linguistic, metaphoric, or narrative skills of the various writers of these books, but with their inadequate grasp of social conditions in their own time—with the limitation of their narrow male perspectives that, as it twisted their values, similarly affected the form and themes of their fiction. To put it simply, if, as we say, literature "reflects" life, then it reflects the values and consciousness of the writer as much as anything else. Those values are decisive as they judge characters, decide their course of action, control their fate. Those values are rooted in a writer's perception of such matters as gender, race, class, religion: who people are and what in the society they may or may not do and think. When one constructs a narrative, consciously or unconsciously, one also makes decisions about characters who live in a world ordered by social class, by race, by gender, by sexual preference. The writer's values control the vision of reality; those values can be judged reliable or not, "true" or "untrue," in an historical context. In other words, this kind of criticism is, like other criticism, judgmental, not relativist.

For example, to keep creating "bitches" rather than women in novels is not only not excusable; in fact—and it is possible to demonstrate this, as Judith Fetterley has with regard to Hemingway's *A Farewell to Arms*[3]—such limited visions cannot create great novels: they do not reflect living characters in their richness and complexity, but rather shadows we do not recognize as people. (The "we" in this sentence includes all who understand that women are never merely "bitches.")

I say this still as preface to Maimie because in this book we have a very special instance of the connections between literature and life. Obviously, Maimie's letters were written very close to the scene, even occasionally to the very moment of an event (as with the pain over the final quarrel with her mother in Montreal); sometimes they have the quality of a tape recording—which is, of course, one quality of the best fiction or autobiography. On the other hand, since the volume stubbornly continues to be letters, and not fiction or autobiography, we are forced to deal with them as such. What happens if we look at them as letters? Like found volumes of diaries, these three boxes of letters were human remains of a person's life.

In 1974, Ellen DuBois showed me copies of several letters by Maimie that Ruth Rosen had shown her. I went to Boston that fall and sat in the Schlesinger Library on the History of Women in America, at Radcliffe College, for two or three days entranced, reading the letters, moved by them on occasion, mainly marvelling. I talked about them with Patricia King, then director of the Schlesinger, who had read all of them, and who was worried about the fact that more and more people were coming in to use them, and that the pages were crumbling into shreds. She was so worried, she said, that she was considering copying the lot and having people read only the copies, though there were problems because of the handwriting and the color of the paper.

I could not read all the letters, but I read enough to know that Maimie was an extraordinary writer of very long letters, that she made what I call "stories" in her letters, and to guess that the letters could be placed in chronological order (many of them were not dated and though their envelopes had been, handling had dislocated them). I guessed too that, placed in order, the letters might provide a whole narrative, not only of the years covered by the writing, but also of the years before. I had read at least one letter with an interpolated story of Maimie's early life in it. And Patricia King and I dreamed about providing the autobiography Maimie did/didn't write.

When Ellen DuBois had given me some of the letters, she had said that they were very significant historical documents. After my first reading, I said that they were also significant literary documents. I was interested in them because Maimie seemed to me a writer, perhaps a lost Agnes Smedley or Tillie Olsen. Reading in the Schlesinger verified that for me, and Patricia King and I wrote a grant proposal to the National Endowment for the Humanities claiming the potential value of Maimie as historical document and literary art. I mention this fact not because NEH won't give funds for the editing of historical documents, but to make clear that from the beginning

Maimie was, at least in my head and Patricia King's, a writer of literature.

It was Patricia King's responsibility, as holder of the manuscript, to produce an accurate typescript for editing and publication. Once we got the grant, she hired people to type the letters and supervised their work. I should say at once that this was not as simple as it seemed, since the names had to be changed throughout the 140 letters because of the terms of Helen Howe's will, and since there was always the question of the handwriting, as well as of the accuracy of the typing.

It was my responsibility, as publisher, to choose the persons who would turn the letters into a book. With Ellen DuBois's help, I chose Ruth Rosen to serve as historical editor and to write the historical introduction. She was a notable expert on the history of prostitution. As textual editor and in-house Feminist Press copyeditor, I chose Sue Davidson. I want to say something here about my choice of Sue Davidson, since I am interested in writing about Maimie as a literary work. Sue Davidson had joined the staff of the Press in 1974. She had been a writer for most of her life, and I believed that it would take a writer to produce the best text we could have. As I look back now, I know that that was one of the two most significant decisions made about *The Maimie Papers.* The other was that we cut sufficiently to produce a single volume at a price that might make Maimie accessible to many readers.

We had two other options, of course. We could have published a two-volume inclusive text that would have sold only to libraries. We could have attempted a briefer—say, two hundred-page—text that was closer to a "selection" than the volume we produced. We never discussed the second option seriously, and Patricia King and I were committed to making Maimie accessible to a wide reading public. The four of us, Davidson, King, Rosen, and I met once in Cambridge in 1975 to discuss the terms of the volume and of the contract that The Feminist Press was by then formulating with the Schlesinger. We actually changed some names, leaving others to be dealt with later by Sue Davidson alone. We outlined what we needed by way of historical introduction. Most important for this discussion, we decided on some general principles for the textual cutting and for reproducing the text. Most of these are described in Sue Davidson's Textual Note. She says, for example, that she cut both whole letters and parts of letters. She also says that she dated the lot before beginning and then realized that they did make a whole narrative, and thus it is quite understandable that she cut so as to avoid having to describe to the reader "what happens." But she does not describe the time it took to do the work or the torment: when so much is fine writing, when so many details are interesting, how do you choose? She had several guidelines from me: to maintain the coherent narrative thread without distorting Maimie's life or character, without losing lively scenes and engaging characters, and without losing important historical information. As if that were not enough, I instructed her to retain the quality of "artlessness," which sometimes meant repetition. We did not want only the purple passages, only the lively incidents, only the big scenes.

I want to conclude this section with the observation that at least one factor essential to being able to accomplish the goals we set for the volume was the generous size we proposed for it. We cut only 30 percent. I wonder whether we could have cut more and retained the quality we have, and I mean literary quality at this moment. I have heard some people say it is too long for use in the classroom; it takes too long for students to read. It takes a long time for faculty to read. Well, what does that tell us? Among other things, that it needs to be valued and read as literature—one can hardly read *Moby Dick* in an evening. One cannot read *Sister Carrie* in an evening, and yet I have given my students that bulky novel. If we are reading this volume as historical document, I suspect that we want its essence more quickly than it is ready to give it to us. If we are reading it as "literature," for which we customarily have patience, it is our problem that we can't think of it as a literary work worth the time it takes to get through it. Of course I should add that not only is the number of words at issue. Also at issue is what I shall call density, not only of description, detail, event, scene, person, but also of analysis and development: development of action and plot, characterization, and social analysis. I would argue that this book has many virtues that we do not expect to find in a collection of letters. I am going to treat the volume now as a whole, a piece of literature made up of a series of letters, without labelling the volume as fiction or autobiography—or anything else.

I said at the beginning that the work is art and artlessness at the same moment, that the letters bring together (in every sentence and in the work as a whole) the connection implicit in the best writing: between literature and life. I think this comes from a number of sources, including one that is central. The source is language, a huge outpouring between two literate persons—though we have only one of those streams, and I am guessing it is the superior one aesthetically. We always know that Maimie is writing real letters to a real person, and so we may feel close to that scene constantly. If we are asked for a "suspension of disbelief," it is of a somewhat different order from that asked of us by premeditated art. What helps is that the single major theme of the first hundred pages, and one that runs as a rich thread through the rest of the work, is honesty, the ability, even the need, to tell the truth about one's life, one's history, in order to be a person, to feel self-respect, to plan for a future, to help others in need. In order to do this, even beyond the motivation and the need—the will to live rather than to subsist or die—Maimie had to train herself to see honestly and to report what she saw, with patient attention to detail, shadings of feeling, and eventually careful social analysis as well.

She gives us a clue to her very early ability to learn from observation when, late in the letters, she describes how early in life she learned middle-class table manners from watching people in restaurants breaking bread rather than biting it (277). It is important to note, of course, that her "honesty" as a reporter of her own feelings and values also allows us to judge her class biases: she labels the man who bites bread "plebeian" and unworthy of her attention; she learns about breaking bread from observing those whose "appearance stamped them as of 'nice' people." There are numerous instances of Maimie's errors as she judges from such surfaces, and sounds like a snob. On the other hand, there are as many examples to be found of her revisions of such views, or of her additional discovery that those with "nice" manners are often without any other redeeming social values. And on many occasions, Maimie can see instantly beyond the surface, as in her meeting the Italian soldiers, and her sympathetic recognition of them as having "the weight of years of toil on their bodies and faces." (305)

I am trying to suggest how Maimie, as a writer, deals with the

446

theme of honesty which is central to her work and integral to her style. She offers us versions of reality, visions and revisions. She is not afraid to revise herself from letter to letter, year to year. In fact, she is not doing that as consciously as my words would make out; she is writing—and living—her way through the years. The letters record, and help to achieve, growth and development.

But the honesty is a literary method too. She keeps saying that she wants at least one person to know the truth: she is tired of pretending, she is wearied by the effort of having to be so many other selves that she does not know who she is. To be honest she has to explain in detail, she has to find the right words, she has to describe the person, the incident, her feelings. Honesty is here a literary method that Maimie shares with many diarists and letter-writers: the lists of groceries and their costs; the doling out of pennies for survival; the endless string of rent checks and pawnshops, descriptions of made-over dresses and retrimmed hats, the dailiness of women's lives. Maimie has to distinguish between reality and desire, she has to sum up, and always she has to ask to be judged by her one-person audience. Did I do the right thing? Was I honest enough? Can you bear my honesty in these letters even when I am reporting bad news about myself? Can you love me when I am disgusting?—disgusting even to myself?

The urgency about honesty—to describe and define who she is as a social creature—makes the volume a revelation about social class in the United States during the early years of the century. Because Maimie is so interested in social distinctions to the point of survival, and because she is writing to someone she regards as having real "class," we can get a grasp of the class-consciousness of a second-generation Jewish immigrant whose life, even by age twenty-five, had already spanned a large range, from the middle to the bottom.

The question of class for Maimie, related to her rage for social identity, is ultimately tied to her gender and of course to the question of education and work for women. She is her father's daughter, one could say. And yet, in a family of three brothers and two sisters, the three brothers are "successful," the two sisters, before they are fifteen, are both institutionalized, and in fact they remain, in Maimie's words, "outsiders" to their own family. The honesty with which Maimie pursues the question of social class, judging

447

herself and each person on a very complex ladder that includes holding a tea cup, literacy and literary taste, work, caring for others, and genuine unselfishness, she applies to women.

With regard to feminist consciousness, the honesty operates through trial and error: she knows, for example, that admitting to having been a prostitute will not get her a job; but she has to learn, through filling out an application, that admitting to being properly married will not gain her employment either. She understands, and interestingly does not dwell on directly, the double standard that condemns prostitutes and not their clients; indeed, that allows her brothers, who have undoubtedly hired prostitutes and who have been most ungenerous to her, to condemn her without redemption for having "fallen." I should like to mention the domestic feminism implicit in her view of herself as a civilizer and educator of the untutored working-class man.

The ultimate backbone of dwelling on honesty rests in Maimie's need to define herself in relation to other people and to useful work. We all need love or friendship (I am not talking particularly about sexuality, though that may be included in the definition); we all need useful work, not only because we need to eat and because our society is organized so that eating is dependent on money, but also because work provides identity, a sense of purpose, a reason for being, that humans also need.

Ultimately, the focus of Maimie's search for truth about herself has a purpose. Like most people, she wants to figure out what to do with her life. As a person caught in a sexist, class-biased world, and one who has fallen to its bottom rung, she has to understand it to climb out. Thus, gender and social class intersect as Maimie tries to learn about the world of work. Hence, her detailed portraits of work are very significant as social history, since she is a participant from the usually silent majority. And we hear first hand how it is to work as a prostitute, to live "in sin" with a single man, or to go out for one-night stands with occasional men; how it is to be an exploited clerical worker, a businesswoman, an entrepreneur, and a social work pioneer far ahead of her time.

The literary value of such portraits comes not only from Maimie's ability to describe; what I have been calling "honesty" might also be called veracity of telling—fidelity to the event, the scene, the detail, the speech pattern. It also comes out of what I have called a "reliable" consciousness: the consciousness that can analyze and make connections. For example: Maimie knows that marriage is a form and a formula; without love, caring, and respect, it is nothing more than legalized prostitution. Or she knows that she is in what we would call a catch twenty-two: with her eye patch, she cannot get the kind of work she is fit to do, even after getting the stenographic training that supposedly would allow her to do work "behind the scenes," rather than in a shop where appearance allegedly matters more. One could elaborate further, especially with reference to her understanding of the difference between the social workers who sent her to prostitution and the kind of social worker she proposes to be.

I have left for last the question of love, friendship, family, and of human relationships more generally, including sexuality. Not because it is of least importance, but because it is, like the questions of honesty, identity, and work, fused within the work. And like them, but perhaps more than any of them, it is fused with the form—the letters themselves. Maimie writes the letters out of a real need, a need that I defined as I wrote the word "therapeutic" again and again in the margins of the first hundred pages of the volume. The need is urgent for Maimie to find a human being who cares for her and for whom she can care: the mutuality is very important here, at least to begin with. She has already found such a person, before the letters begin, in Herbert Welsh. But he is a social worker of that Christian school that Maimie can deal with only hypocritically; he is also a man. He may have known, as Maimie knows certainly, that she needs a woman to love her and whom she can love. She knows that women for their own health need to be woman-centered, whatever their sexual preference. It is unhealthy for women to feel unloved by a woman (or women); it is unhealthy for women not to love women. Early in the letters, Maimie says again and again that she cannot trust women, has not been able to love women, and of course we know about her eleven-year alienation from her mother. Yet she is fiercely loyal to and caring of her sick sister, her sister-in-law, and such other women in need, including Mrs. Garrick, the old lady mistreated by her actor son. But the love she wants—and I am reminded of Agnes Smedley[4] here—insists upon the kind of understanding that includes forgiveness of all that may be disgusting or disquieting.

She wants a mother's love, and she finds it when she is twenty-five in the forty-year-old mother Fanny Quincy Howe.

In the early pages of the letters, in 1910 and 1911, and even into 1912, Maimie is centered on her own need for understanding and hence love from Fanny. She talks about wanting to know about Fanny in more detail so that, presumably, she can love her—love being connected to understanding. I don't think that Maimie can "love" Fanny: this, indeed, is a literary relationship. It is not surprising to me that the tone of Maimie's letters alters as she approaches the close of the decade and gains her independence (both financial and moral) from Fanny. But before that happens, however, in the center of the volume we can find the climax of these letters: the place in which two kinds of female relationships are counterpoised to Maimie's relation to Fanny and to each other; those between Maimie and her mother; and those between Maimie and the "girls" she begins to befriend, especially Stella. Letter 93, March, 1915, written five years after the start of the correspondence, begins "My mother is here" (p. 247ff). This letter and several subsequent ones return us dramatically to the earliest and most profound theme of the letters—to honesty, sincerity, truth-telling—and to Maimie's need to understand why her family has cast her out, why she has become the "outsider," why they don't love her, why she doesn't love them, and how to live without that love. Interestingly, it is not at the end, but a little past the middle of this decade of letter writing that the climax occurs, since the bulk of the letters were written between 1910 and 1918.

The only point I will take the time to make is that here Maimie is different: I think it would be possible to demonstrate that she writes better (that's another way of approaching the same problem I have approached here: as a group of letters written over a decade, it might be possible to look for evidence of "literary" growth, if one defined what that meant precisely) in the second half of these letters. But I am more interested in the growth of her consciousness, in her cumulative ability to analyze, and, further, to act on that analysis. Maimie could not have rescued girls in Philadelphia in 1910 through 1912, not only because of her own status in Philadelphia. Only in Canada does she feel "free." She means "free" of stigma, since she has not been a prostitute but rather a successful businesswoman in Canada. She could not have rescued "girls" in Philadelphia because, as we learn through the pages of the early letters, she despised and looked down upon them even as she despised herself. She could not even have dealt with her mother; there, indeed, in the one recorded early meeting, she makes public mockery of her mother at a family funeral. In these later letters, she may never come to understand her mother, or to love her, but she comes to understand some of the social dimensions of the questions she asks about her and about her own family. She also learns to teach her mother something about herself; that she has no money or source of income from "men," and that rescuing "girls" is useful work.

Indeed, and here Maimie's work—which is, finally, loving and rescuing girls—is useful not only to the "girls" being rescued; it is also useful to Maimie's need to love and be loved by women; it is also essential to the conclusion of this volume of letters. For I don't believe that the letters cease because Maimie gets married, and because her husband thereafter becomes the emotional center of her life, rather than Fanny Quincy Howe. After all, Ira, even as "husband," is hardly new to her life or to the letters. We will probably never know, of course, unless we find more letters, but I prefer to think that Maimie's correspondence with dozens of other Stellas—or Maimies—replaced the correspondence with Fanny. I cannot believe that Maimie stopped writing. She has all the earmarks of the "addict" to the word, the scene, the character, the idea.

Many of us dream of finding more literature by Maimie, of filling in the details of her later life from the clues discovered by Ruth Rosen and Patricia King, of bringing to her life story some sense of closure. Yet, the volume of letters offers the closure of art: the open ending. The narrative, the development of what I have called a reliable consciousness, of what may be called a character that has depth and that grows in understanding, and the ability to analyze herself and the world around her, has had the space—and the detail—in which to become literature. As literature, the book can be closed.

Florence Howe
New York, New York
October, 1996

1. This essay was written as a lecture for a Modern Language Association three-week seminar held in the summer of 1978 on the campus of the University of Alabama. The lecture reported also on Pat King's early search for Maimie's later life, omitted here. I am grateful to the participants—among them Nancy Porter—for swift and interesting responses to the lecture. I am grateful to Susan Cozzi and Susannah Driver for urging me to allow the publication of this essay now, and to both of them for editorial advice. The errors that remain are my own.

2. From the blurb Doris Lessing provided Virago on the occasion of their publishing an edition of *The Maimie Papers* in 1978.

3. Judith Fetterley, *The Resisting Reader: A Feminist Approach to American Fiction* (Bloomington: Indiana University Press, 1978).

4. See *Daughter of Earth* (New York: The Feminist Press, 1973).

INDEX

Bureau and, 233, 234, 238; cigar store for the Arons family and, 157-58; closing of mission, 408-10; decision not to return to, Maimie's, 101; divorce, Maimie's, 308-9; financial assistance from, 127, 132, 135, 143, 146, 332, 404-5; incentive provided by Maimie, 79-81; invalid, Maimie treated as, 390; Italian reservists and, 305-7; letter to Maimie, 366; mail-order business of, 238, 239; as Maimie's "beau," 273, 274; marriage to, 386, 387; marriage to, possibility of, 113, 242, 308-10, 319, 340; Mary Antin, visit to, 159-67; mission and, 382, 404-5, 408-10; Montreal, possibility of going to, 186; possibility of Maimie's returning to live with, 295-96; registration papers, problems with, 414; relationship with Maimie in Montreal, 238-39, 244; Stella Phillips and, 279-81; 286-87, 300; summer house, 392-97; venereal disease contracted by, 286-88, 291-92

Benjamin, Elaine, 309
Benjamin, Libbie, 396, 405
Benjamin, Lina, 78
Benjamin, Roseanne, 396, 404
Benjamin, Sonya, 396, 404
Bernhardt, Sarah, 58
Berthe C. (girl in mission), 364
Birthday, Maimie's, 148-49, 401
Birthday party, 402-3
Blemmer, Carl, 87
Blockley Hospital (Philadelphia Hospital), 280, 282, 290, 301
Boat accident, 127-28
Books and reading, 22, 85-87, 94, 95, 168, 171, 187, 190, 196, 198, 358, 391; in childhood, 192, 369; in mission, 317, 337, 339, 343, 353, 357-59; See also Poet-

ry; and specific books and magazines

Borrowing money, 14, 16, 29, 31-32, 39, 47-48, 96, 136, 256; advance from employer, 139; for Business Aid Bureau relocation, 226, 231; for cigar store for Arons family, 157-58; for the Goldstein's store, 203-6; from Mrs. Howe, 133-134, 143, 203-6, 226, 231; from moneylender, 140, 144-45; for mother's Atlantic City stay, 139-40; See also Pawning of personal property

Bosses and managers, relationships with, 150-54; credit for form letters taken by manager, 129-30, 150, 152; discrepancy in Mr. Kaufmann's books, 212-14; See also Sexual advances and assaults

Boston, possibility of going to, 75, 77
Brook, Donald, 302-3
Brothels ("public places"), xxv-xxvi, 77, 263
Brown, Nina, 184-88, 190, 197-98, 200, 203, 210, 212, 234, 239-40
Brown, Wistar, III (attorney), 242, 304, 339, 351, 378, 382
Brownie (dog), 115-20
Burial of Caroline Pinzer, 412-13
Burns on arms, 388-91
Business Aid Bureau (B.A.B.), xxx, 216-38; closing of, 243-44; equipment for, 218-19; forced to relocate, 219-23, 229; Ira Benjamin and, 233, 234, 238; McKim Agency and, 236, 237; Multigraph Sales Company and, 217, 222-26; multigraphing letters, 217, 218, 228-30, 237; sex discrimination against women in business, 219
Business school, 109-10; See also Secretarial school

Jones, Albert (husband), xxii, 10, 11, 31, 36, 79, 391; deceives Maimie regarding money, 48, 54; divorce from, 242-43, 304, 308-9, 326, 351, 376, 378, 379, 382; jobs held by, 15-16, 20, 23, 38-39, 51, 92-94, 108; ordered out by Maimie, 51, 54-55, 56, 59; marriage to, reasons for, xxvi-xxvii, 10, 51-52; mother-child relationship between Maimie and, 46; layed off or unemployed, xxvi-xxvii, 29, 32-33, 54; used as cloak by Maimie, 52, 54; visited by Maimie in Atlantic City, 69-72; wages earned by, 15-16, 20, 41, 45-46

Judaism, 54, 172, 190, 387, 407

Kaufmann, Mr., 183-84, 206, 211-14
Kelsey, Mary, 285-86

Lauterman, Dr., 286-88, 299
"Lea, Miss" (benefactor), 105-8
Letters: to Mrs. C., 384; to Helen Howe, 367-71, 379; to Miss Huntington, 386-400, 403; to Miss Payson, 397-400; to Mr. Welsh's friends, 327-30, 333-37; *See also* Writing letter
Letters from Mrs. Howe, 68; emotional support from, xviii-xx; first letter, 103; as friends, 82-83
Letters to Mrs. Howe, 49, 68, 99, 102; as diary, xviii, 32; as incoherent and confused, 8-9; silence, reasons for, 403
Letters from Mr. Welsh, 93; return of, 65, 66, 71, 82
Letters to Mr. Welsh, 84, 86, 110, 172, 258-65, 403; corrected for grammatical errors, 120-21; as diary, 12
Library, public, 85-87, 187, 192

Life of Henry Stanley, 88
Literature, *see* Books and reading; Poetry; *and specific authors, books and magazines*
Loans, *see* Borrowing money
Lonesomeness, feelings of, 121, 174, 180-81, 189, 374, 375
Lowe, Hazel, 263, 310-11
Lower classes ("plebeian people; the half-bred and half-educated"), xxxviii-xxxix, 19, 149, 277; *See also* Working-class women
Lucey, Mr., 213-14
Lulu, 245
Lynn, Miss, 212

McCoy, Frances (roommate and fellow worker), 168-79, 185, 228
MacKenzie, Mrs., 245-47
McKim Advertising Agency, 236, 237
Magdalen Home, 196
Maids, *see* Domestic service
Manners, 79; table, 35-36, 45, 277
Margaret McD. (girl in mission), 365
Marriage, xxvi-xxvii, xxviii-xxix, 81; to Ira Benjamin, 386, 387; to Ira Benjamin, possibility of, 113, 144, 242, 308-10, 319, 340; Jewish, 78, 146
Married women, employment discrimination against, 34
Mateer, Miss, 331, 332
Mayfield, Georgette, 263
Meredith, George, 95
Militarism, 388
"Mimi," xxxix, 372-73
Mission, Maimie's, xxxi, xxxiv-xxxvi, 246-47, 261-62, 289, 293, 294, 313-14; accusations about Maimie by "Creeping Jesus," 338, 345-47; books and magazines, 337-39, 357-59; in Brin-

Prostitution (prostitutes), xiii-xiv, xxi, 245; economic need (poverty) as cause of, xxv, xxvi, xxx-xxxi; family life and, xxxi-xxxii, 274, 336-37; family's rejection of Maimie for, xxiv, 23; Maimie on, xxvi; Maimie's halfway house (mission) for, *see* Mission, Maimie's; in New York City, 84; possibility of Maimie's return to, 42, 60, 65, 66, 68-69, 74, 75; "rescue work" approach to, 253-54; types of, xxvi

Public library, 85-87, 187, 192

Puppies, selling of, 21, 30

Purim (Jewish holiday), 115, 121-23

Ramsey, Ruth, 373

Reading, *see* Books and reading

Records, 337, 342-43

Red-light districts, xxv-xxvi

Reform school, xxii, 196

Reformers, social, xxxiii-xxxiv

Religion, 12, 54, 178, 254-55, 406-7; militarism and, 388; mission and, 340, 344; Welsh and, 12, 54, 73, 407; *See also* Church attendance; Judaism

Religious conversion, xxxiv, 12, 54, 320, 407

Rent, 74, 111, 132, 183, 266; for Business Aid Bureau office, 219-20; difficulties in paying, 14-16

Rescue Band, 346-47

"Rescue work," 253-54

Ronayne, Dr., 203, 205, 210-11

Rosh Hashona, 100

Rothwell, Miss, 293

St. Louis, Missouri, 11

San Antonio, Texas, 11-12

Sanford, Edith, 375

Santa Claus, 110-11

School, 192, 416; *See also* Business school; Secretarial school

Secretarial school, xxx, xxxii, 73, 74, 90-91, 105-12, 123-25

Sedgwick, Anne Douglas, 349

Sedgwick, Ellery, xxxvii, 252, 258

Self-esteem (self-worth; self-respect), Maimie's, xxiv, xxxii, xxxix, 32

Self-improvement, Maimie's quest for, xv, xxxiii; *See also* Secretarial school

Settlement house, *see* Mission, Maimie's

Sex discrimination: in business, 219; in employment, xxx, 215

Sexual advances and assaults, 193, 246; at work, xxx, 140-41, 143, 154, 215

Shakey, Mr., 223-25

Shevuoth (Jewish holiday), 132-33

Silverman, Mr., 127

Sloan, Frank, 45

Smith, Mrs. (benefactor), 377

Social elite (the socially elect; aristocratic families; "nice" people; well-bred people), xxxiii, 22, 27, 28, 277

Social reformers, xxxiii-xxxiv

Social workers (social work; welfare work), xxxiv, xxxv, 301, 380; *See also* "Rescue work"

Soldiers, 246-47, 280, 293-94

Stella C. (girl in mission), 364-65

Stenographer, 106; *See also under* Employment

Stenography, 123-24; Suiffen's offer to teach Maimie, 73-74; *See also* Secretarial school

Stephens, Mr., 229, 236, 237

Stockton, Frank, 87

Suiffen, Mr. (Welsh's secretary), 7, 14, 17, 41, 56, 70-73, 86, 90, 100, 123, 124, 289, 313, 314

Summer house, 384, 392-97, 404-5

Syphilis, 280, 287-88, 290